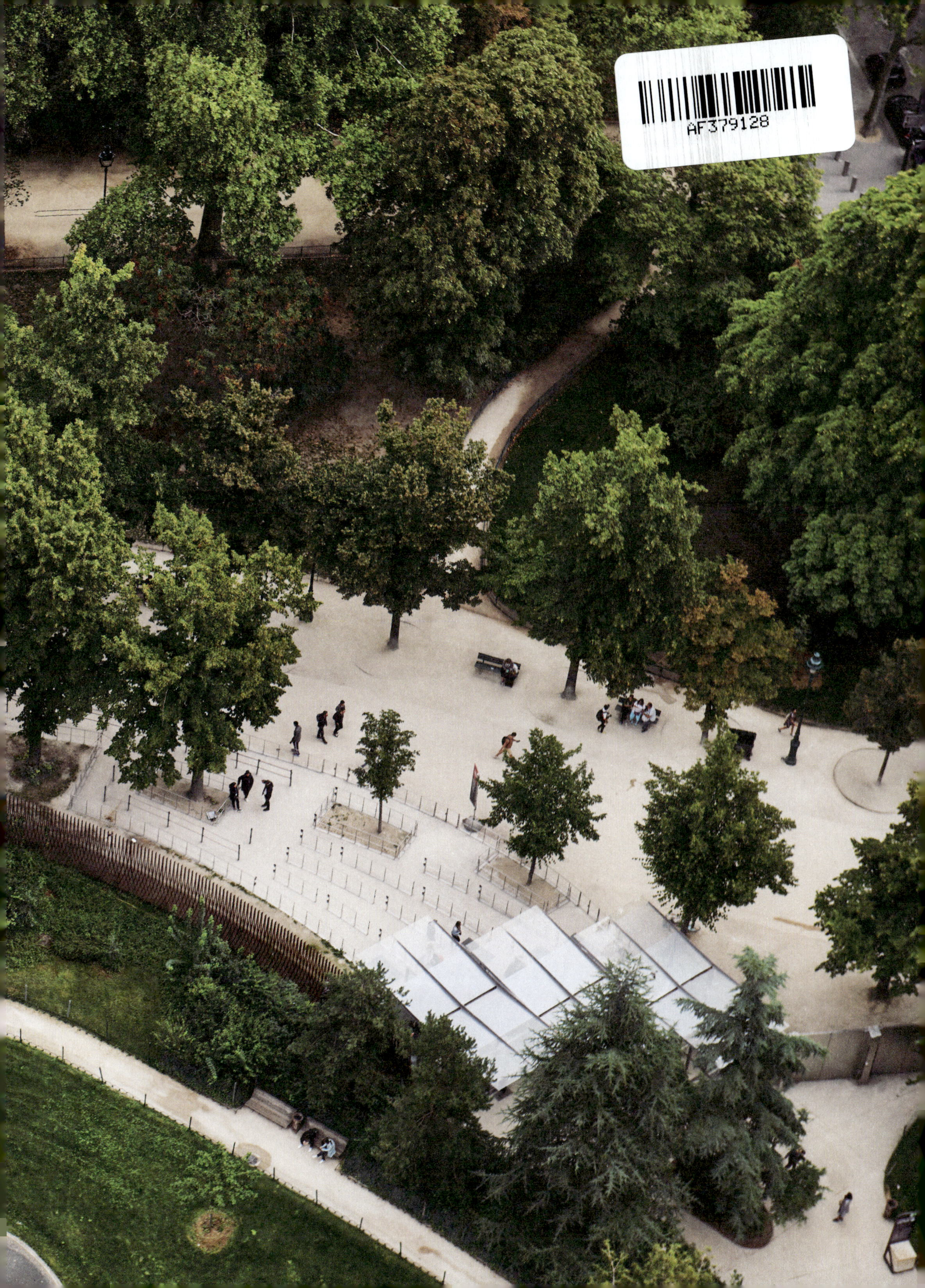

AF379128

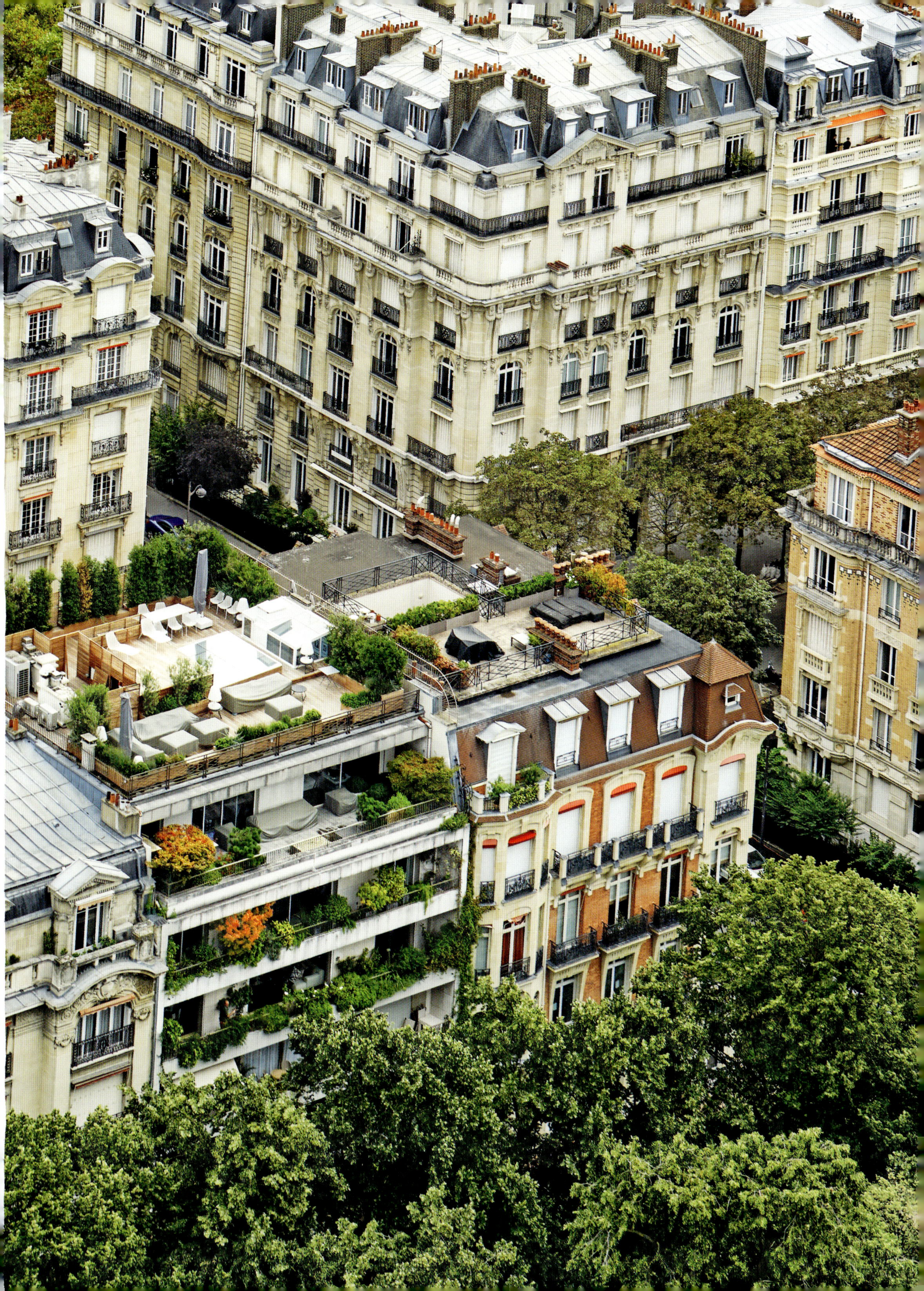

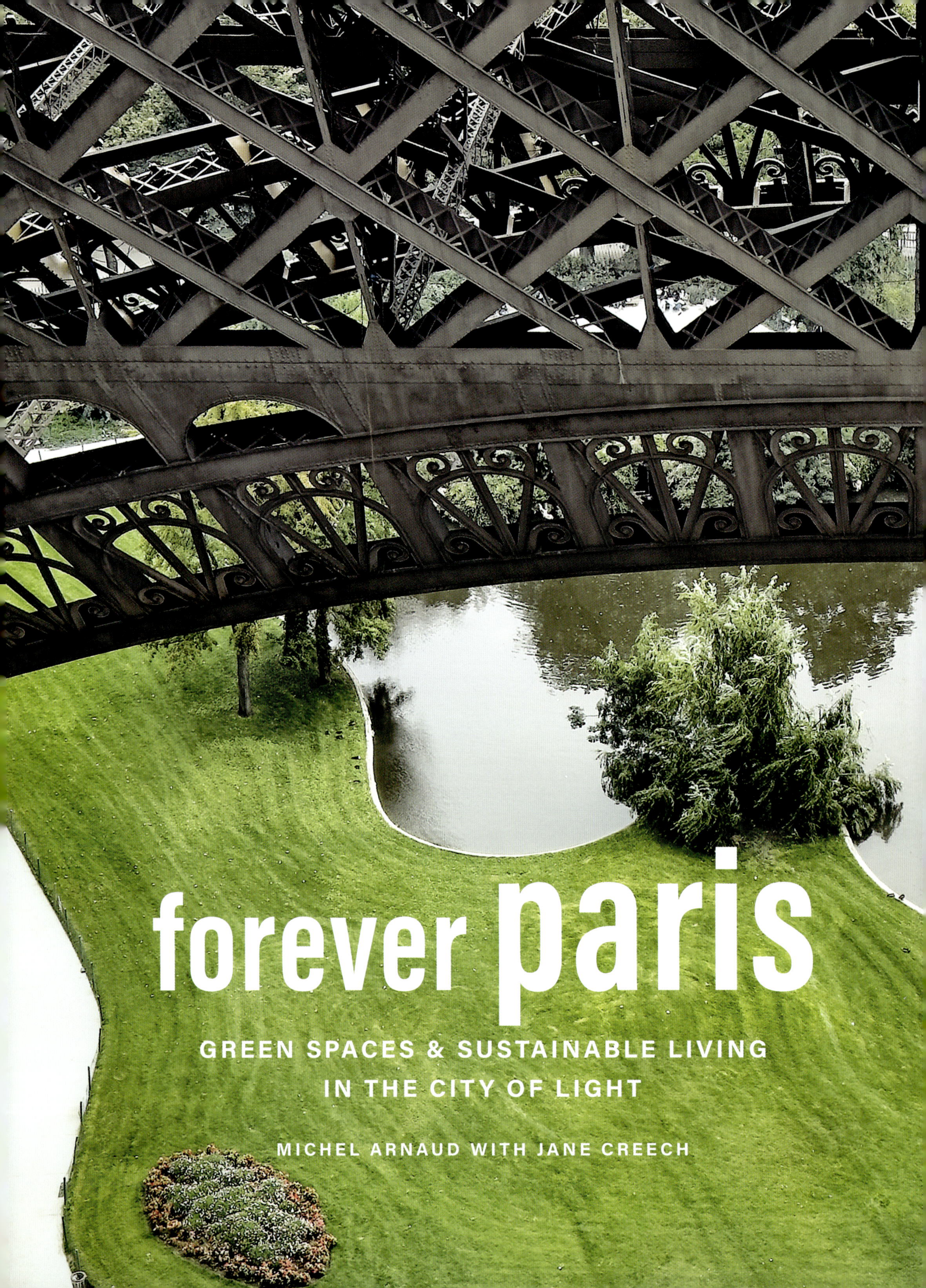

forever paris
GREEN SPACES & SUSTAINABLE LIVING
IN THE CITY OF LIGHT
MICHEL ARNAUD WITH JANE CREECH

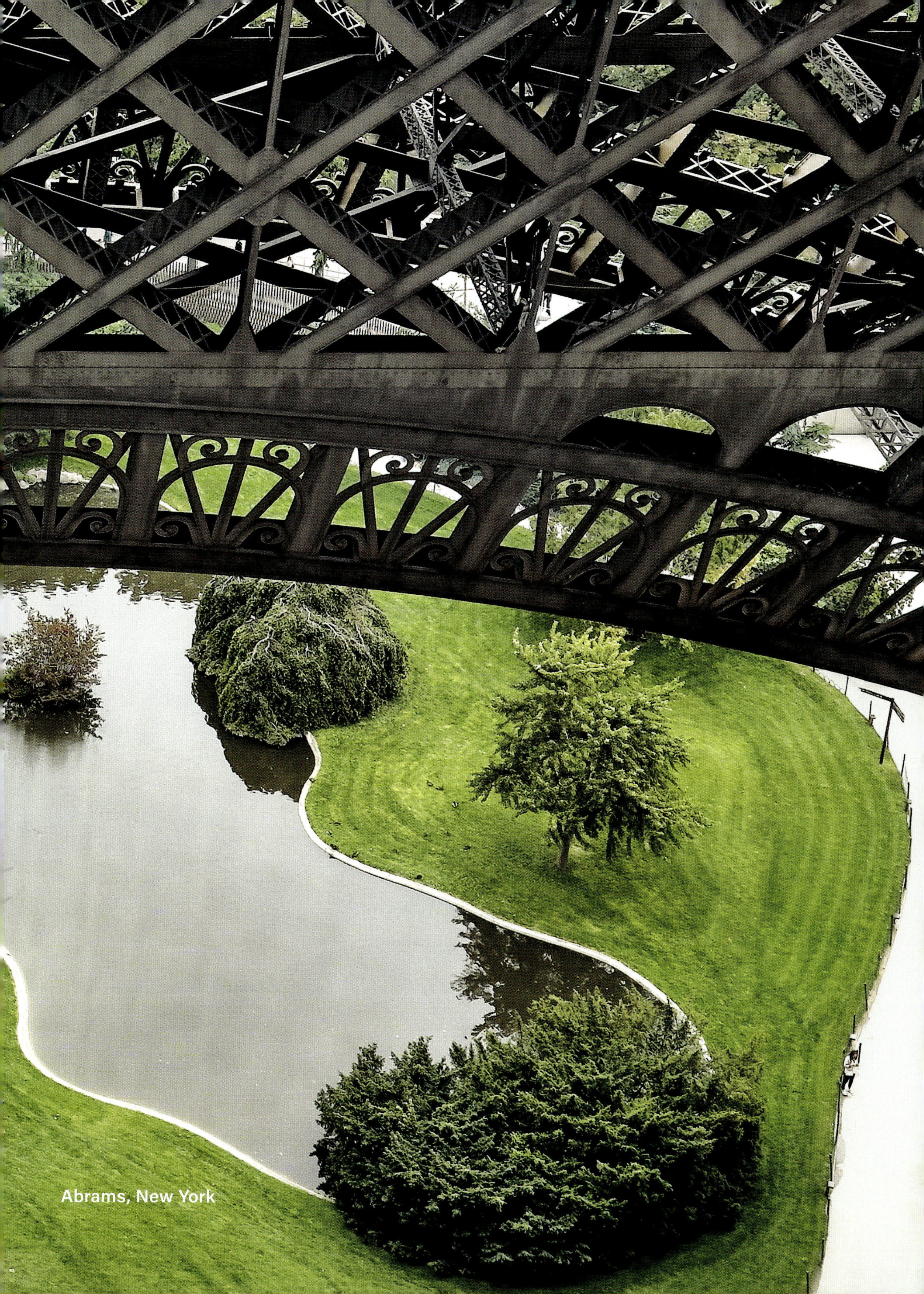
Abrams, New York

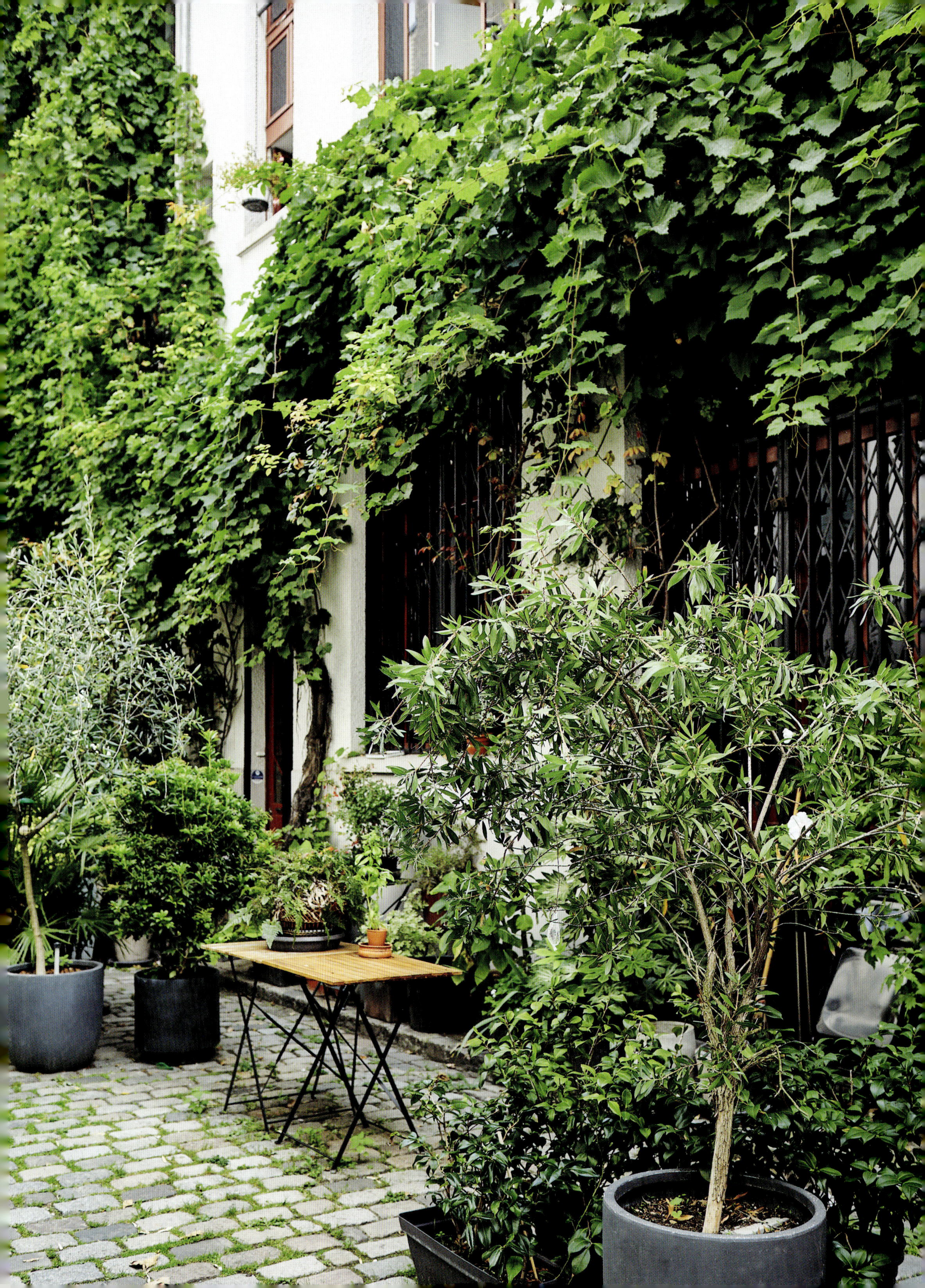

# contents

# preface by Michel Arnaud

## Toward a Garden City/*Vers une ville-jardin*

This book aims to be a witness of the transformation of Paris toward a greener future. It is not the first time that Paris is a trailblazer embracing change. We saw it in the seventeenth century when Henry IV completed le pont Neuf—a truly revolutionary idea in bridge construction and urban planning that was copied by the major cities of Europe. We saw it when Baron Haussmann, under the guidance of Napoleon III, transformed Paris, for hygienic and political reasons—a Paris that we can still recognize today. At the beginning of the twenty-first century, the then new mayor, Bertrand Delanöe, started a quiet revolution, organizing new initiatives to reduce traffic and to change the lives of Parisians with projects such as Paris Plages. Started in 2002 and continuing every summer on the banks of the Seine, it gives Parisians who cannot go out of town on vacation a chance to relax in the center of the city. Delanöe also proposed a program named Vélib' (now Vélib' Metropole) that gives Parisians access to bike sharing, and he developed a plan for a nonpolluting electric tramway that now services more than a million riders a day throughout its entire Île-de-France system. Not only have these initiatives been expanded by the new administration of Anne Hidalgo, the present *maire*, or mayor, of Paris, but she has also implemented further reductions in cars by the urgent and radical greening of Paris, a change that gives nature the priority. As this book shows, the city's approach to becoming a garden city not only considers the gardens and public spaces of the past but also focuses on new projects that are reinventing the cityscape.

My grandmother lived in a small village on the outskirts of Paris where she had a little farm with chickens, vegetables, and fruits. She supplemented her meager retirement with income from the farm. While it may seem romantic, it was a hard life. Some of my fondest memories of that time are visiting her and helping her at harvest time to pick the raspberries from her garden. My cousin Anny and I moved along the rows of plants, filling the little boxes with the ripe fruits. We were also eating the fruits of our efforts. My grandmother sold these boxes of berries at the local market, or *marché*, along with other vendors from the farms nearby. You could say they were the predecessors of what is now the farm-to-table food movement. Years later, her farmhouse, which dated to the seventeenth century, was transformed into three side-by-side residences, occupied by my aunt, uncle, cousins, and their families.

It is fascinating to see how examples of sustainable living are seeping into the Parisian lifestyle as well. New enterprises are taking over and adapting the old railroad stations of the Petite Ceinture, or Little Belt railway, that encircled Paris. In addition, city gardeners are planting their own vegetables along the unused historical railway tracks. The recycling of furnishings, and now fashion, are part of a circular economy.

For a brief time, my twin sisters and I lived with my Aunt Janne and her husband Yves, who had been a chef-owner of a noted Parisian restaurant. I experienced firsthand what it took to work in the City of Light, as I lived in Paris a few years before I moved to London. In 1968, I was in Paris to witness the student revolution that was changing the country's culture

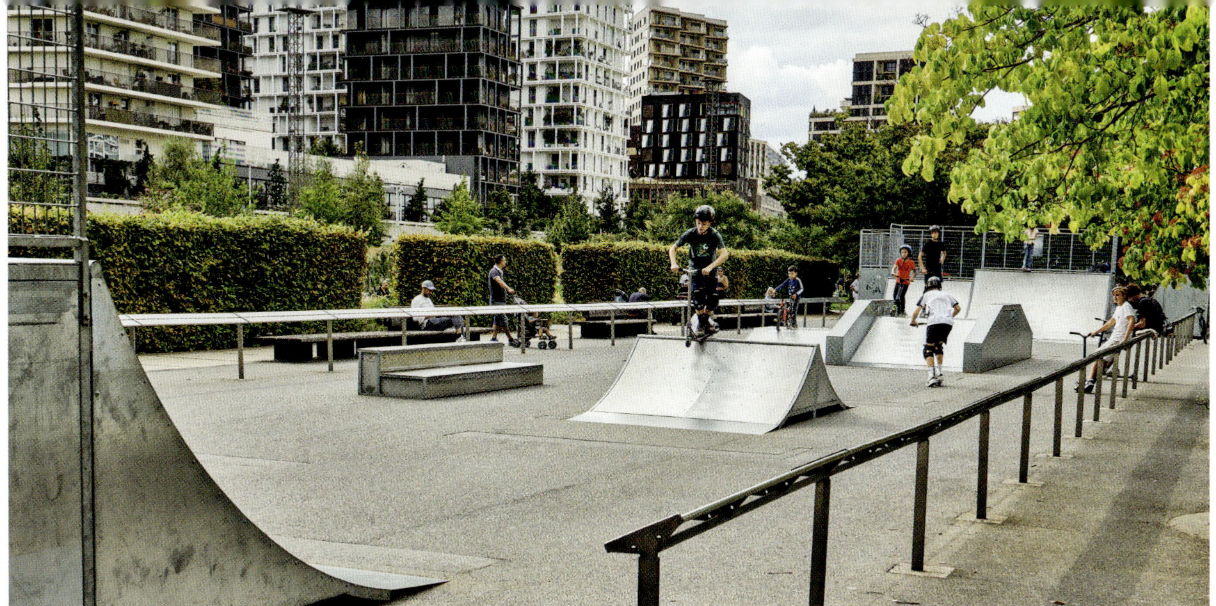

The skateboard park in parc Martin Luther King in the *écoquartier*, Clichy-Batignolles.

and, arguably, its politics. Since that time, I have returned to Paris many times, not only to visit family but also for work. For more than twenty years, I traveled, first from my home in London and then later from New York, four to six times a year for weeks at a time to photograph the seasonal fashion shows for *Vogue* and *Harper's Bazaar*. Visiting Paris today, I sense that same urgent call for change as I did in 1968. However, now the issue at hand is the *urgence climatique*—the climate emergency. Again, a new generation is part of the cultural change. They are creating businesses and ventures that prioritize the environment and sustainable living practices. This time, these younger entrepreneurs and innovators do not have to fight "city hall" for support. The City of Paris, led by Anne Hidalgo since 2014, is taking an even more active stance by reducing traffic, roadways, and spaces for cars; by making room for alternative forms of transportation such as bicycles and trams; by creating more green and open spaces for residents to breathe fresh air; and by encouraging the revitalization of old buildings, infrastructure, and open places for pedestrians. There is a plan for the *végétalization,* or greening, of Paris as an effort to help cool the city and make a more livable city for all Parisians.

We are living in a time of extraordinary change. We are forced to reckon with our past behavior and the consequences that our activities have had and are having on our planet. I agree with John Kerry, who was the first special presidential envoy for climate in the United States when he said, "We do stand next to another abyss. It is the test of our own times, a test as acute and as existential as any previous one. It is about

survival." I am not a scientist, but I believe in science. I am, as most of those behind a lens are, an observer. I believe that our cities are a direct reflection of our times. The fact that a major city has taken on the role of leader of our present time and circumstances struck me as remarkable and worth documenting. These changes have not happened immediately but incrementally, over time. In fact, parks, gardens, green spaces, and public spaces have been created in Paris since Charles V included the Louvre gardens next to his residence there. The culmination of the changes is now adding up; for example, the newly finished Clichy-Batignolles–parc Martin Luther King, a significant project named after the American civil rights leader, took more than fifteen years to complete. It is the most recent large park created in the city.

Paris was my muse in 1969. Before I left for London, I made a series of photographs. A few of the images from a traveling exhibition, *Parisians' Paris*, are published here for the first time. The photographs that I took then feel as if they are encased in a time capsule created by my views of the town. But the photographs I have taken over the last year feel alive and vibrant. This project has made me examine the city in a fresh way. To be sure, it is a view of Paris that some may not recognize—even those who live there. I hope it is one that all who love Paris, as I do, will follow to see how one of the greatest cities in the world has set out to change itself, once again.

Now, go for a walk,
Michel
2024

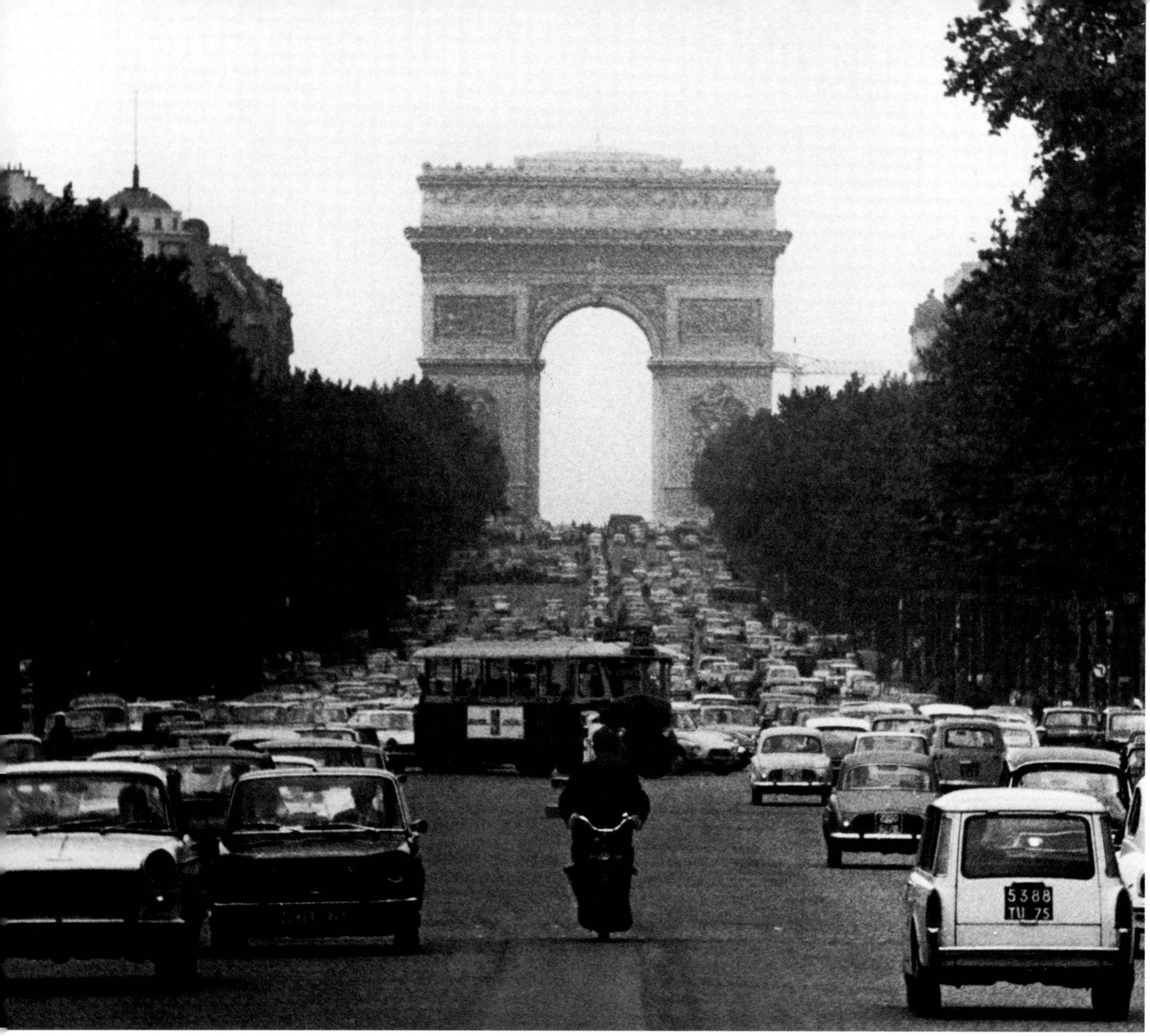

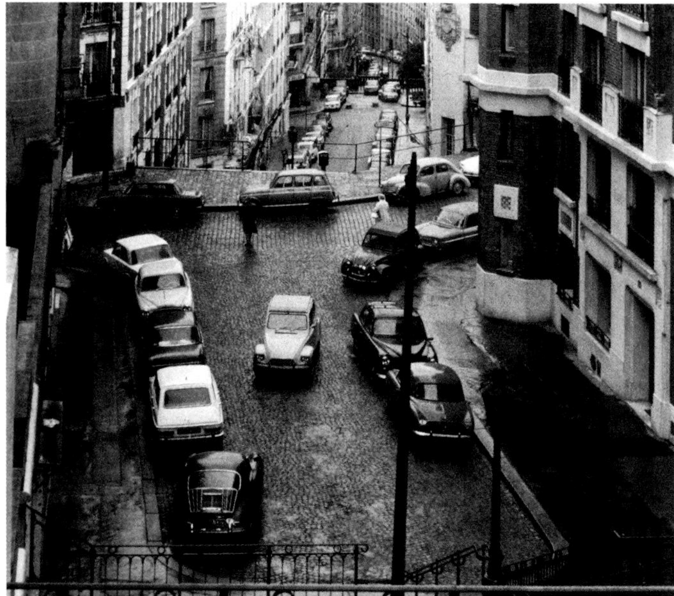



**ABOVE**
A view of the Champs-Élysées looking toward the Arc de Triomphe. The traffic circle around the arch was notoriously congested, as was the grand boulevard.

**LEFT**
Cars dominated the cobblestone streets of Montmartre, the Parisian neighborhood. A Citröen 2CV, in the middle of the street, was a popular car in France in the 1960s.

**OPPOSITE ABOVE**
La place de la Concorde in 1969. Traffic encircles the Luxor Obelisk, or l'Obélisque de Louxor.

**OPPOSITE BELOW**
Cars parked along le quai de la Seine on the Right Bank in 1969.

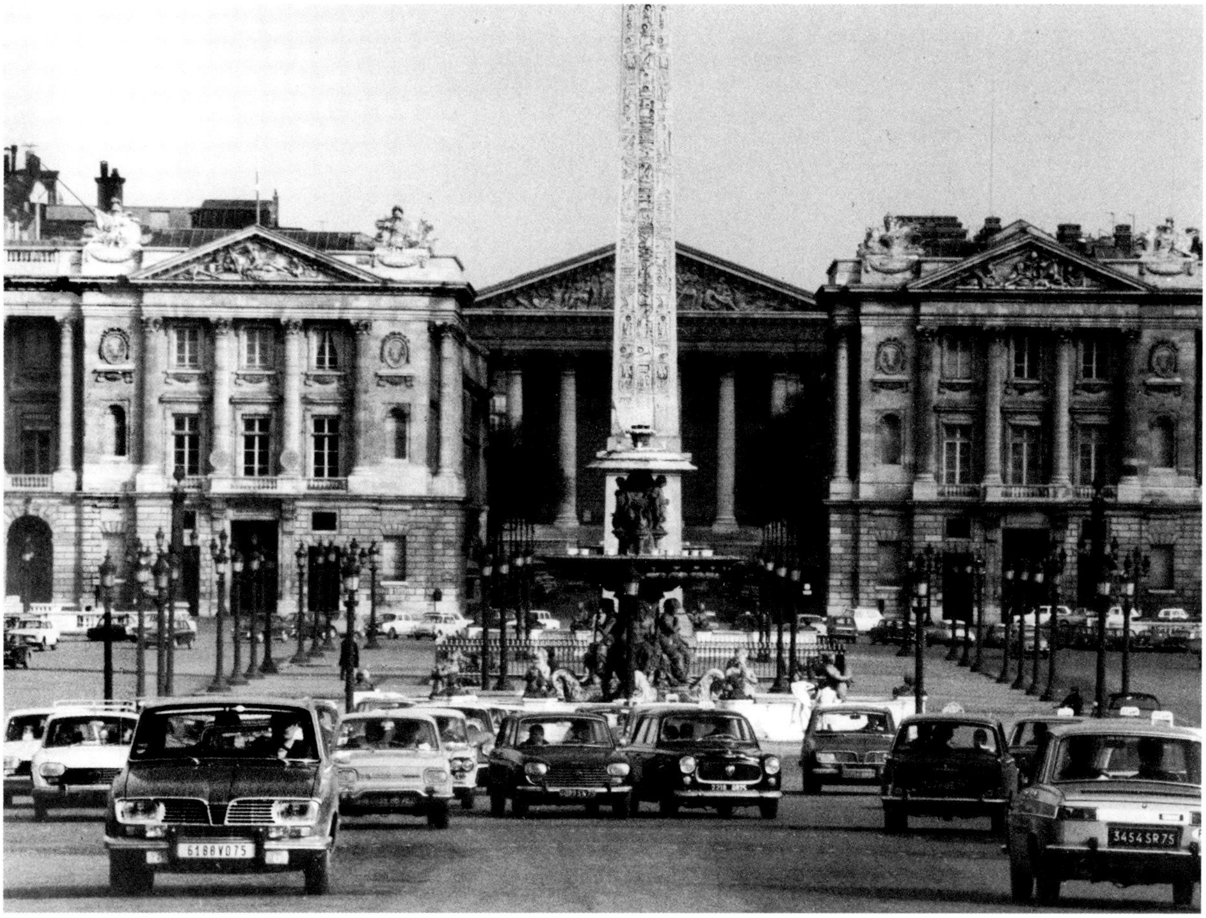

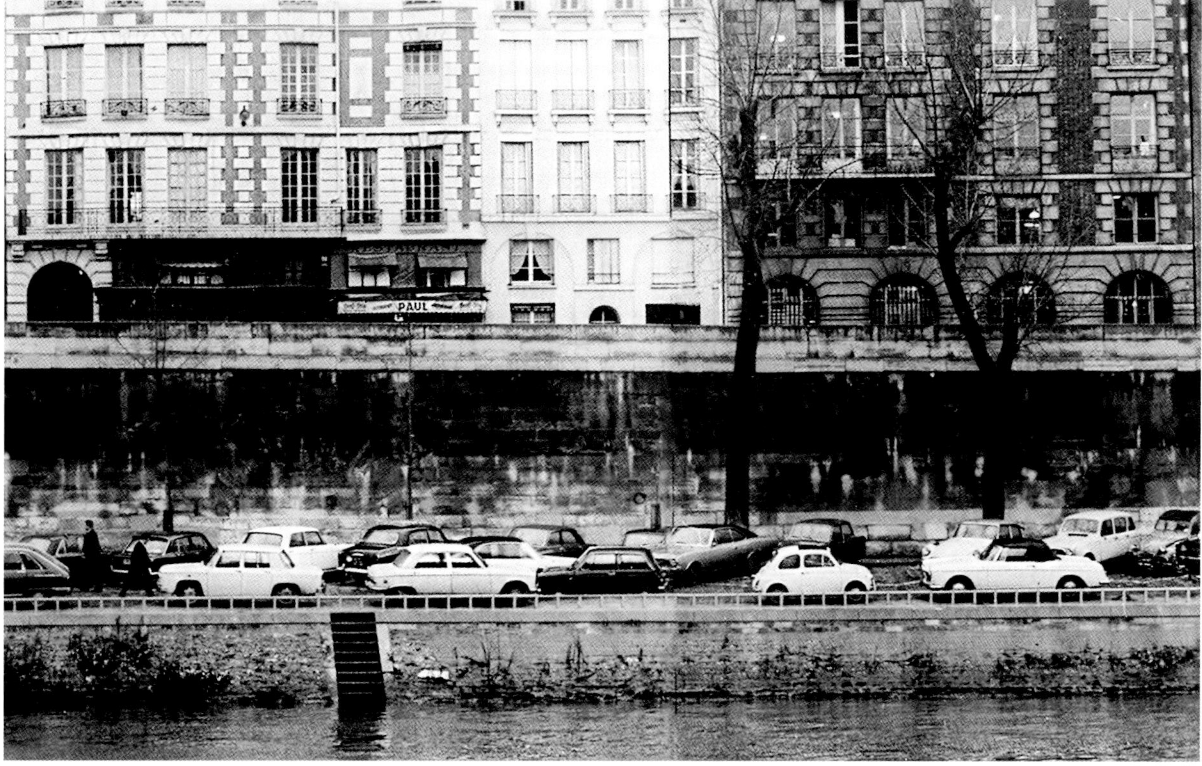

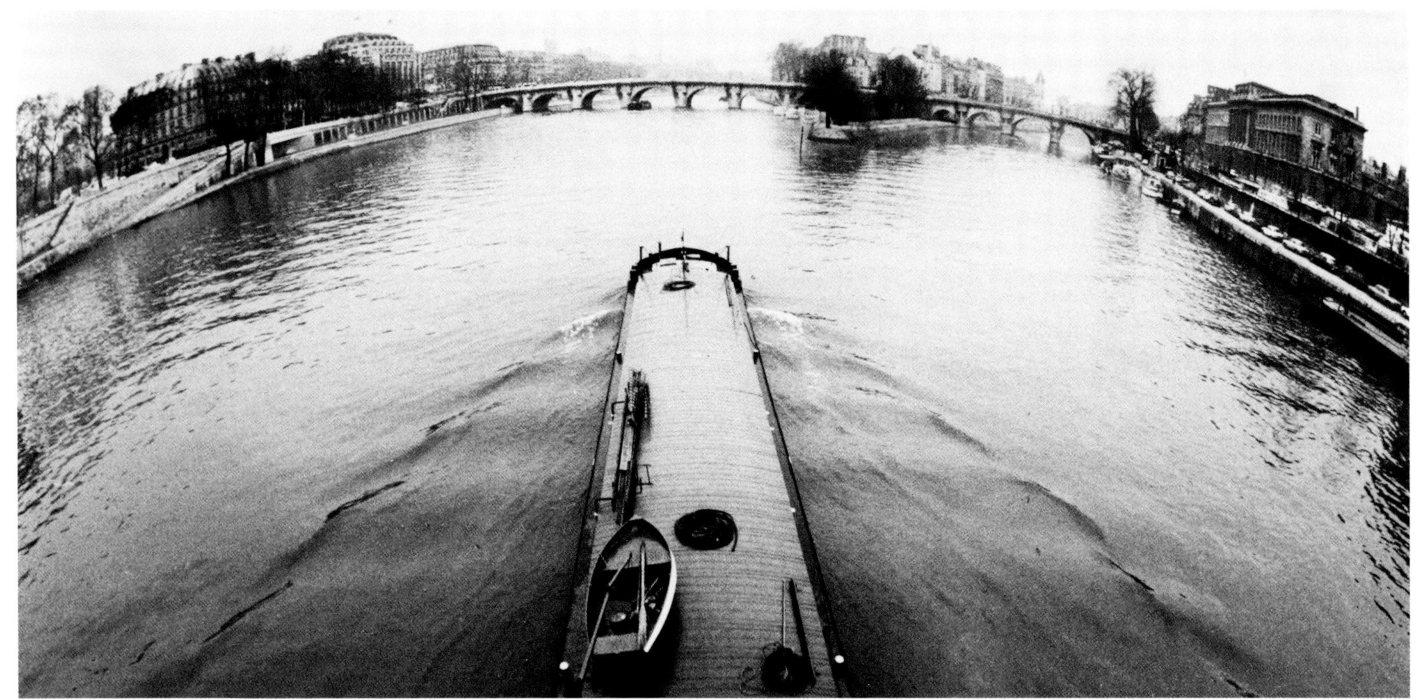

A river barge headed toward le pont Neuf, which crosses over the Seine River. It was finished under the reign of King Henry IV in 1607.

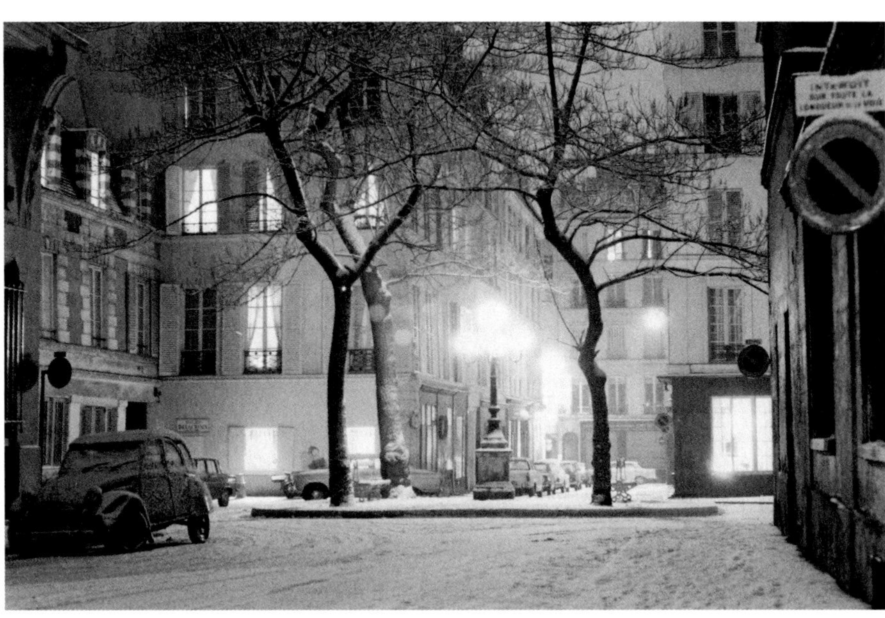

Place de Furstenberg, Paris's smallest square, was photographed in the snow.

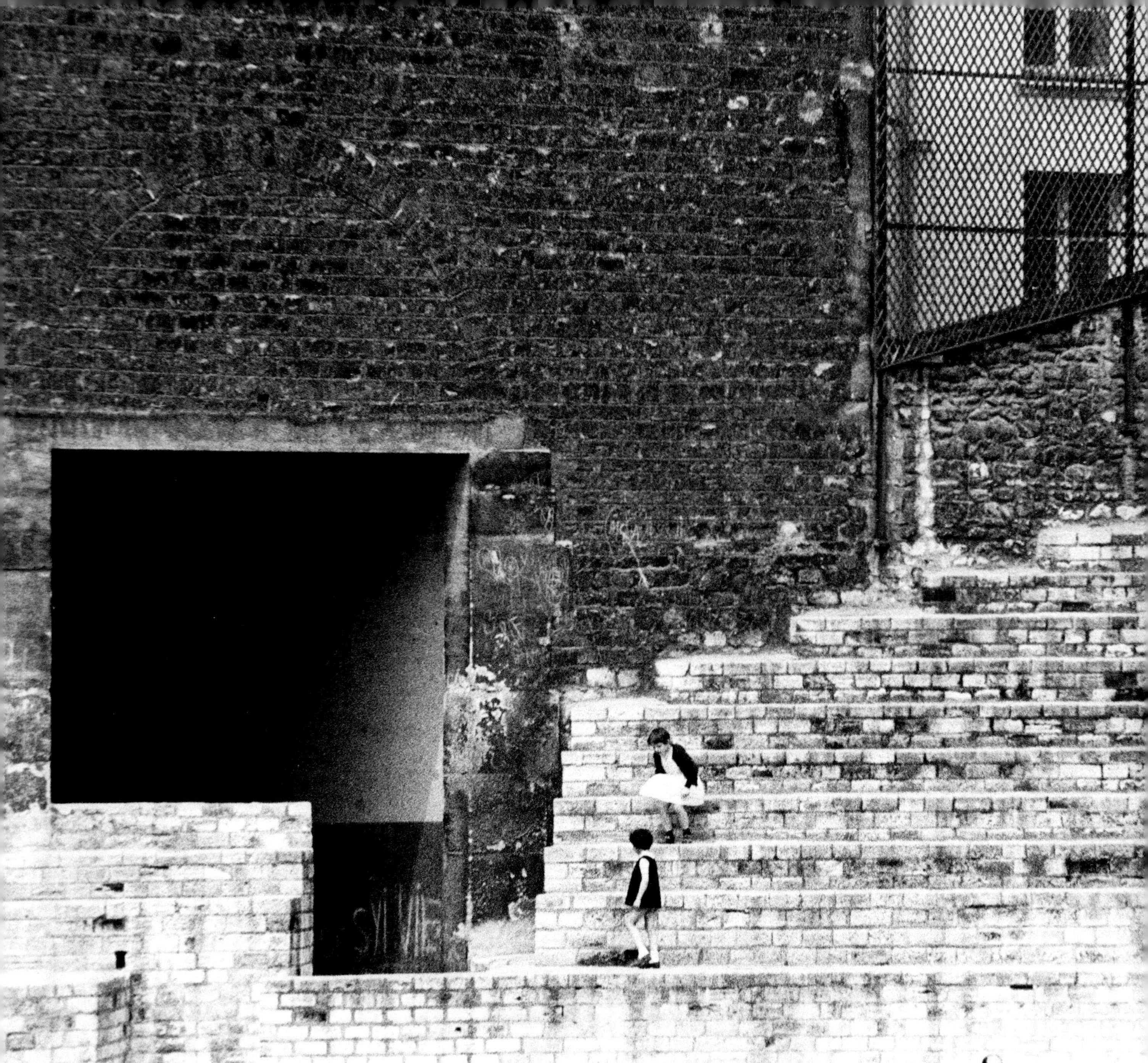

Children playing in Montmartre.

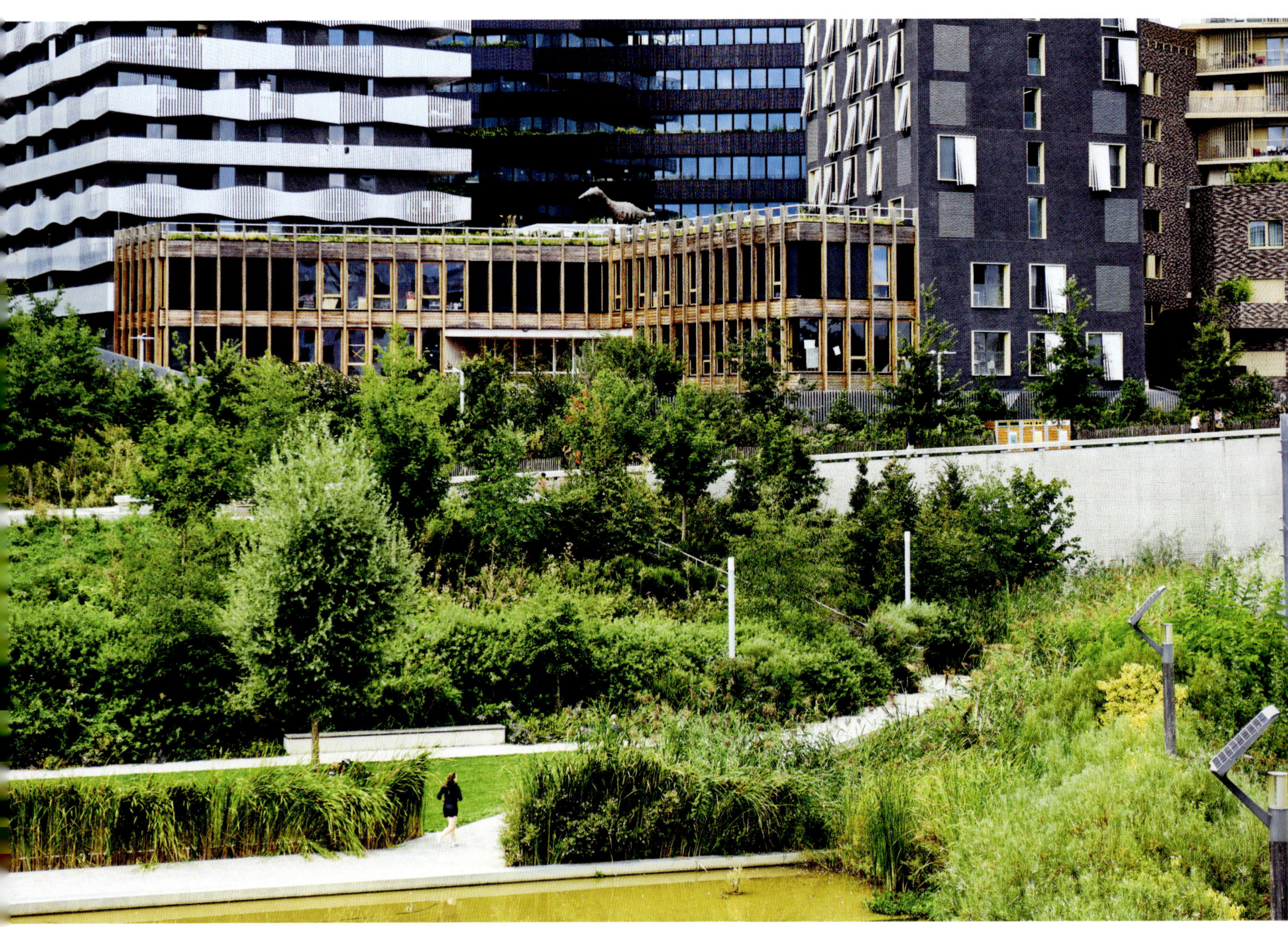

Looking west across parc Martin Luther King, at the elementary school of the *écoquartier* Clichy-Batignolles in the 17th arrondissement.

# a conversation with Christophe Najdovski

C hristophe Najdovski is Paris's current deputy mayor in charge of green spaces, biodiversity, animal condition, and the greening of public spaces. He has held this position since 2020. He was elected Paris city councillor in 2001. Najdovski became deputy mayor in charge of early childhood in 2008 until 2014. He was then deputy mayor of transport, mobility, roadways, and public spaces between 2014 and 2020. Since 2020, more than 550 kilometers (342 miles) of biking lanes were created. While tramways, metros, and buses are mainly the responsibility of the Île-de-France region, the Paris City Council also contributed. The new tramway loop around Paris transports about 340,000 people a day according to a 2022 report. Impressive work indeed. I was most interested to speak with him about the efforts in the greening, or *végétalization*, of the streets and parks of Paris. Our conversation that took place on February 20, 2024, has been edited and condensed for clarity.

**Michel Arnaud:** These days there is controversy about the term "green city."
**Christophe Najdovski:** Yes.

**MA:** Do you consider Paris a "green city"?
**CN:** It is difficult to answer definitively one way or another without hesitation. Of course, the answer is not entirely affirmative or negative. [Paris] is in the process of becoming [a green city]. At least, the [city's] ambition is to become [a green city]. All major cities around the world are deeply marked by the history of their country. Cities have inevitably been shaped over the decades by the prevailing culture of the time and ideas of the moment.

It's true, there is the idea to try to transform the city—to adapt it to the challenges of the twenty-first century. Beyond the question of adaptation, there is a sense of an urgency. That is why the transformations are being carried out hastily, which inevitably sparks controversies. Obviously, if we had an unhurried course, it would be much less subject to criticism. By provoking reactions and implementing bold projects, controversies are inevitable.

**MA:** Can you give us an example of the new greening projects in Paris that stand out?
**CN:** A very beautiful example is the large park, [Clichy-Batignolles] Martin Luther King, which is the latest park to be built in Paris. It is quite surprising that this park was constructed on a former rail yard that belonged to the SNCF (France's national state-owned railroad company). It was the last available land in Paris. The park, which covers 10 hectares (or nearly 25 acres), was the subject of an international competition in 2002. The contest for the landscape design was won by the well-known French landscape architect Jacqueline Osty, who is a leading figure in urban planning. She designed the park with a diversity of ambiences, which makes the composition modern, and [her design] blends well with the environment. Martin Luther King Park is a signature project of great quality and a place that is highly appreciated.

In 2020, I was elected to oversee green spaces. Urban projects are now conducted over a relatively long period of time. The Martin Luther King Park was planned and decided about fifteen years ago. And for the last almost four years, we have been putting the finishing touches on the park. We were able to create an orchard. We planted fruit trees—which was not done in public places until recently—on one of the last parcels that was still being developed and landscaped. We planted fifty-eight fruit trees, making it the largest area planted with fruit trees in central Paris. We have apple trees, pear trees. There are also blackberry and raspberry bushes.

**MA:** Will people be able to pick the fruit from the trees?

**CN:** Yes, in fact, the plants are starting to bear fruit—which is both poignant and beautiful. It is a return of nature in the city.

**MA:** Can you talk more about this return of nature to the city. This is an important point.

**CN:** In my current role, we are responding to a very strong social demand from citizens who live in the city to have more nature present in the city near one's home, and that's what we are trying to do—a demand that was intensified by the COVID lockdown, as only a privileged few were able to leave the city for a house in the countryside. The vast majority of those in the city were confined to minuscule apartments.

Another mandate that we are trying to fulfill is the idea that nature is no longer confined only to green spaces, but that it overflows and permeates the entire city. That's why we are carrying out greening projects in more than just public spaces but also in the streets. We have several programs: One is called *rues aux écoles* (renamed in 2024 after this interview to *rues aux enfants*), where the streets leading to public or private schools are pedestrianized and replanted when the below-ground systems allow it. In Paris, we have a very congested underground with infrastructure such as the metro, electricity, gas, district heating, telecoms. In short, it's a maze of everything you can imagine. When the underground network allows it, we can plant trees, develop green spaces, and remove car parking.

Rue Charles Baudelaire is an example of what we are doing in terms of streetscape transformation. The street is not very far from la place de la Bastille in the 12th arrondissement, next to le square Trousseau in the Aligre district. On that street, there are two schools, an elementary and middle school, and a kindergarten. Often the streets are not particularly famous streets; initially they are quite ordinary. On rue Charles-Baudelaire, we closed the street to cars and planted fourteen fruit trees and other plantings. We changed the color of the asphalt from dark to light to reduce the heat of the street. Rue de la Providence in the 13th arrondissement has been completely transformed. Before, there was an iron fencing barricade that separated and constrained the movements of parents to a narrow sidewalk in front of the school. We removed the fencing, leveled the street with the sidewalk. By greening the space with a bed of plants, we have truly transformed the landscape of the street.

There is support from the Parisian population for these projects, as two-thirds of Parisians do not own a vehicle. There is still a quite passionate relationship with cars. It's not something I need to explain to you, especially in the United States, where it's even stronger.

The program of planting fruit trees in the streets is starting slowly, but continues; they are planted in several places. We have some principles of development in terms of the plant's life cycle. Whenever possible, we have automatic watering for the plantings, so they are aesthetically pleasing. Plant growth follows the seasons. Inevitably, the growth is less spectacular in winter when it's dormant than in spring and then in summer, when it can also turn yellow. That's just how it happens. With these automatic watering operations, we try to maintain a landscape that is presentable despite everything. We have many examples [where the plants are supported] such as rue d'Arbalète, in the 5th arrondissement. Also, in the western Parisian districts, which are known to be very mineral [concrete and stone] areas in the 8th arrondissement, for example, rue de Moscou and rue de la Bienfaisance. These streets are not well known, and these projects are a relatively modest size, but today, they offer a streetscape that was unanticipated, undreamt of.

**MA:** I have heard that you are working on incorporating urban forests into the cityscape as well.

**CN:** We have more remarkable projects that are always in public spaces and notably embody the concept of urban forests. The idea is attributed to the French landscape architect Michel Desvigne, who has led projects of this type in Paris, but also in different Japanese cities. And we have been inspired by his work to carry out a quite radical transformation of la place de Catalogne, which is located next to the Montparnasse train station. Today we have a "mini forest" that has been planted with nearly five hundred trees on a square that was completely concrete. Place de Catalogne was designed by Ricardo Bofill in the early 1980s. It was a square made entirely of concrete, stone, and asphalt—it had become a heat island—with a fountain by the artist Shamai Haber. The fountain never worked [properly] in thirty years. It was also an energy sink in terms of electricity and water consumption. Finally, we said to ourselves, let's keep some elements of the fountain and reuse it. Since the subsoil allowed it, we completely removed the asphalt on an area of 4,000 square meters [43,000 square feet] to plant trees and install benches. Following the model of a micro forest, we reconstructed a forest floor, including a forest soil. [The new forest] gives a whole new perspective to the place. The plantings are underway and will be completed by the end of March 2024. If you come in the spring, it will be quite spectacular to see this transformation.

**MA:** Very exciting! Are there other projects you would like to mention?

**CN:** We have some projects that are ongoing. Porte Maillot, for example, is also an important [revitalization]. We are working [on] the historical perspective of the Tuileries axis, Arc de Triomphe, Arche de la Défense. Before, there was a roundabout on Porte Maillot Square, but now, we have removed it to create an alignment with the historical perspective. We are bringing the bois de Boulogne into Paris, with an extension of the woods. It is a very interesting landscape.

Another project is an urban forest in the east of Paris that will be named the bois de Charonne. The Charonne district, which was annexed by Haussmann in the 1860s, is a working-class neighborhood of the 20th arrondissement. The forest will be alongside the Petite Ceinture railway. This mythic disused line is our Parisian version of New York's High Line. We will connect the park of 3.5 hectares [or 8.6 acres] with more than two thousand trees that are currently being planted. These trees are transplants; in fact, any tree planting is a transplantation. They are quite spectacular, since they are conifers and pines that are already 10 to 15 meters high [32 to 49 feet high]. This planting will radically change the urban landscape of the district along with the mysterious aspect of the Petite Ceinture, which is a wild and timeless place.

**MA:** Speaking about the Petite Ceinture, what are your thoughts about the projects that reuse the old railway stations?

**CN:** We have pursued these projects with the SNCF to help those stations find a new life. Presently, we are accepting bids for the old station at Avron. The model for these projects very often has a leisure component and a restaurant to create a viable business model. Sometimes, there is a local project which is about the community.

**MA:** Those projects are revitalizing older buildings.

**CN:** Yes, absolutely. Yes. We are in the process of remaking the city. Today, the city has evolved by rebuilding itself so that it can develop again. We're bringing abandoned areas back to life. We encourage those initiatives.

**MA:** What is the story of Paris Plages? It seems to be a very popular program.

**CN:** Bertrand Delanöe initiated Paris Plages in 2002 in a single location. The project's aim was twofold: to rescue the Seine riverbank from being an expressway and to bring in sand to create a beach to remake Paris *sur Seine*. Over time, we've aimed to replicate this idea at other sites, such as le bassin de la Villette, providing leisure spaces for those who can't afford vacations. The bathing area at bassin de la Villette has been a success thanks to improvements in water quality. We used to transport sand in by boat to reduce the ecological impact, but it became costly and energy consuming. Now, we're exploring more sustainable options like using wood chips from tree removals from Paris parks. We are using local resources, promoting reuse, and transforming what could be waste into a new material to meet our needs.

We are opening more sections of the Petite Ceinture to the public to increase accessible green spaces. Land being scarce, we're repurposing existing areas like the Petite Ceinture, opening it section by section. We're connecting it to parc Georges-Brassens in the 15th arrondissement for a green continuum [throughout the city]. Last summer, parc Georges-Brassens underwent renovations that showcase successful ecological restoration efforts.

While we're also creating new parks, we won't have many more opportunities to create large parks like Martin Luther King. But as I've mentioned, there are urban *végétalization,* or urban greening projects, like bois de Charonne and Petite Ceinture [still in progress]. I also want to talk about the future Python-Duvernois park in the 20th arrondissement, a very difficult area near la porte de Bagnolet. It used to be one of the poorest neighborhoods in Paris. This park will be finished in spring 2024, and it's located near le boulevard périphérique. Large road infrastructures and housing were demolished to make way for new constructions, including social housing, business activities, and sports. This type of development is a part of the rebuilding of the city through urban renewal. We are indeed rebuilding the city.

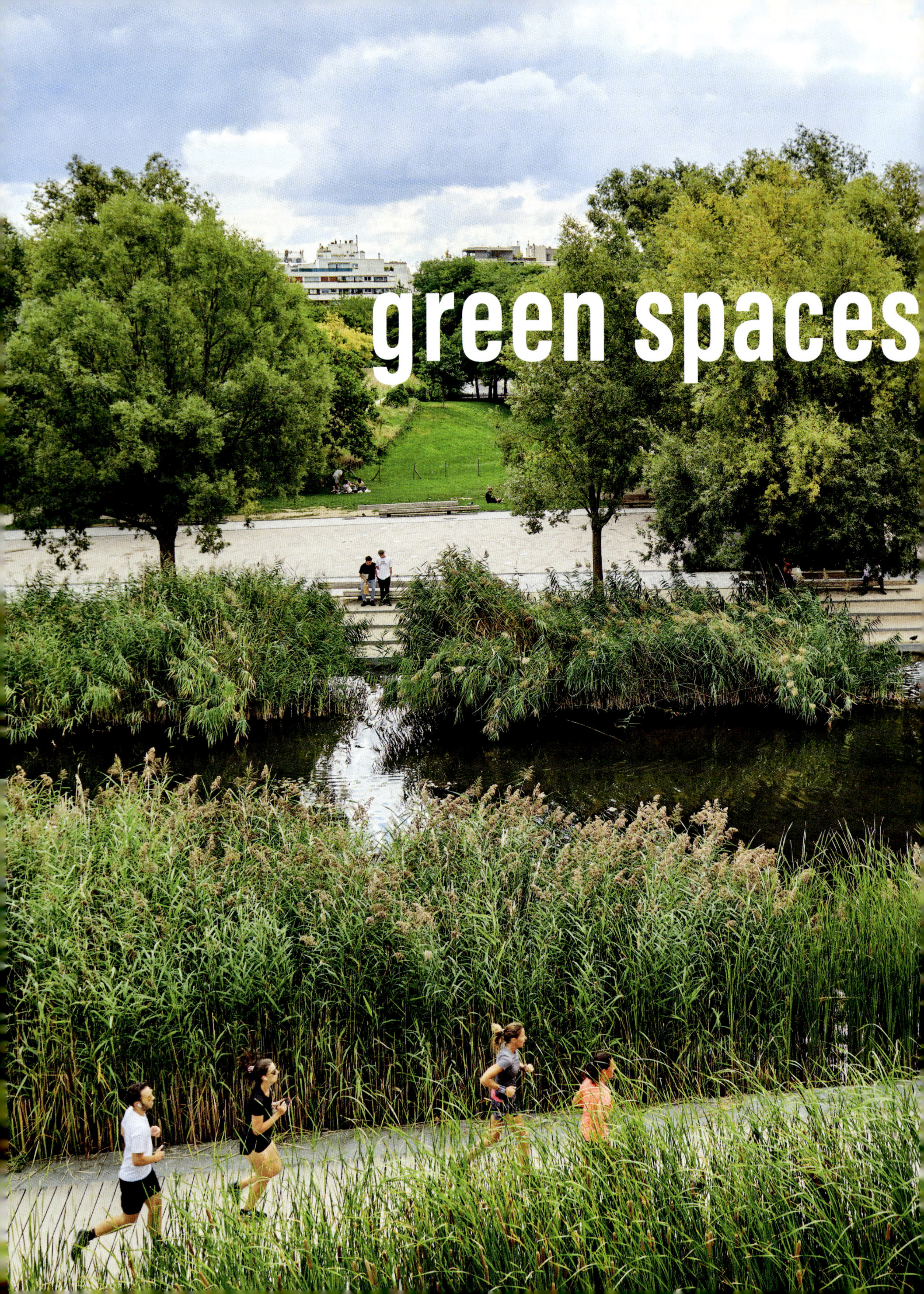
green spaces

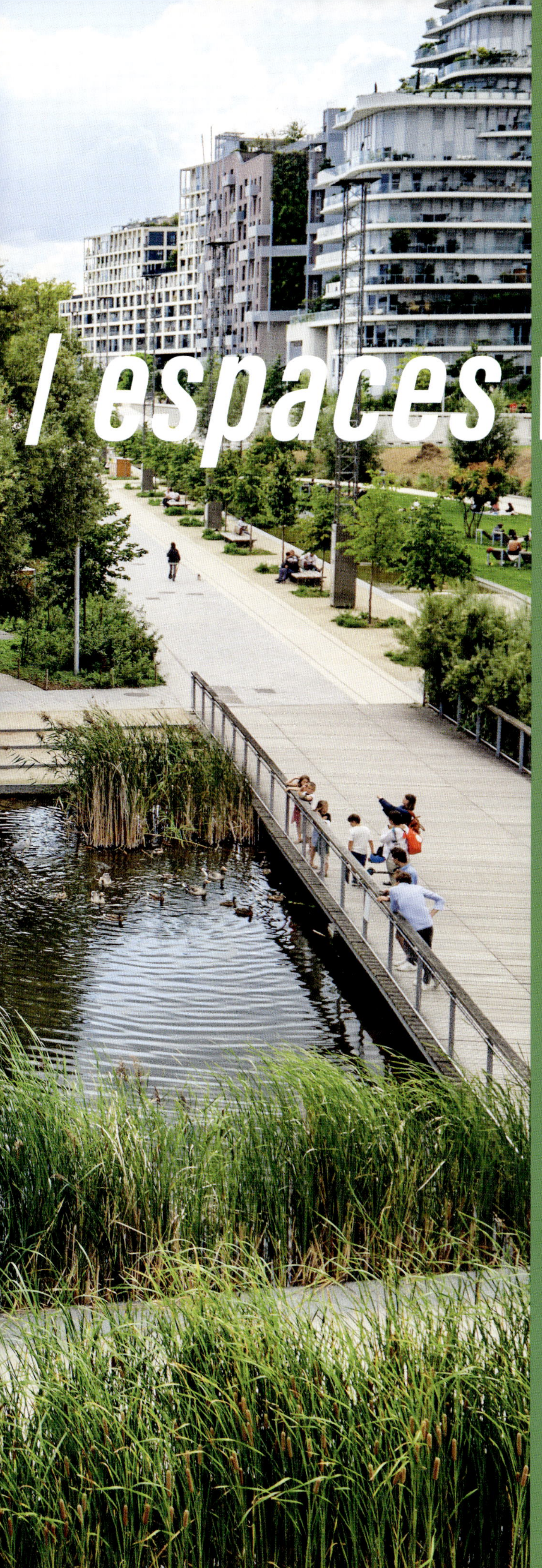



# les espaces verts

The plan for more green spaces in Paris is not a new one. From the city's early beginning, monarchs, emperors, presidents, mayors, and Parisians themselves have been pursuing ways to bring more nature into the city. From Catherine de' Medici in the sixteenth century, who commissioned le jardin des Tuileries, to Napoleon III in the nineteenth century, who transformed royal hunting grounds into the city parks bois de Boulogne and bois de Vincennes, to more recent mayors of the twenty-first century like Bertrand Delanöe and Anne Hidalgo, who have amped up green space projects including adding eighty thousand trees to the cityscape. Previous generations considered outdoor public spaces as the source of fresh air, as gathering places, and as sites for relaxation and entertainment. Today, in the context of the climate crisis, green spaces are one tool used to bring down the temperature of the city. Green and public spaces have expanded to include infrastructure such as green walls and streets, urban rooftop farms, and new eco-neighborhoods.

A marsh at parc Martin Luther King.

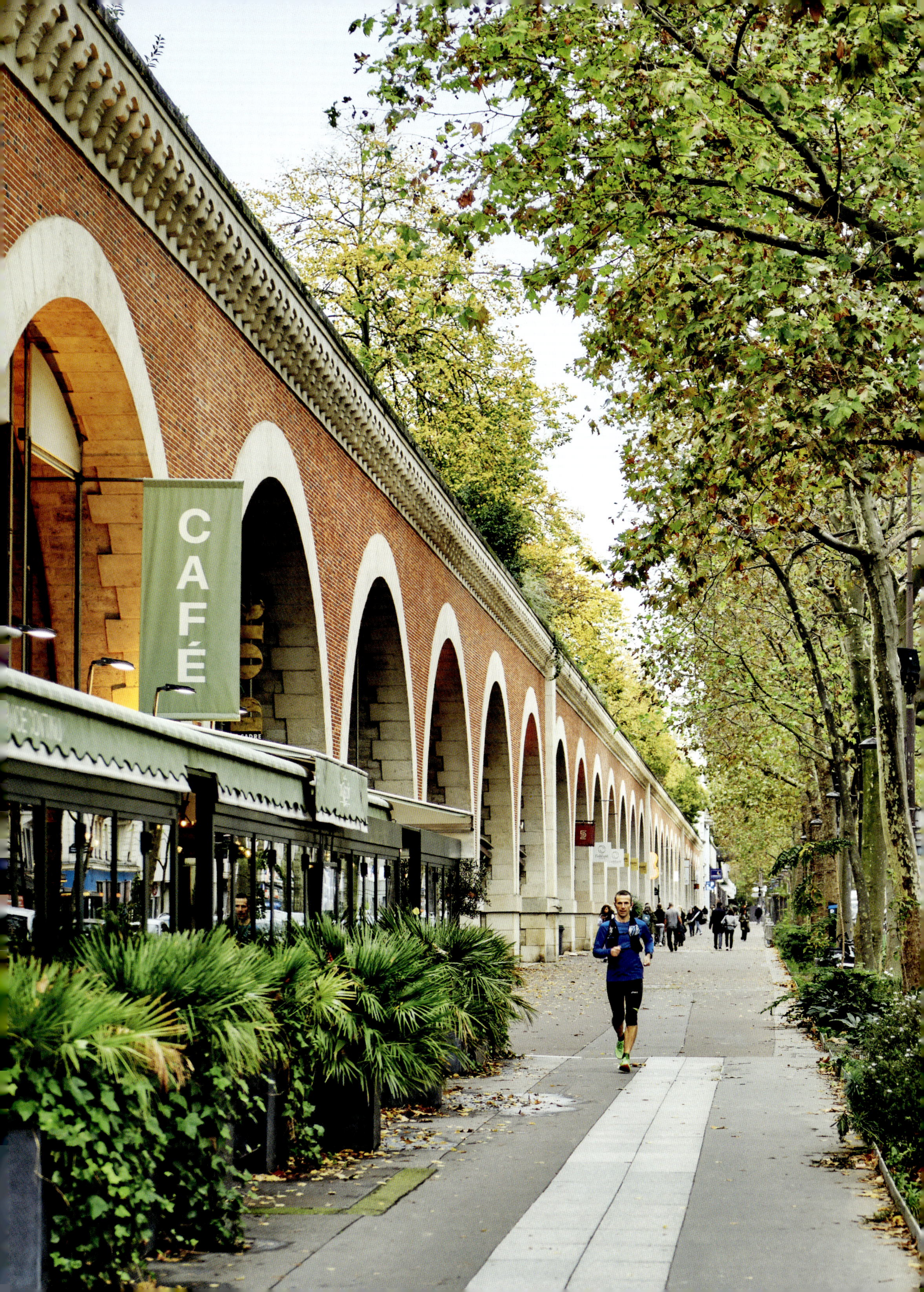

CAFÉ

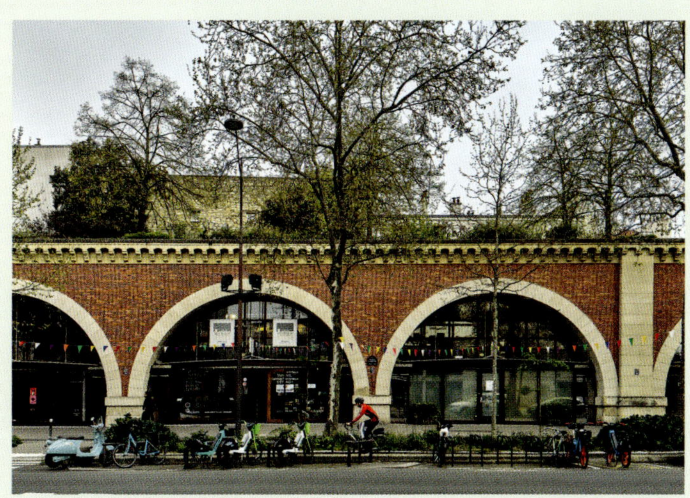

Sixty-two brick arches of the old railroad trestle now support the Viaduc des Arts, a collective of artisan studios and shops, as well as cafés and restaurants below, and the plantings of la coulée verte just over thirty-two feet above. Architect Patrick Berger worked with the owner, SEM Paris Commerces (formerly Semaest), to design the unique spaces.

## *Coulée Verte René-Dumont, La Promenade Plantée*
## The Green Corridor, A Promenade of Plants

### 12th Arrondisement
### 1987–1993

The 1993 opening of la coulée verte René-Dumont, also known as *la promenade plantée,* or the planted walkway, started a revolution. It was one of the first urban projects to transform an abandoned railway into a public park. The narrow corridor of plantings was commissioned by the City of Paris and designed by a team of architects led by Philippe Mathieux and landscape designer Jacques Vergely. The park begins above street level on the remaining structure of the early nineteenth-century Vincennes railway train trestle, near la place de la Bastille. The park descends to street level at le jardin de Reuilly. From there, other sections flow through the old train tunnels to where the path ends near le boulevard périphérique. Along the almost three-mile walkway, which is completely car free, there are varied types of garden design styles, from formal trellis work and a reflecting pond on the raised platform to the rose and vegetable gardens, a hedge maze alongside the path, and more ground cover on the lower sections. More than 150 different types of plants are grown on the path. Gardeners are constantly updating and maintaining the plants. Mathieux designed the outdoor furnishings, such as lighting, benches, garden sheds, and, at the terminus, a spiral staircase. The trees on the lower section, including the native European hop hornbeam, provide a lush, shaded respite to runners and walkers, while the upper sections give an intimate view of the neighborhoods that the park crosses over. Since the park's opening, the concept of converting a railway to a trail has spread to other countries throughout the world, including the United States, Spain, and New Zealand. The success of the design is how it connects the disparate elements of the neighborhood while creating a unified experience. There is a relationship with the cityscape, but also moments when the natural world seems to take over. On a hot summer day in August, walking through the shady park's green alleyway is a true pleasure.

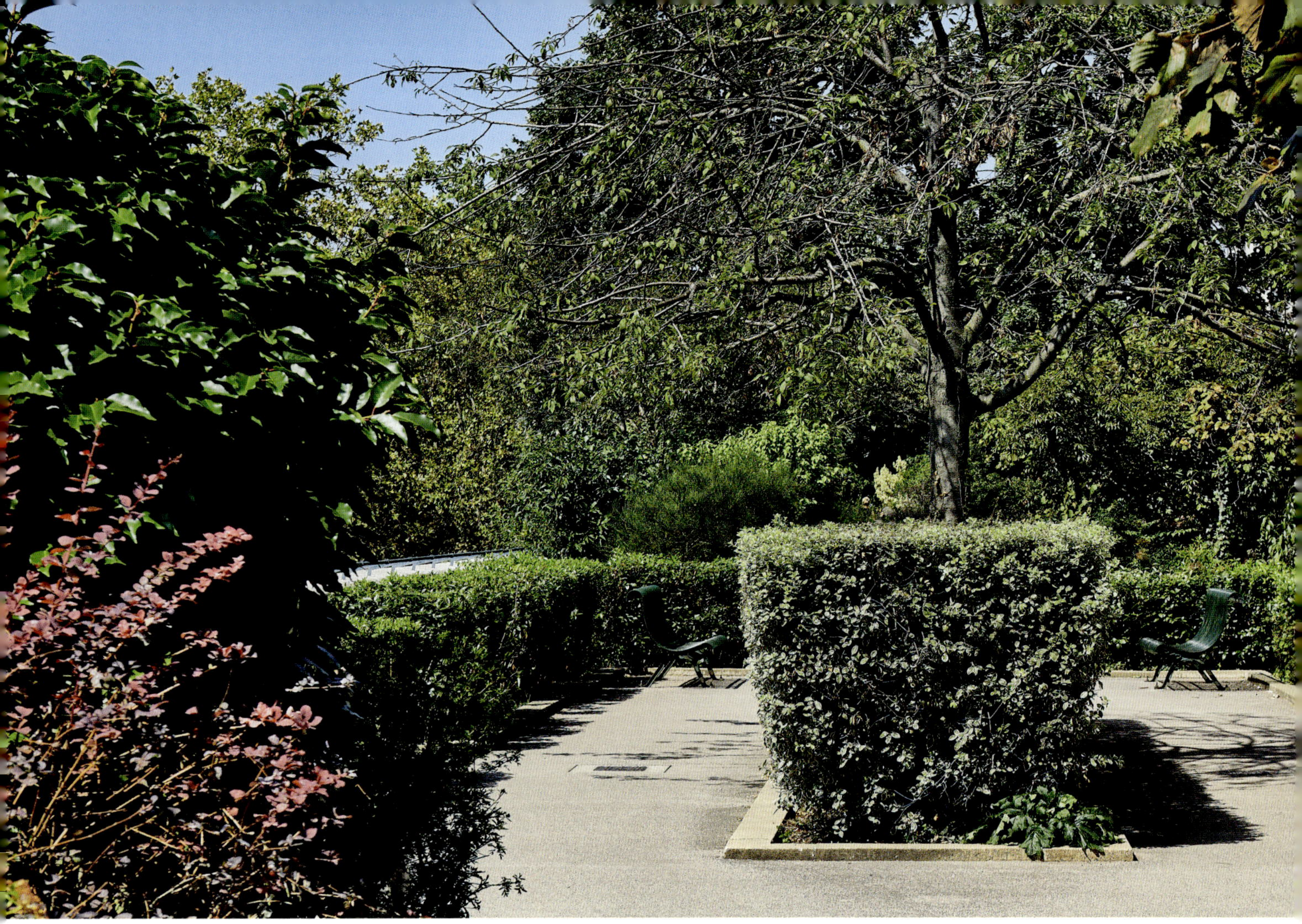

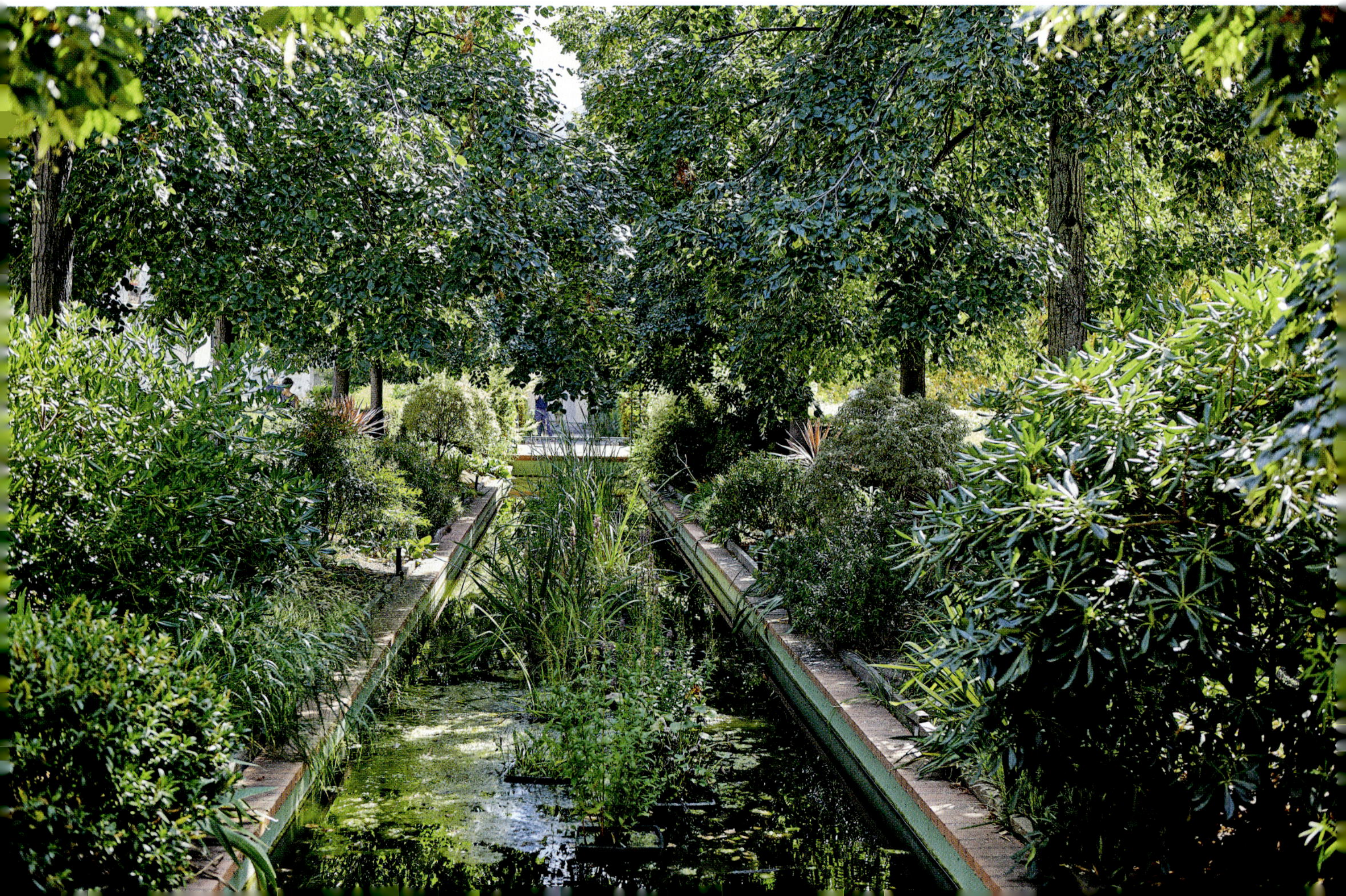

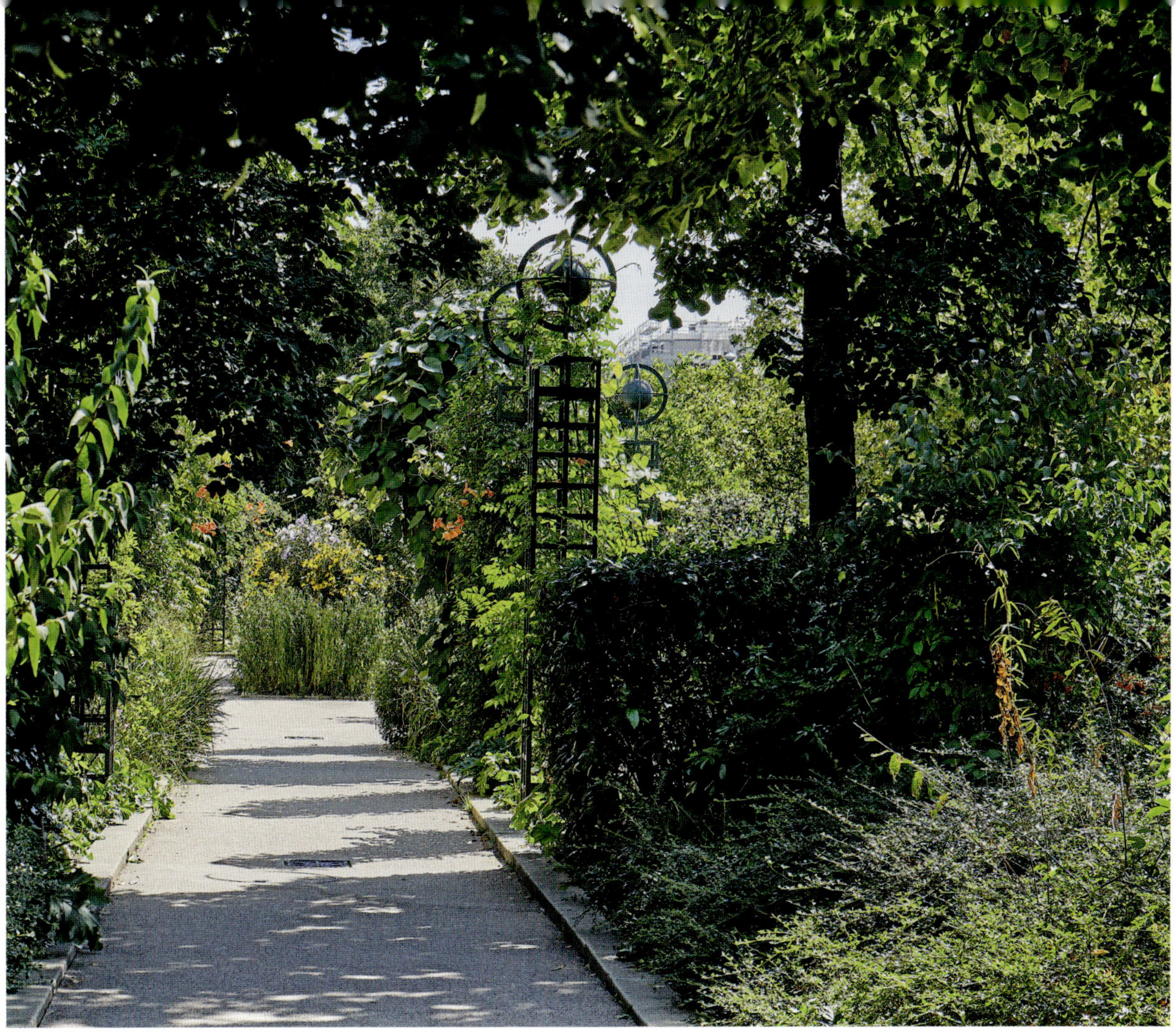

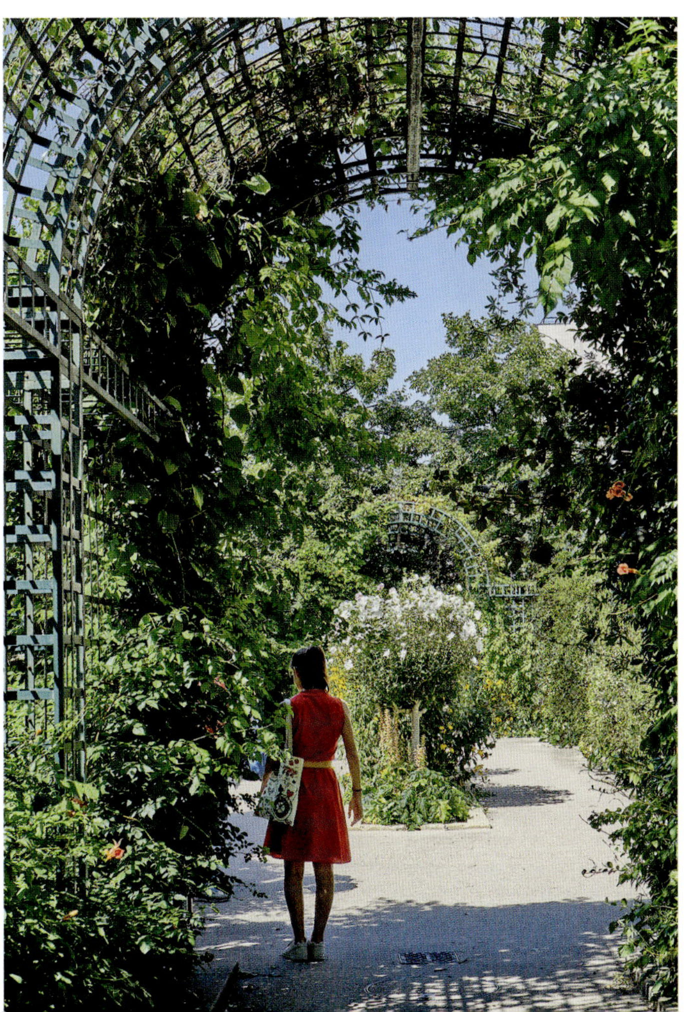

One elevated section of the park features metal archways where a variety of vines and climbing plants, including trumpet creeper vine, or *vigne trompette*, grow. In the center of the path are flower beds with acanthus and cornflowers, which are known as *la marguerite jaune*. Trimmed hedges and small trees are placed in other beds. The long, narrow brick-and-tile-lined reflecting pool is a water oasis and a visual refuge from the urbanscape. The shaded environment allows for cooler temperatures for the plants surrounding and in water, such as water lilies and grasses.

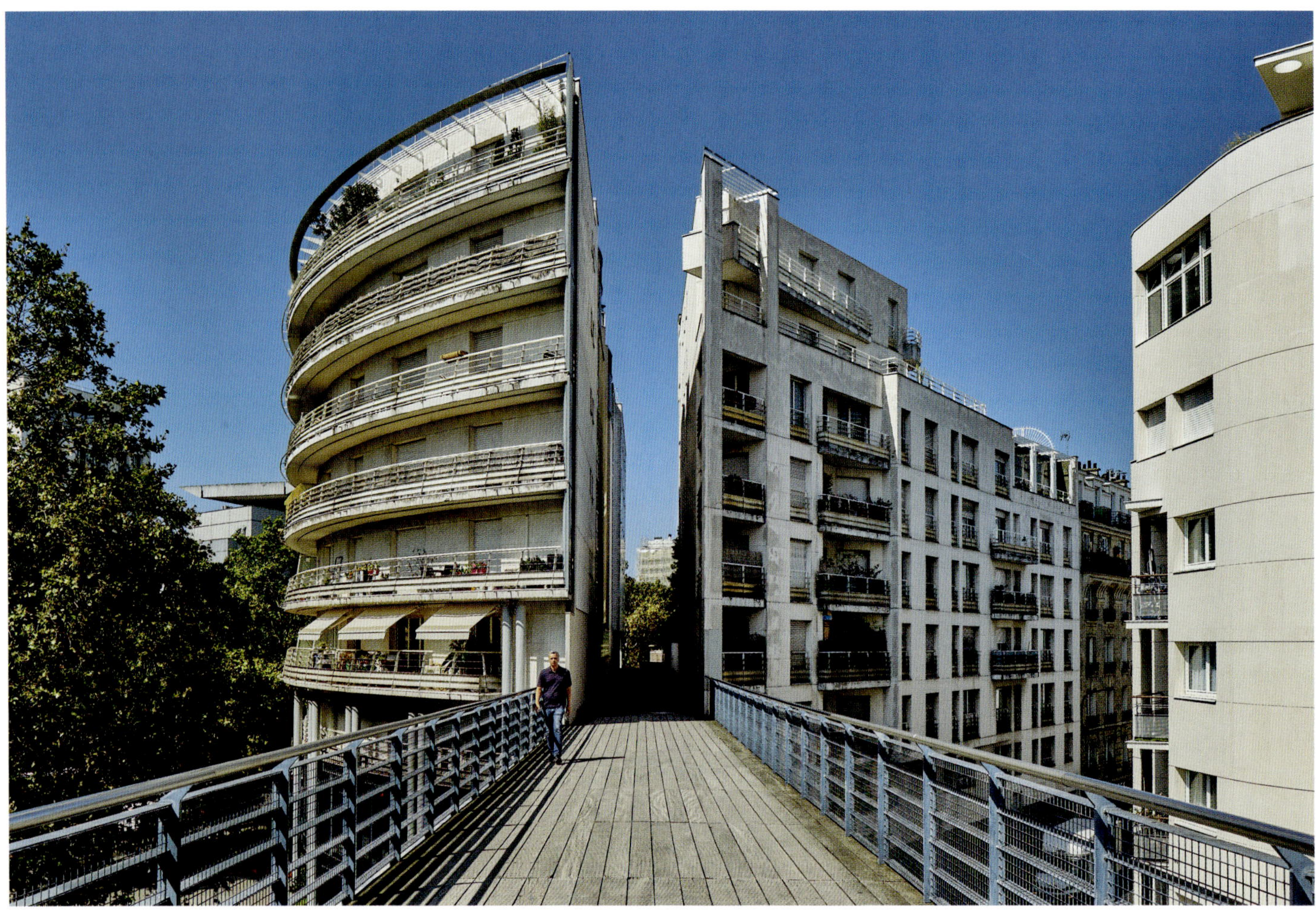

ABOVE
Two contemporary buildings intersect with the pathway of la coulée verte. Both were designed by the architects Wladimir Mitrofanoff, Le Cuong, and Rémi Las Fargeas. The first, a seven-story structure, is located at 147–149 Avenue Daumesnil and has two parts that appear to be split in half by the path. The curved façade faces one of the longest avenues in Paris. The flat side of each creates a corridor around the walkway's bridge over rue Montgallet and rue de Chareton.

RIGHT
Farther down the avenue, at the corner of rue Rambouillet, the old brick train trestle intersects with the new passageway, leading to the second modern addition to la coulée verte at 129 avenue Daumesnil. The 1995 building replaced a dilapidated section of the railway and became a connection point between old and new moments in time.

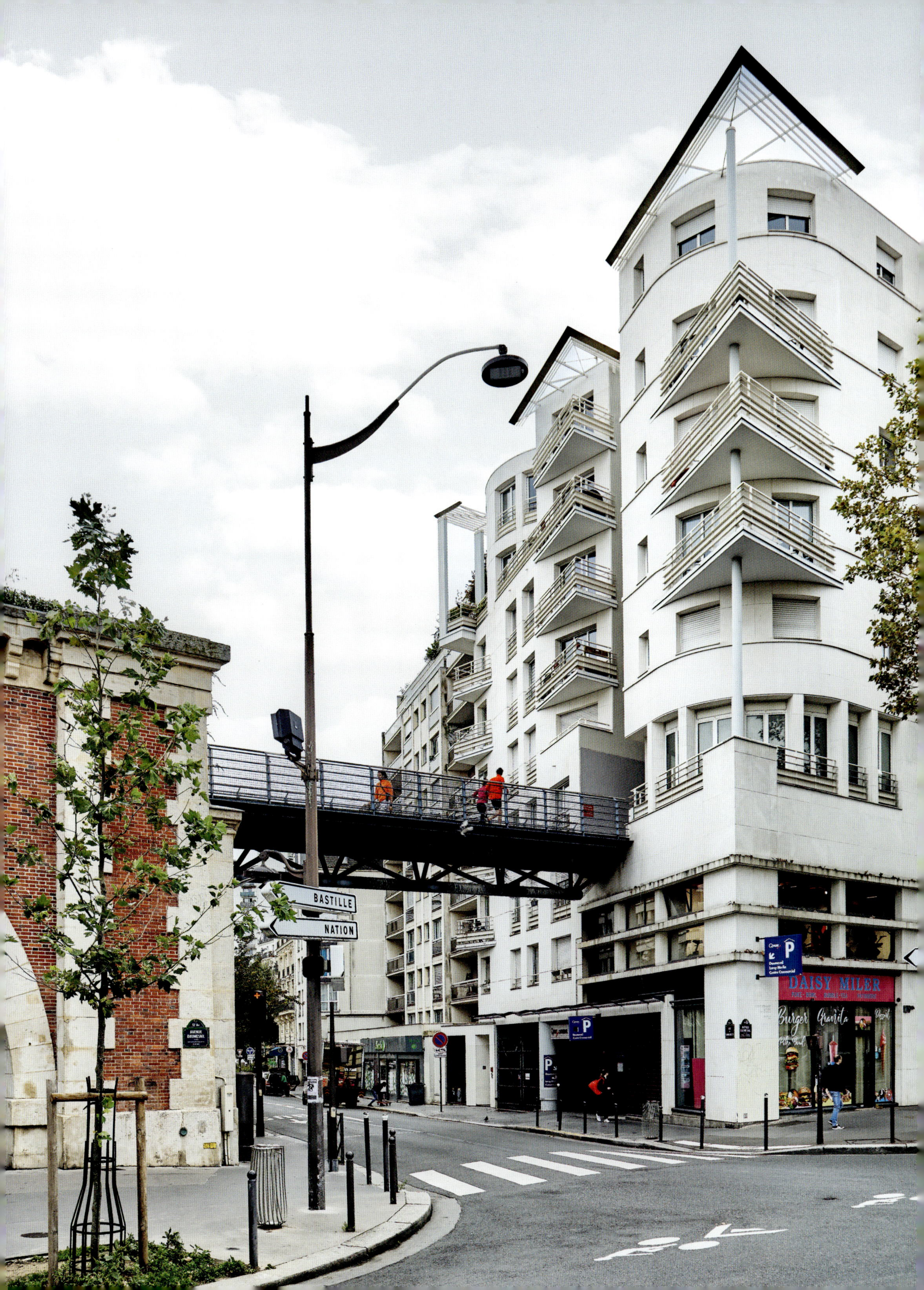
BASTILLE
NATION
AVENUE DAUMESNIL
DAISY MILER
Burger  Granita
P

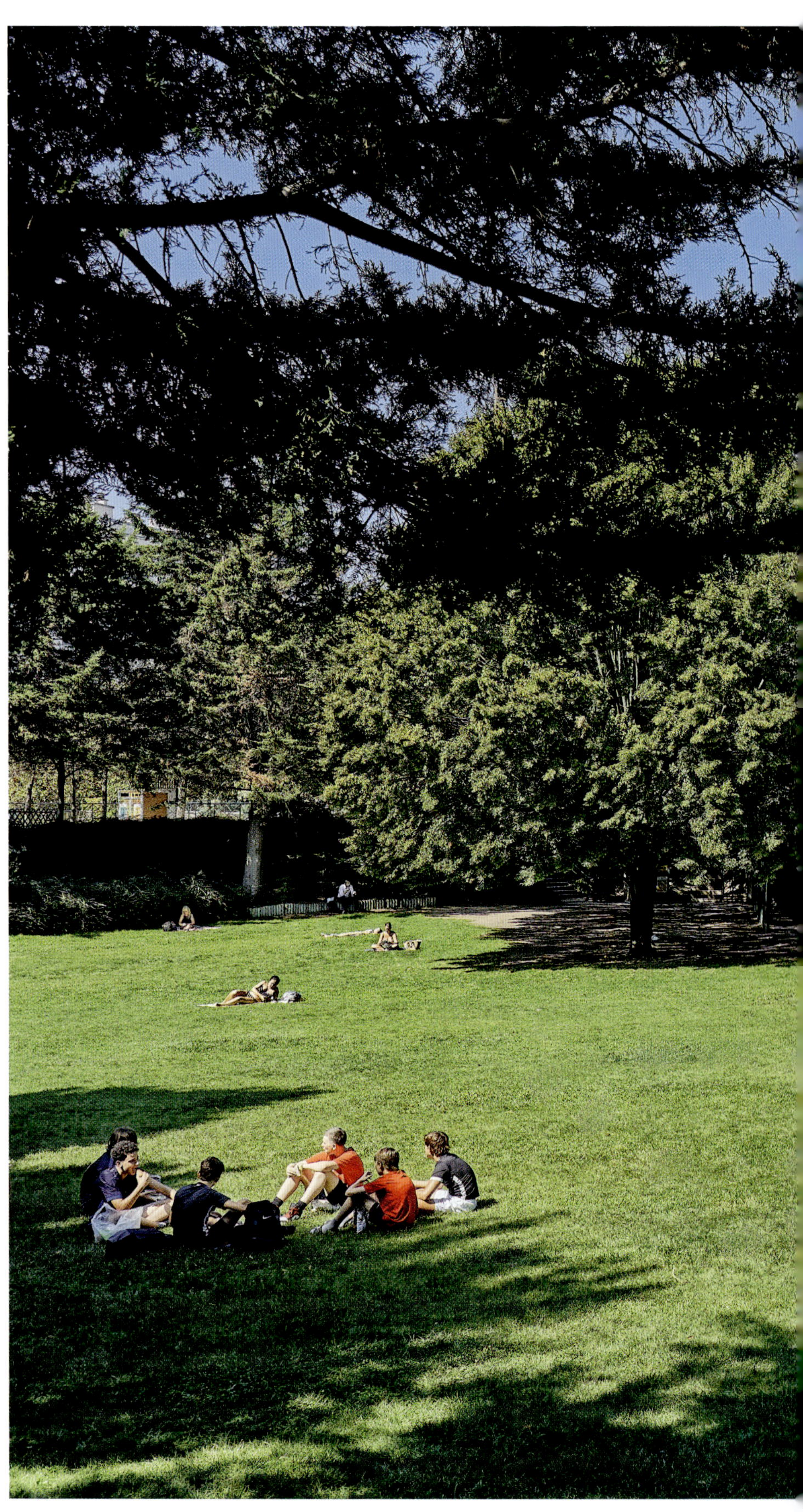

Jardin de Reuilly–Paul-Pernin was built
in five years, between 1993 and 1998.
It is located between the Viaduc des
Arts and l'allée Vivaldi, where la coulée
verte descends from the railway bridges
to street level. A curved suspended
footbridge passes over its open lawn,
where visitors gather to relax and picnic
on the grass.

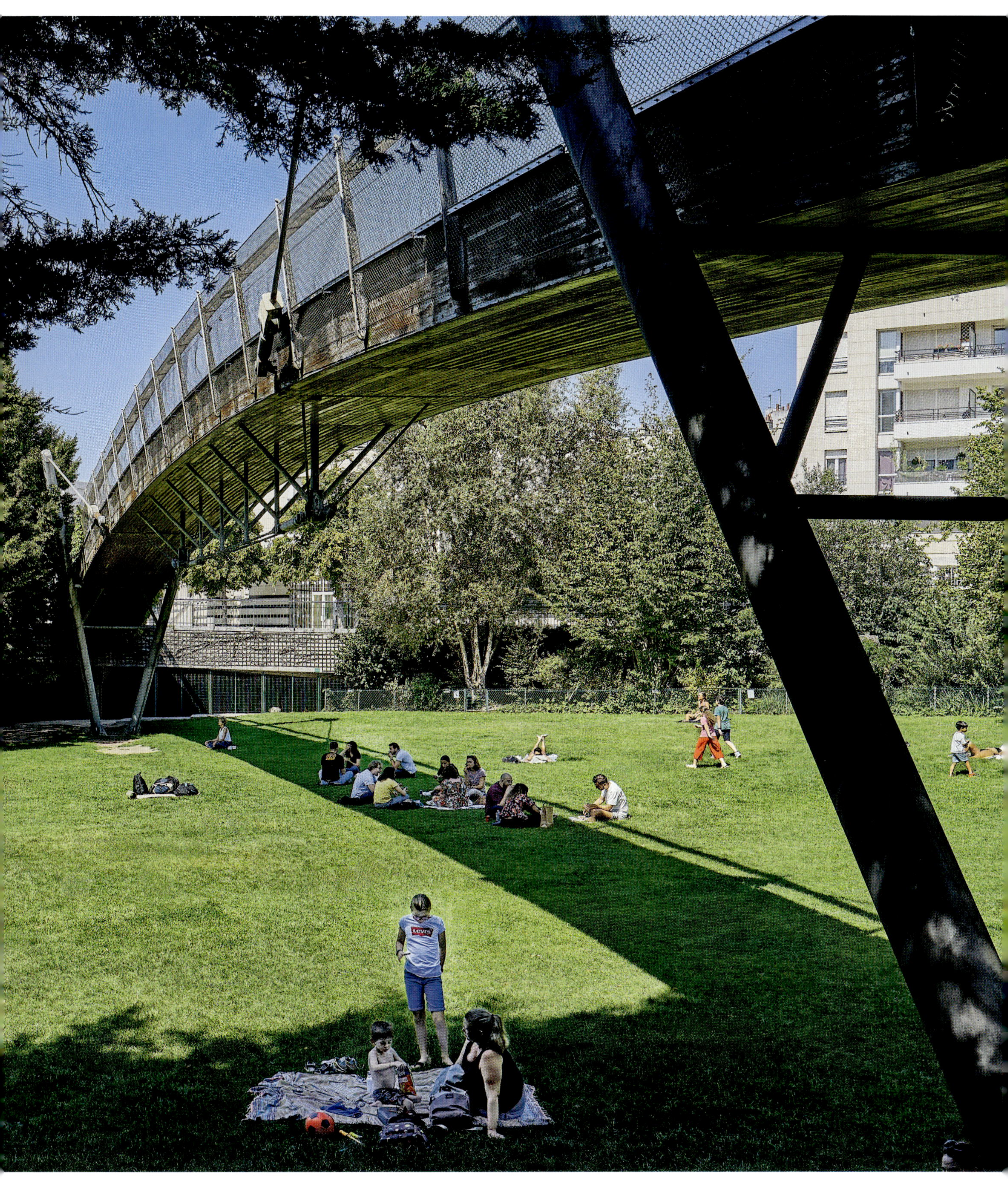

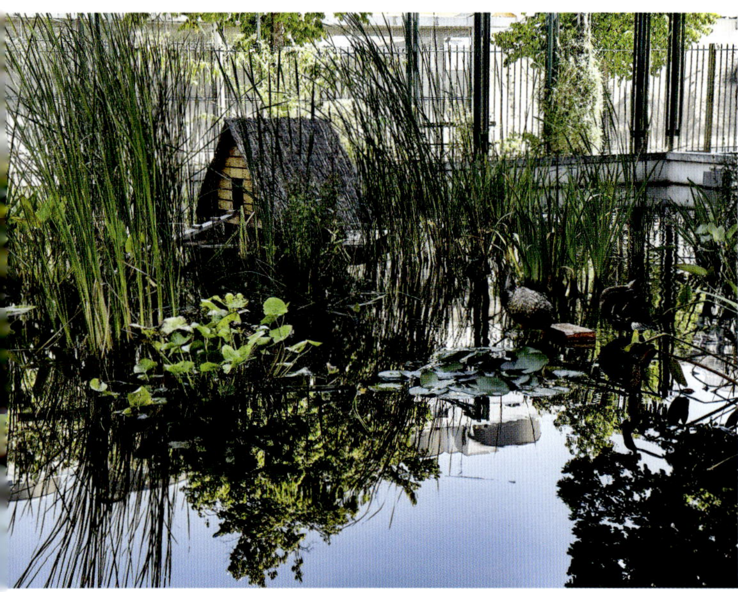

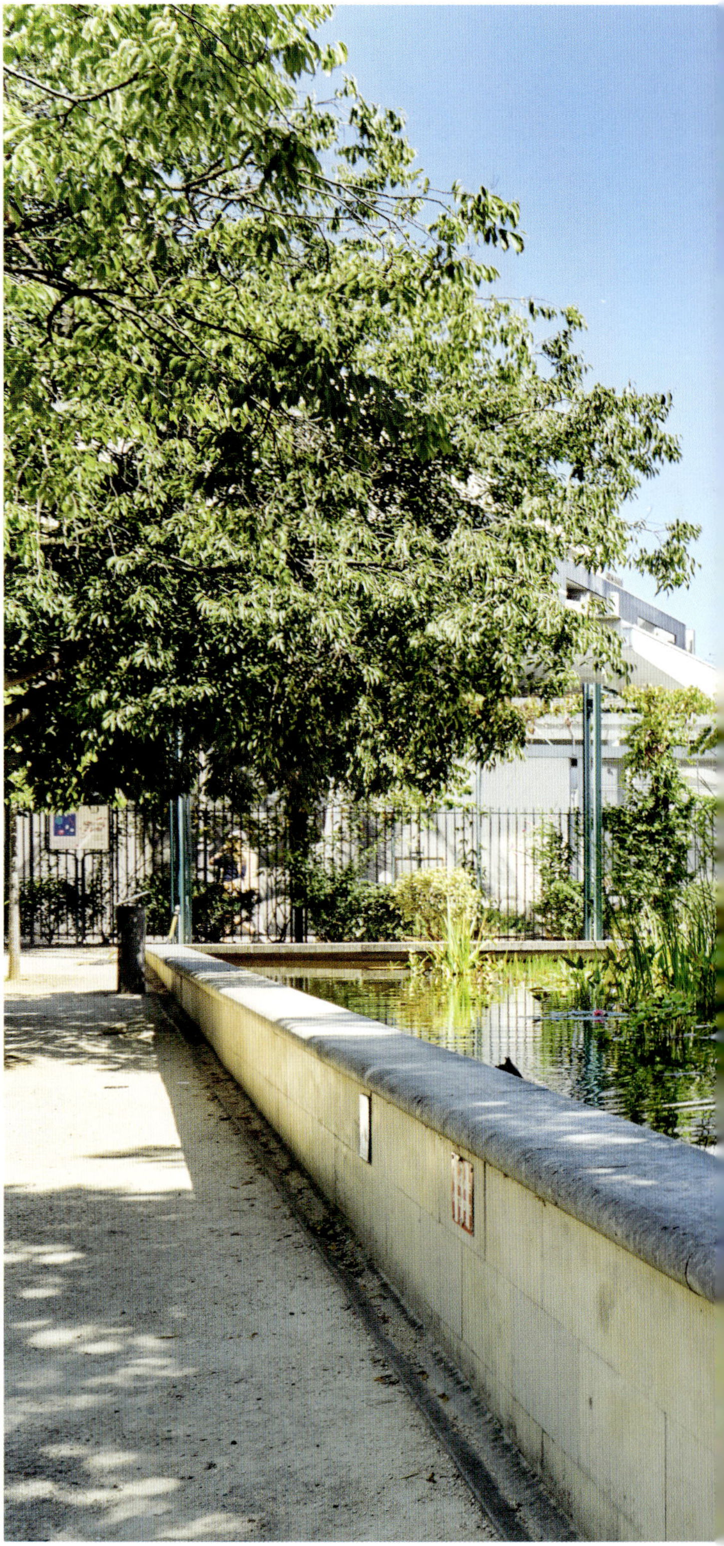

Close by the lawn at jardin de Reuilly, there are playgrounds and an indoor swimming center. A protected habitat for ducks and other waterfowl is near the basketball courts. The pond's ecosystem also includes *aselles aquatiques,* a type of lily pad.

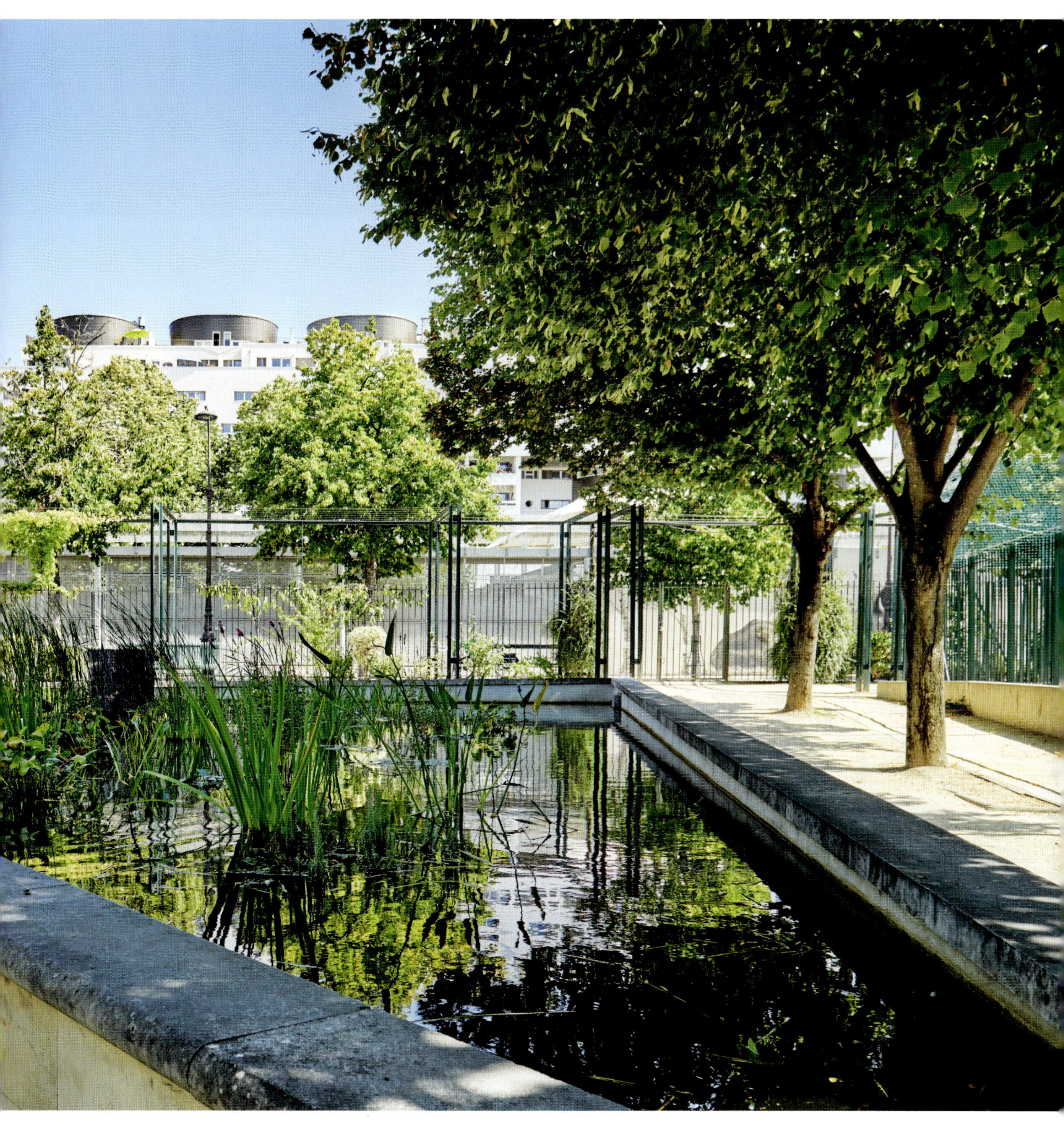

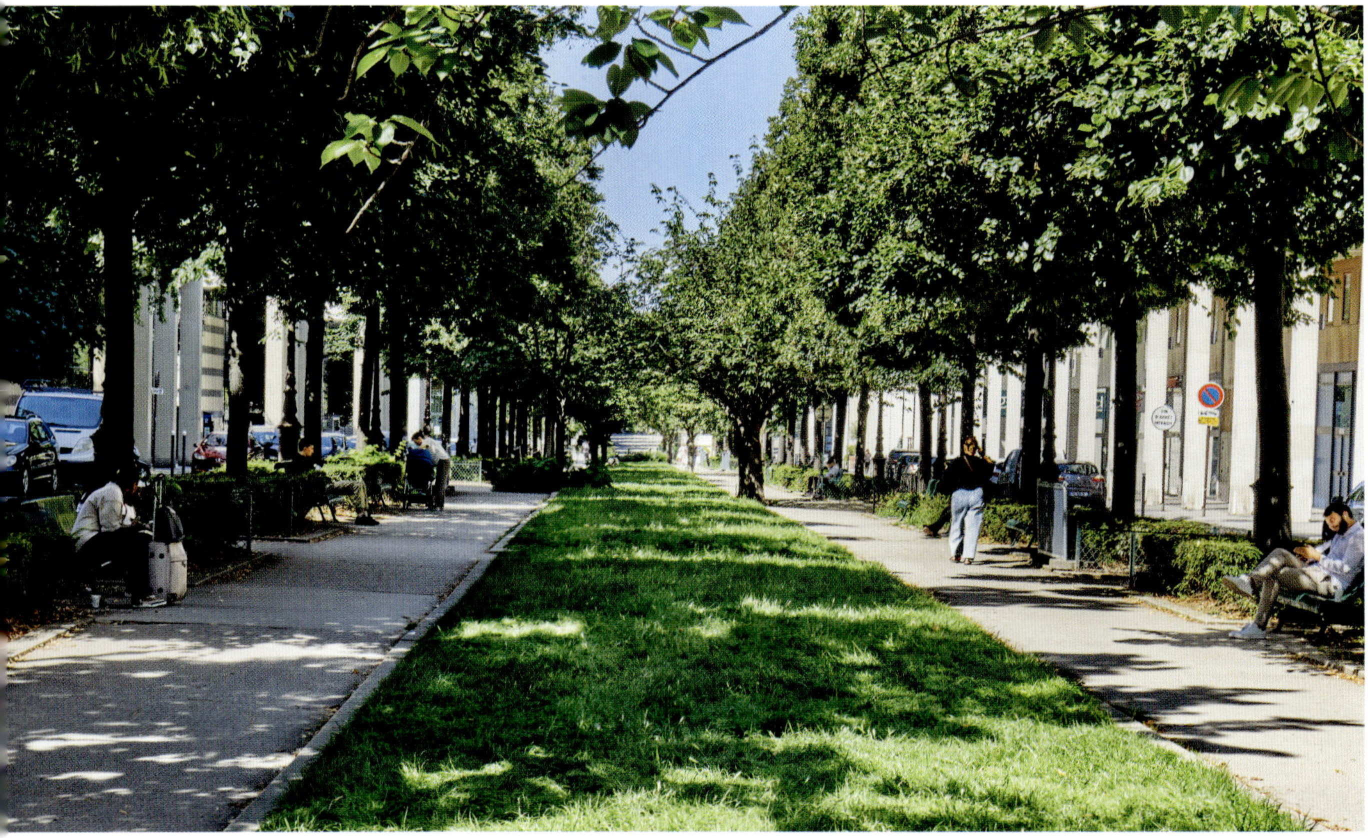

**ABOVE**

Built in the 1980s, allée Vivaldi, named for the Italian composer Antonio Vivaldi, has a border of symmetrically placed trees with center beds of grass. On either side of the alley are rows of modern commercial buildings and roads. This part of la coulée verte is very structured, which is a contrast to the verdant overgrown sections. The alley connects two sectors of the park, le jardin de Reuilly and the paths leading to the train tunnels. The alley of trees gives a feeling of enclosure, leading the walker into or away from the tunnels.

**RIGHT**

Artist Caroline Laguerre's graphic art in red, yellow, and blue acrylic paints is a tribute to dogs.

**OPPOSITE**

Laguerre was commissioned by the mayor's office of the 12th arrondissement to make paintings on the barricades that divide the walkway. This piece is titled *Timelapse*.

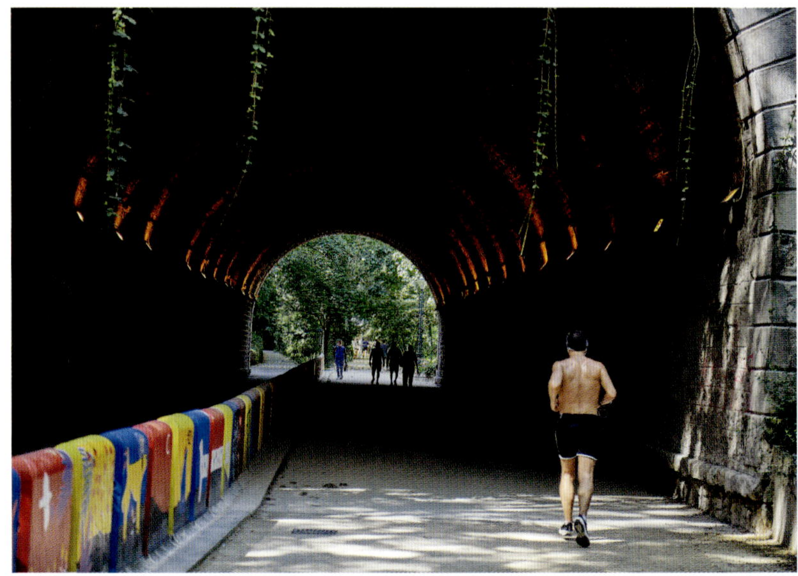

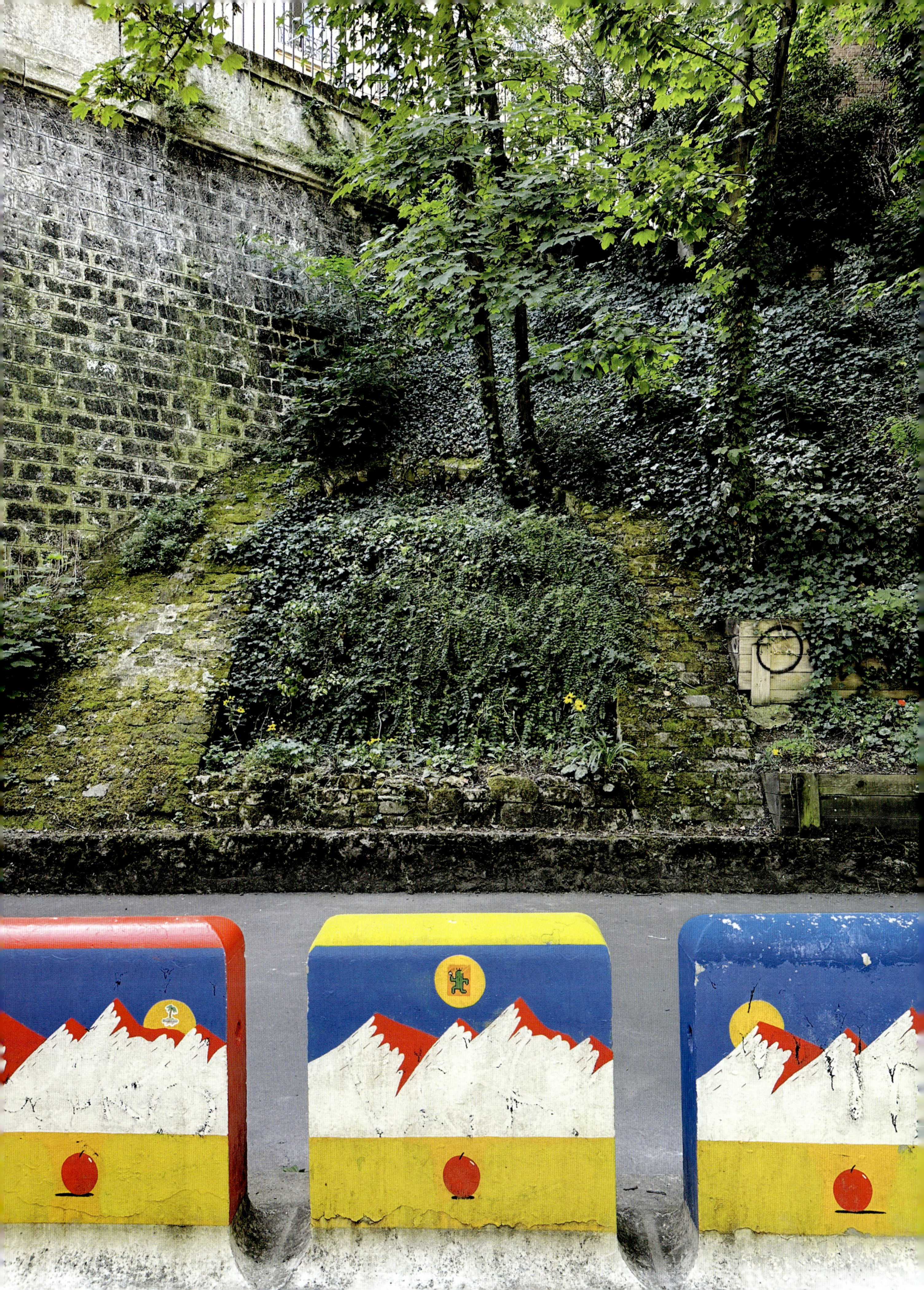

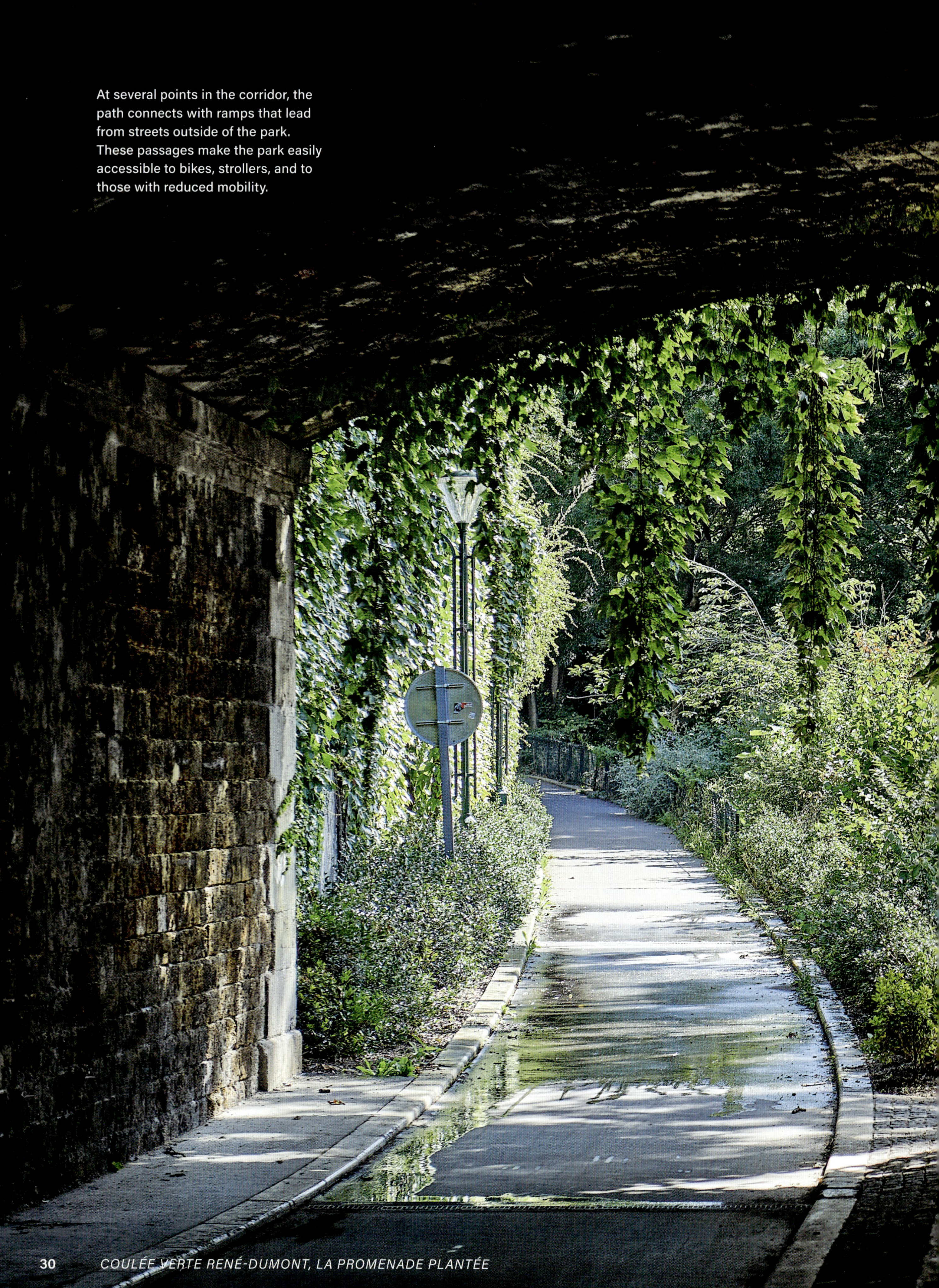

At several points in the corridor, the path connects with ramps that lead from streets outside of the park. These passages make the park easily accessible to bikes, strollers, and to those with reduced mobility.

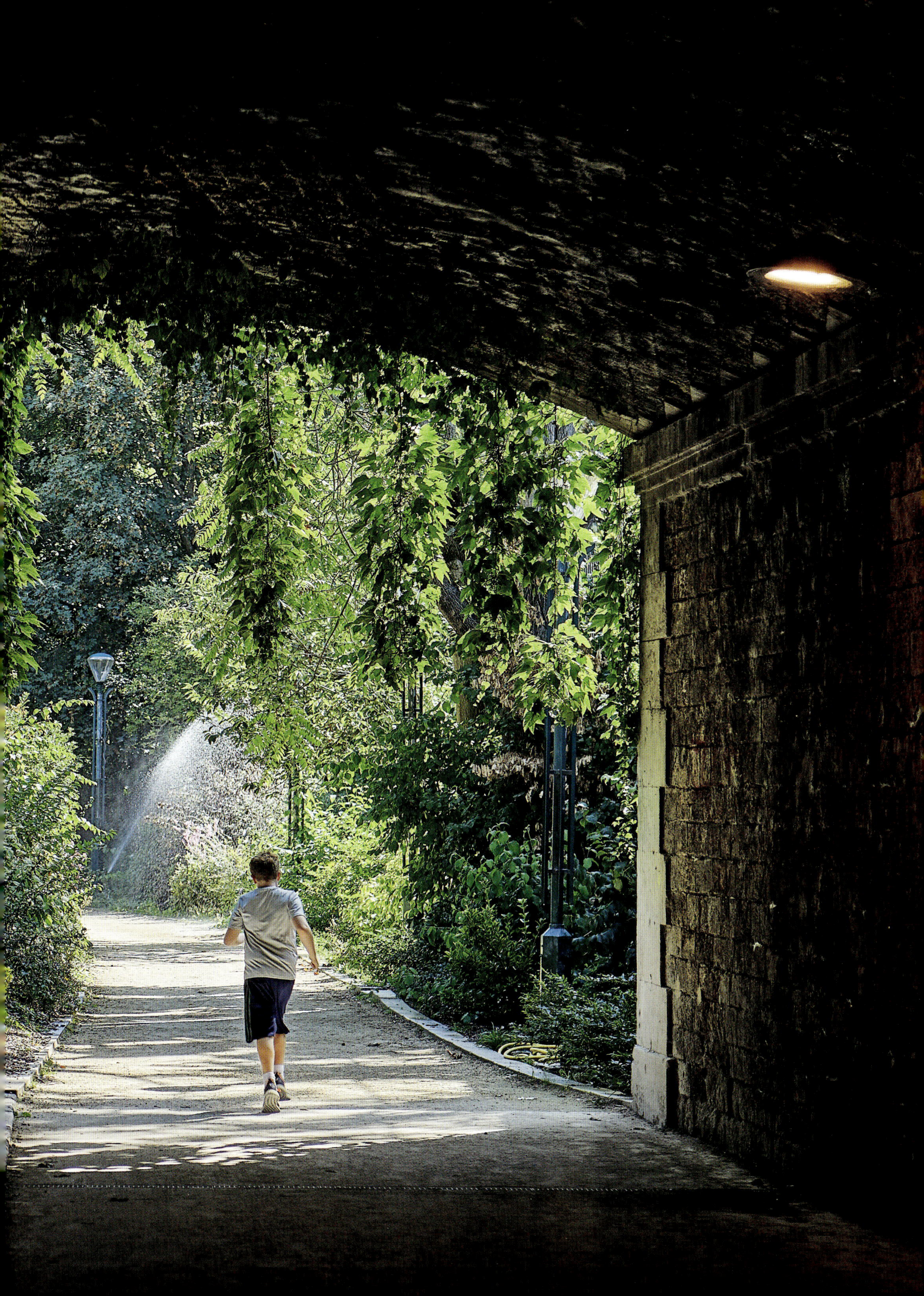

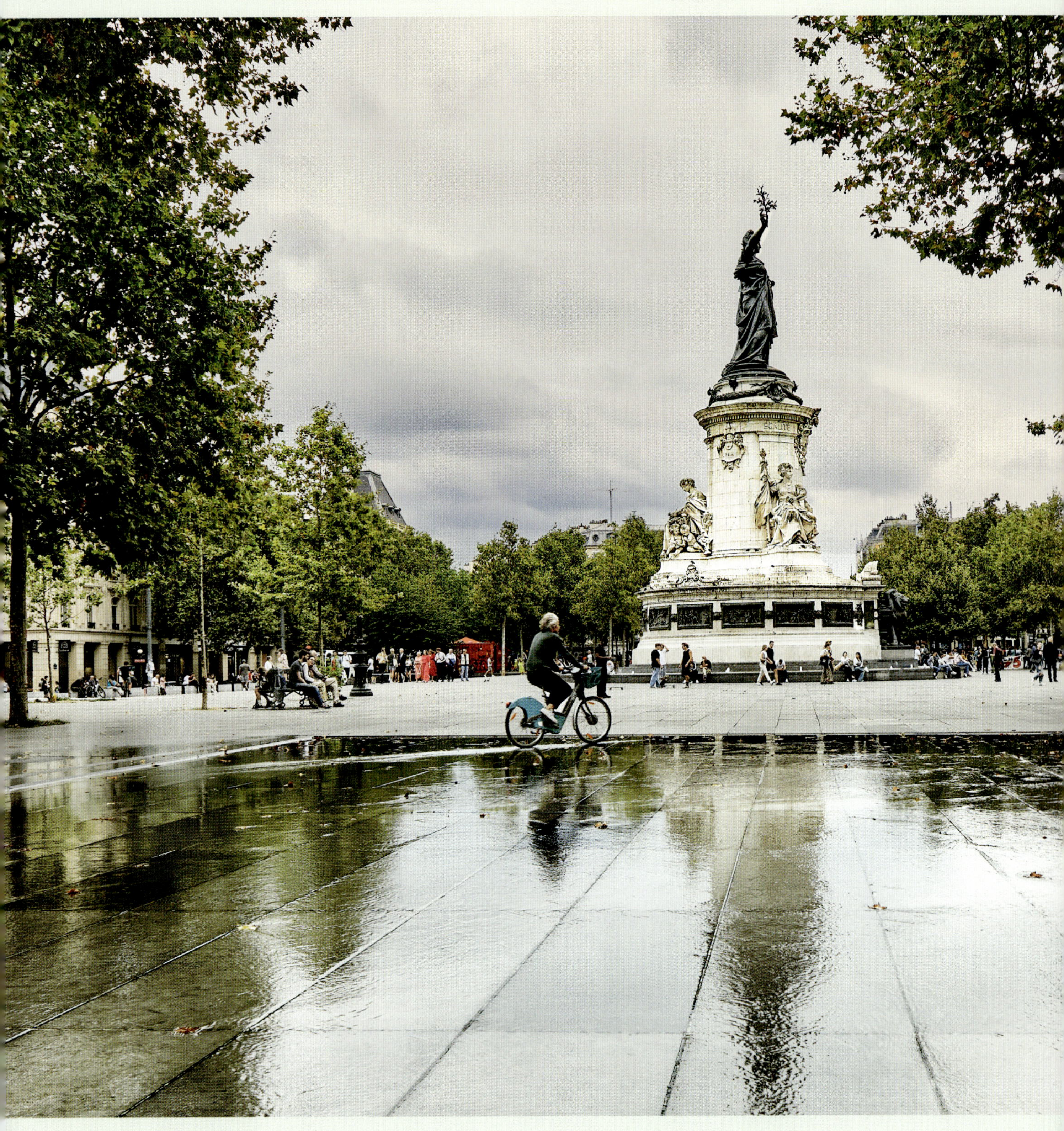

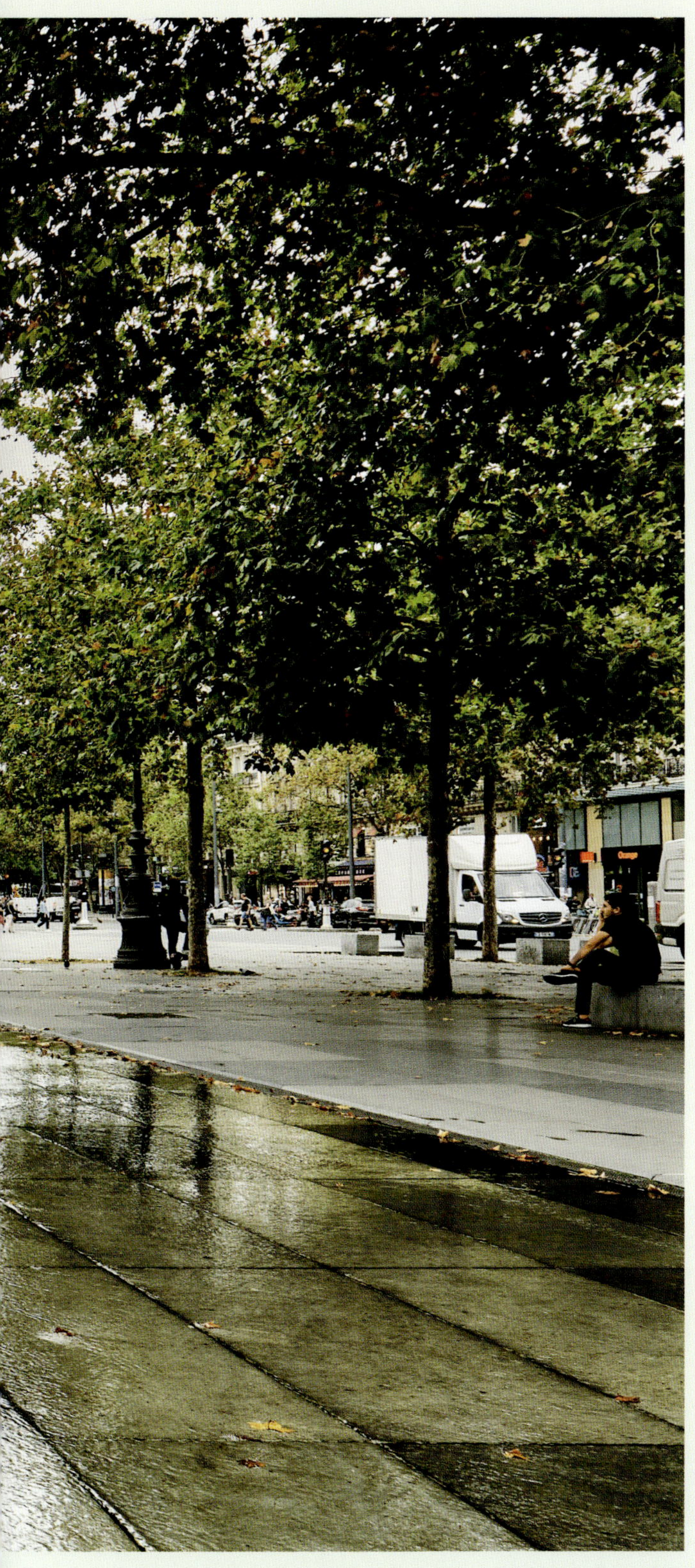

A cyclist rides across the shallow reflecting pool at la place de la République. The nineteenth-century Monument à la République still stands in the center of the square.



## *Place de la République*
3rd, 10th, and 11th arrondissements
1879, latest redesign in 2013

La place de la République has always been a gathering place: a place to protest, a place to mourn, a place to celebrate—a hub of activity. The square exists on the edges of three neighborhoods, or *arrondissements*. Before it was created and officially named in 1879, a fountain provided water to the cattle going to the slaughterhouse nearby. The large square was part of Baron Haussmann's plan to build open areas and expand the city beyond its center. The fountain was replaced with the Monument à la République, represented by a young woman, Marianne. It was later centered between two streets that bisected the long rectangular place. In modern times, place de la République developed into a public transportation tangle of subway lines below ground. Above ground, the square became known for the traffic that whirled around the monument. In 2013, the French architecture and urban design firm TVK was commissioned to rethink the site with pedestrians in mind and with the objective to diminish the role of cars. Streets on both sides of the monument were closed and incorporated into the walkable areas. Additional honey locust and plane trees were planted. Benches were placed under the newly planted trees. A pavilion with glass walls and a reflecting pool was built on one end. The new design encourages the public to stop and take in the open space. It's possible to cross the square on foot, on bicycle, or on scooter. More than ten years after the redesign, la place de la République continues to offer a shady respite and place for reflection.

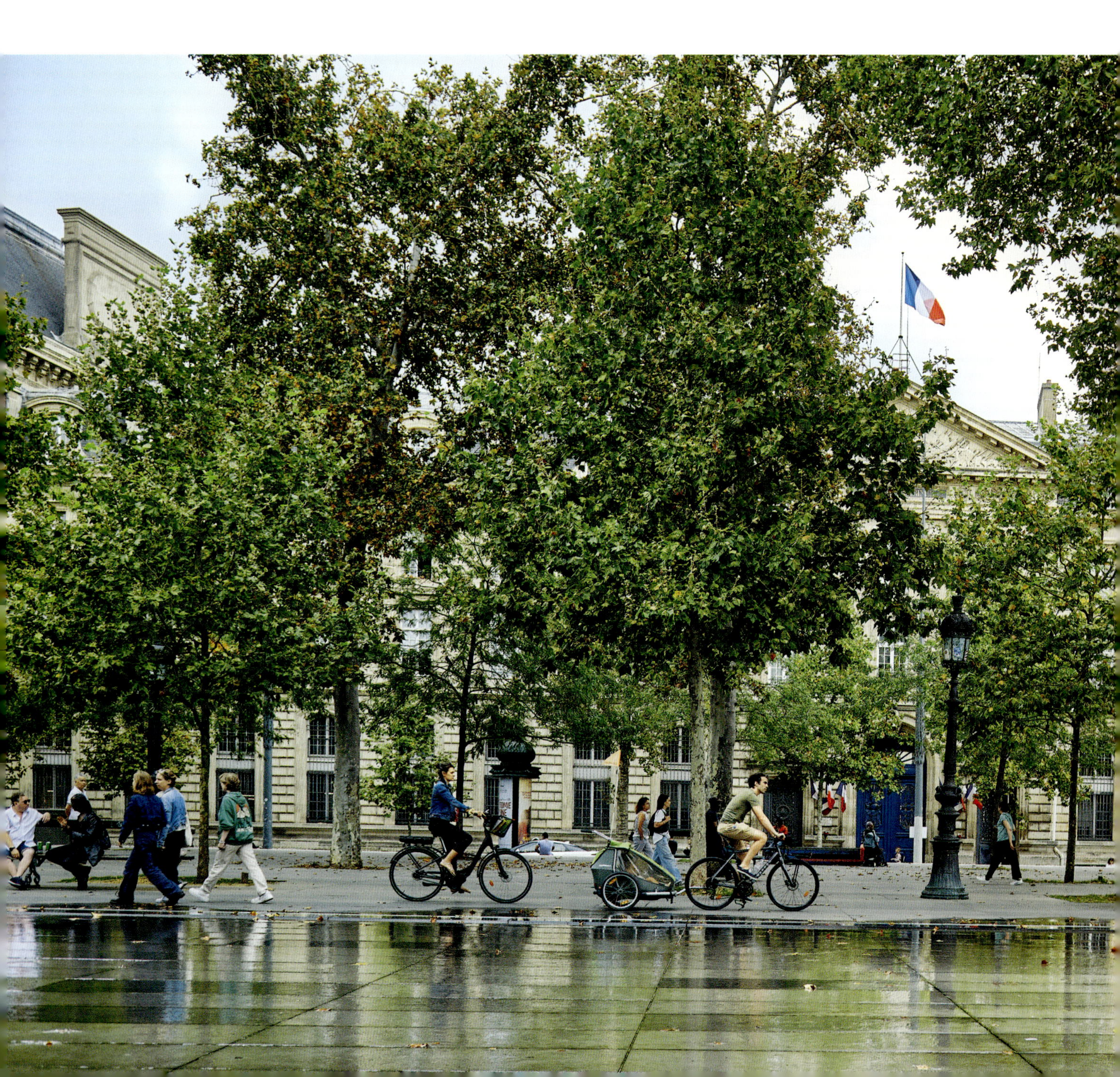

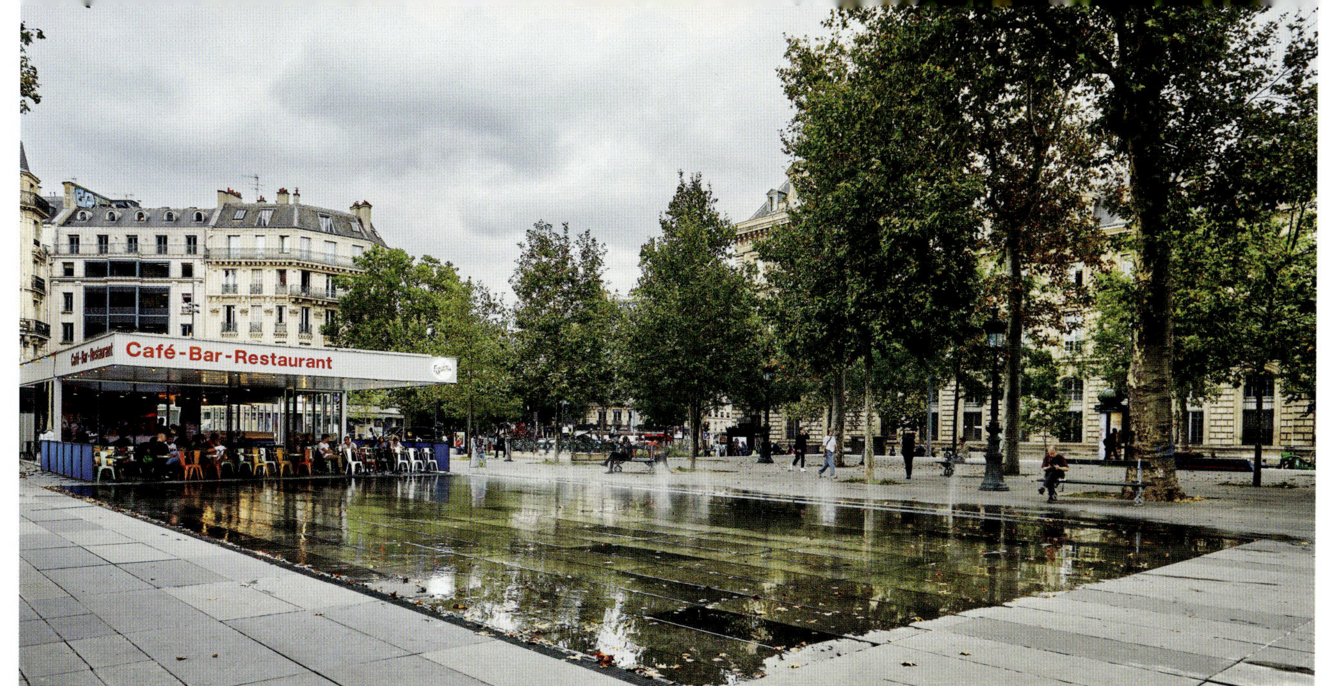

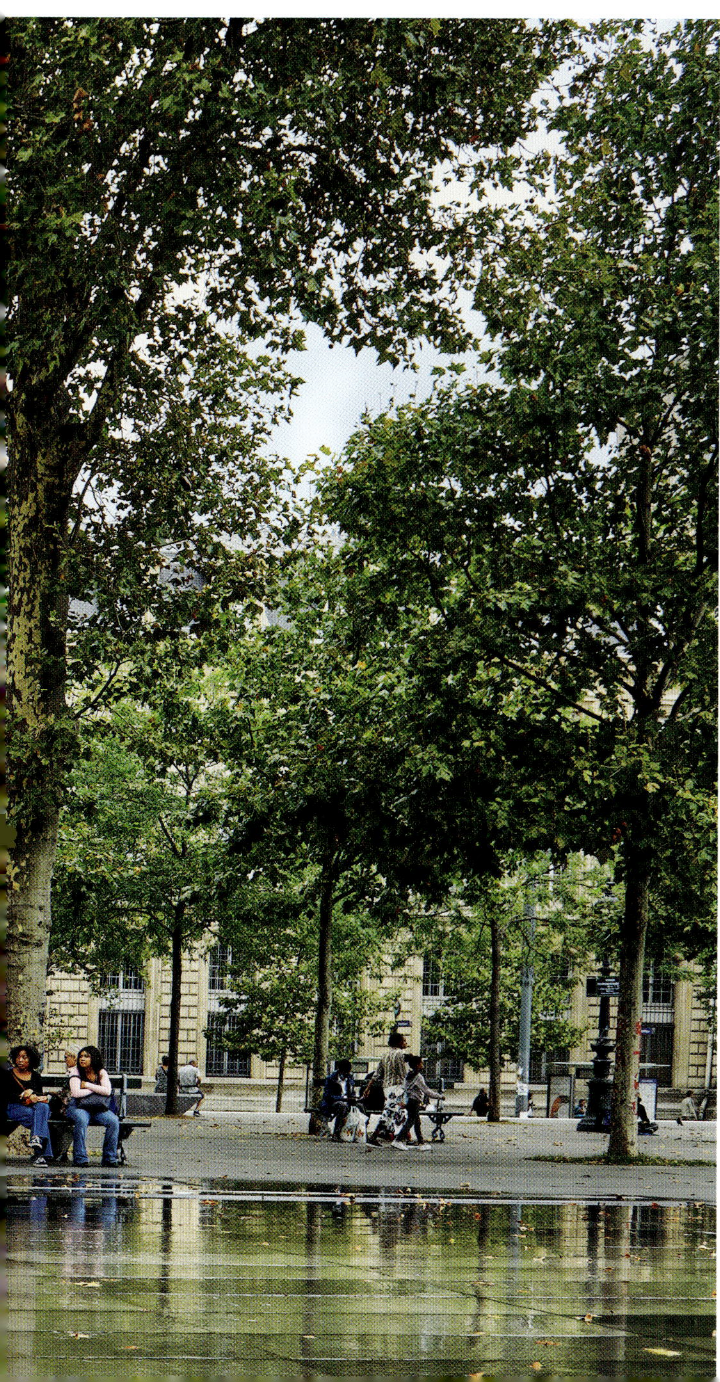



**LEFT**
More than 150 trees are planted on the square, providing shade against the background of la caserne Vérines, a former miliary barracks that once housed 3,200 soldiers.

**ABOVE**
At times, the multipurpose pavilion has been a café, a bar, a restaurant, and an event space. After the 2015 terrorist attacks in Paris, the pavilion was renamed after the city's Latin motto, Fluctuat Nec Mergitur, which means "it is tossed by the waves but does not sink." In good weather, tables and chairs are placed under the cantilever roofline and around the exterior glazed-glass side walls.

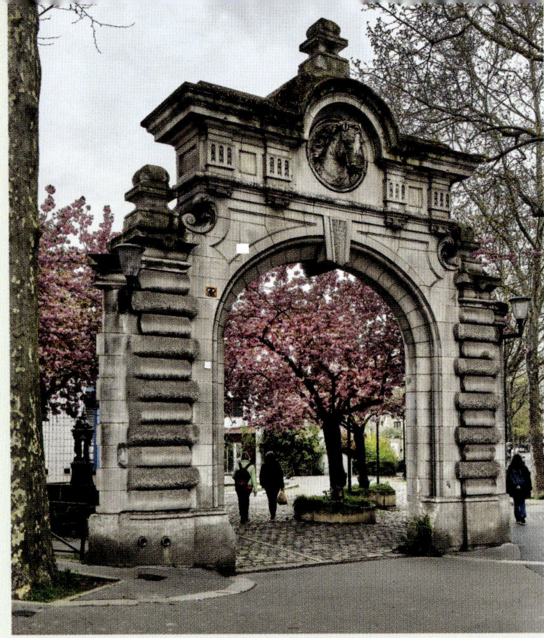

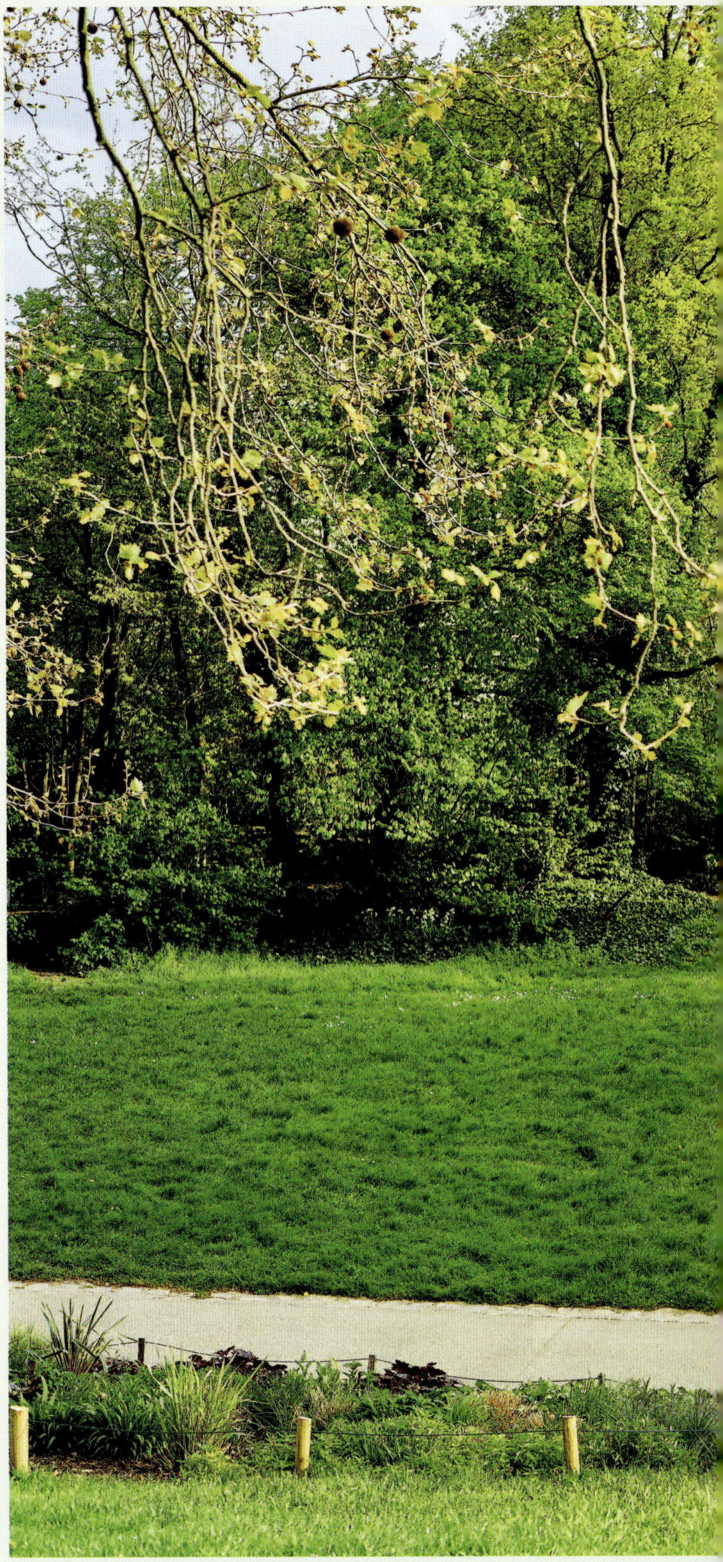

## Parc Georges-Brassens
15th arrondissement
1982, redesign completed in 2023

There's a stone arch near la rue Brancion that marks one entrance of the newly updated parc Georges-Brassens, which is named for the singer and poet who lived nearby on rue Santos-Dumont. Centered at the top, above the keystone, is a horse's head—soot accentuates its sculptured shape and adds to its animation. The arch shows its age and gives a clue to the park's past use as a horse and fish market as well as a slaughterhouse. The steel, wood, and glass structure of the horse market stalls still stands, as does the bell tower of the fish market. Only now, the nineteenth-century marketplace is used for a different type of product; on weekends, tables are set up to sell rare and old books. Wide grass lawns surround the paved pathways of the bell tower and the new basin. The hillsides of the park are wilder—a forest of trees and dense scrubs feel overgrown—but in fact they are well kept. Pathways meander through these sections. Upon a glance upward, contemporary buildings are not far away; they frame the perimeter. Long ago, before the Vaugirard slaughterhouses, and before the neighborhood attracted artists (such as Marc Chagall and Chaïm Soutine, among others who lived nearby in the artists' studios known collectively as The Beehive), vineyards grew. Today, vines that were planted in the 1980s grow pinot noir grapes for wine produced by Clos des Morillons. There are plans to connect parc Georges-Brassens to the Petite Ceinture, which is a few blocks away from the current park's edge, adding to the continuum of green spaces around Paris.

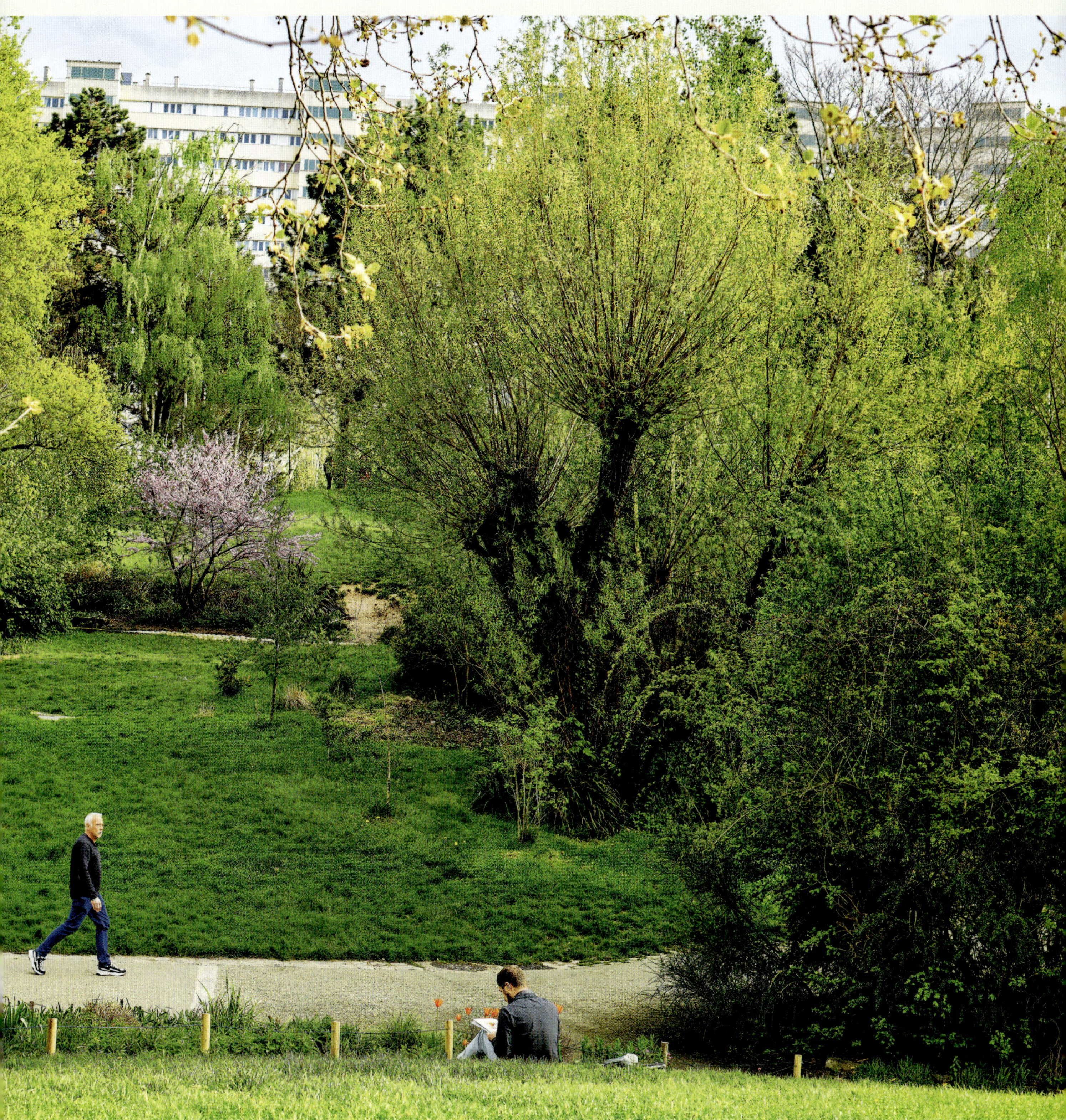

**ABOVE**
The nine-hectare (or twenty-two-acre)
park has a varied landscape, from open
lawns to wooded sections.

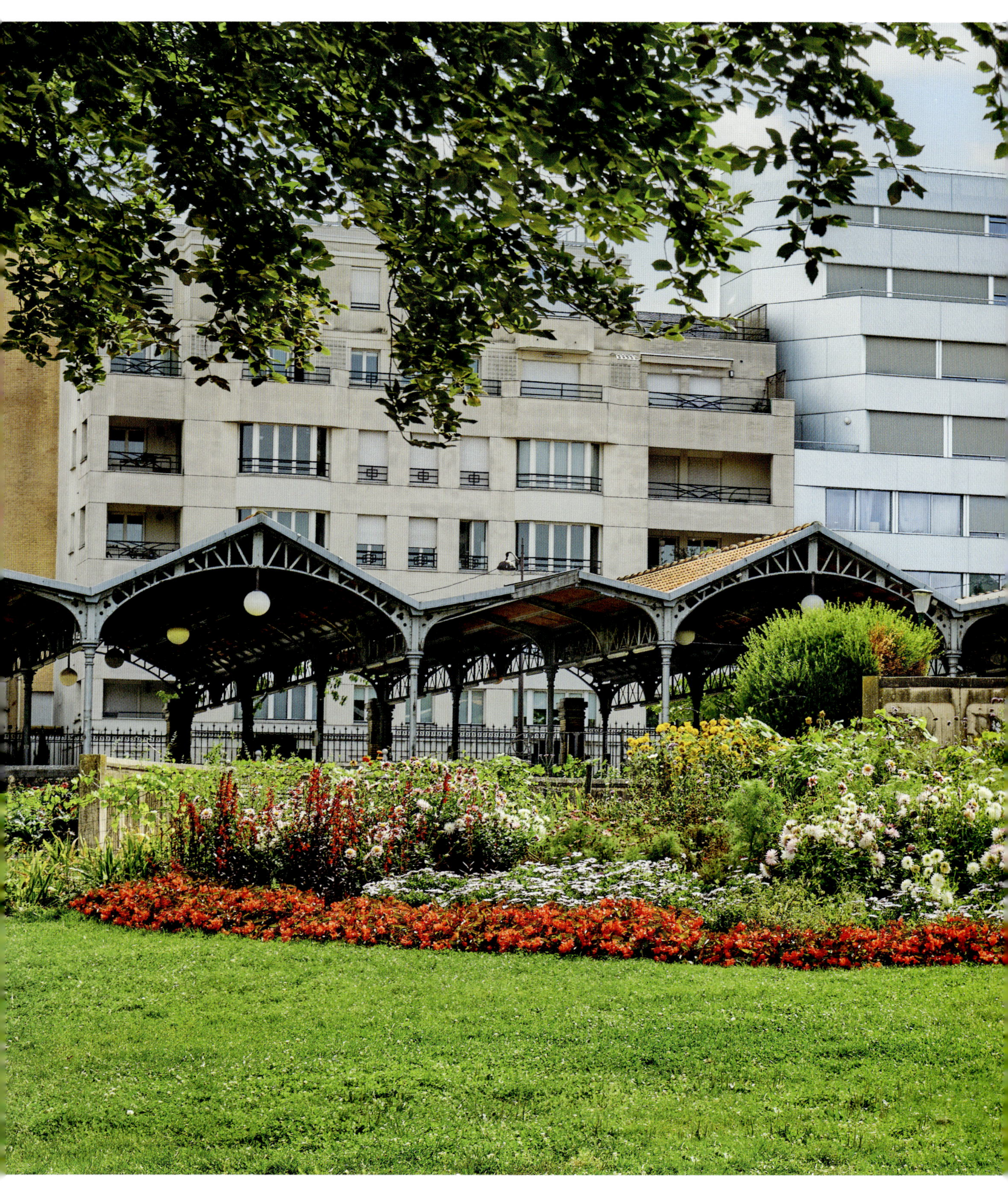

  PARC GEORGES-BRASSENS

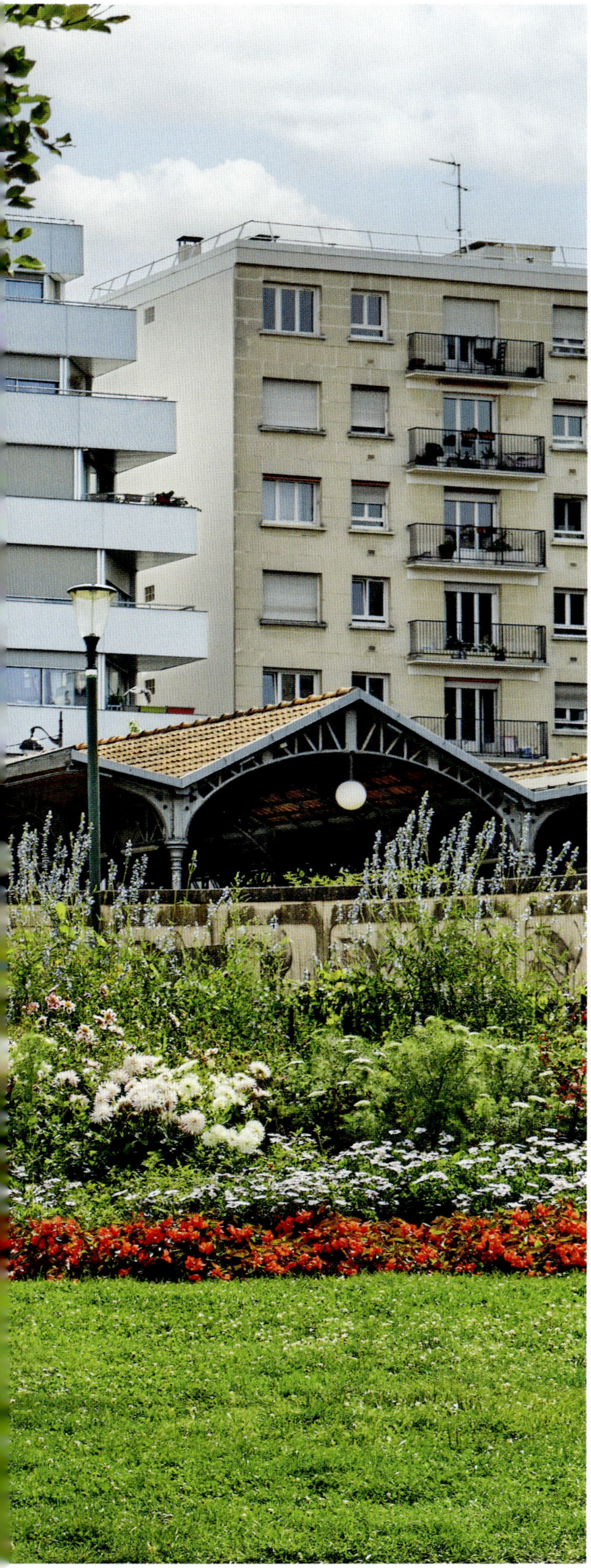

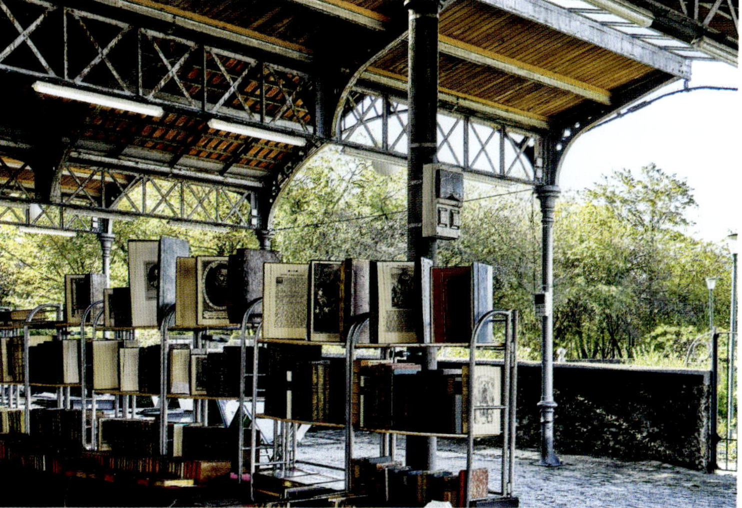

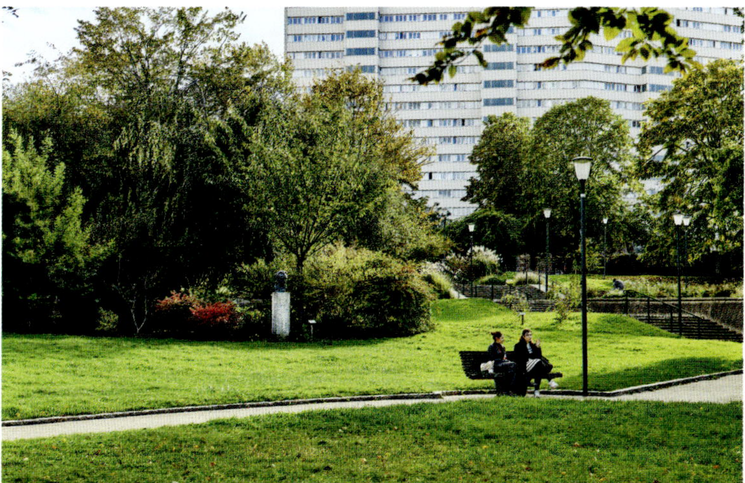

LEFT
New apartment buildings serve as a
backdrop to the old horse market, or
*halle aux chevaux*, at the side entrance
of the park. The open pavilion is made
of a series of pitched, tiled roof lines that
extends down the block. Mixed beds,
planted with flowers in various heights
and colors, divide the marketplace from
the lawns of the park.

TOP
On Sundays, an antique book *marché*
is set up under the wooden ceiling
of the nineteenth-century cast-iron
structure. Books are displayed on tables
and racks.

ABOVE
Stairs to other terraced sections of the
park lead up the hills toward larger trees
and down toward the lawns, where
visitors sit on a park bench or picnic
in the grass. A 1989 bust of Georges
Brassens by André Greck is installed
close to one of the park's lawns.

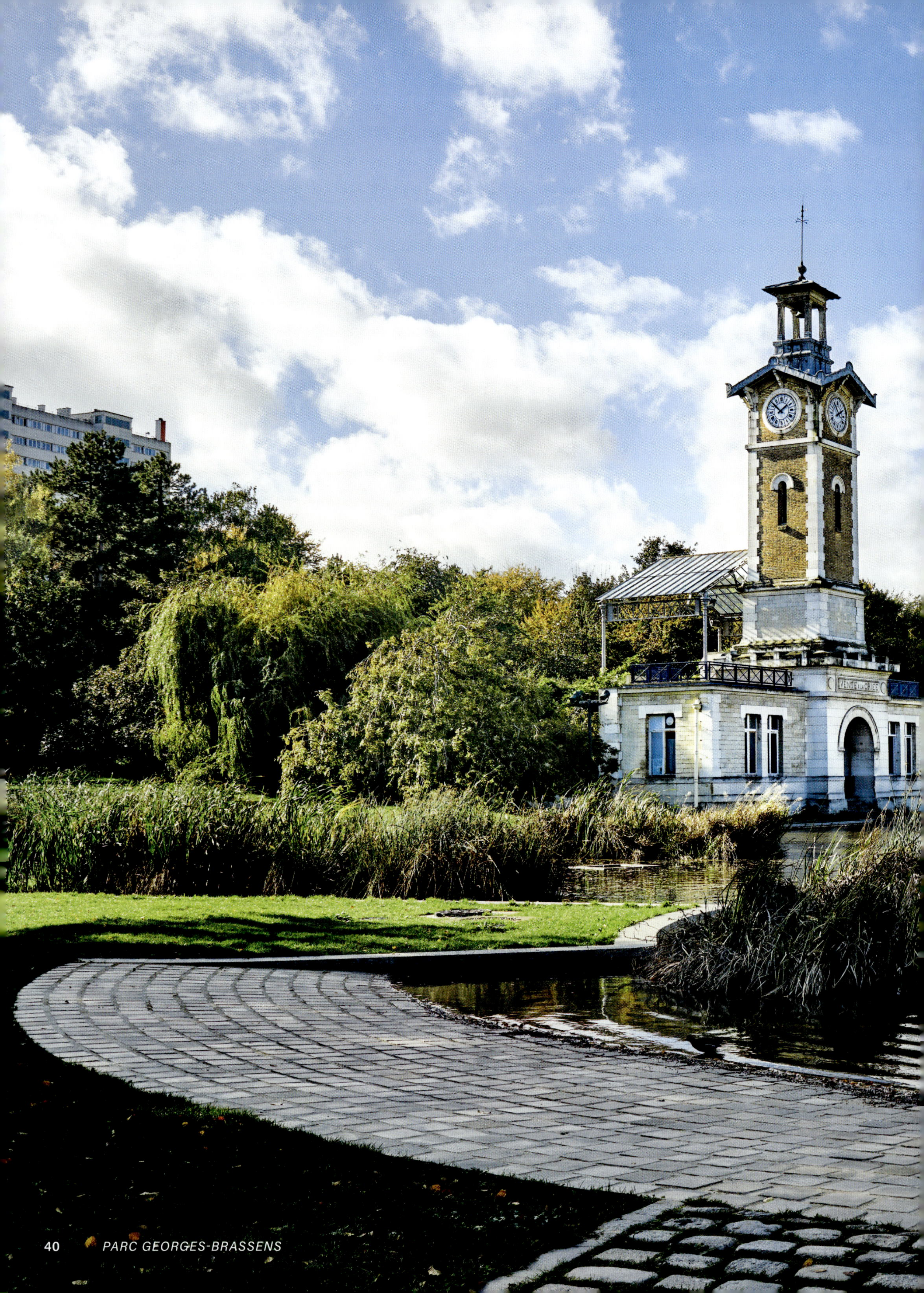

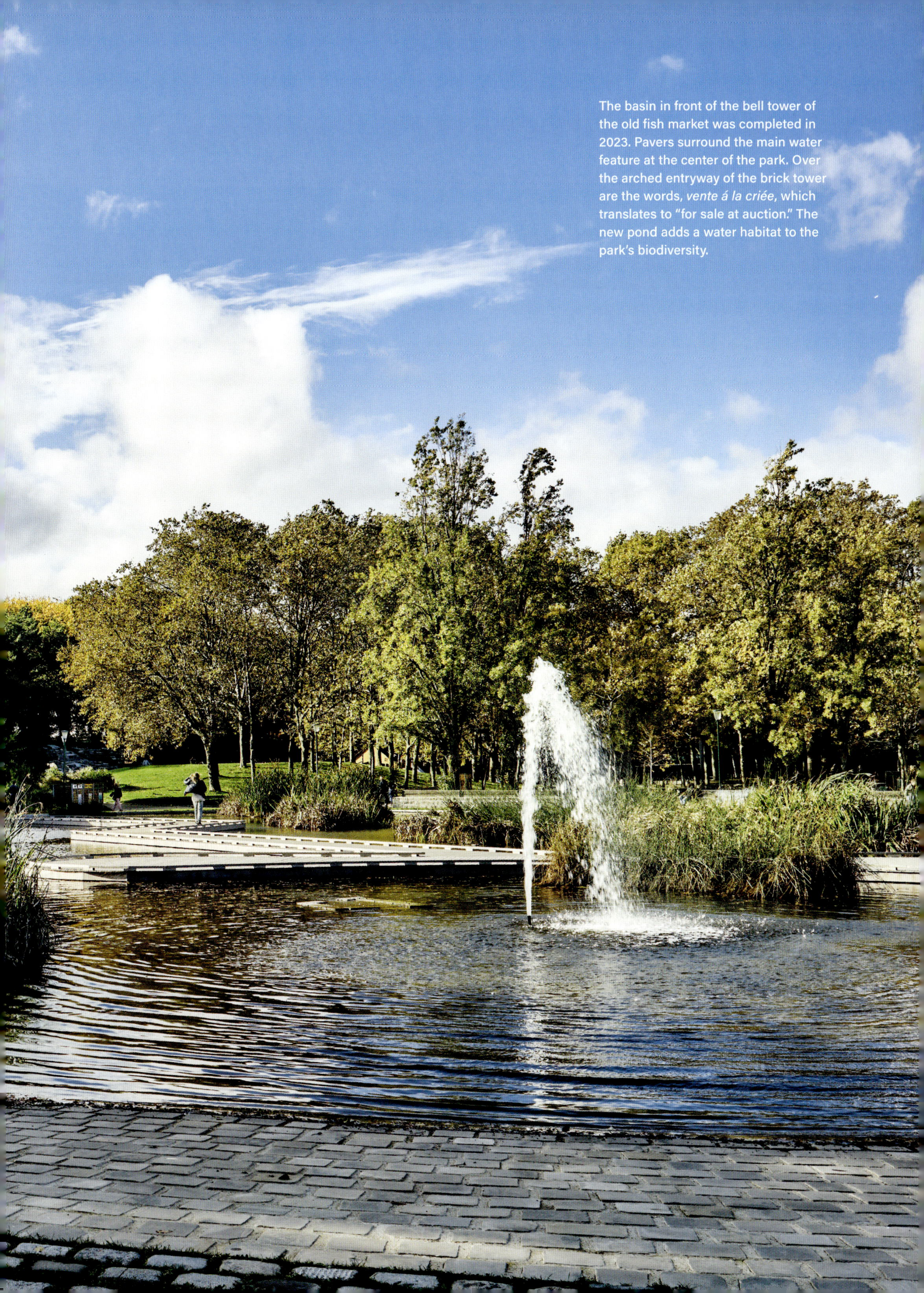

The basin in front of the bell tower of the old fish market was completed in 2023. Pavers surround the main water feature at the center of the park. Over the arched entryway of the brick tower are the words, *vente á la criée*, which translates to "for sale at auction." The new pond adds a water habitat to the park's biodiversity.

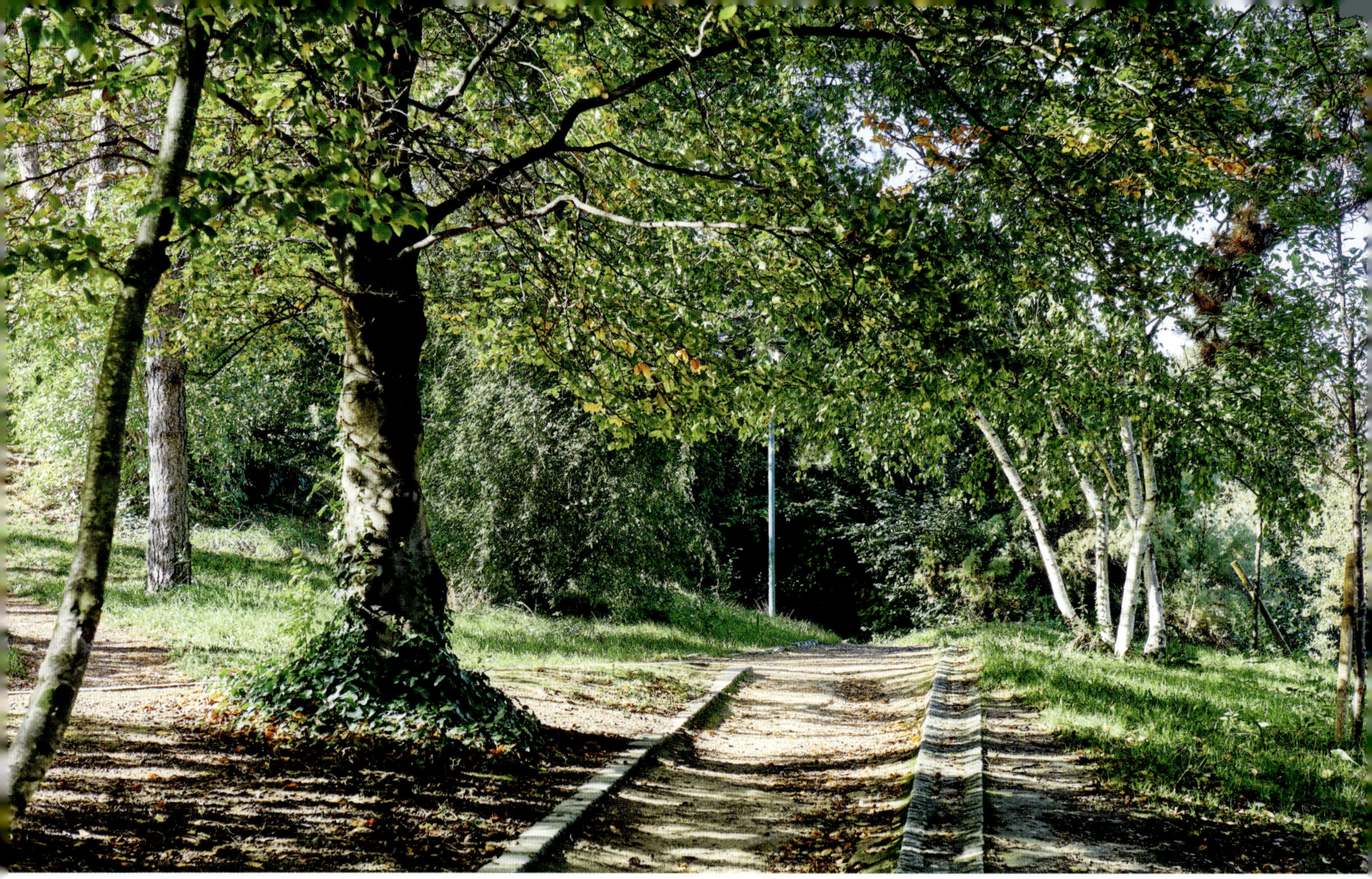

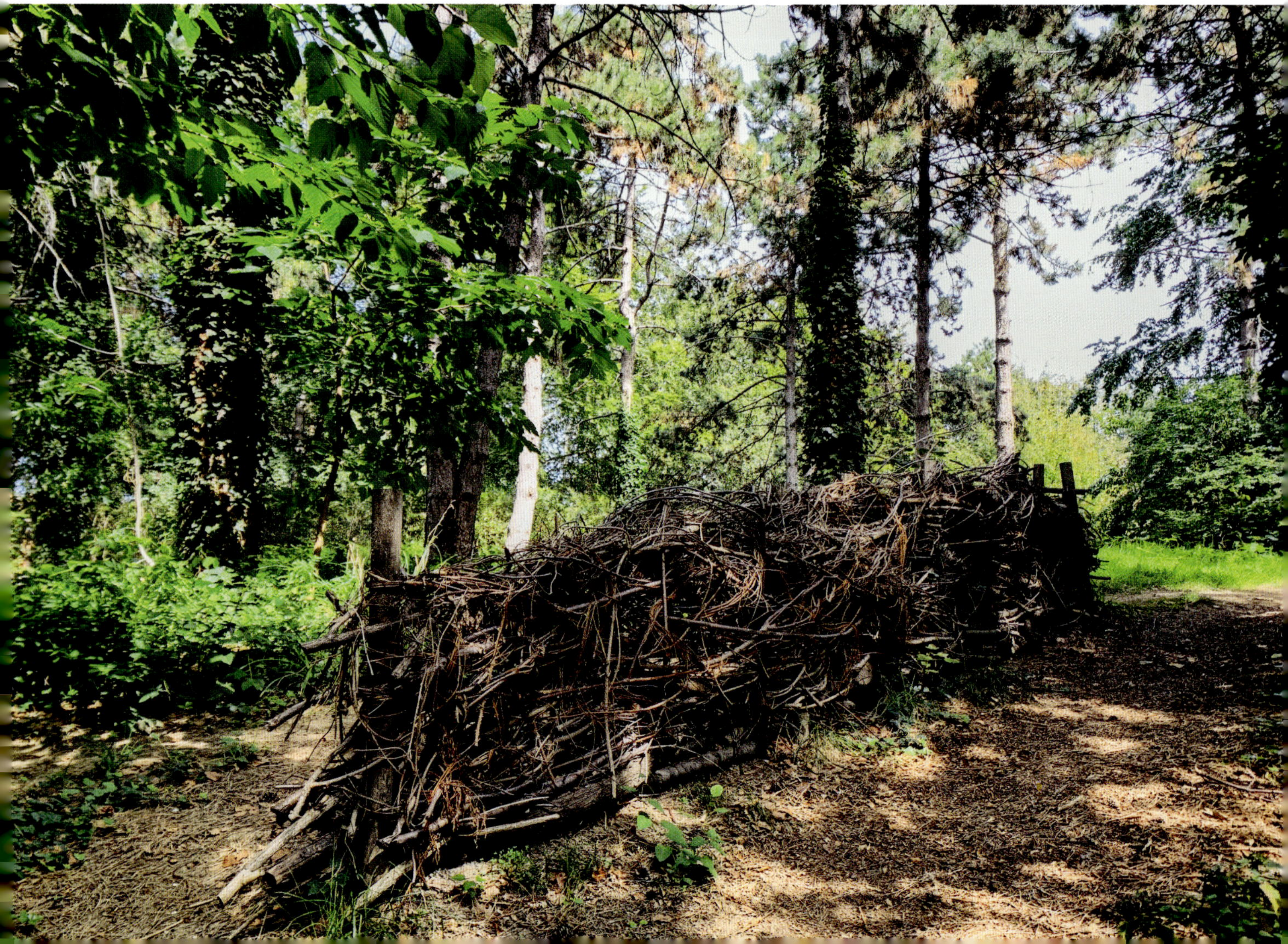

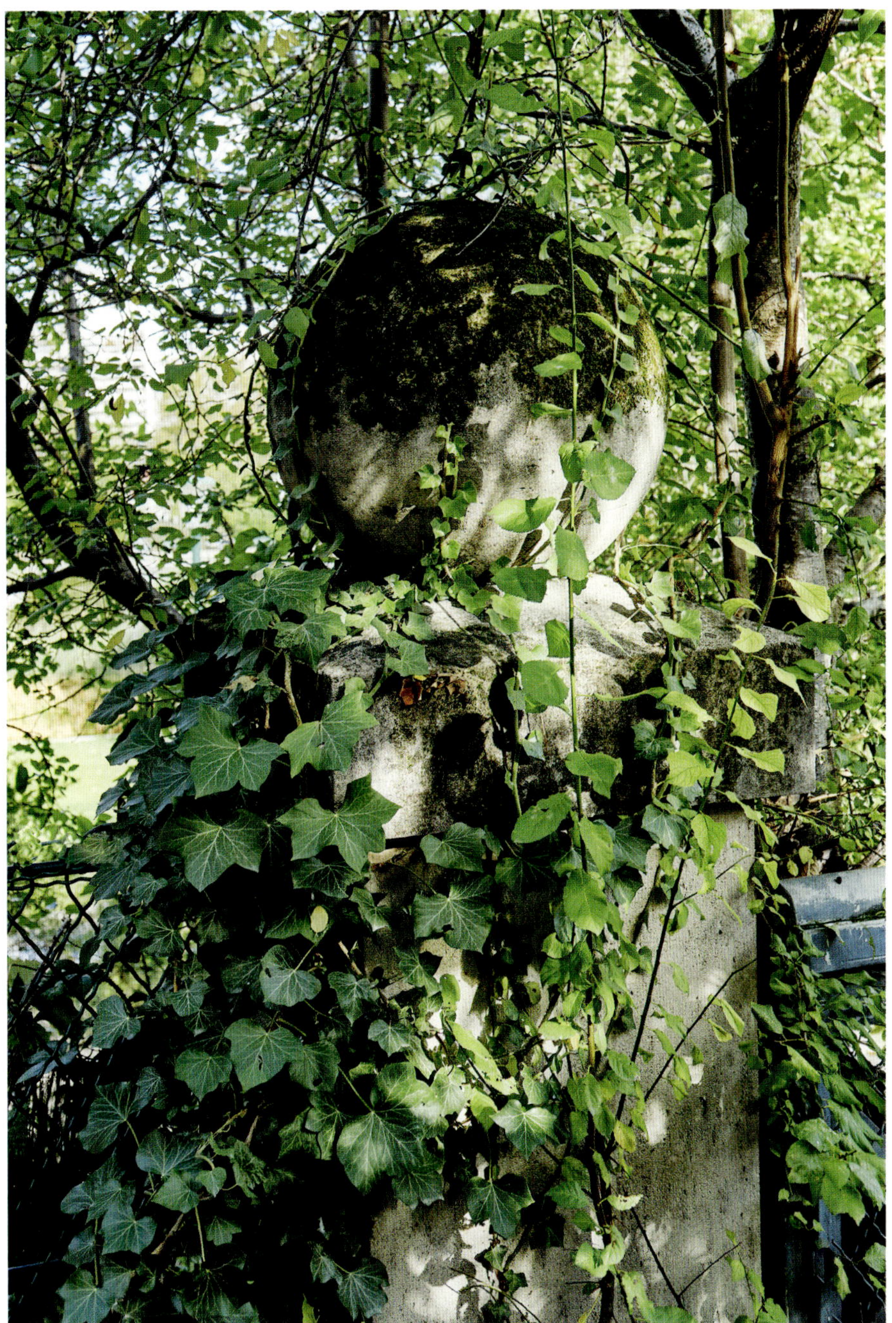

OPPOSITE ABOVE
Pathways, edged in pavers, lead away
from the center of parc Georges-
Brassens through an informal wooded
section of the urban park in the 15th
arrondissement.

OPPOSITE BELOW
A dry hedge, or *haie sèche*, is made
from fallen limbs as well as vines and
shrubs. As the wood decomposes, more
branches can be added on top. Small
animals, insects (including bees), and
fungi make their homes in the hedge
and live off it. The hedge can also be
used as a directional guide to lead
walkers through the park's forests.

ABOVE RIGHT
A cement garden sculpture now covered
in ivy adds an ambience of romance.

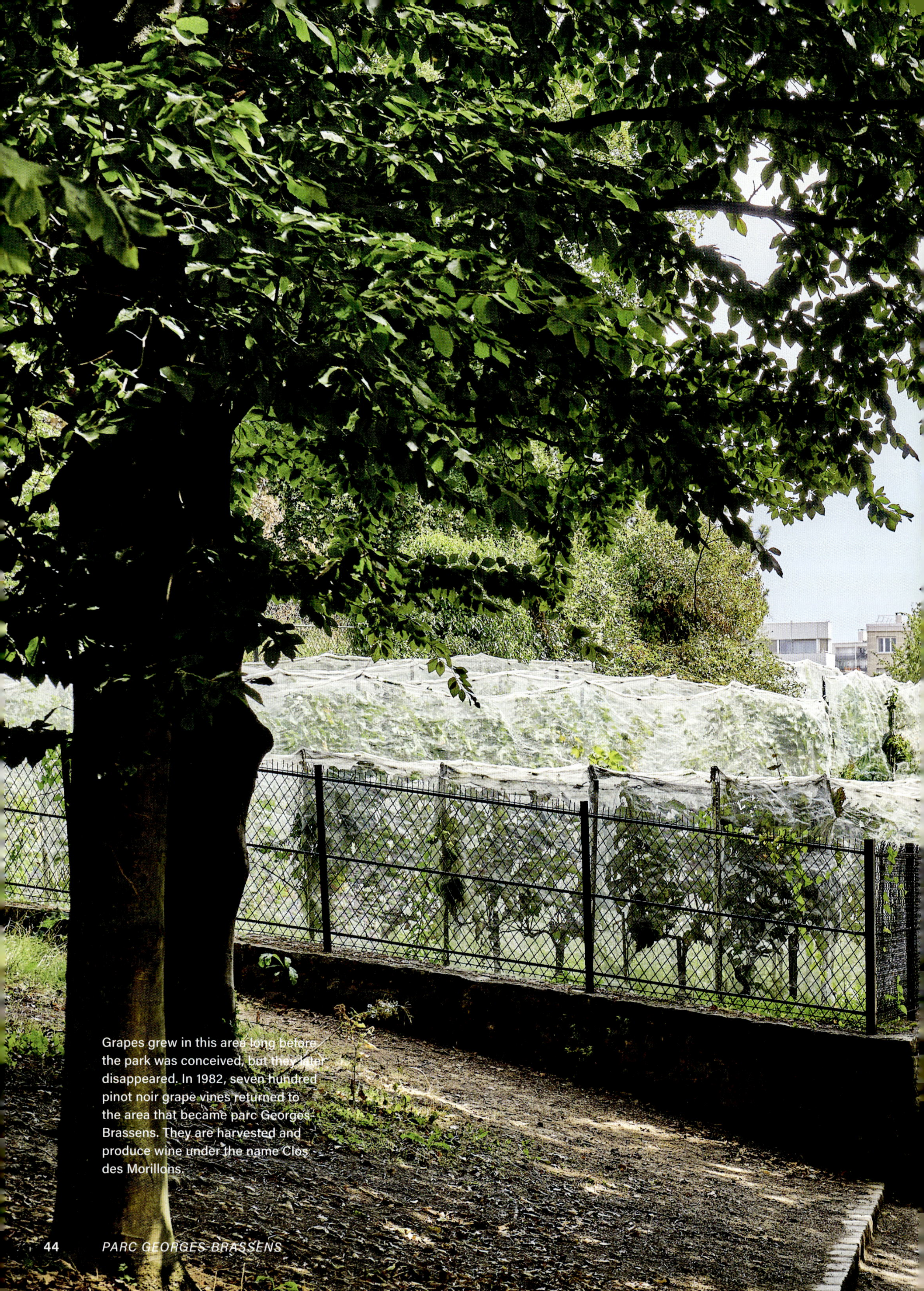
Grapes grew in this area long before the park was conceived, but they later disappeared. In 1982, seven hundred pinot noir grape vines returned to the area that became parc Georges-Brassens. They are harvested and produce wine under the name Clos des Morillons.

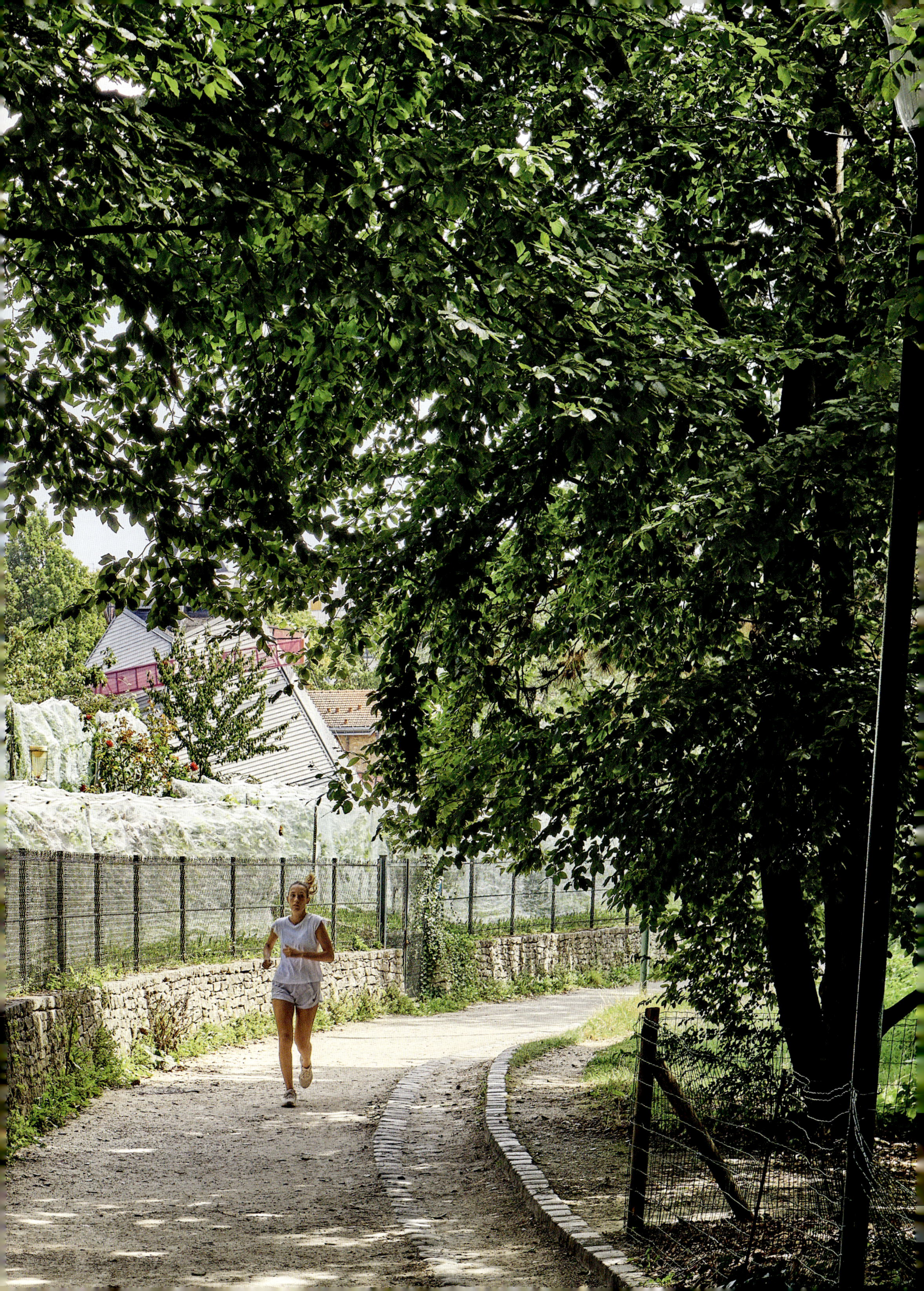

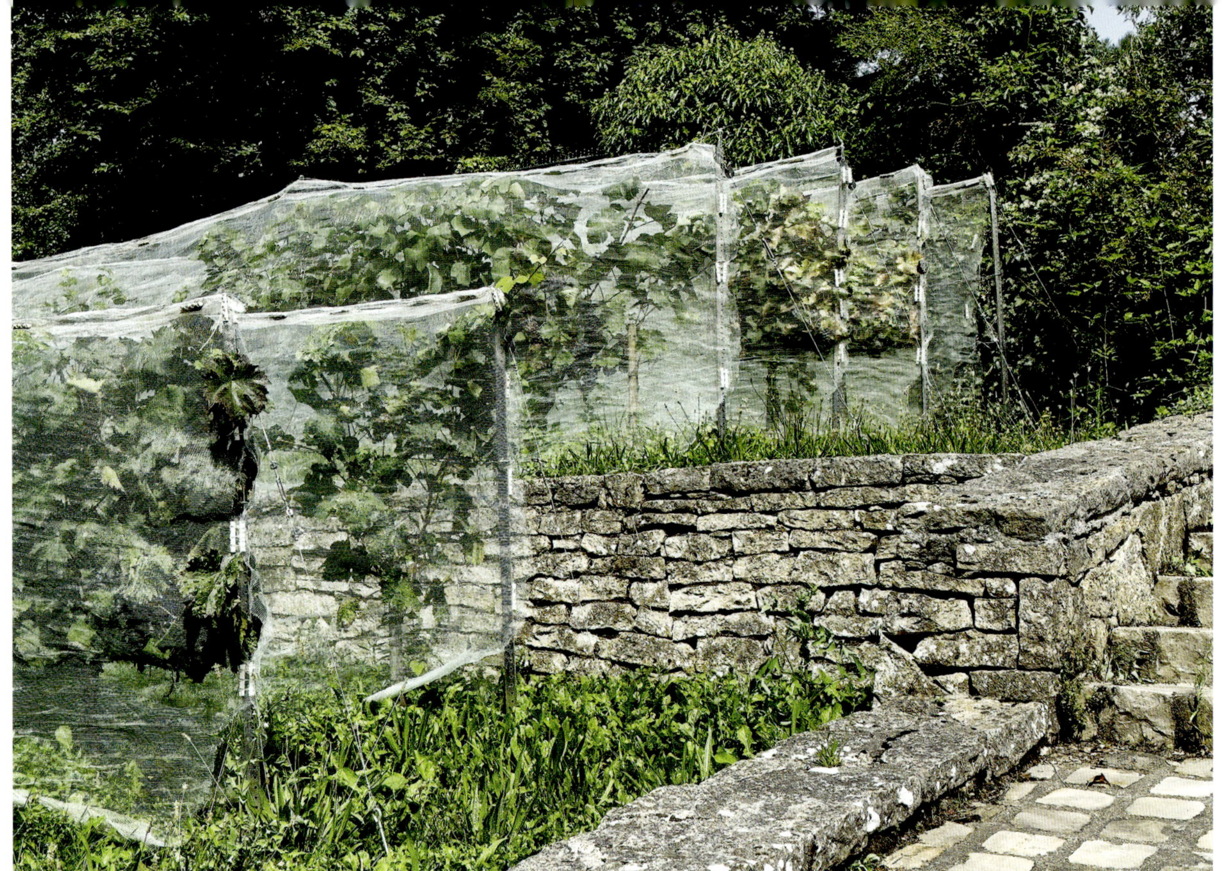

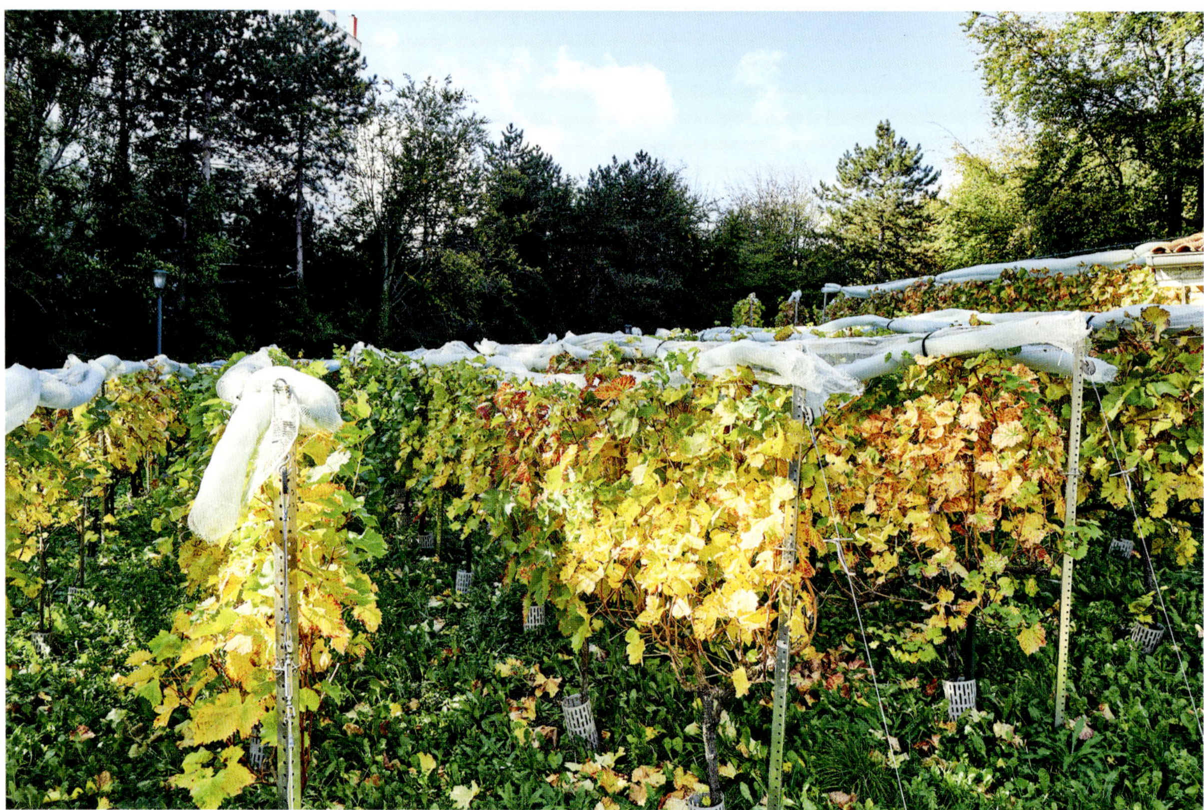

In the summer, the grapes are protected
from the birds by a white diaphanous
fabric. In the fall, when the leaves turn
yellow, the fabrics are rolled up for
harvesting the fruits off the vines.

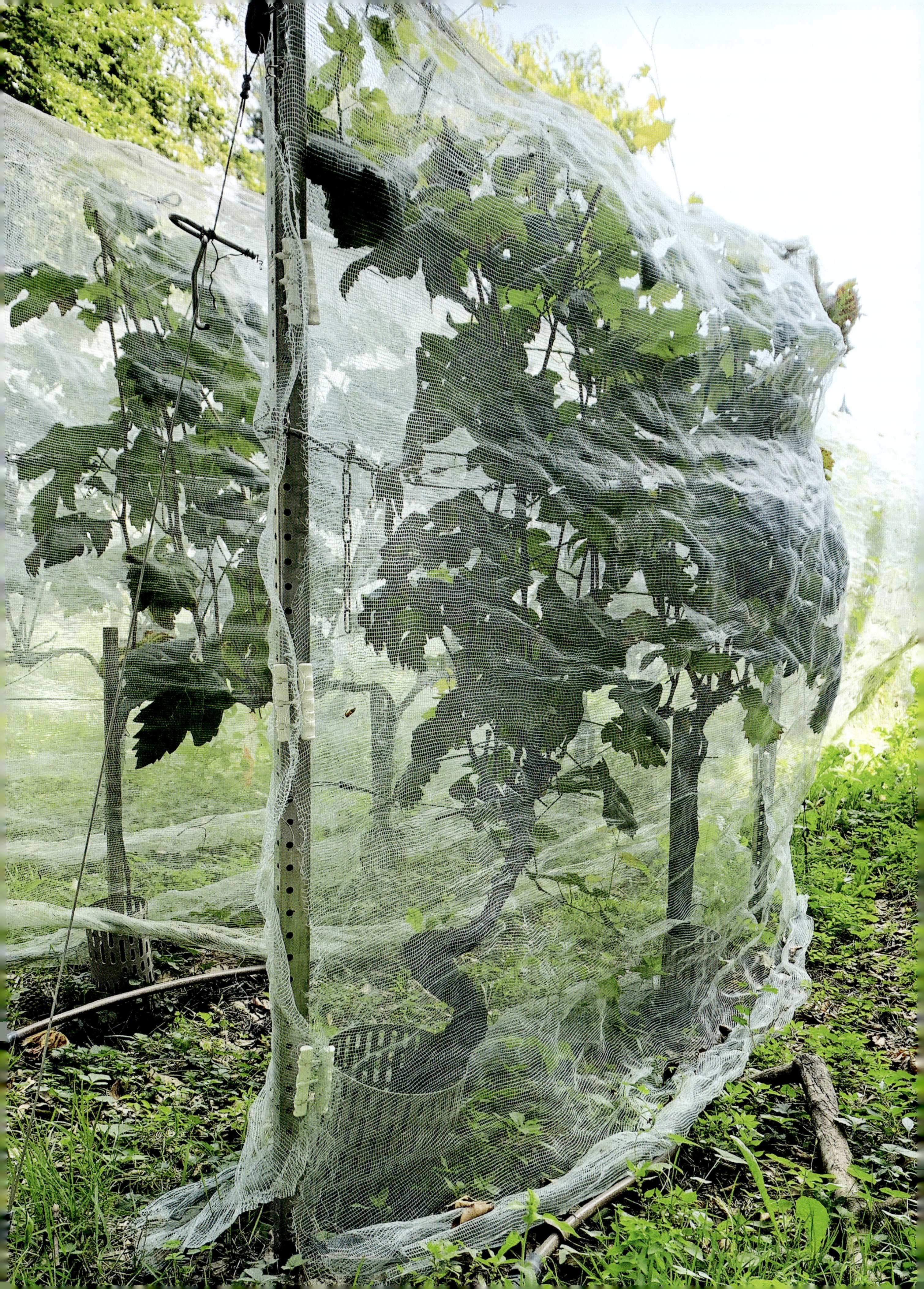

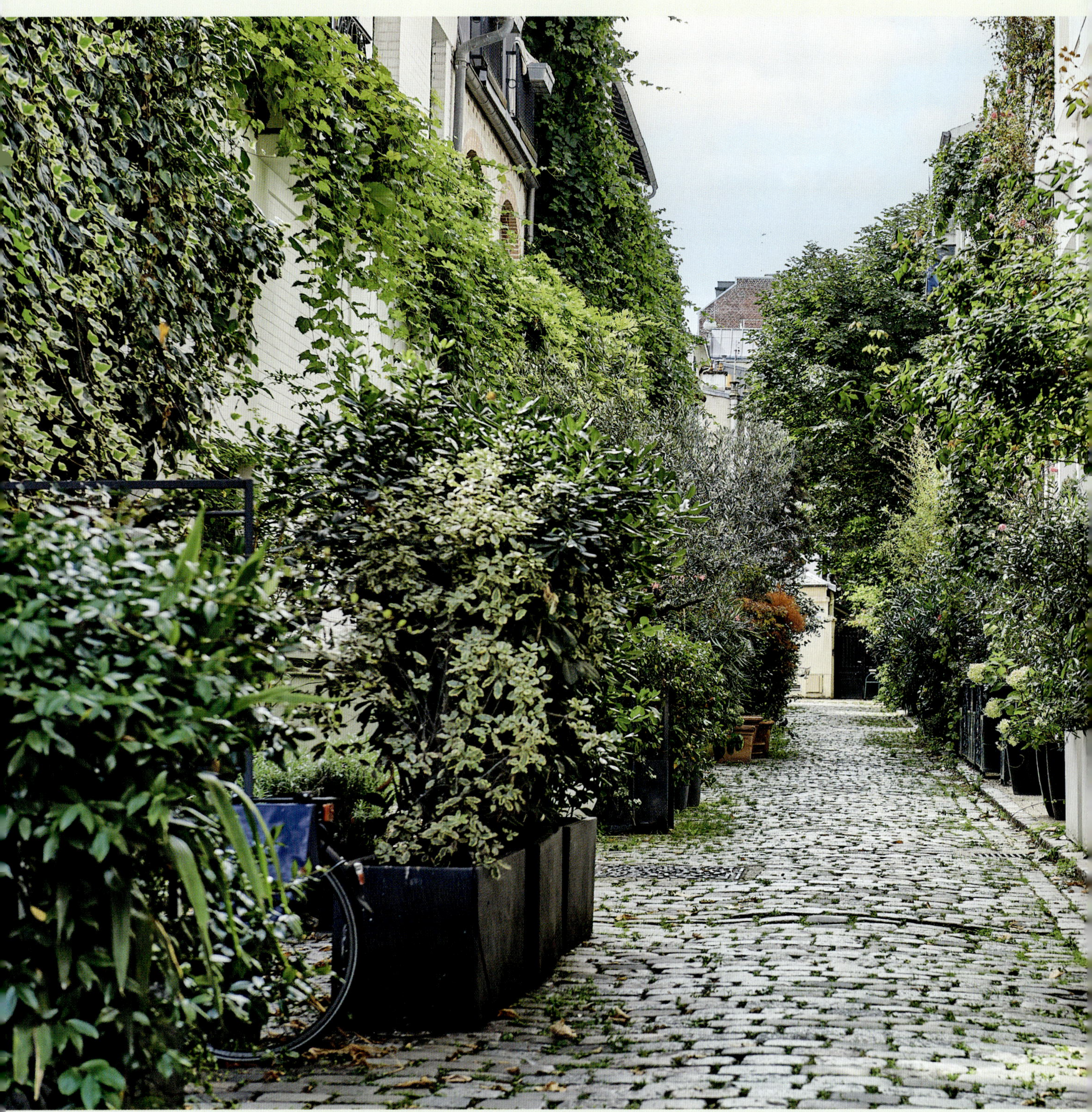

ABOVE
Looking toward la rue Santos-Dumont
in late summer, blooming trees and
plants on both sides of the street almost
obscure the houses on the cobblestone
alleyway. Residents have installed chairs
and tables outside to take advantage of
the garden.

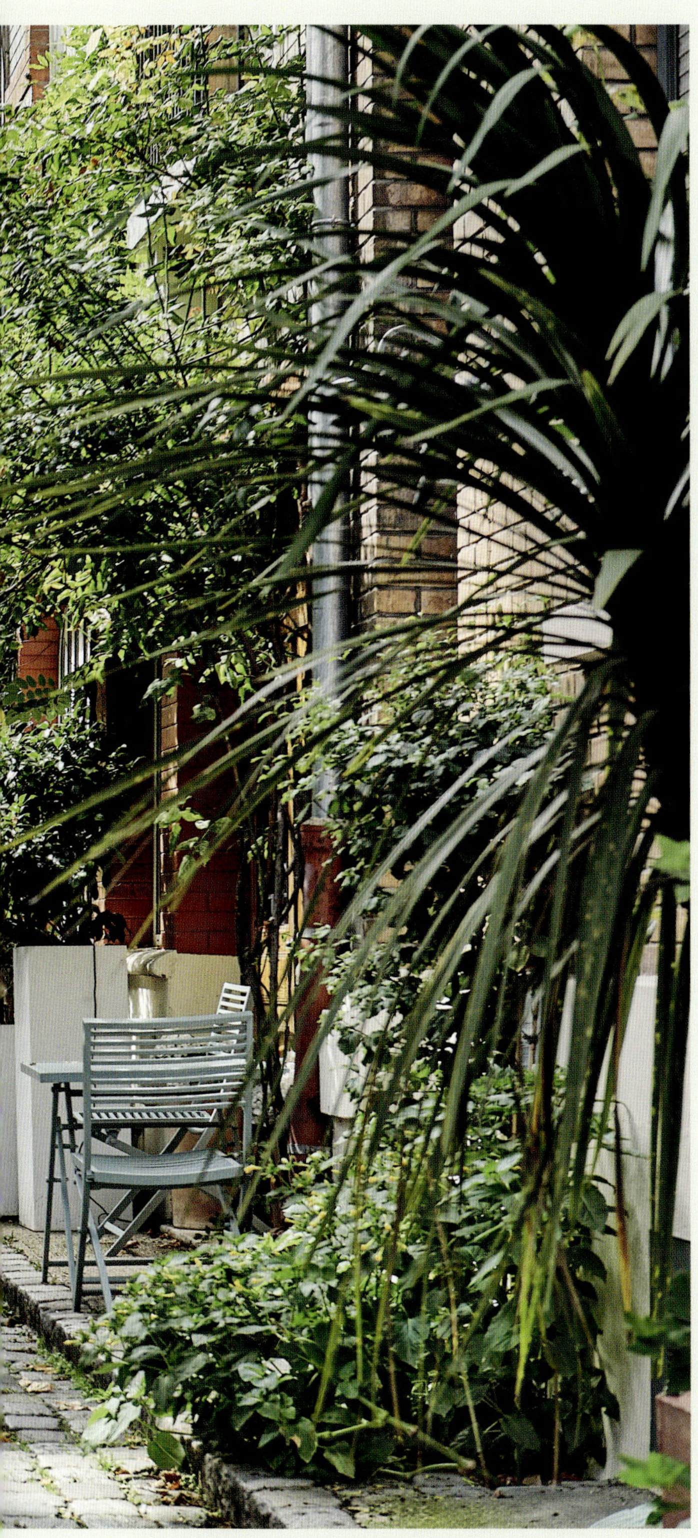



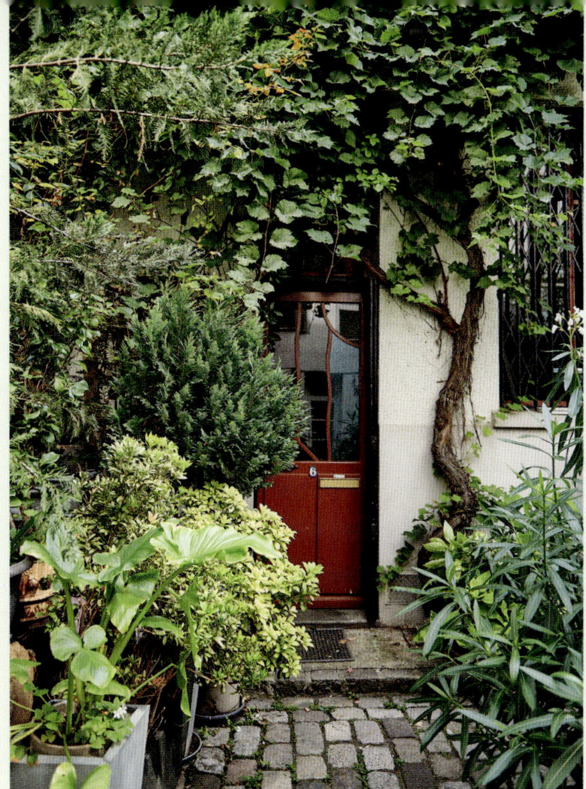



## Villa Santos-Dumont
15th arrondissement
1926

A mere five-minute walk from parc Georges-Brassens, villa Santos-Dumont is a small alley that finishes at a dead end, or *impasse*. Named in 1943 for the early twentieth-century aeronautical inventor Alberto Santos-Dumont, who once flew one of his early flying "experiments" around the Eiffel Tower, the street is paved in cobblestones and lined with twenty-five small houses that are two or three stories tall. However, the street's beginning was founded in the arts. A sculptor, Louis-Raphaël Paynot, bought the land in 1889 and made his family home there. Years later, in the 1920s, his son developed the property to include two parallel rows of individual residences. At the time, the occupants were artists and craftspeople whose work benefited from the large iron multipaned windows. Today, the architecture is hidden behind layers of plants; some long established in the ground and some planted in vessels of all shapes and sizes. Residents have created their own gardens with small palm and olive trees, morning glory and grape vines, topiaries, flowering roses, and oleander. The bucolic feeling of the past has been preserved. At the same time, a modern container garden thrives, bringing nature to a small, quiet part of a busy metropolitan city.


A path leads to the glass and metal entrance of one of the original 1920s-built houses on villa Santos-Dumont, where a well-established grape vine grows vertically.

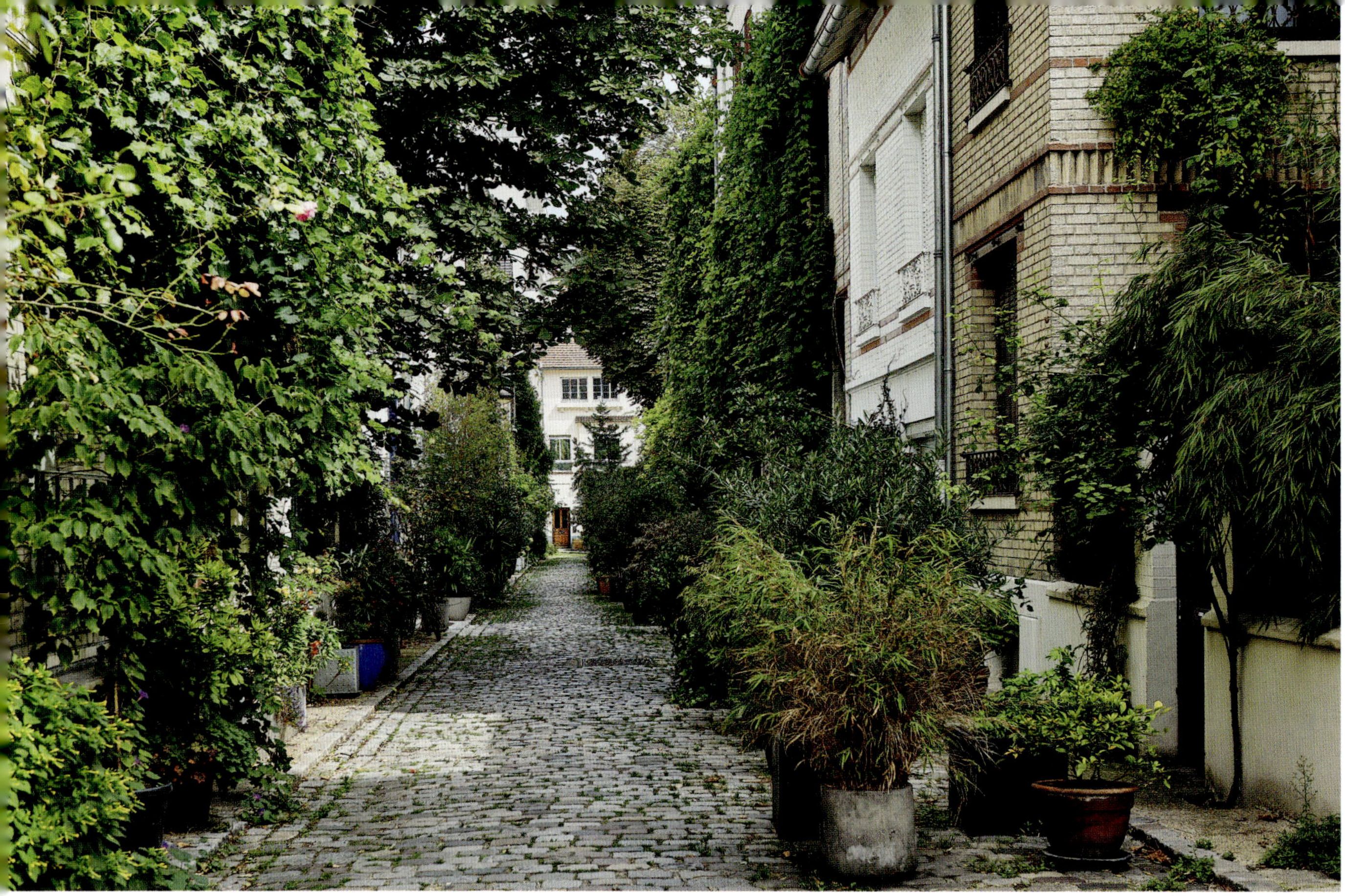

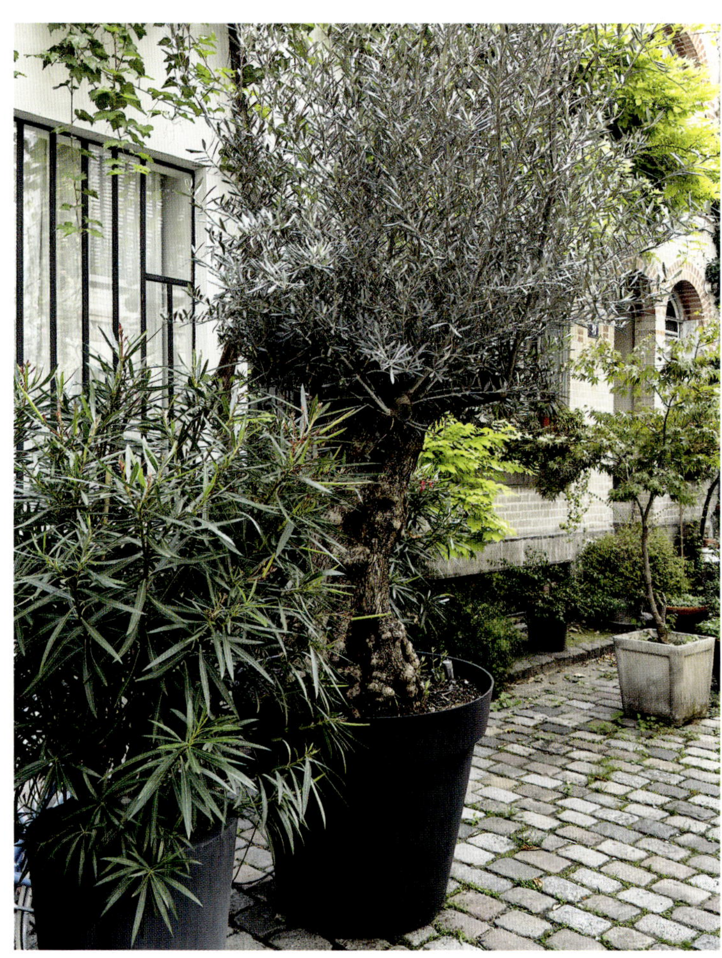



**ABOVE**
Several of the houses were built for their original owners, including number 25 at the end of the alley, which was designed for the American artist Malvina Hoffman in the 1920s and is now the address of Hôpital de Jour Santos-Dumont.

**RIGHT**
A small olive tree is successfully maturing in the three-foot-high pot. These trees are native to the Mediterranean.

**OPPOSITE**
Ivy climbs over vines planted against the *maisonette*'s façade. The planters are full of oleander and lavender. A horse chestnut tree, known as a *marronnier d'inde*, provides plenty of shade. Wistera and bamboo also grow in the garden next door.

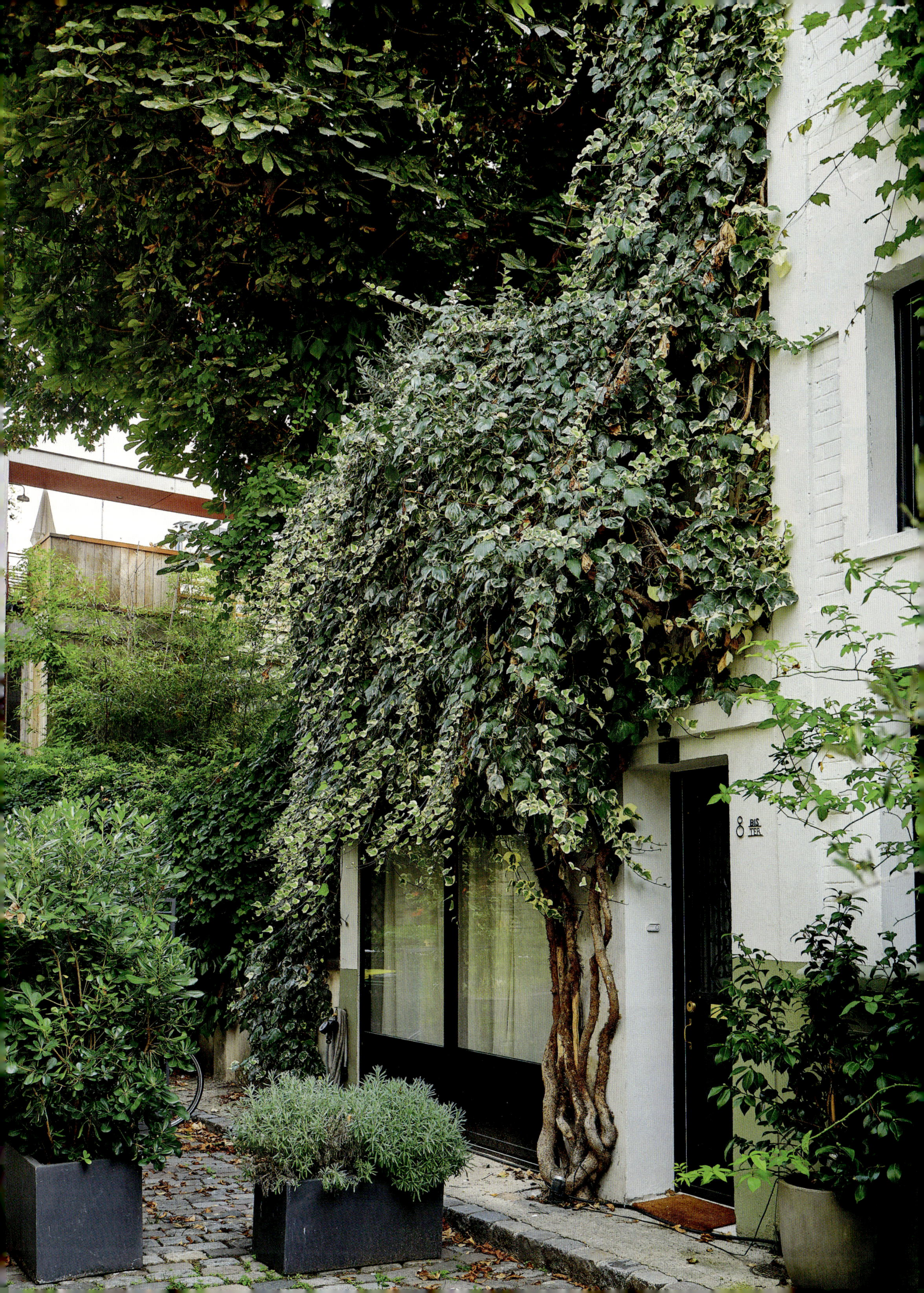

## *Écoquartier de la Gare de Rungis* and *Jardin Charles-Trenet*

13th arrondissement
2014

In 2004, a new eco-district, gare de Rungis, was imagined for an unused freight station in the 13th arrondissement. The area was once a distribution center for merchandise, much like the market Les Halles that distributed food products until it was taken down in the 1970s. Trains brought in freight from other regions in France. The new concept had three environmental goals: first, reduce the energy consumption of the new area by using solar panels; second, reduce the car traffic inside the district by reducing the public and private parking, to be replaced by alternative transportation; third, manage rainwater to offset useable water. The rainwater is harvested from the building rooftops, stored and treated, then used throughout the site for watering gardens and in plumbing for offices and university residences. This system reduced the need and usage of drinkable water by fifty percent because the water is not used for the sewage systems. The only people who can drive in the district are those who live in the neighborhood, except for one street: Rue Annie-Girardot is open for traffic. An international design competition was held for the new buildings for the new neighborhood. The public garden Charles-Trenet honors the French singer and composer whose songs were popular beginning in the 1930s. The design of the garden alternates between its structured sections and its natural sections that are perhaps a nod to the wildness of the old Petite Ceinture railroad nearby.

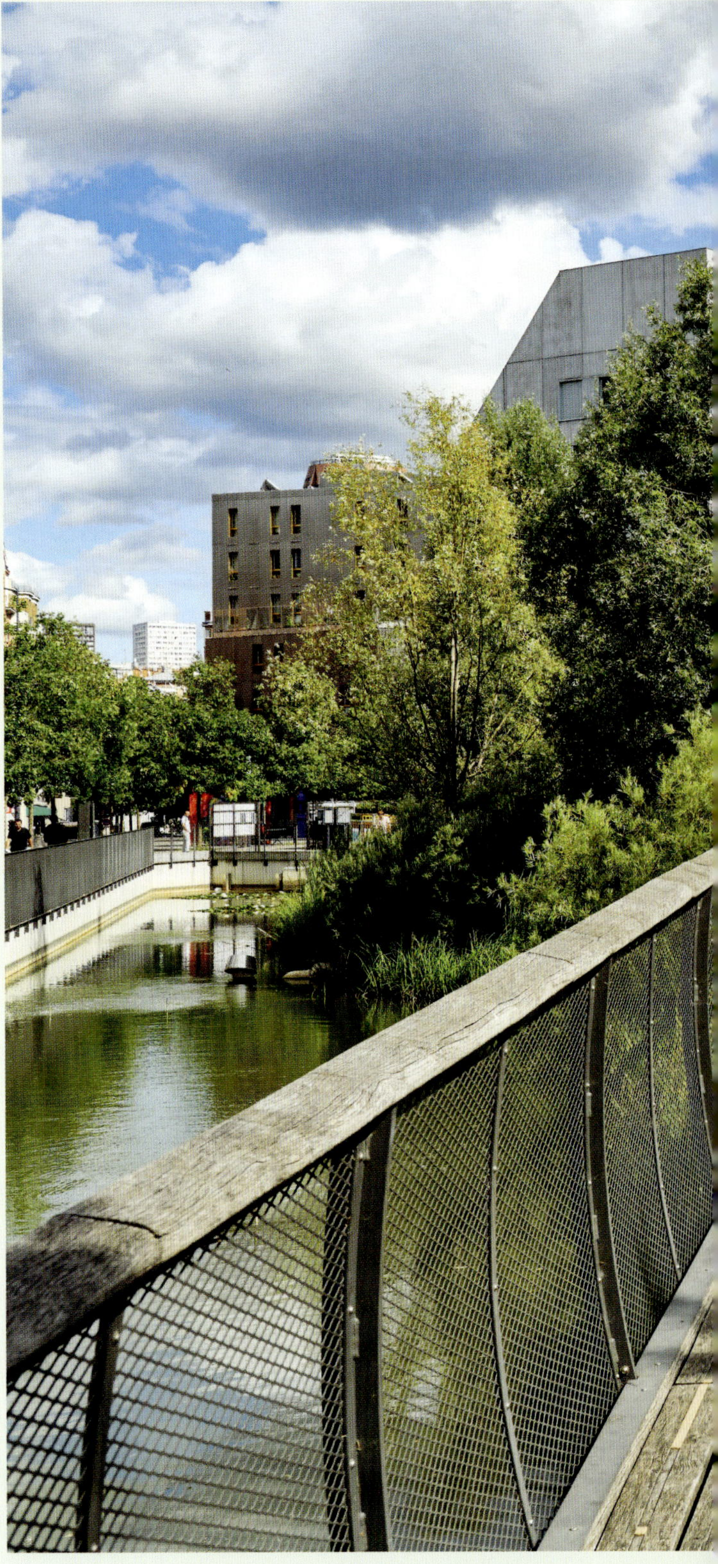

A wooden pedestrian bridge traverses jardin Charles-Trenet from la rue Brillat-Savarin, up the hill to the apartment buildings known as the Polyèdres, designed by architect Anne Démians.

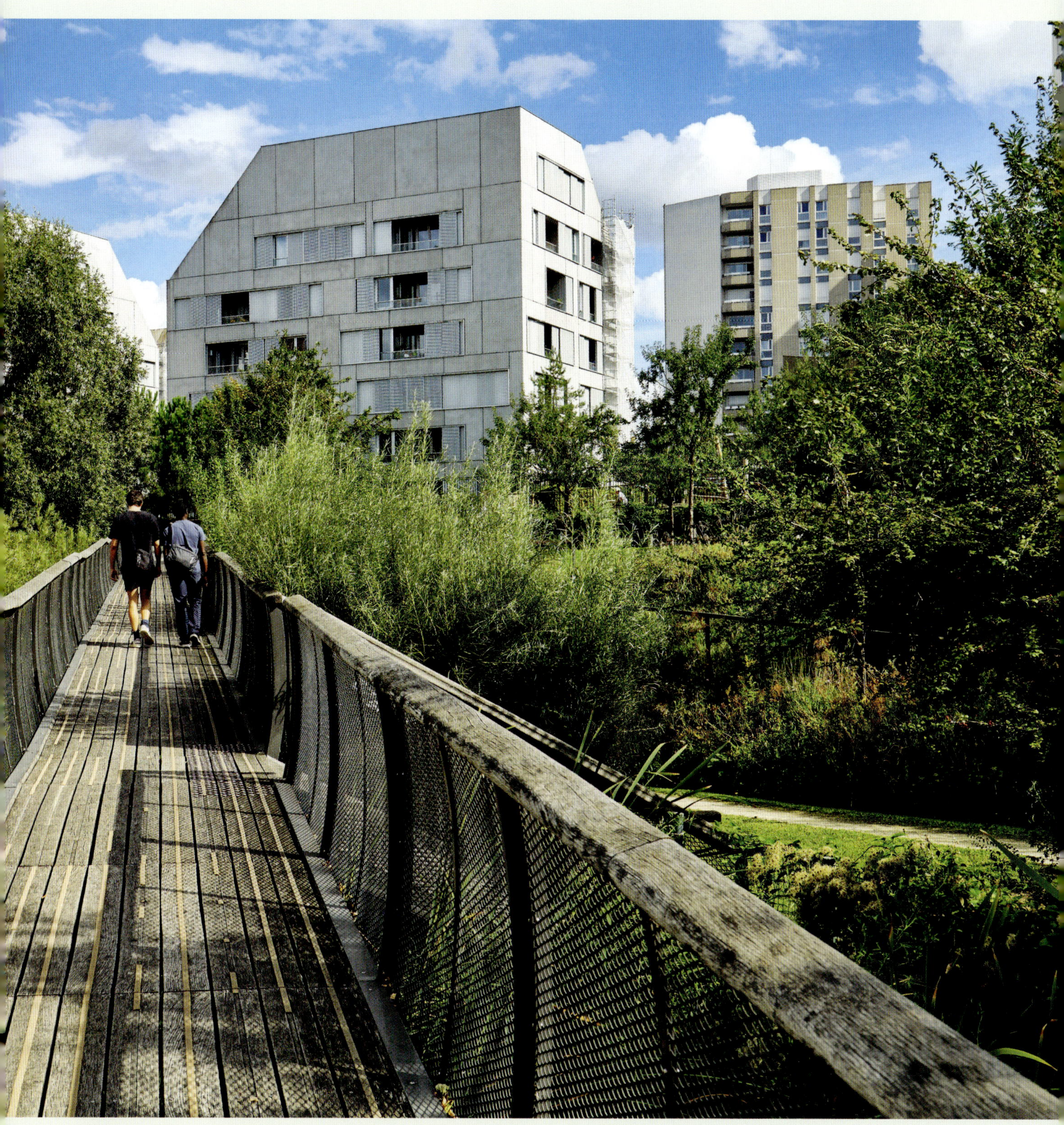

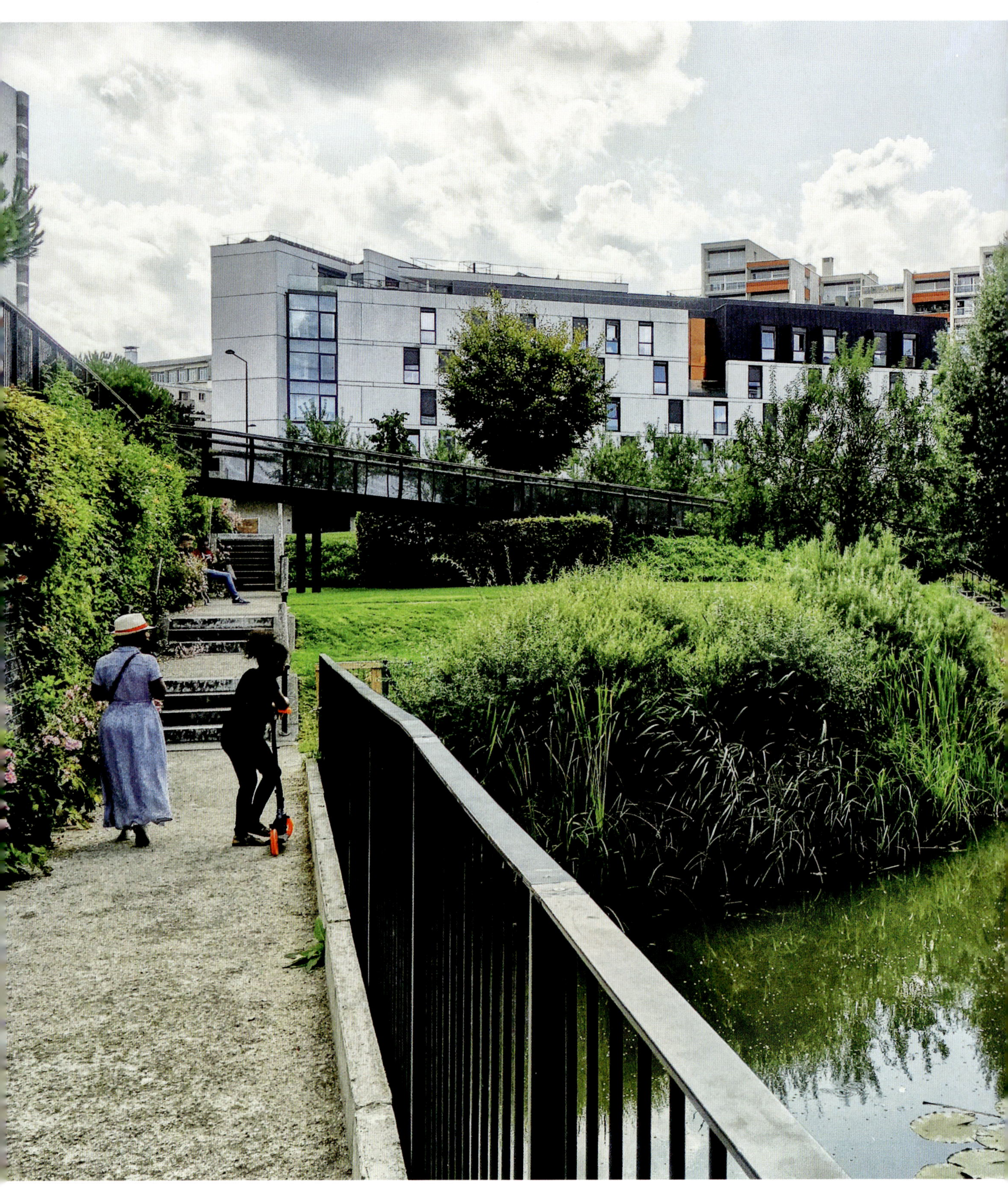

 *ÉCOQUARTIER DE LA GARE DE RUNGIS* AND *JARDIN CHARLES-TRENET*

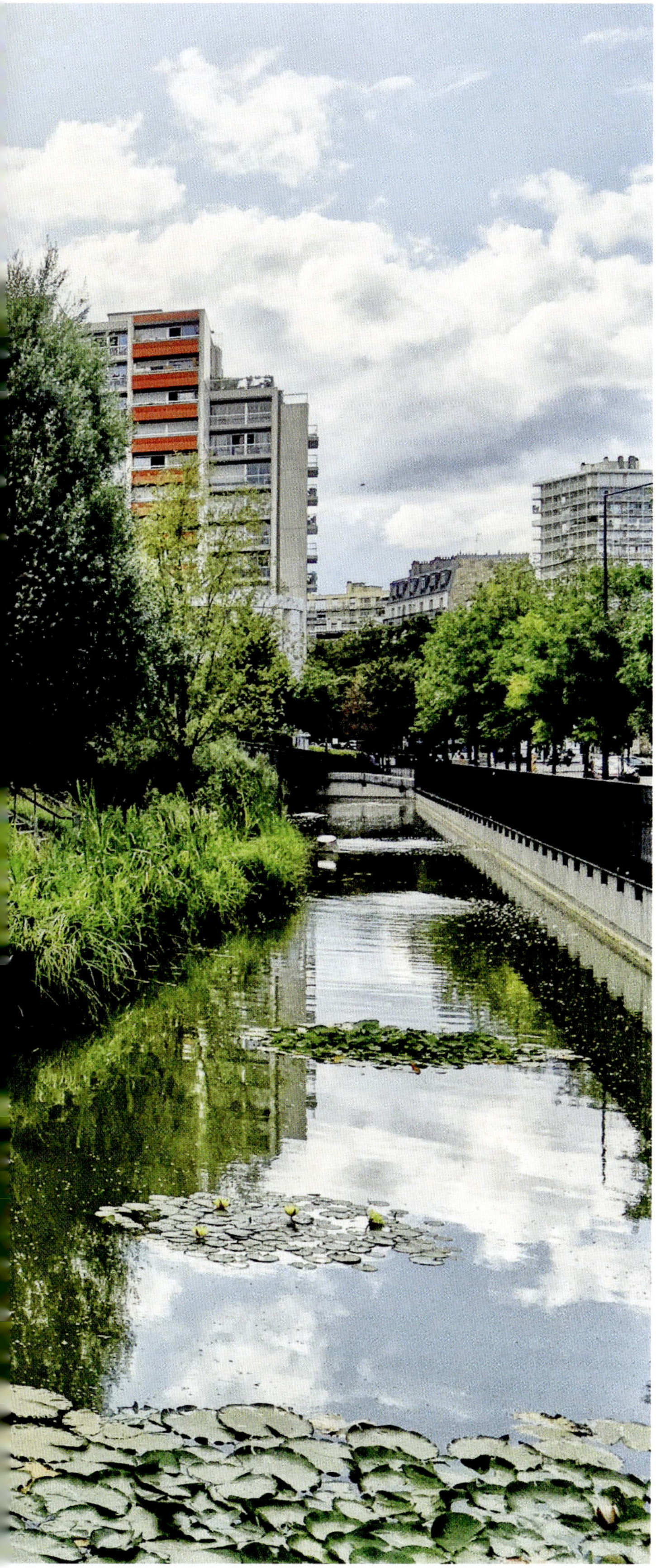

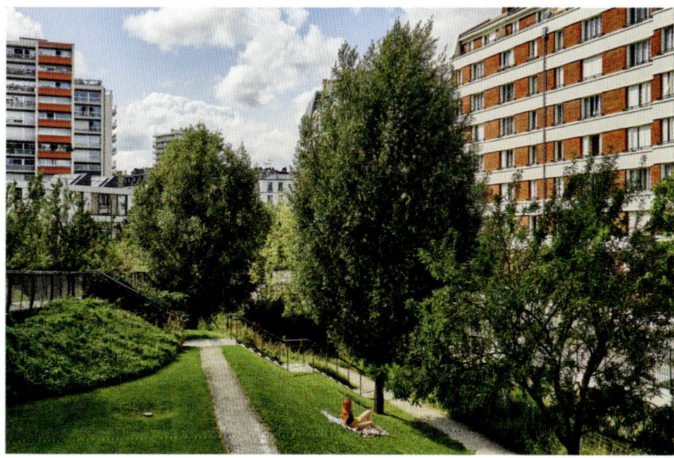

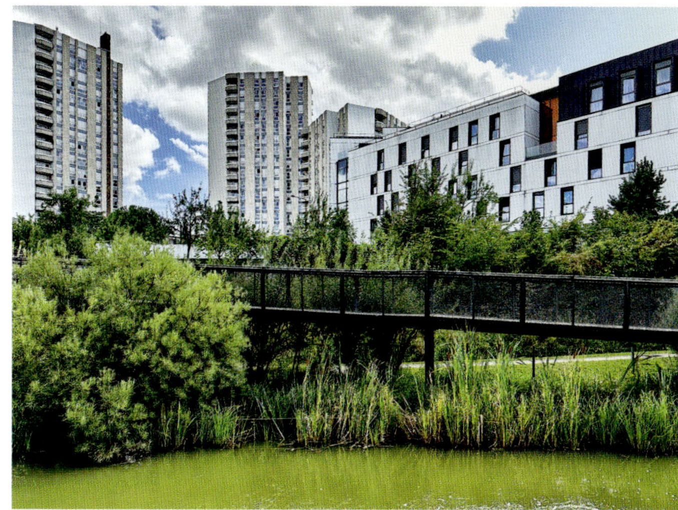

**LEFT**
A terraced pathway, next to the retaining wall—now covered in vines—gives access to the upper section and beyond to the children's playground at the top of the park.

**TOP**
A lawn for sunbathing or relaxation extends down near the wetland plantings by the water. The trees also provide shade for hotter days.

**ABOVE**
Landscape architect, or *paysagiste*, Michel Pena planned the park with a new body of water, creating wetlands along the water's edge—adding to the biodiversity of the site. The bridge allows a gradual ascent to the upper lawns, and pathways are carved through the landscape of trees and shrubs.

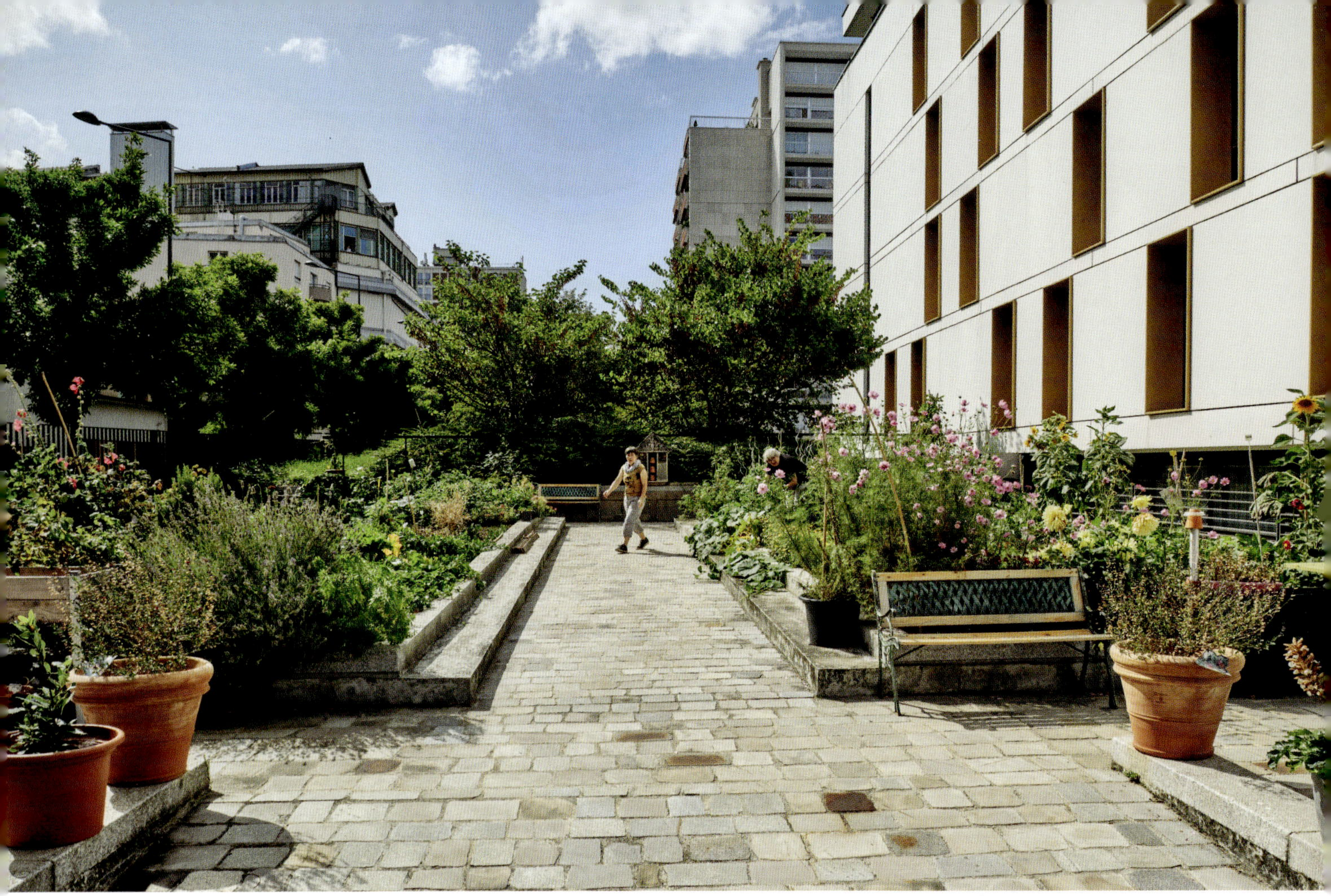

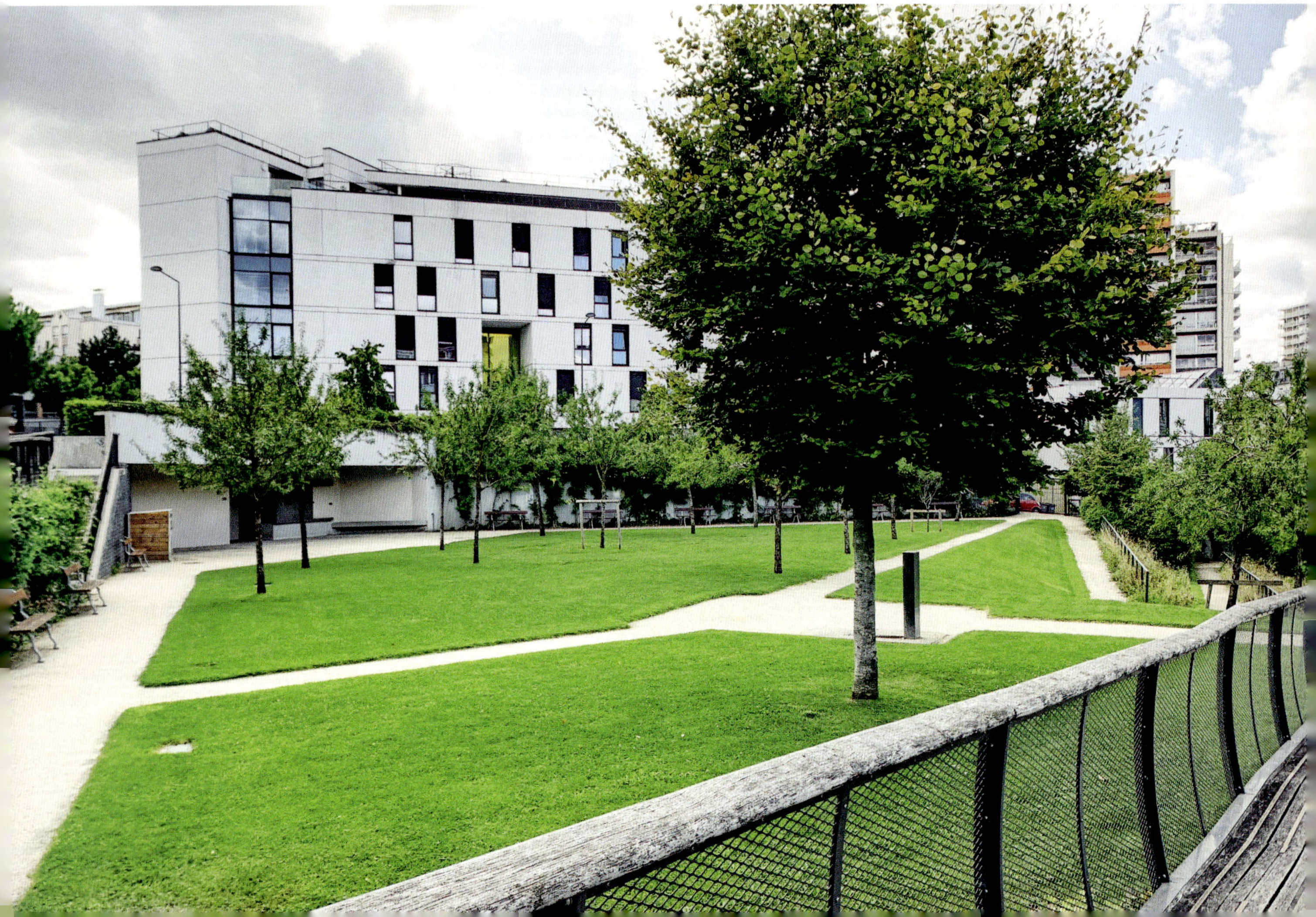

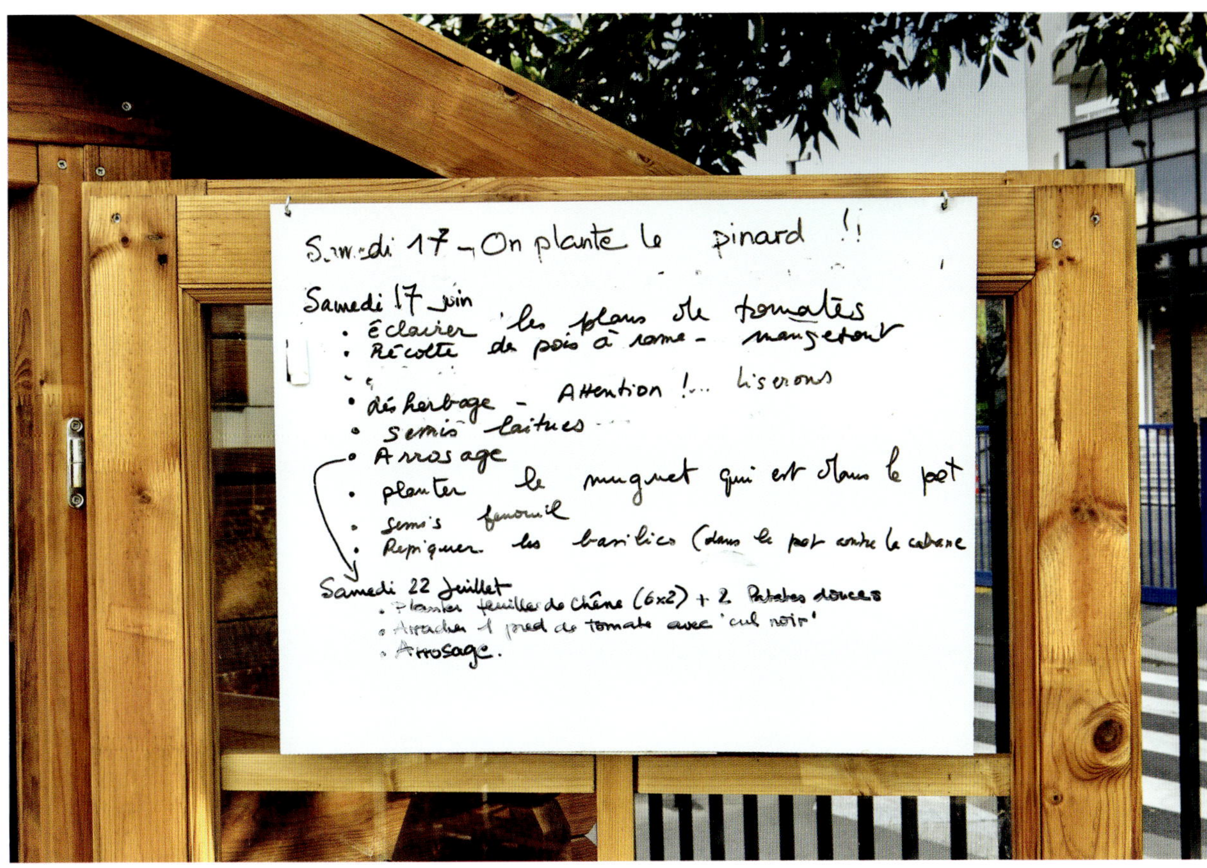


**OPPOSITE ABOVE**
Near the back of the development is a community garden with beds for growing fruit, vegetables, and flowers.

**OPPOSITE BELOW**
Fruit trees, which flower in the spring, are planted on the lawn in front of EHPAD Annie Girardot, an assisted living community for Alzheimer patients, designed by the architectural firm Lazo & Mure.

**ABOVE**
A list of gardening activities is posted on the shed door.

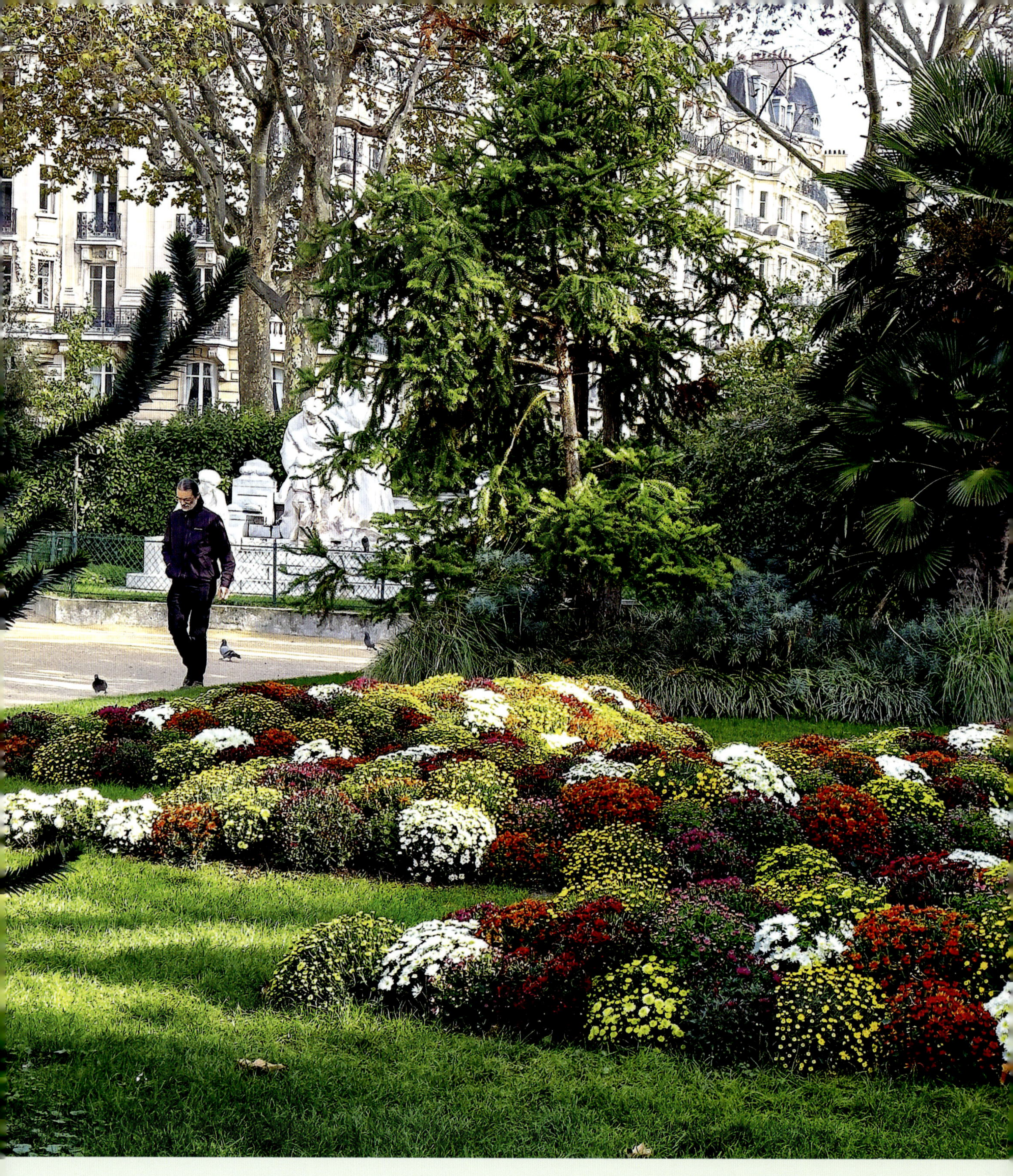

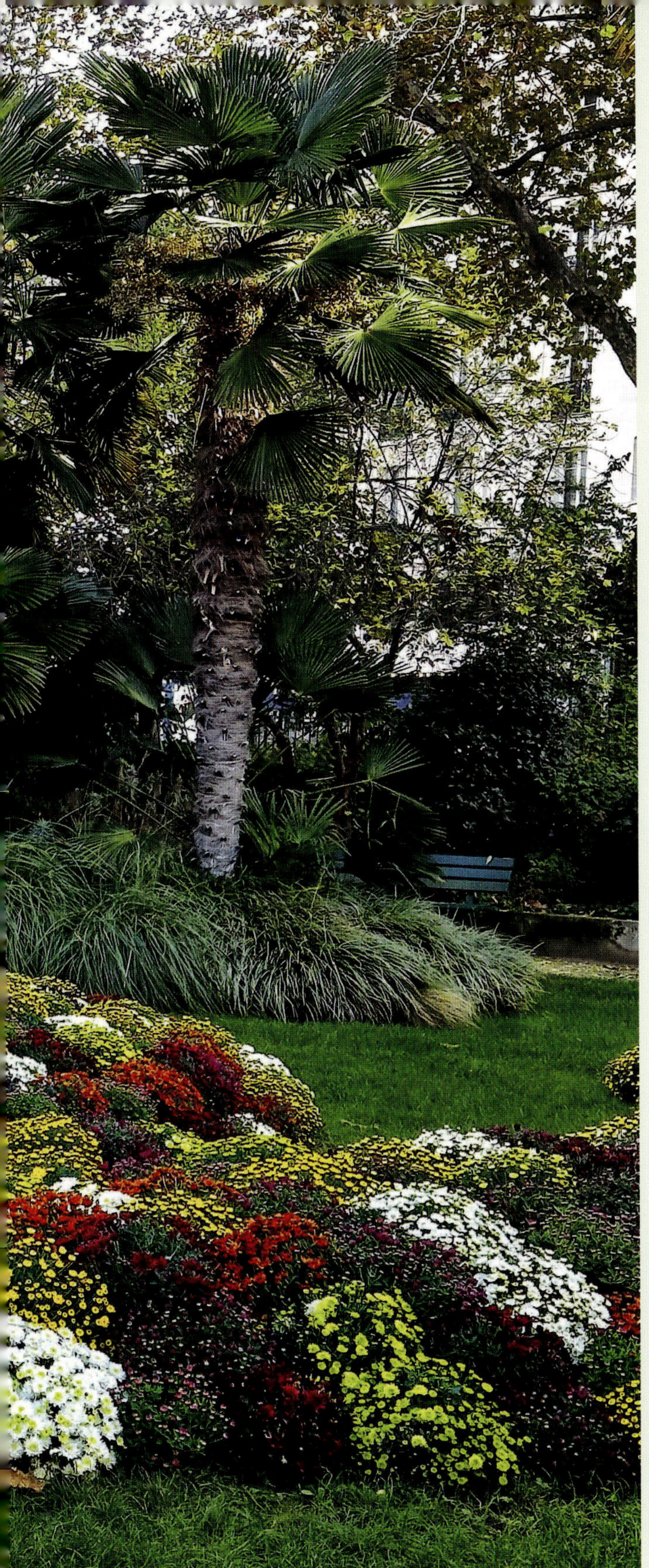

## *Square Boucicaut*
7th arrondissement
1873

Square Boucicaut, located just in front of Le Bon Marché, Paris's first department store, has a history of survival. The garden was originally called square Le Bon Marché, and it coincides with the first iteration of the iconic *grand magasin*, or department store, building on the corner of rue de Sèvres and rue Velpeau. The park was much different then; several rows of aligned trees surrounded a triangle-shaped lawn with statues and decorative urns placed throughout. Later, the garden was named for the store's genius retailer and creator, Aristide Boucicaut. A white marble sculpture of his wife and business partner, Marguerite, and her friend, Baroness Clara de Hirsch, honoring their role in philanthropy, still stands there. In the 1960s, the site was excavated to make room for an underground parking garage. Trees on the edges near the sidewalks survived the demolition, including a *margousier*, or Indian Lilac, planted in 1699, and mentioned on Paris's list of remarkable trees. While the triangle shape of the original lawn remains, the garden is smaller, hemmed in by busy streets. Those old trees lean over slightly, protecting the park and its wide, winding *alleé* that has rows of park benches. A carousel, a playground, and one hundred trees and more plantings have been added over the years. The City of Paris also created a pond with its own ecosystem that includes insects, mollusks, and various birds.

Some plantings are decorative and seasonal. In the autumn, a parterre of multicolored mums brightens the park. The white marble statue of Madame Boucicaut is behind a row of trees.

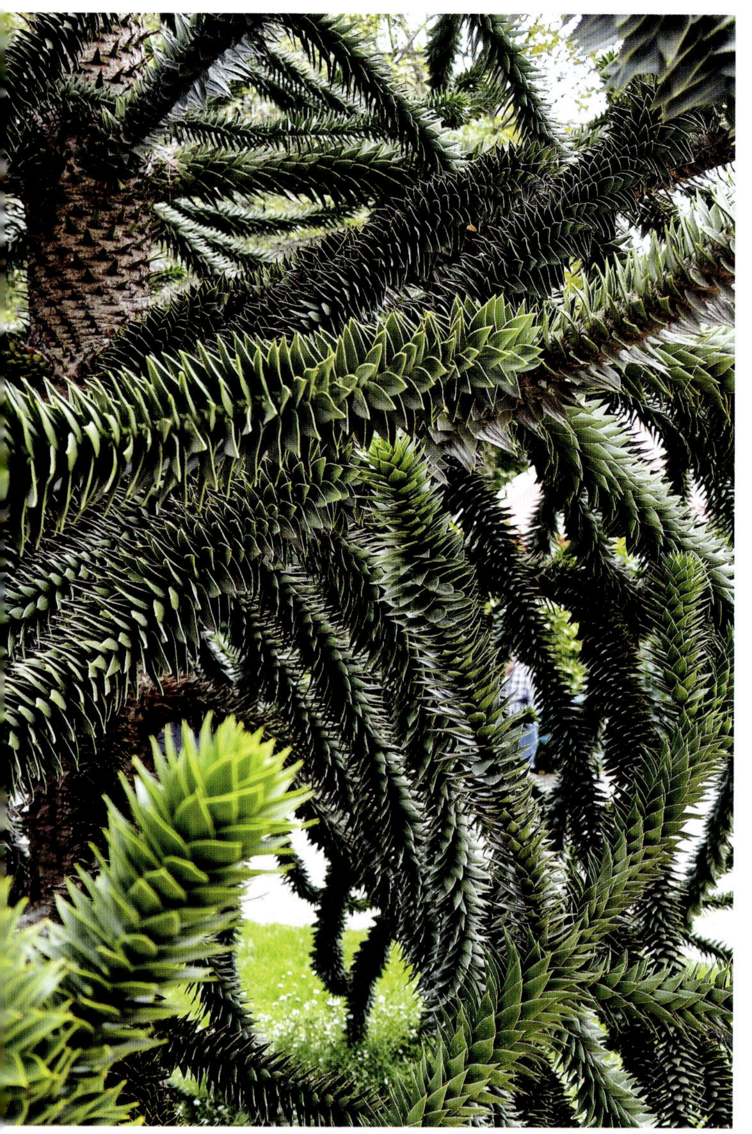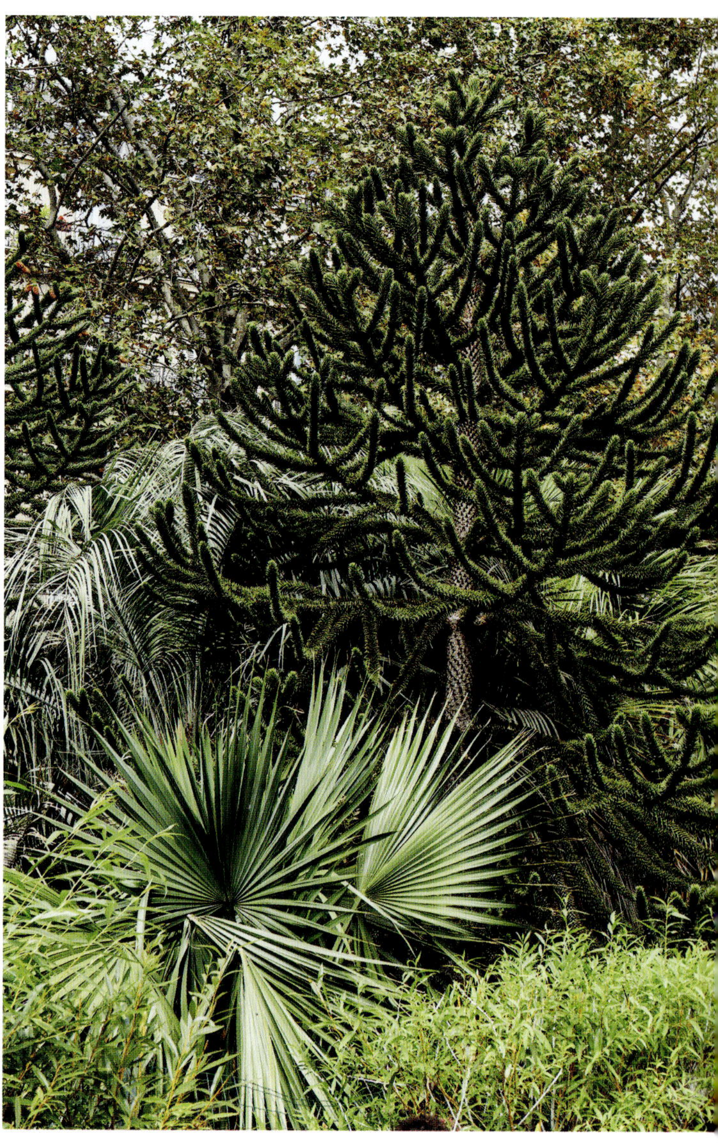

Native to South America, a monkeypuzzle tree, or *désespoir des singes*, is an evergreen conifer. Its spindle-like branches, with their flat pins, draw attention among the other plantings. In the summer, a bed of flowers surrounds the base, giving it a colorful stage.

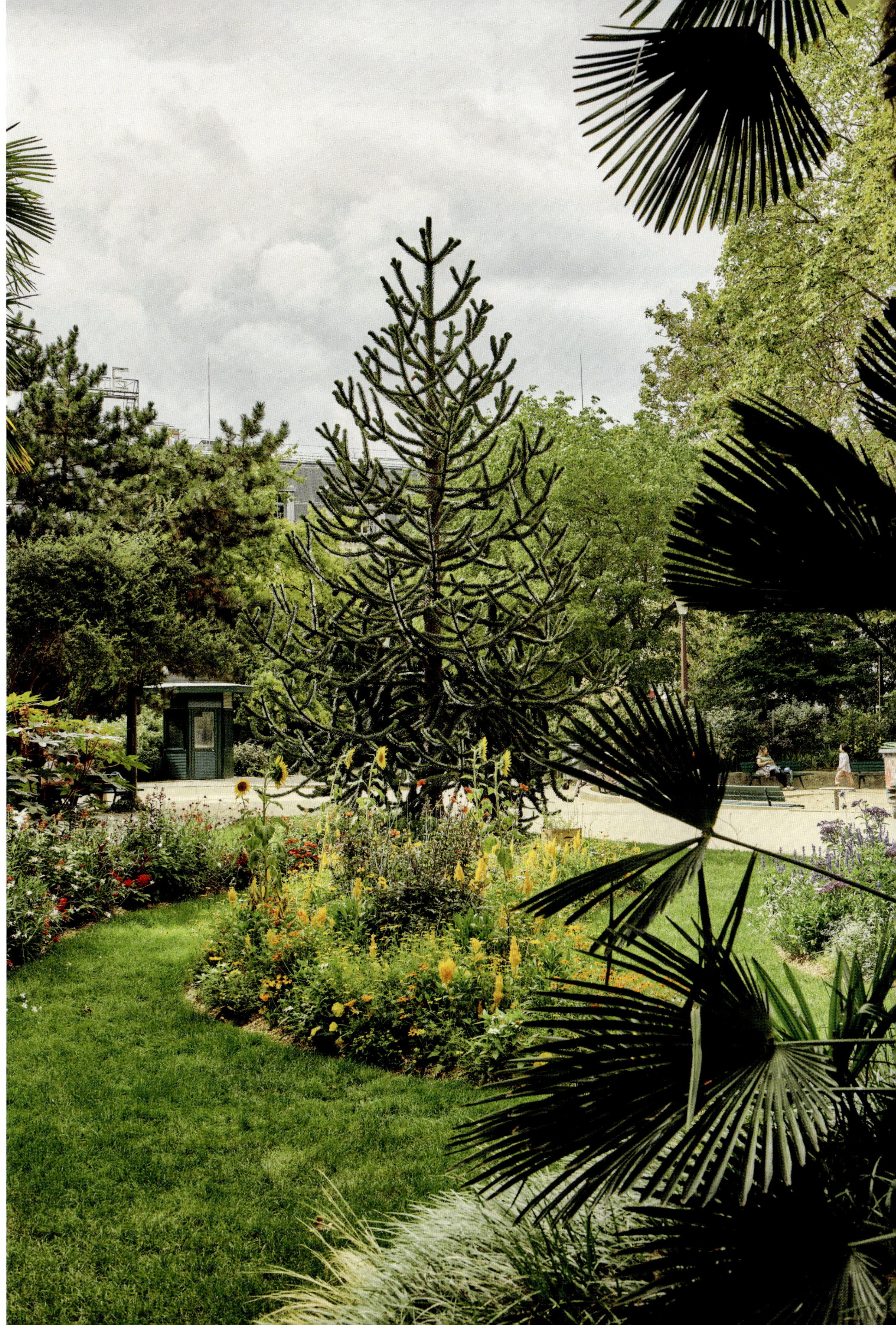

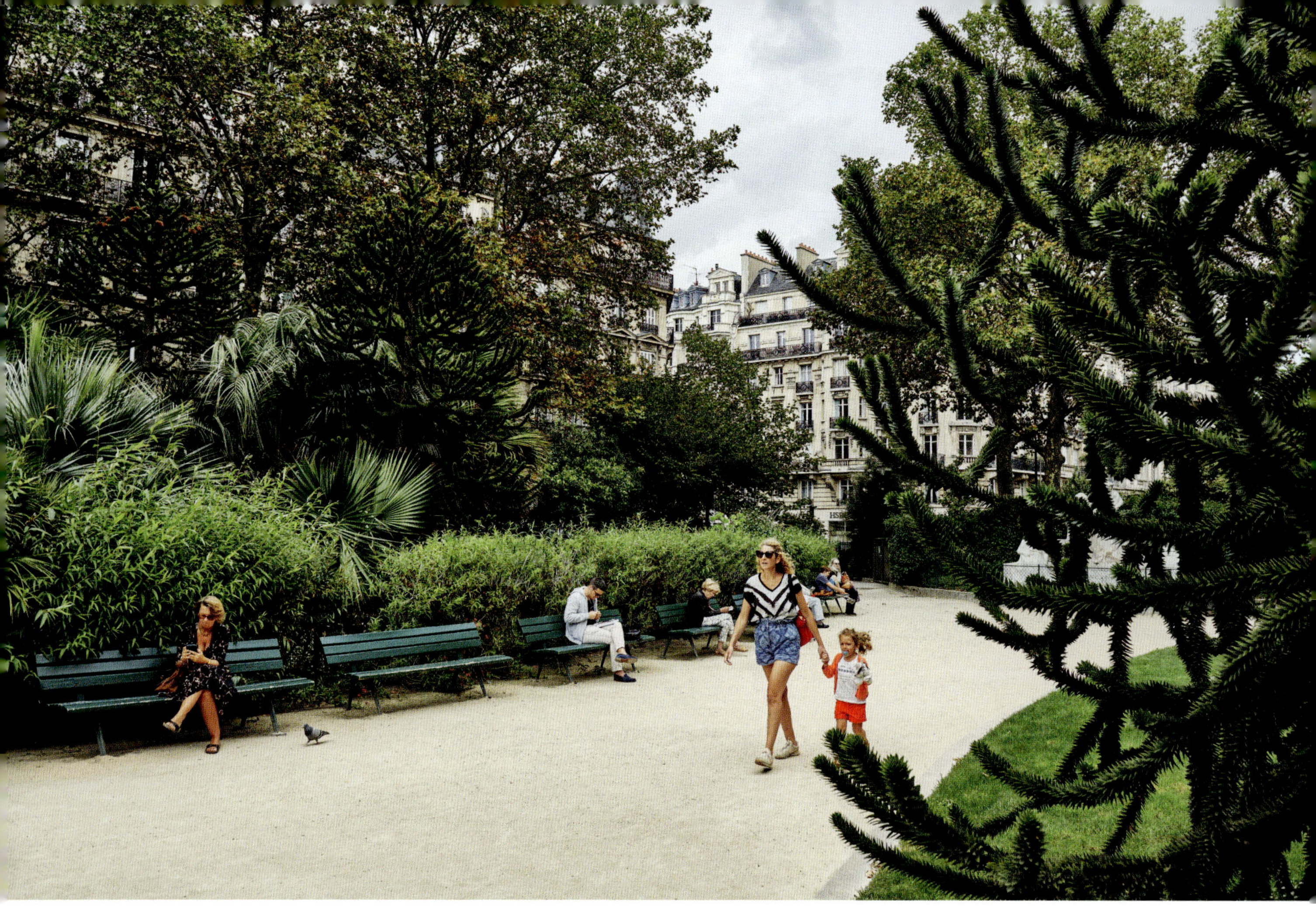

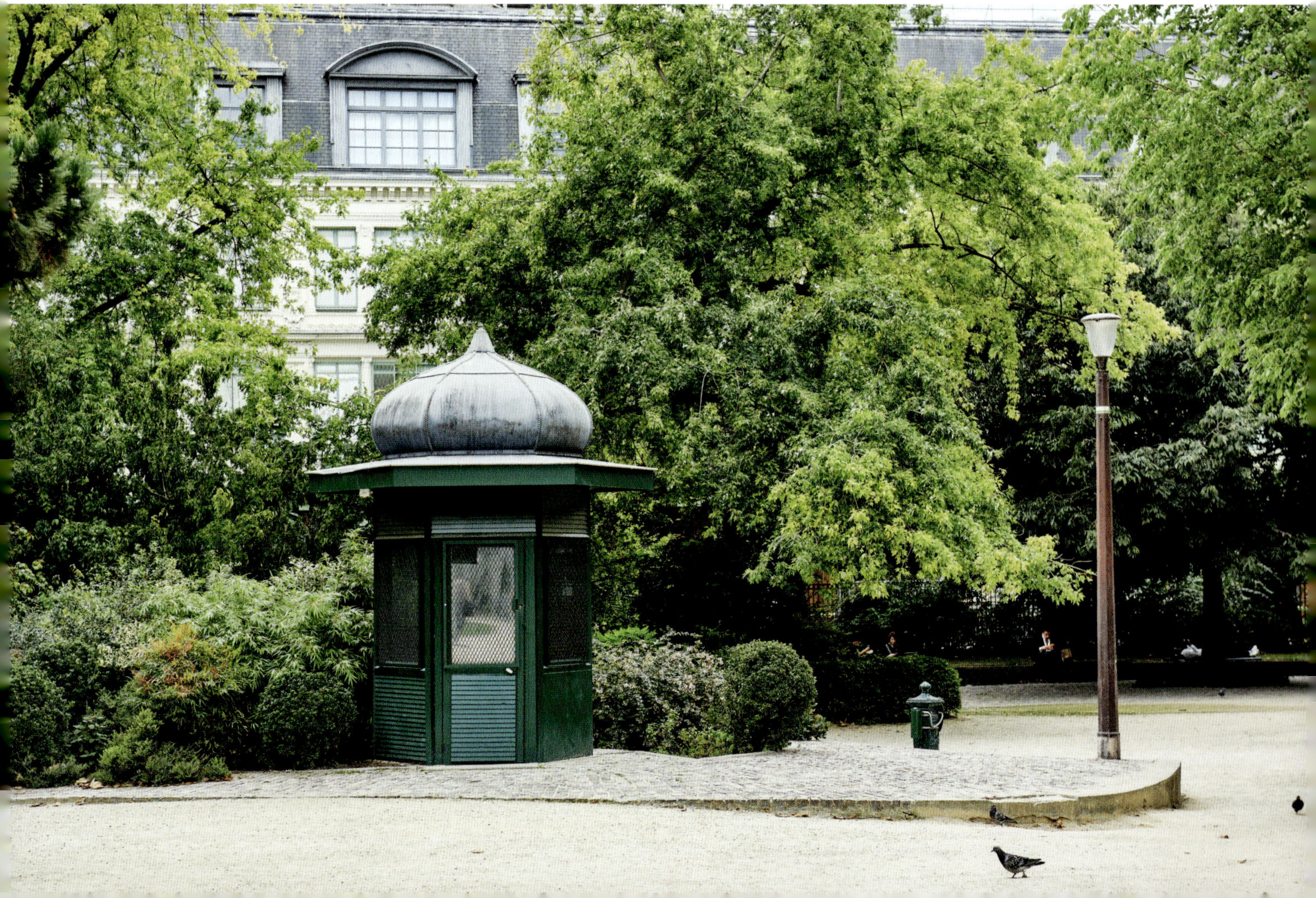

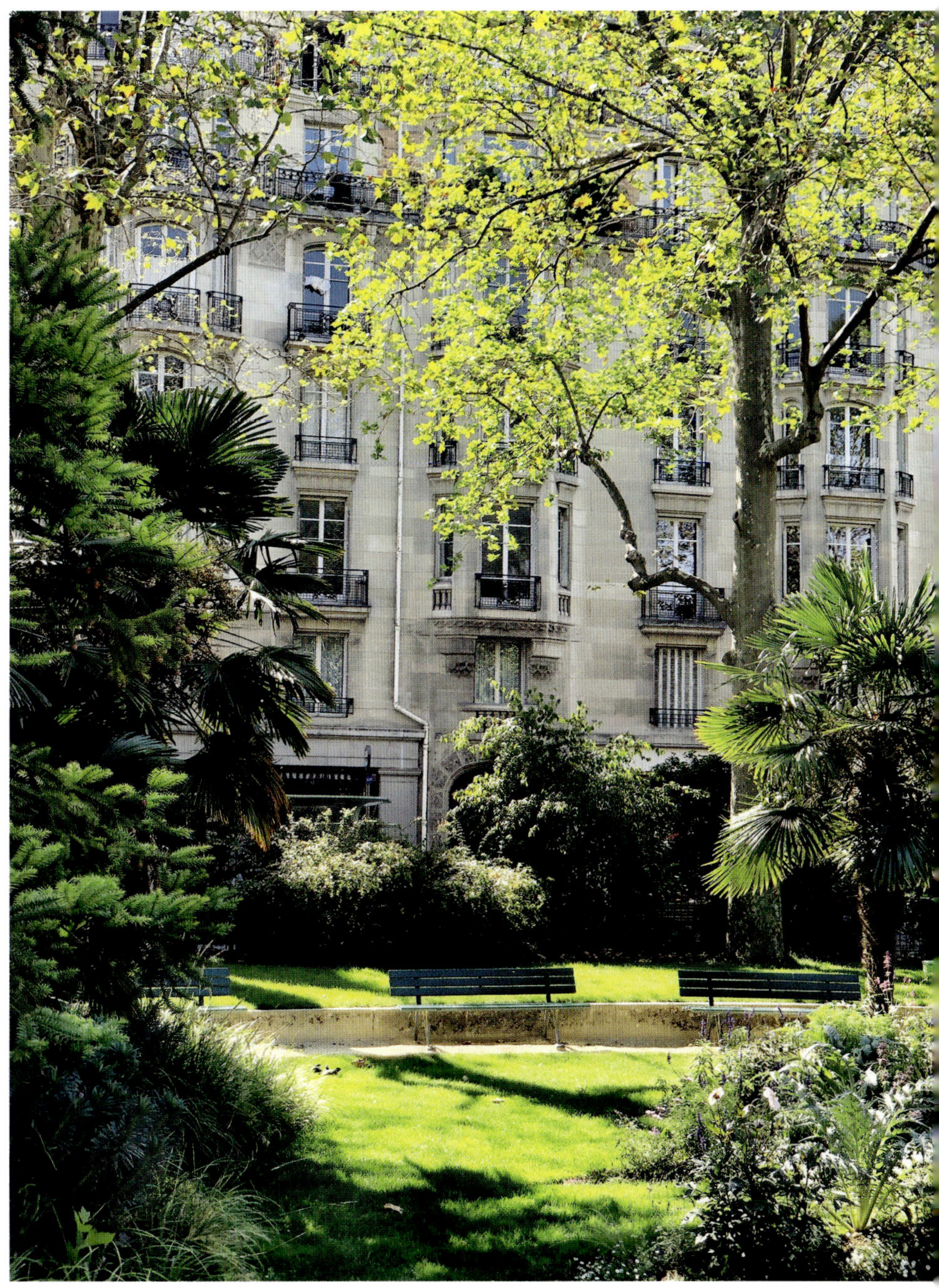

OPPOSITE ABOVE
Layers of trees of varying heights, from
the shorter palmettos to towering plane
trees, are a backdrop to the rows of
park benches.

OPPOSITE BELOW
Under the direction of Baron
Haussmann, all *mobilier urbain*, or street
furniture, was standardized and painted
dark green, including the benches
and kiosks, such as the domed one
standing near la rue Velpeau entrance of
square Boucicaut.

ABOVE RIGHT
Square Boucicaut has been transformed
from its origins in the style of an open
public square to the feeling of an
intimate hidden garden. It only took 150
years or so.

# Square Roger-Stéphane

7th arrondissement
1933

t is very easy to miss le square Roger-Stéphane. Unlike square Boucicaut, which sits on a very visible triangle of one of Paris's well-known neighborhoods and is a few minutes' walk away, square Roger-Stéphane is off a tiny carless street. It is a well-kept secret, surrounded by a mixture of modern architecture and buildings from the 1750s. The square and the street that leads to the park were originally named for Juliette Récamier, who is famous as the beautiful muse of political and cultural France in the eighteenth century. The garden is built on the ruins of l'Abbaye-aux-bois—the site of her last salon—which was destroyed in 1907. In 2007, the park's name was changed in the memory of resistance fighter Roger Stéphane. Over the years, dead trees were felled and replaced as part of maintaining the park. The density of the trees and plants add to the cool temperature of this serene location.

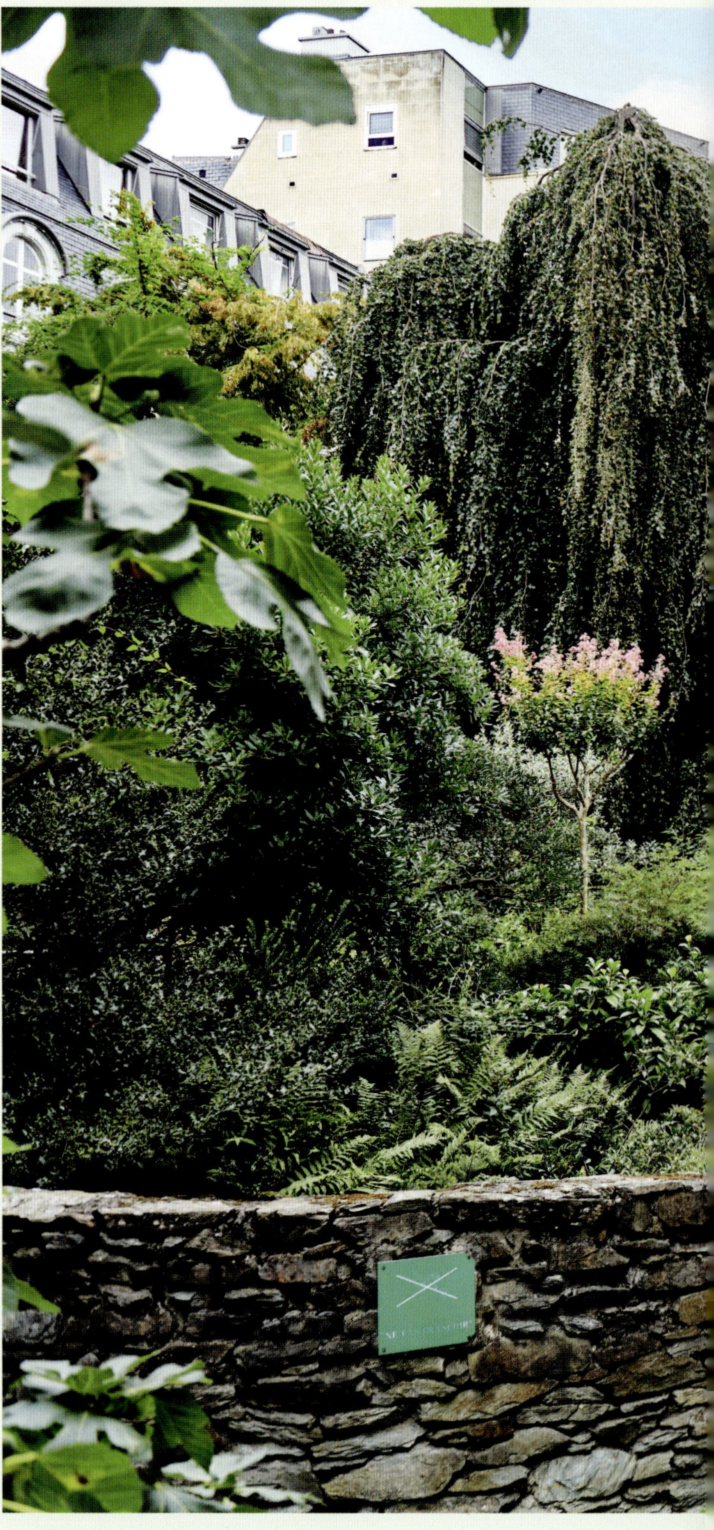

A fig tree at the entrance welcomes visitors. The sloped walkway past the rhododendrons was made from a combination of pavers and blocks of stone. Many of the terraces of the 1970s apartment building overlooking the square are also filled with plants.

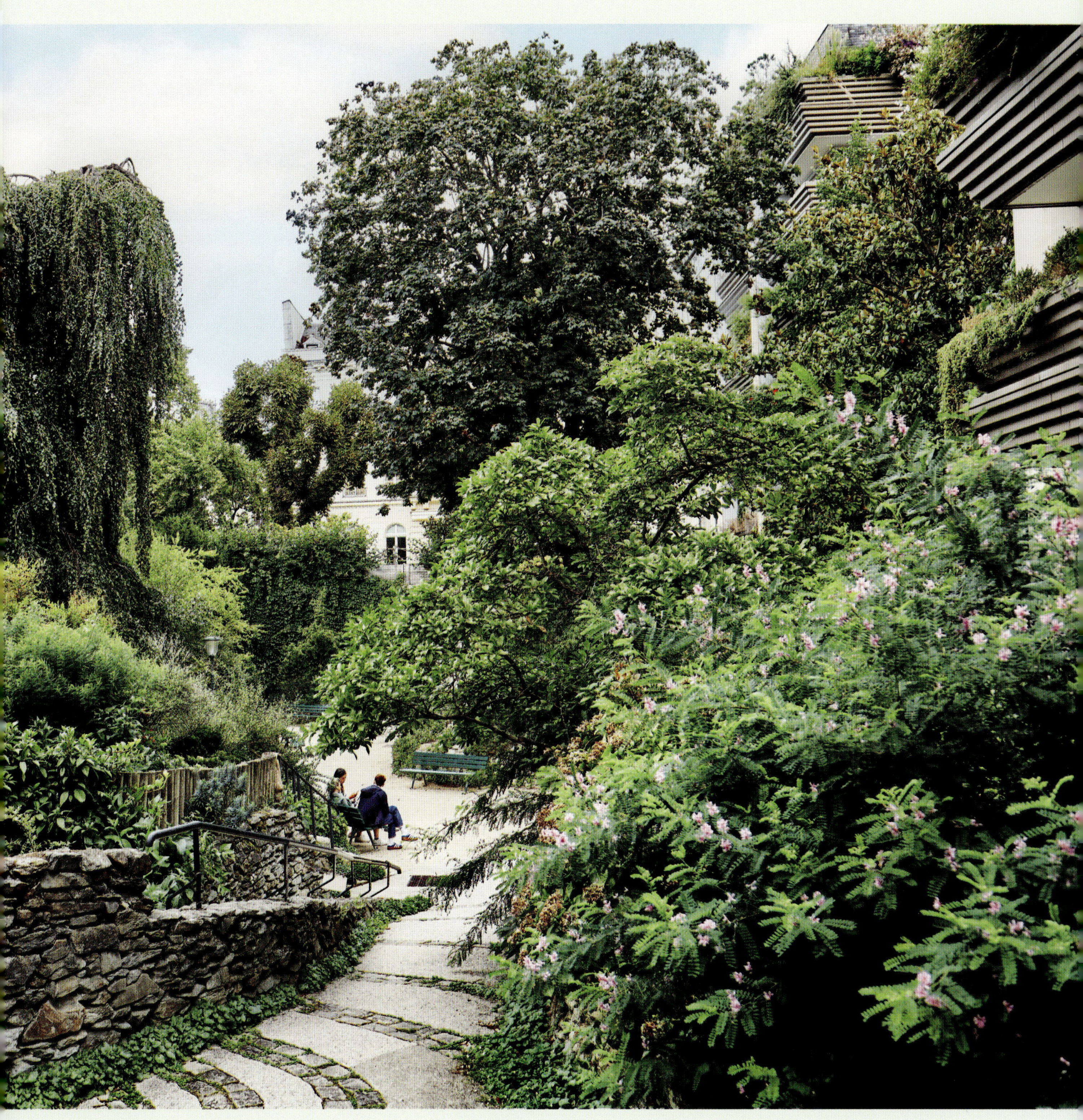

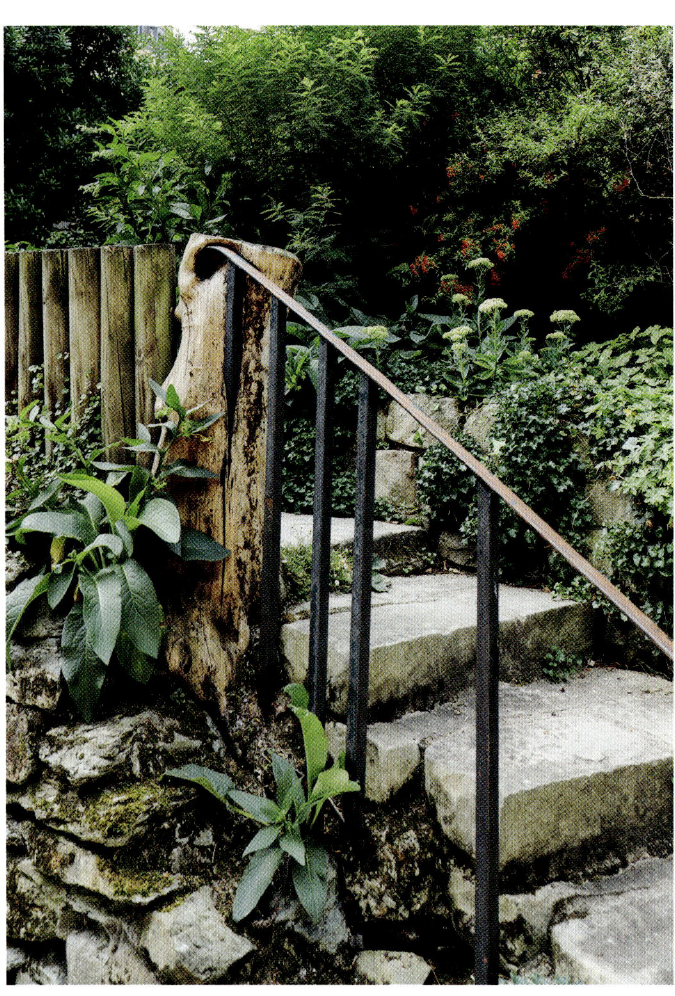

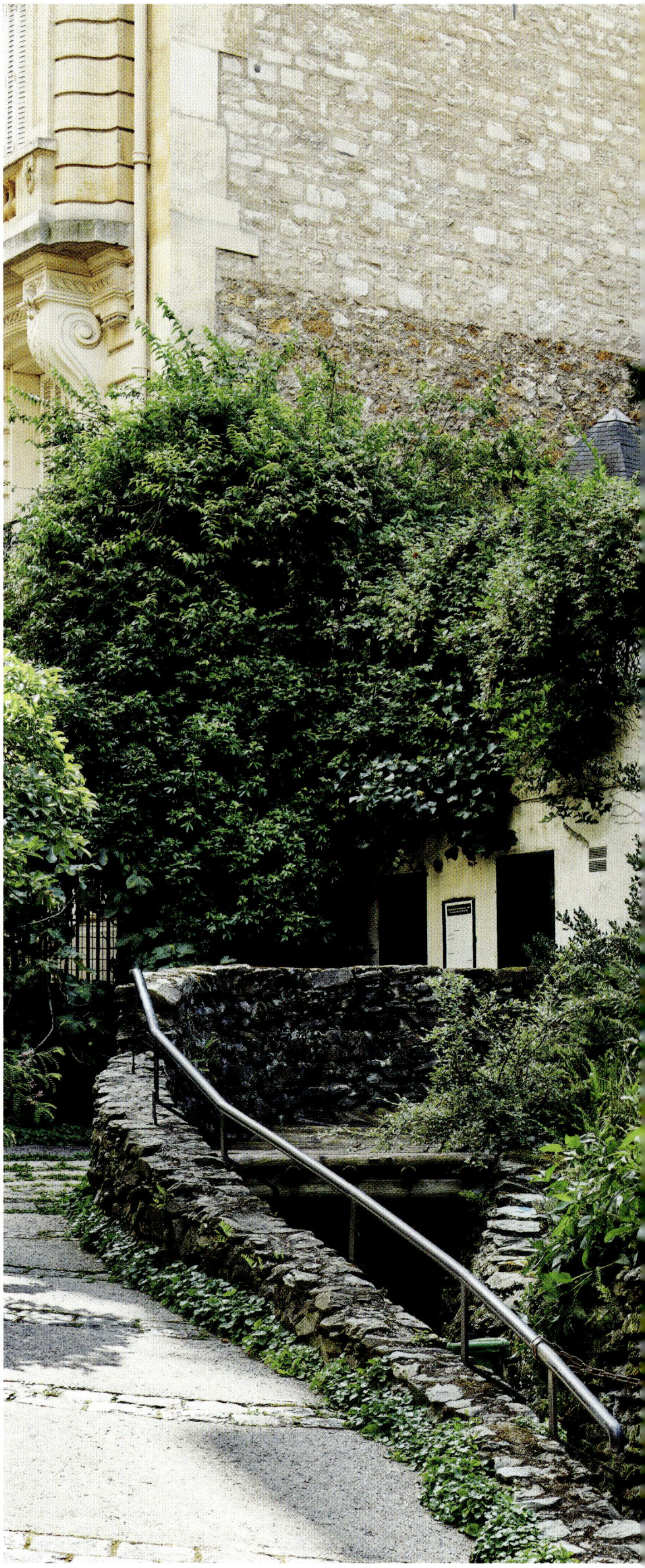

ABOVE
The trunk of a tree grew around the iron
handrailing and was later incorporated
into the wooden garden fencing.

RIGHT
A curved rock wall of the garden leads
down to the main section and to an
upper terrace of plantings. A shed is
hidden from view by the overgrowth of a
variety of trees and plants.

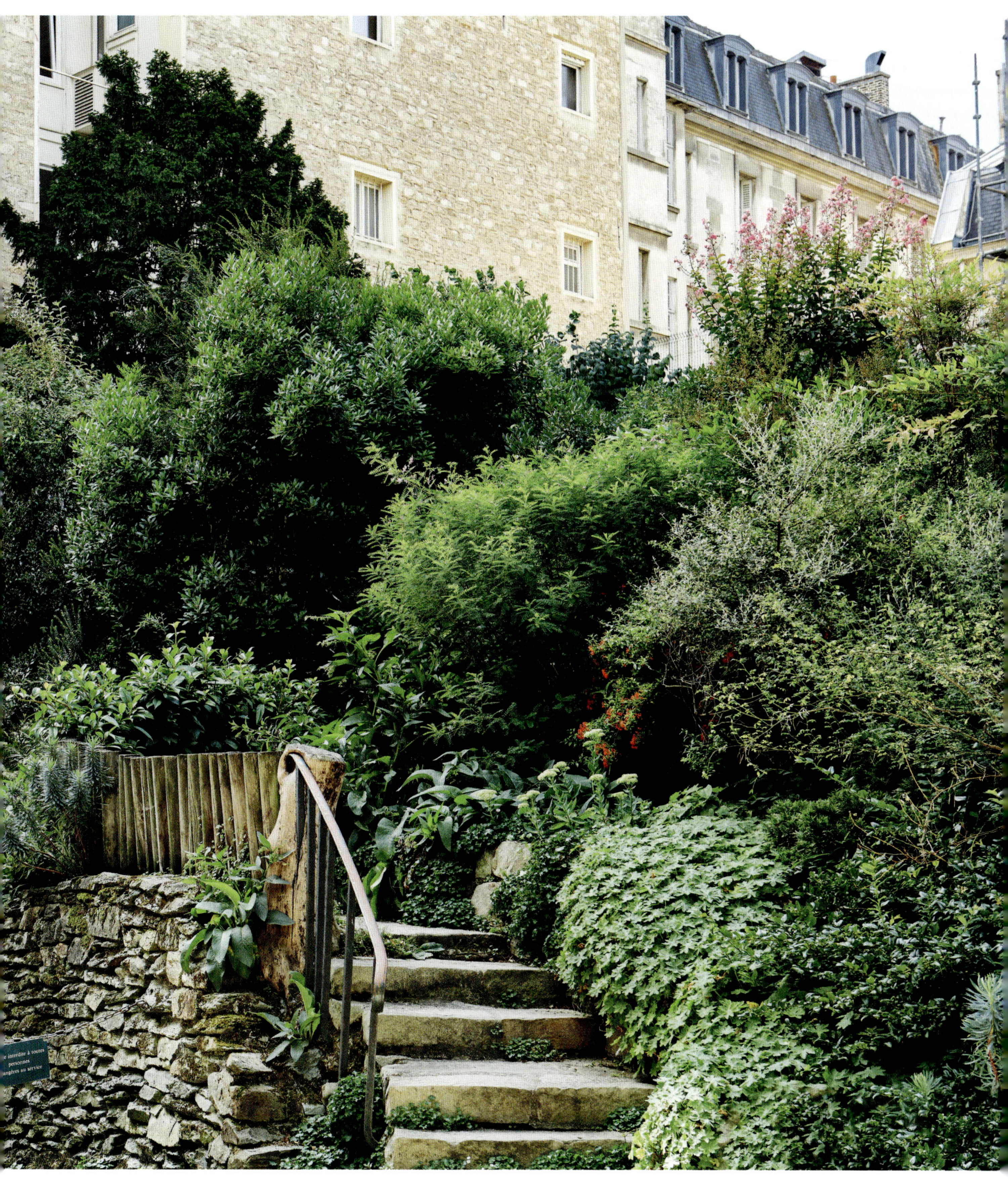

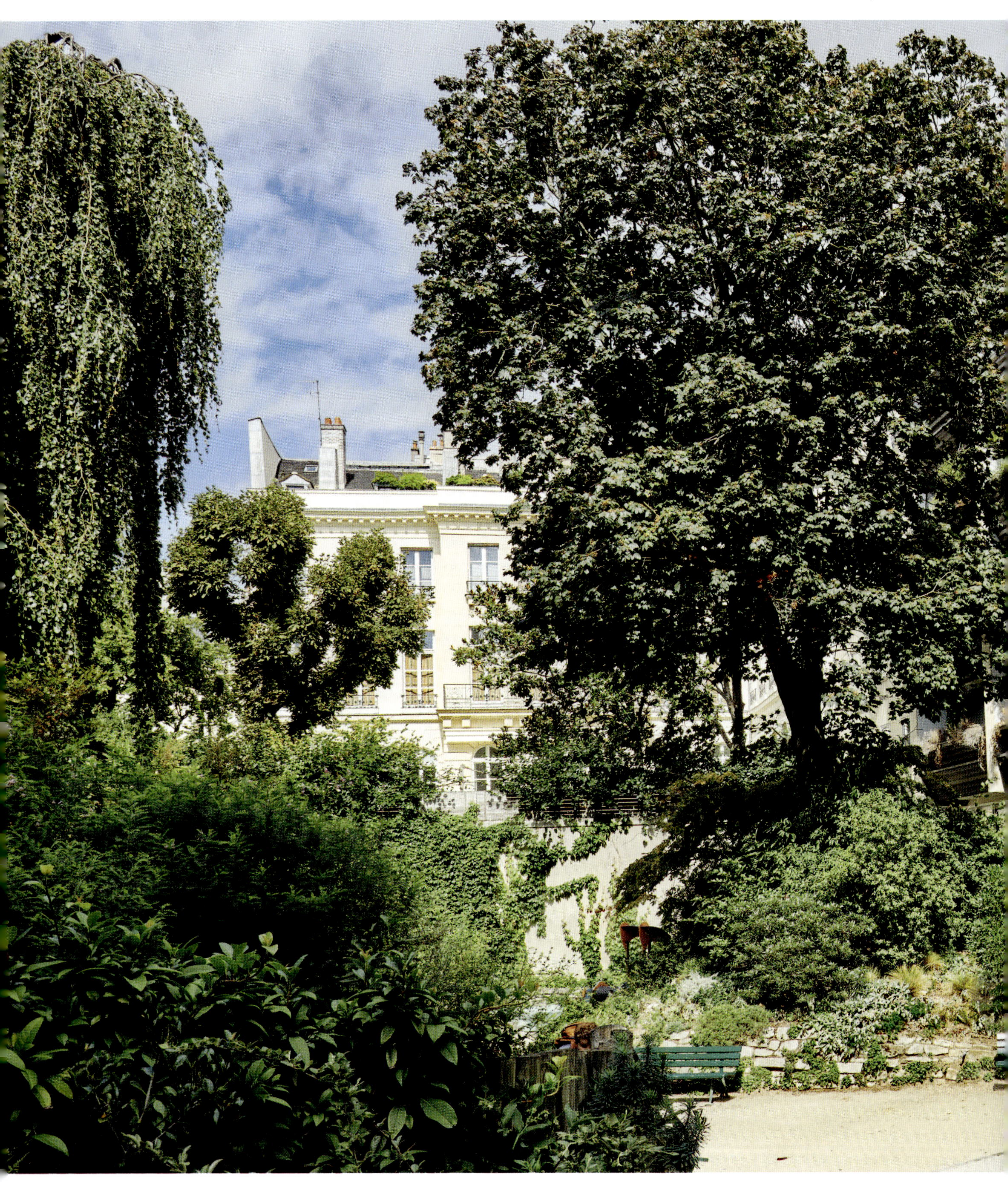

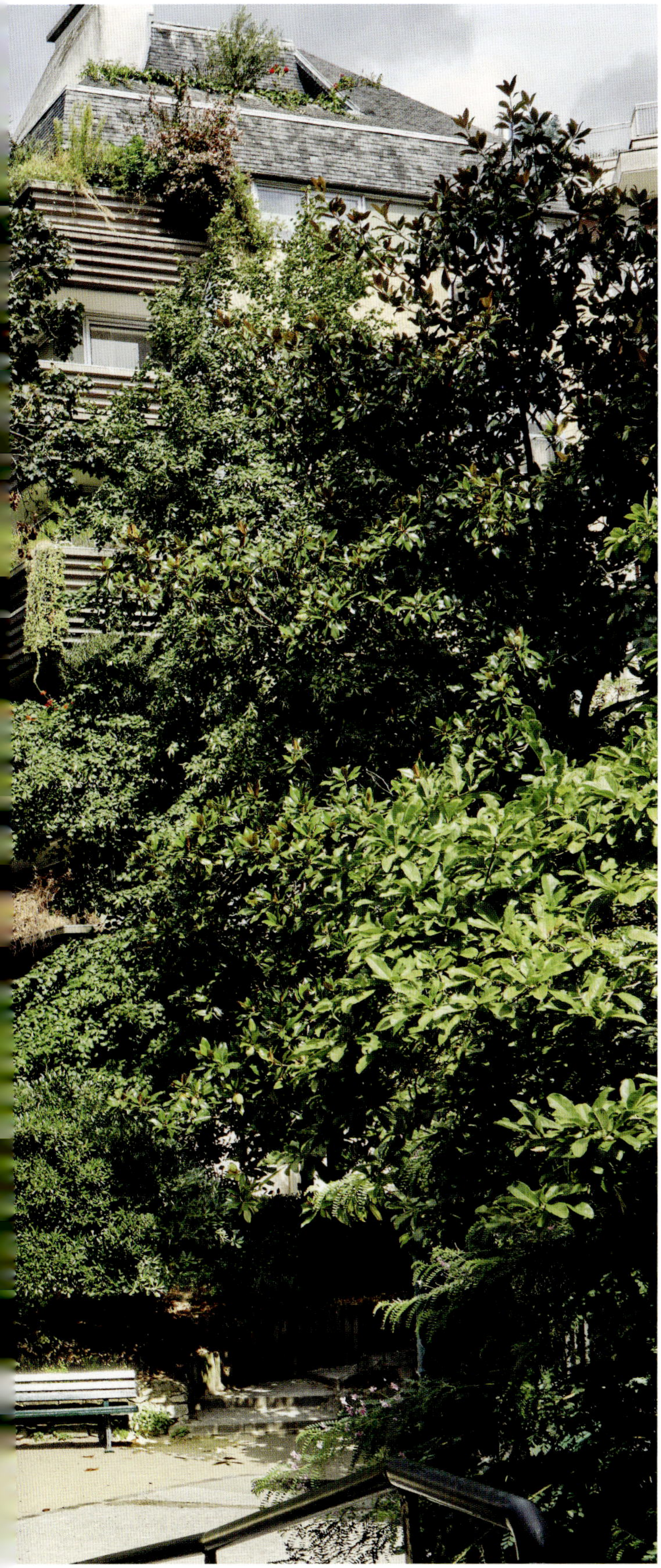

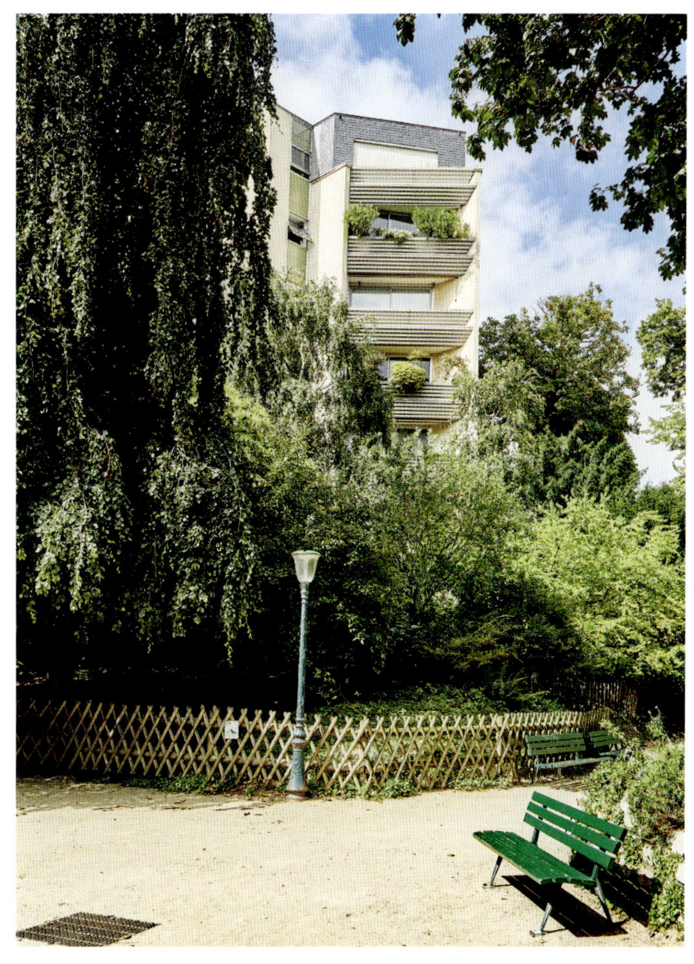

**LEFT**
A plane tree also has a large presence
in the garden, as does a magnolia. The
back garden wall is covered in ivy.

**ABOVE**
The square does not have a lawn; only
benches are used for seating. The
contrast between the surrounding
architecture from the eighteenth
century and the 1970s adds to the
garden's allure.

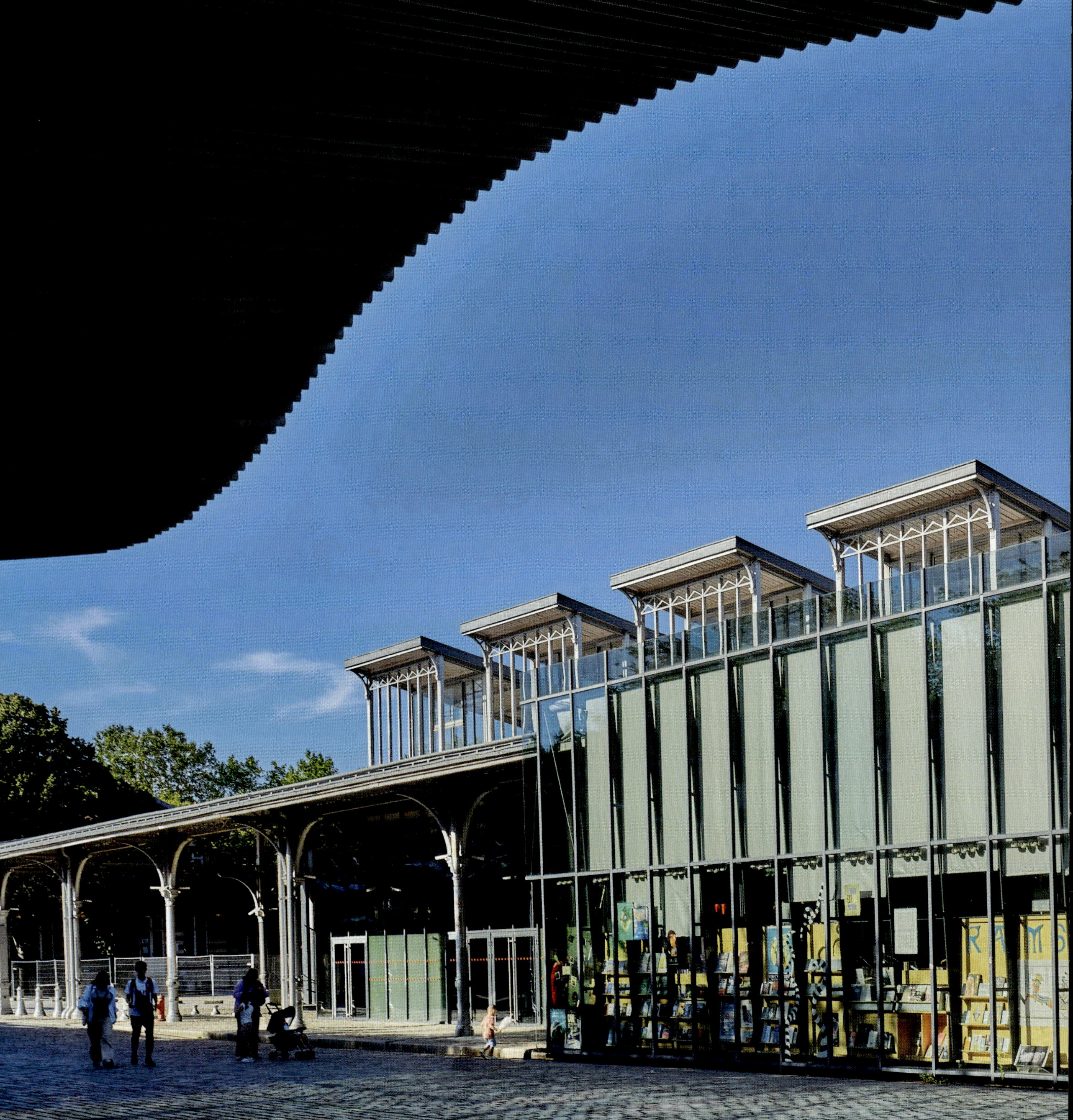



**ABOVE**
The contemporary canopy shades the walkway alongside the old cattle market, commissioned by Baron Haussmann from architect Jules de Mérindol in 1865. The Grande Hall de la Villette is a center of activity and contains a bookstore, restaurants, and exhibition halls.

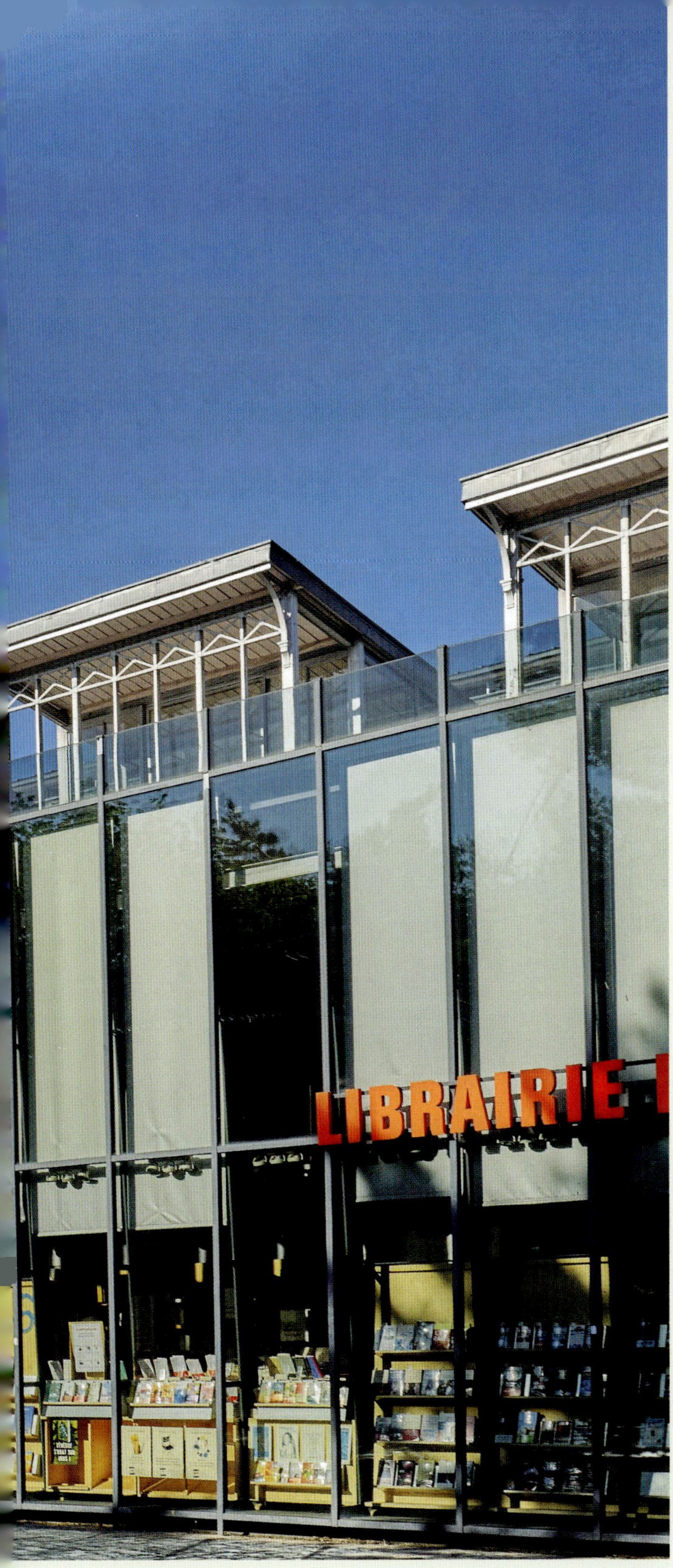

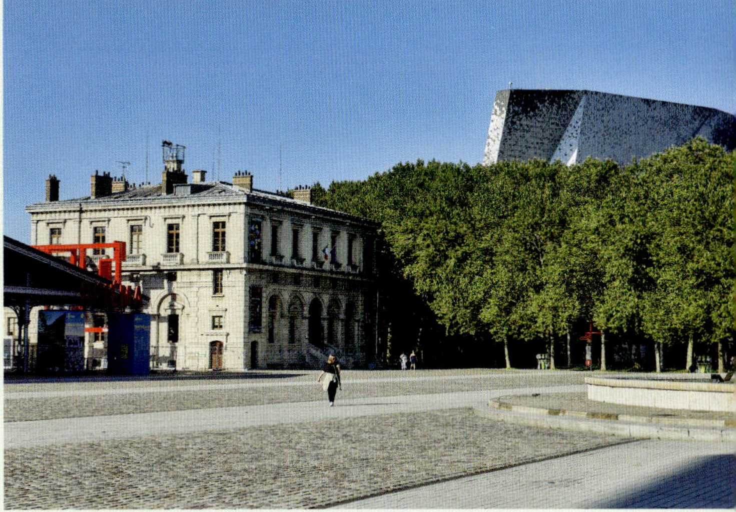



## *Parc de la Villette*
### 19th arrondissement
### 1982–2016

n 1982, La Villette was one of the last large areas in Paris—137 acres, or 55.5 hectares—that was awaiting a renewal. It became part of President François Mitterrand's Grand Projets plan. Since Napoleon III, in the mid-nineteenth century, the site was home to a cattle market and slaughterhouse that, as the process of producing meat changed, eventually outlasted its use. Architect Bernard Tschumi won the competition to reconceive the site. His plan was not a typical urban park. Tschumi took the approach that culture, not nature, should lead the design. Thus, the park has multiple museums, performance centers, sculptures, gardens, and twenty-six follies that take a different vision of nature in the city. The remaining buildings of the old cattle market were looped into the design and now house the Grande Halle de la Villette and the Théâtre Paris-Villette. In 2015, architect Jean Nouvel created a new symphony hall for the Philharmonie de Paris with more than 2,400 seats as well as rehearsal spaces, adding an exhibition center and restaurant to the grounds. In the summer, the open green spaces are transformed into an outdoor movie theater. Visitors can stroll along the banks of le canal de l'Ourcq, which bisects the park, or view an outdoor art exhibition, or take their children to one of the playgrounds. It seems at parc de la Villette, *tout est possible*.

**ABOVE RIGHT**
A diagonal row of trees separates Jean Nouvel's Philharmonie de Paris concert hall from the Pavilion Janvier with Folie Janvier at its side, as well as la place de la Fontaine-aux-Lions in the front of the Grande Halle de la Villette.

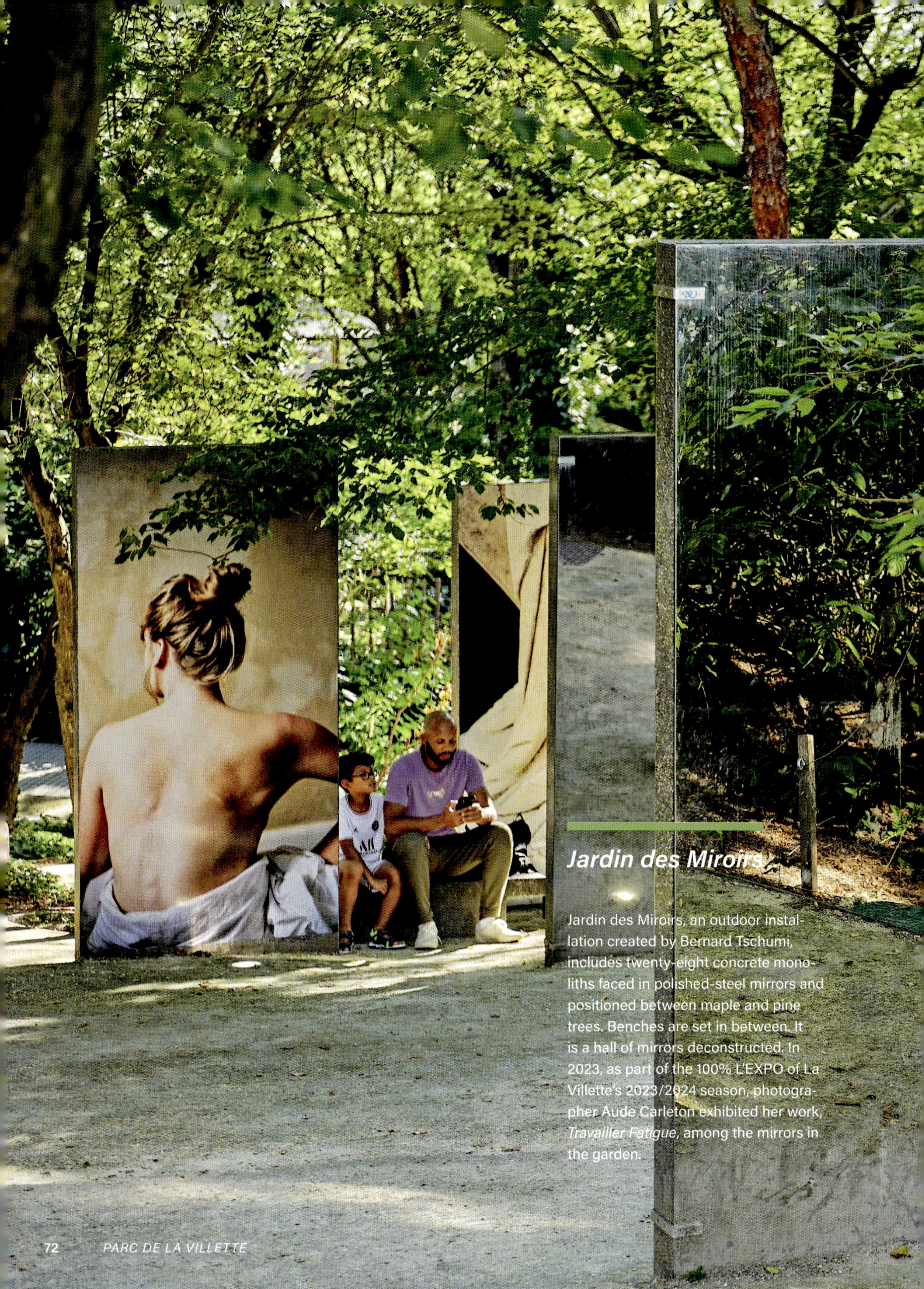

## Jardin des Miroirs

Jardin des Miroirs, an outdoor installation created by Bernard Tschumi, includes twenty-eight concrete monoliths faced in polished-steel mirrors and positioned between maple and pine trees. Benches are set in between. It is a hall of mirrors deconstructed. In 2023, as part of the 100% L'EXPO of La Villette's 2023/2024 season, photographer Aude Carleton exhibited her work, *Travailler Fatigue*, among the mirrors in the garden.

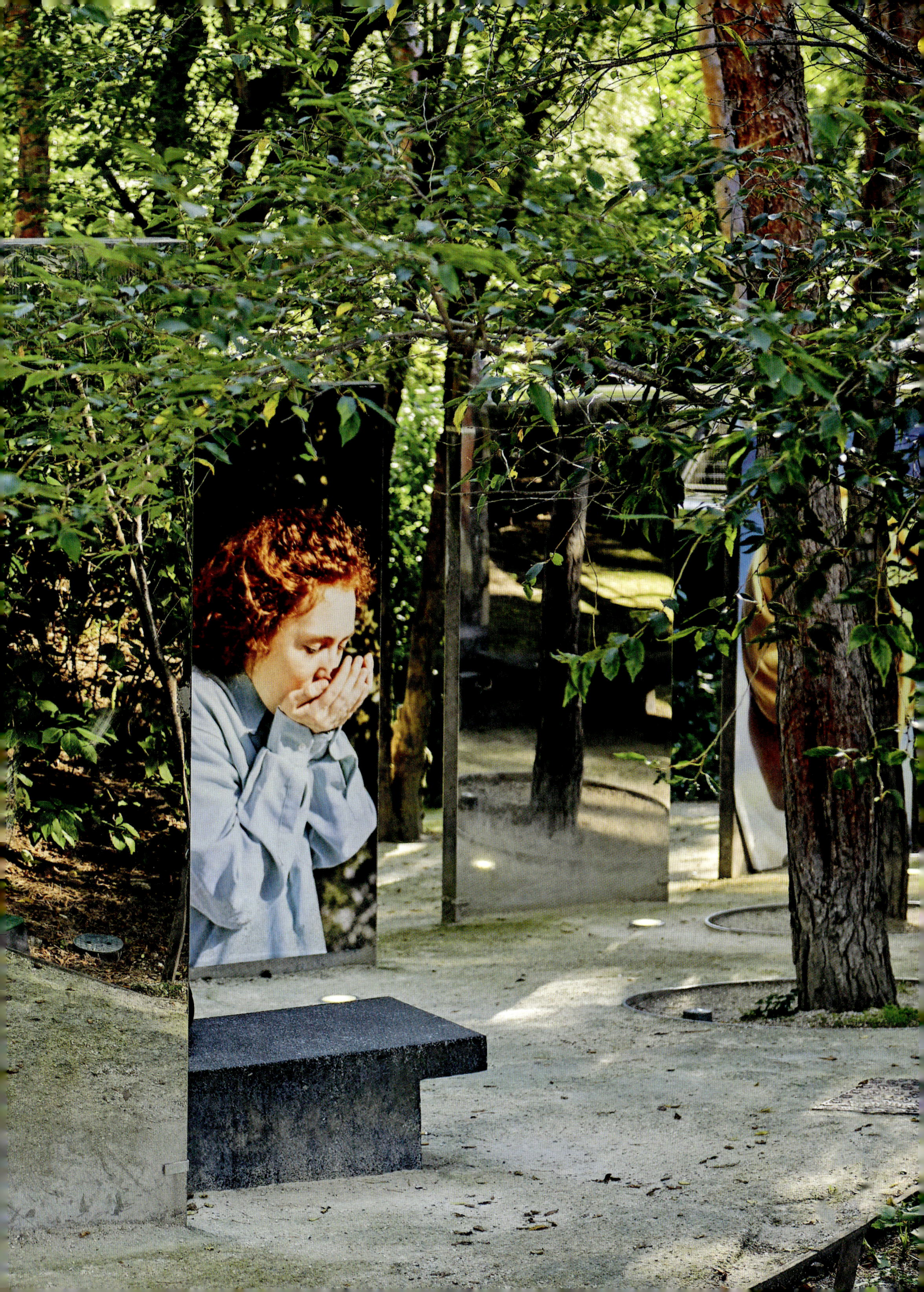

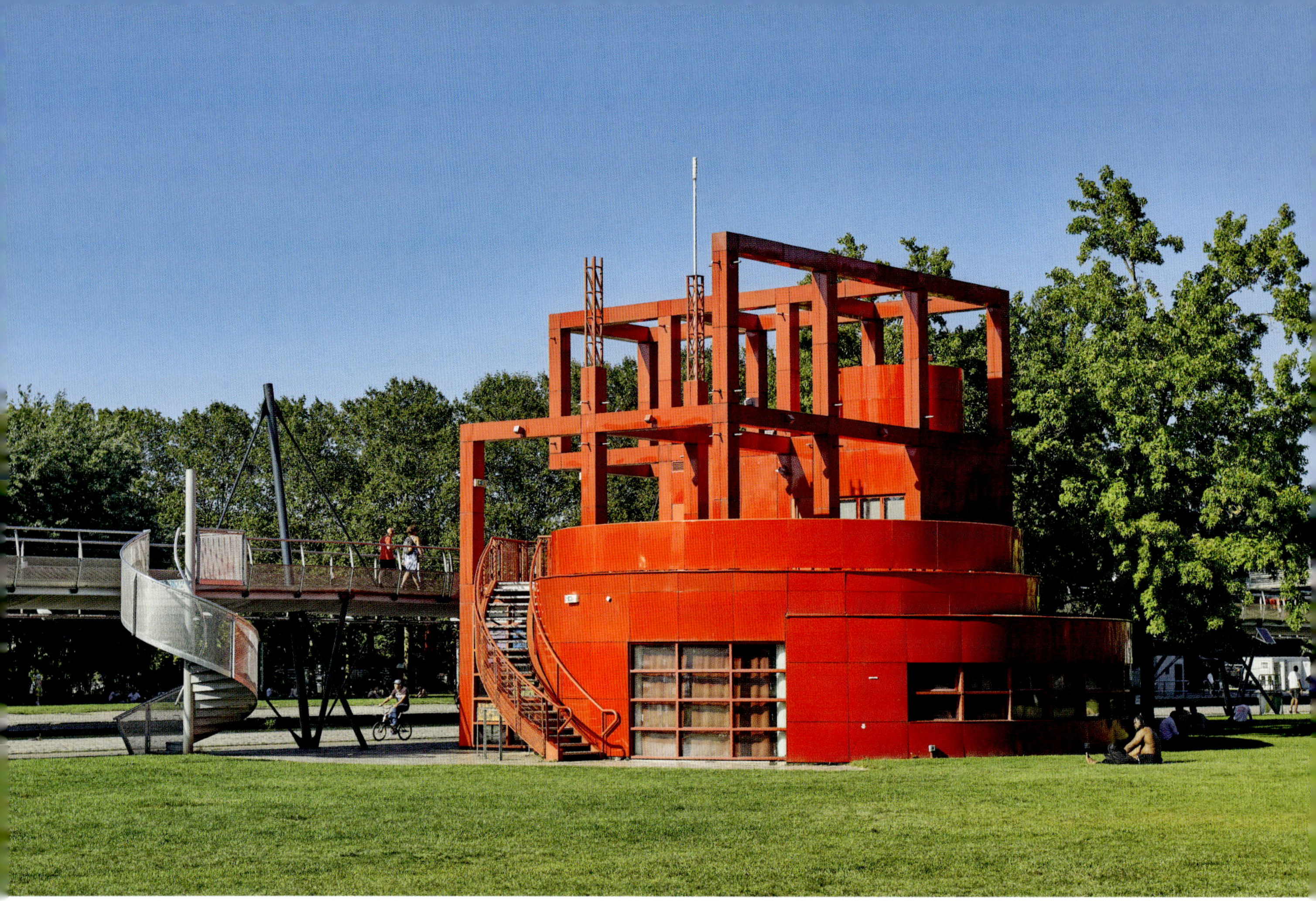

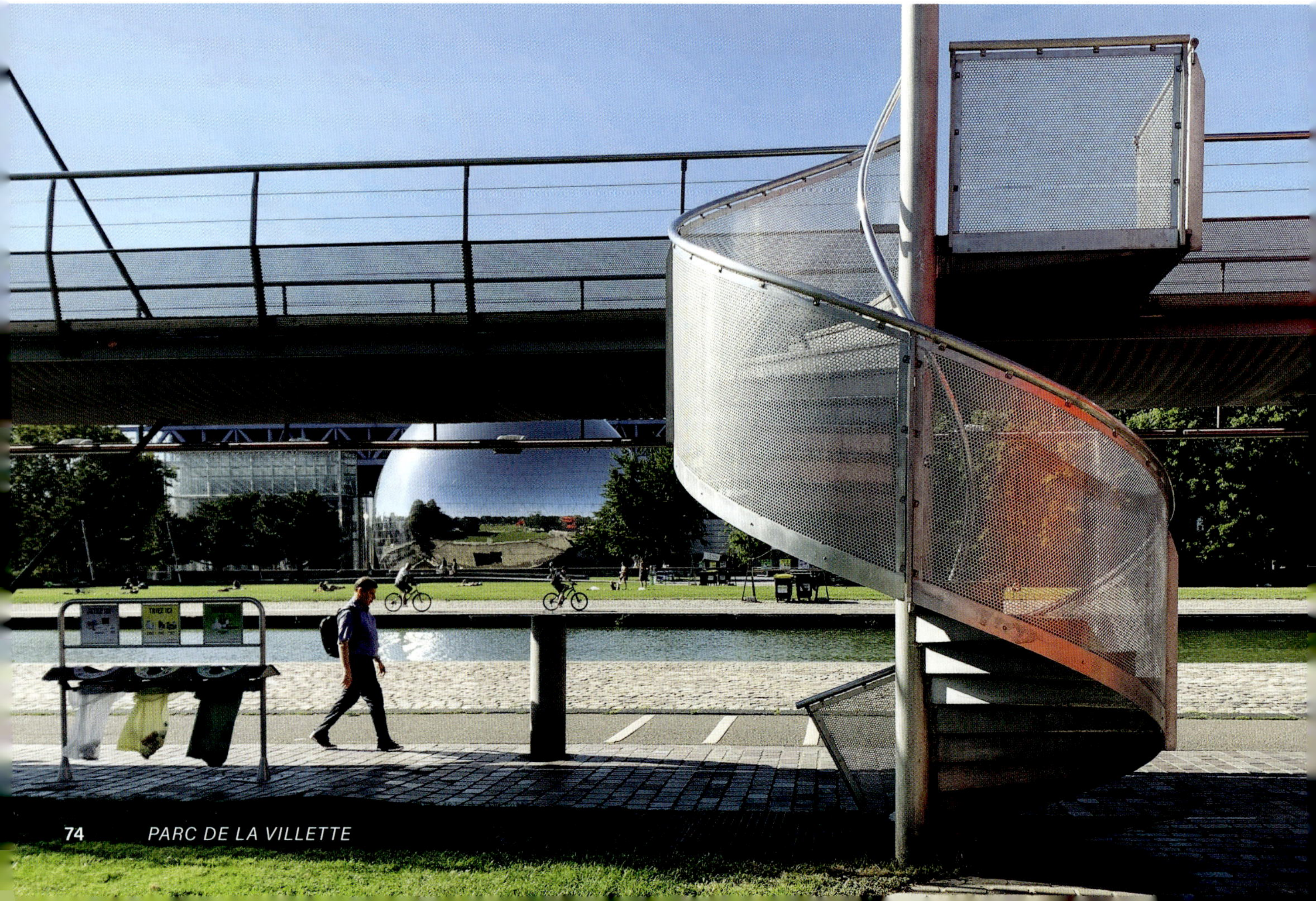

   PARC DE LA VILLETTE

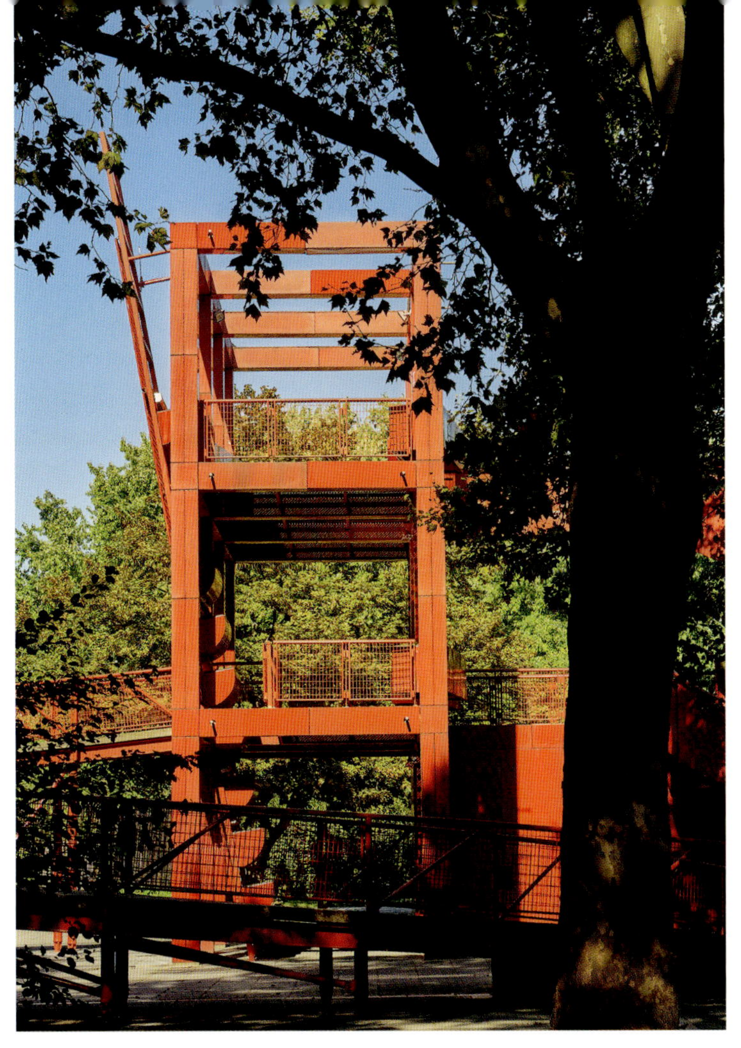

Petite Folie is next to le canal de l'Ourcq, which divides the park site.

## *Folies*

Tschumi designed twenty-six red *folies* (follies) to be placed throughout the grounds of the park. Most garden follies are playful and decorative, but these offer a way to navigate through the park. Each one has a specific name and purpose; they are united by their red color.

**OPPOSITE ABOVE**
Petite Folie is next to le canal de l'Ourcq, which divides the park site.

**OPPOSITE BELOW**
Past the raised walkway along the canal, the Géode, a geodesic dome, shimmers in the background. It is part of the campus of the Cité des Sciences et de l'Industrie and was designed by architects Adrien Fainsilber and Gérard Chamayou.

**LEFT**
Folie Belvédère has a ramp and is also used as a viewing station.

**BELOW**
Folie des Fêtes houses a space for meditation.

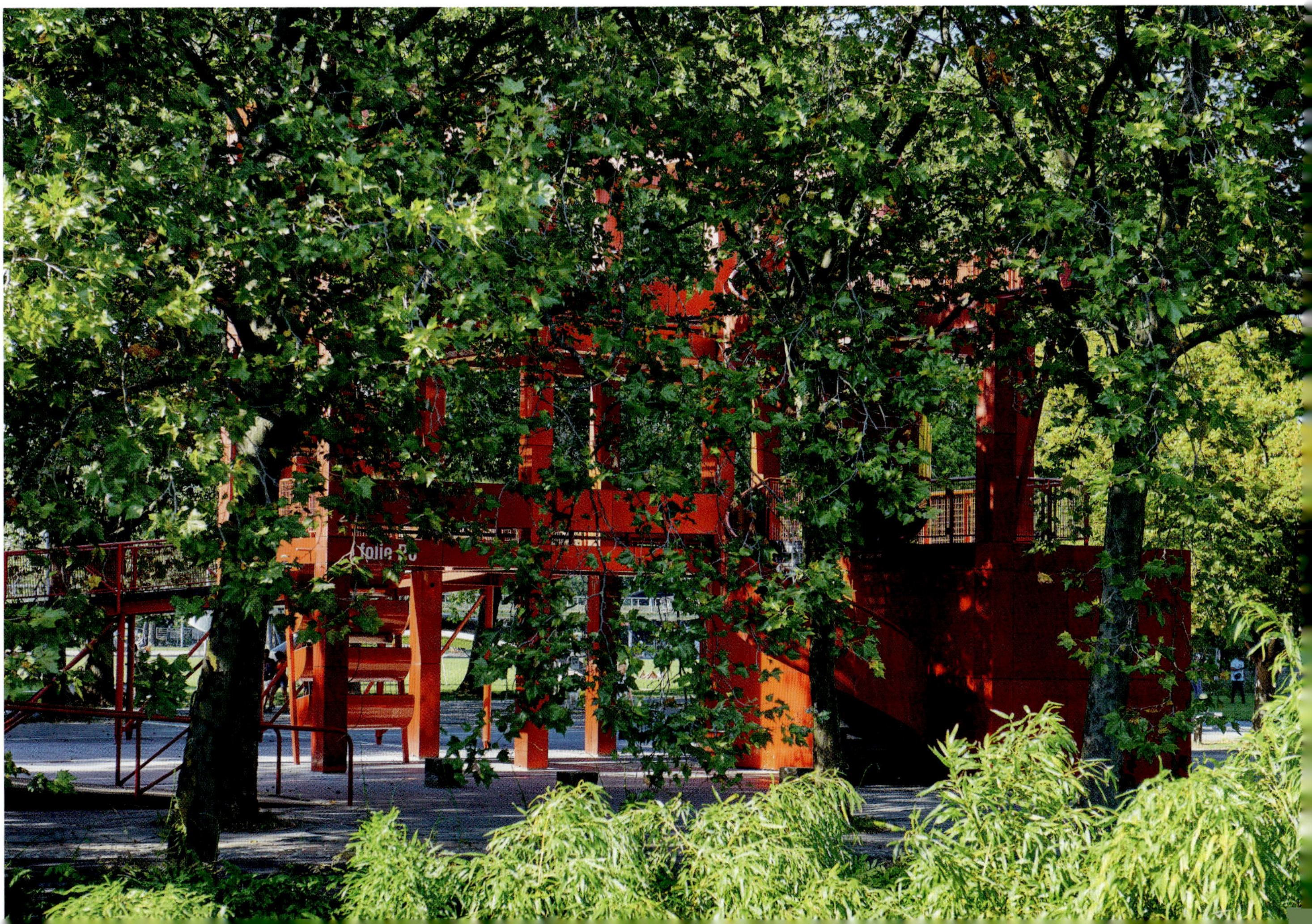

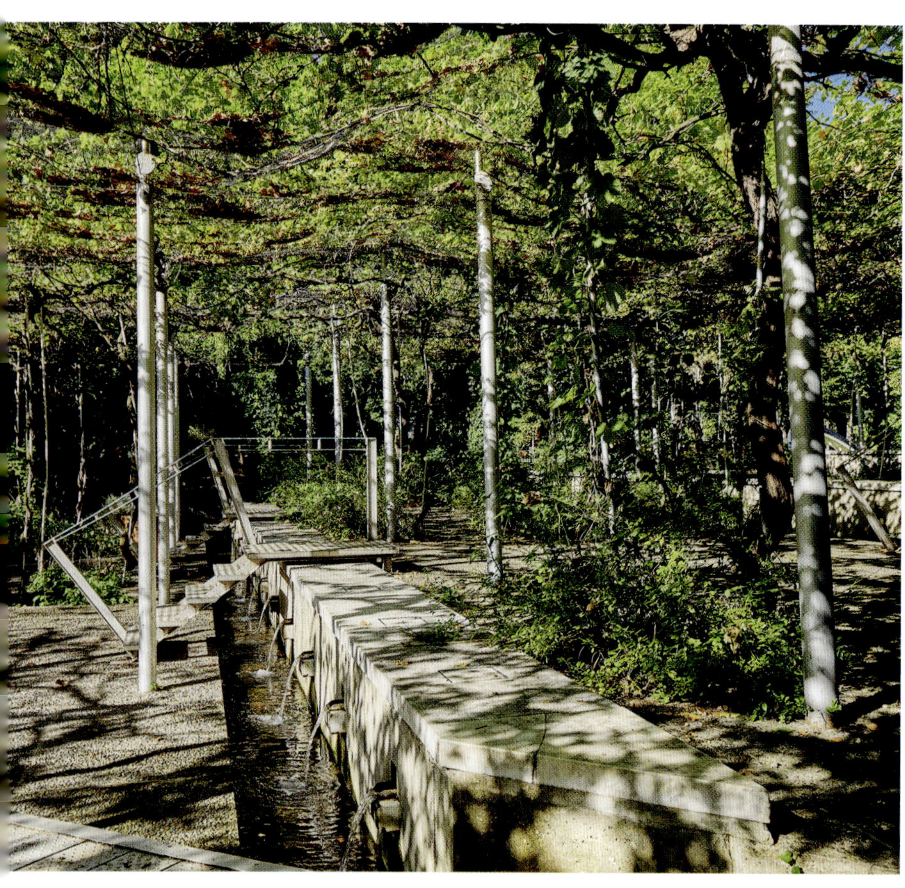

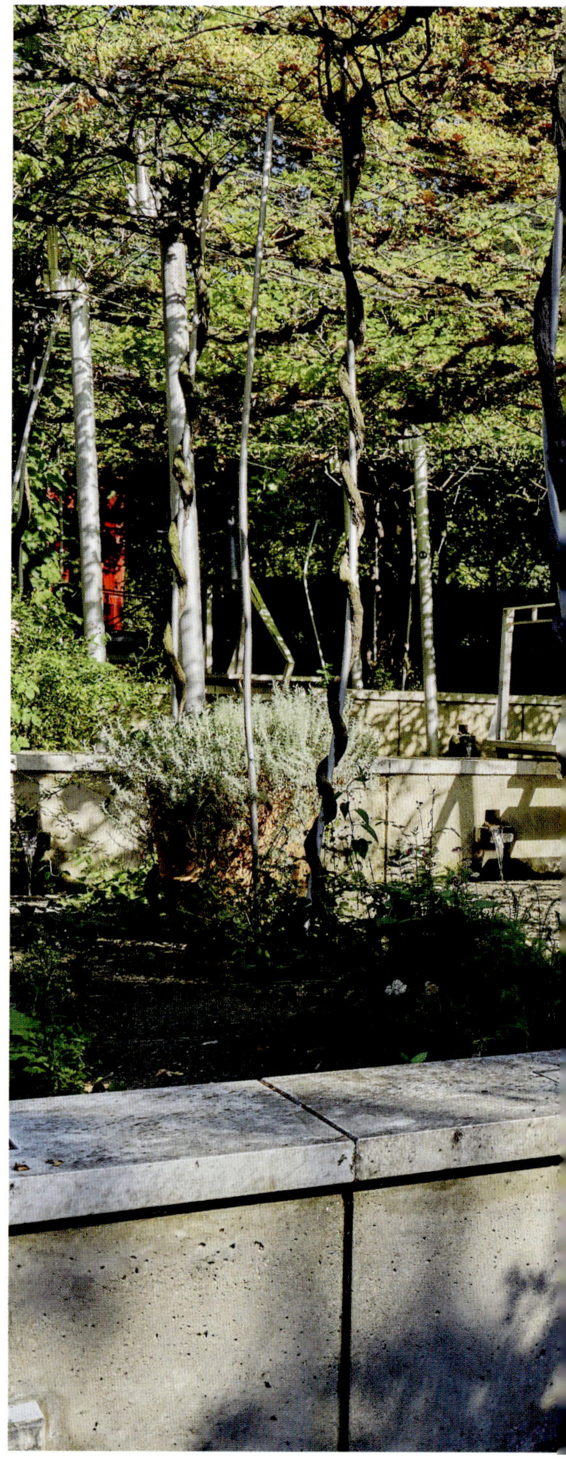

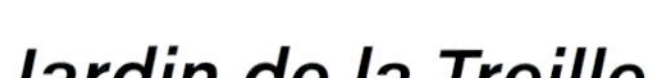

## Jardin de la Treille

**ABOVE**

Le jardin de la Treille, or the Trellis Garden, is a collaboration between nature and designer. While architect Gilles Vexlard designed the foundation of walkways, fountains, and a structural trellis, nature has created the canopy of vines that float above.

**RIGHT**

Within the concrete base are ninety small fountains, which bring the element of sound to the experience.

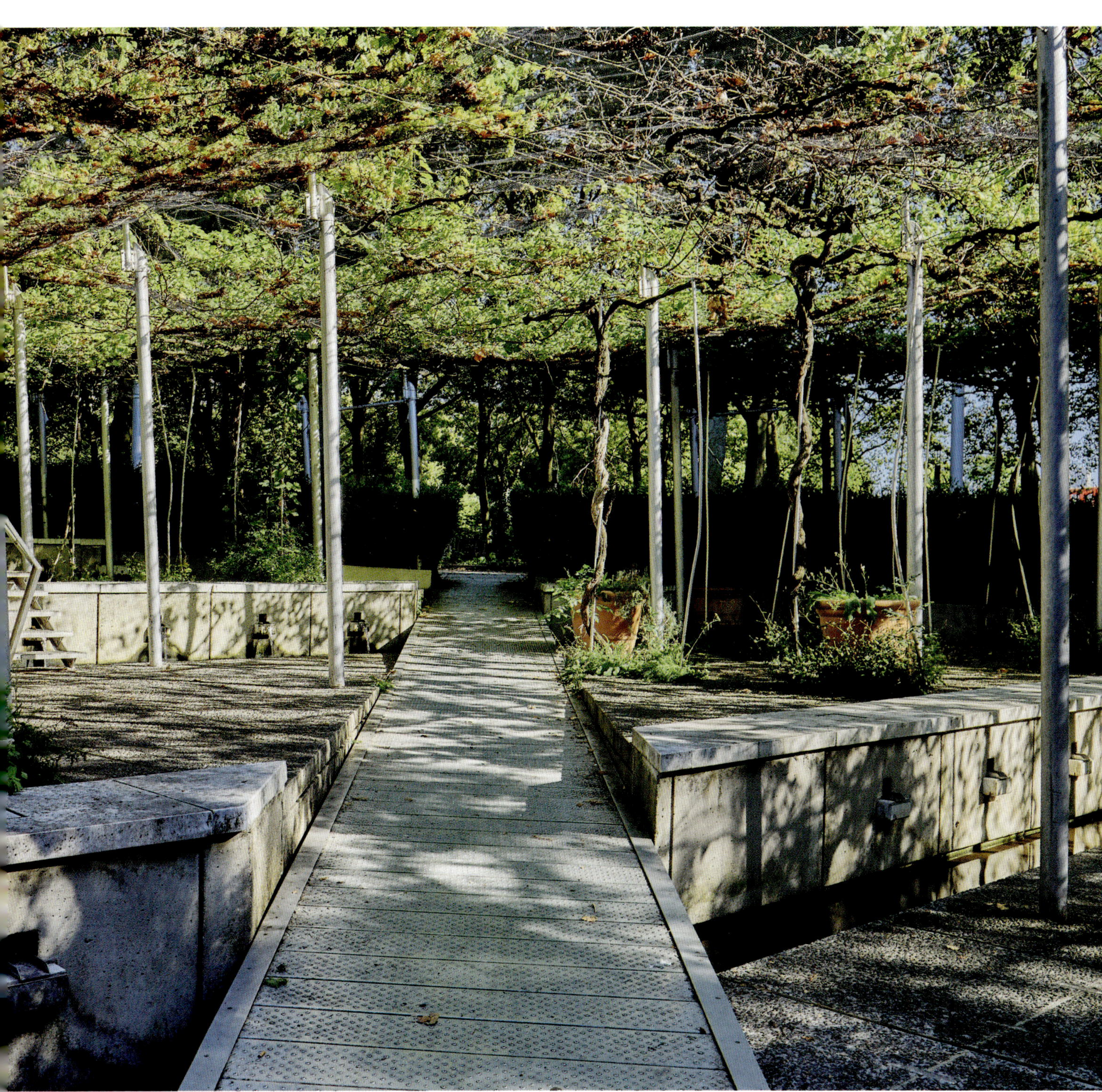

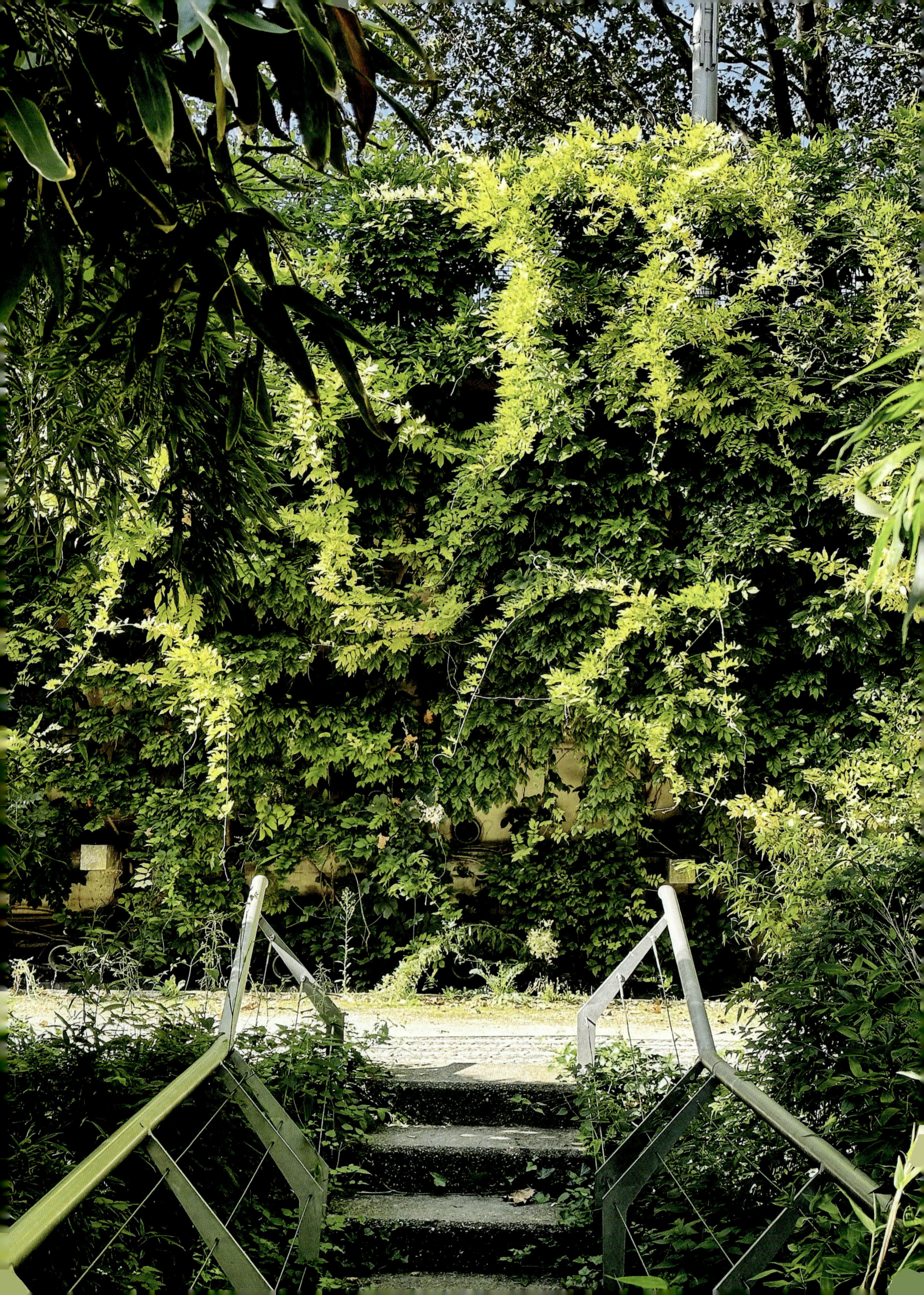

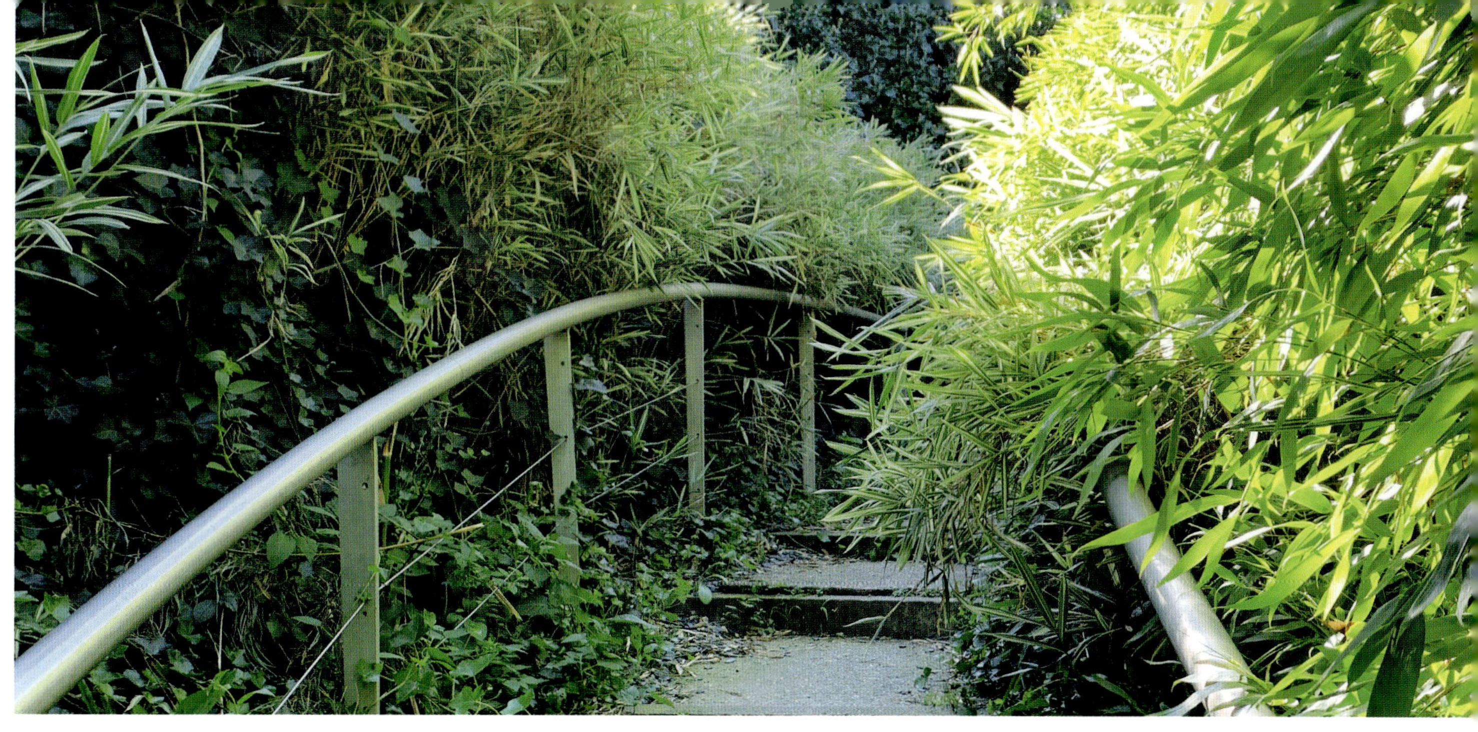



# Jardin des Bambous

**OPPOSITE**
The garden wall is also a "heat wall" that absorbs the sun's warmth to keep the temperature warm for the bamboo. It is covered in a variety of vines, including summer lilac and wisteria.

**ABOVE**
To enter le jardin des Bambous, or the Bamboo Garden, you descend a winding stepped pathway through thickets of bamboo on either side.

**RIGHT**
Le jardin des Bambous is below street level. A pedestrian bridge, or *promenade cinématique*, enhances the feeling of being completely enveloped by one of the largest examples of bamboo in France. The garden design is a collaboration between landscape designer Alexandre Chemetoff, sound architect Bernard Leitner, and artist Daniel Buren, who worked his fascination with stripes, made with black and gray pebbles, into the floor surface.

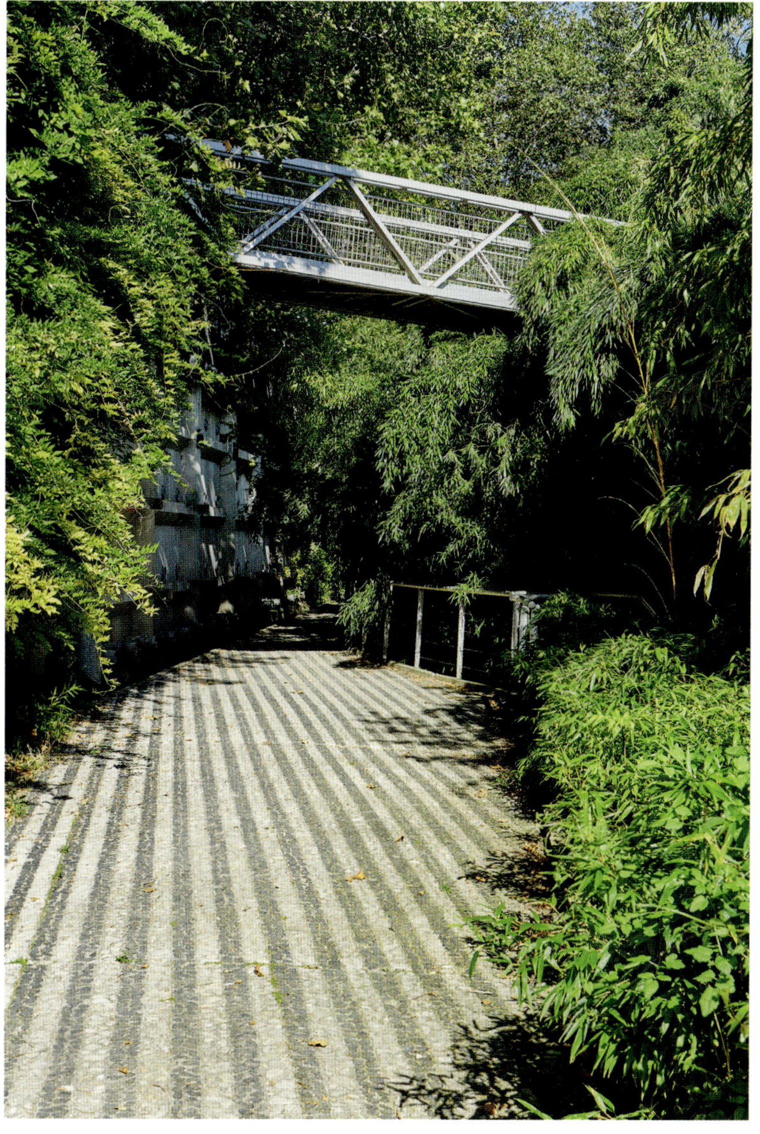

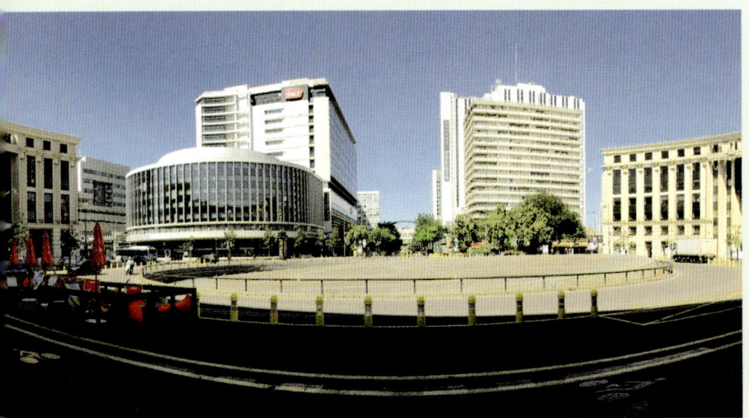

## *Place de Catalogne*
### 14th arrondissement
### 2024

We take for granted that forests have always and will always be part of our existence. Most of us have never witnessed the beginnings of a forest. However, a few lucky Parisians will watch an urban forest grow from the start, from their apartment windows, disrupting their view of la tour Eiffel. La place de Catalogne is not far from la gare Montparnasse. Built in the 1980s, the concrete plaza, with a fountain named Le Creuset du Temps, designed by sculptor Shamai Haber, had become a heat island with traffic circling it. As part of the city's official climate action plan, the Plan Climat de Paris, Anne Hidalgo, *la maire* (mayor) of Paris, made the decision to redesign the place, changing the neighborhood. The plan closed part of the road circling the site, redirecting the flow of traffic away from the residential buildings. Water was already there because of the existence of the fountain. The concrete was broken up and removed, then the process of building a forest floor began. Trees varying in type and height were brought in, and they were planted with their root systems intact and with dirt from their first homes. More than 470 youngish trees were planted in place of concrete. The pigeons and other birds were thrilled. On one visit, they walked and pecked along the forest floor and flew among the saplings. Neighbors leaned against the temporary barriers that protect the forest as it is established. "Where will they place the benches?" one neighbor asked as he waited patiently to gain entrance to the newly formed green space.

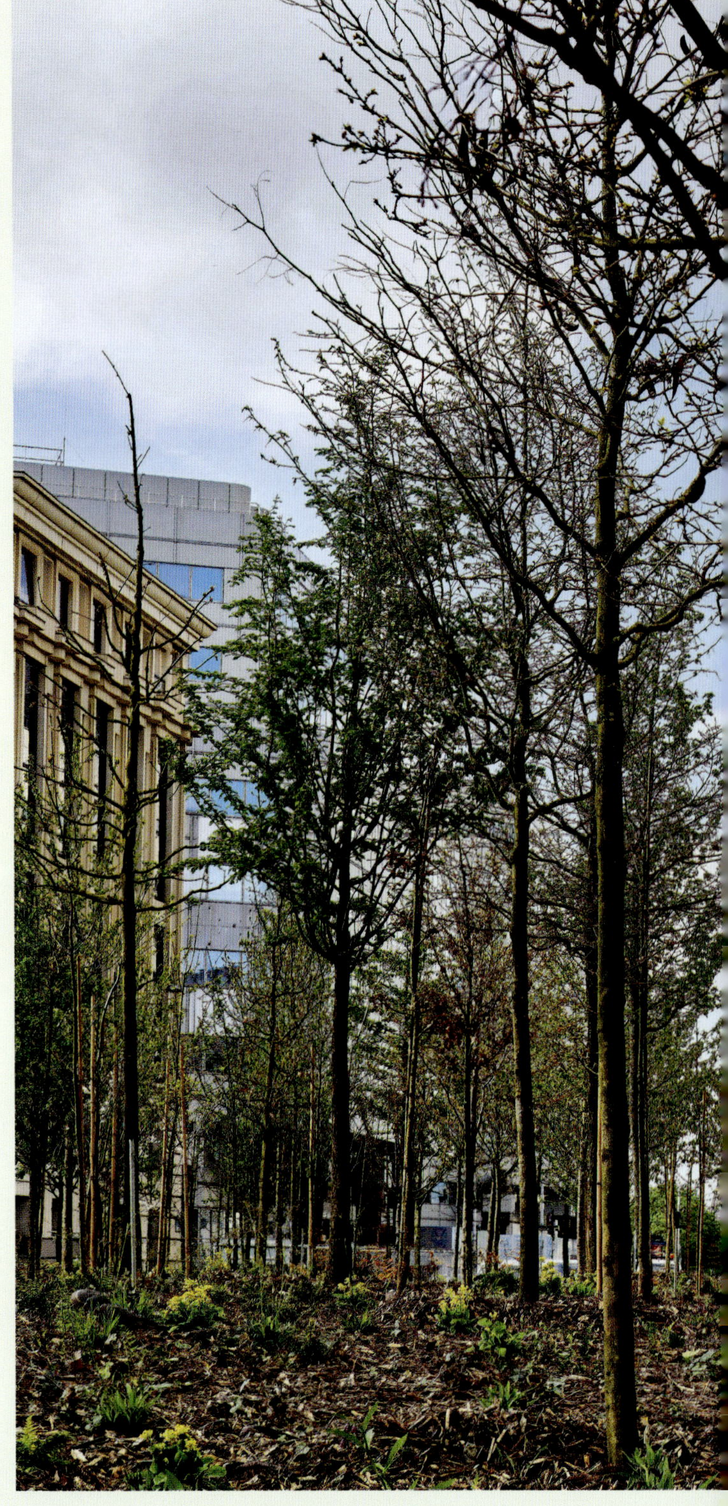

**ABOVE LEFT**
A before photograph of place de Catalogne that shows how the space was dominated by concrete before the forest was installed.

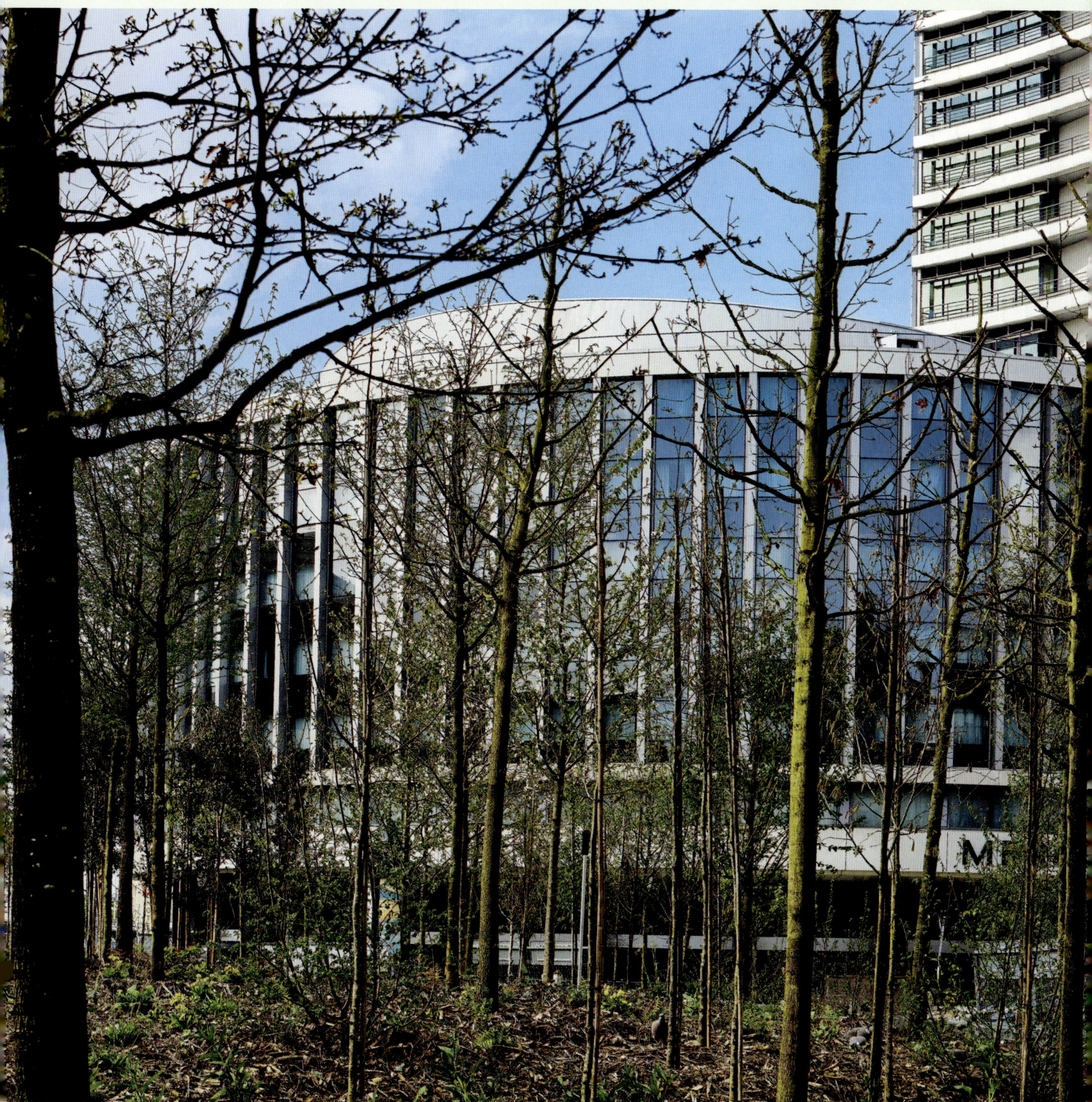



**ABOVE**
Already the dense plantings of trees
are shielding the residential buildings
from the commercial buildings across
the plaza. Indeed, the whole view has
changed; even now, la tour Eiffel is
barely visible.

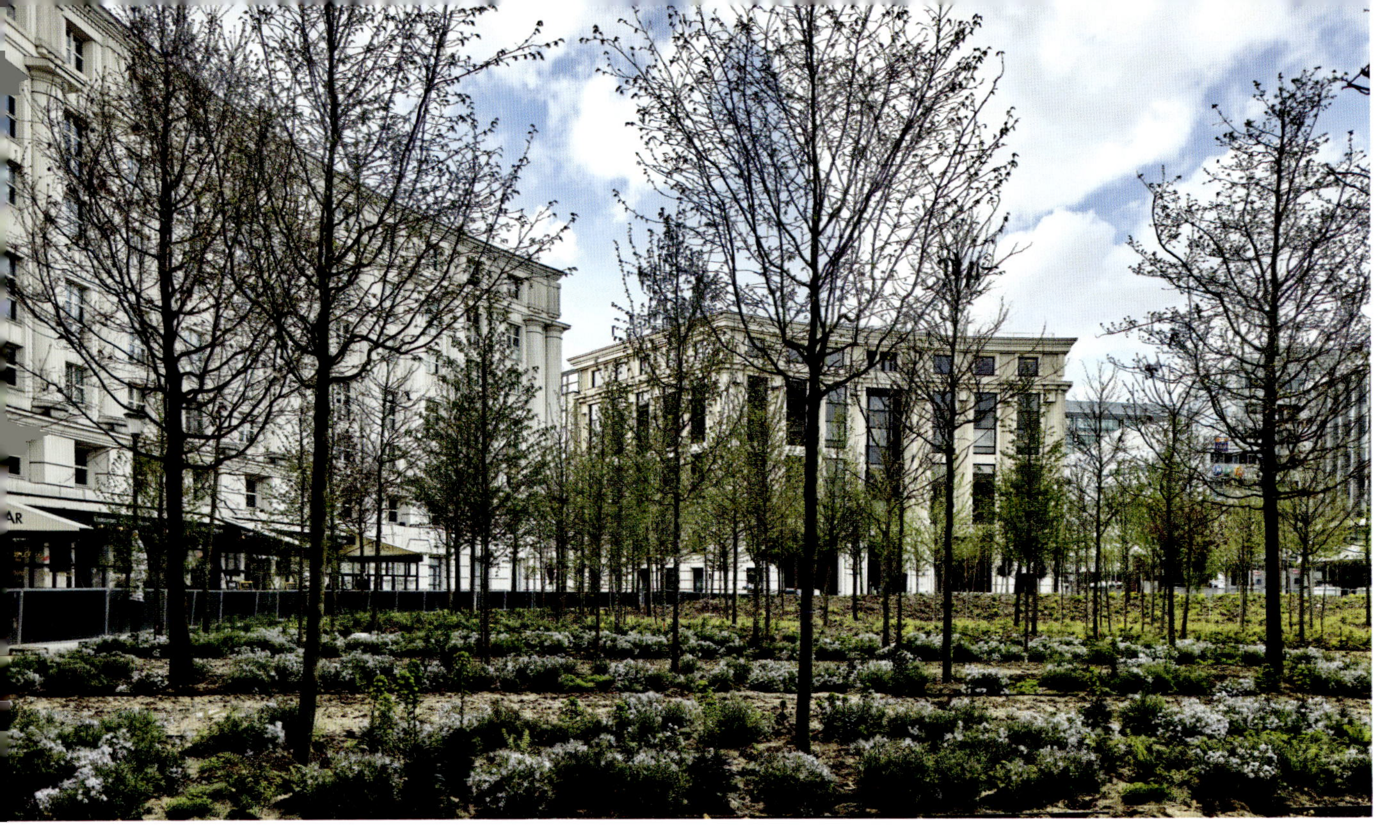

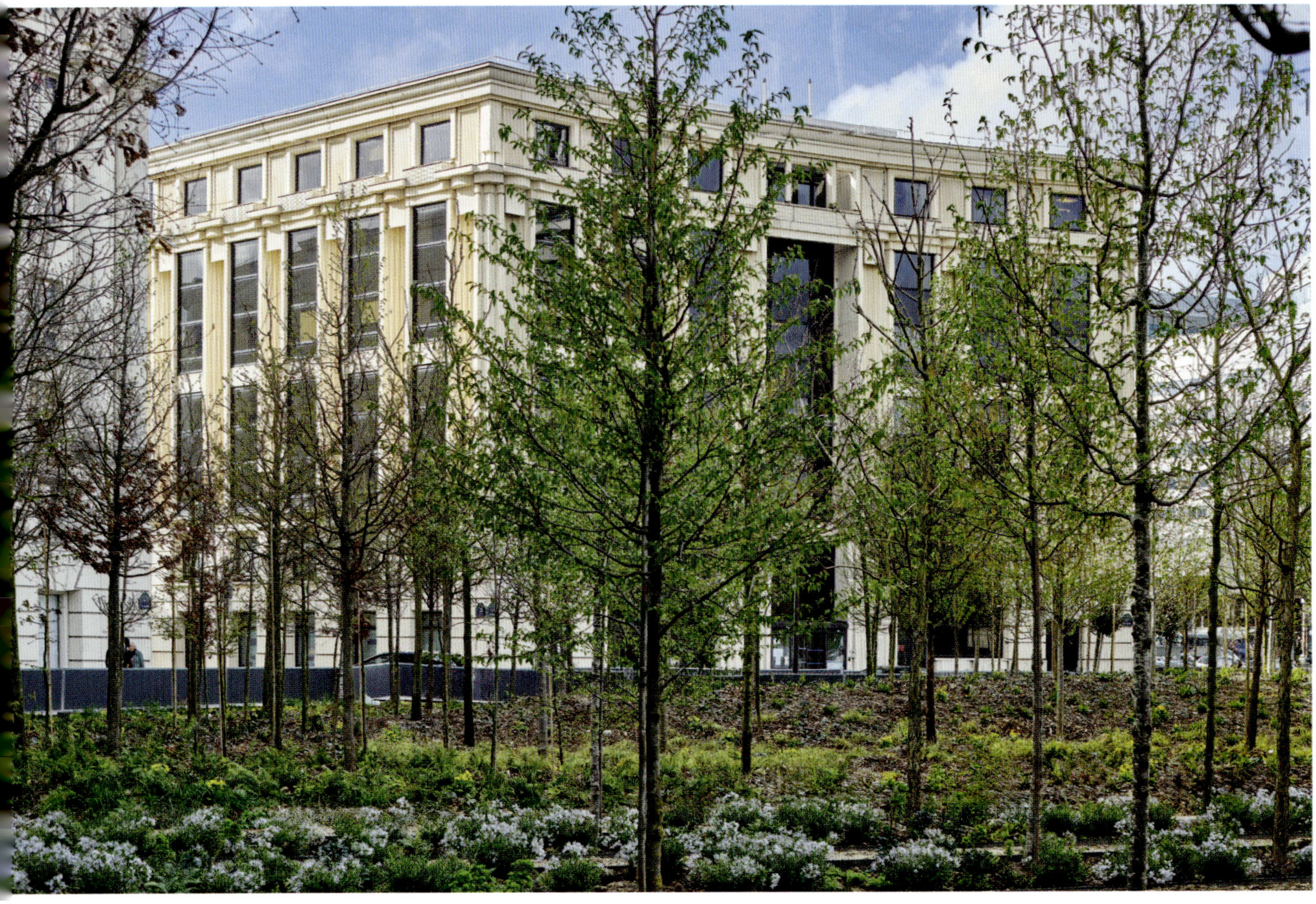

    *PLACE DE CATALOGNE*

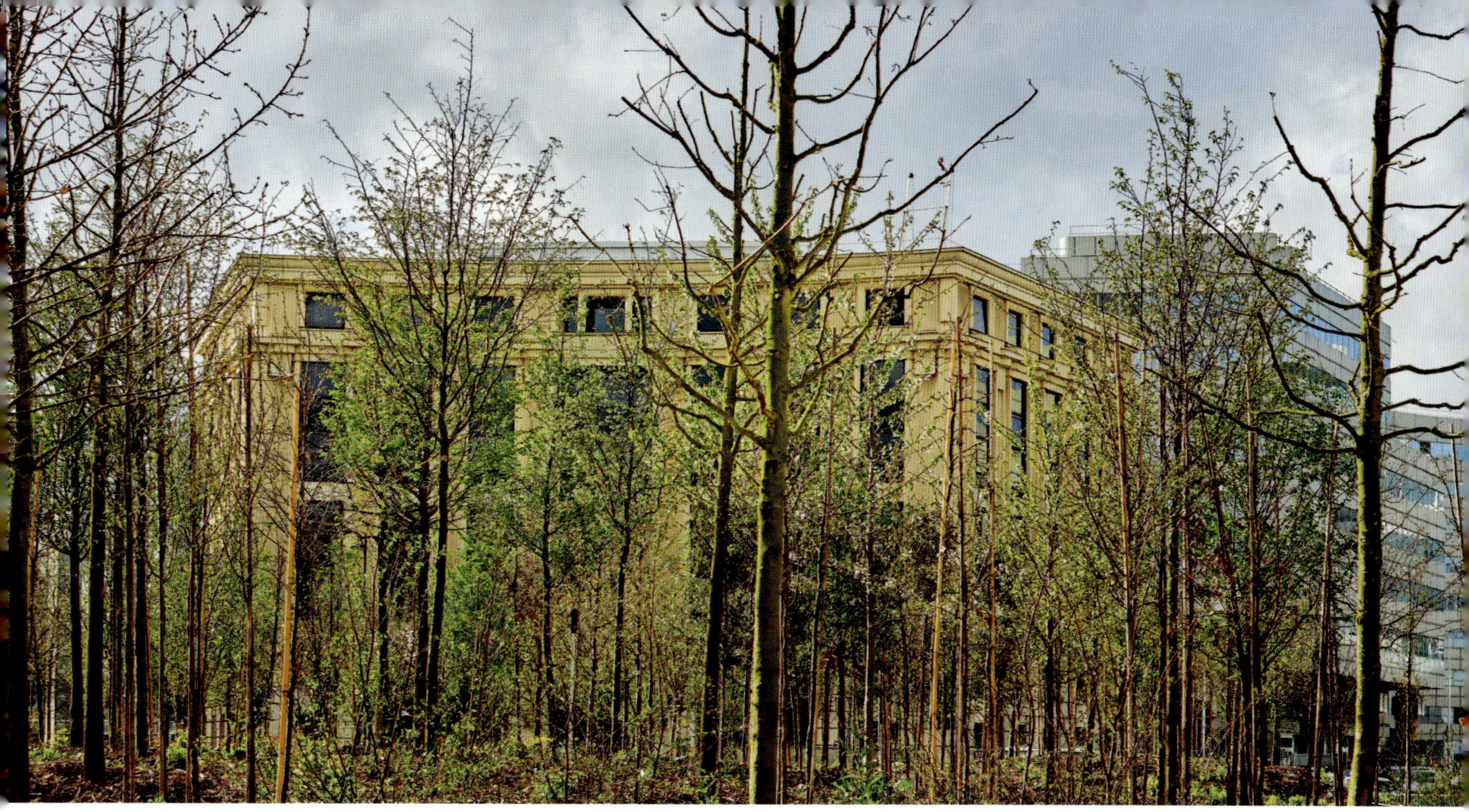

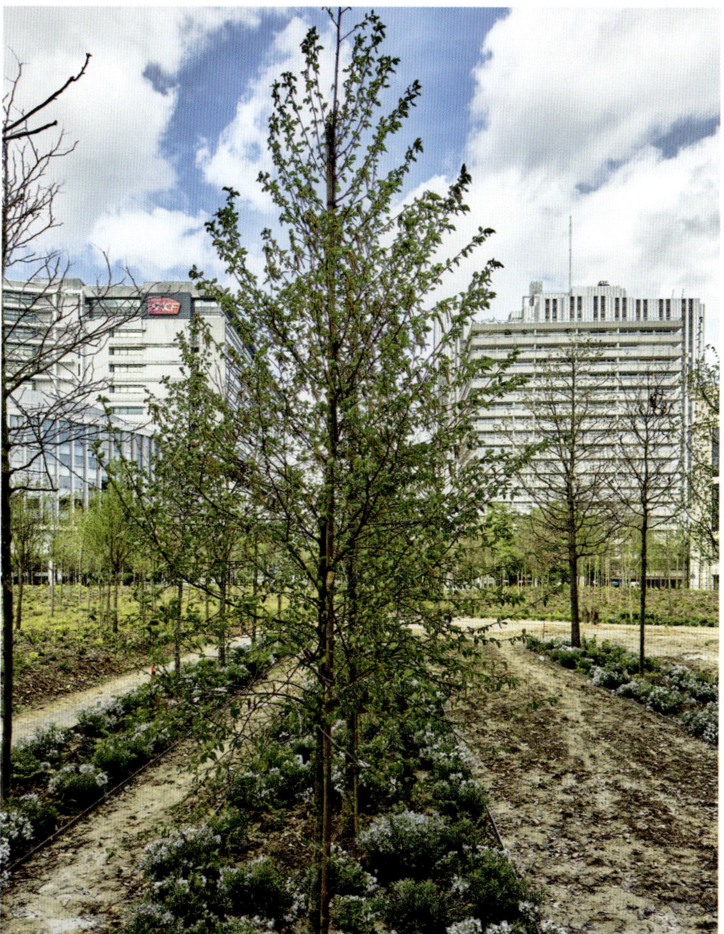



**OPPOSITE ABOVE**
Eventually, the tree canopy will reduce the temperature of the site by four degrees, but for now the heat will be absorbed by the plantings.

**OPPOSITE BELOW**
There is a mixture of size and type of trees planted in the forest. All are prepared to withstand the rise in temperatures.

**ABOVE AND LEFT**
In some sections of the park, trees are planted in beds with other low-growing plantings. In other sections, the plants of the forest floor are planted in a more natural way, to re-create the randomness of nature.

## *Murs Végétaux*
### 2nd, 5th, 8th, and 15th arrondissements
### 2013, 2021

Green walls, or *murs végétaux,* are scattered throughout Paris. No matter how these plant installations are applied to structures, they all bring an element of surprise. While the concept of the wall of plantings did not originate in France, it was French botanist-researcher Patrick Blanc who took the idea to another level, inventing a system that made it possible for plants to be grown without soil. In 1986, his first project, an interior wall of plants at the Cité des Sciences et l'Industrie at La Villette, created in collaboration with architect Adrien Fainsilber and engineer Peter Rice, opened to the public. Since that moment, the greening of buildings has become an international design phenomenon. While many living wall projects are commissioned for private clients, institutions, and corporations, the City of Paris has also placed vertical gardens on city infrastructure. Plant walls bring not only beauty and a connection to nature to a city corner but also filter the air and keep the building and the surrounding neighborhood cooler.

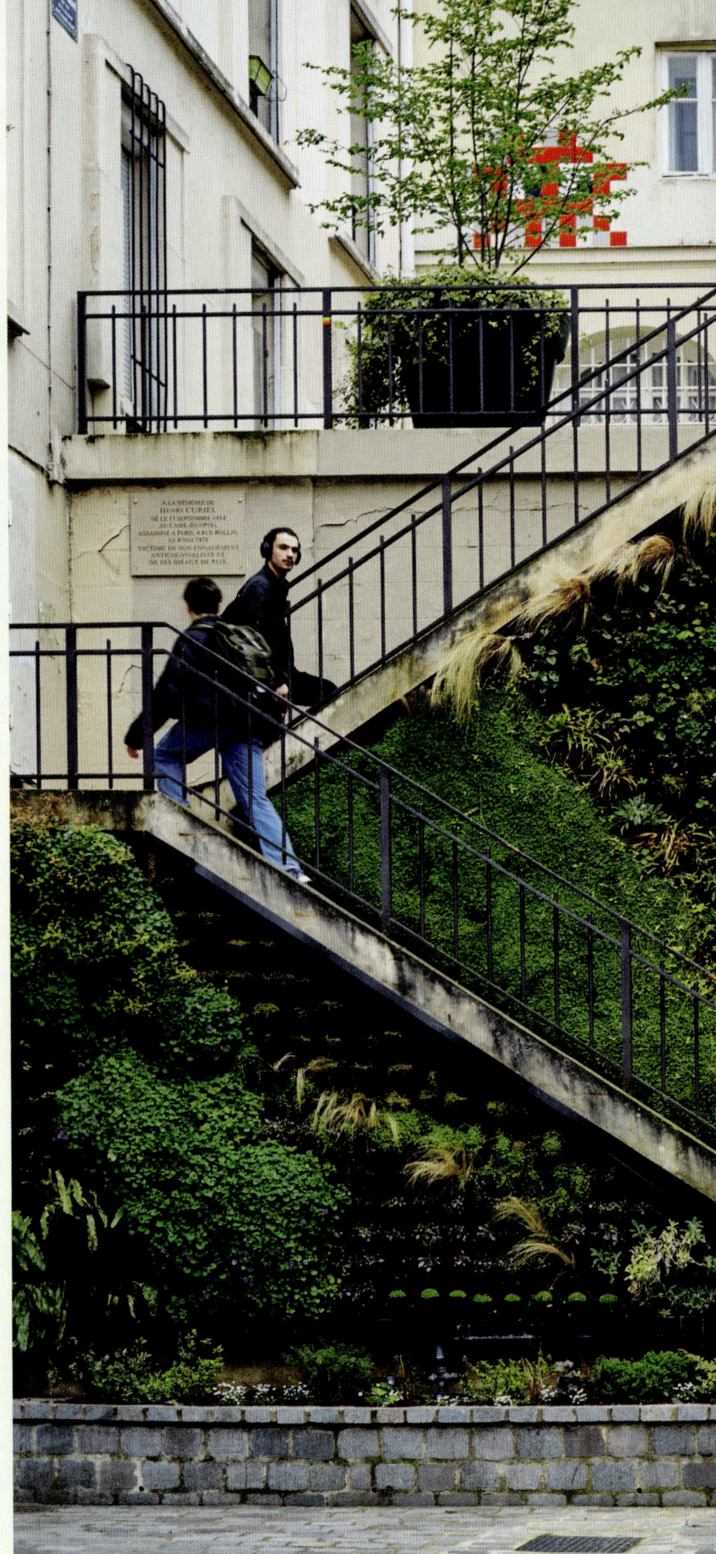

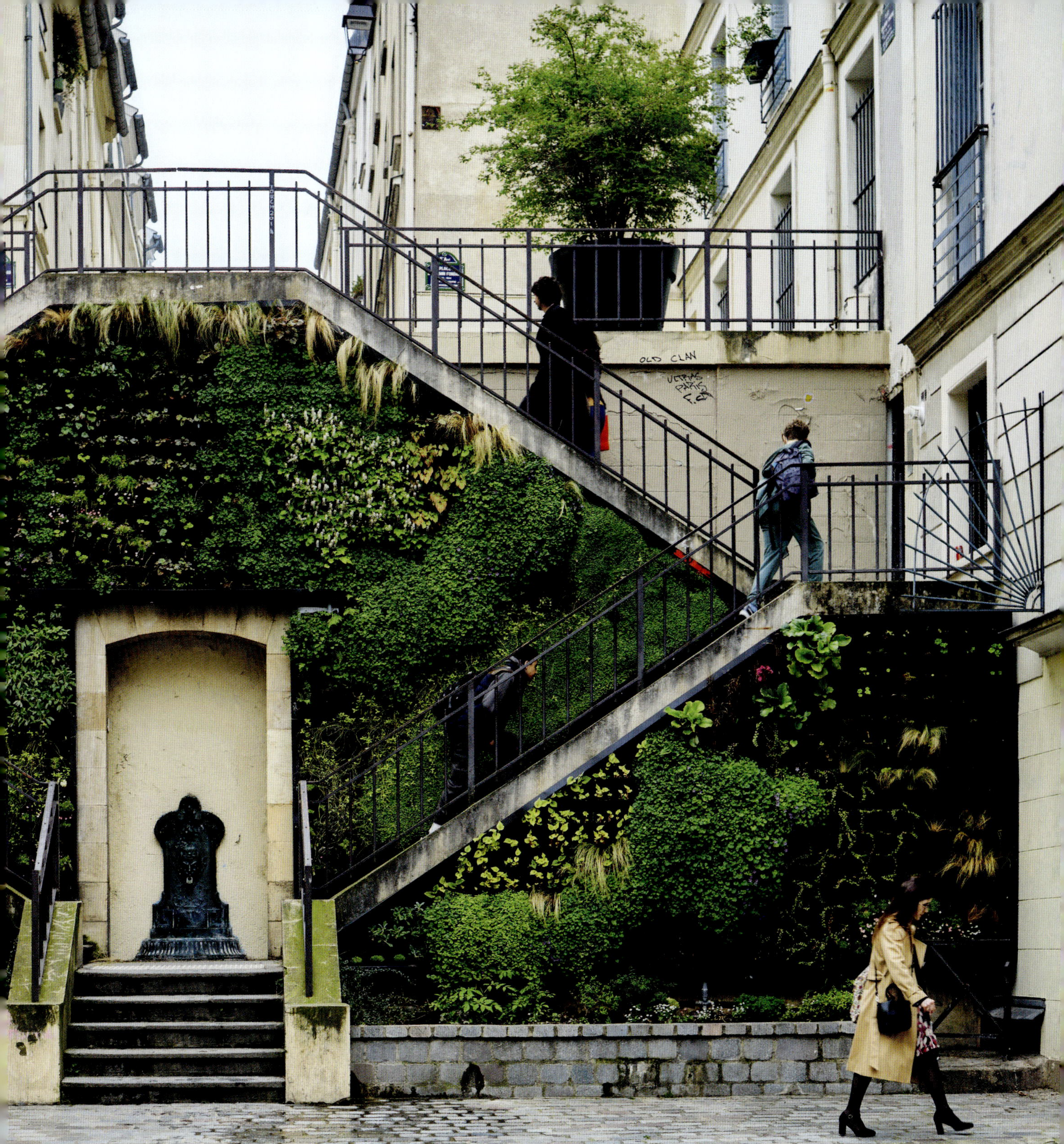

## Rue Rollin

Off la rue Monge in the 5th arrondissement, set back from the road, is an *escalier végétalisé*. The staircase leads up to la place Benjamin-Fondane, where the narrow old street, rue Rollin, continues. The green wall-growing system was installed as part of the City of Paris's plan to add more green spaces to the streetscapes. Plants grow in small containers of soil and are watered through an irrigation system. In the middle of the archway, there is a wall-mounted water fountain, similar to the nineteenth-century Wallace drinking fountains that were once found throughout Paris.

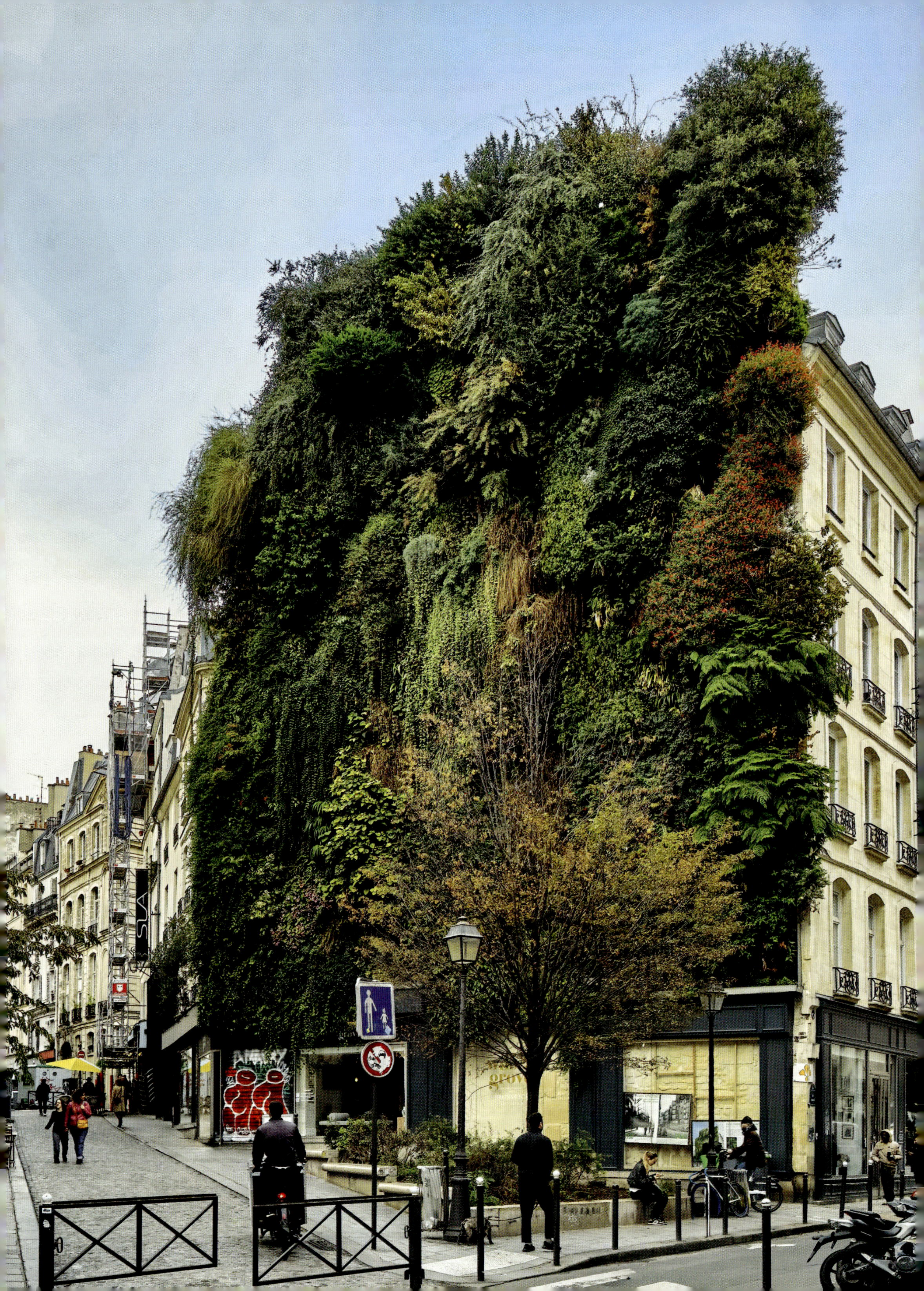

# Oasis d'Aboukir



Walking around the corner of rue d'Aboukir and rue des Petits-Carreaux in the 2nd arrondissement, it is startling to look up and see the majestic Oasis d'Aboukir. A combination of 237 different types of plants is placed together artistically in the vertical garden, designed by Patrick Blanc.

# Villa M



Plants growing over an old building on a quaint side street in Paris is charming. But the designers of Villa M, a modern hotel on busy boulevard Pasteur in the 15th arrondissement, updated that idea in 2021. In the process, they have captured the spirit of better health by creating a garden with medicinal plants. Eventually, the hotel will exist behind the vertical plantings. Industrial designer Philippe Starck has made his mark on the city, and Villa M is no exception. Here, as creative director, he has partnered with healthcare-professions association Groupe Pasteur Mutualité, architectural firm Triptyque, and landscape architects Coloco to create a holistic approach that considers the environment—inside and out. Indented tracks on the façade's metal structure are a space where vines can grow from the street to the roof. In addition, container gardens with their watering systems are positioned on the terraces.

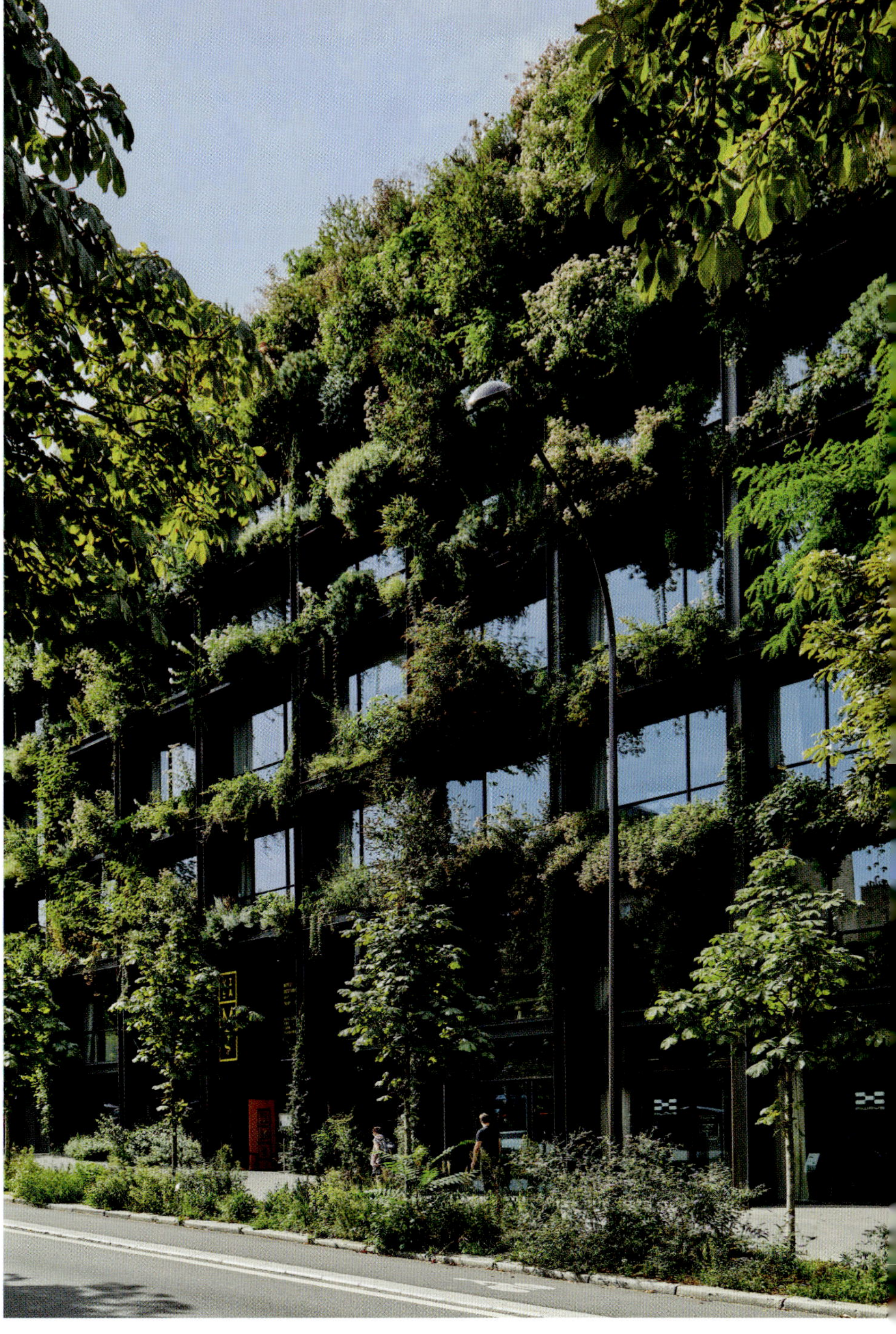

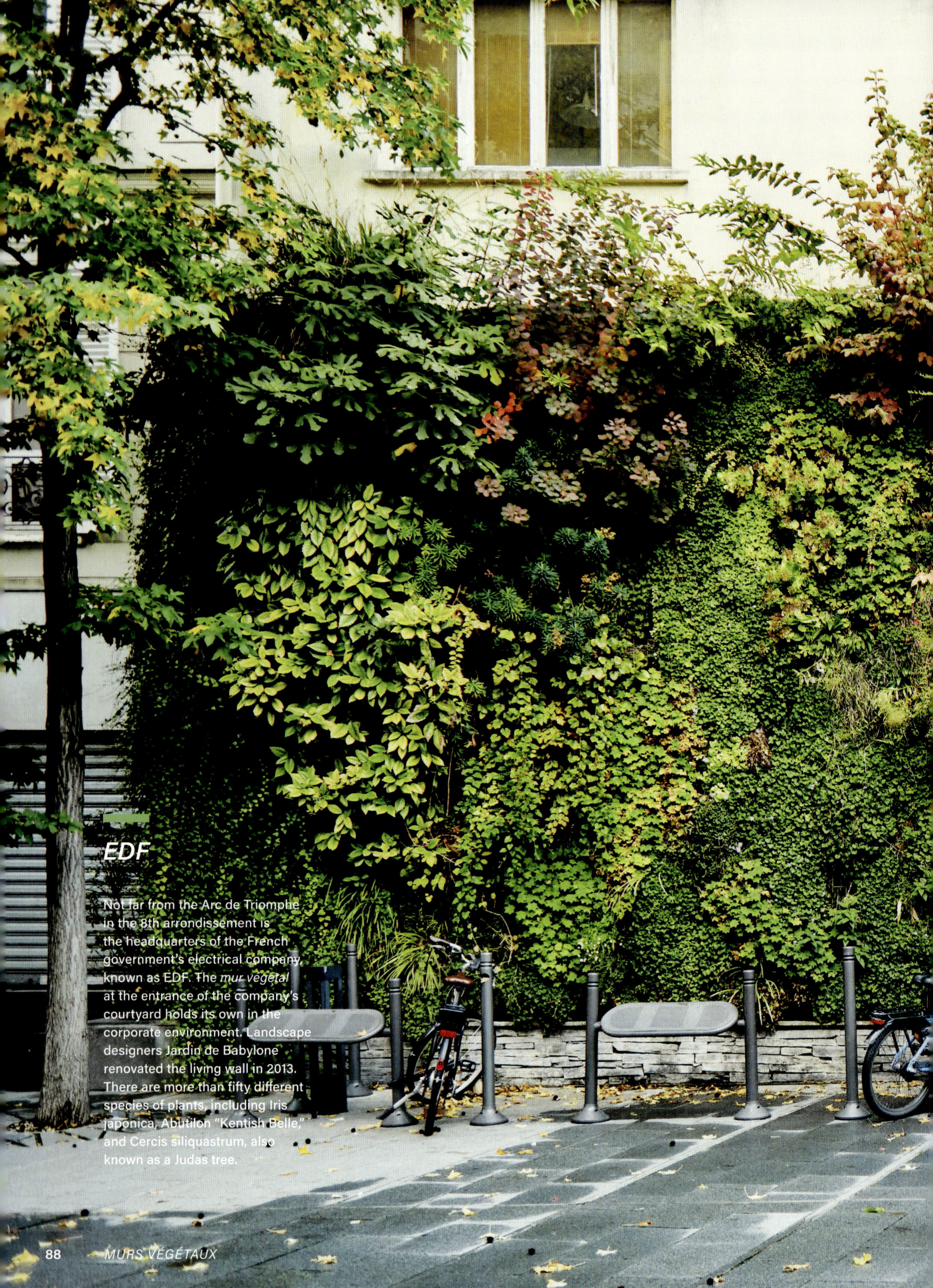

## EDF

Not far from the Arc de Triomphe in the 8th arrondissement is the headquarters of the French government's electrical company, known as EDF. The *mur végétal* at the entrance of the company's courtyard holds its own in the corporate environment. Landscape designers Jardin de Babylone renovated the living wall in 2013. There are more than fifty different species of plants, including Iris japonica, Abutilon "Kentish Belle," and Cercis siliquastrum, also known as a Judas tree.

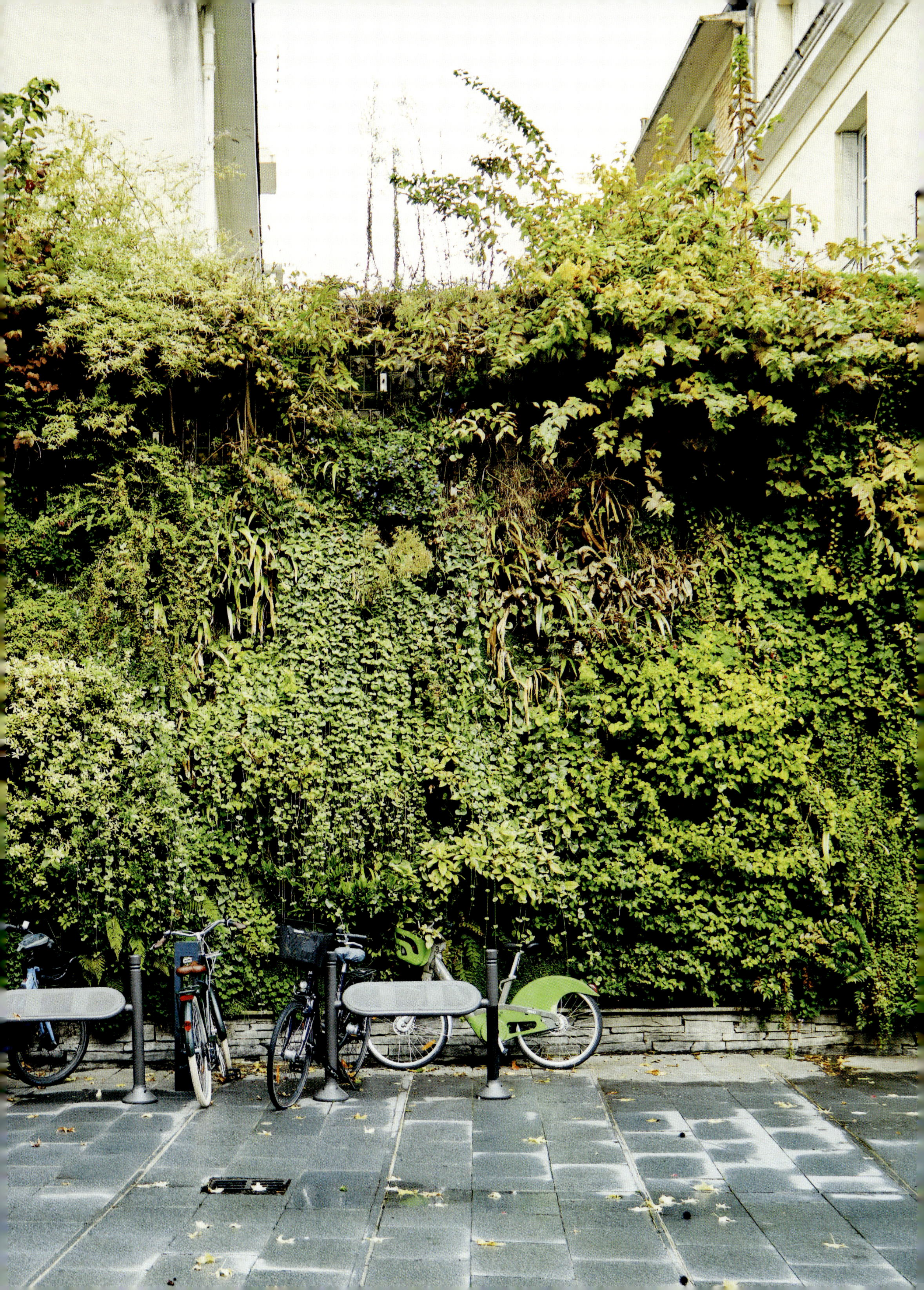

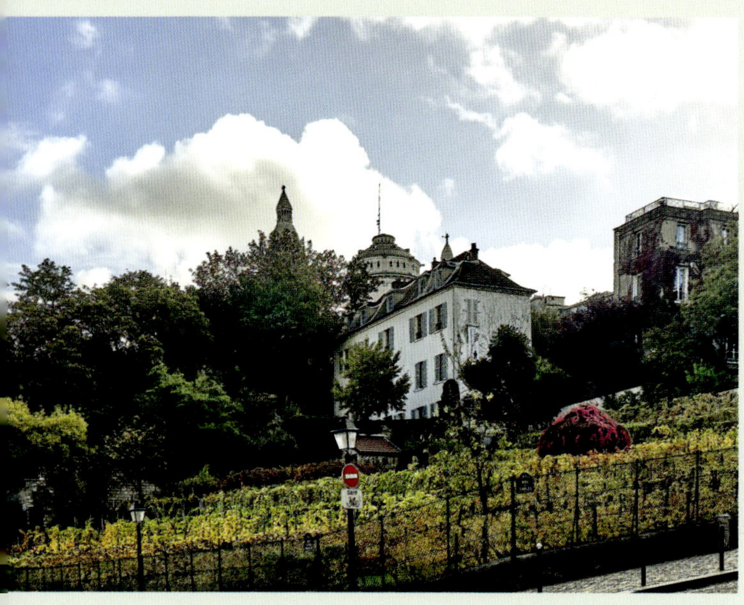

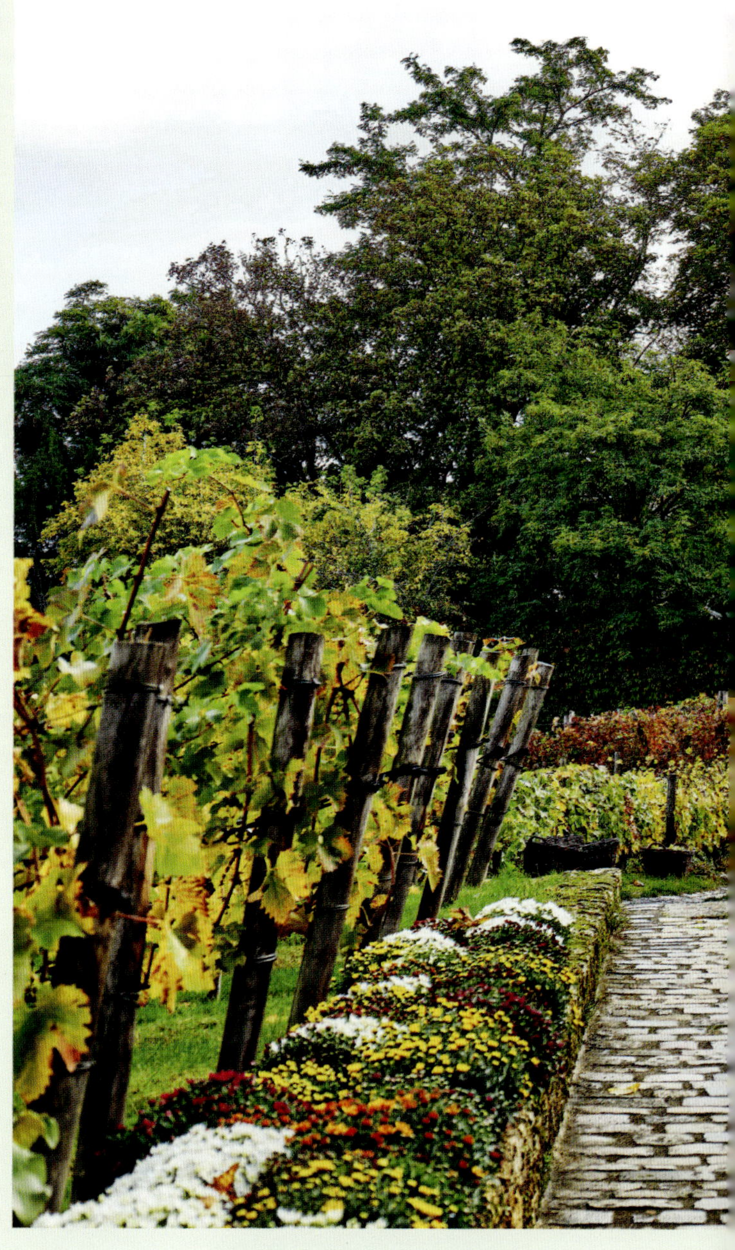

## Vignobles de Paris
18th and 19th arrondissements
1933, 2023

While there is an abundance of wine through-out the French capital, there aren't very many vineyards—there are ten vineyards within the city limits, including one at parc Georges-Brassens (page 36). During Roman times, grape vines grew in the rural area that is now Paris. Wines were made and sold locally. Many factors led to the demise of the city vineyards, including wars, plant diseases, and development of new buildings. In the 1930s there was a movement to restore the winemaking tradition. The recovery has been slow, but it is fitting that Parisian vineyards are starting to gain attention, and that a natural resource is being established and protected in the capital. Each year since 1934, the Fête des Vendanges de Montmartre, a wine festival, celebrates the harvest-ing of grapes in early October. Of course, grapes aren't only for drinking but also for eating. A new vineyard has been established in the 19th arrondissement that grows table grapes.

## Clos Montmartre

**ABOVE LEFT**
The Clos Montmartre vineyard takes up a full street block. More than 1,760 *vignes*, or vines, are planted and growing on the picturesque hillside using organic methods and pesticides. The vineyard produces 2,000 bottles of wine per year.

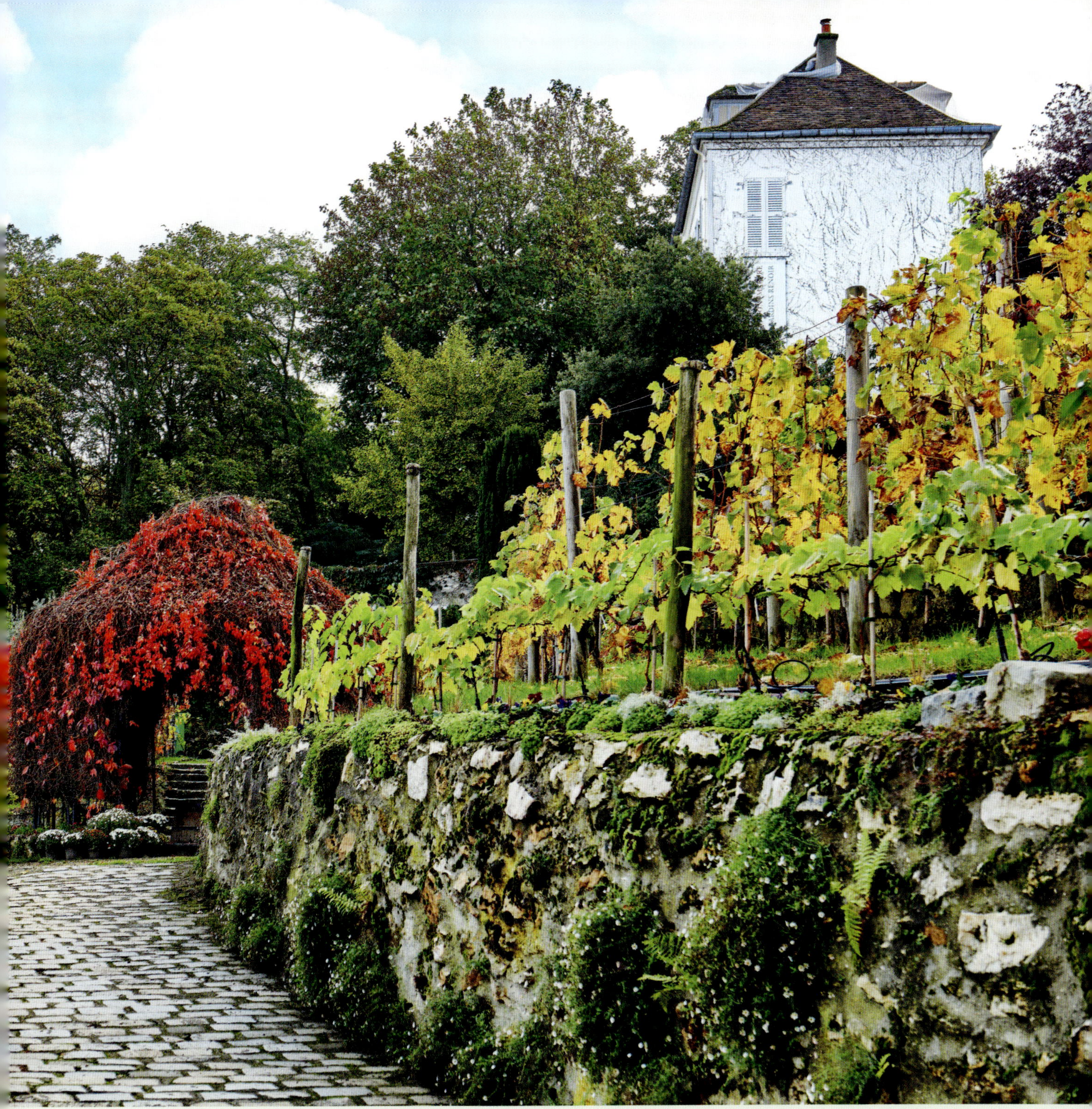



**ABOVE**
The vineyard is one of the oldest in
Paris. Grapes have been grown in this
location since the twelfth century. At one
time, the Basilica of Saint-Denis owned
the vineyard. Cobbled pathways and
rock walls separate sections.

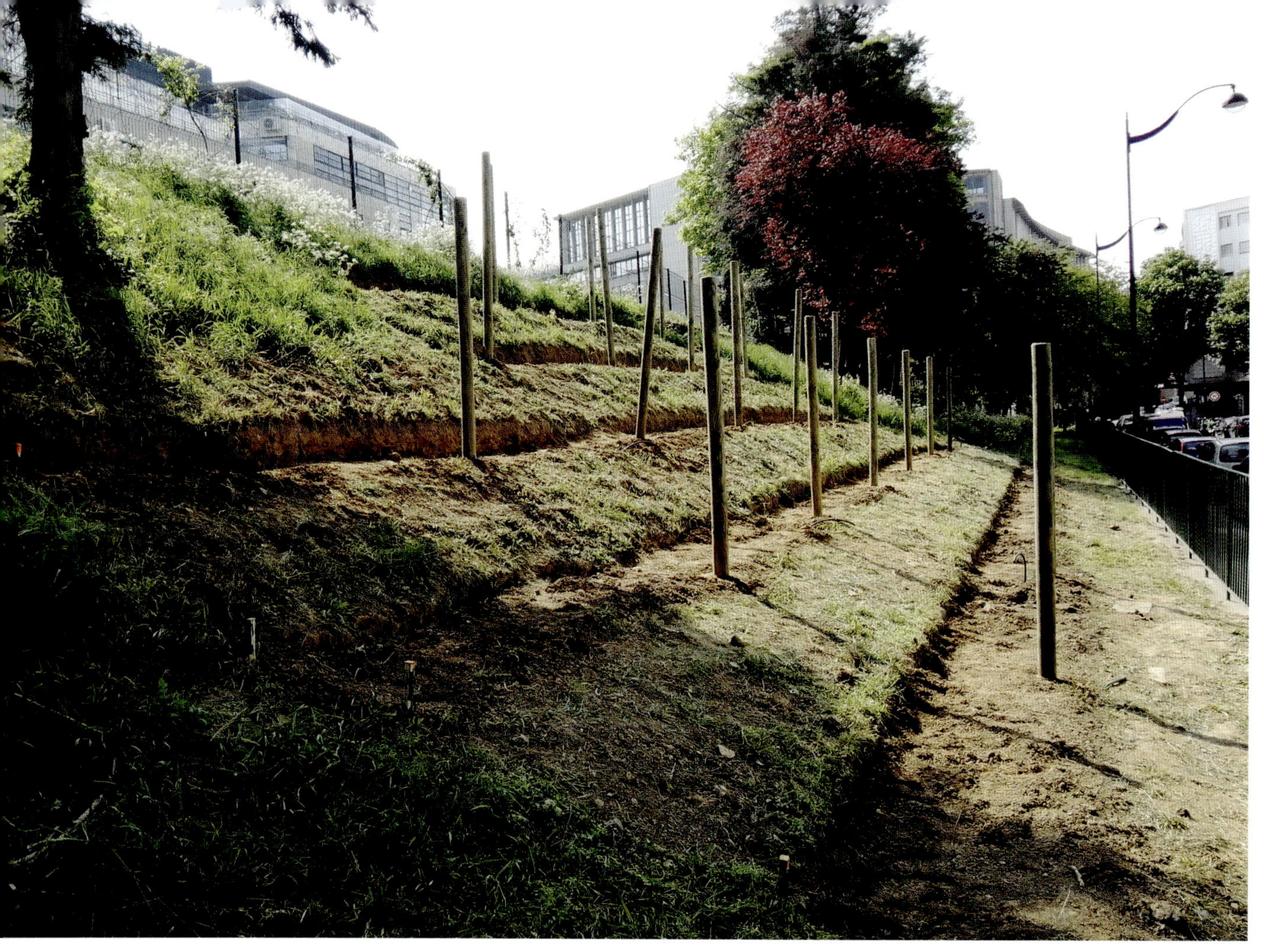

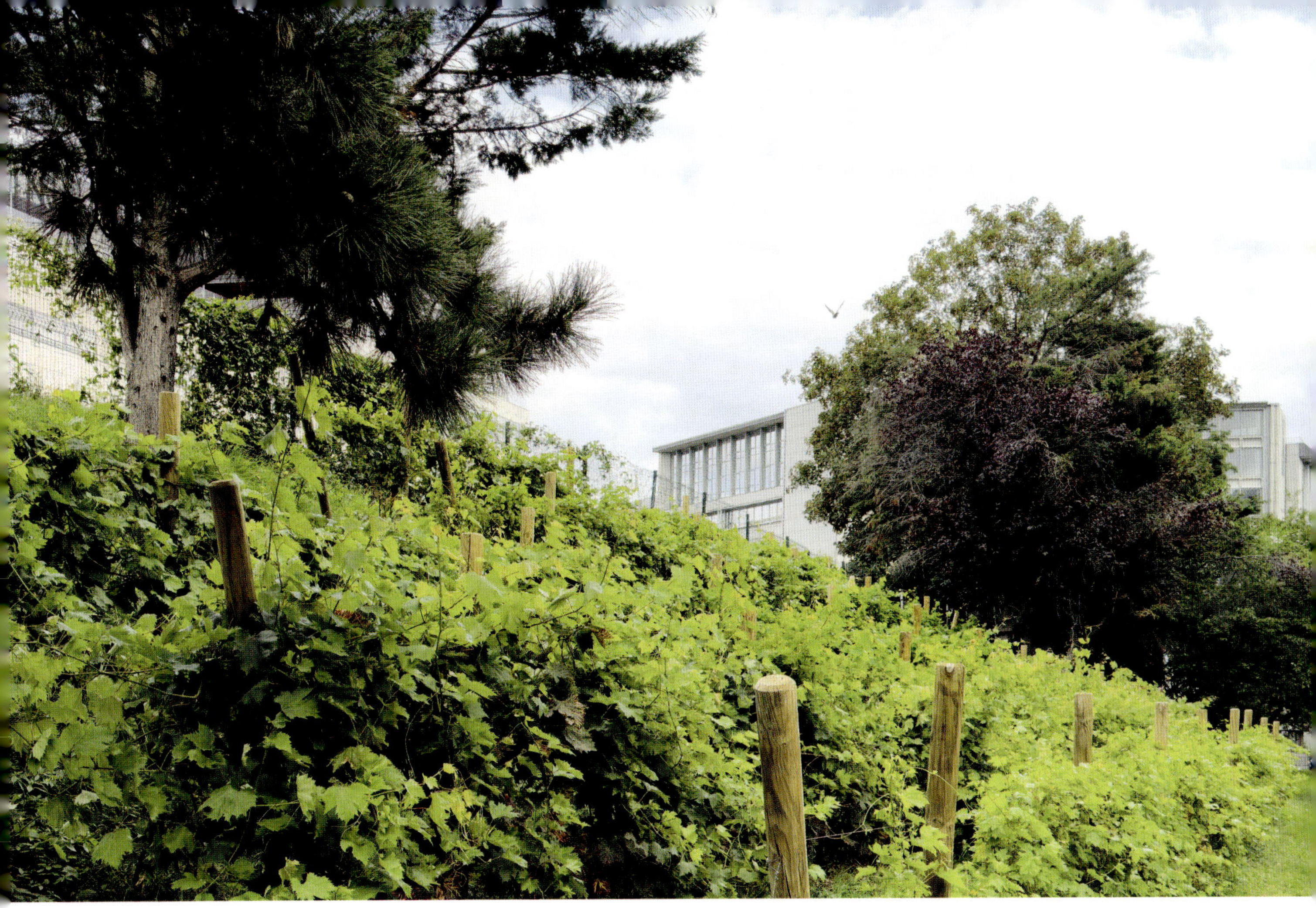

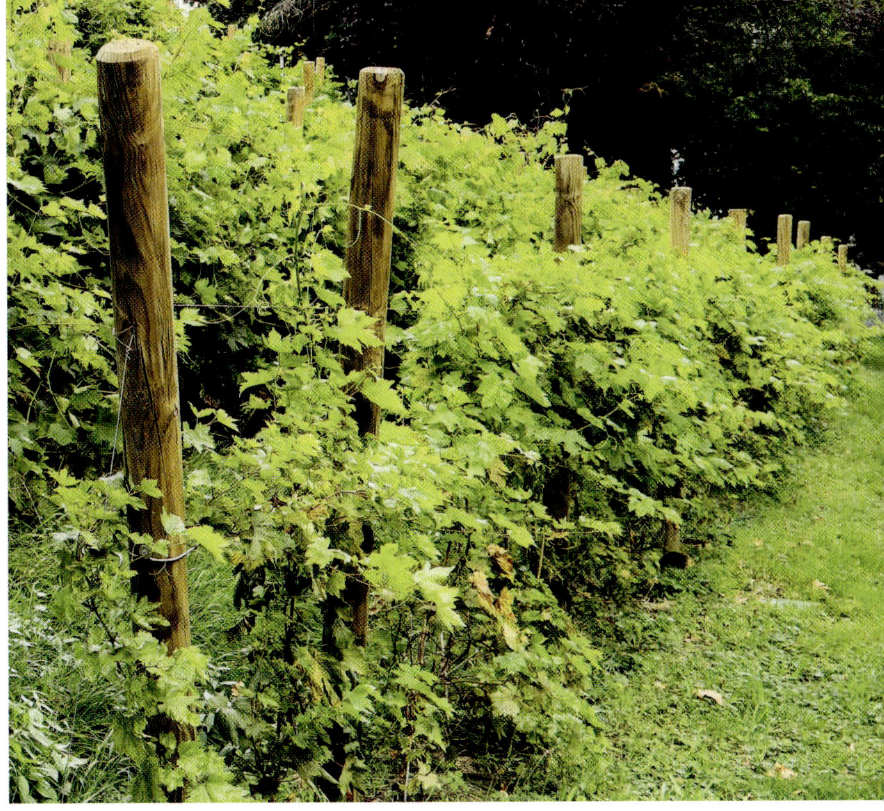

## Rue André-Danjon

One of the youngest vineyards in Paris: This small urban vineyard on rue André-Danjon grows on a sloping hill across the street from an apartment complex. It is located off the Petite Ceinture in the 19th arrondissement. These young vines produce table grapes, and they were planted in 2022 by the mayor's office of the arrondissement and produced their first grapes in 2023.

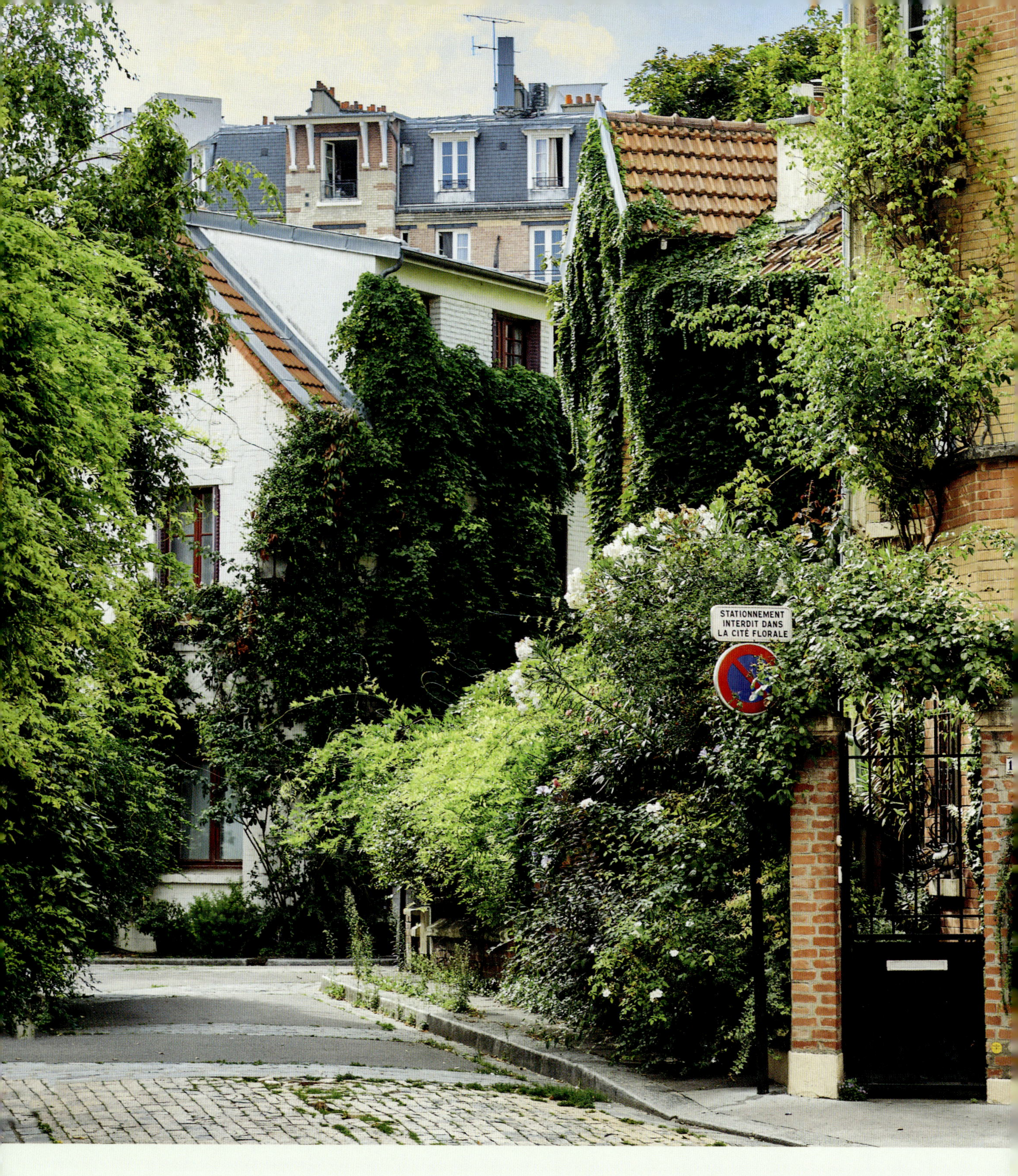
STATIONNEMENT
INTERDIT DANS
LA CITÉ FLORALE

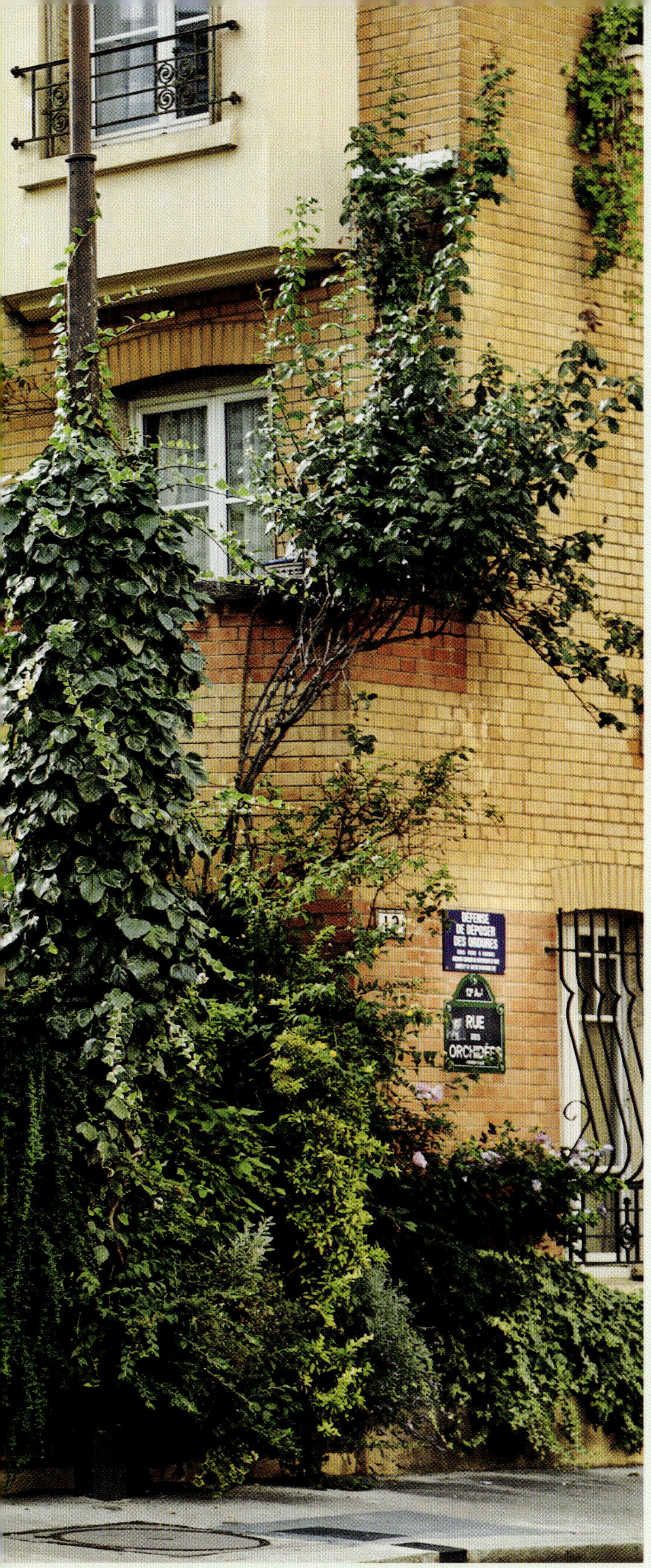

This two-toned brick house was built in 1928 on the corner of rue des Orchidées and rue des Glycines. An interior garden is behind the iron gate and brick column entrance. Even the lamppost is covered by plants.

## *La Cité Florale*

13th arrondissement
1928)

La Cité Florale is located on a triangle bound by three larger streets: rue Auguste-Laçon, rue Brillat-Savarin, and rue Boussingault. The older enclave of small, mainly brick houses is the epitome of charm: The modern city seems to disappear when walking its six narrow brick-paved streets. All are named for flowers: rue des Iris (iris), rue des Liserons (bindweed), rue des Glycines (wisteria), rue des Volubilis (queen's wreath), rue des Orchidées (orchid), and square des Mimosas (mimosa). But it was the meadow that the tiny district was built on that determined its design. At the time, the land was not stable for larger buildings. It was often flooded by the Bièvre river, which was eventually redirected and covered over. Each of the more than fifty residences have a garden, and each one displays a passion for plants. Some homes have plants in containers and pots, and others have fully grown trees, old vines, and ivy-covered walls.

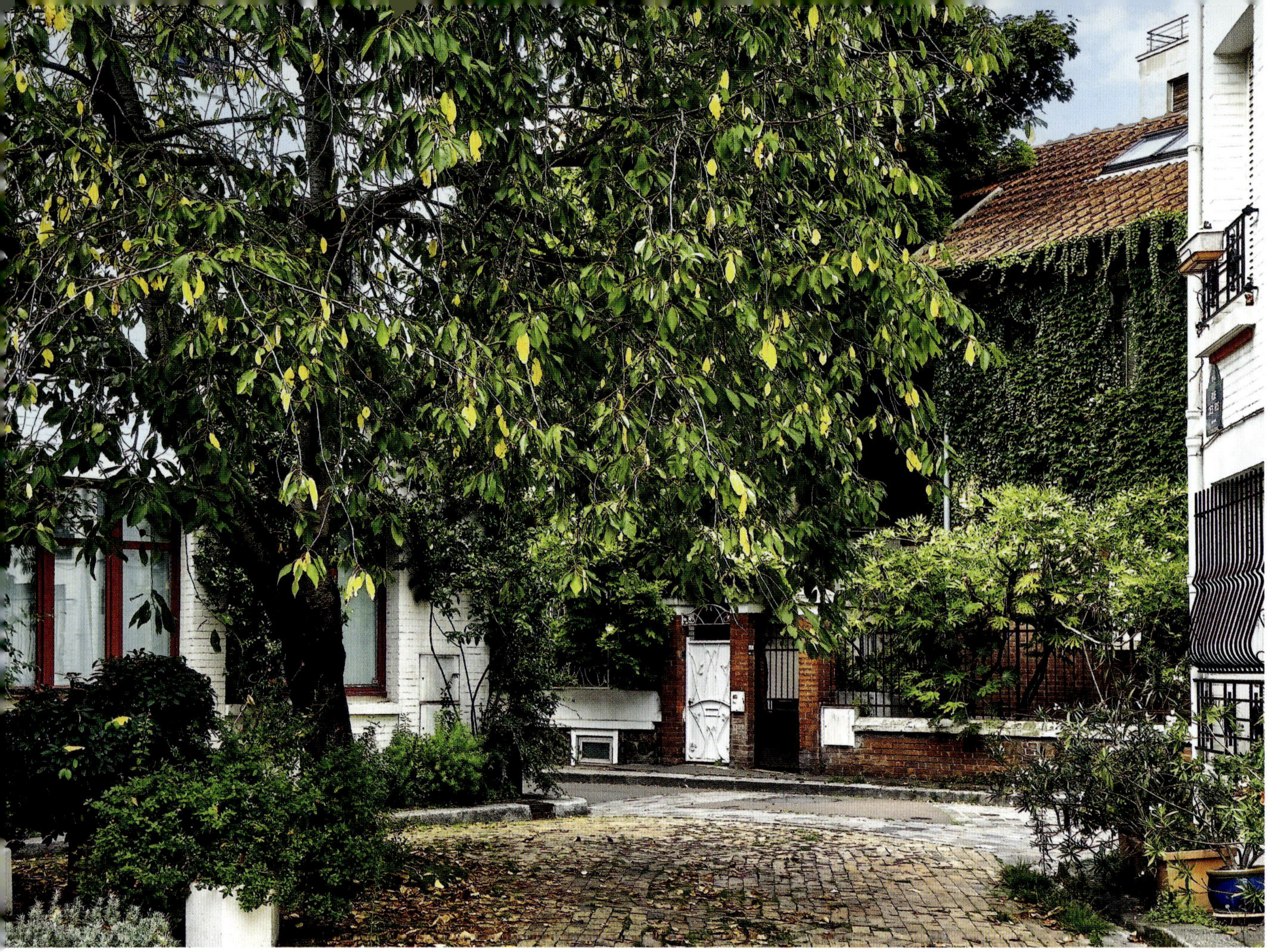

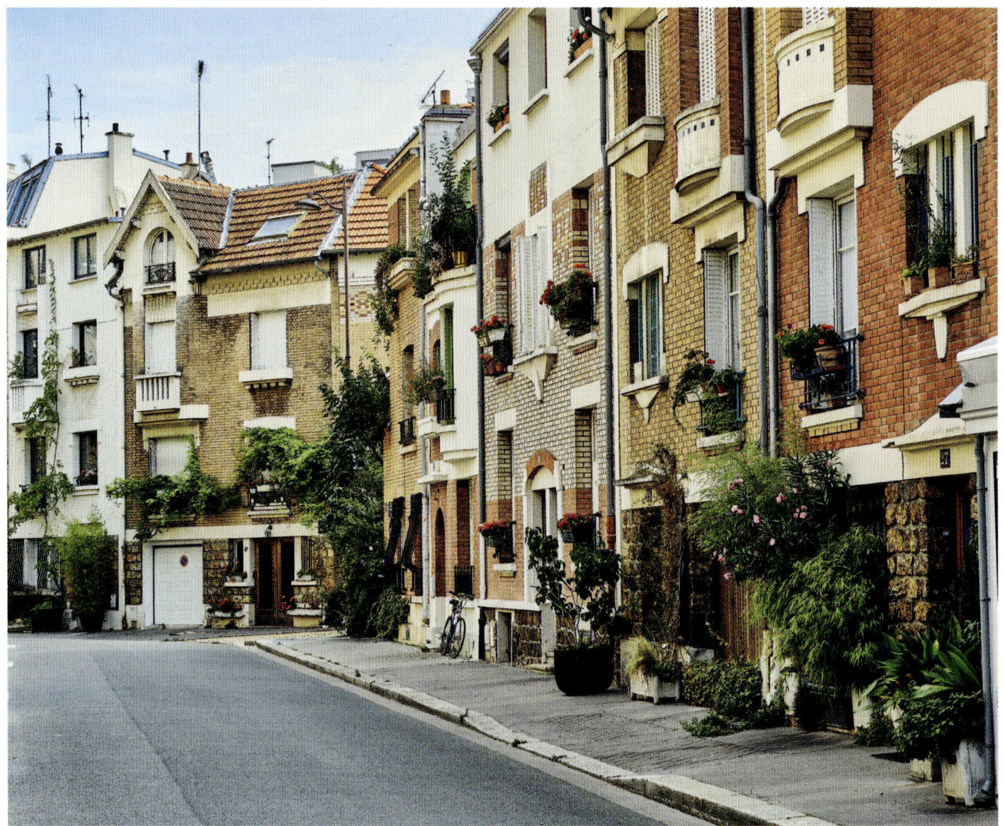

 *LA CITÉ FLORALE*

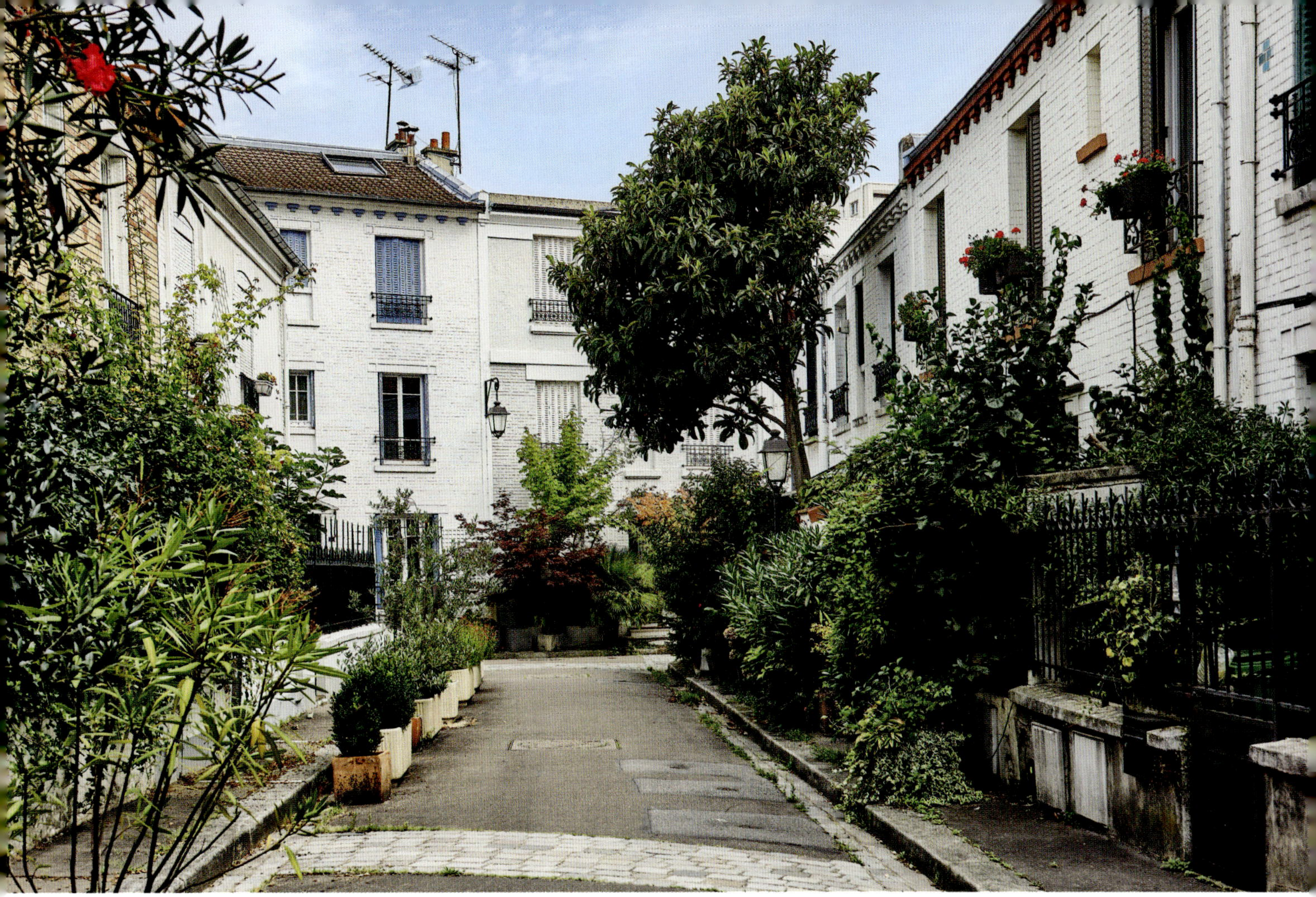

**OPPOSITE ABOVE**
A large tree shades the courtyard on the corner of rue des Iris and rue des Glycines.

**OPPOSITE BELOW**
The streetscape of rue des Orchidées includes houses with a variety of rooflines, materials, and styles, including a mansard roof and traditional red ceramic tile. Over the years, houses in Cité Florale have been updated and added on to with changes such as additional terraces for plants.

**ABOVE**
Most of the brick houses on this side of rue des Iris have been painted white, which gives a unified look and background to the green plants and trees growing on the street and in the window boxes.

**RIGHT**
An ivy-covered house from 1932 was updated in 2022—ninety years later. The six-pane windows face the larger rue Brillat-Savarin.

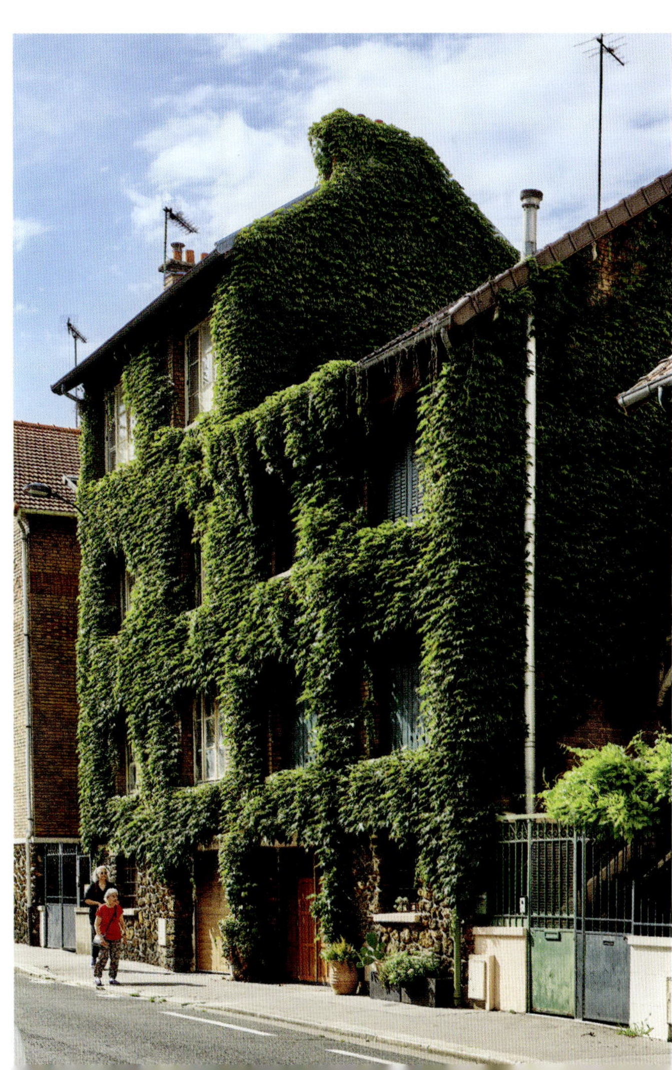

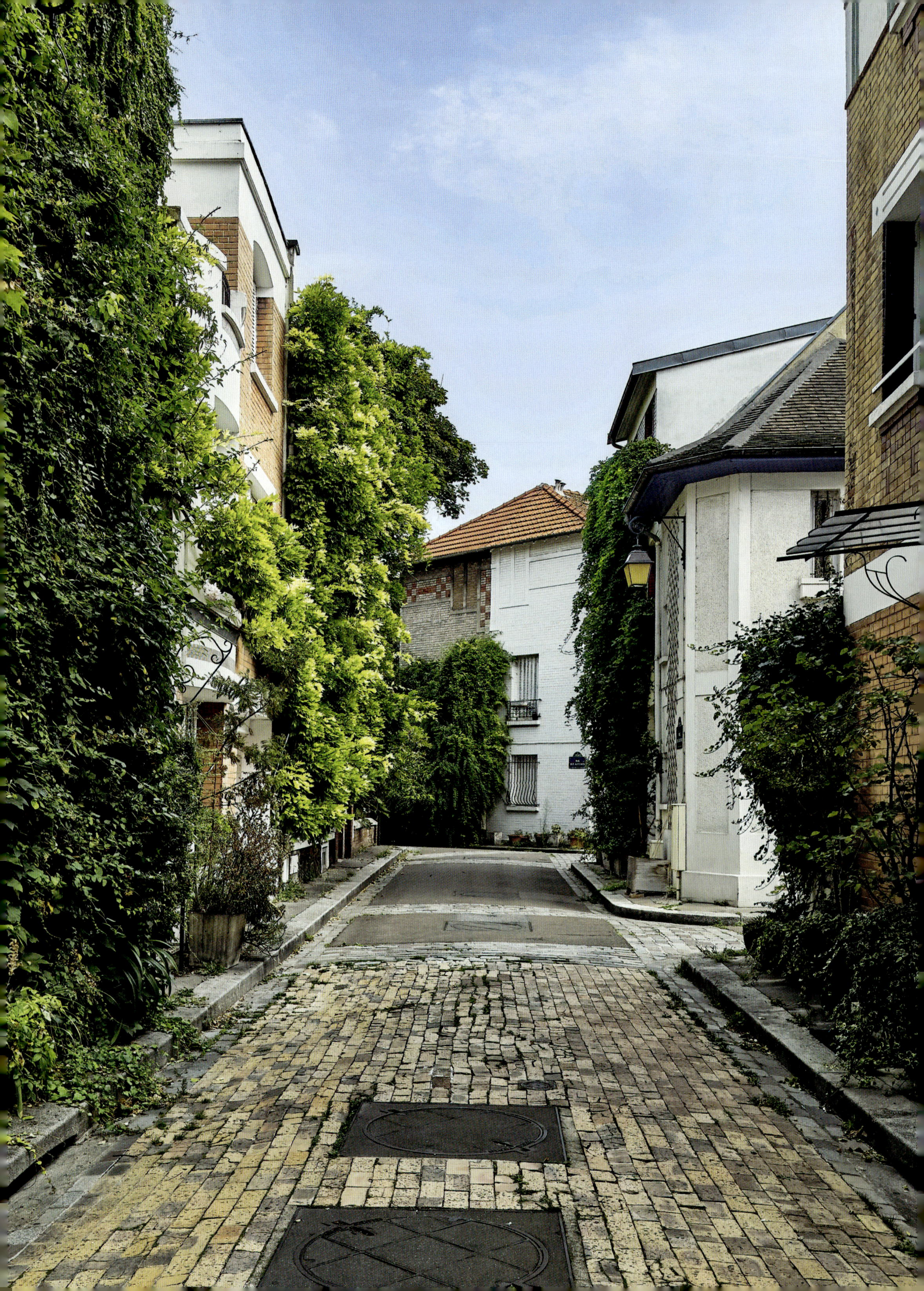

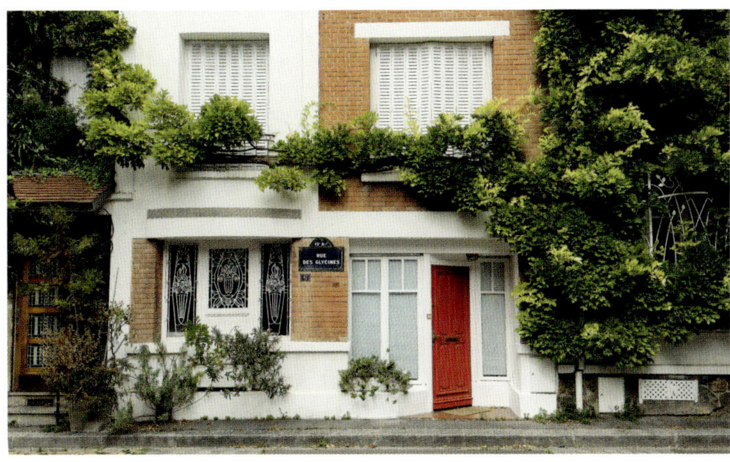

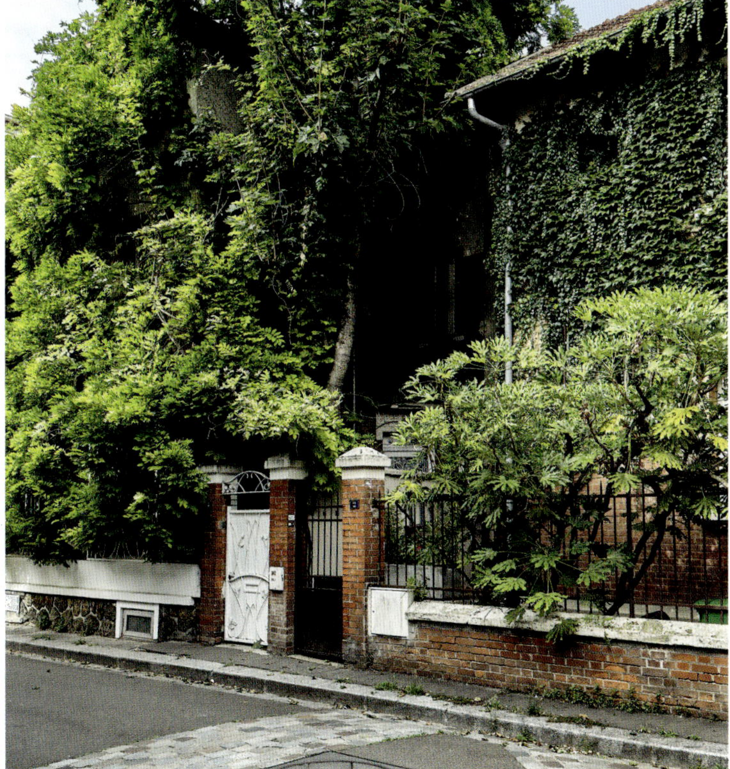

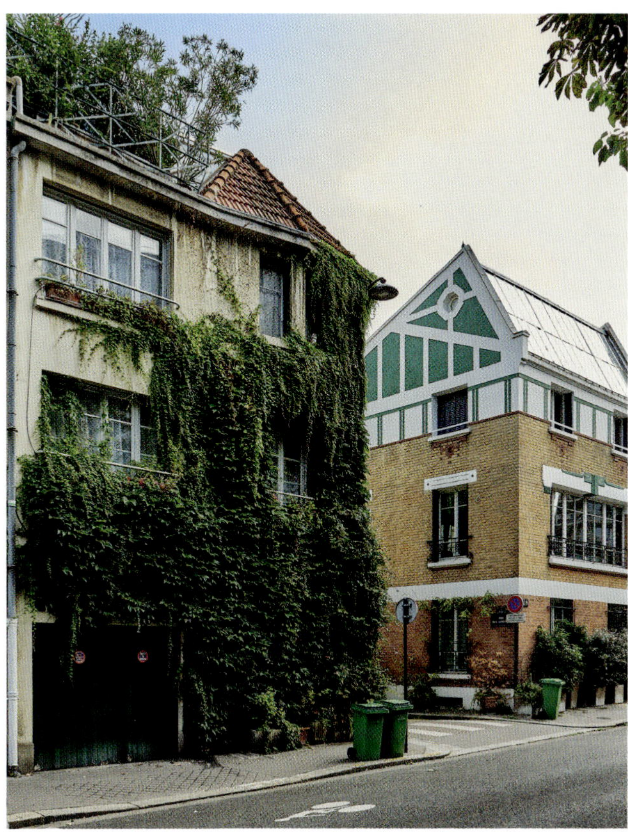

## Four Views of *Rue des Glycines*

**OPPOSITE**
The large three-story house at No. 11 sits on the corner of rue Glycines and rue Auguste-Lançon. A metal and glass awning is positioned over the home's alley doorway.

**ABOVE LEFT**
No. 6 has *vignes de glycines*, or wisteria vines, growing across the façade and over the red front door. Baskets of flowers appear in the designs of the window guards.

**BELOW LEFT**
The two-story at No. 2 rue des Glycines was built in 1926. The house at No. 4 just next door is completely covered in growth from two trees in the front garden. Even its white metal doorway has a decorative floral motif.

**ABOVE**
The house at No. 8 was built in 1927. Windows peek out from behind the greenery.

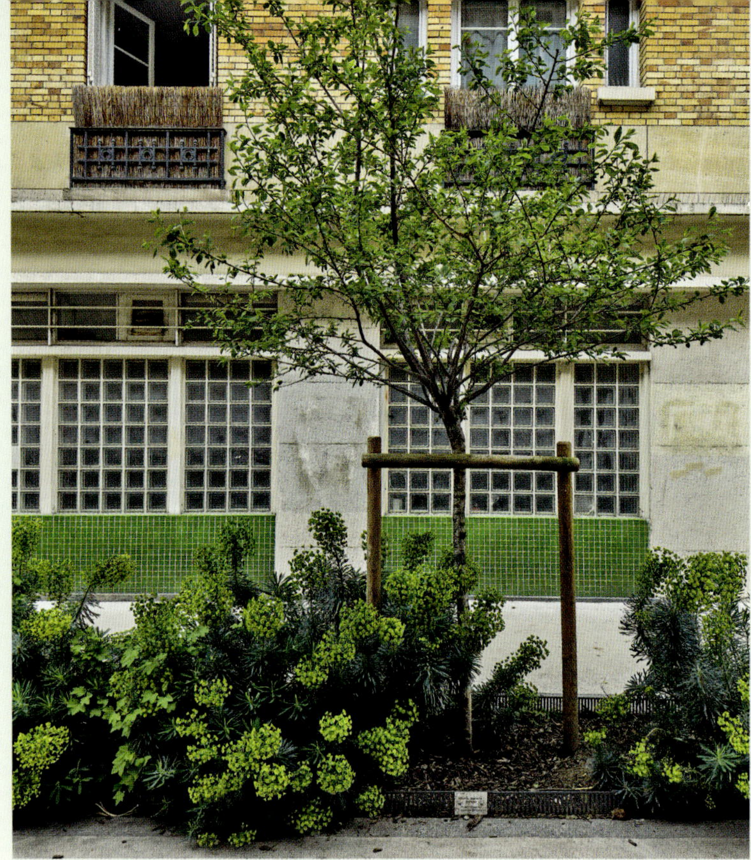

## Rues aux Enfants

5th, 7th, 12th, and 13th arrondissements
2020

In 2020 the Paris mayor Anne Hidalgo started a program to change the streets in front of schools. Many of the school streets had narrow sidewalks with barricades at the entrances, which made the dropping off and picking up of students congested, unsafe, and unhealthy, as cars were usually on the streets at the same time. So instead, the mayor's office began to transform these streets by eliminating car traffic from the street all together, filling in the roadways to the level of the sidewalks and adding beds with trees and plants. Each project is slightly different and is modified to the site. As of 2024, when the program name changed from *rues aux écoles* (or streets to schools) to *rues aux enfants* (or children's streets), there are more than two hundred projects that have been completed all over the city; there is at least one project per arrondissement. The gardens are organized with water systems and set up with new plants that are cared for until they are well established. Now, instead of cars running down the street in front of a school, children run and play in front of their neighborhood school. Soon they will be able to pick an apple from the tree that grows there.

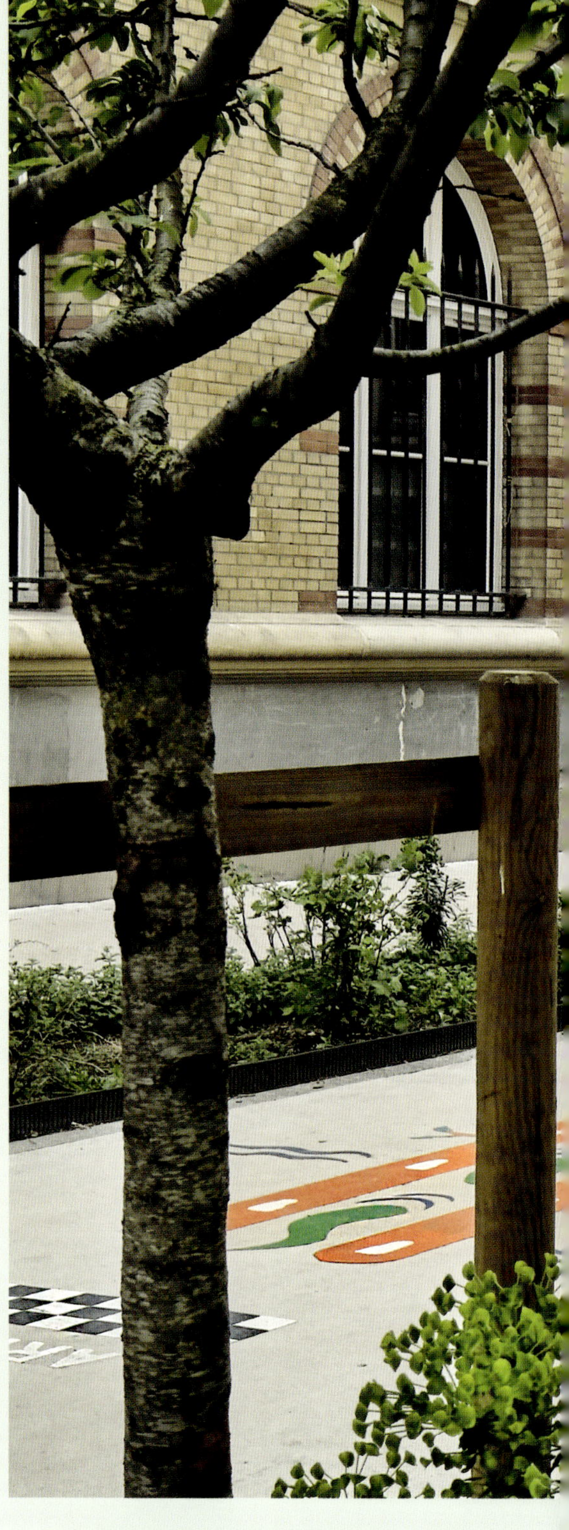

## Rue Charles-Baudelaire

**ABOVE LEFT**
In front of one school on rue Charles-Baudelaire, two rows of garden beds were planted with different fruit trees, including several *grand Alexandre* varieties of apples.

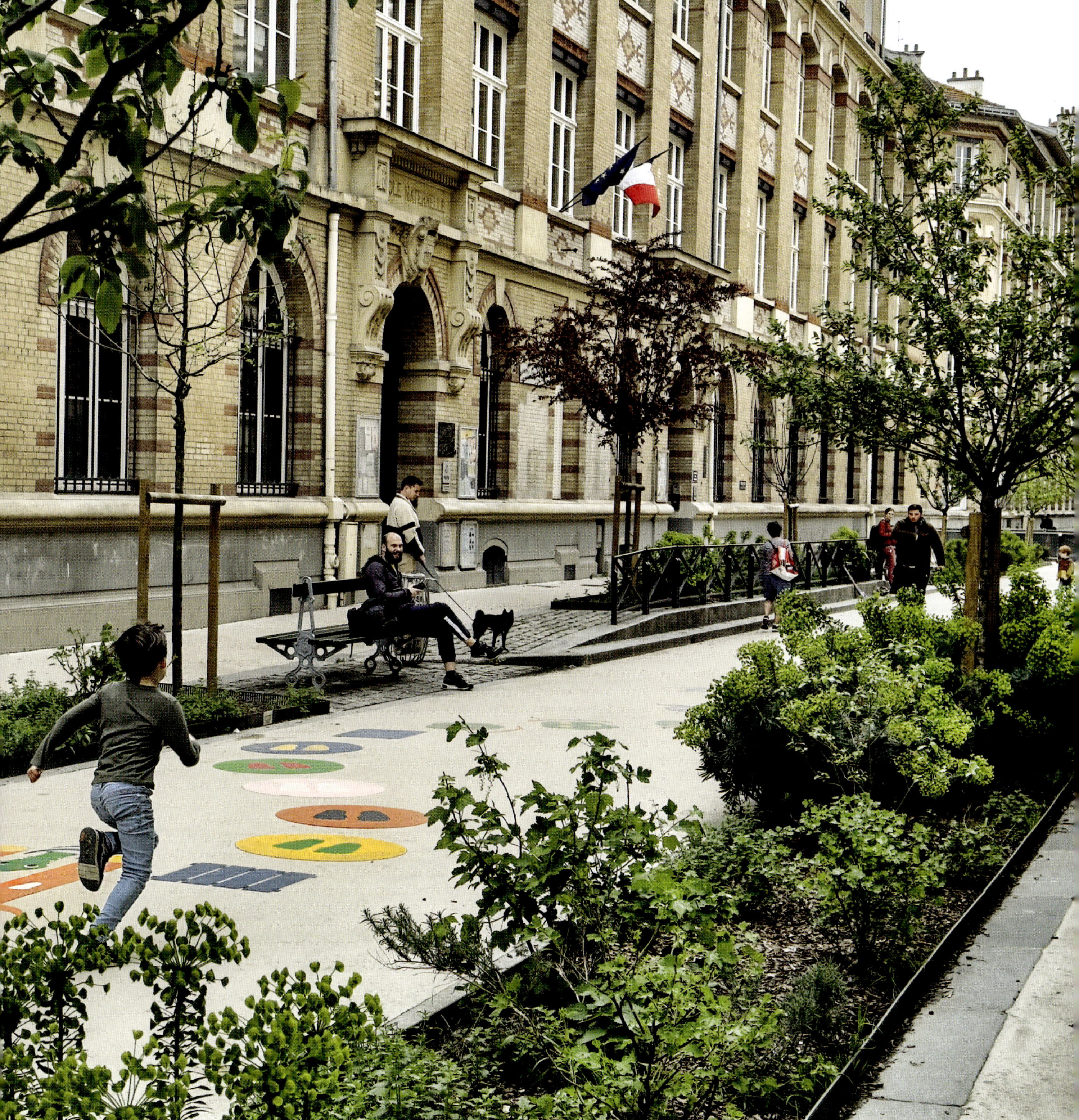



**ABOVE**
Rue Charles-Baudelaire is a long street
in the 12th arrondissement that was able
to be pedestrianized. Running is totally
allowed on this street. Games similar to
hopscotch are embedded in the sidewalk.
Benches are installed for parents.

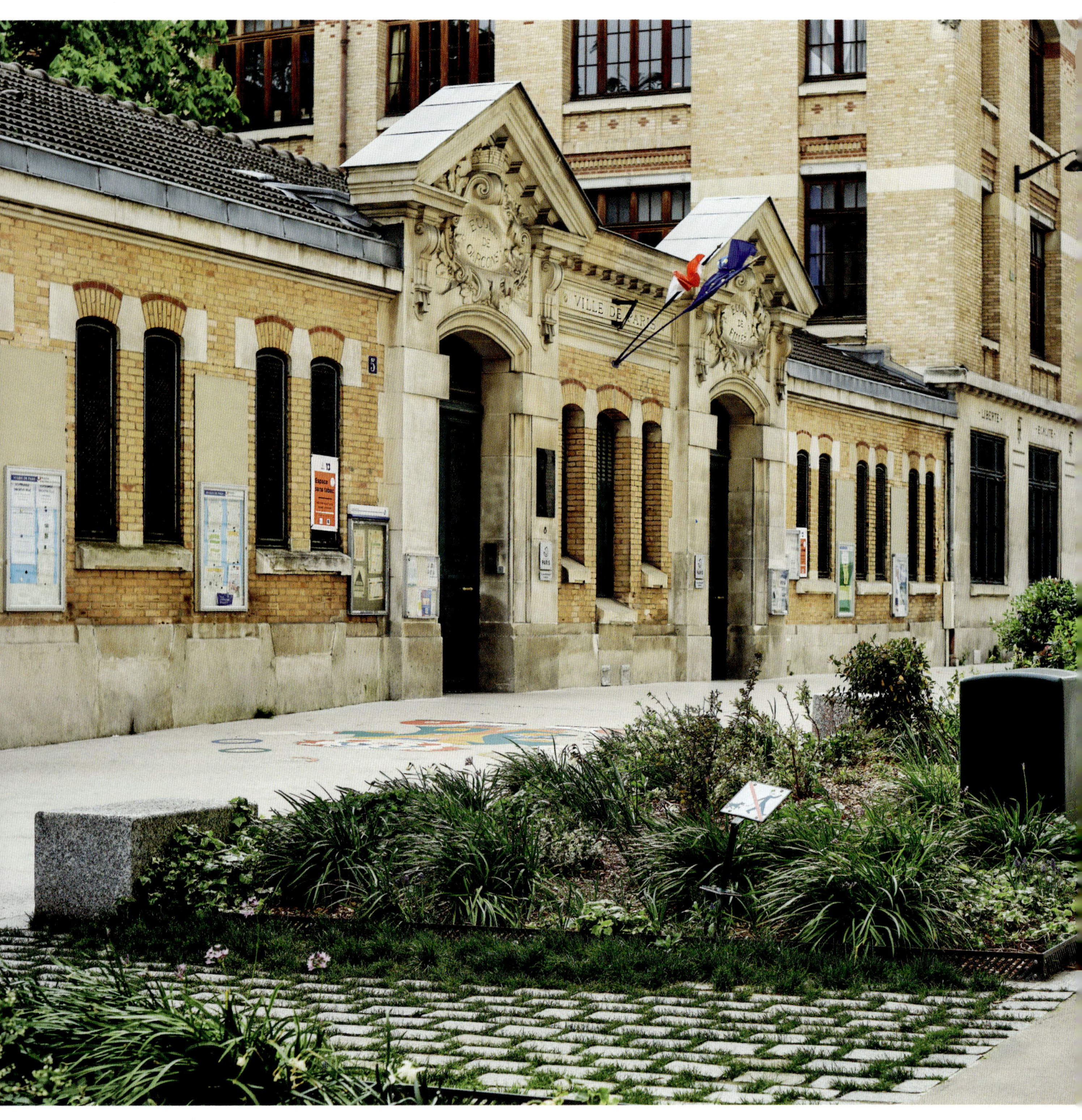

VILLE DE PARIS
LIBERTÉ
ÉGALITÉ

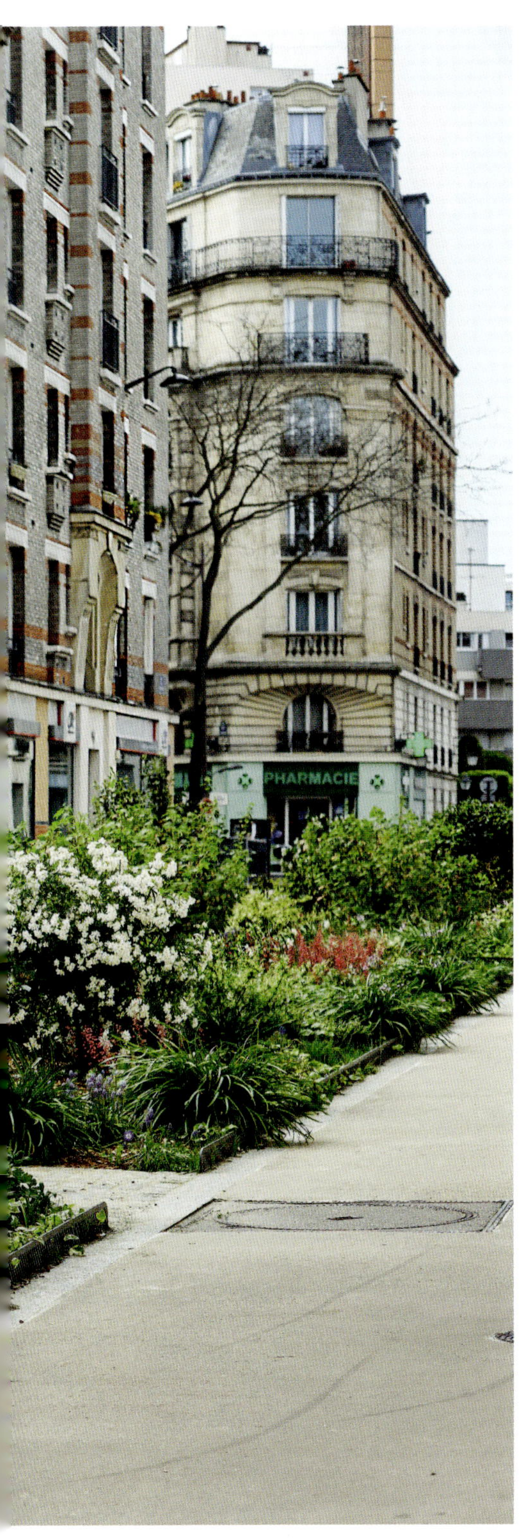

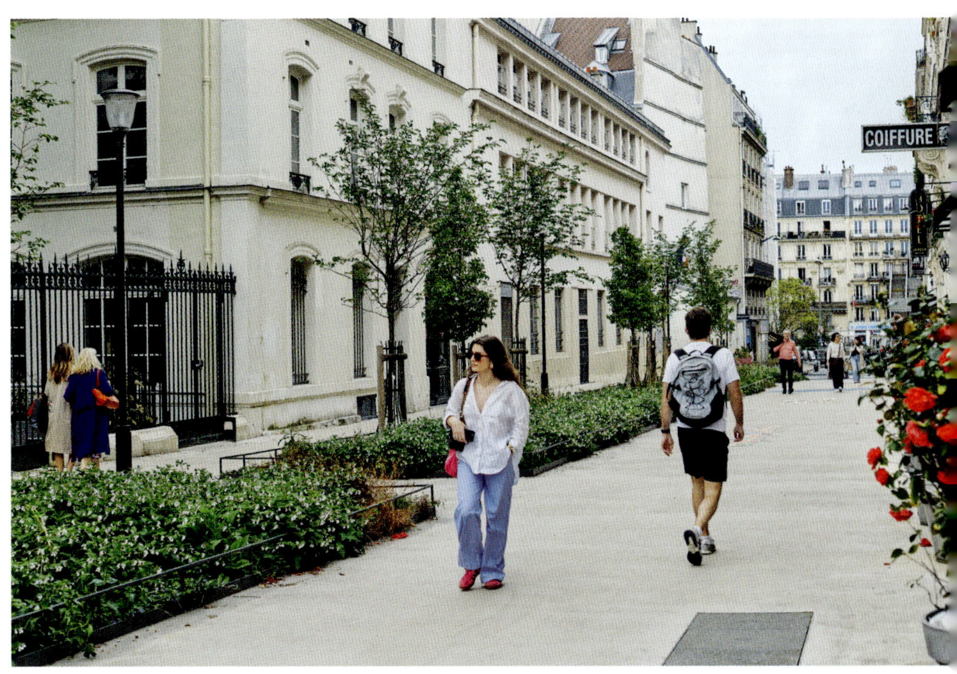


## Rue de la Providence

**LEFT**
Rue de la Providence in the 13th arrondissement is a short street. The beds in front of the school contain low scrubs and bushes. A box with a water supply is installed in the middle of the garden. Marble benches are placed throughout. While the gardens in front of the schools have similar elements, each one is unique.

## Rue du Sommerard

**ABOVE**
On rue du Sommerard in the 5th arrondissement, three beds of plants were planted in front of the school. The pedestrian street is far wider, safer, and healthier, not just for the children and parents who use it but for everyone who walks there, which includes hotel guests, shoppers, and residents.

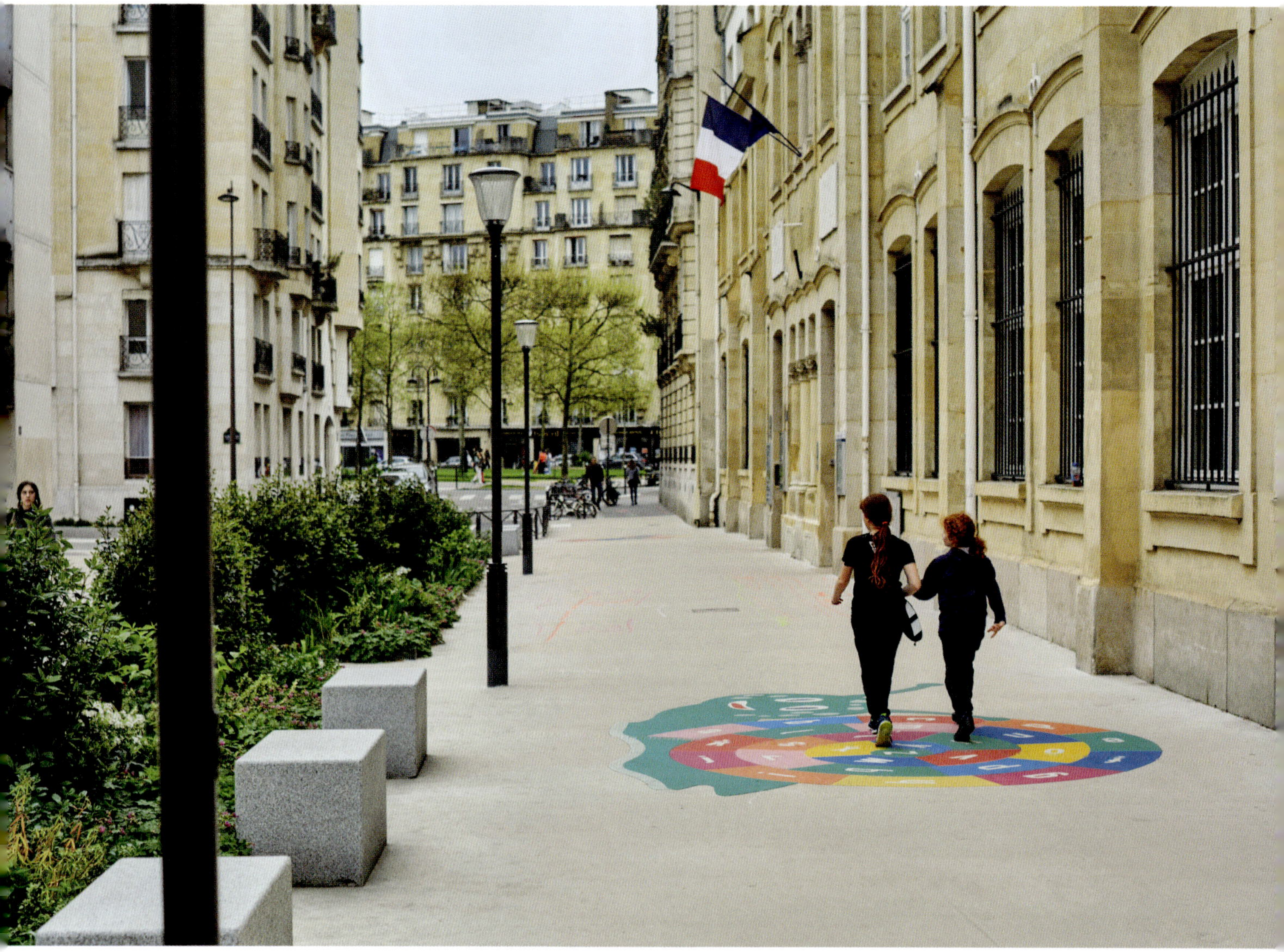

**ABOVE**
The streetscape has been transformed not only with the plantings and seating but also with additional streetlamps. Instead of one lamp per block, there are now six.

**RIGHT**
A view of rue Eblé in the 7th arrondissement before its transformation. Cars and a barricade lined the street.

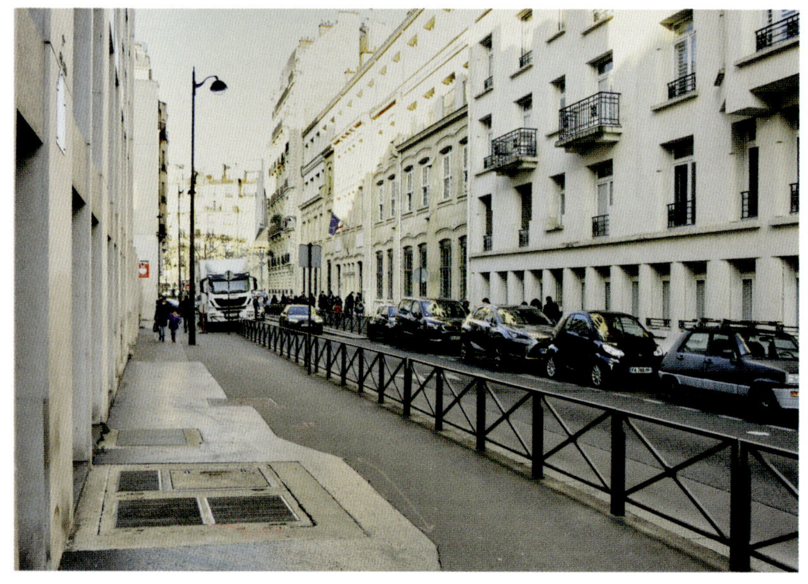

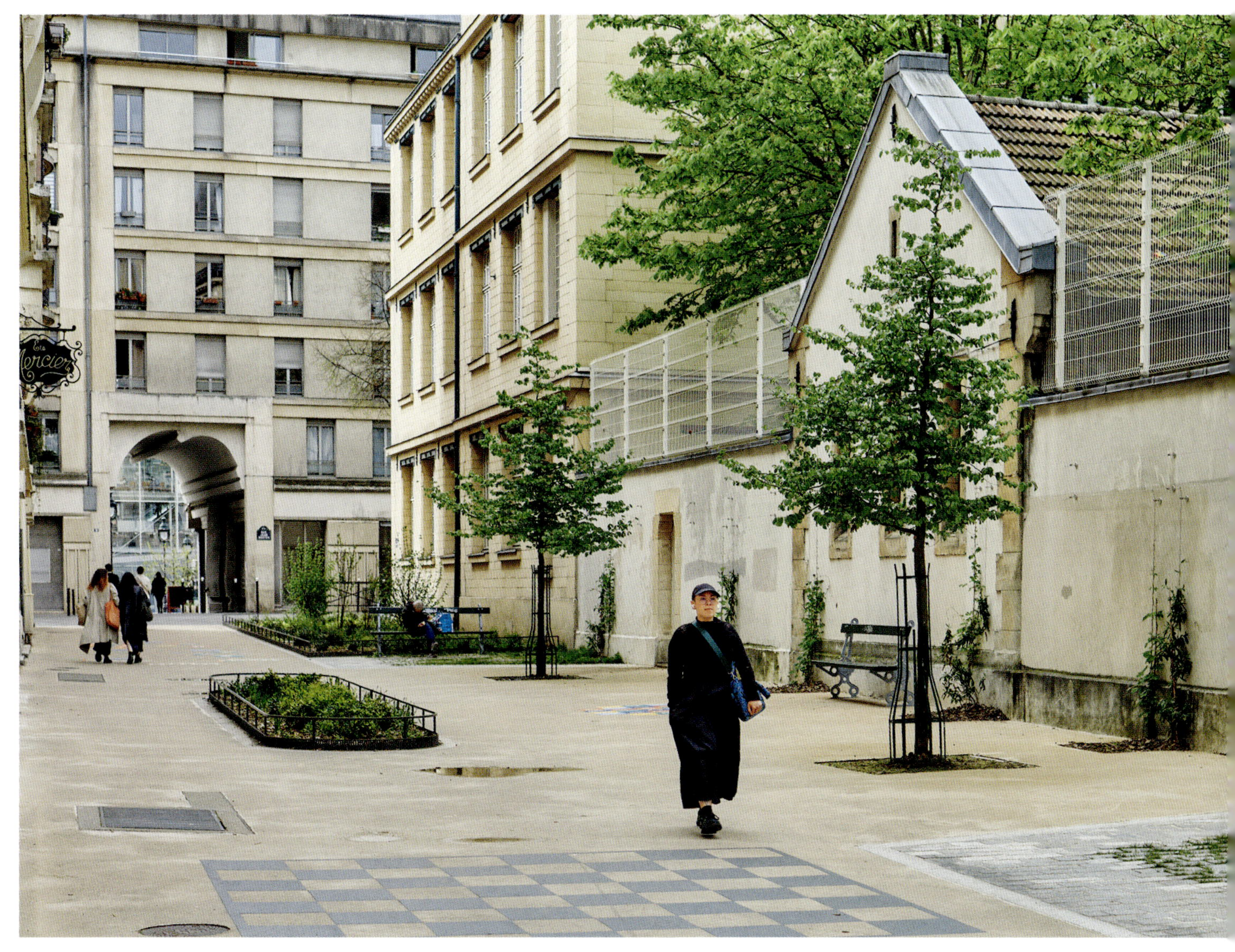

## Rue Guillaumot


In the 12th arrondissement, an elementary school was hemmed in by two major streets: avenue Daumesnil and boulevard Diderot. So a decision was made to turn a small back street located just behind the school, rue Guillaumot, into an expansive pedestrian space. This street also services visitors to the library on the corner.

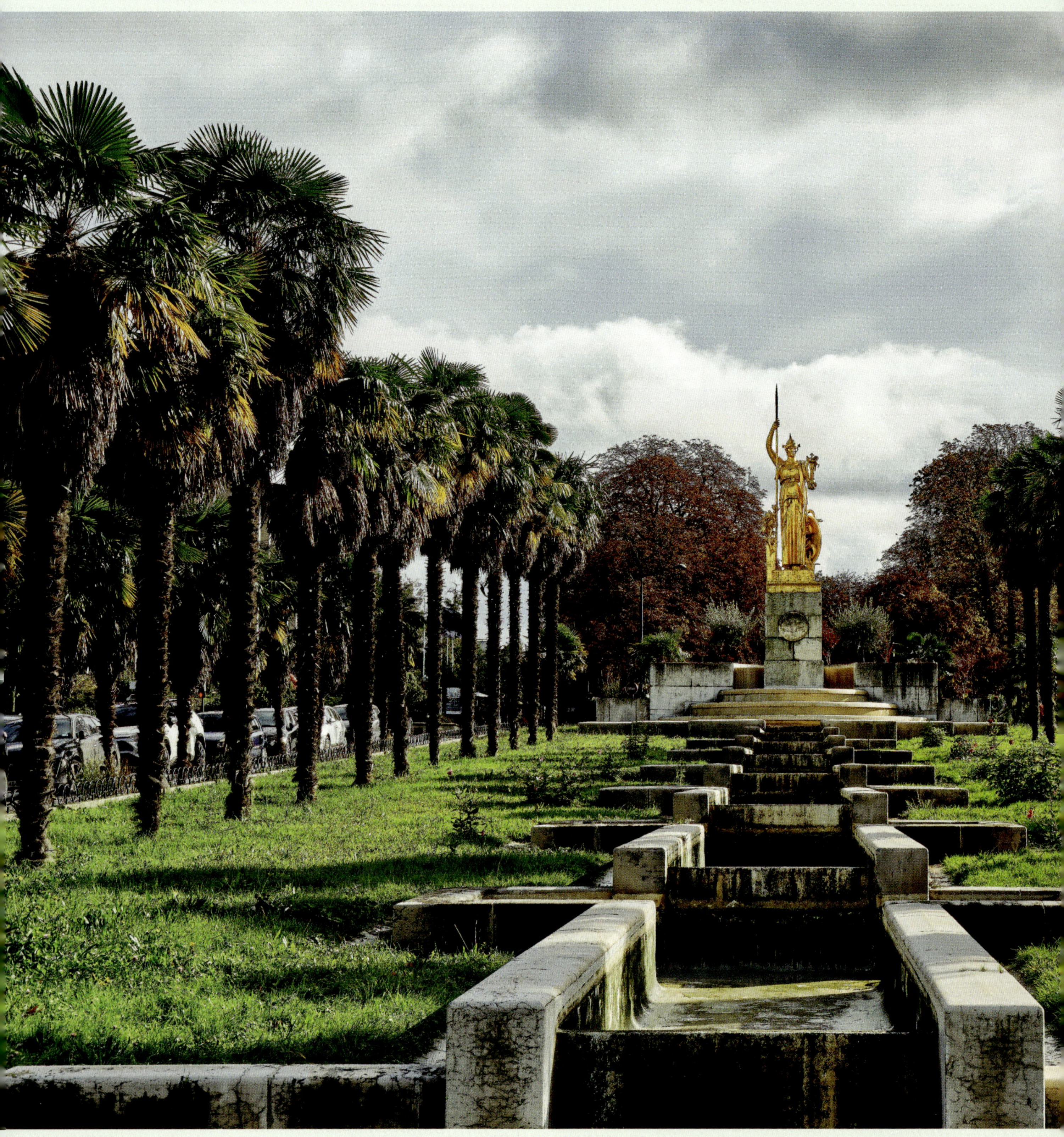

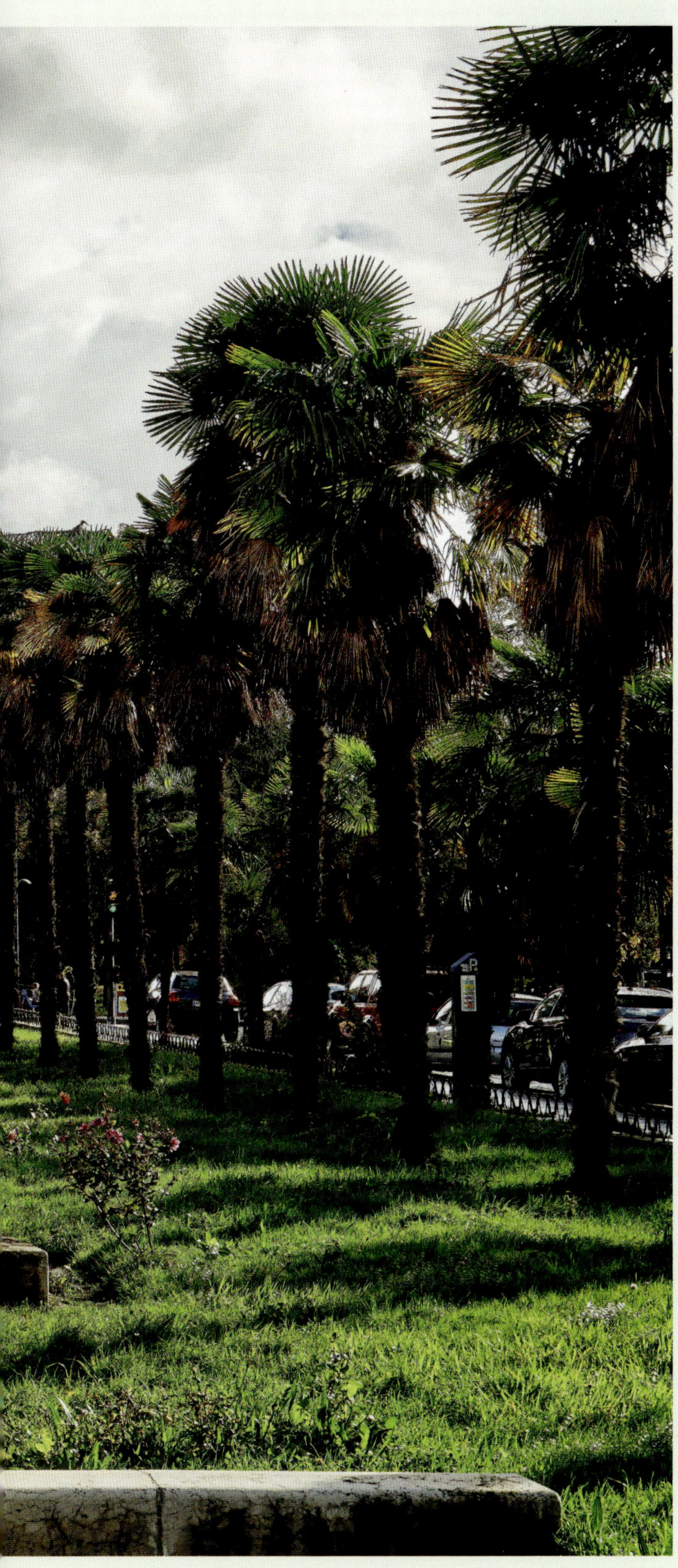



## *Fontaine de la Porte Dorée*
12th arrondissement
1931

Palm trees in Paris? At avenue Daumesnil, near le Musée national de l'histoire de l'immigration, there is a different type of *allée des arbres* (aisle of trees): Windmill palm trees surround la fontaine de la Porte Dorée. The space was initially planned as part of the site of the 1931 Paris Colonial Exhibition. At that time, a row of palm trees lined the Porte d'Honneur. As the building, designed by architect Albert Laprade, transformed to hold the collection of the Musée national des Arts d'Afrique et d'Océanie, so did the plaza. In 1935, it was renamed place Édouard-Renard, and a new tiered fountain appeared, designed by the architect Louis Madeline, while the palm trees disappeared. Years later, the collection of art, objects, and artifacts moved to the new museum at le Musée du quai Branley–Jacques Chirac. In 2007, the current museum was inaugurated. It's program and grounds were finally completed in 2013. These days, palms have returned to line a lawn of grass that surrounds the fountain. Its new name is le square des Anciens-Combattants-d'Inochine. While palm trees are not native to the region, they've been arriving for a long time and were cultivated indoors in places such as Louis XIV's Orangery at the Palace of Versailles. Lately, various types of palms—from short, stocky palmettos to tall, graceful palms—are being planted not only in huge containers for Paris Plages but also in the courtyard of the Petit Palais and in the 19th arrondissement, near le jardin Curial.

Overlooking the aisle of palm trees and the fountain is a golden statue of Athena, made by sculptor Léon-Ernest Drivier in 1931.

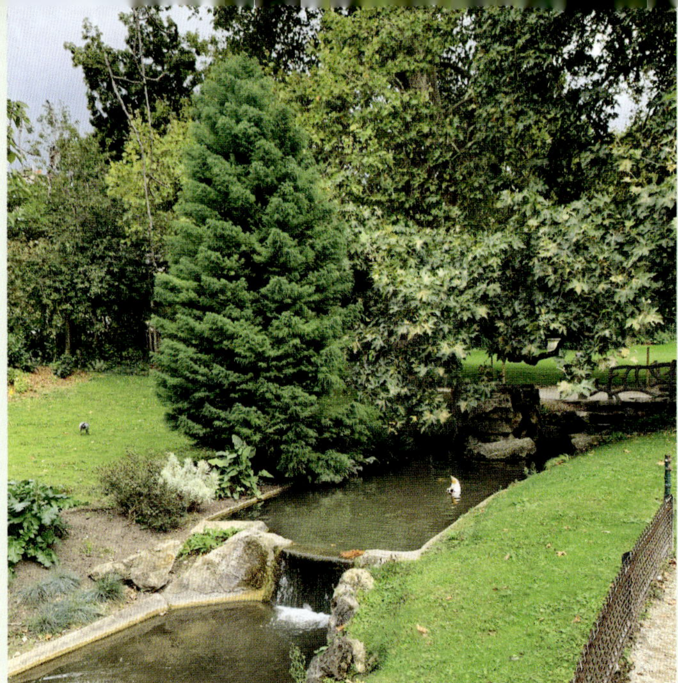

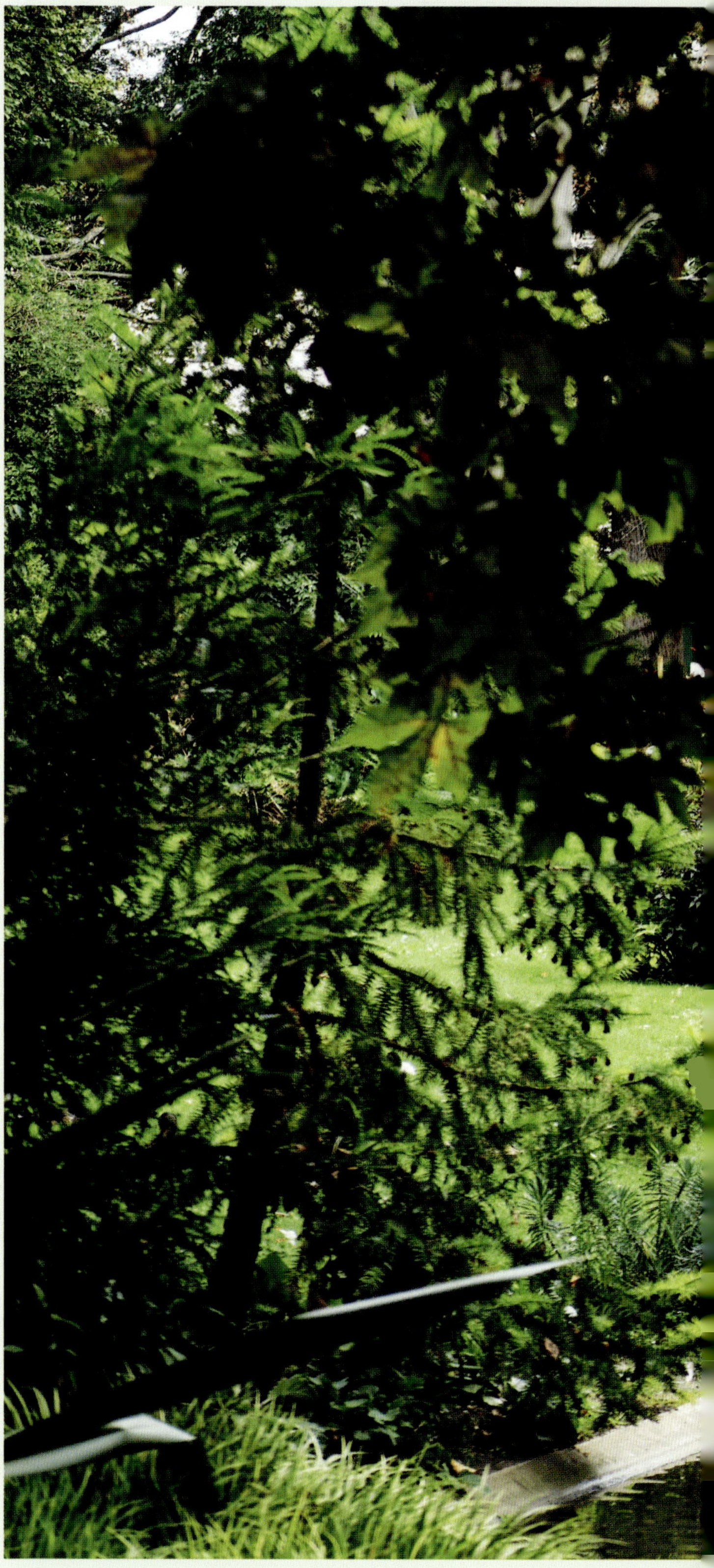

# *Square des Batignolles*
## 17th arrondissement
## 1862

Le square Batignolles is the archetype of an ideal Parisian neighborhood park. It has courts to play pétanque, a babbling brook, huge beautiful old trees, a little free library, rows of benches, a children's playground, lawns for picnics, clever gardening displays, and an arts space. Located in the north of Paris, the village of Batignolles was incorporated into the city limits in the 1860s. The park was created by engineer Jean-Charles Adolphe Alphand as part of Baron Haussmann's new Paris plan in 1862. For many years, the area was impacted by the large train station, depot, and market nearby, which later fell into disuse. That area has now been renovated as a new park known as Clichy-Batignolles–parc Martin Luther King. Although they exist near each other, the two parks are very different in terms of scale and design, but each pays homage to naturalistic English parks of the nineteenth century. Le square Batignolles's plan includes an oblong walking path that is bisected by l'allée Barbara, named for the French singer popular in the 1970s. These paved walkways meander around several ponds and among the giant trees, including a *platane commun* (common plane tree) and a *platane d'Orient* (Oriental plane tree) deemed remarkable by A.R.B.R.E.S, an organization that seeks to preserve and protect important trees throughout France. The trees were planted in 1840 and 1872.

**ABOVE LEFT**
More than four hundred ducks feel at home in a cascading stream and ponds in le square Batignolles.

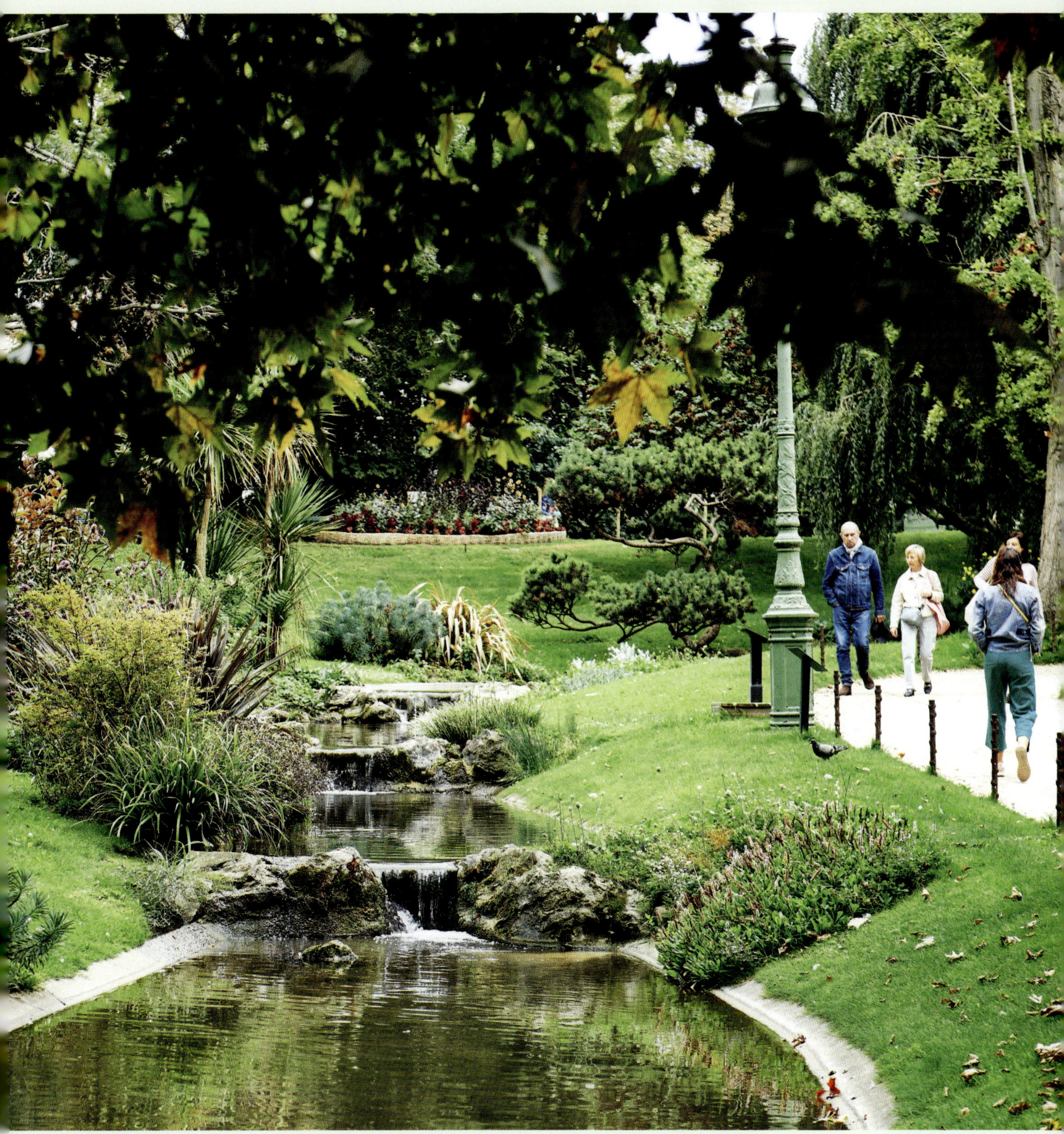



**ABOVE**
Various tiers of the landscape
surrounding the stream add to the visual
dynamics and biodiversity of the park.

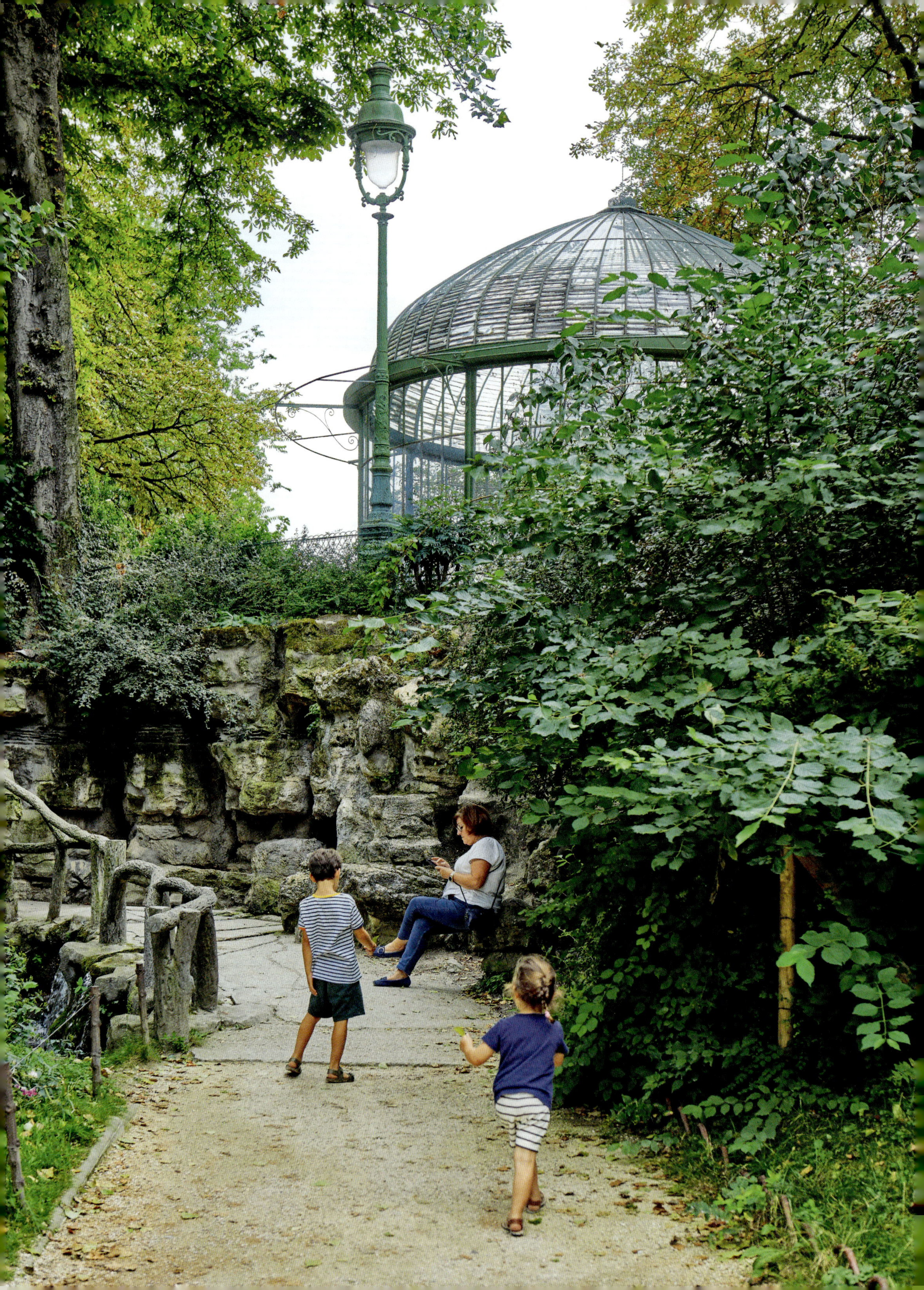

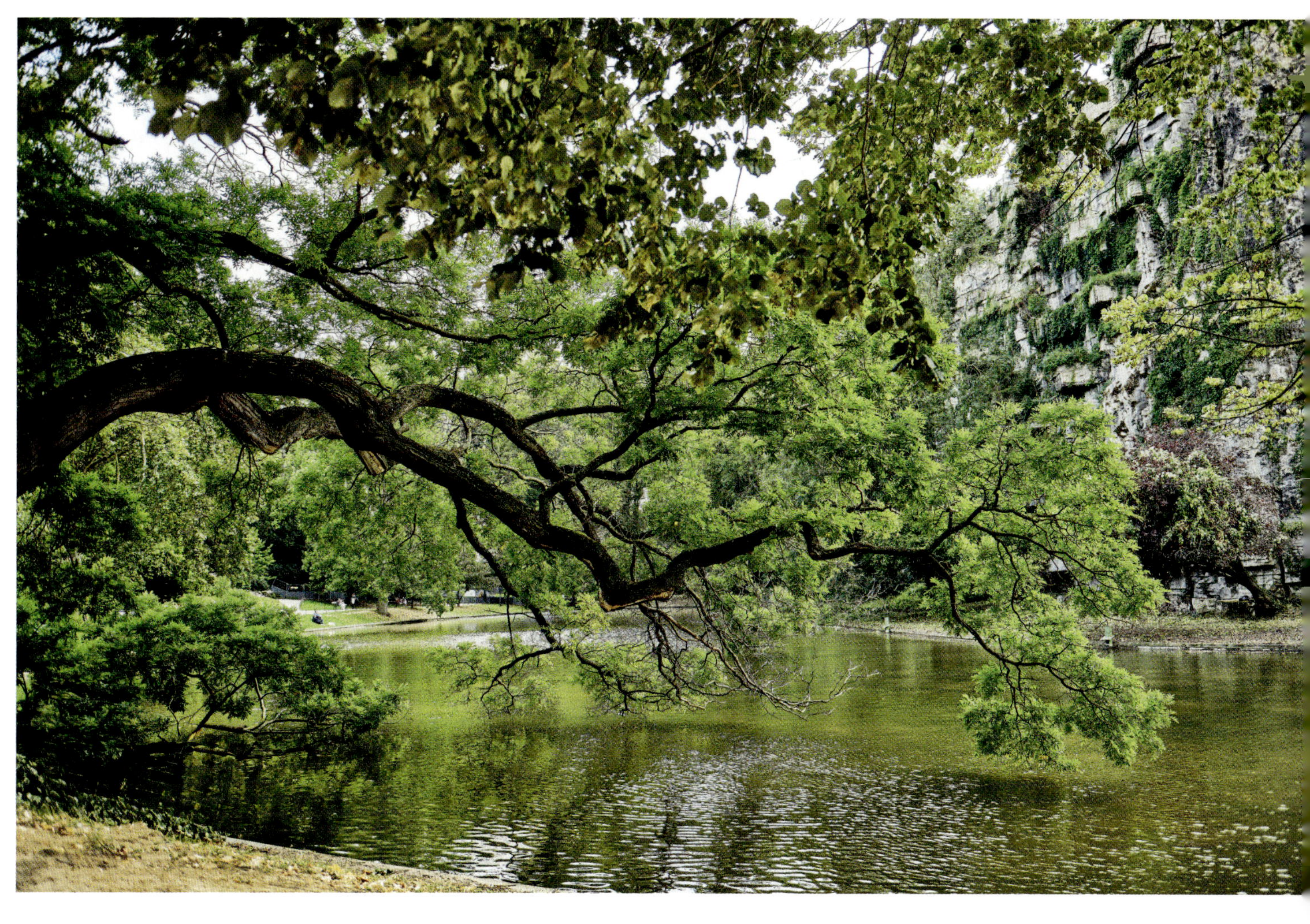

OPPOSITE
A round glass-and-metal *serre*, or
greenhouse, was installed on a rocky hill
in the garden. It is being used as an art
space that is managed by Le K.A.B.

ABOVE
The limbs of the old plane tree stretch
out over one of the ponds of the park.

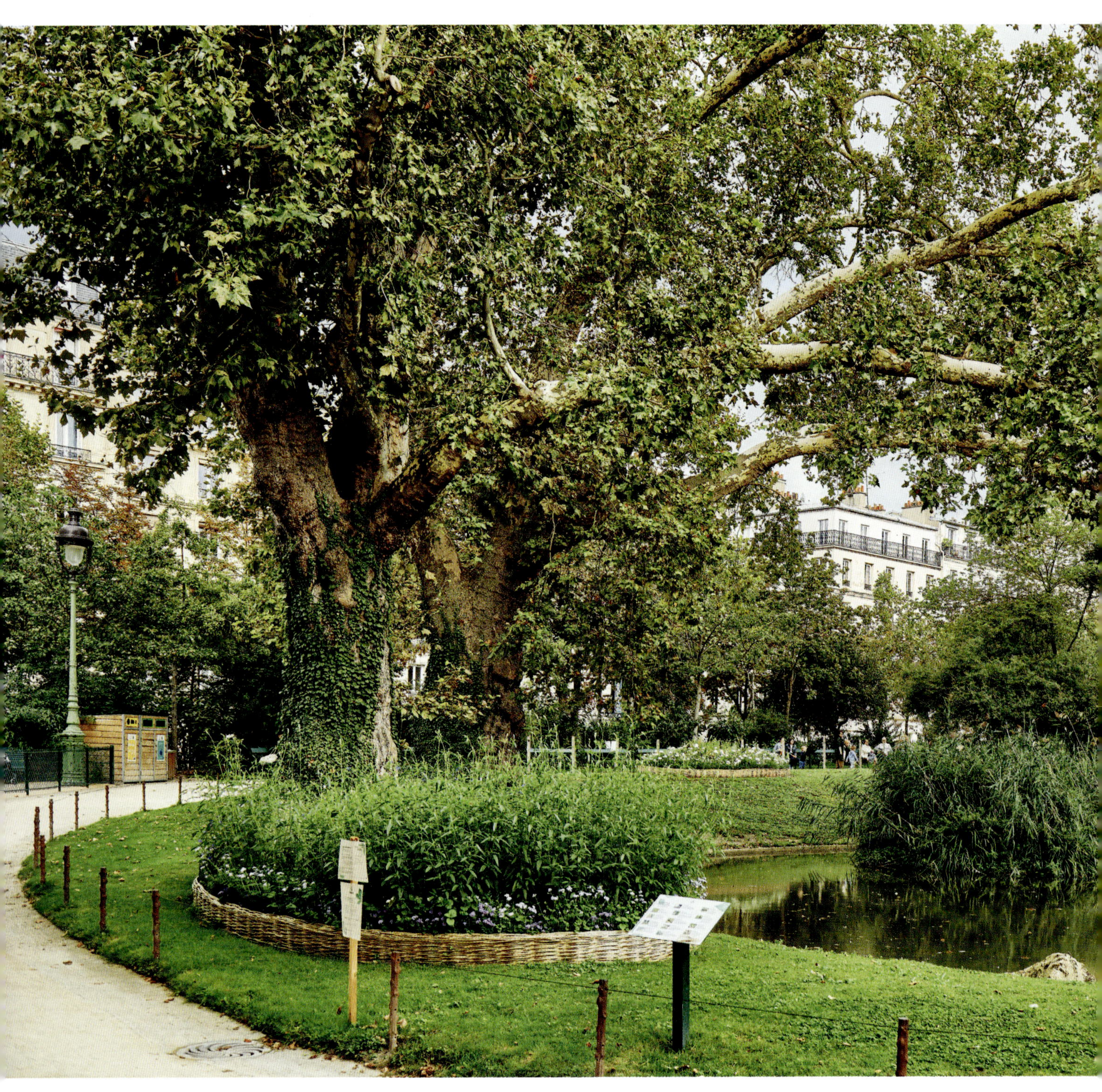

 *SQUARE DES BATIGNOLLES*

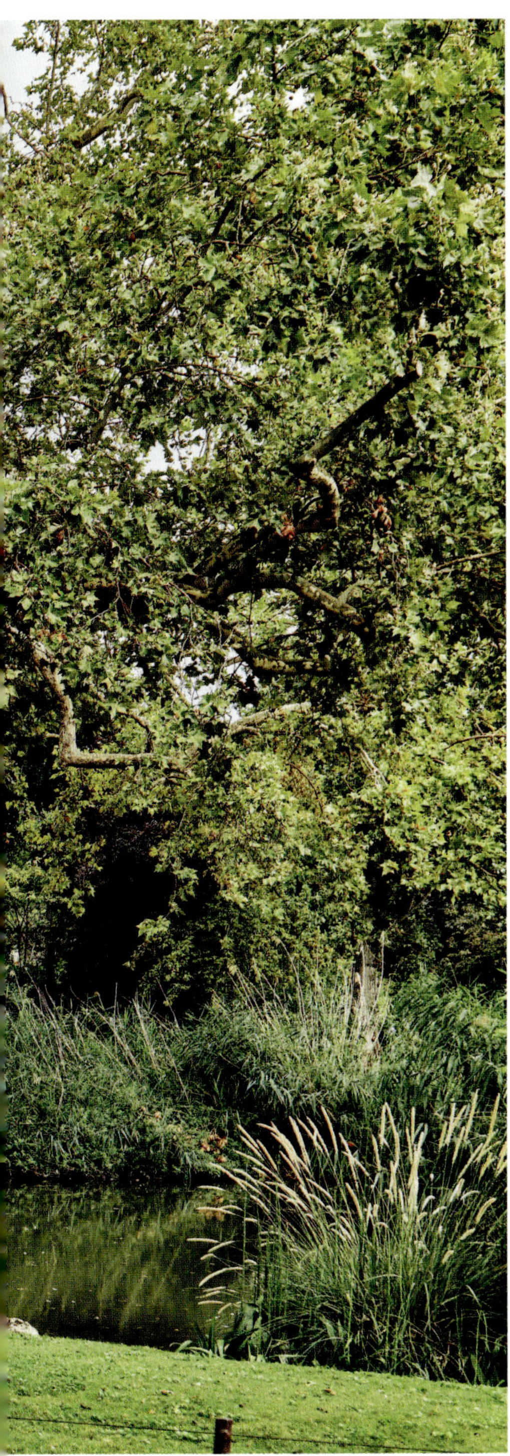

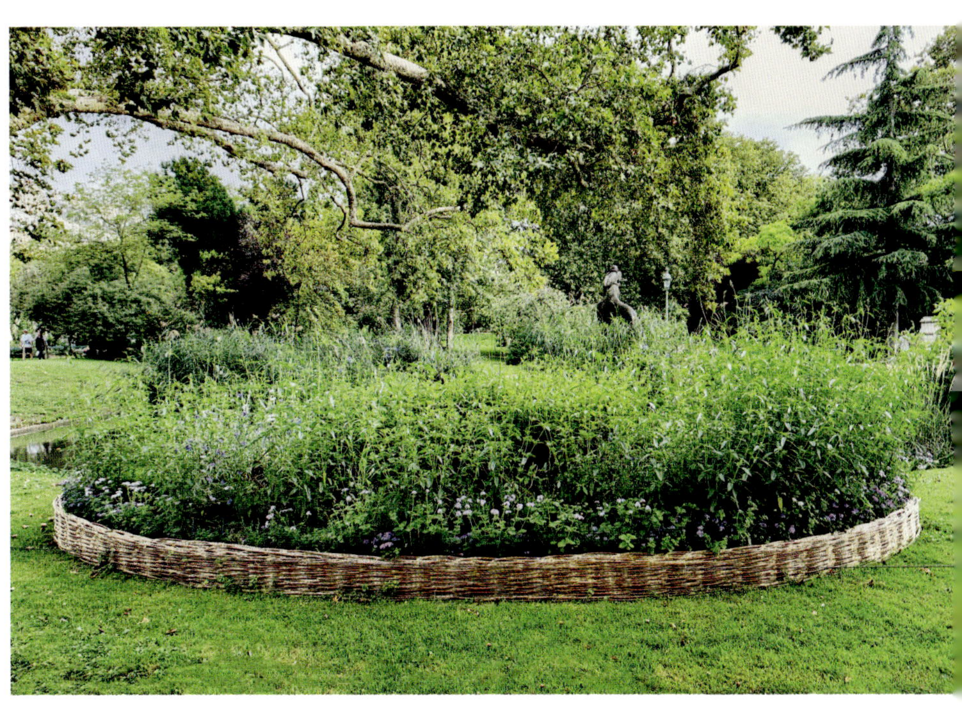

LEFT
A block of residential buildings on the
park's border serves as a backdrop to
one of two plane trees in the garden
designated as an official remarkable tree
of France by A.R.B.R.E.S.

ABOVE
There are seven "baskets" of flowers
throughout the garden. These woven-
bordered beds hold *scabieuse* (or
sweet scabious), *bourrache* (or borage),
*verveine de Buenos Aires* (or Argentinian
vervain), and *agastache du Mexique* (or
Mexican giant hyssop), among other
flowers. The plantings in the beds are
rotated three times a year.

## *Écoquartier Clichy-Batignolles* and *Parc Martin Luther King*

17th arrondissement
2023

What if there was a chance to build a neighborhood from scratch? Clichy-Batignolles is the kind of project that few people imagined in an old district that was a village long ago. The area, all 54 hectares (or 133 acres), is at the edge of le boulevard périphérique, a major highway that loops around the city. The former railyard and storage facility, holding trains not in use, was one of the last large open spaces in Paris. The yard was built in the 1860s, and while other developments started to spread at the time, such as le square des Batingolles, the area became increasingly separated from the city by dozens of railroad tracks and, in the 1970s, by the RER, a commuter rail line. After two failed bids to host the 2008 and 2012 Olympics, both of which included schemes for reworking Clichy-Batignolles as the athlete's village, the question of the area's future arose. The ZAC Clichy-Batignolles was created to transform the railway yard into an *écoquartier*. (ZAC is an acronym for *zone d'aménagement concerté*, or an urban development zone.) The guiding themes of the design would be "a presence of nature, density, and energy conservation." The aim would be toward carbon neutrality, using solar panels and geothermal energy sources. Nature would provide protection against a heat island effect. Martin Luther King Park was part of the first phase of development in 2007. Designed by landscape architect Jacqueline Osty, the park has elements of water and wind. It is organized in sections representing the seasons. As the process progressed, political leaders and teams from the City of Paris, urban planner François Grether, developers including P&Ma, and other architects and builders all worked together using a collaborative studio model. The public was invited to participate in the project reviews. The plan included residential buildings, student housing, and housing for the elderly. Aiming for social diversity and inclusiveness, goals were set: Half of the new apartments are dedicated to social housing, twenty percent are subject to rent control, and thirty percent are available at market prices. Everything that makes a city livable is here: home, work, play, food, and nature. The last piece of the project—planting an orchard of fruit trees—was completed in 2023.

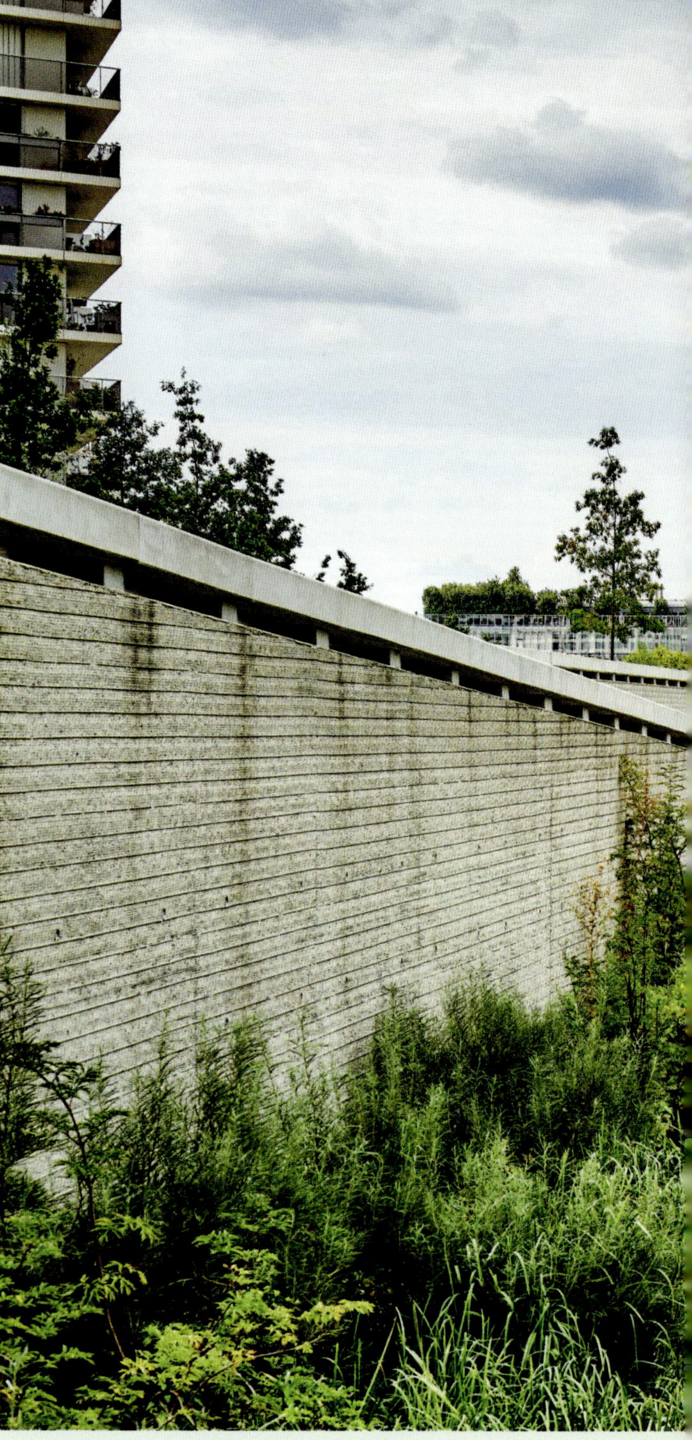

On a hot day, sitting by the water is delightful. The entrance of Clichy-Batignolles écoquartier is an example of the layers of landscaping, from the retaining walls of the terraced garden to the water plants and grasses along the creek-like basin that runs parallel to the old tracks embedded near the paved walkway. One day these new young trees will provide even more shade for the platform-like wooden seating. In the background, Renzo Piano Building Workshop's Palais de Justice rises above the park.

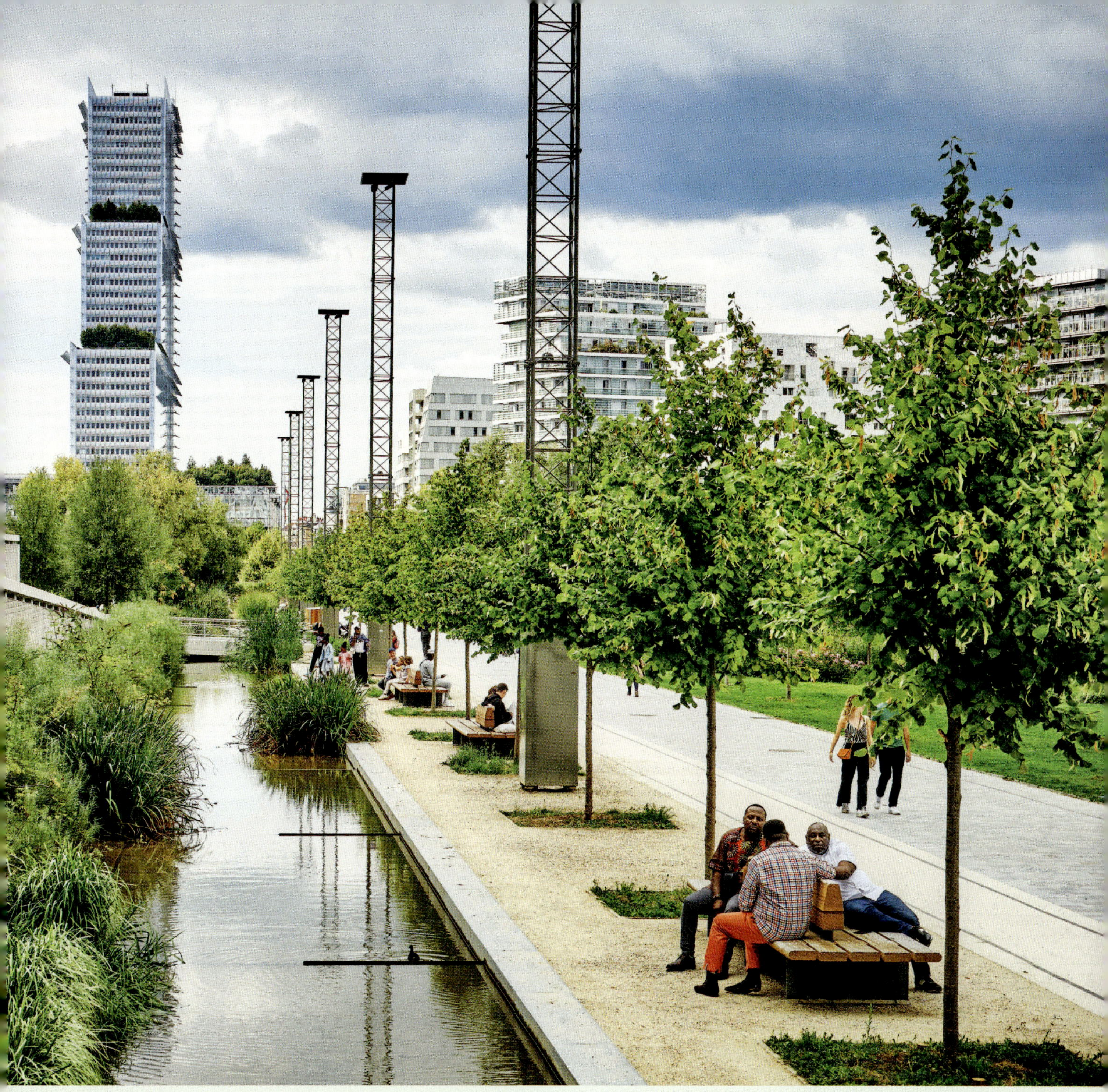

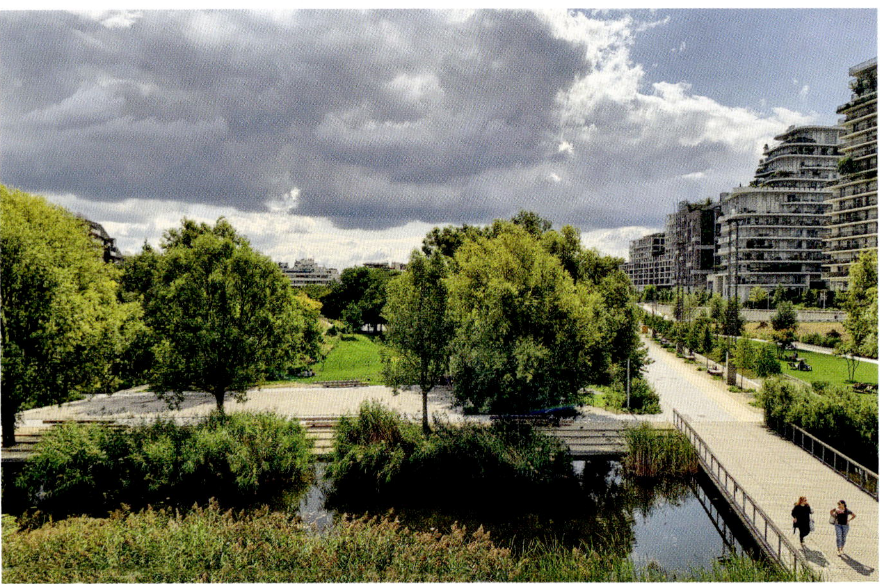

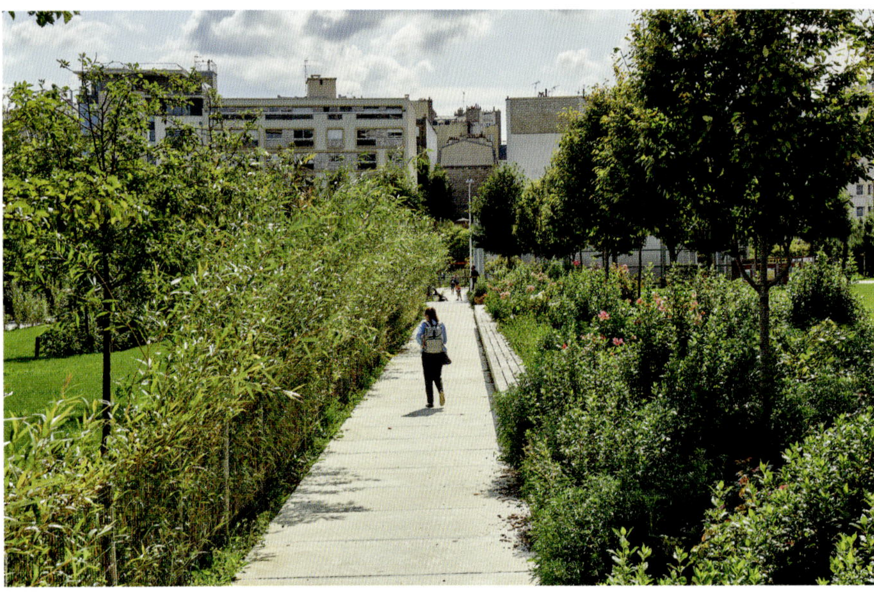

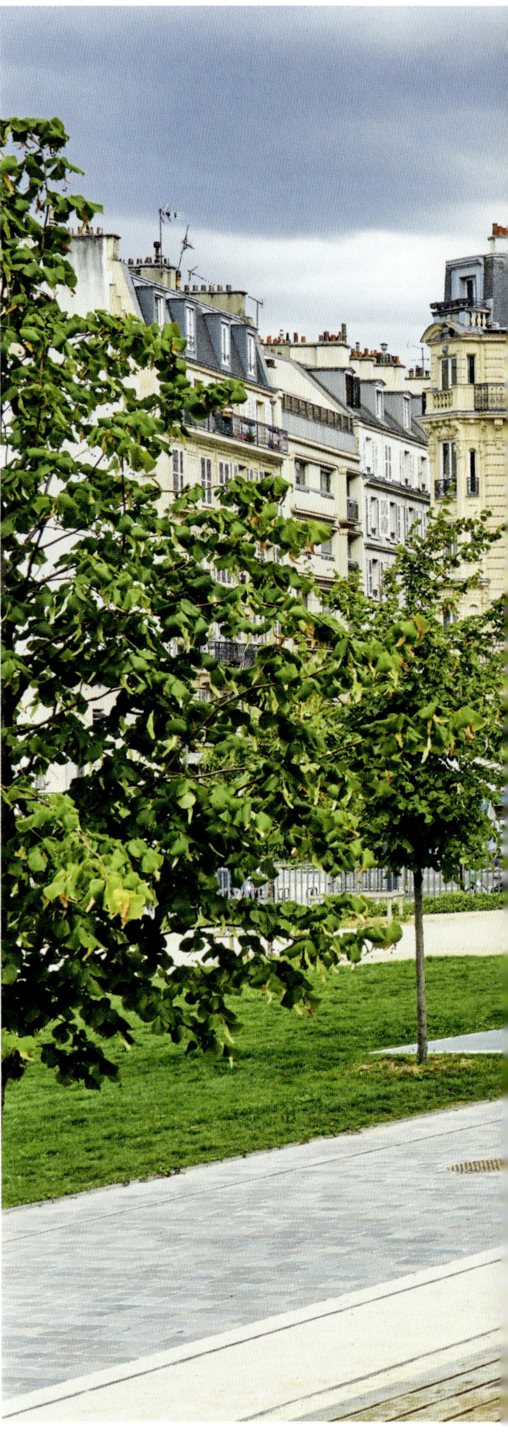

**TOP**

The park is the center of the neighborhood. The buildings are grouped in a line around the center. Another important Jacqueline Osty idea is the placement of water in the park. A large basin is in the center and the plants in this area are inspired by *été*, or summer.

**ABOVE**

A stand of bamboo and a row of trees create a corridor on the south side of the garden. A long built-in bench is a resting place. One of Osty's primary ideas was to divide the park into sections by season. The plantings of this park section are inspired by *printemps*, or spring.

**RIGHT**

Rue Cardinet is the southern border of parc Martin Luther King. The older, traditional architectural style of the buildings that line the street highlights the contrast between the newer architecture of 2012. Each new tree is given its own square of dirt. There are no sidewalks to rein in or divide the park.

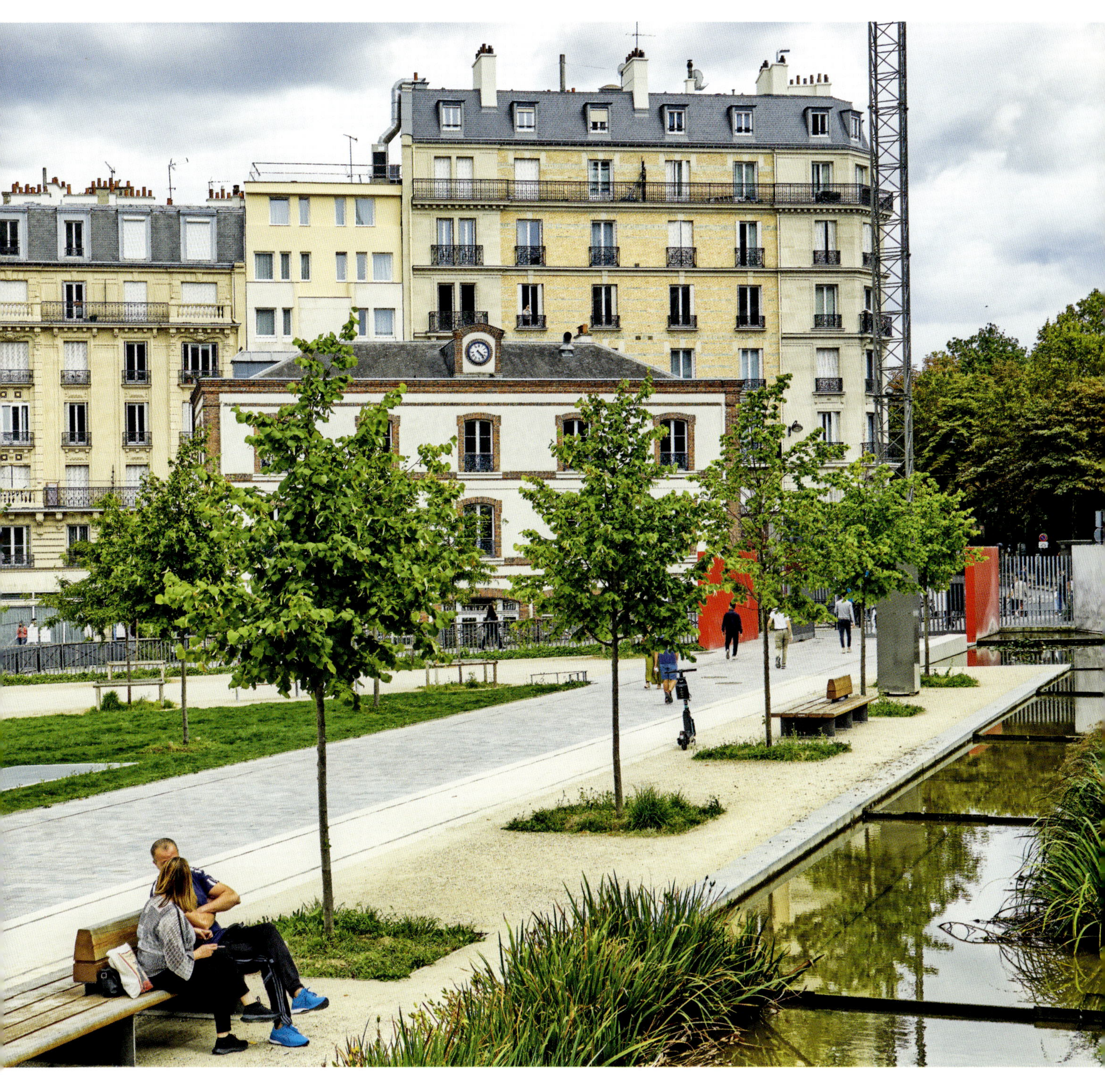

The western sector of Clichy-Batignolles's cityscape has a few answers to the questions of measuring successful communities and neighborhoods. Each building has a combination of uses, all designed around the lives of the residents. The project was divided into lots, with architects working both individually and in collaboration, not only with aesthetic appeal in mind but also with the shared resources of the site. The result is harmonious.

**LOT 01:** One entrance of the district begins on the corner of rue Cardinet (on the far left). The corner building was conceived with both residential and commercial spaces in mind, as well as a courtyard garden and a metro station below. It was designed in collaboration by Gaëtan Le Penhuel Architectes & Associés, Saison Menu & Associes Architectes Urbanistes, and SUD Architectes, with landscape architect Emma Blanc.

**LOT 02:** Next door, there is another residential building, this one designed by Biecher Architectes. On the same lot the apartment building UNIC rises. It is the architectural firm MAD's first apartment building in Europe.

**LOT 05:** A commercial office space named Season was designed by Jean-Paul Viguier et Associés and Agence Search.

**LOT 04B:** Near the large basin, AAVP and Aires Mateus's building, known as Emergence, has 50 rent-controlled and 120 affordable housing apartments.

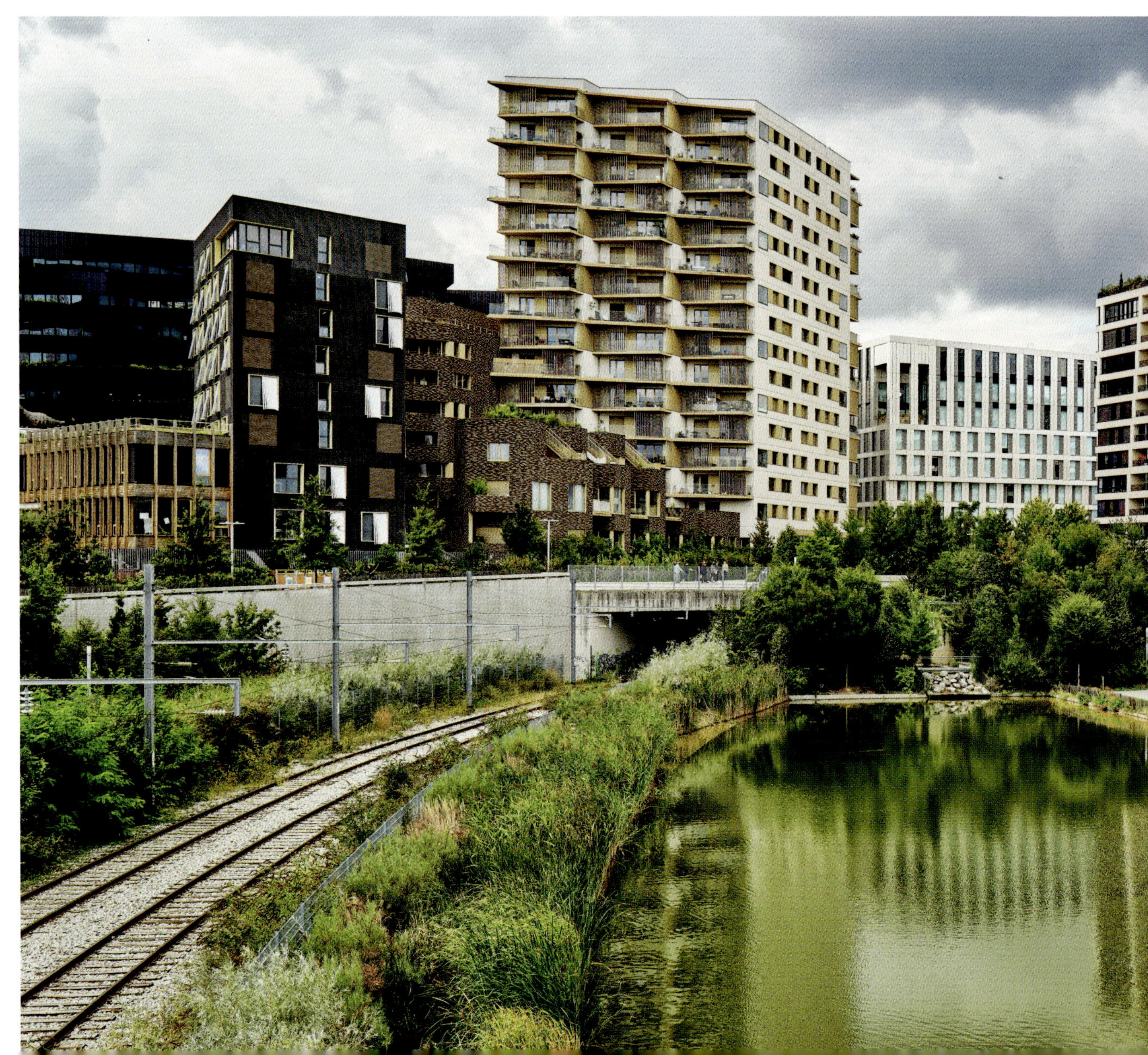

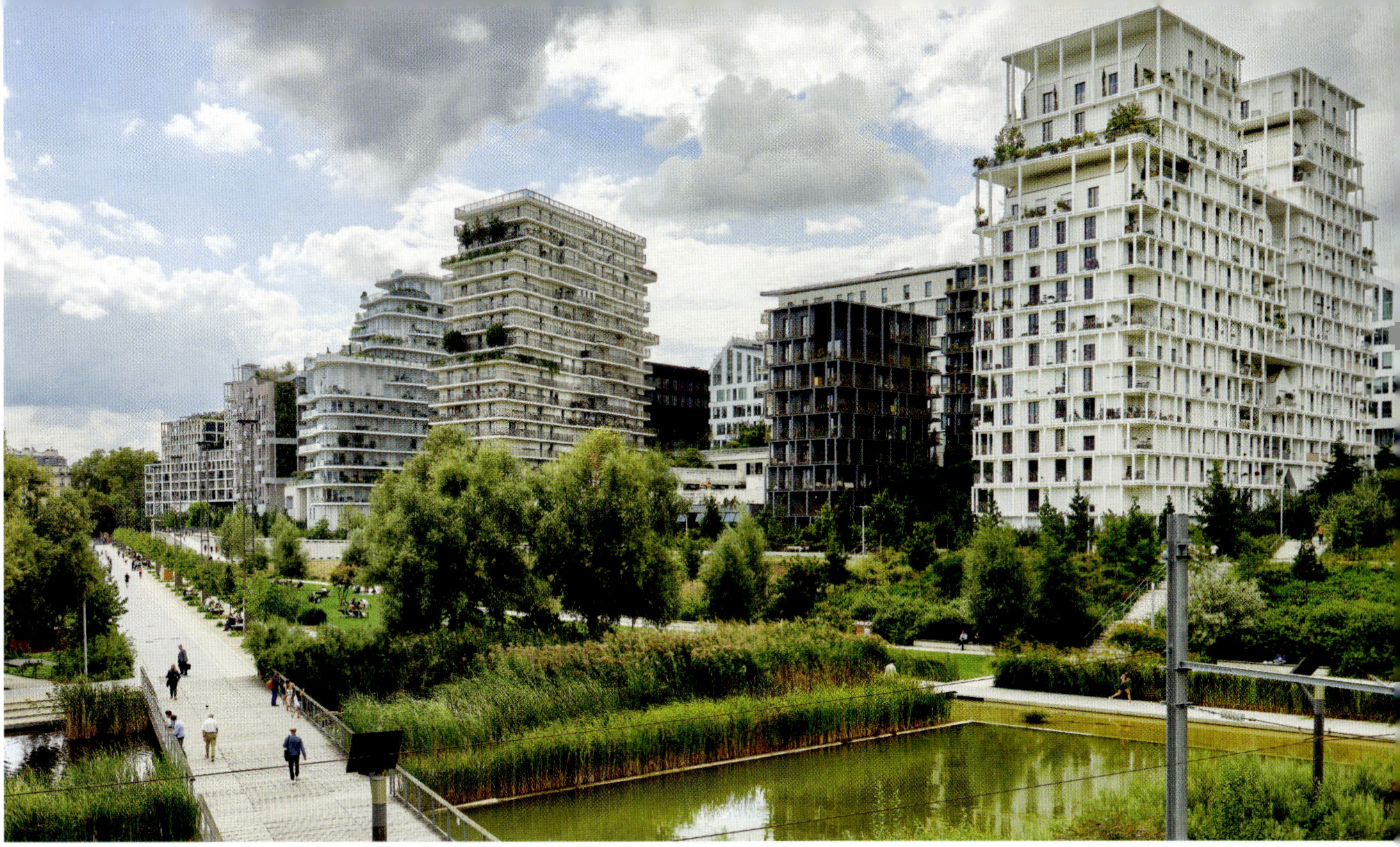

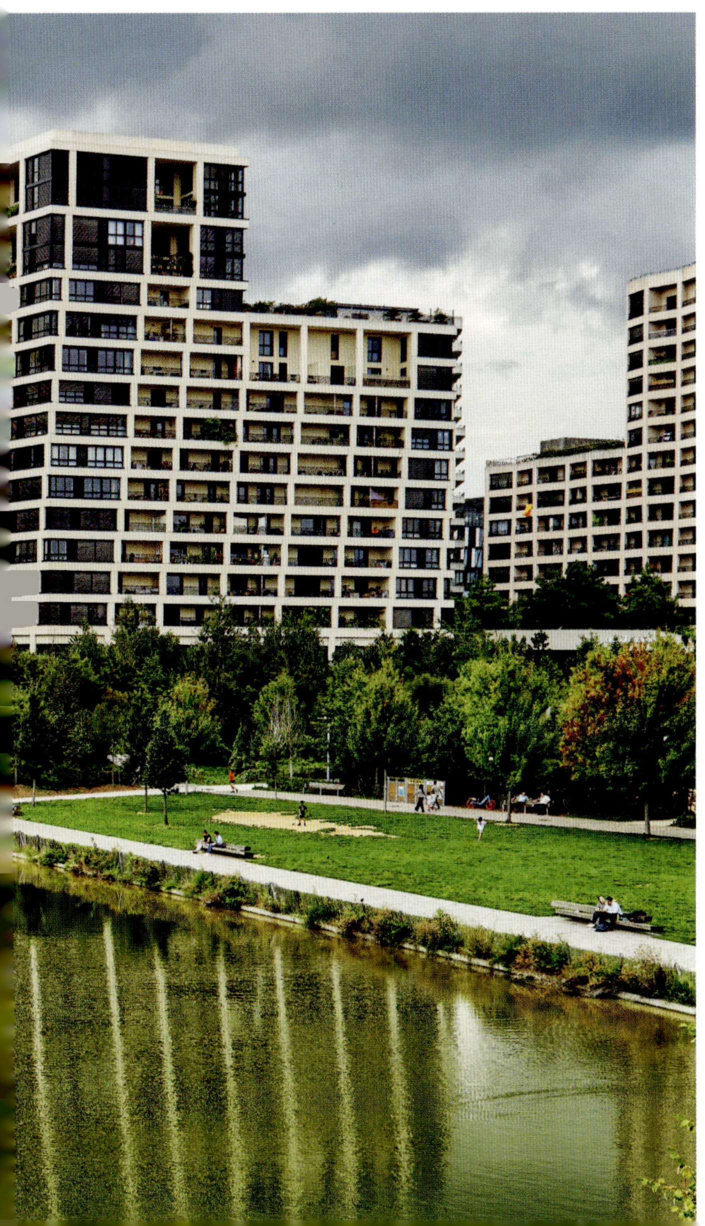



Farther along the western edge of the park are buildings that consider entertainment, working spaces, and the education of the neighborhood's children. The mixture of architectural styles and building materials creates a vibrant streetscape.

**LOT 06A:** Designed by Querkraft and SAM Architecture, these buildings (on the far left) have a mixed program including a daycare, housing for migrants, social housing, and commercial spaces.

**LOT 06B:** Fresh Architectures and ITAR Architectures designed this building for rental apartments and affordable housing. Balconies face the water.

**LOT 09:** Located along the commercial corridor near the train tracks, this building is used for office space. The team of architects included firms Baumschlager Eberle and SCAPE with Alessandro Cambi, Francesco Marinelli, and Paolo Mezzalama.

**LOT 08:** The architects TVK and Tolila + Gilliland designed this residential building and its entertainment spaces, including a movie theater.

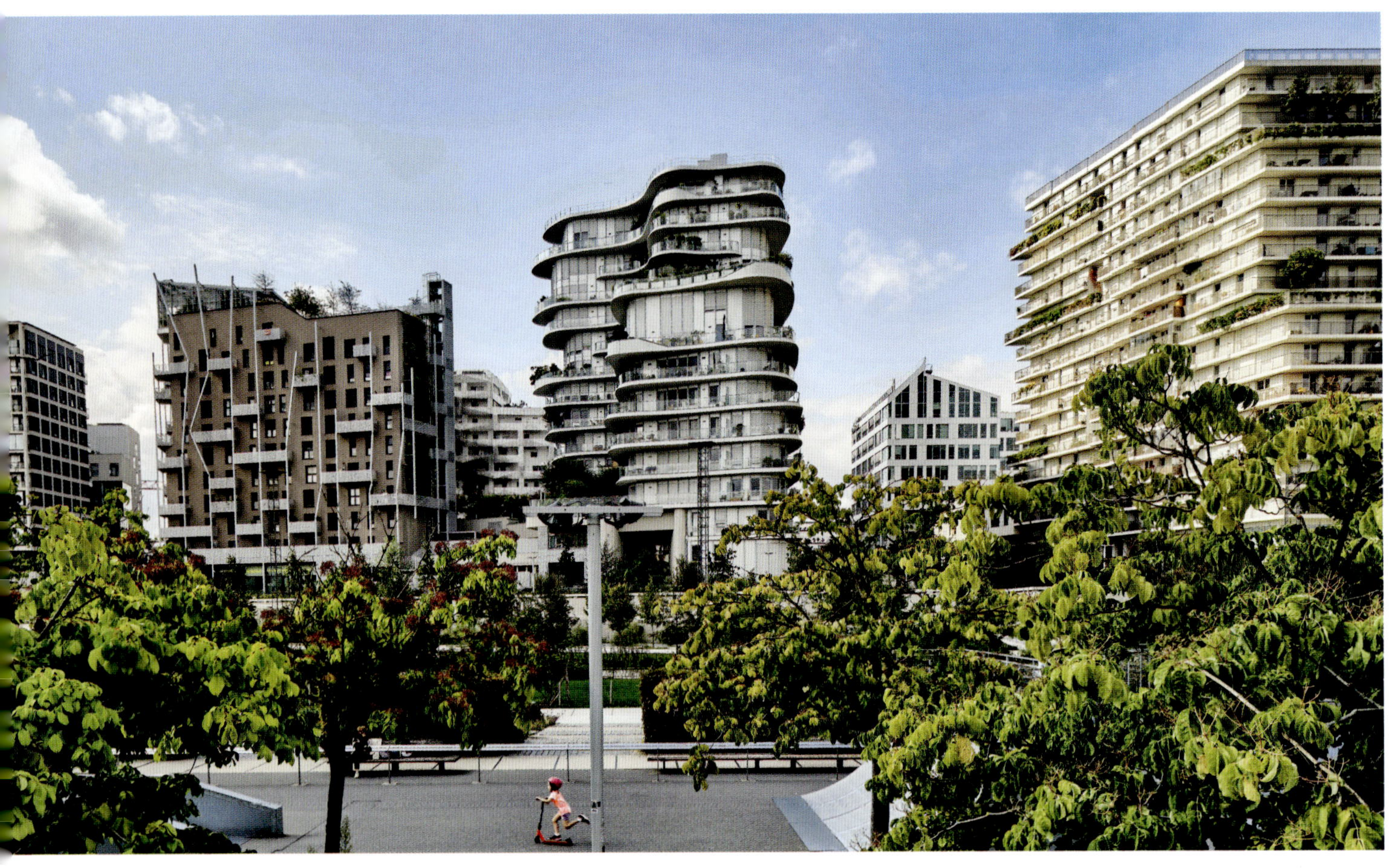


ABOVE
Designed by MAD architects, UNIC
(in white, center of photo) was the
first building in the city of Paris that
achieved the Passive House standard,
which makes it energy efficient by using
airtight insulation and windows, among
other material specifications. Each of the
thirteen floors has a terrace of varying
heights, giving the appearance of an
undulating surface. UNIC shares a site
with a neighboring building designed
by the Parisian firm Biecher Architects
that features a greenhouse, roof garden,
a green wall (or *mur végétal*), and an
exterior elevator made for taking in the
city views. While they are very different,
their proximity suggests a dialogue
of similarities (the variety of their
terraces) and their differences (the color
treatments of each façade). Access to
the metro and a shared garden and lawn
complete the site.

OPPOSITE
A wood boardwalk with the marsh
wetland grasses on each side
moves toward the building known as
Emergence (at left), which has more
than 170 apartments. The motif of the
iconic shape of a house is repeated
throughout the design: at the entrance
and on the terraces of both this building
and the one next door, which is black.

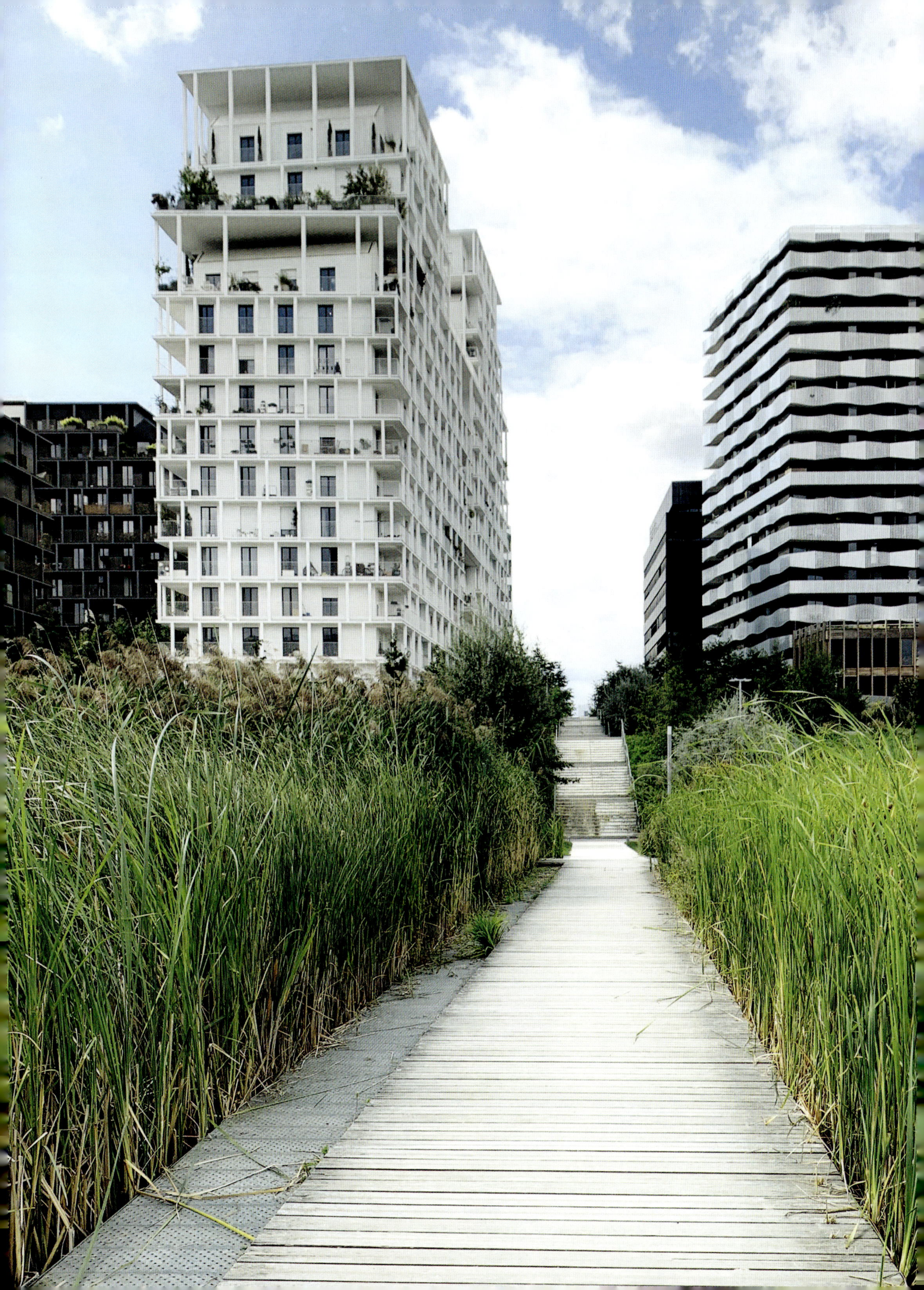

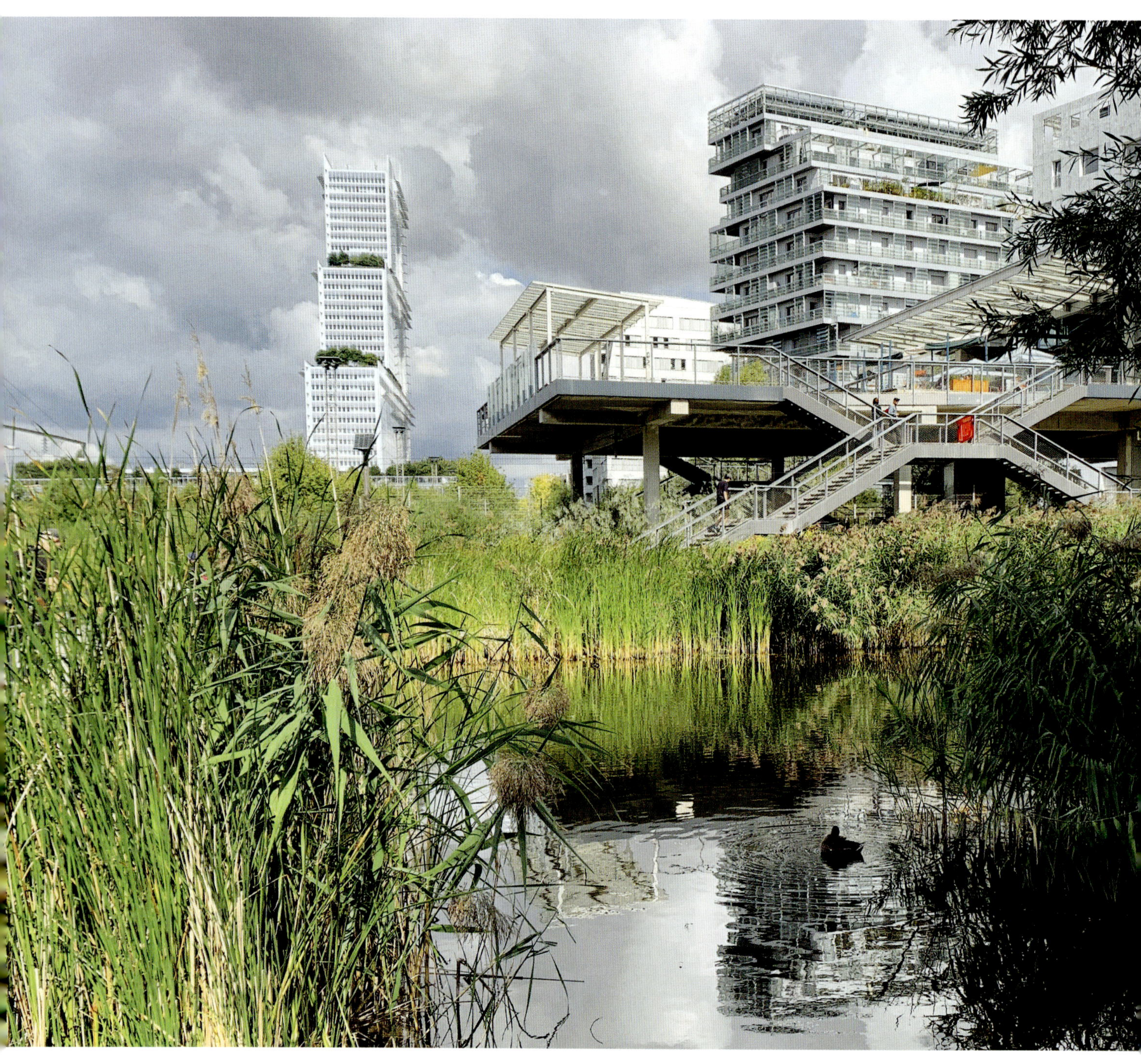


A northeastern view from parc Martin Luther King includes the Palais de Justice de Paris, designed by Renzo Piano's firm, on the left, and buildings on the lots in the eastern sector on the right. Piano is well known for the design of the Centre Pompidou art center in Paris. A viewing terrace of the restaurant Hoba looks out over the tall marsh grasses.

More than 7,500 residential units are available across the entire site, and they offer much-needed housing to the 17th arrondissement. The distinct design of each building gives not only a pleasing aesthetic experience but a feeling of individuality for each place. The eastern sector of the quarter has ten lots:

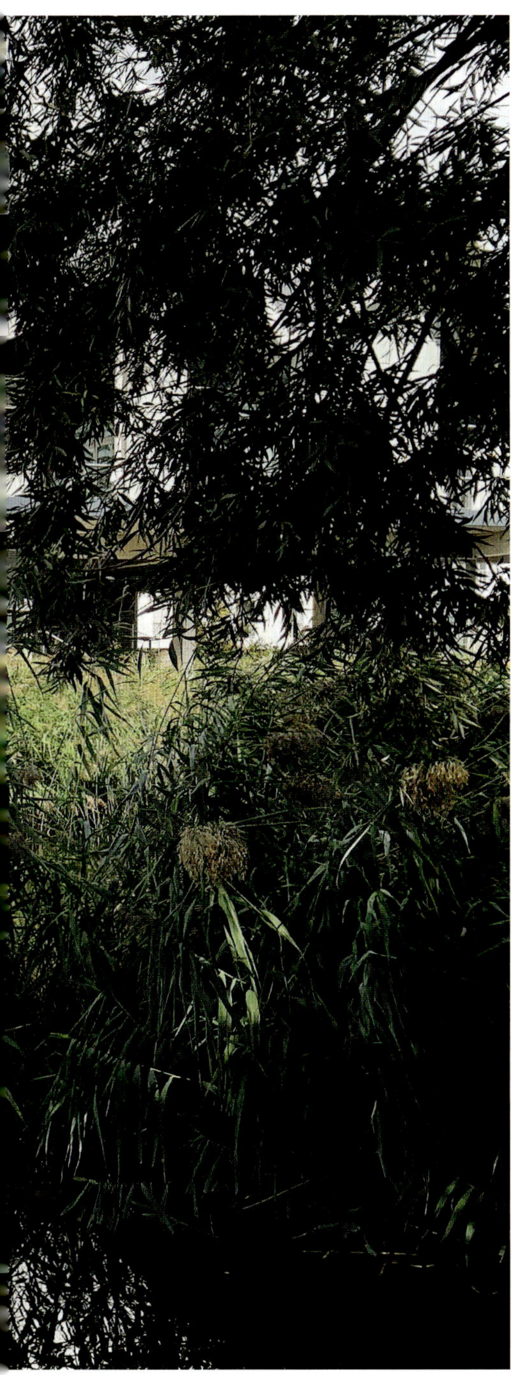

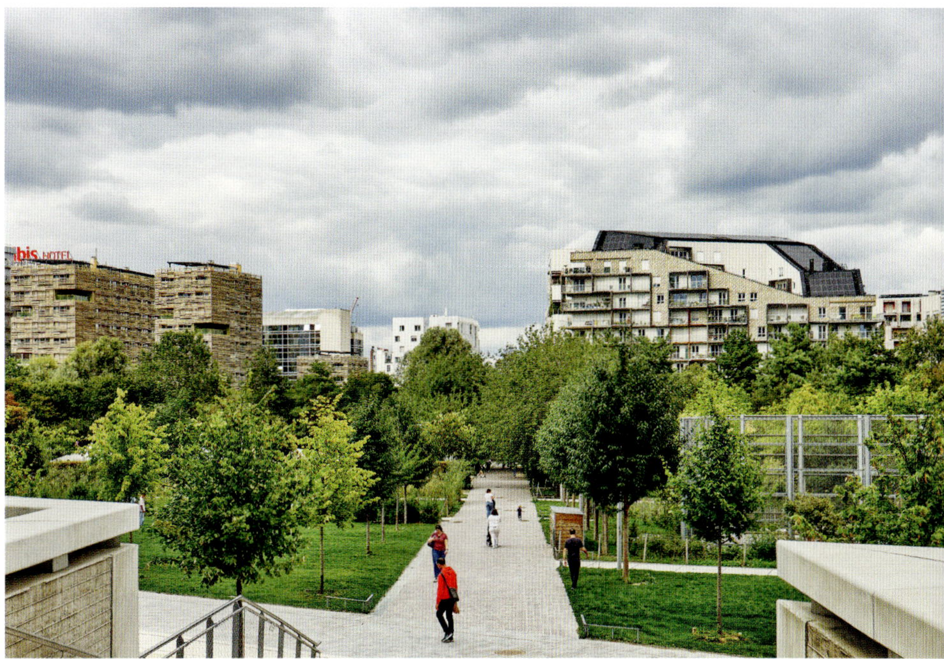

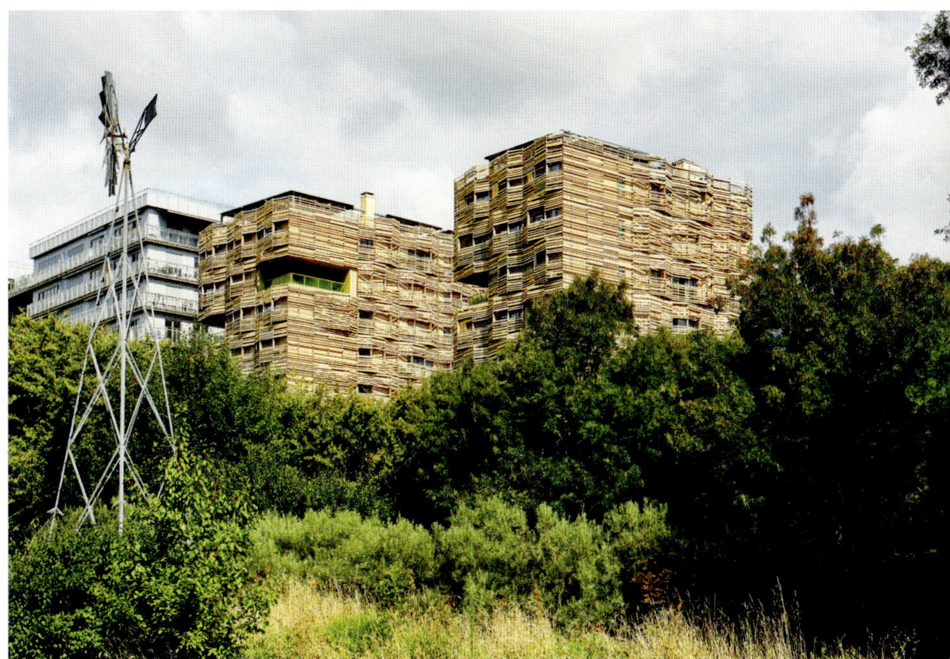



**TOP**
Lot E2 was designed by Périphériques Architectes in 2008 and has 117 apartments, some of which overlook parc Martin Luther King. The building has a center well along with a solar panel system on the rooftop. Balconies are framed in wood to reduce the heat from the sun while allowing light into the rooms.

**ABOVE**
LOT E4: The Ibis Hotel is the tenant of one part of this two-building project designed by Atelier Philéas. The other building holds 150 apartments for student housing. The woven façade and the almost neon green color of the building stand out and at the same time integrate with the natural environment.

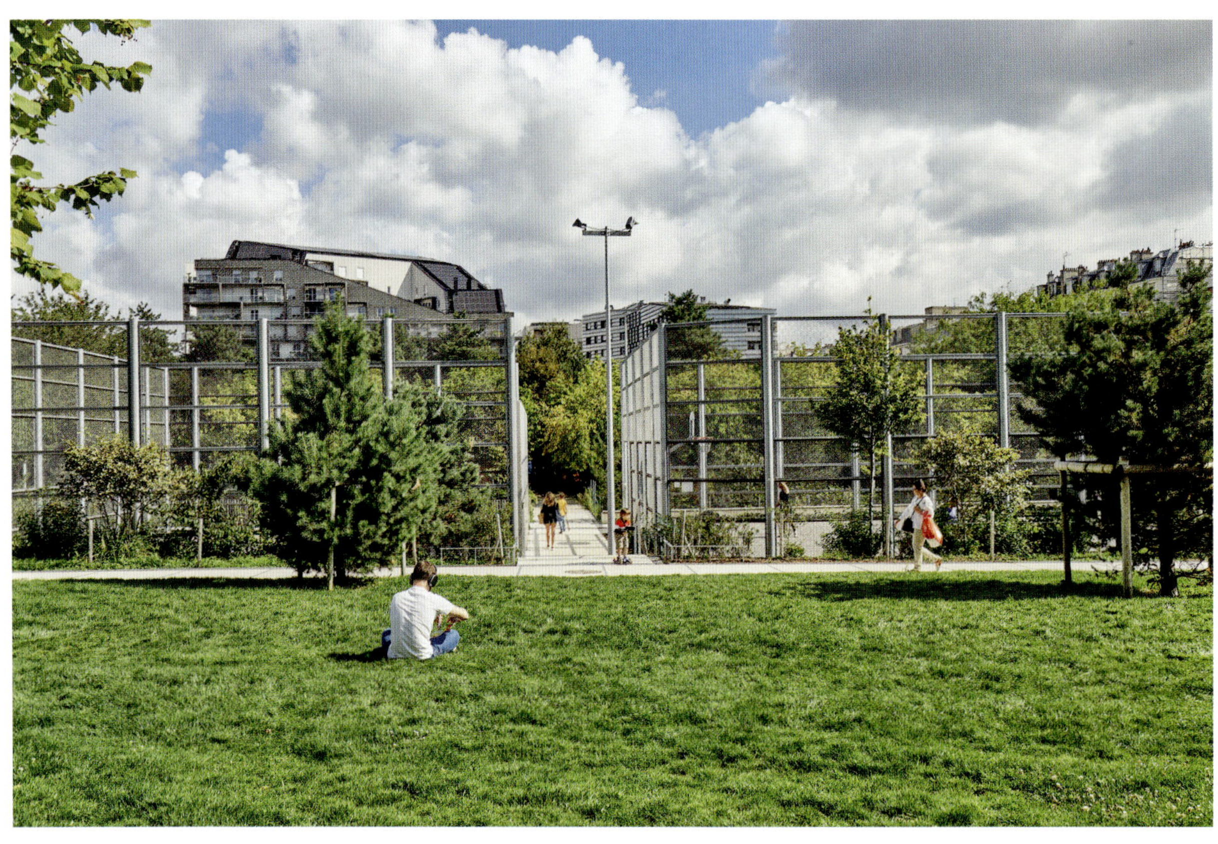

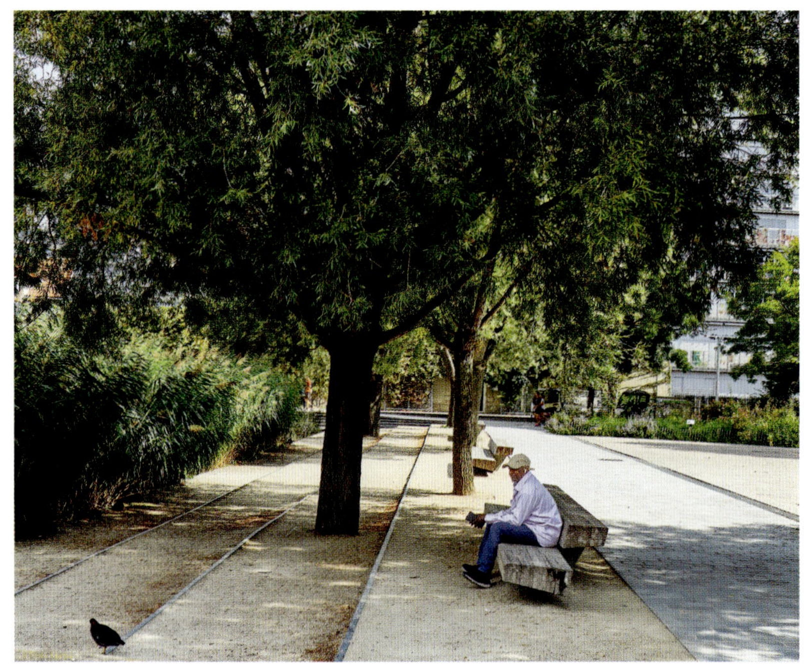

**ABOVE AND OPPOSITE ABOVE**
Sports are at the heart of the Clichy-Batignolles development. Runners are everywhere. The terrain is flat and without many obstacles such as curbs to trip over. Basketball courts for pickup games at all levels are in the spring section of the garden. The skateboard park ramps are impressive for their size and sculptural look, but kids on scooters are not intimidated.

**RIGHT AND OPPOSITE BELOW**
The old rails of the train yard still exist in Martin Luther King Park. In some places, they have been filled with a combination of dirt and sand that is typical of Paris walking paths. These iron lines draw a connection to an industrial past. They are reminders of what was here before. In other places, pavers fill the areas between the rails. They are used as tiers for downhill paths to prevent water runoff.

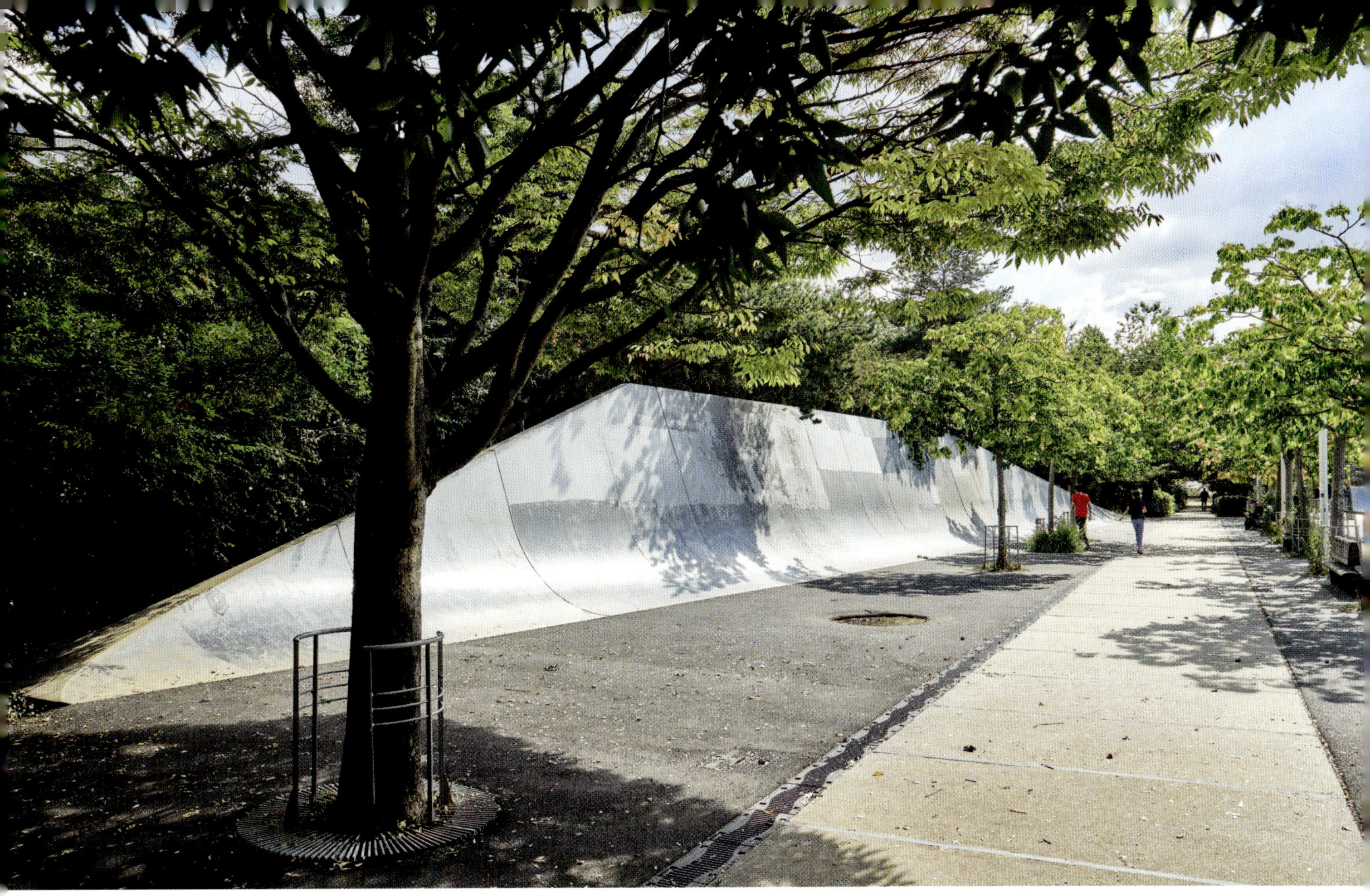

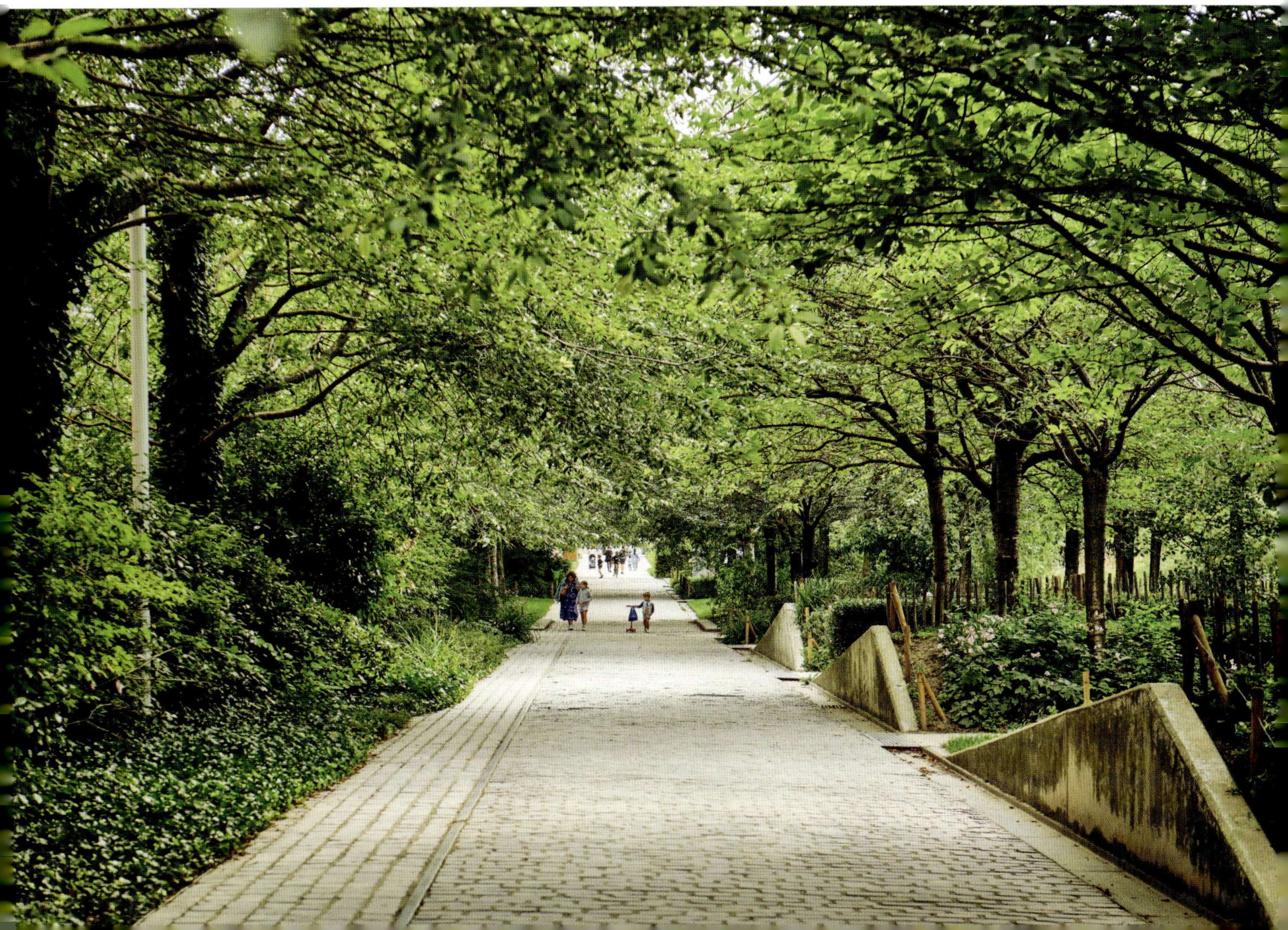

## Parc Éco-Responsable Cité Internationale Universitaire de Paris

14th arrondissement
1921

Walking through the hilly parc Montsouris, arriving at the campus of la Cité internationale, it's possible to catch your breath. The landscape is remarkably flat, organized, and expansive. The thirty-four-hectare (eighty-four-acre) campus first opened in the 1920s. The garden was designed by landscape architect Jean-Claude Nicolas Forestier in collaboration with architect Lucien Bechmann, who designed the overall campus. Forestier was known for his designs of the gardens at the Champ-de-Mars, bois de Bologne, and bois de Vincennes when he worked for the City of Paris. The garden plan was inspired by visits to American cities and university campuses: A large lawn is surrounded by *maisons* representing different countries; some of the *logements* were built by legendary architects, including Le Corbusier, and they still provide places for international students and researchers to live and study together. An alley of lime trees that stretches from one end of the campus to the other breaks at the grass lawn. Formal French topiaries of varying geometric shapes and sizes are placed along the edge of the great lawn and in front the Maison Internationale building. Additionally, there are examples of naturalistic garden design styles in contrast to the formal ones. The open spaces are used as a place of relaxation and gathering spots. Panels of educational information about the three thousand trees, one hundred plants, and more than fifty bird species that live in the garden are installed throughout. Each summer art exhibitions are also mounted in the park.

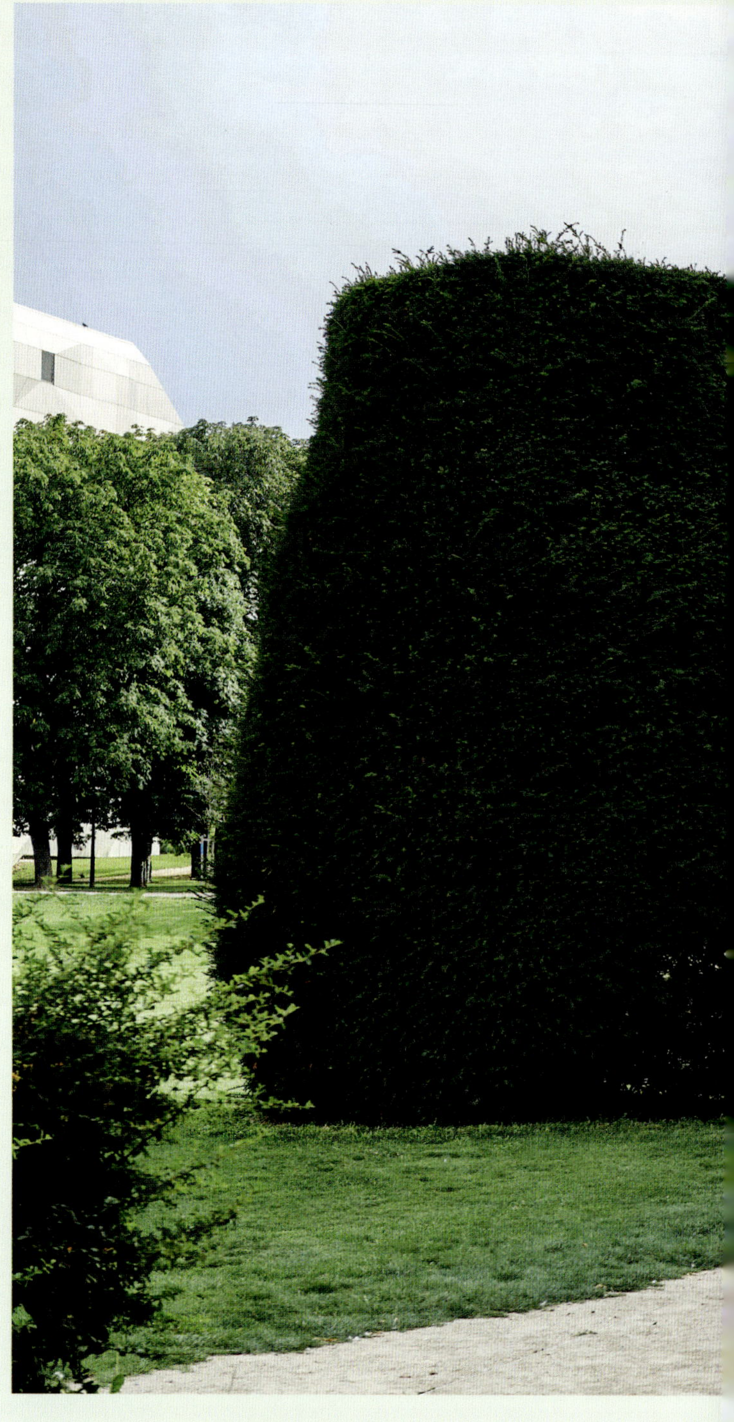

A line of topiary trees in geometric shapes borders the garden path of the park of la Cité internationale universitaire de Paris.

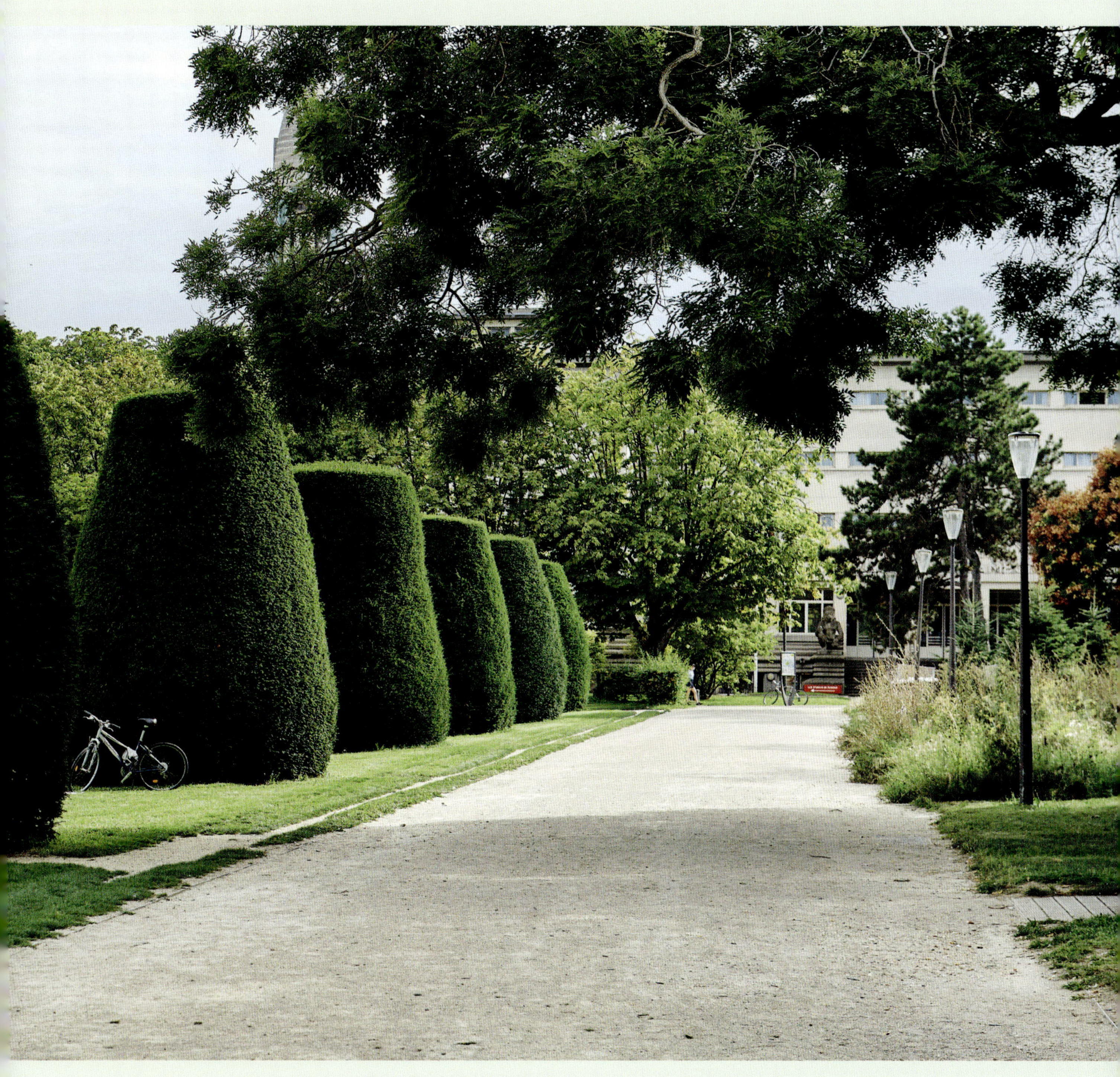

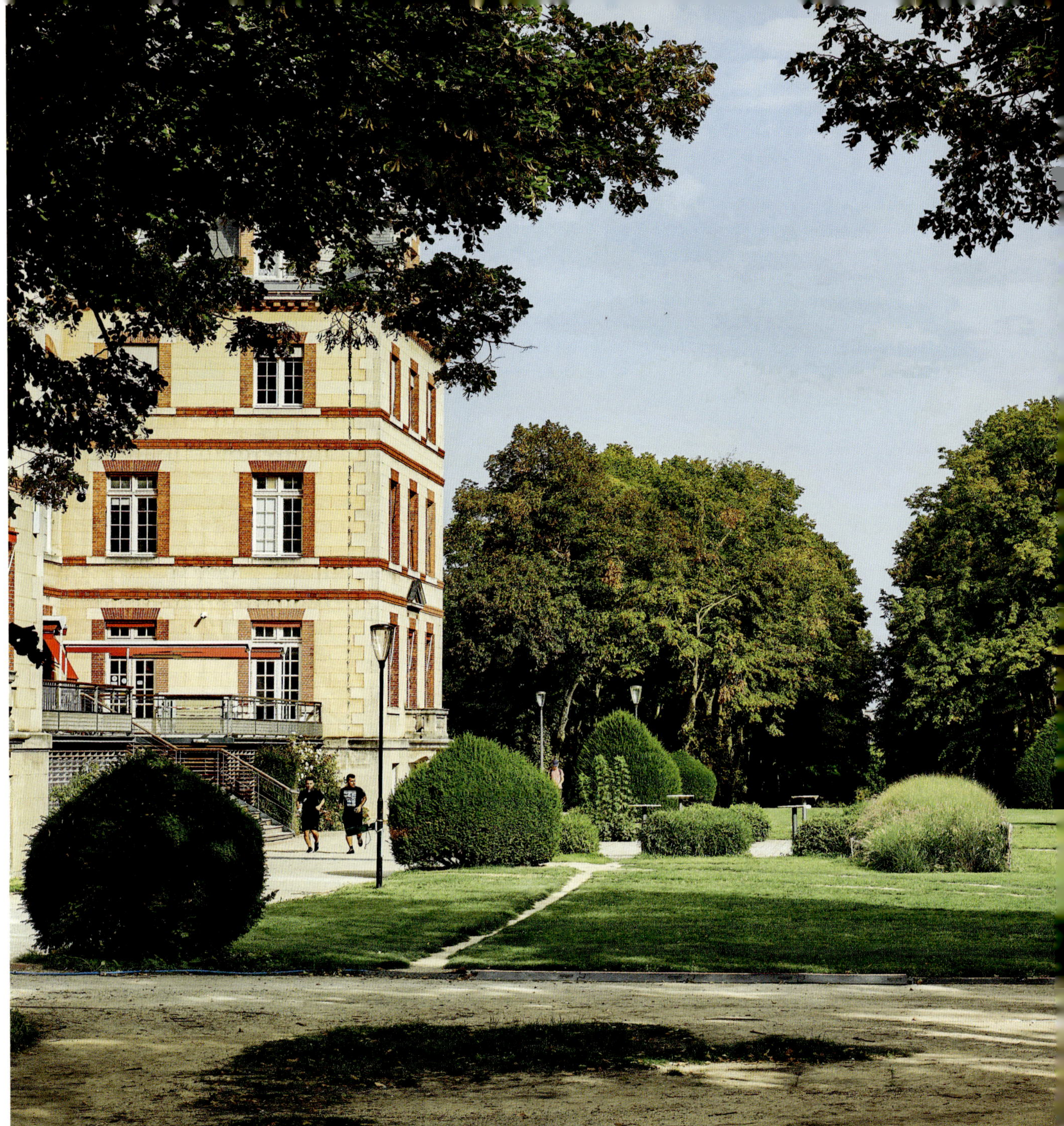



**ABOVE**
A view through the alley of lime trees to
the *grande pelouse*, the large lawn of the
campus grounds.

**OPPOSITE**
A screen of wild grasses with wooden
fencing at the entrance of the Maison
Internationale's garden terrace is a
contradiction to the architecture's
precise symmetry.

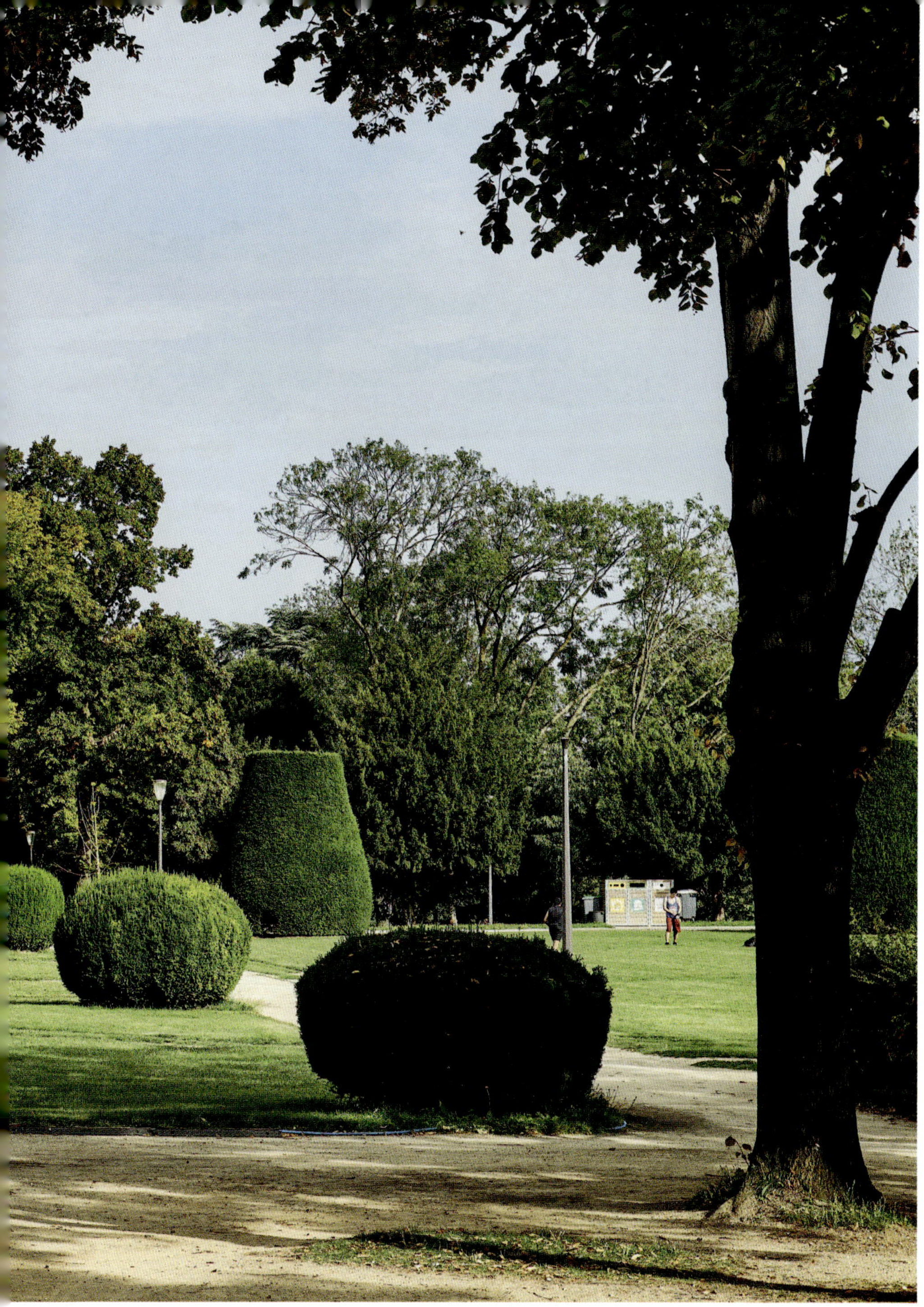

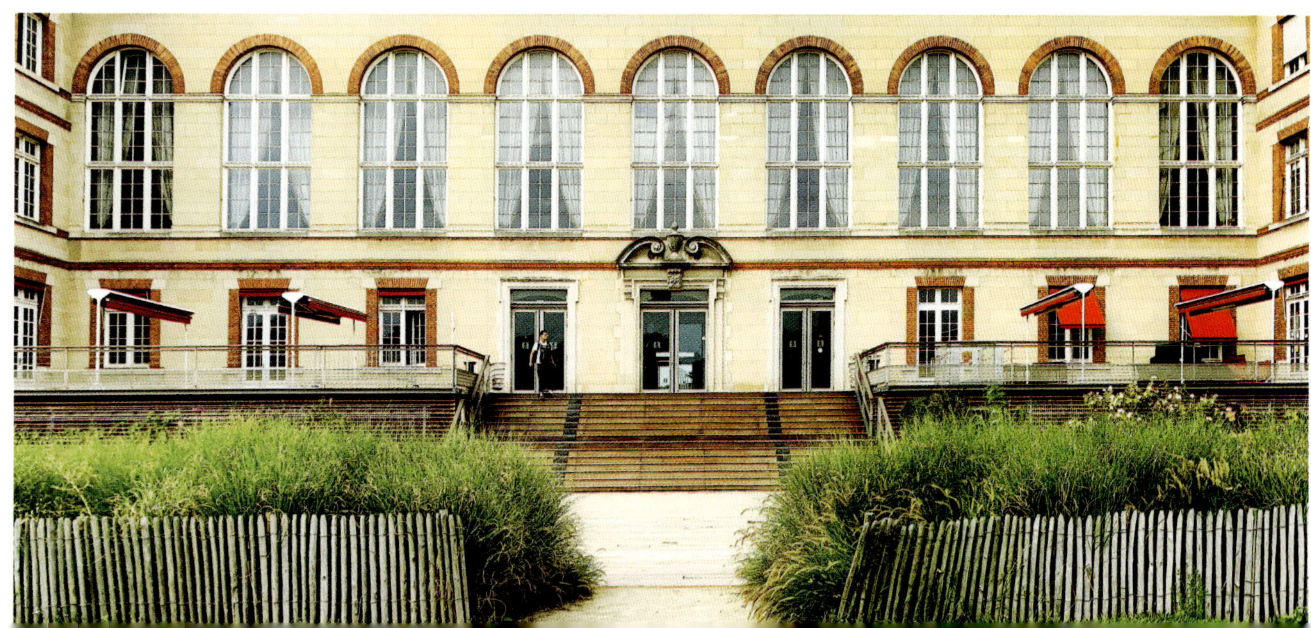

RIGHT
Both the Maison de l'Île-de-France,
left, which was completed in 2017, and
l'eglise du Sacre-Cœur de Gentilly, built
in the 1930s, can be seen above the
great lawn and the treetops of the park.

BELOW
Each summer the Cité jardin
participates in the exhibition called
*Jardins du Monde en Mouvement*,
which invites artists to make and install
artworks in the park. In 2023, Maria
Ibanez Lago's work titled *The Miroir of
the Canopée,* a combination of natural
and artificial elements, was on display.

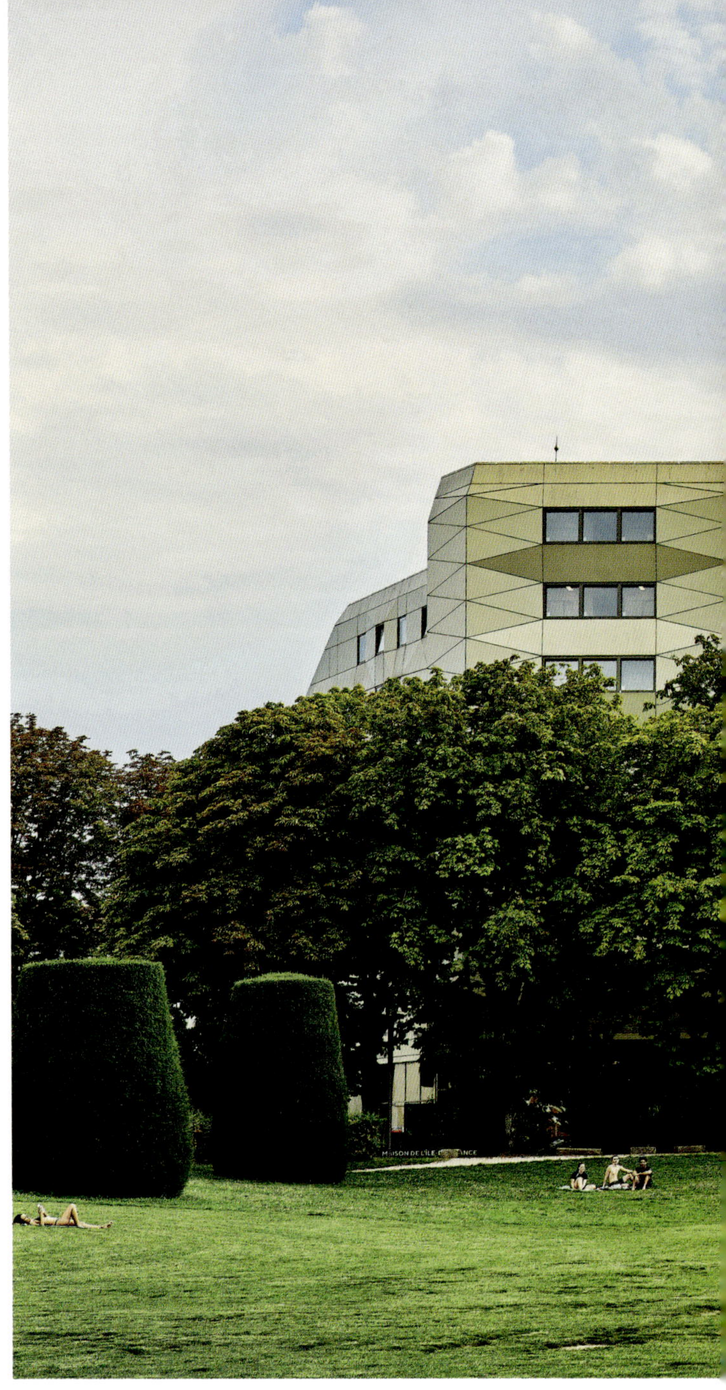

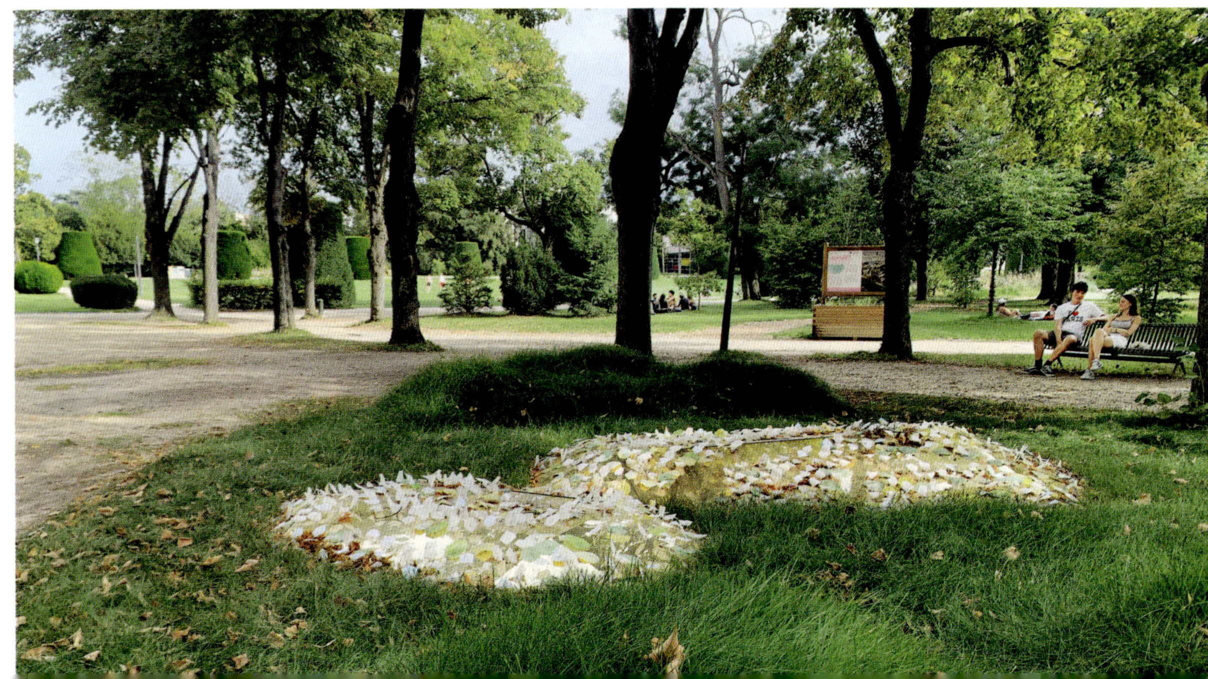

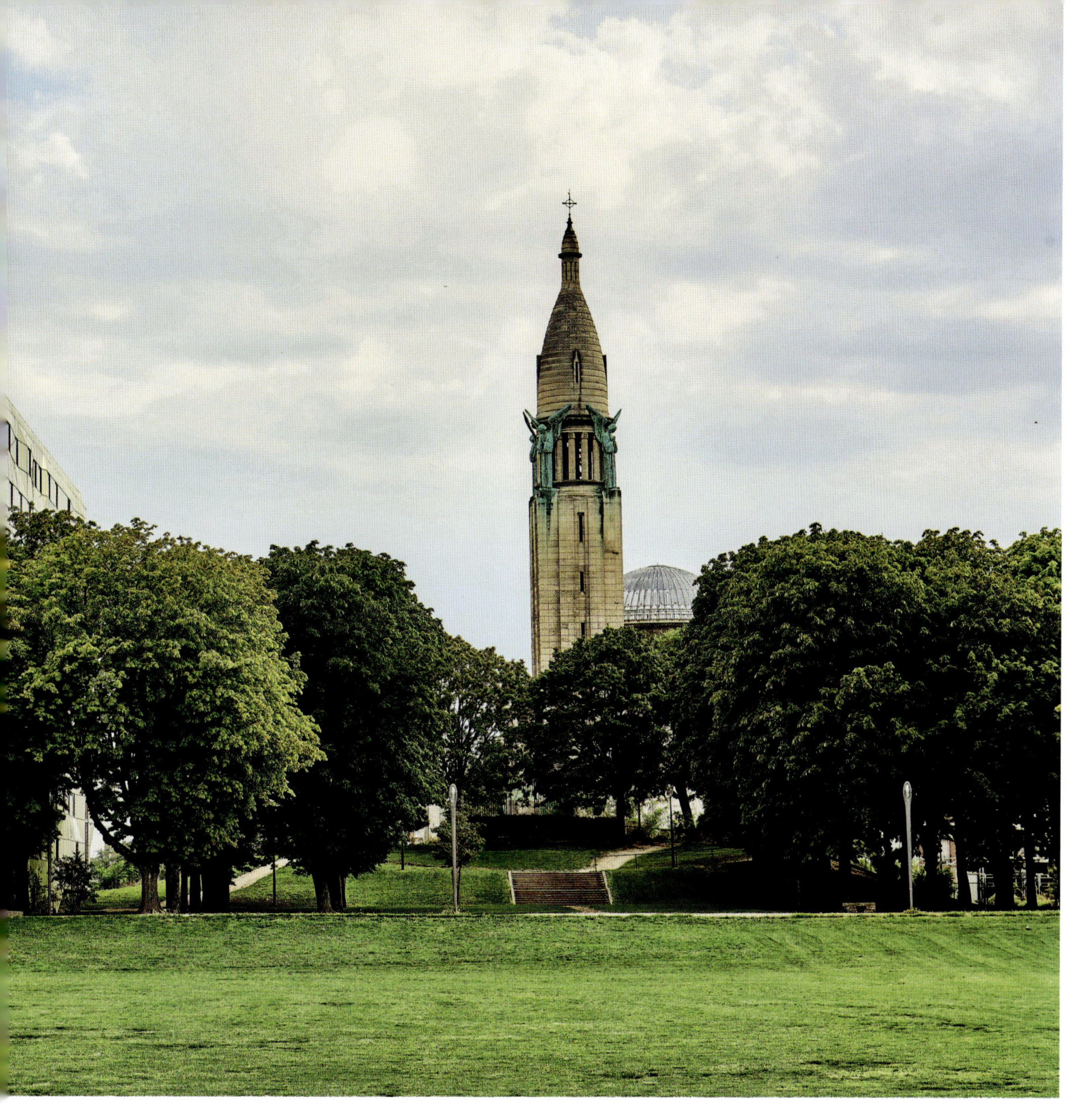

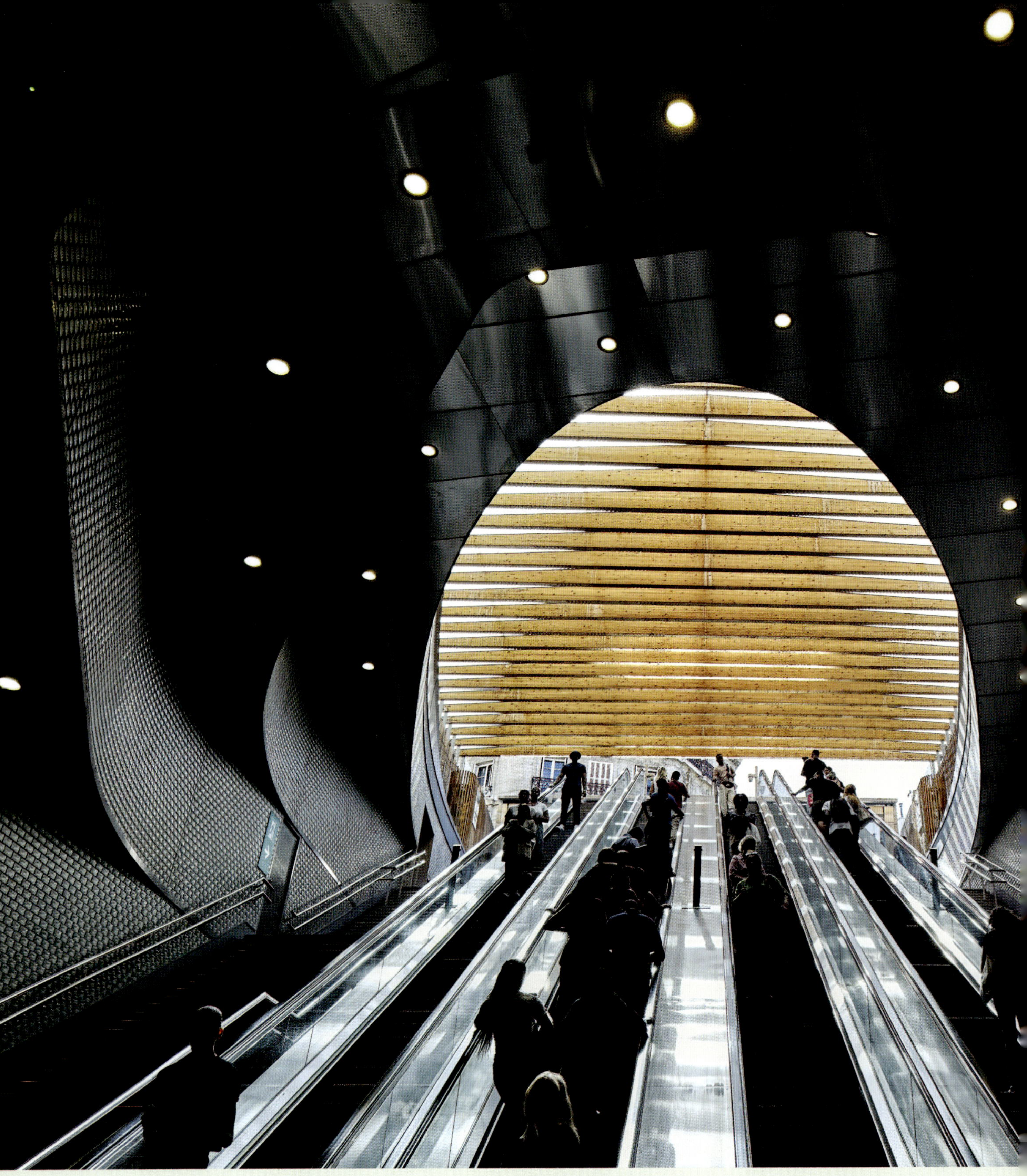

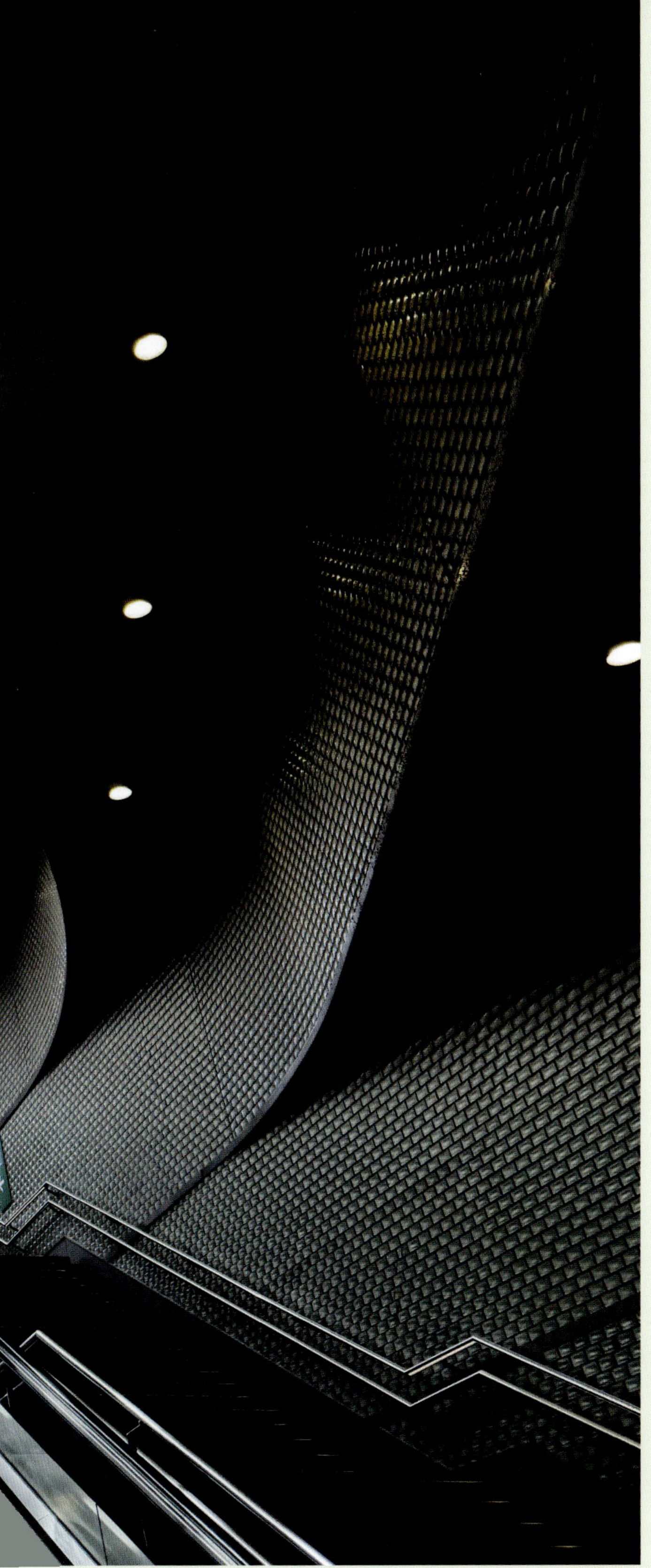

## *La Canopée* at *Forum des Halles*

1st arrondissement
2016

The area of the former marketplace of Paris, Les Halles, has many associations for many Parisians and visitors alike. Once the primary food market and distribution center of Paris, the nineteenth-century iron-and-glass *halles* were razed (or destroyed, as some might say) in 1971. The replacement structure was considered visually offensive and at best mediocre. As the site, renamed Forum des Halles, became more of a shopping mall and a transportation hub for the subway and the RER commuter rail line, the neighborhood suffered, as did the remaining historic buildings, such as the sixteenth-century Saint-Eustache church and the Bourse de Commerce, a stock exchange. Architects Jacques Anziutti and Patrick Berger proposed an elegant solution to unify the site and all its competing elements: transportation, shopping, restaurants, cultural spaces, and a garden. Berger was inspired by the site itself, by the circulation of the people moving through the city, by wind, by trees and their leaves. The structure acts as protection against the weather and stabilizes the temperature of the spaces underneath, which helps to use less energy.

A glance of la Canopée as seen coming up the escalator from the subways below. The yellow-gold color of the glass panels is one of the most discussed aspects of the project, which was completed in 2016.

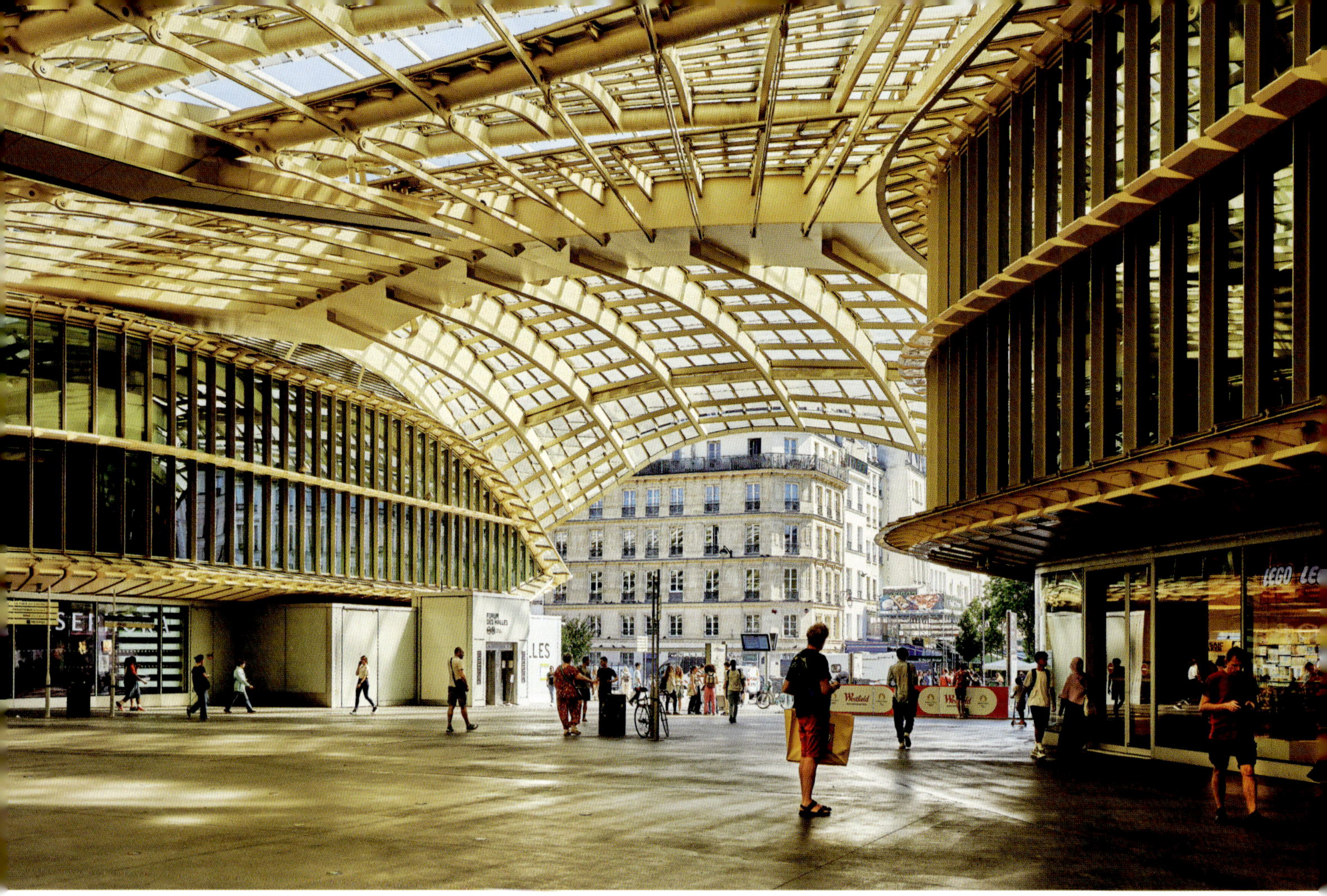

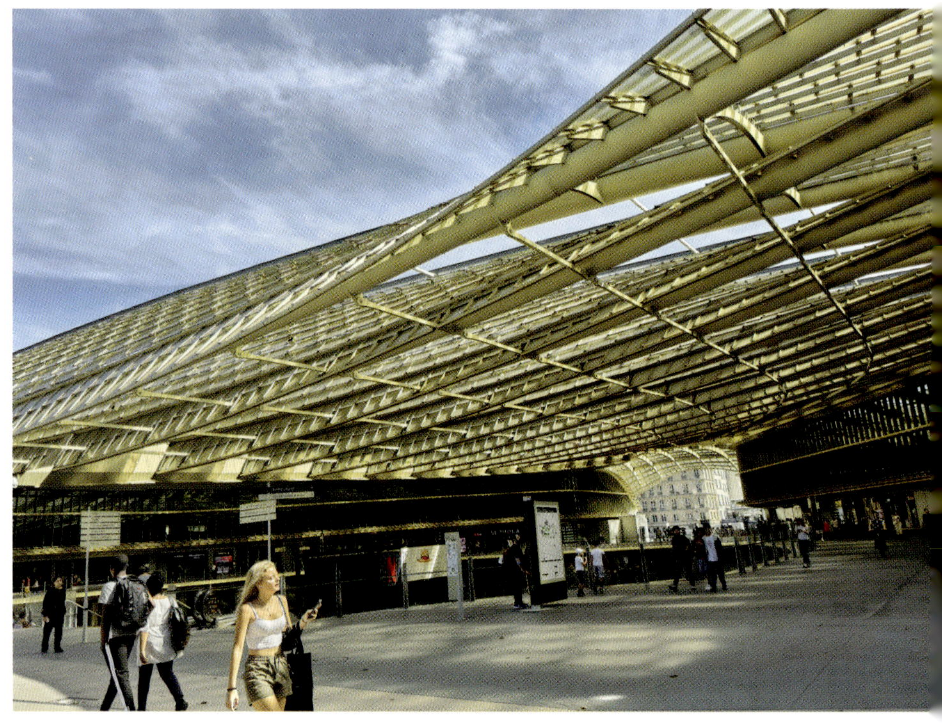

**ABOVE**
Two-story buildings on the street level
are part of the site's redevelopment.
Several cultural centers, all involved with
dance and music, occupy these spaces,
such as La Place–Centre Culturel Hip-
Hop and a branch of La Maison des
Pratiques Artistiques Amateurs (MPAA).

**RIGHT**
Spaces between the glass panels of the
canopy allow for the circulation of air
throughout the building. The canopy
covers 140 meters (460 feet) in length
and is 24 meters (79 feet) high. It seems
to float above the site.

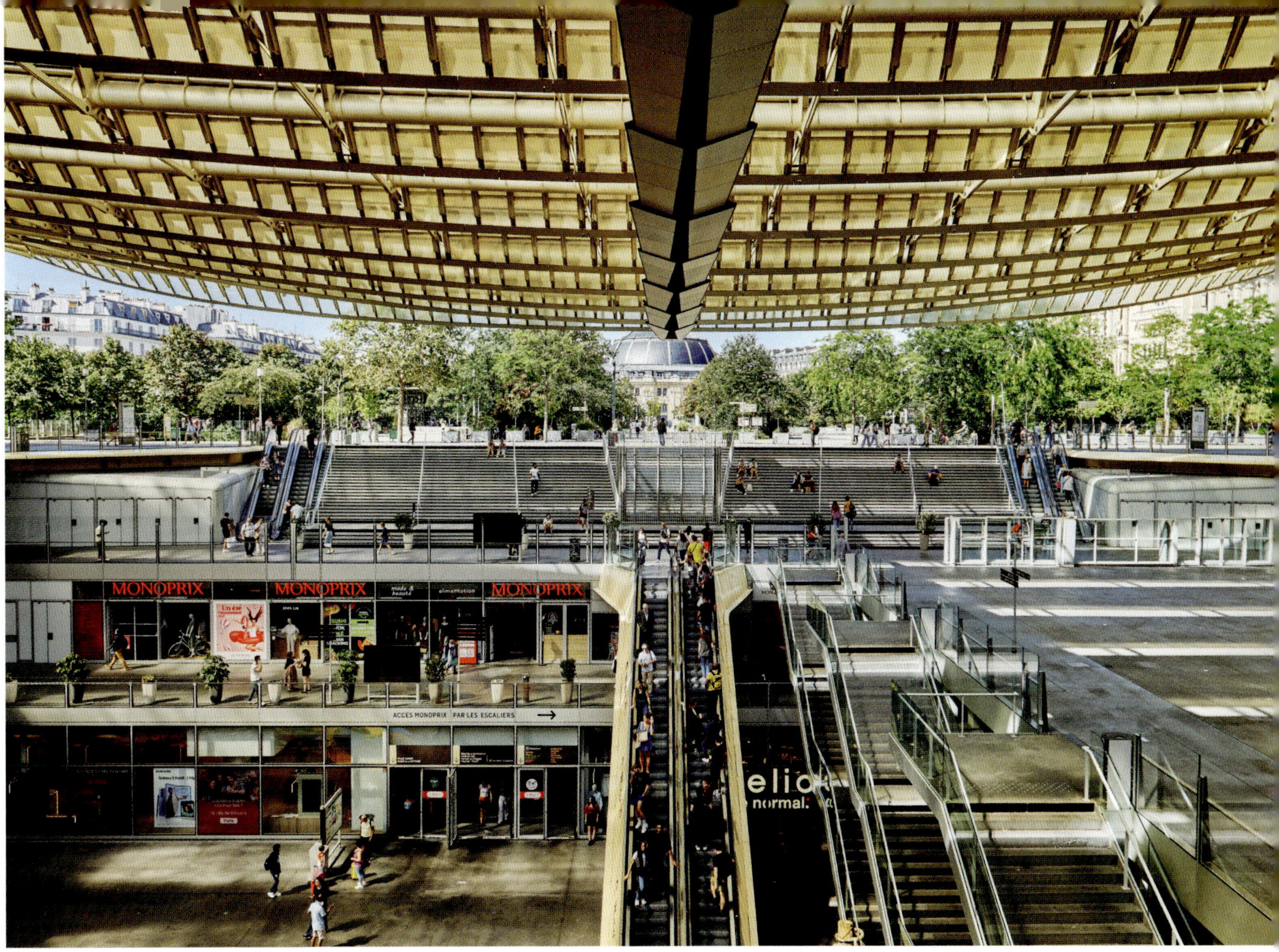

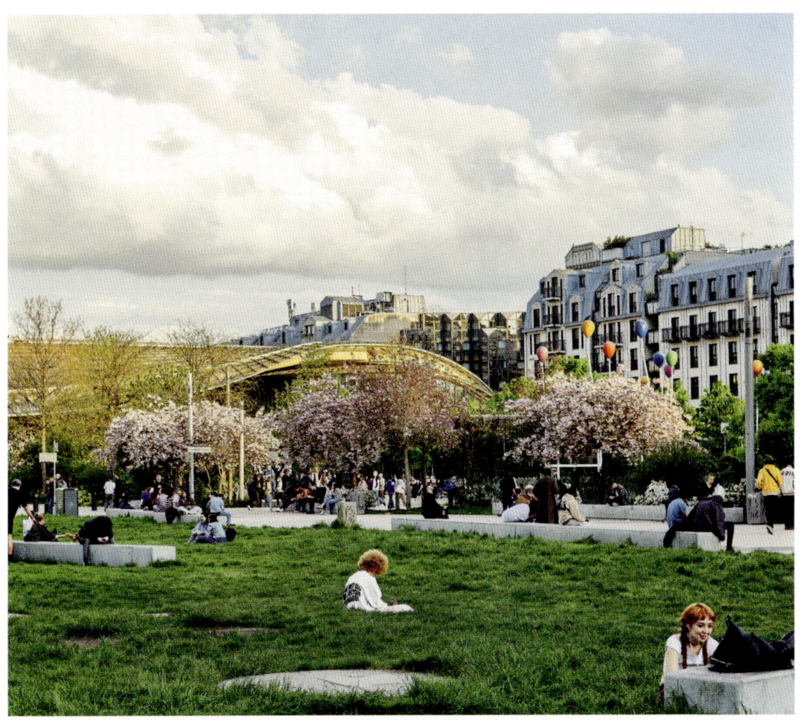

**ABOVE**

The park's trees are one of the first things commuters see as they arrive at the street level. Stairs and escalators help keep the flow of people moving smoothly. Three metro stations service the hub, including Châtelet–Les Halles, which is one of the largest and busiest in the Paris subway system. Commercial spaces and retail shops are on the lower levels.

**LEFT**

The area surrounding la Canopée also received a much-needed renovation. A new park, named for Nelson Mandela, was built on the open plaza, and grass lawns replaced concrete. In the spring, the roofline disappears behind the flowering trees near its entrance.

# URBAN FARMING

## *Plantation Paris*
18th arrondissement
2018

Of course, it's the cityscape surrounding the roof of a warehouse at l'Arena Porte de la Chapelle, home to Plantation Paris, that makes an immediate impression. Looking over Paris's iconic rooftops at nearby Montmartre's Sacré-Coeur is magical. While rooftop gardens and terraces are not new news in the city, urban farming on a grand scale only recently officially became part of the City of Paris's climate action plan, in 2018. At 7,000 square meters (75,000 square feet), Plantation Paris's urban farm is enormous. The roof has two greenhouses for growing and preparing a variety of organic vegetables. The glass-covered Grange and a terrace are used for yoga classes and other events. Sarah Msika and Sidney Delourme founded the business, and each brings their expertise in art, food, and sustainability to the program. They put together a group of investors and began the complicated building, permitting, and permissions process at the height of COVID. They are committed to sustainable practices, for example, zero plastics are used in their work flow, delivery of produce to clients and restaurants are made using bikes, and they use their own produce at the events they host, which keeps things very local.

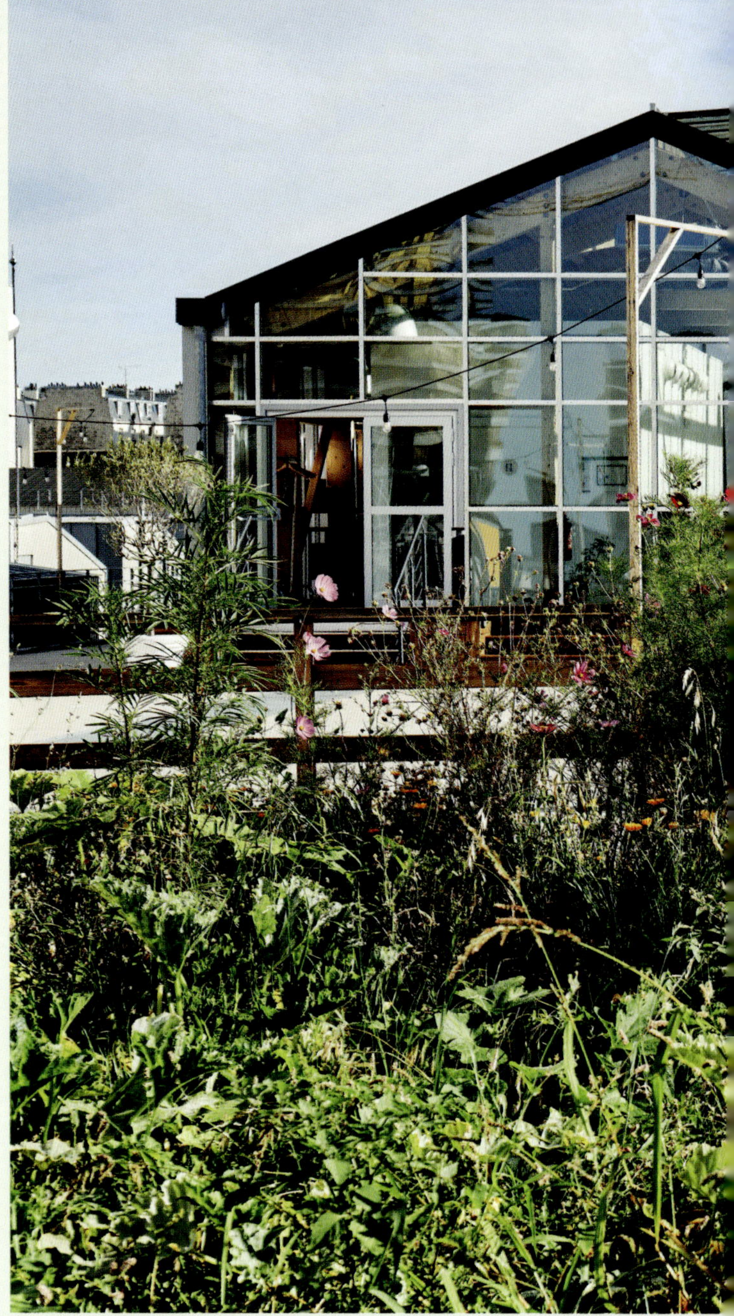

**ABOVE**
Flowers are planted at the terrace in front of the Grange event center at Plantation Paris.

**OPPOSITE**
On-site events provide another revenue stream for the business. Staff organize the events for and with clients. The interiors are made with materials from France, including the wood beams and supports.

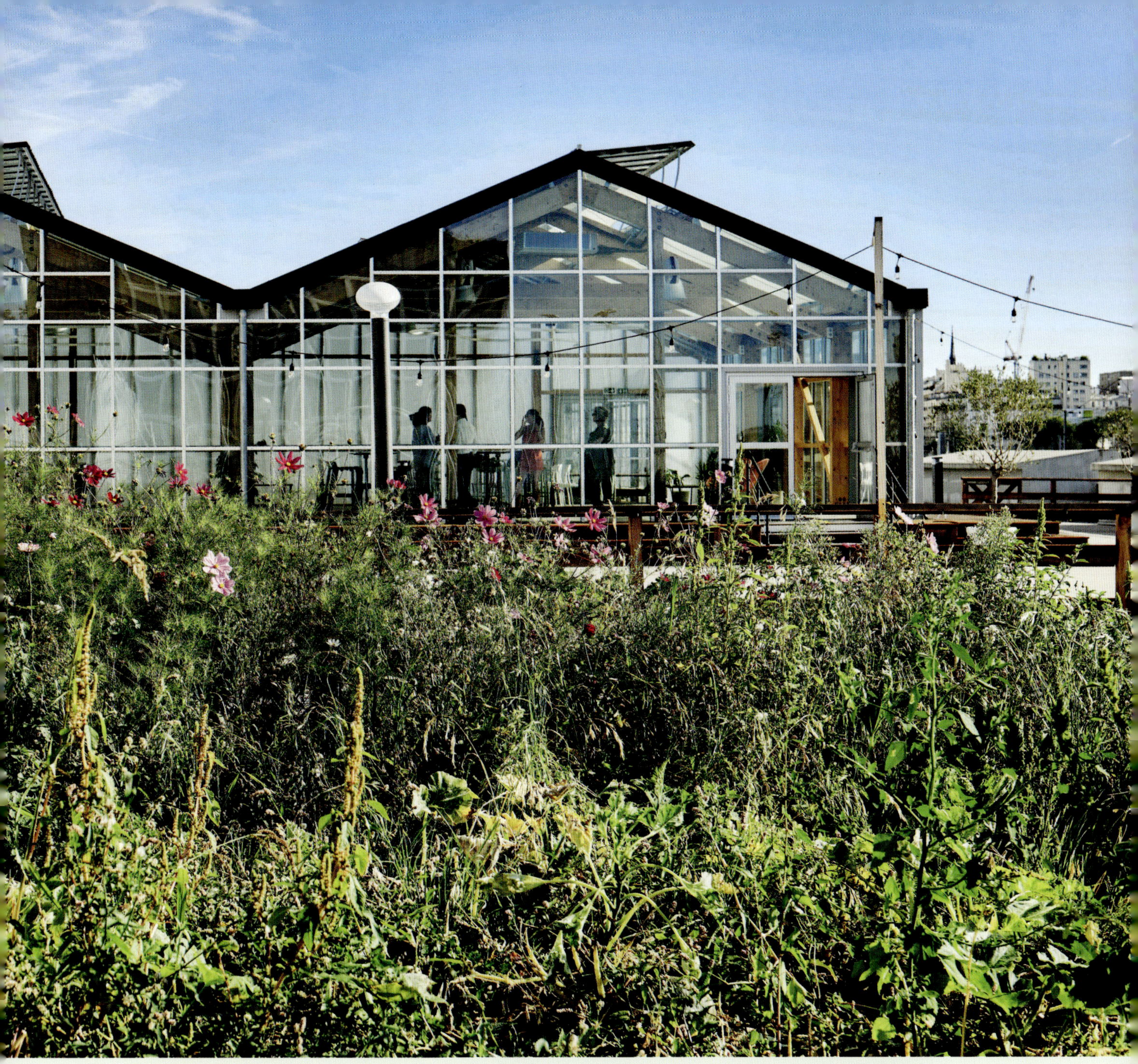

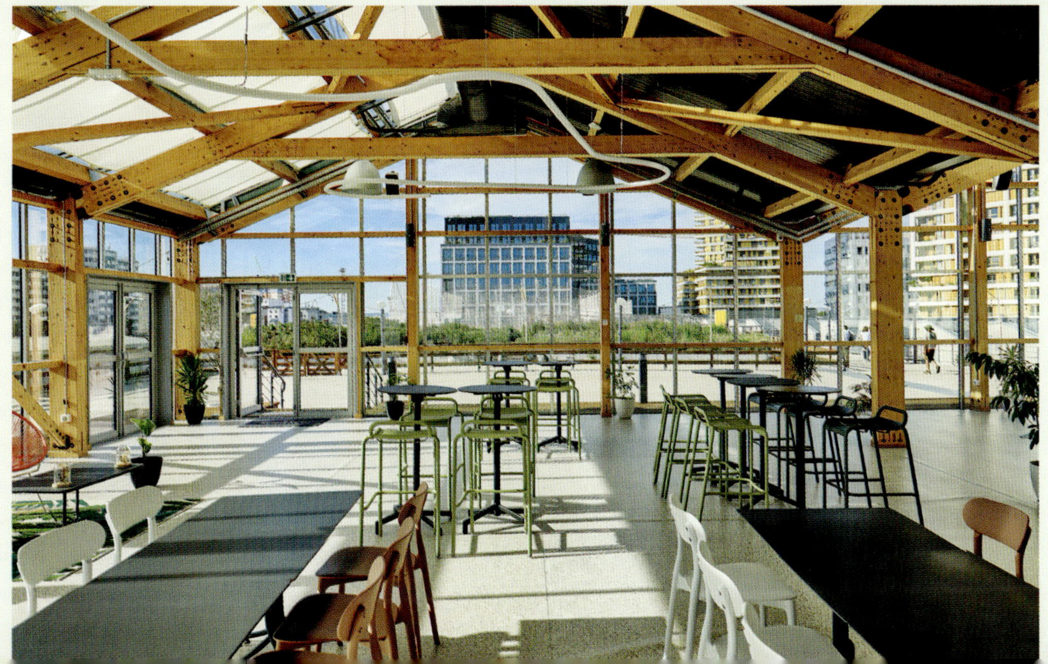

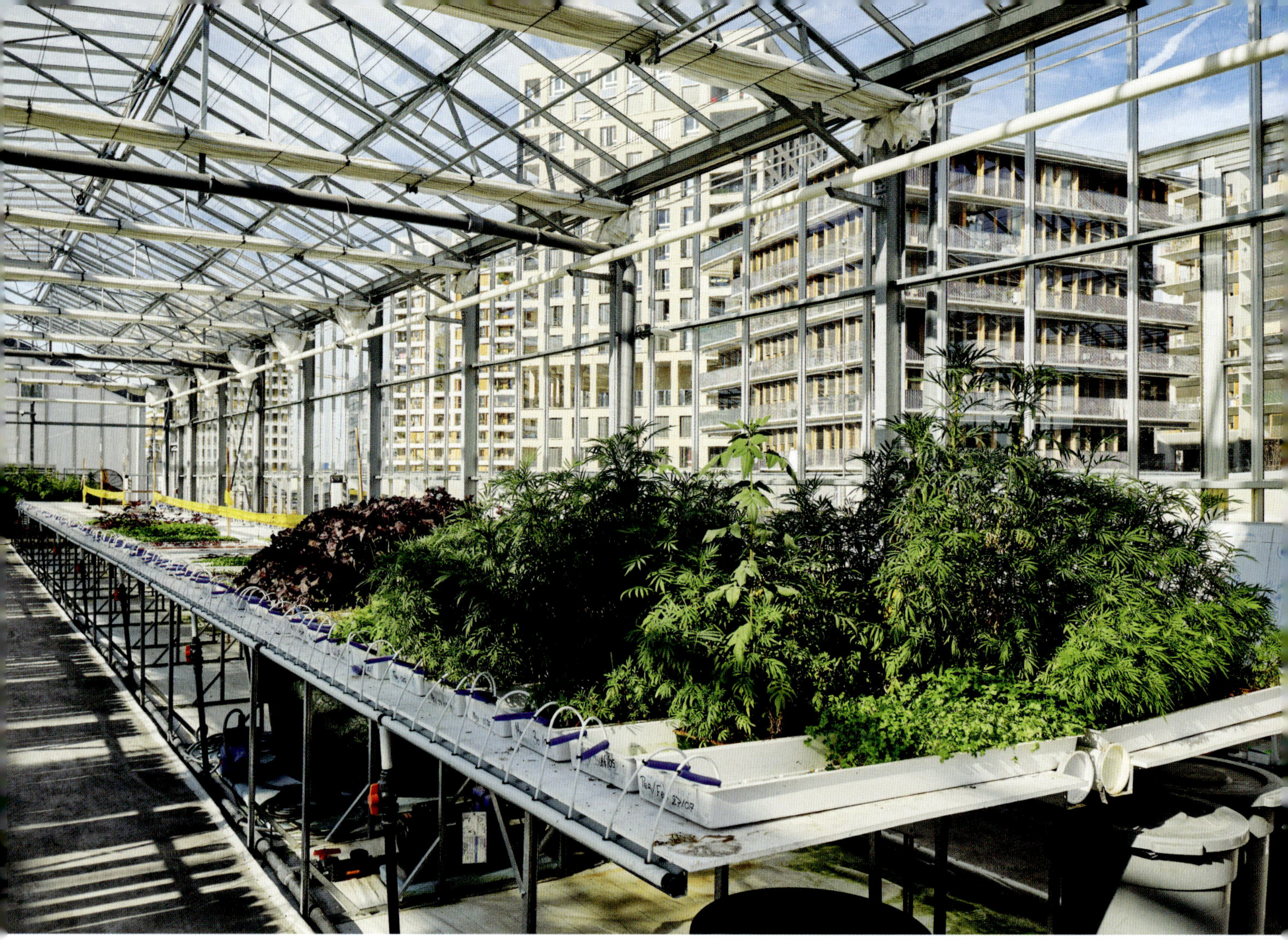

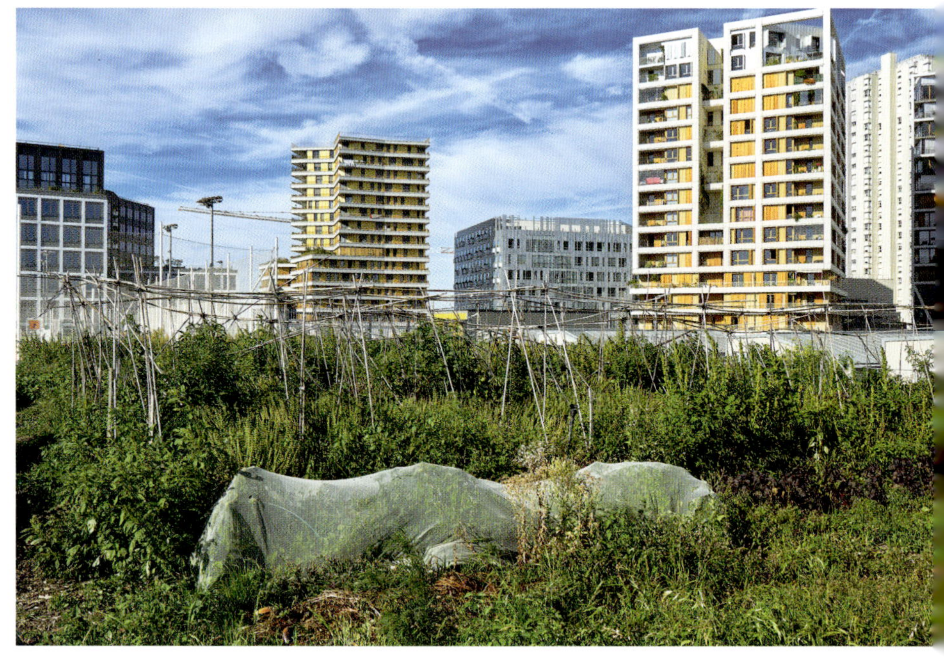

ABOVE
The greenhouse structures are for
planting and preparing produce for their
restaurant and chef clientele.

RIGHT AND OPPOSITE BELOW
Against a truly urban setting, all the
vegetables on the rooftop are grown
using organic techniques. The creation
of the farm also brought new agricultural
jobs to the city. A small staff manages
the garden and harvests the vegetables.

OPPOSITE ABOVE
Montmartre's Sacré-Coeur Basilica is
part of the skyline around the farm.

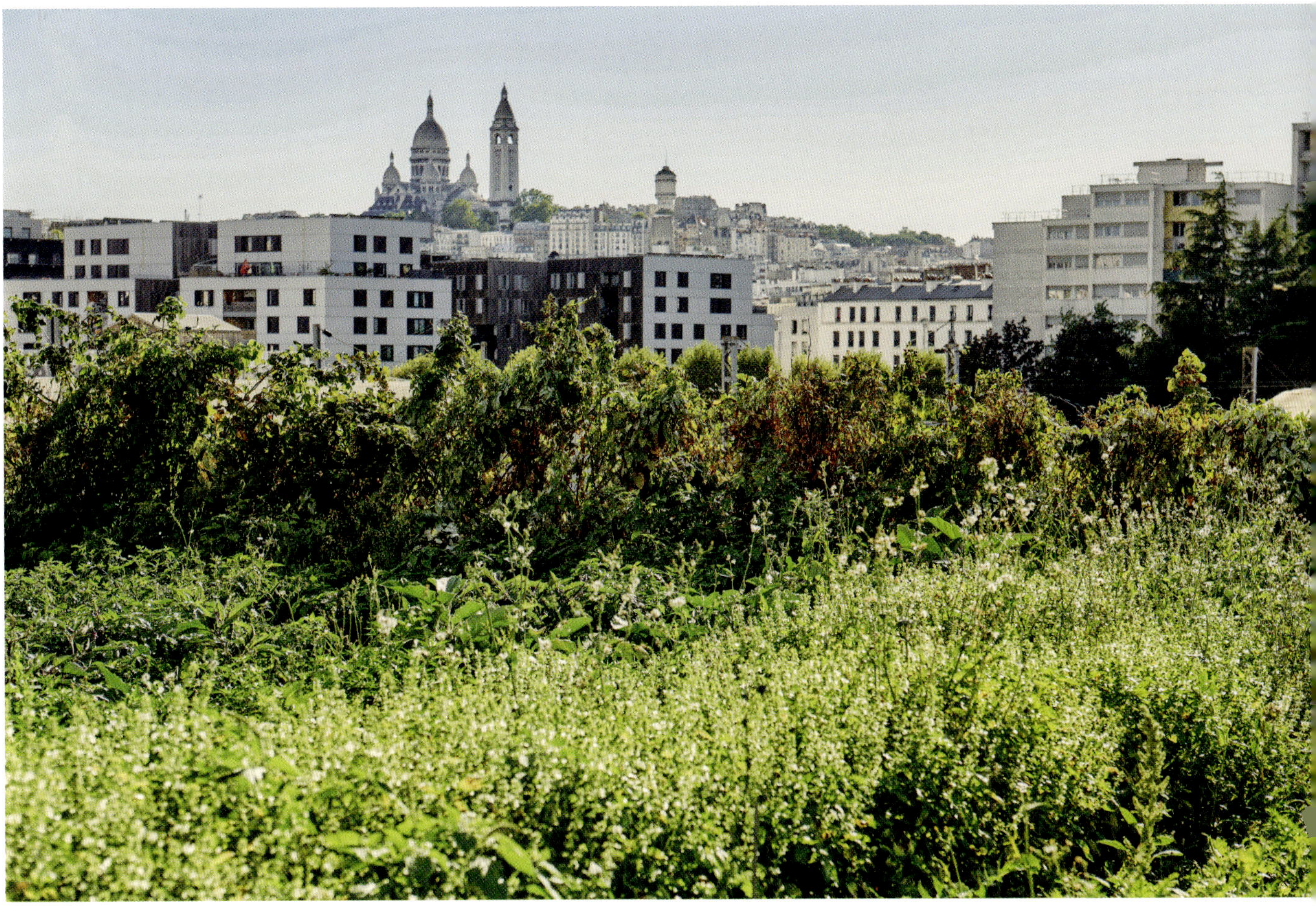

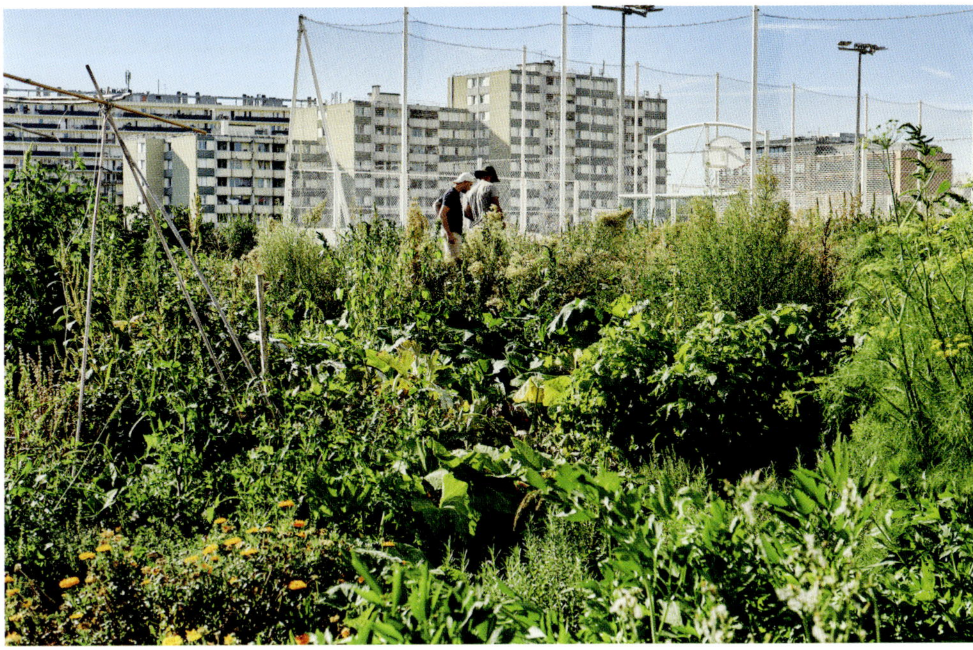

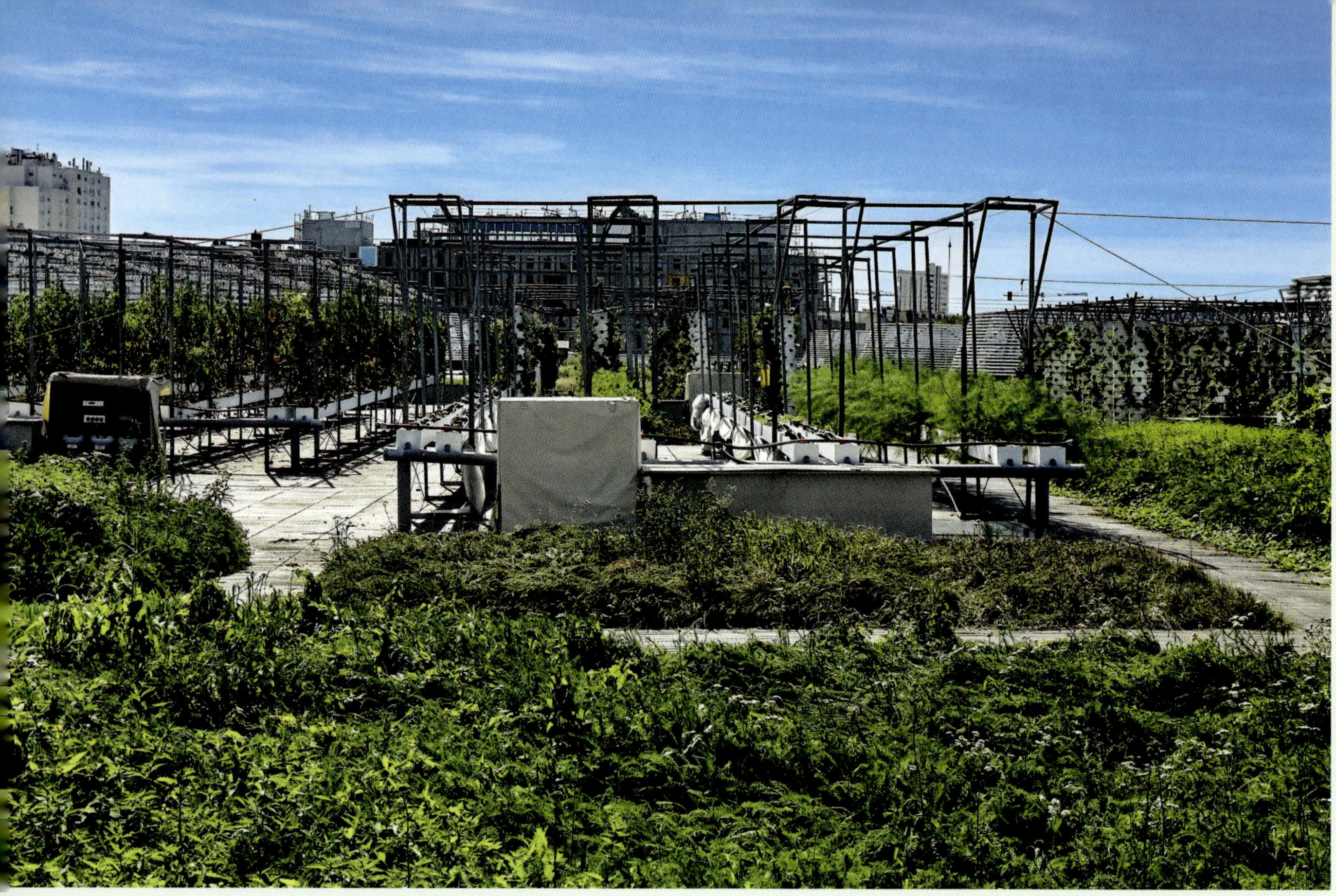

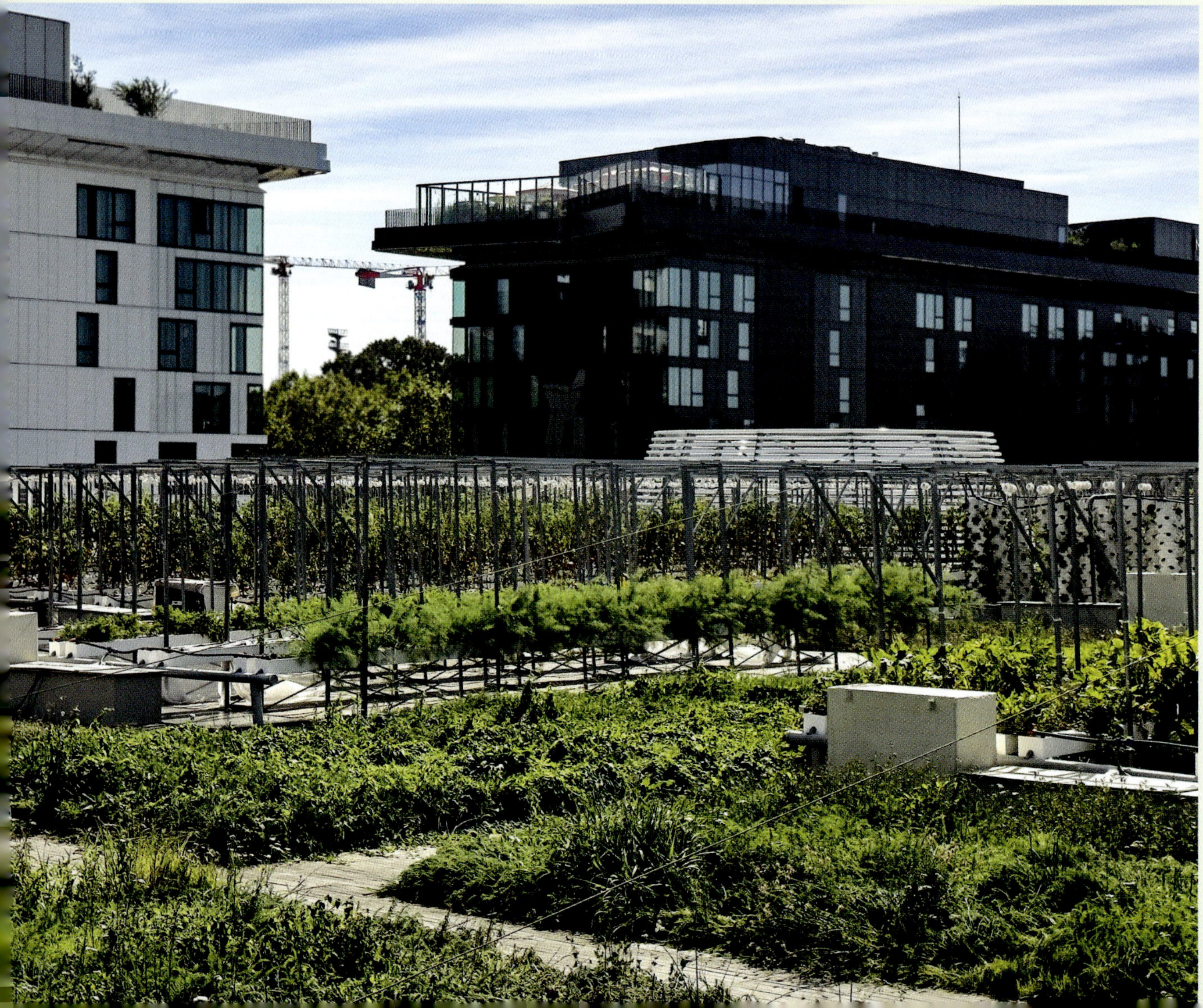

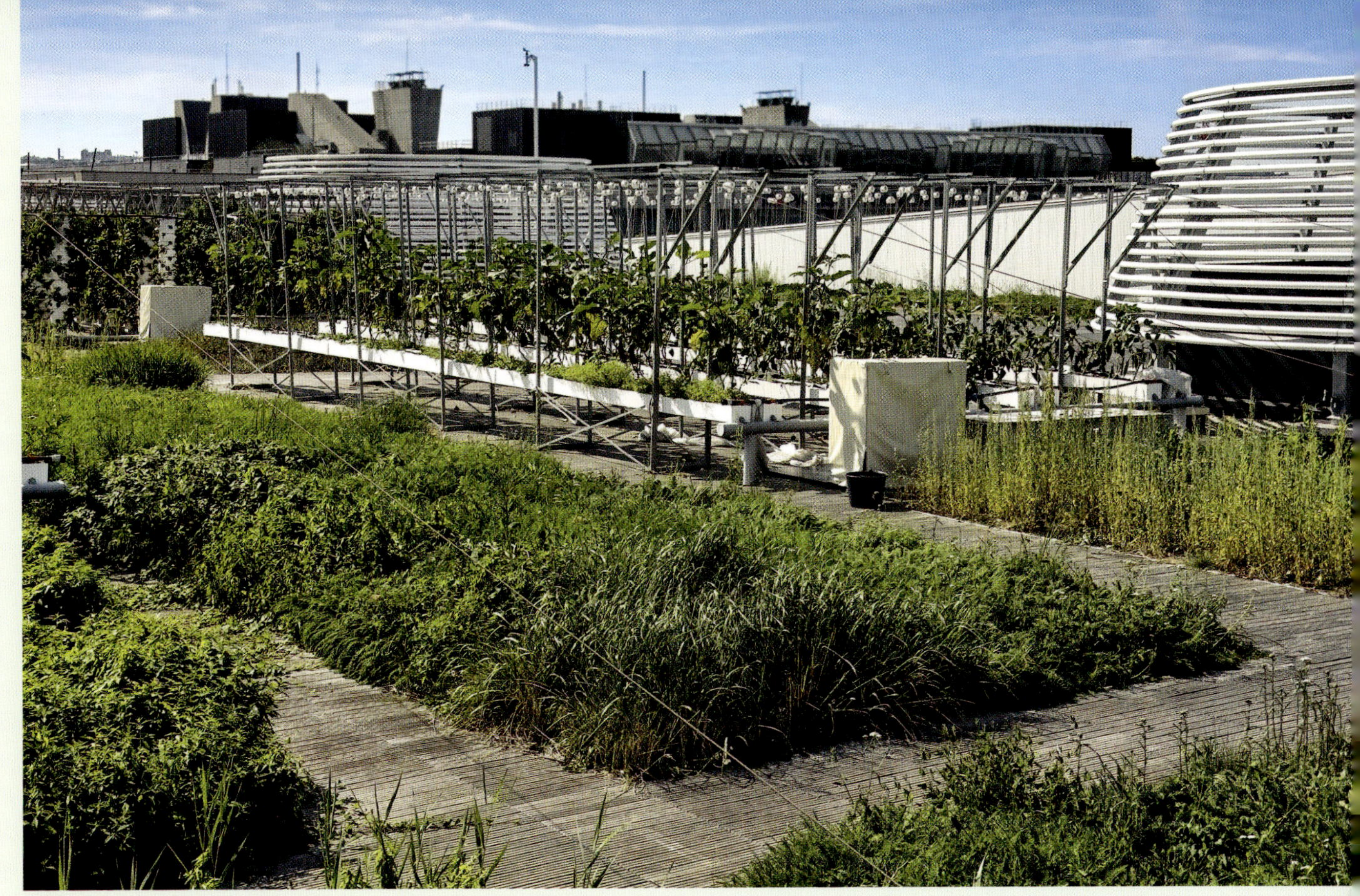

## *Nature Urbaine* at *Paris Expo Porte de Versailles*
15th arrondissement
2020

The urban farm on the rooftop of the exhibition hall pavilion 6 at Paris Expo Porte de Versailles is more than 14,000 square meters (151,000 square feet), making it one of the largest urban farms in Europe. Nature Urbaine was founded by Pascal Hardy and Antoine Juvin, each of whom is well known as an expert in sustainability and agriculture sectors. The plants are grown using hydroponic and aeroponic systems. The farm produces a variety of vegetables including tomatoes, greens and lettuces, and raspberries, to name a few. Tours are given to the public, and there are more than 150 plots of land offered for rent to Parisians to grow plants on their own. A restaurant, Le Perchoir Porte de Versailles, shares the rooftop with the farm. The vegetables on the menu are grown just next door. Nature Urbaine's founders hope this farm will serve as a model for growing and supplying food in the city, reducing the carbon footprint of food distribution.

**OPPOSITE ABOVE**
Vertical gardening in aeroponic columns and hydroponic gutters adds to the growing capacity of the farm.

**OPPOSITE BELOW**
A wooden path delineates the planting beds. Parisians who rent a plot for gardening also receive advice from the master gardeners of the farm.

**ABOVE**
A variety of growing systems and structures have been installed on the rooftop of the exhibition space.

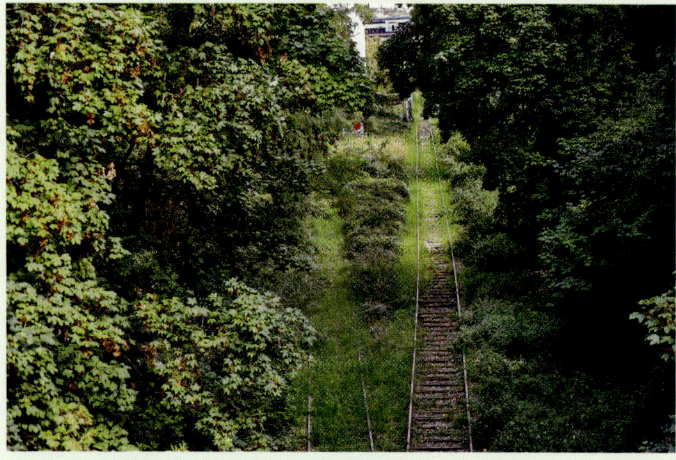

## *Petite Ceinture*

13th, 15th, 18th, and 19th arrondissements
(1852)

Starting in 1852, the Petite Ceinture (or Little Belt) was a rail line that circled the outer edges of the Paris city limits. It carried people, goods, livestock, and produce to and from markets, and to and from neighborhoods. Ridership decreased in the early 1900s as the metro subway lines were developed, and as the processing of livestock changed, so did the moving of stock to slaughterhouses. But the tracks were never removed, and the SNCF, the national rail company, retained the ownership of the properties. The railroad lines are all above ground, but tunnels and new streets grew above these tracks in some locations. The stations also remained and became canvases for Parisian street artists. As human activity left, nature and animals thrived along the tracks. Beginning in 2007, SNCF and the City of Paris started to invite business proposals to take over the abandoned stations and convert them into contemporary spaces such as restaurants and music venues. In some cases, these entities were allowed to buy the old station properties. The city also recognized the railway as a natural environment. Preserving and protecting the habitat of the Petite Ceinture became part of the Paris Biodiversity Plan. While it is exciting to see a wild part of Paris reemerge and open for walking and running, the impact of our presence will be felt by the plants and creatures that live there. The balance between these worlds is a fine line, with a future to be determined.

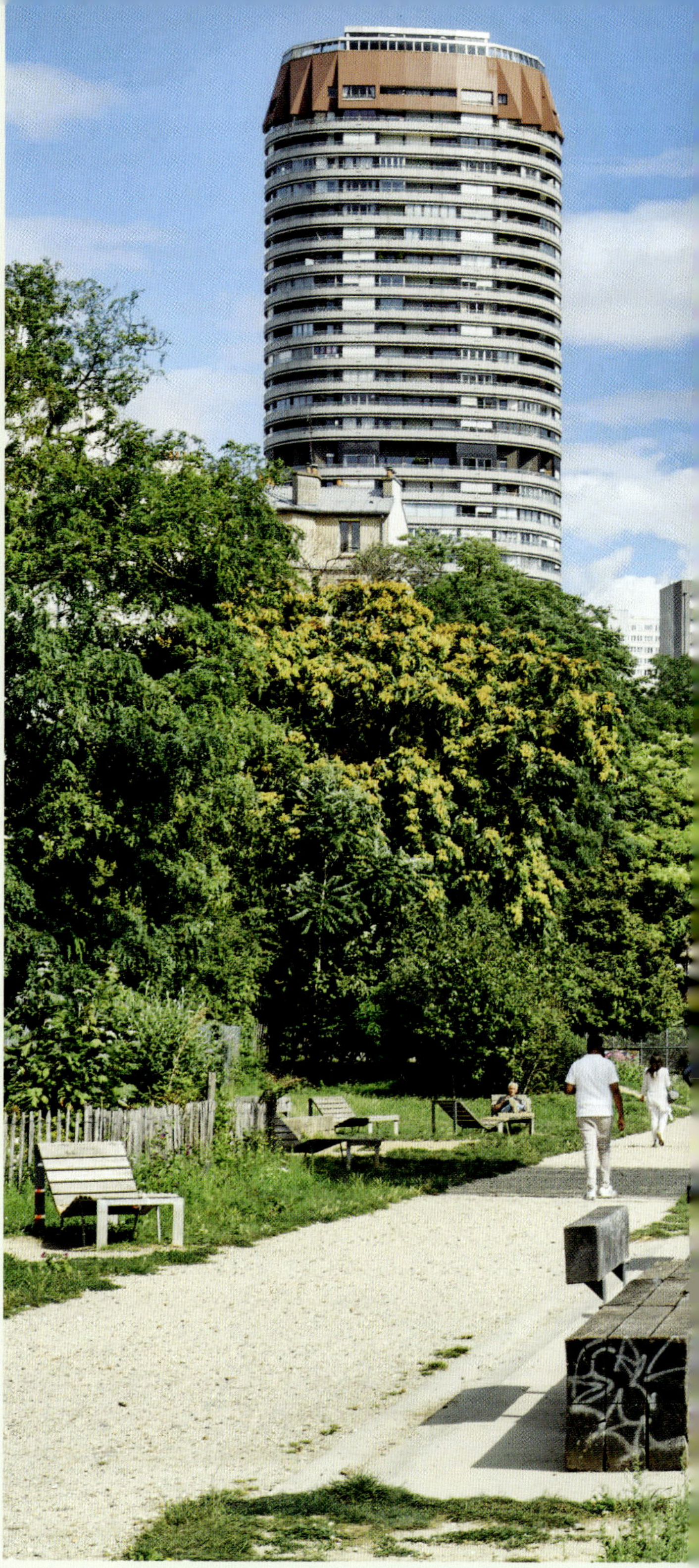

## *Parc Georges-Brassens*


The grass-covered tracks of the Petite Ceinture near parc Georges-Brassens in the 15th arrondissement.

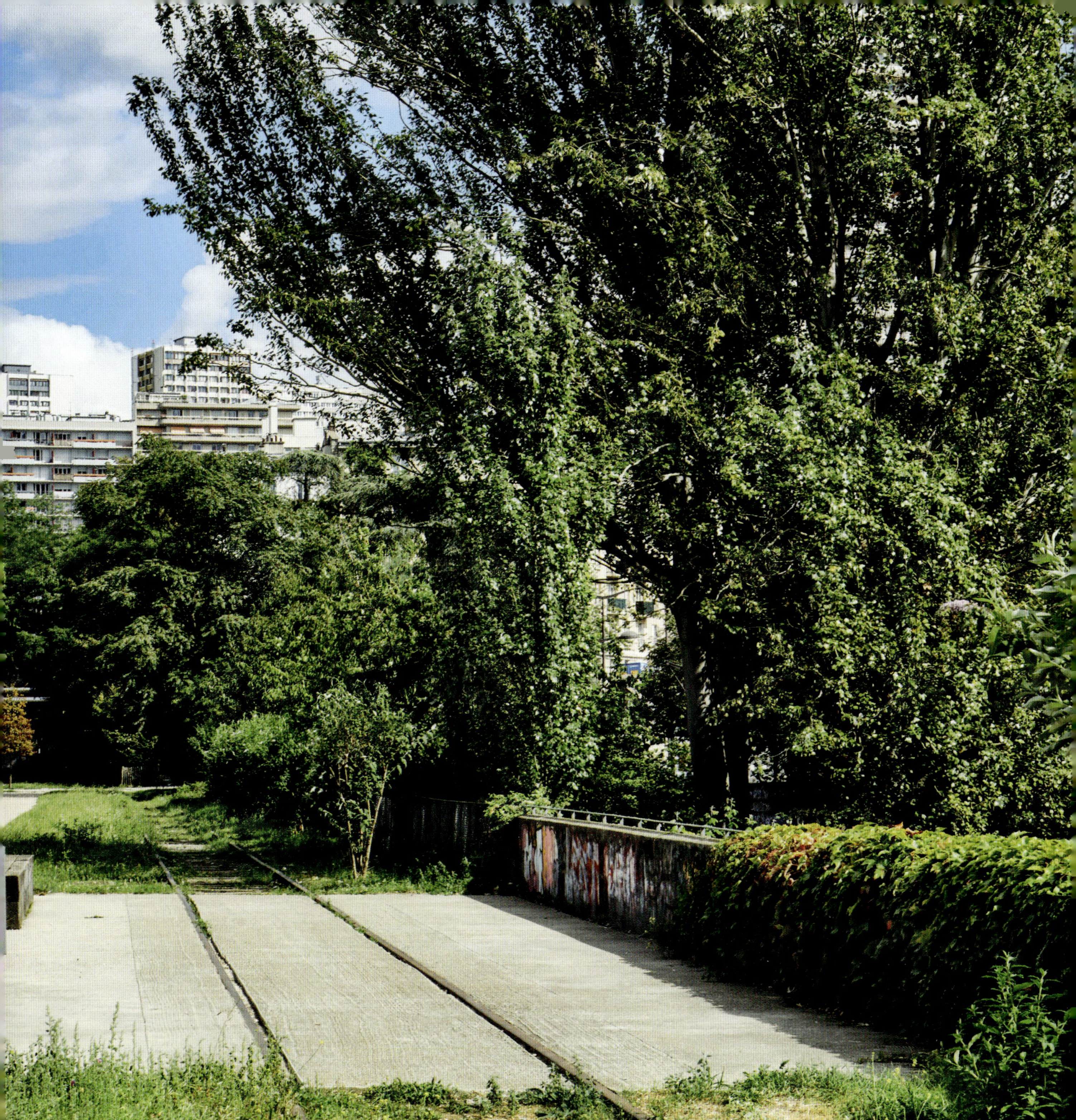

ABOVE
A section of the railroad track in the 13th
arrondissement that has been reclaimed
as a walking path.

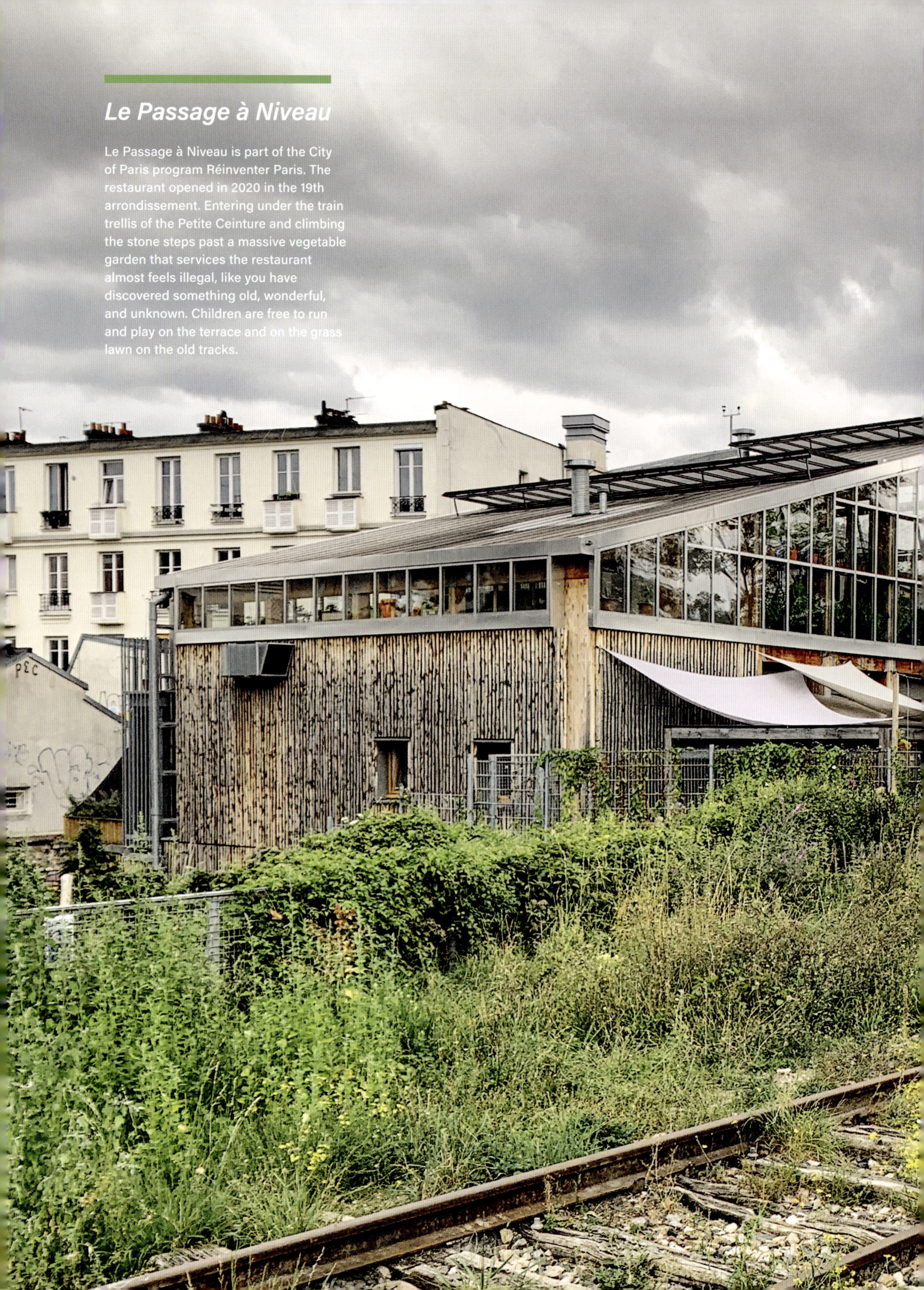

Le Passage à Niveau

Le Passage à Niveau is part of the City of Paris program Réinventer Paris. The restaurant opened in 2020 in the 19th arrondissement. Entering under the train trellis of the Petite Ceinture and climbing the stone steps past a massive vegetable garden that services the restaurant almost feels illegal, like you have discovered something old, wonderful, and unknown. Children are free to run and play on the terrace and on the grass lawn on the old tracks.

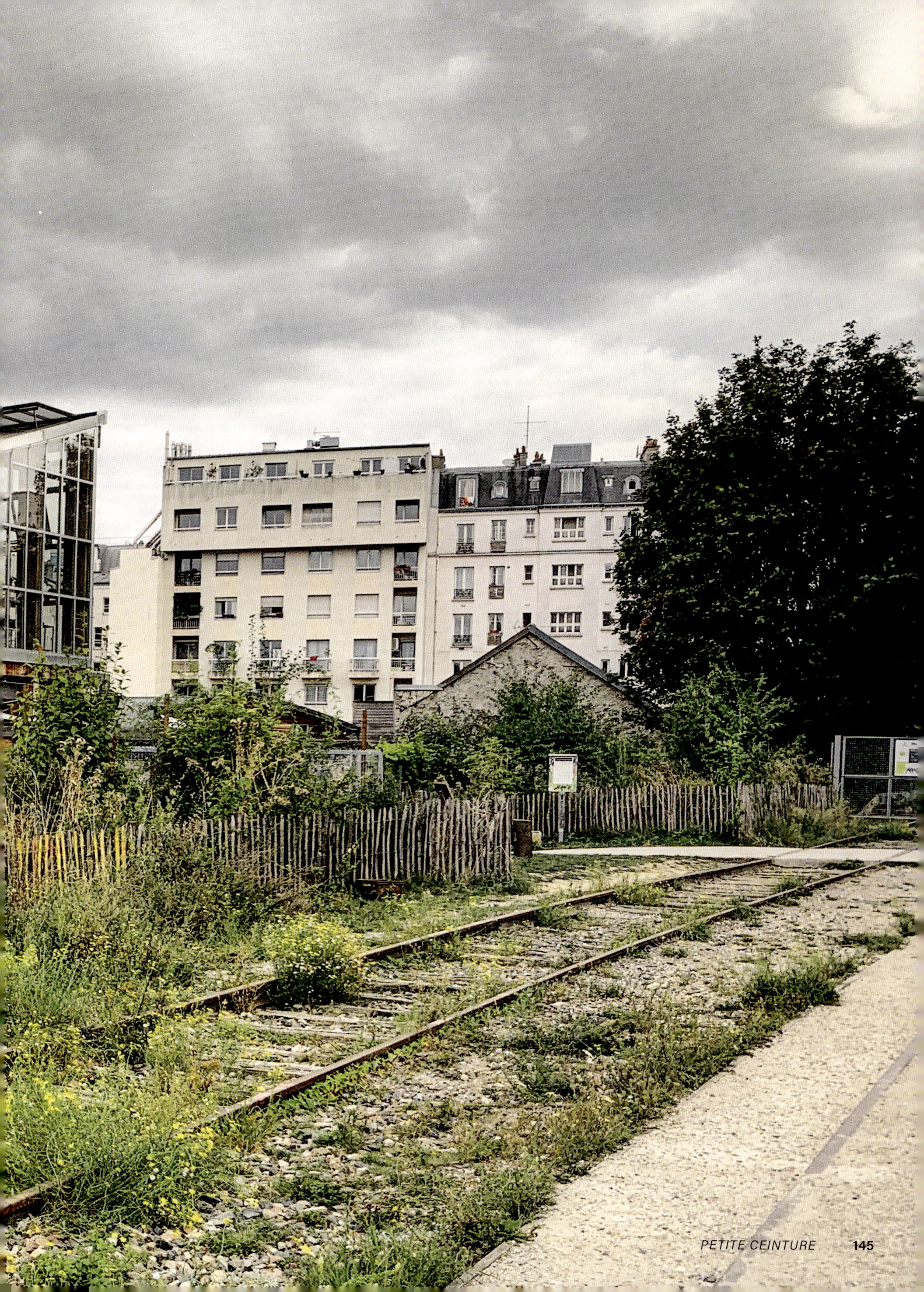

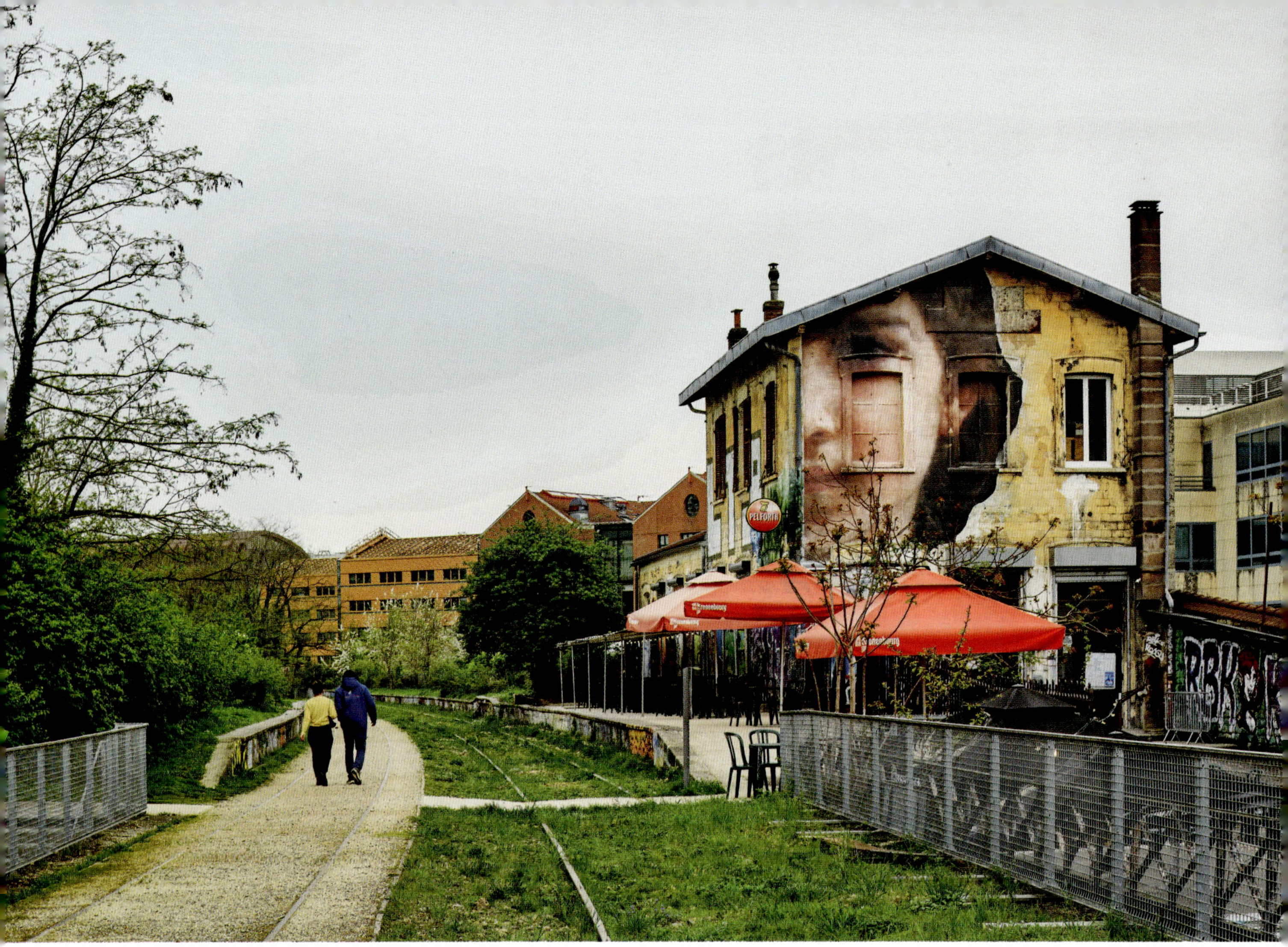

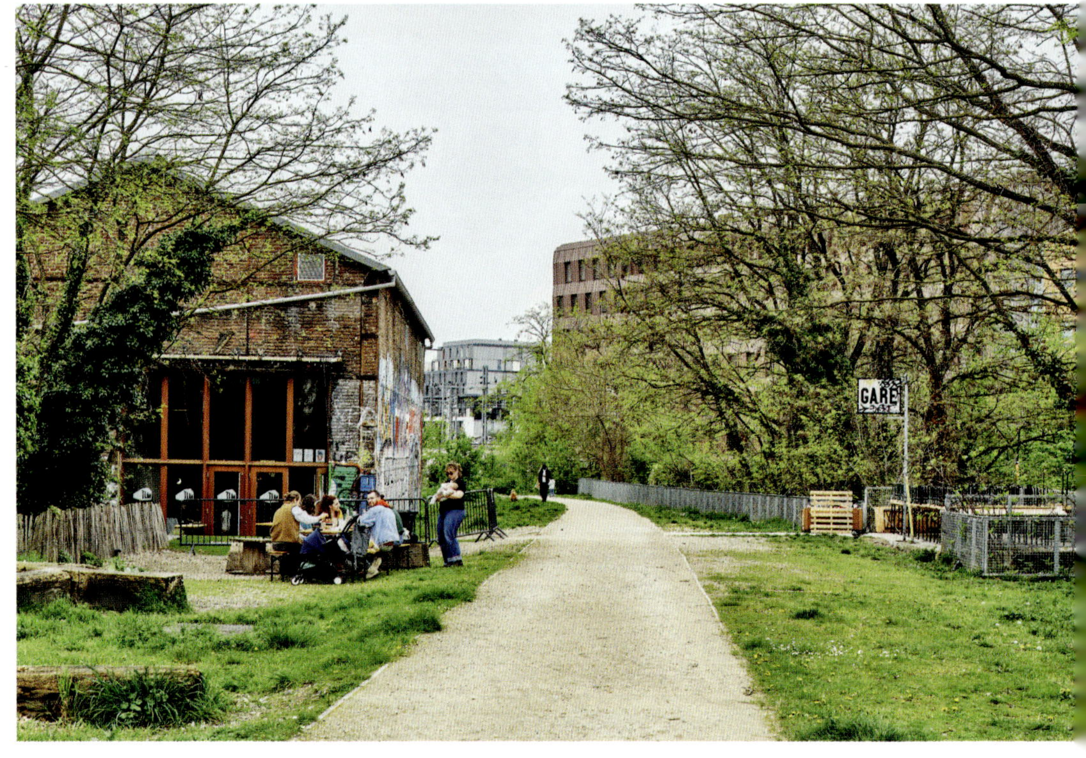

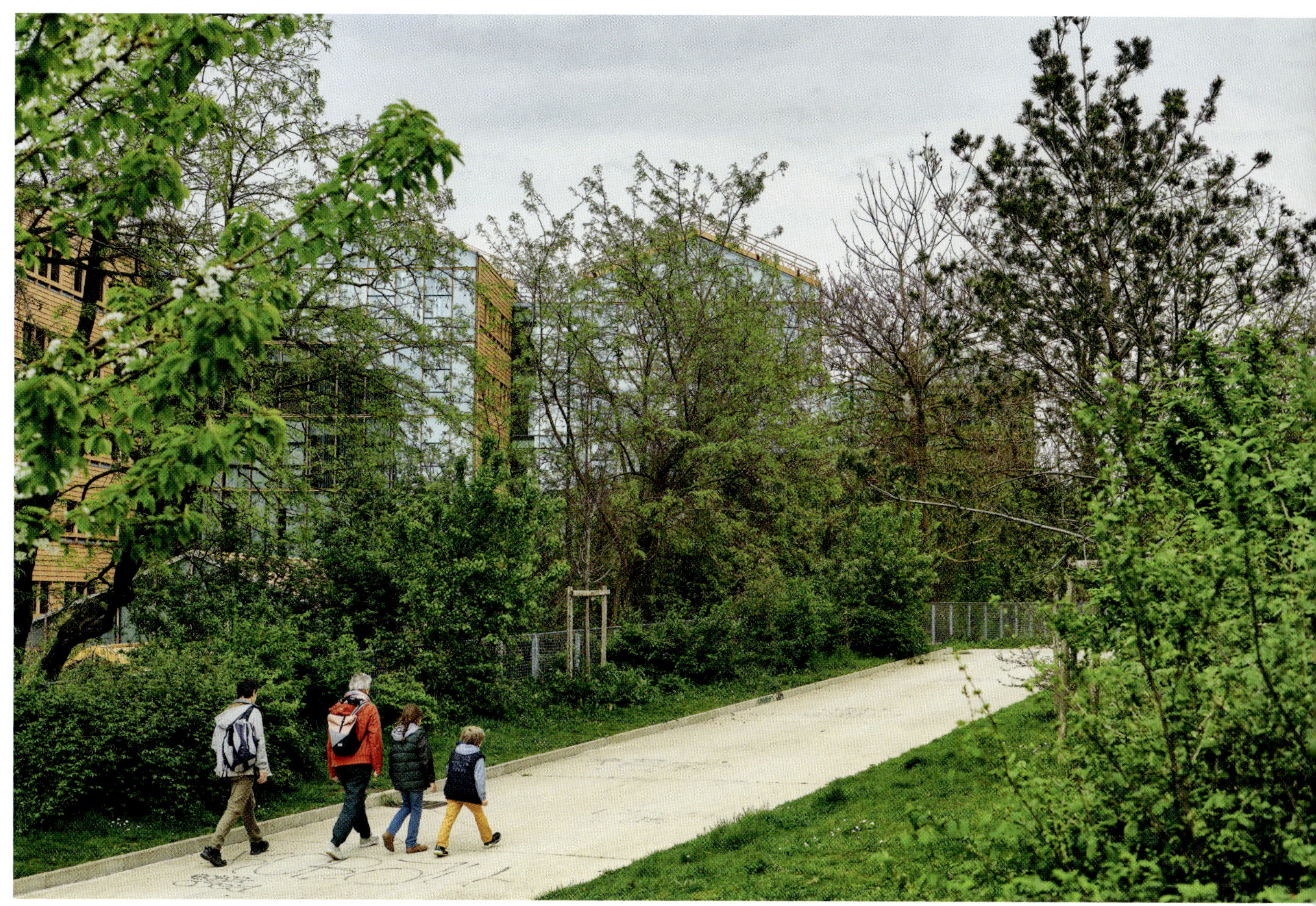

## La Gare–Le Gore

**OPPOSITE ABOVE**
La Gare–Le Gore, a jazz club, near l'avenue de Flandre entrance, was purchased by street artist Julien de Casabianca in 2017. His work from the *Outings* project graces the exterior walls. The old station platform has been turned into a terrace with seating.

**OPPOSITE BELOW**
One of the old railway's hangars has now been redesigned as a *tiers-lieu* (or third space) called Le TLM, a restaurant, music performance space, workshop, and conference venue. The collective Au Fil du Rail applied to use the space through the city's program to reactivate the Petite Ceinture.

## Quartier Rosa Parks

**ABOVE**
In the 19th arrondissement, the Petite Ceinture goes through le quartier Rosa Parks. Both the area and the train station are named for the American civil rights activist. Following the old tracks up a ramp, it's easy to notice the recently planted trees and scrubs such as holly, plum, and hawthorn trees.

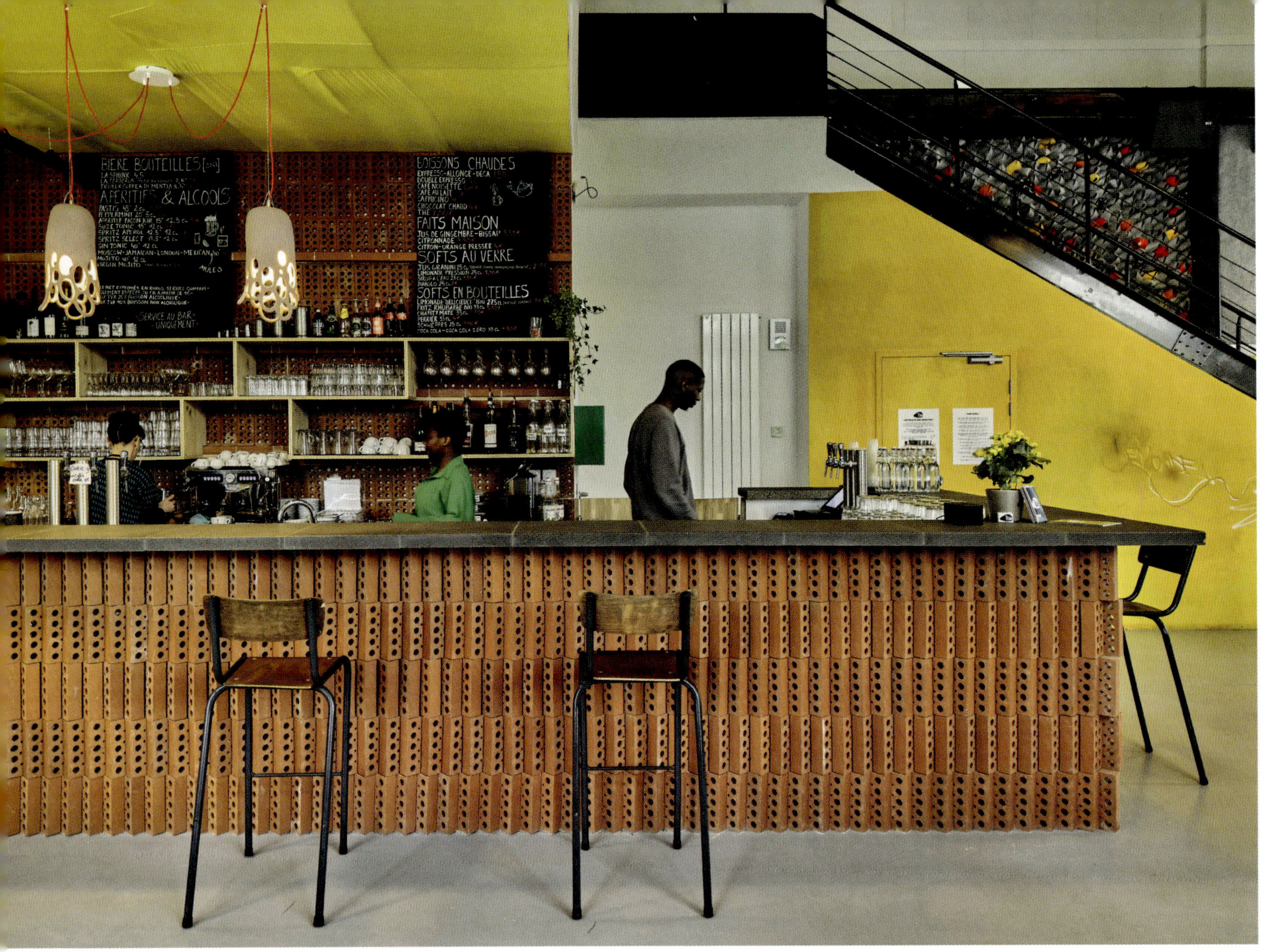

## Le TLM

All the materials used to create the interiors at Le TLM were found or recycled. For example, the wooden and metal chairs came from old hotels throughout France, and the curtains came from a Jay-Z concert at fashion house Louis Vuitton.

**ABOVE**
Each part of the design, including the building, has its own story. The red bricks of the bar's base were left over from another project.

**RIGHT**
Felt around the performance stage helps with sound management. Even the sound system is secondhand.

**OPPOSITE**
The yellow material of the ceiling had a previous life as a *montgolfière*, or hot-air balloon. The tracks and steel beams from the original construction were left exposed.

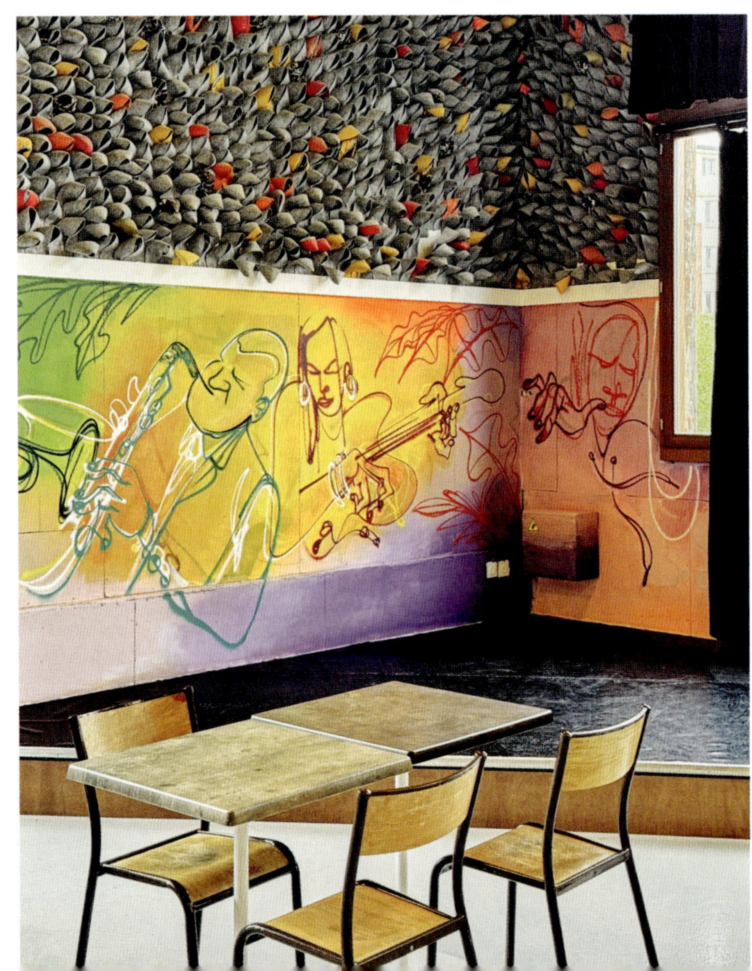

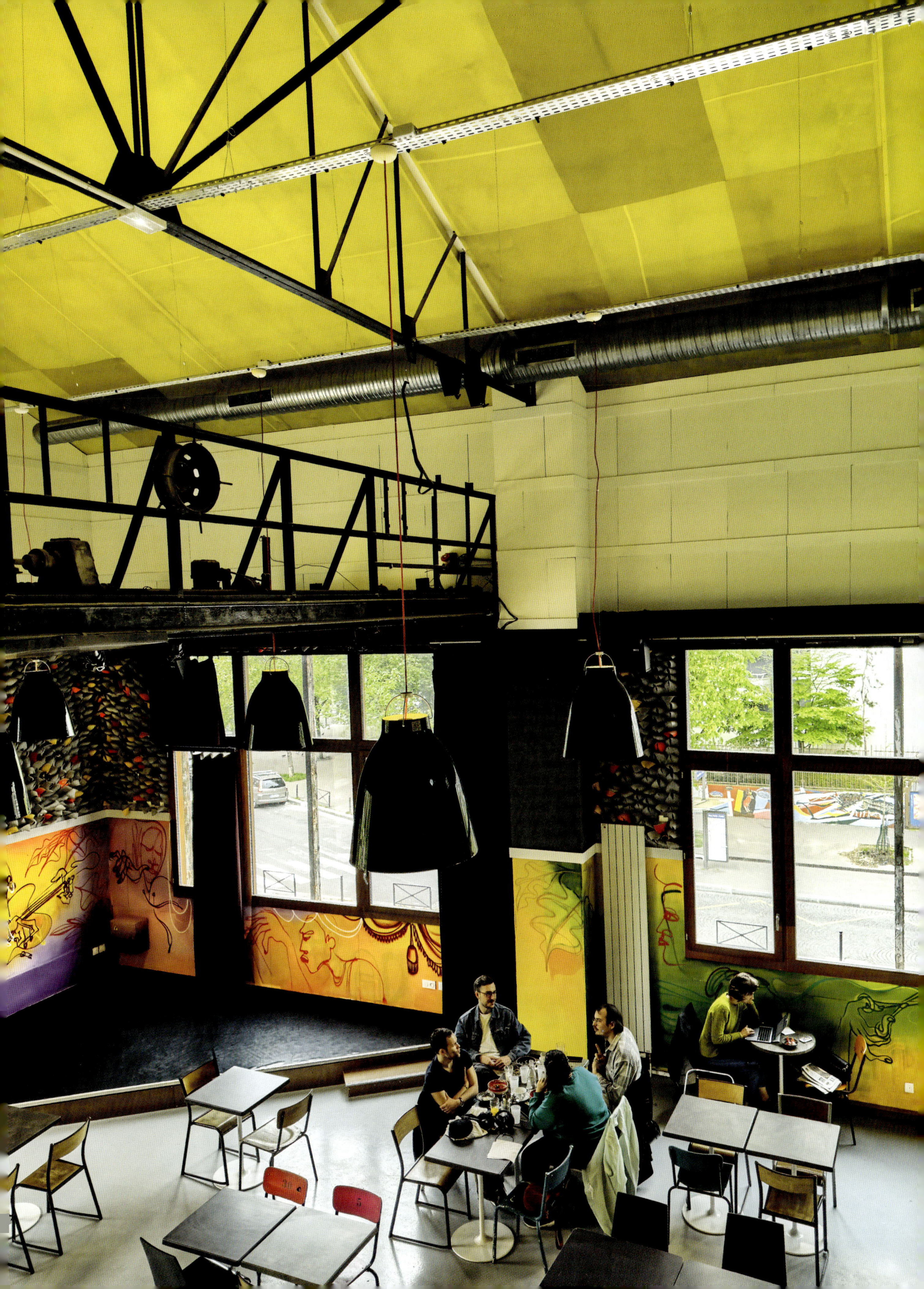

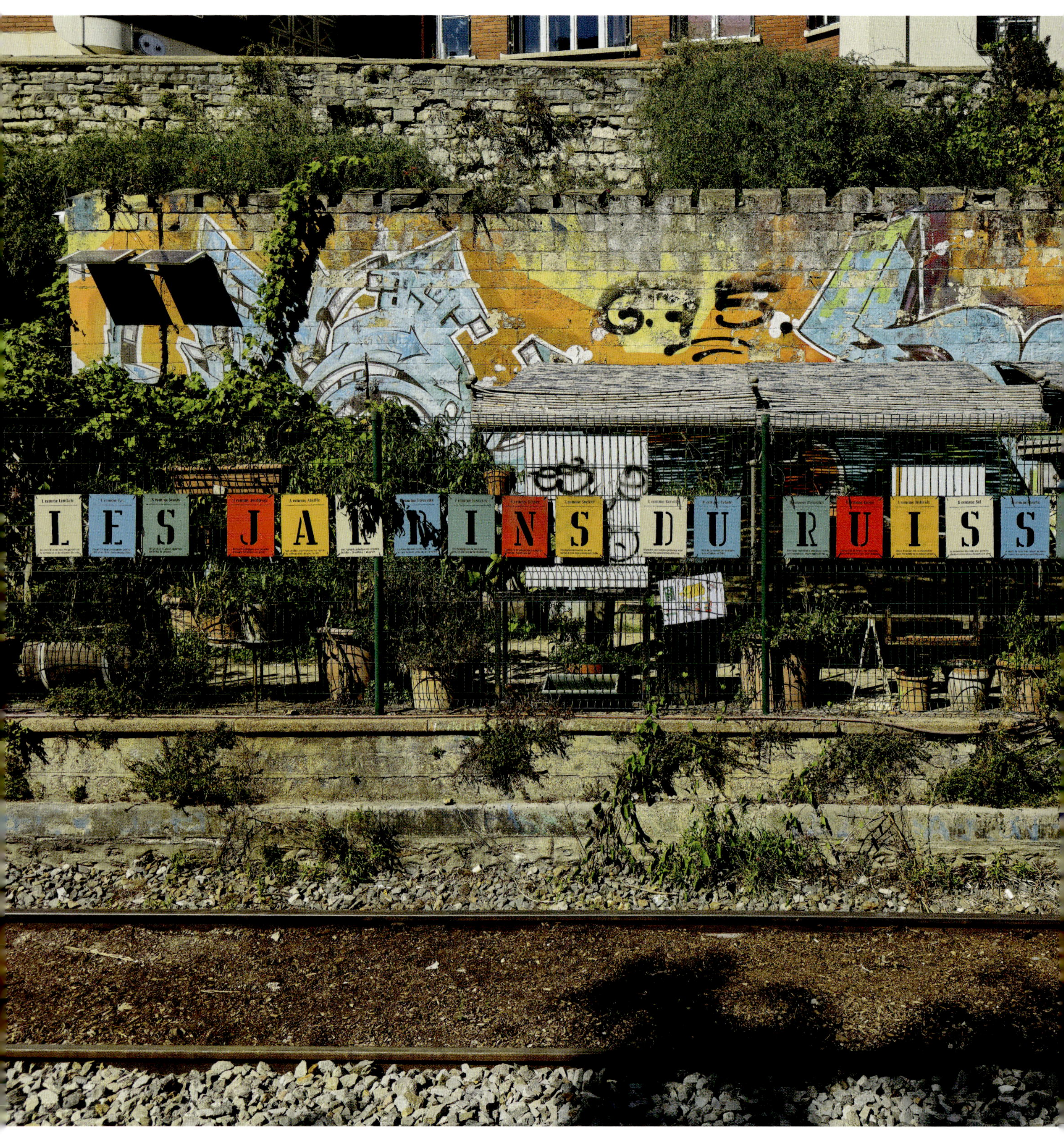


LES JARDINS DU RUISS

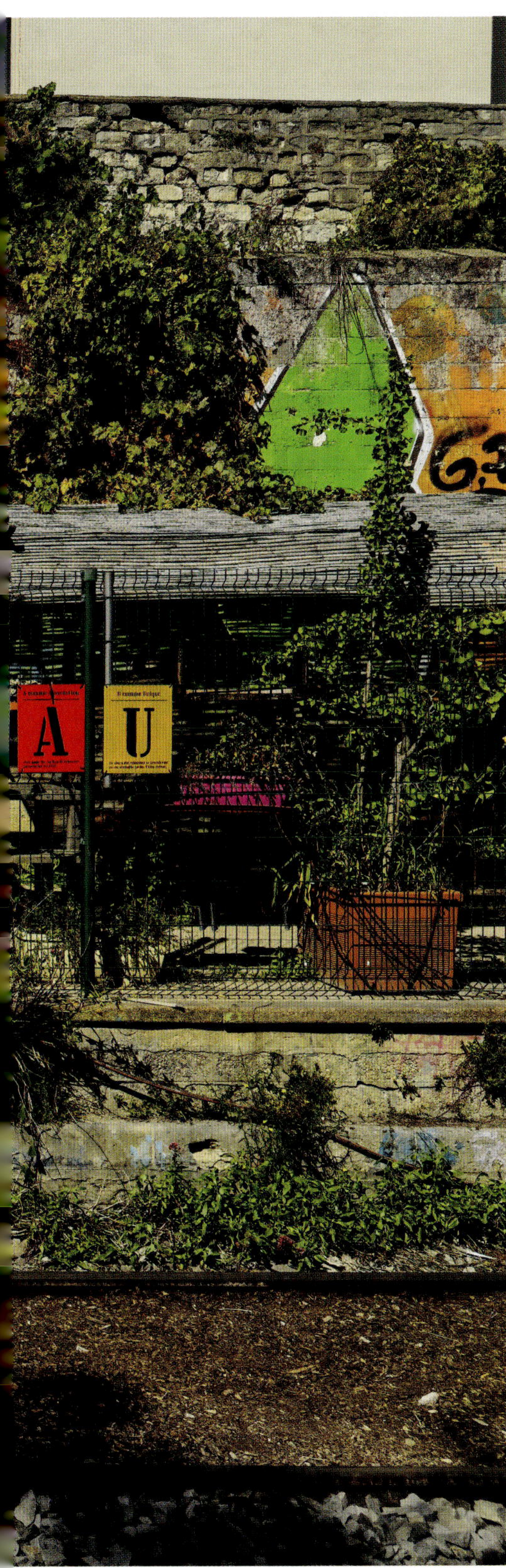

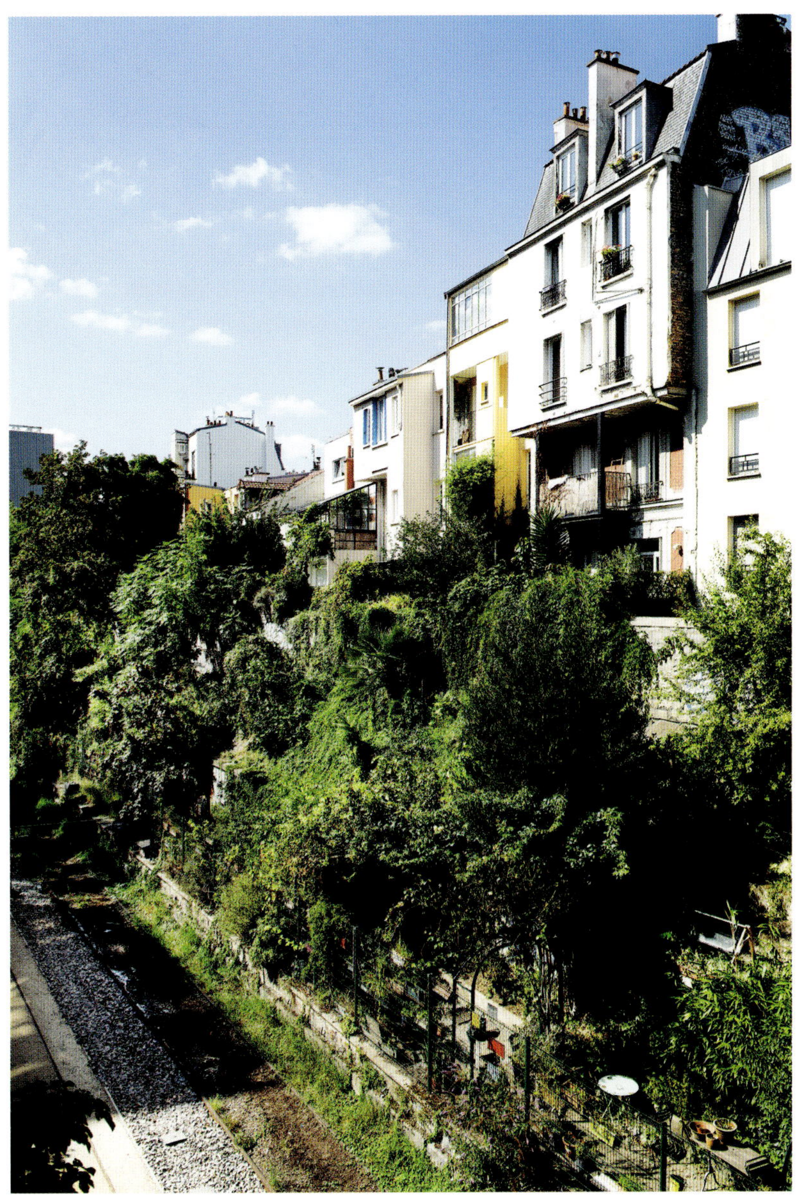

## Les Jardins du Ruisseau

Les jardins du Ruisseau is a community garden first built along the Petite Ceinture in 2004 near la porte de Clignancourt, in the 18th arrondissement. A group of residents came together with the support of the city to rescue the site, owned by SNCF, and to transform it into a shared garden with a strong educational component.


The buildings that face the busy boulevards des Maréchaux offer protection to the garden, which is behind the buildings and below street level. Over the years, the plantings have grown to provide a shady habitat in a very urban neighborhood.

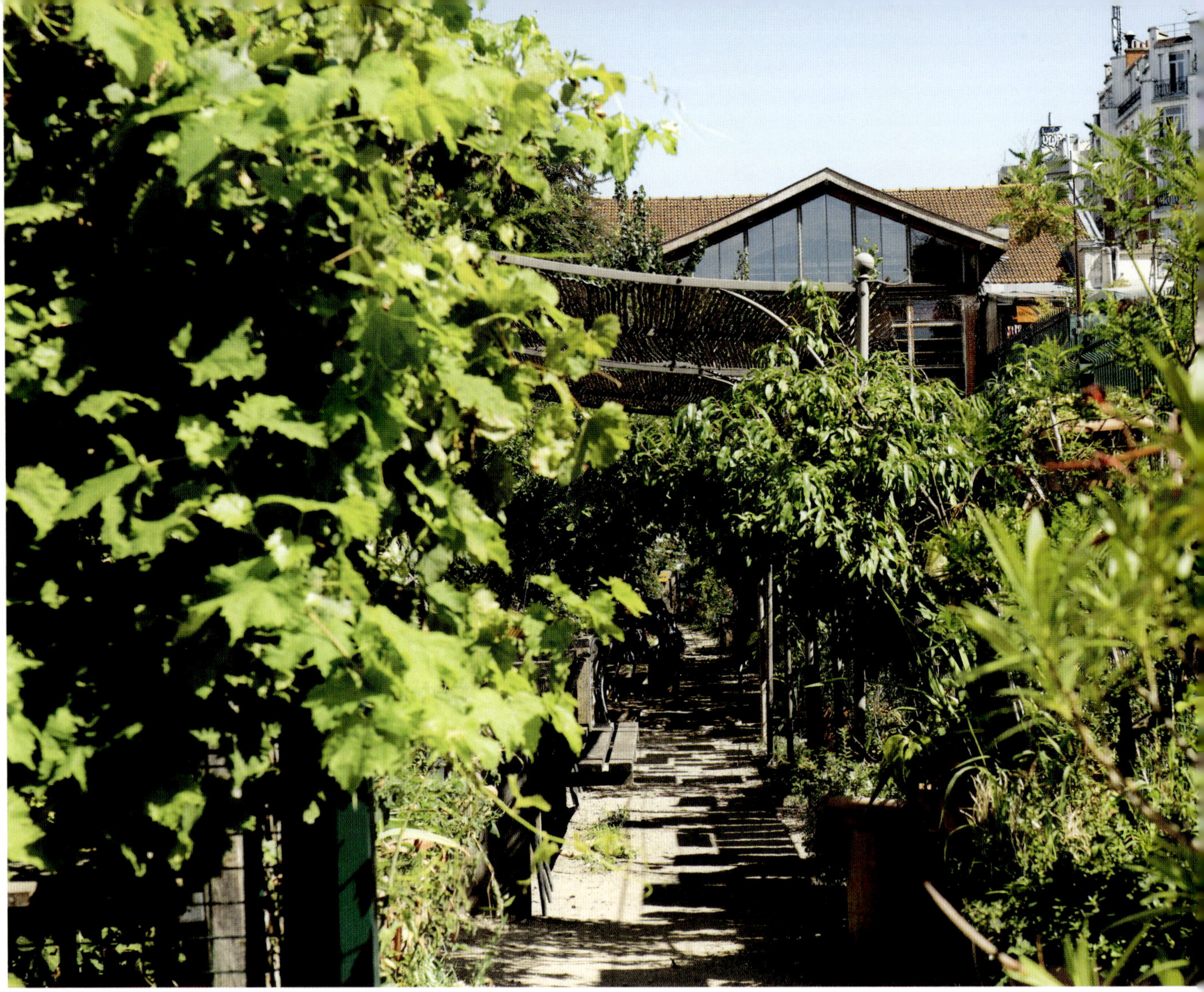

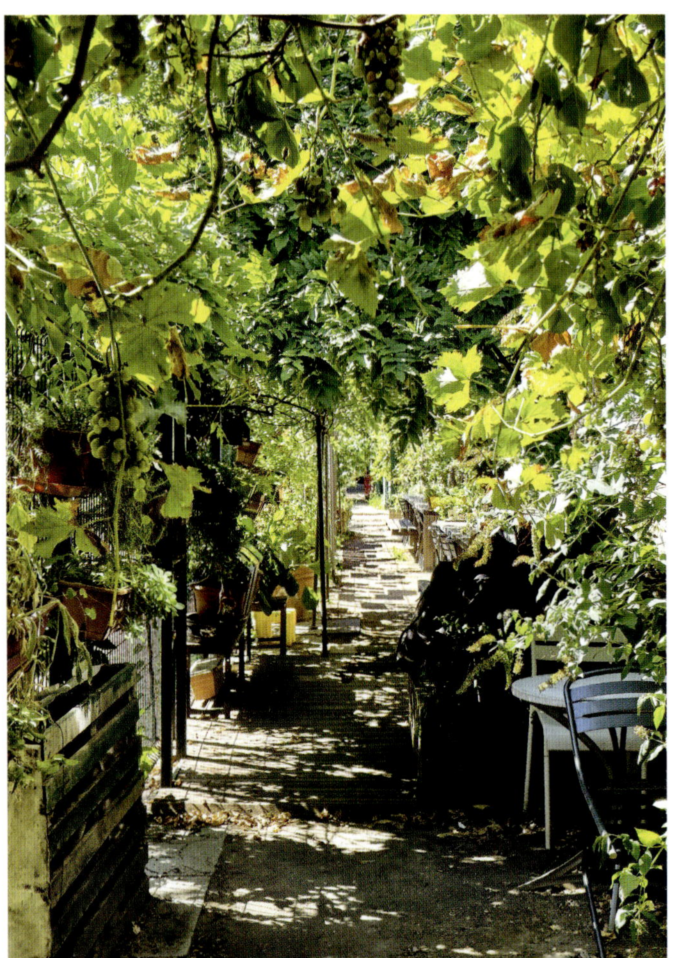

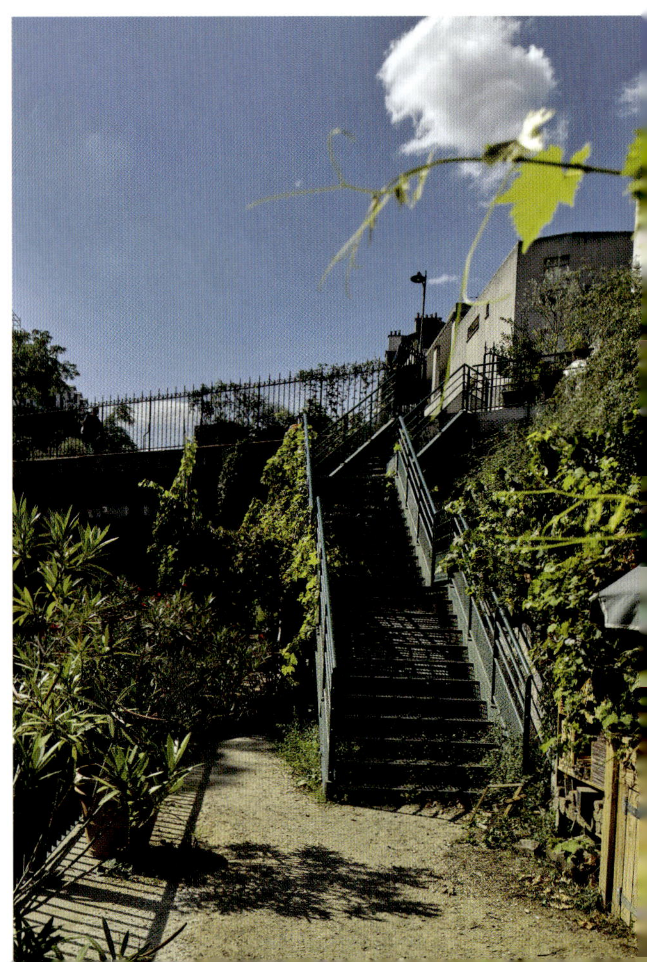

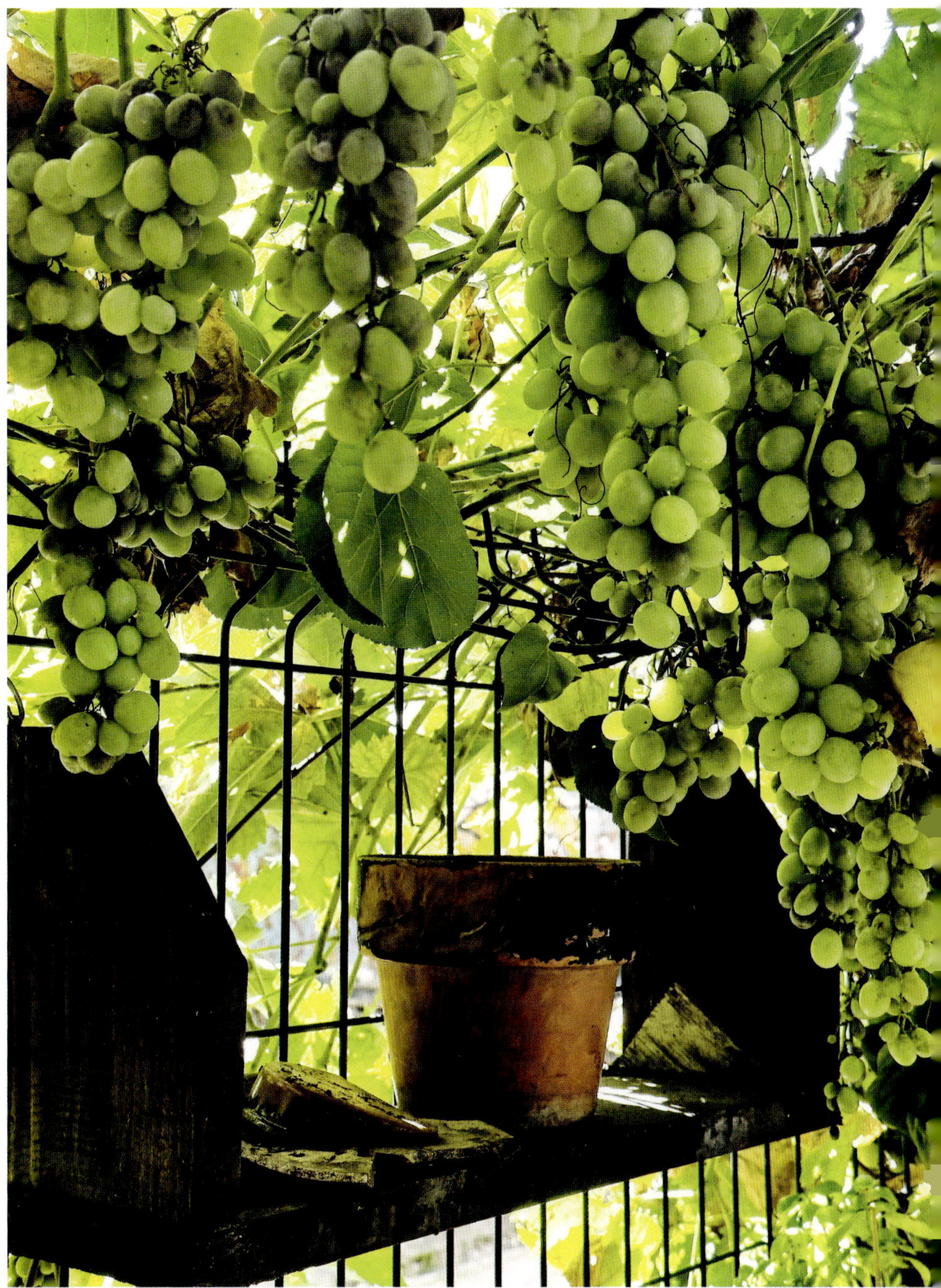

OPPOSITE ABOVE
The old train station has been transformed into La REcyclerie, a *tiers-lieu* (or third space) with a restaurant and coworking space that also has the garden across the tracks.

OPPOSITE BELOW LEFT
It is possible to sit in les jardins du Ruisseau under the grapevines and listen to the birds who live there.

OPPOSITE BELOW RIGHT
The access to les jardins du Ruisseau is a staircase off la rue du Ruisseau at la villa des Tulipes. Even on a very hot day, the temperature among the plants is much cooler than the street above.

ABOVE
The garden is always a work in progress, with plants, pots, and tools in a consistent rotation of use and disuse. Grapes and pears are among the fruits that grow there.

# Reclaiming the Waterfront

1st, 4th, 10th, 11th, 13th, and 19th
arrondissements
1891–2023

Access to the waterfront has dominated the history of Paris from its early beginnings. The city grew from l'île de la Cité, on the banks of the Seine. As the city transformed, the water that flowed through it and around it was constrained and redirected; the riverbanks were covered in concrete, and roadways and cars dominated. Living by the water in Paris became more expensive in the center of the city, and in some areas, as the river's edge became more industrial, it became a less desirable place to live because of water pollution. In 2002, the City of Paris began to act with a new program, Paris Plages (or Paris Beach), to bring more Parisians to the banks of the Seine. The program expanded to other locations in different arrondissements. Also, the city began to limit the cars on the *quais* (or docks) of the river, which, in the 1960s, had become congested by traffic. These sites were turned into walking paths and gardens. While the Seine is the most well-known of the Parisian waterways, le bassin de la Villette, le canal Saint-Martin, and le canal de l'Ourcq, among others, offer residents and visitors the chance to sit, walk, or ride a bike in a green or public space near the water. These transformations also broaden the diversity of the plants and wildlife that live near or in the water. The Seine has played a part not only in the natural resources of the city, or in commercial transportation and the travel industry, as tour boats offer excursion down the river, but also in its cultural life. During the 2024 Olympics, the river was at the center of the opening ceremony. For the first time since the 1900 Olympic games in Paris, athletes swam in the Seine as part of the competition.

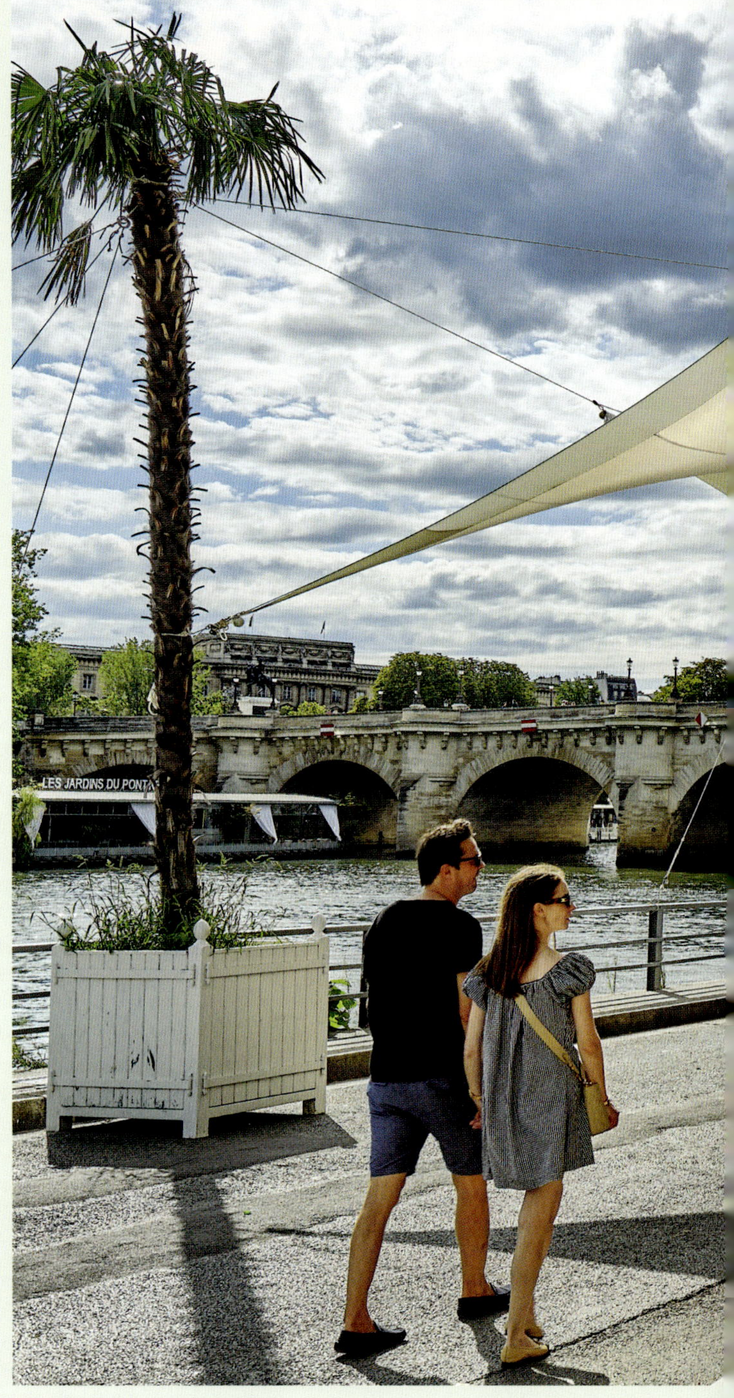



## *Paris Plages*

Paris Plages, or Paris Beaches, is a summer program of the City of Paris. Palm trees, shade canopies, and beach chairs are installed along the waterfront from July to early September each year.

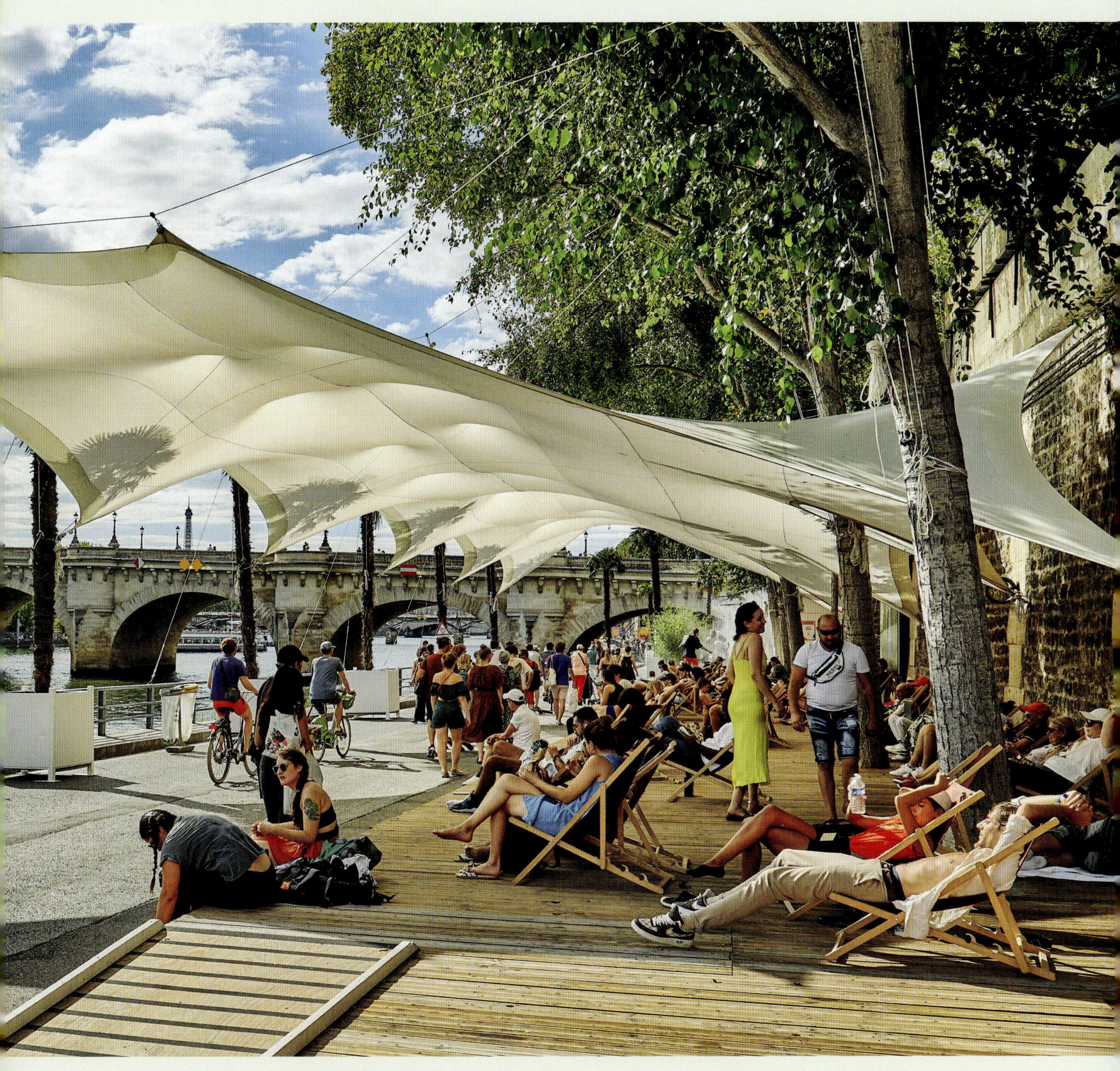

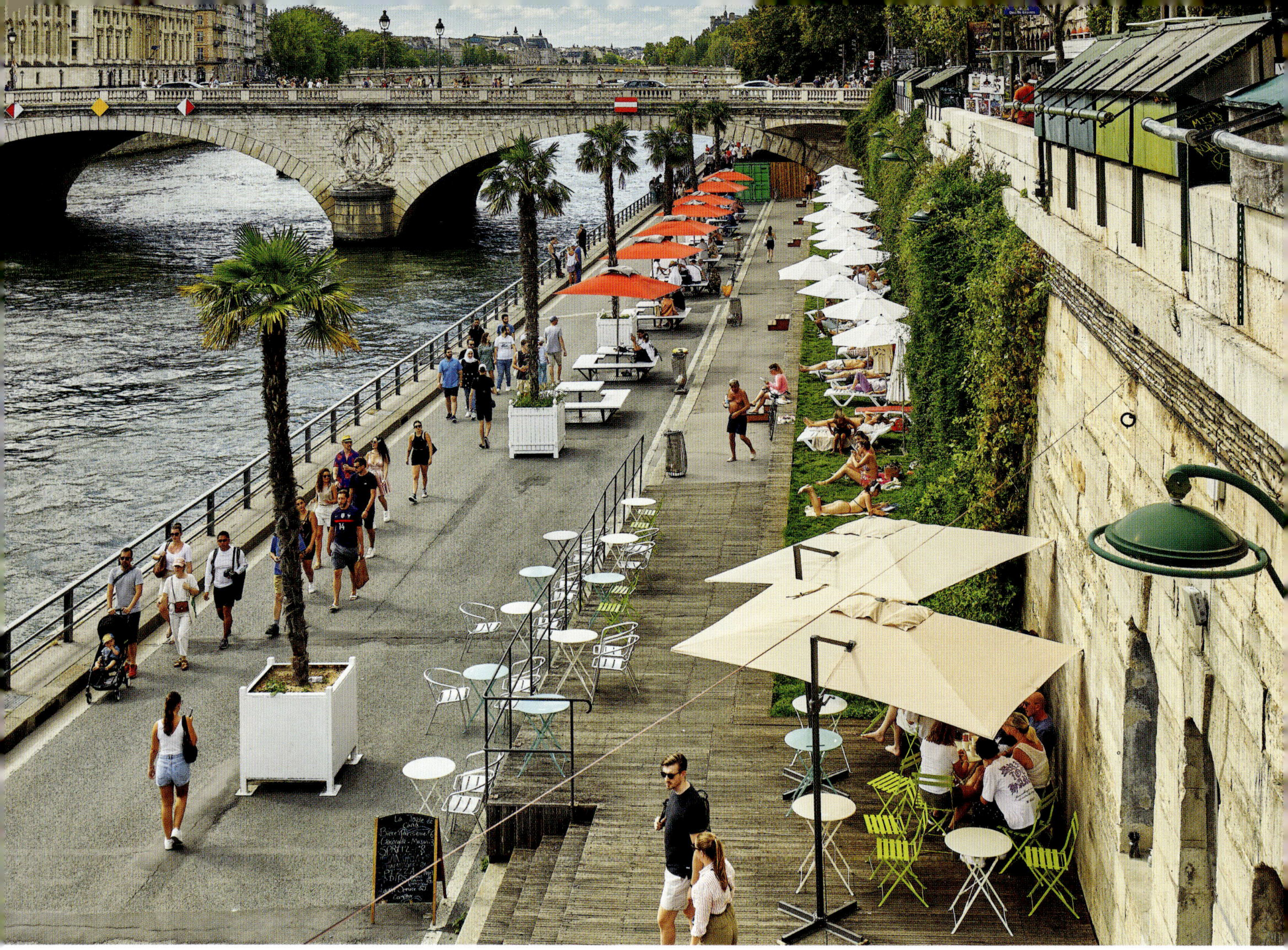

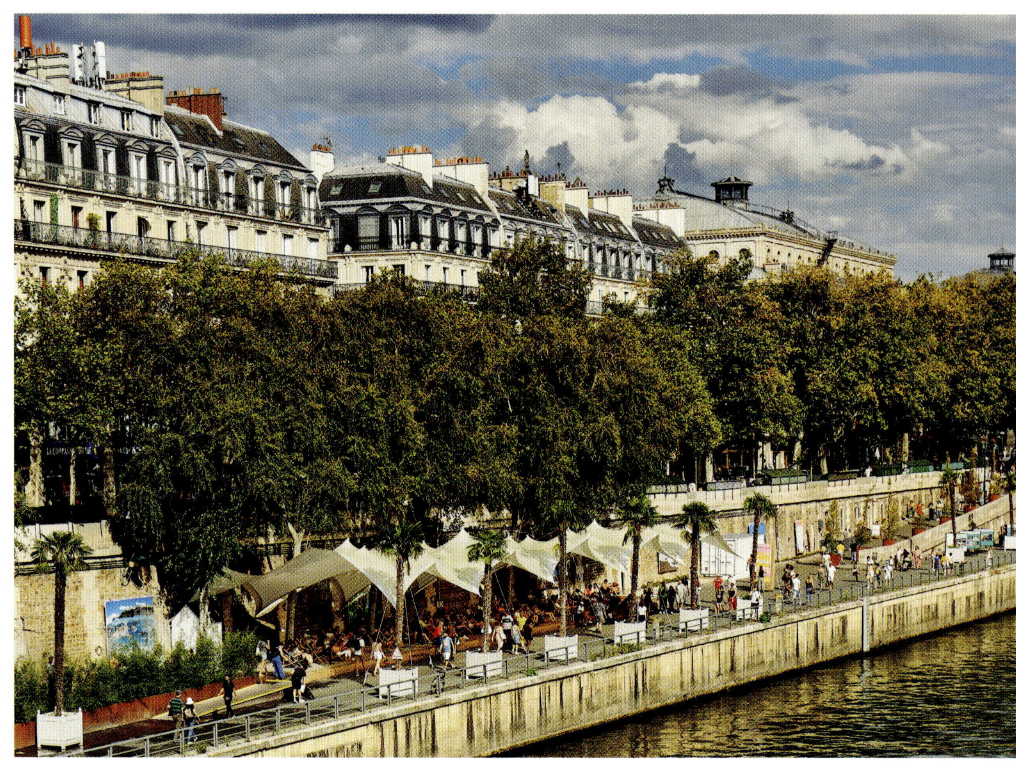

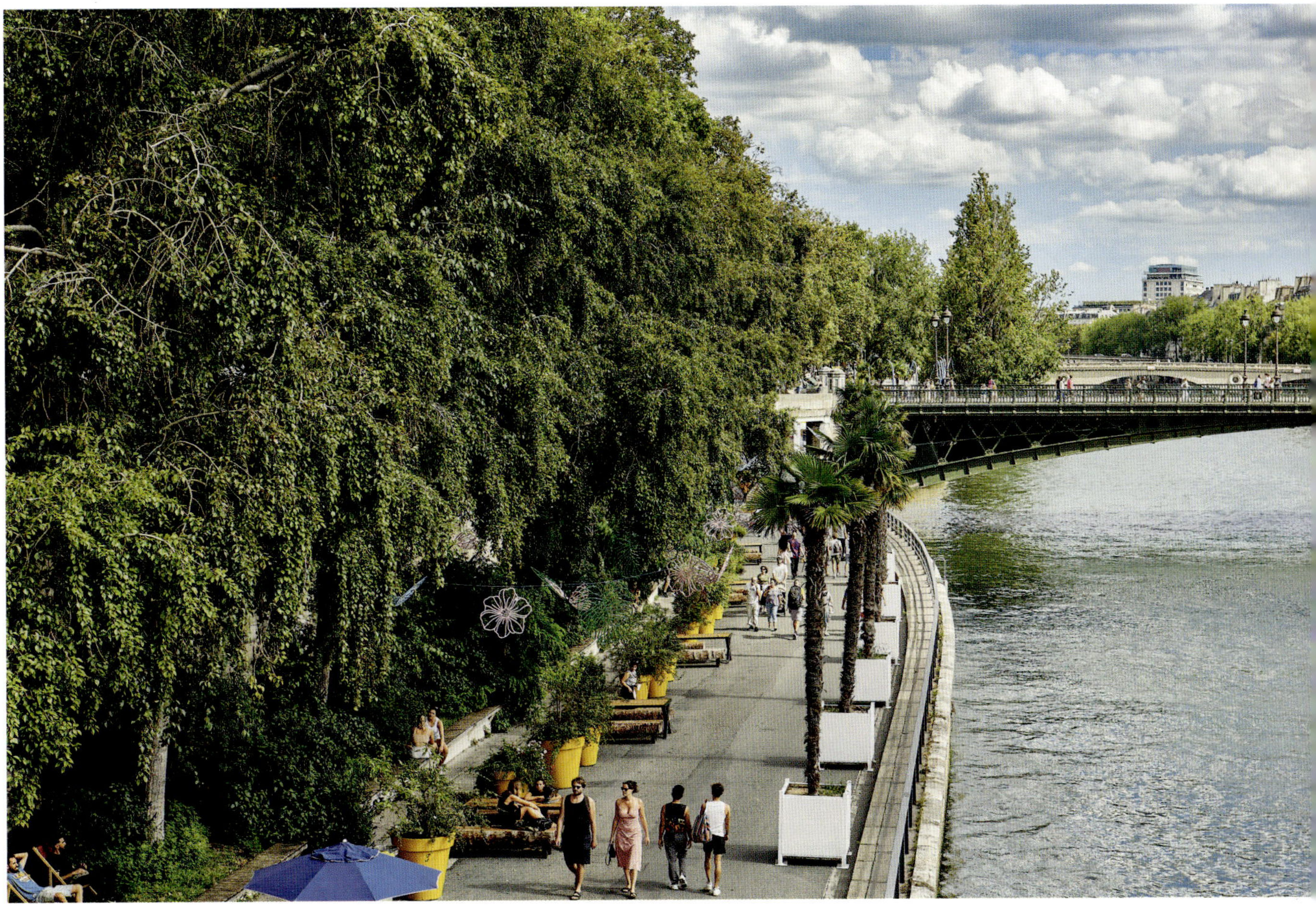

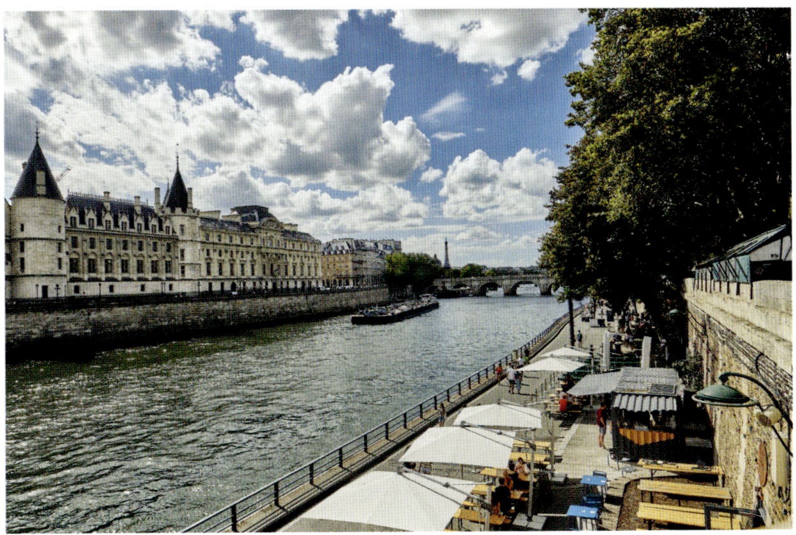

OPPOSITE ABOVE
Restaurants and food trucks are also set up along the Seine riverbanks during Paris Plages.

OPPOSITE BELOW
The beaches on *les rives de Seine* (the banks of the Seine) are on the right bank of the river, from le pont des Arts to le pont de Sully.

ABOVE
On the lower and upper sidewalks, palm trees and other plants in pots add shade and improve the spaces.

LEFT
The fourteenth-century buildings of la Conciergerie, part of the Palais de Justice complex, and la tour Eiffel in the distance bring a sense of history to the Paris Plages program.

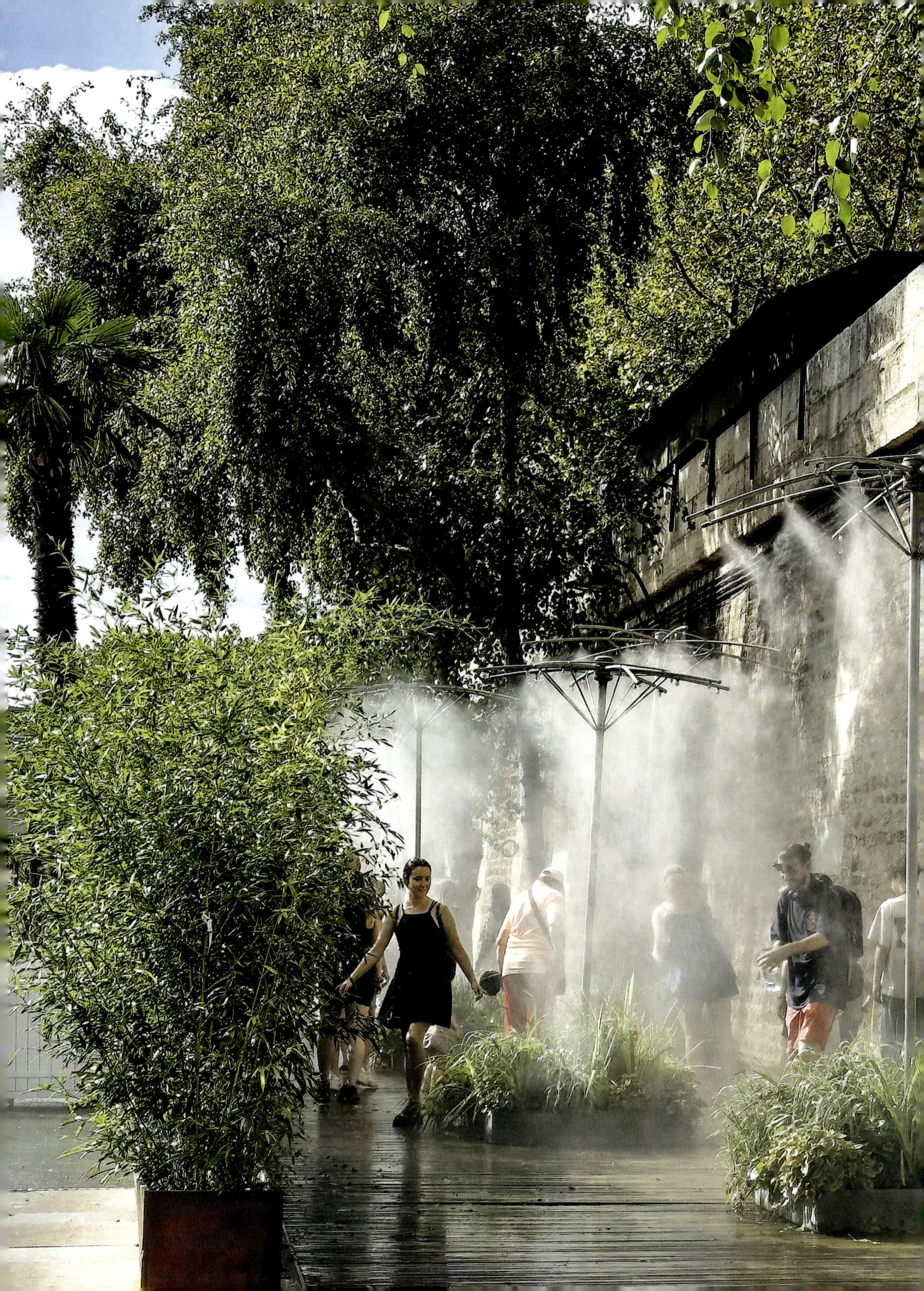

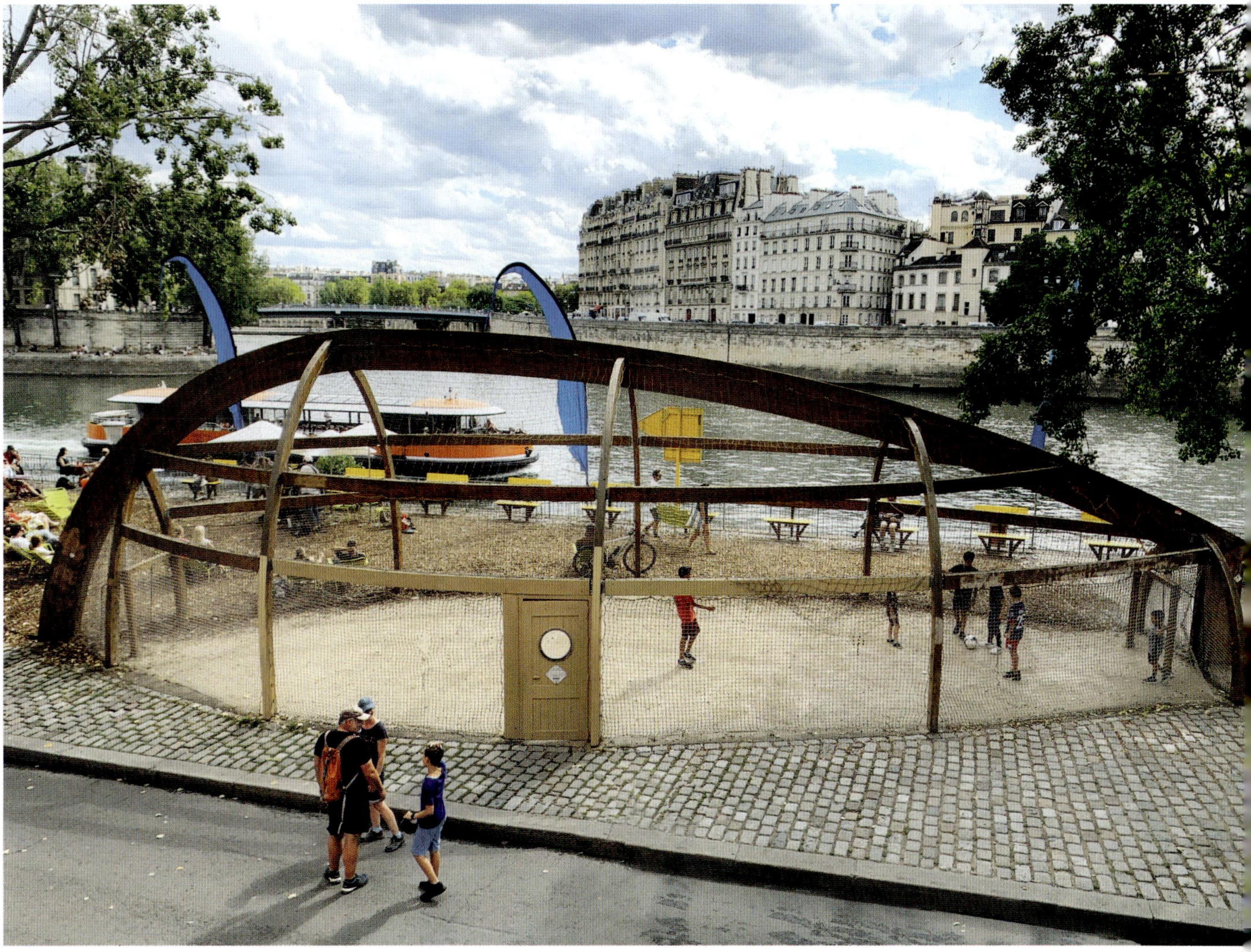

OPPOSITE
Misters are put up to keep everyone
cool on a hot summer day.

ABOVE
An enclosed outdoor soccer play area
near la voie Georges-Pompidou.

RIGHT
Sunbathing is encouraged on the Paris
Plages on the Seine.


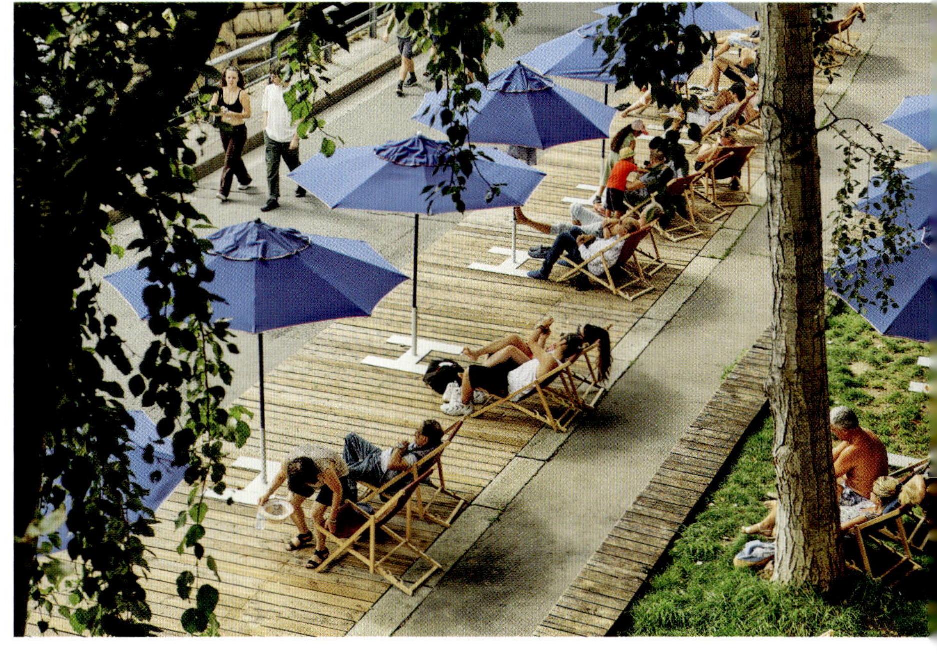

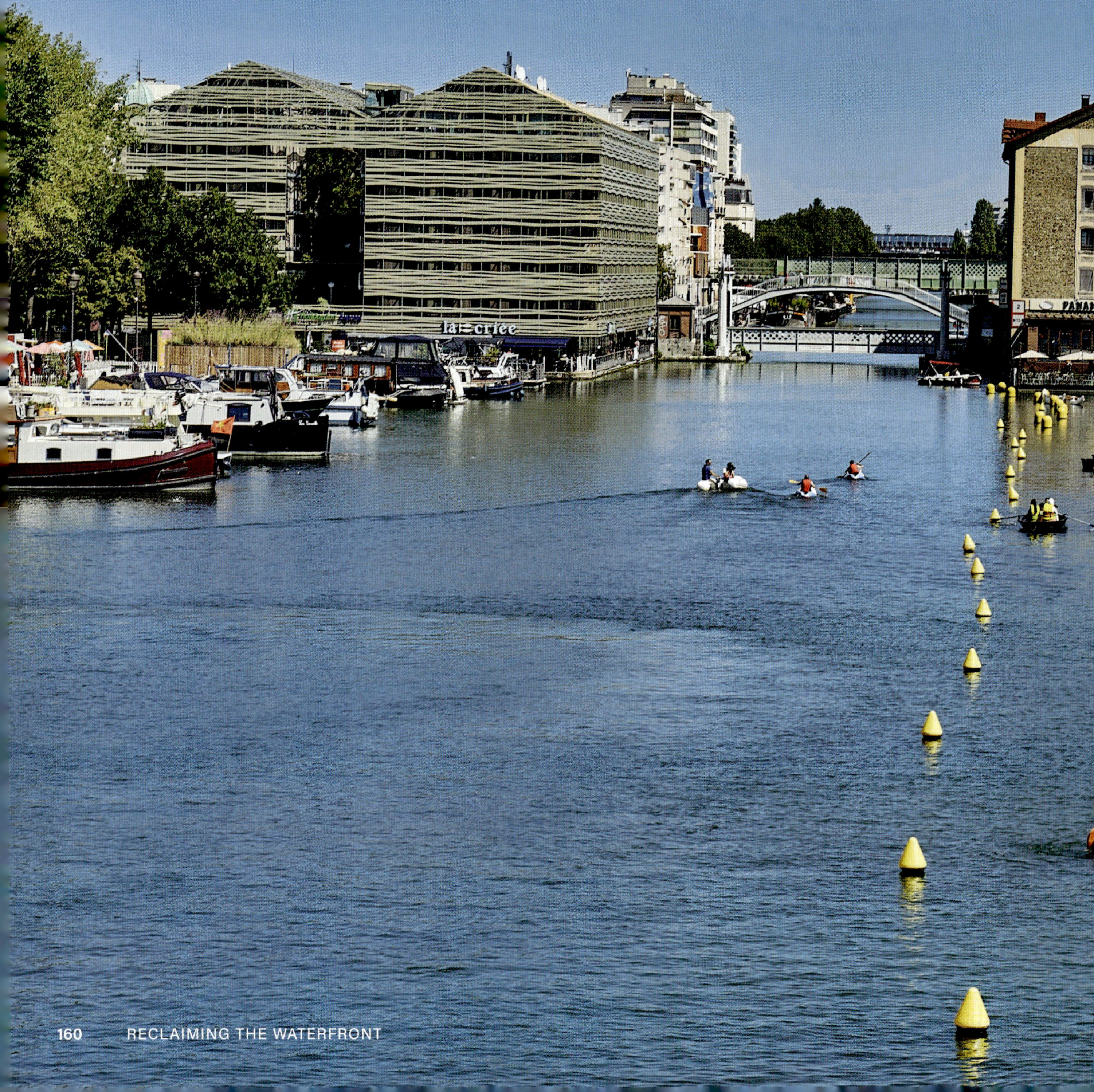

A second Paris Plages location is at le bassin de la Villette in the northern 19th arrondissement. The basin was first filled in the early nineteenth century as a source of drinking water, and there were leisure activities along the shore for residents nearby. It became a commercial center for boats transporting goods through the canal systems of Paris. Now the recreational activities have returned: Yellow paddle boats are on the water.

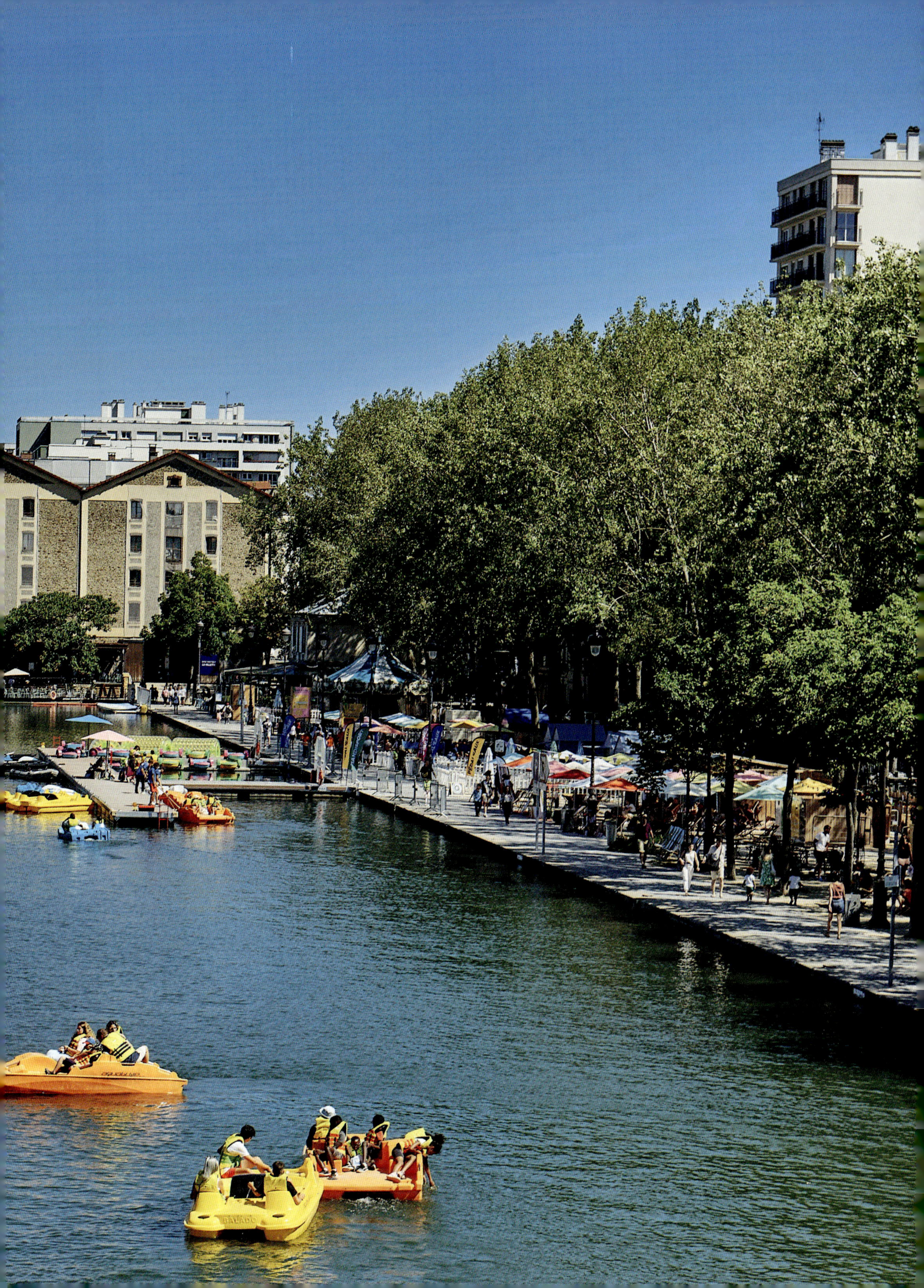

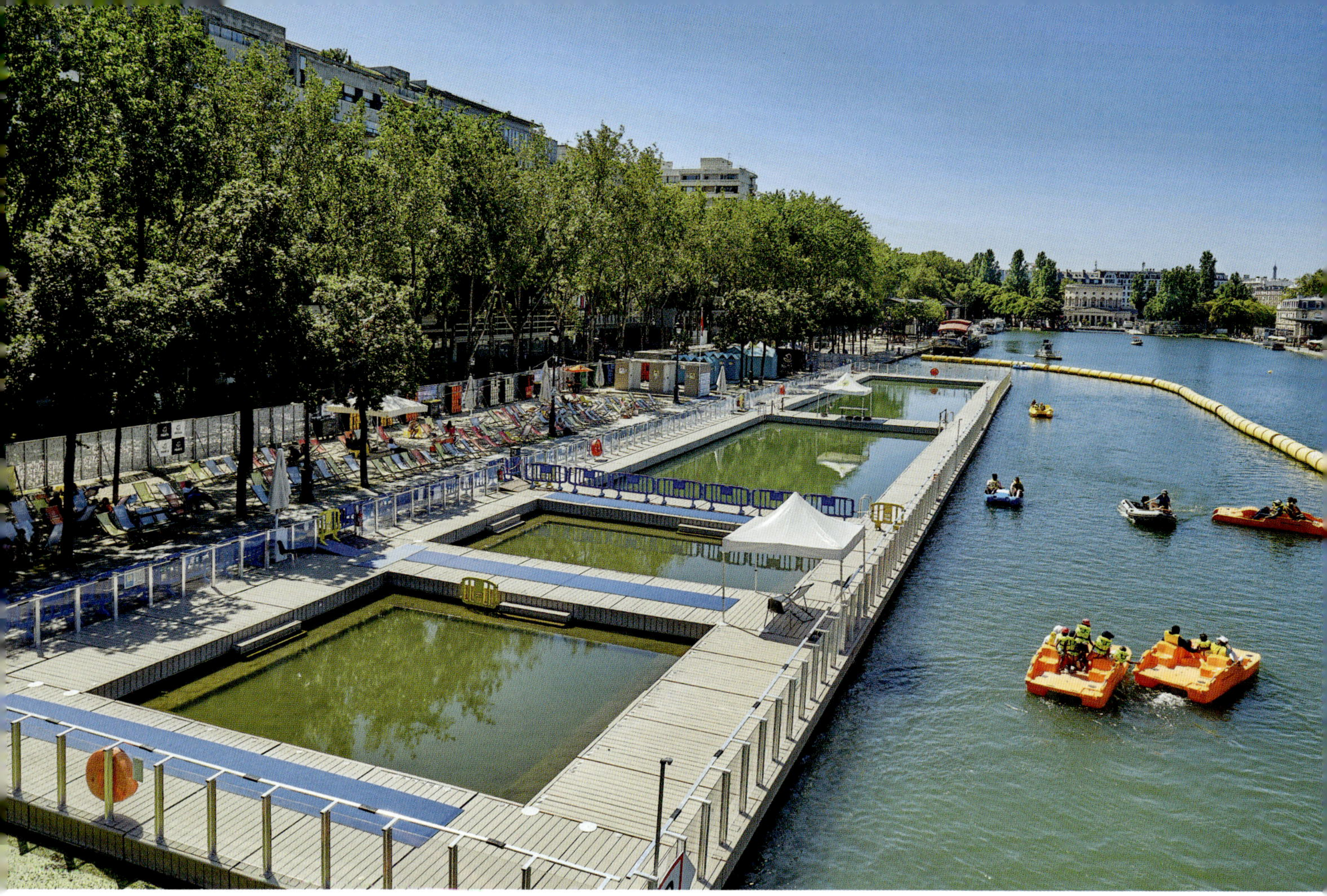

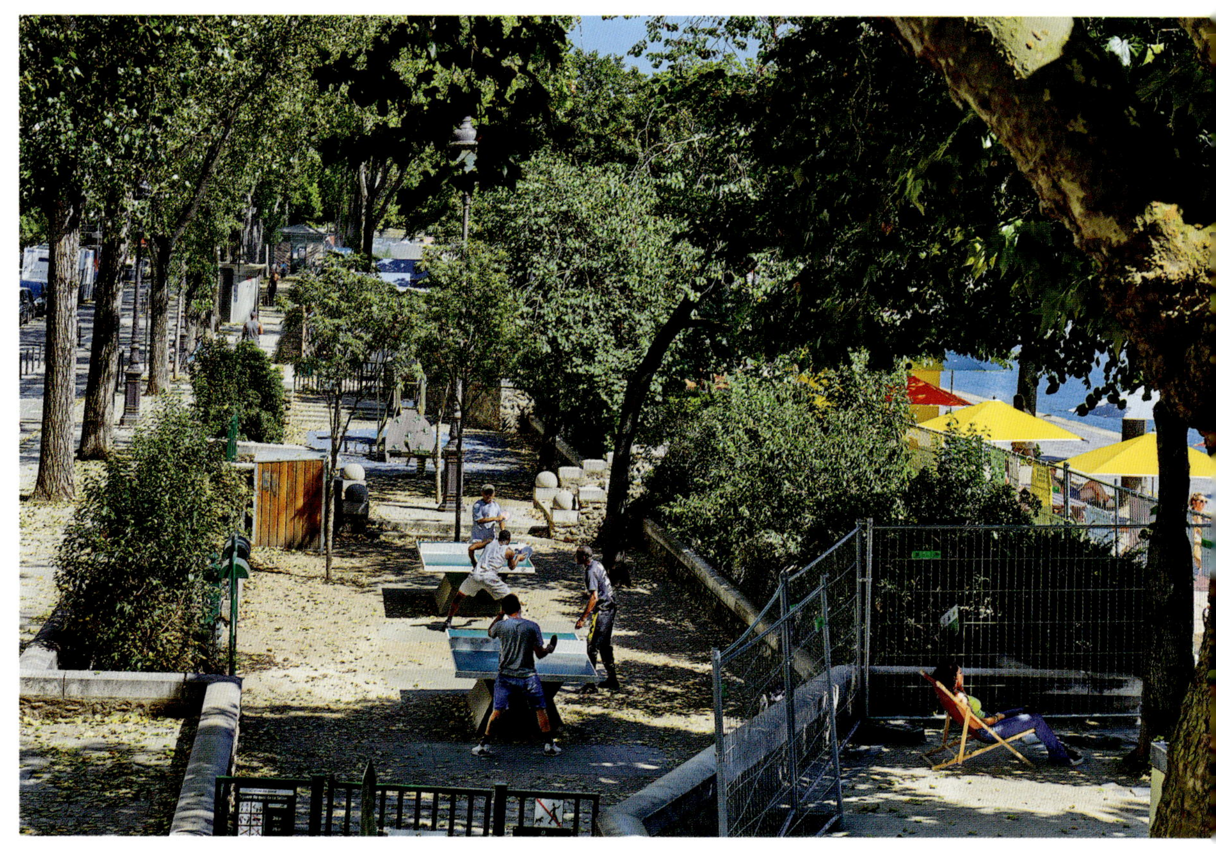

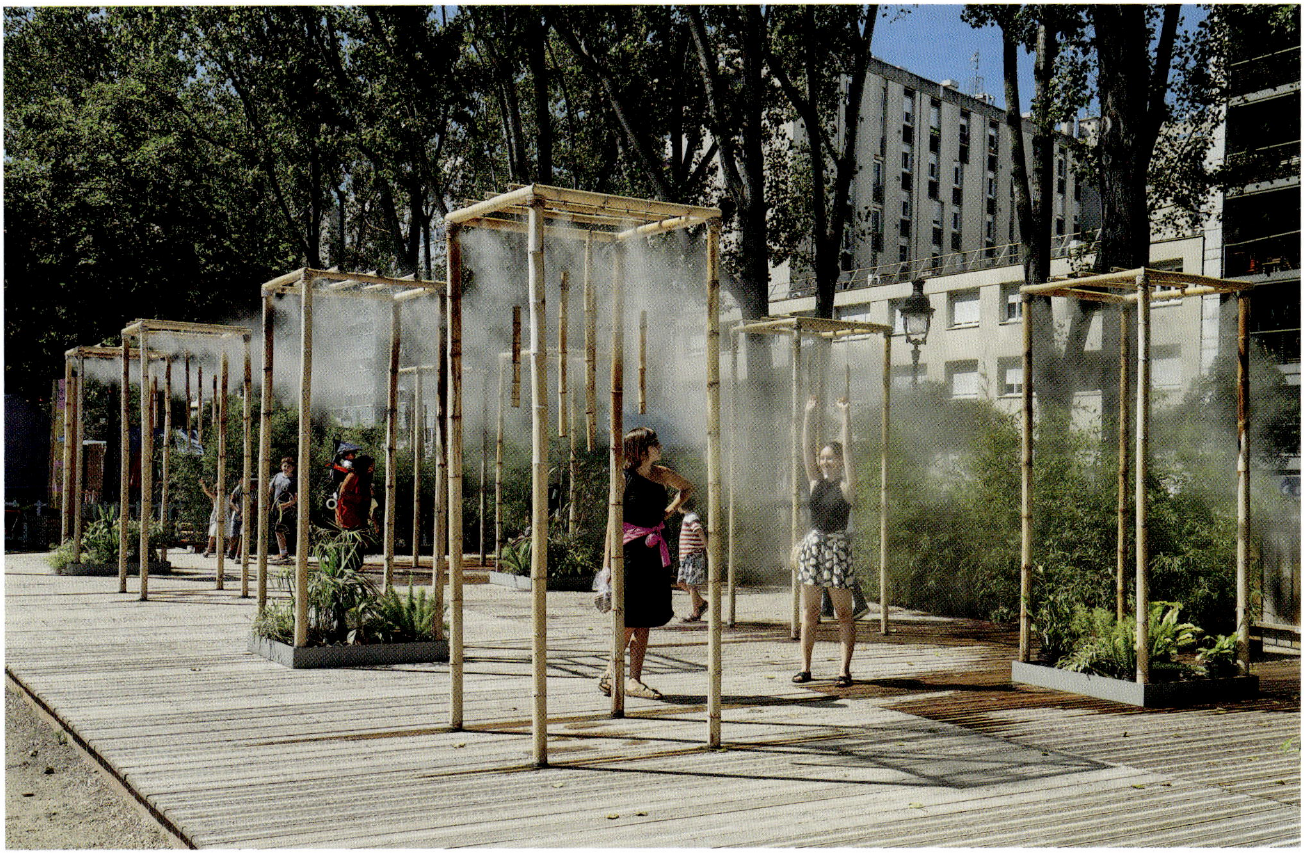

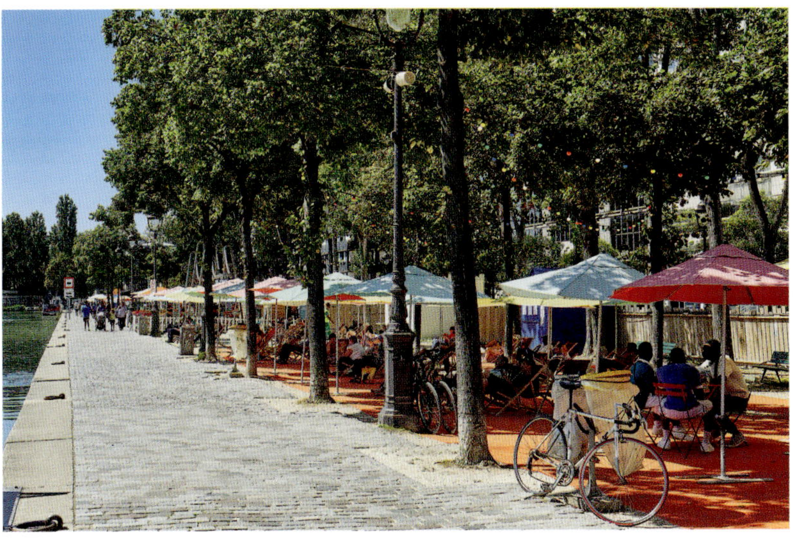



**OPPOSITE ABOVE**
Floating swimming pools in le bassin de la Villette are open during the summer months as part of the Paris Plages program.

**OPPOSITE BELOW**
Ping-Pong tables were also installed in the park.

**ABOVE**
Activities are on both sides of the basin. A footbridge over the water allows people to easily go from one side to the other. The cooling stations provide mists of water automatically.

**ABOVE LEFT**
Just like on the beaches of the Seine, food carts, tables, and chairs are set up waterside.

## *Canal Saint-Martin*

Le canal de l'Ourcq connects to le canal Saint-Martin and continues to the Seine river. Canal Saint-Martin was dug in 1826 and is known for its system of locks and a tunnel where the canal goes below ground.

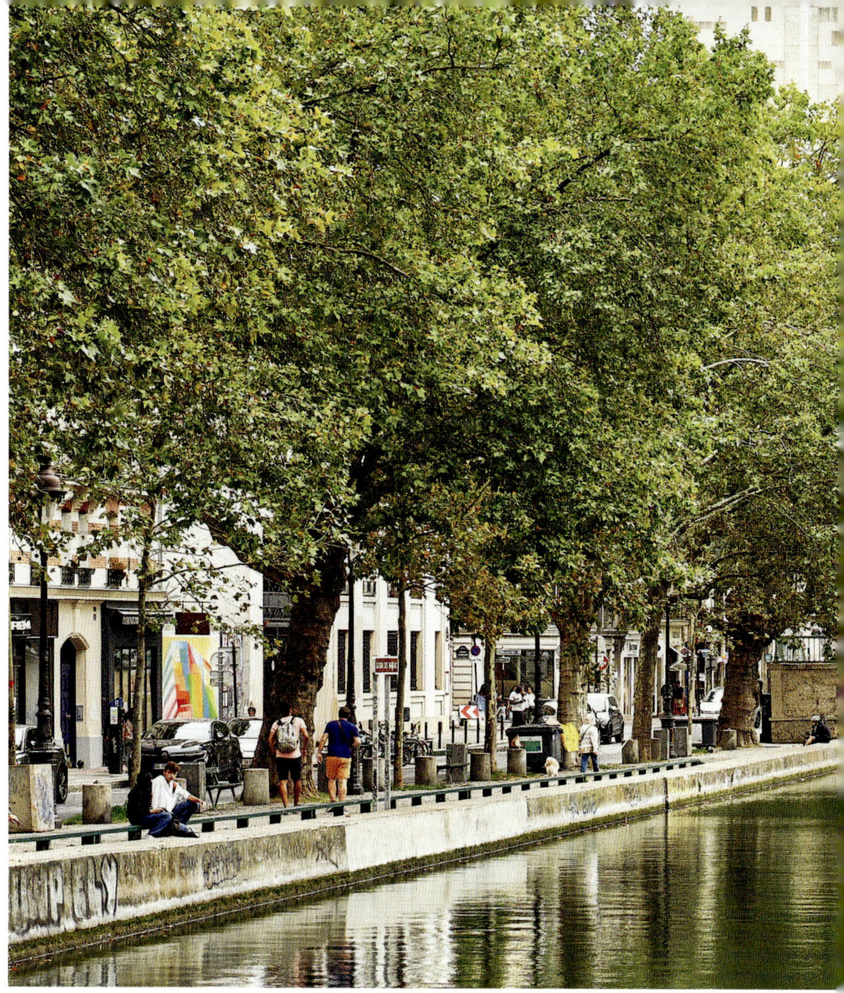

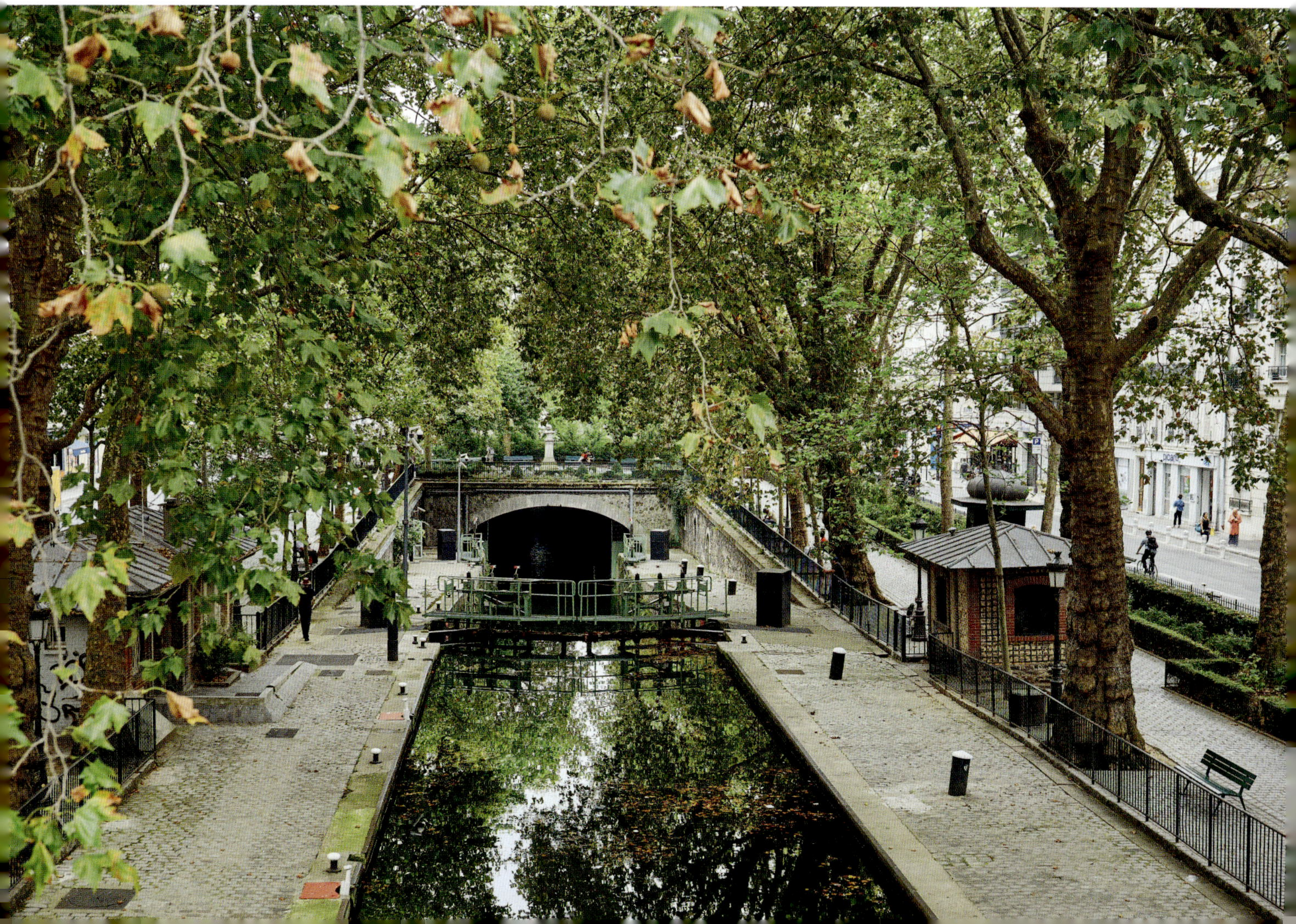

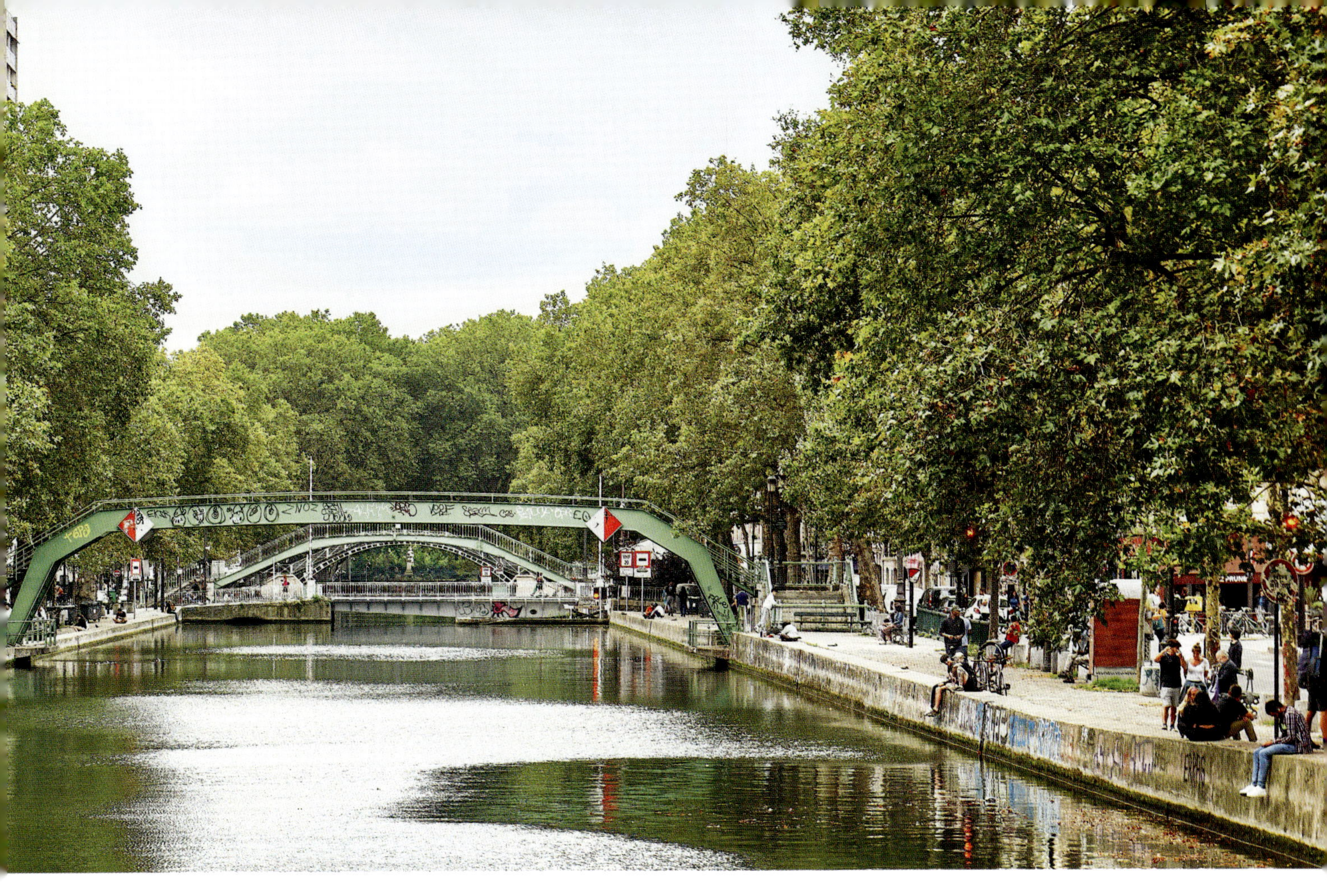



**ABOVE**
One of the ten bridges over le canal
Saint-Martin at quai de Jemmapes in the
10th arrondissement.

**OPPOSITE**
Rows of plane trees line the banks of
the canal. This double staircase bridge,
known as la passerelle des Douanes, is
located at le square Frédérick-Lemaître.

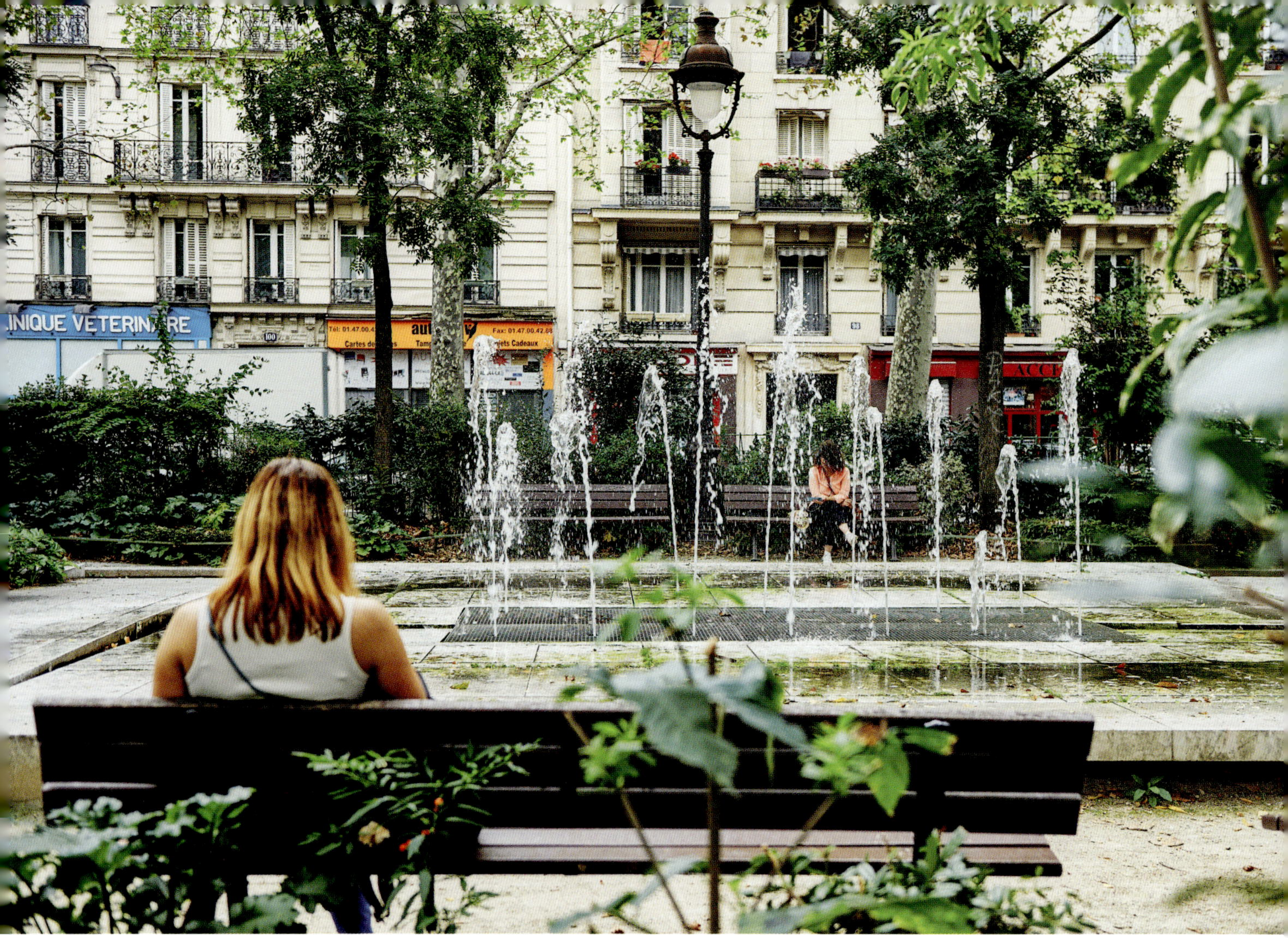

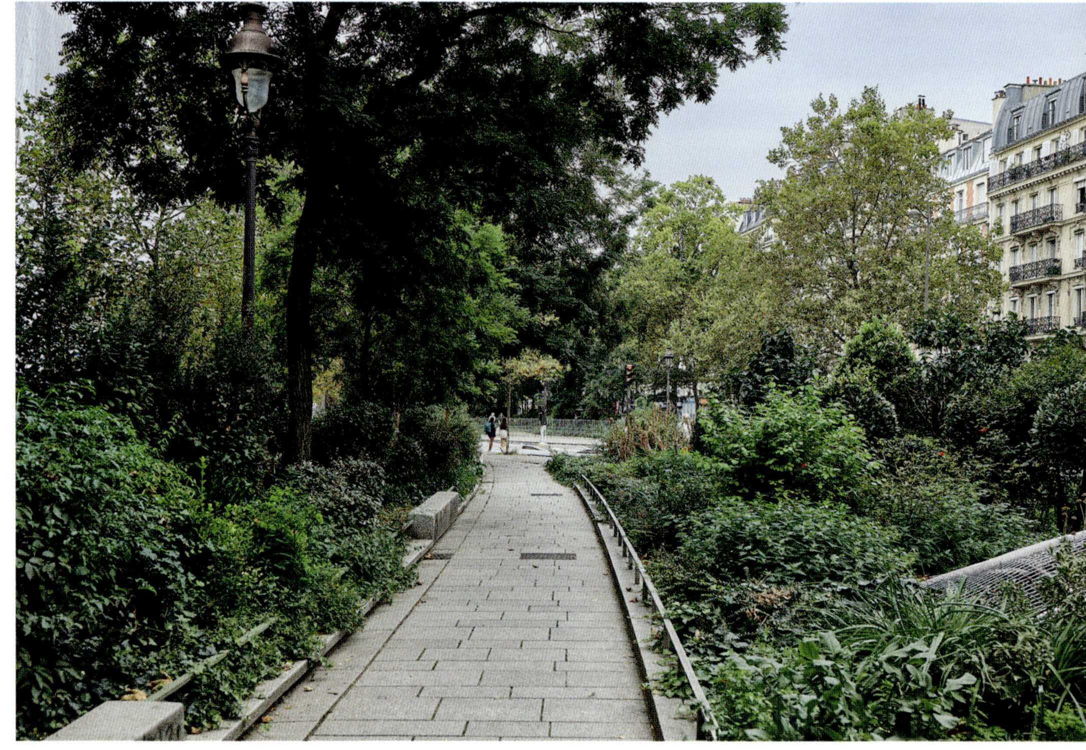

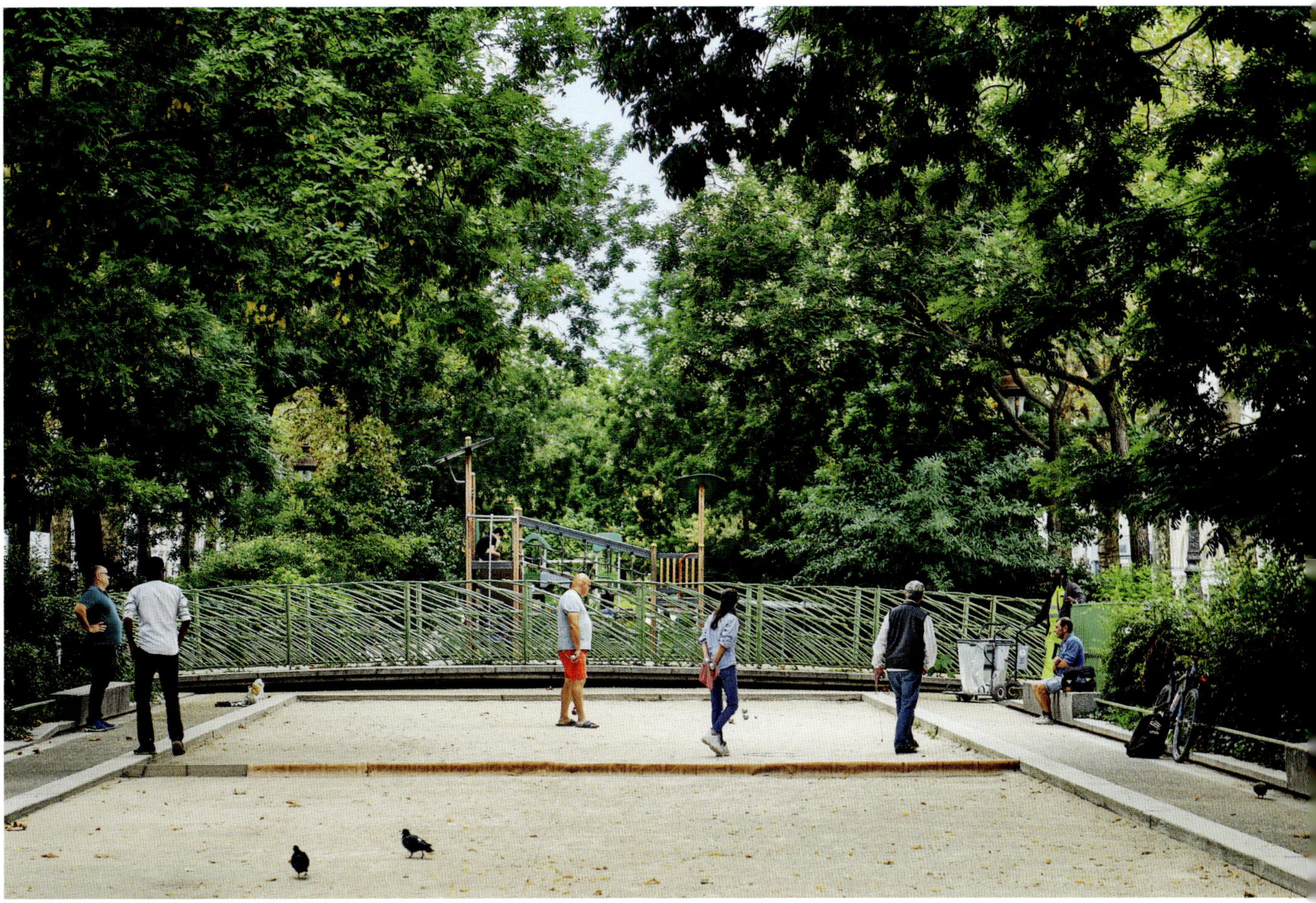

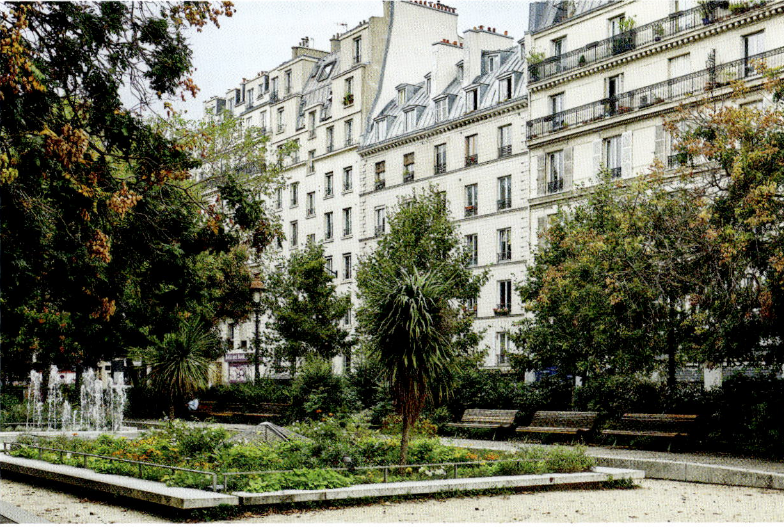

La promenade Richard-Lenoir–jardin May-Picqueray was first created in 1860 on the covered part of canal Saint-Martin that goes underground at l'avenue de la République to la place de la Bastille. Each of the four sections of the park references the canal below street level, with either a fountain or a pyramid-shaped skylight in the flower beds.

**OPPOSITE ABOVE**
The contemporary fountain alludes to le canal Saint-Martin below ground. The garden is an island of green between two streets.

**OPPOSITE BELOW**
The four park sections have a variety of plantings.

**ABOVE**
The park also has a pétanque court and a children's playground.

**ABOVE LEFT**
The canal can be seen below from the skylights in the center of the garden beds.

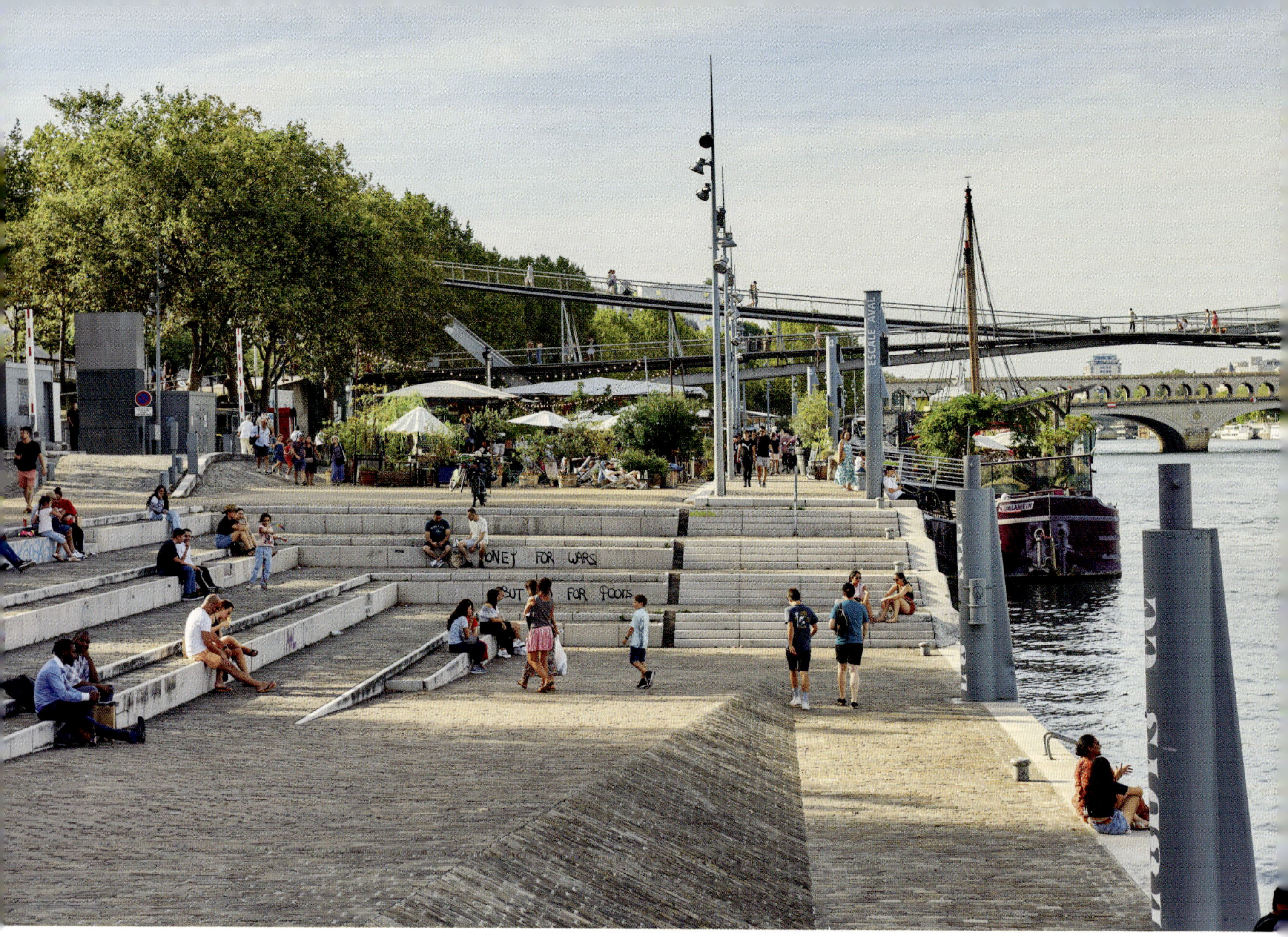

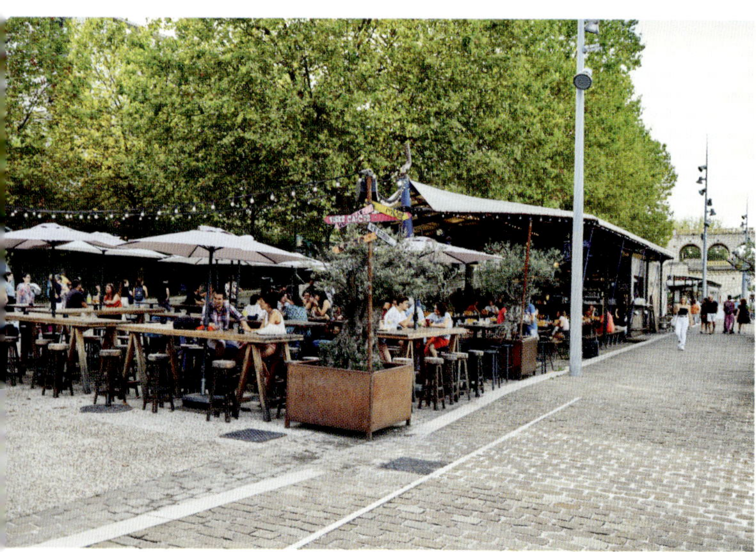

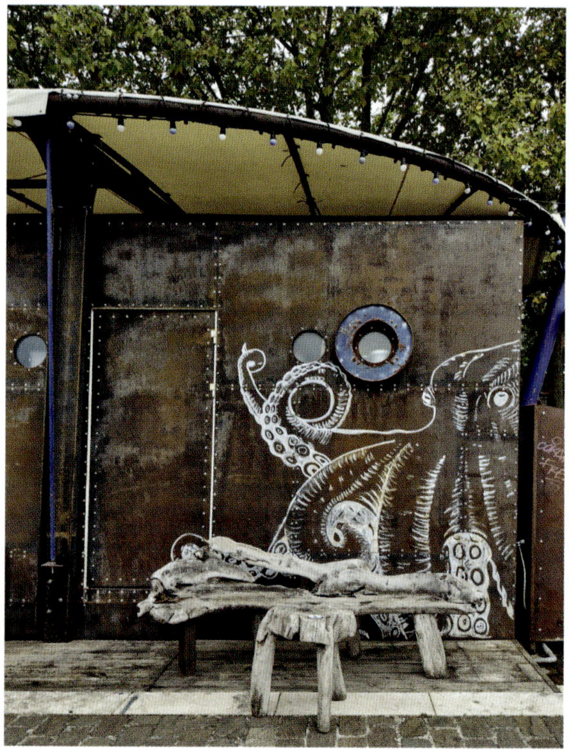

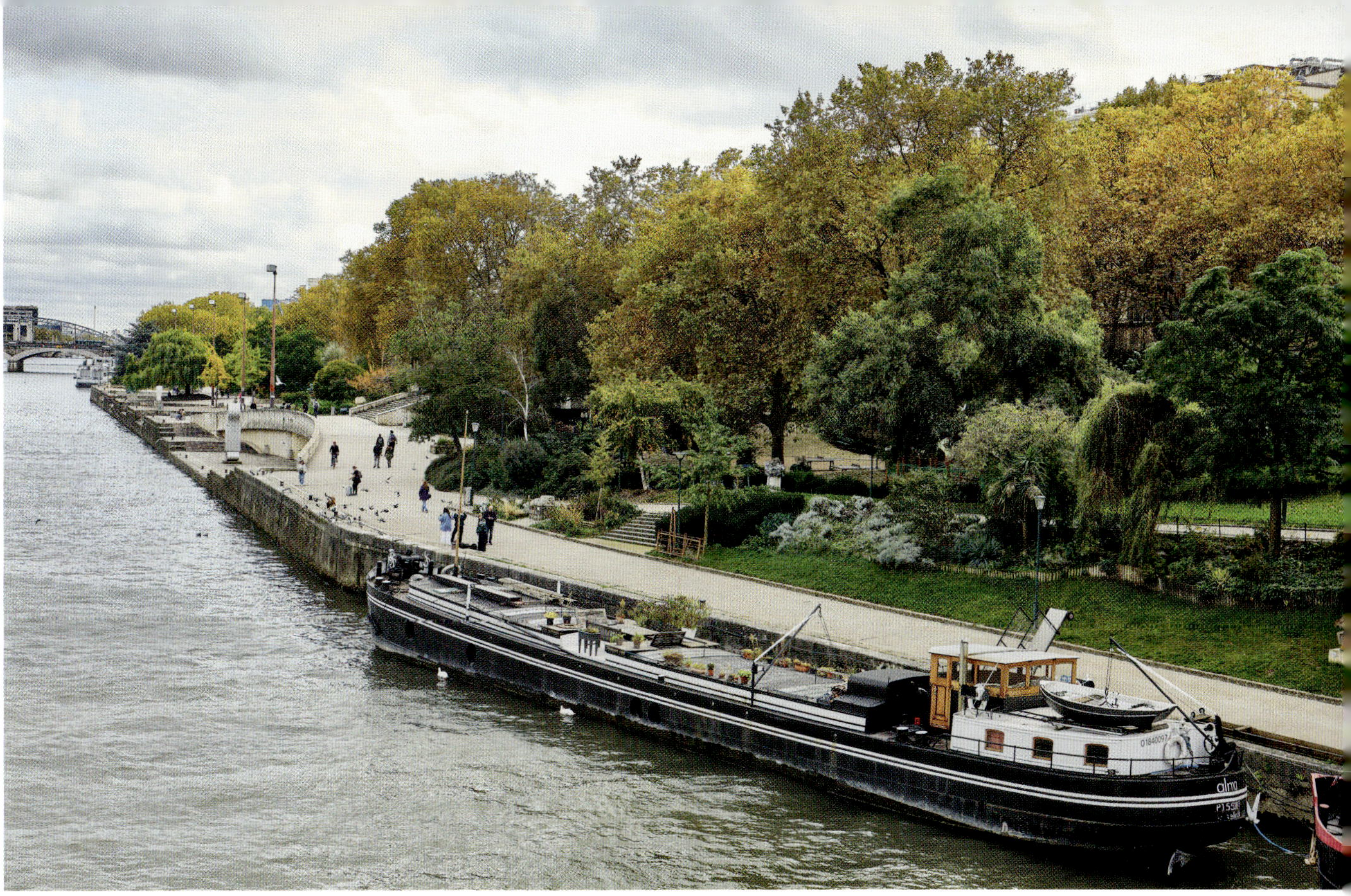

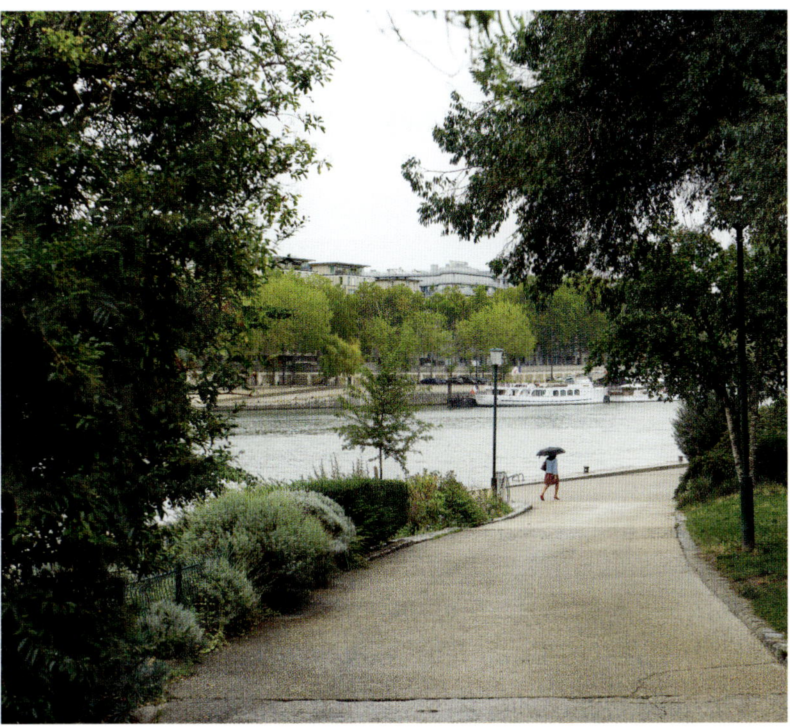



## *Quai de la Seine*

**OPPOSITE ABOVE AND BELOW LEFT**
Along le quai François-Mauriac, in front of la Bibliothèque nationale de France, there is a lot of new activity. There's a new seafood restaurant and bar along with a barge with a swimming pool named piscine Joséphine Baker. It is a popular spot with bike riders. This district called Choisy–Jeanne d'Arc–Seine in the 13th arrondissement went through a City of Paris beautification program named Embellir Votre Quartier.

**OPPOSITE RIGHT**
A weathered bench made of driftwood was placed against a painting of an octopus at the seafood restaurant.

**ABOVE AND LEFT**
Le jardin Tino-Rossi on le quai de la Seine's left bank was named for the famous singer of the 1940s and 1950s. This riverside garden in the 5th arrondissement is both intimate and monumental. It was built as an outdoor sculpture park, with works by artists such as Constantin Brâncuşi and César Baldaccini. The treescape includes plane trees, cherry trees, a poplar, black pines, and magnolias.

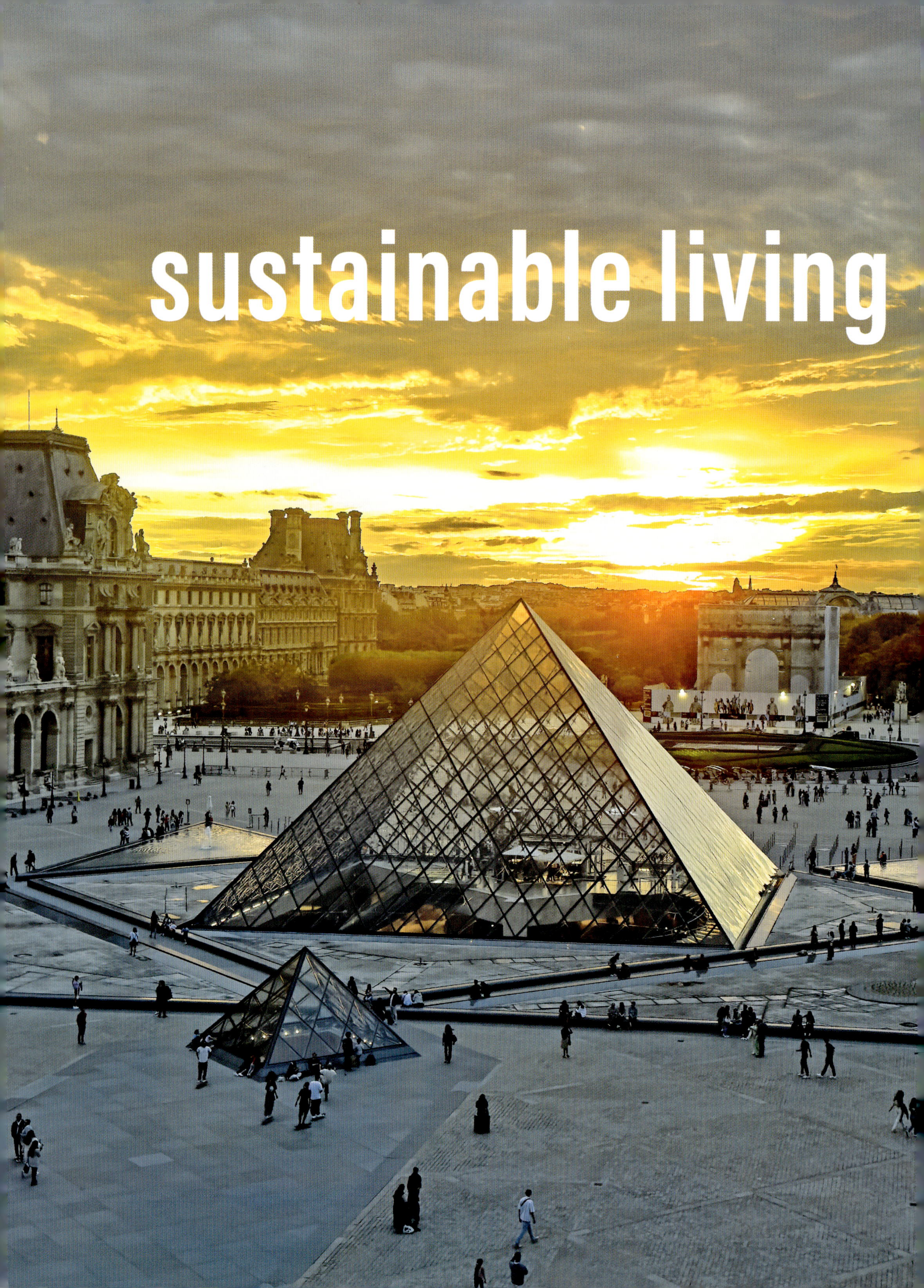

sustainable living

# / la vie durable

What does sustainable living look like in Paris? In many ways, Paris has had the qualities of a sustainable city for a long time. Existing architecture has been adapted and reused for centuries. Second-hand fashion and furnishings have been sold at Paris flea markets in Saint-Ouen-sur-Seine since the 1860s. The city has been ahead of its time by supporting and providing space for its famous outdoor markets. Paris has always been one of the most walkable cities. These days the city is in the process of becoming an even more livable place. Bike lanes are replacing car lanes, which reduces air pollution. There are now more biofuel buses and electric trams. Food entrepreneurs are creating urban farms on the city's famous rooftops. Vegan and vegetarian restaurants of all kinds are flourishing. Natural wines whose producers are paying attention to organic growing processes, ingredients, and worker protections are appearing in wine bars and on restaurant wine lists. Designers are rethinking and recycling fashion and a circular economy. The people behind these stories are making a difference, each in their own way. This is only a start, and it is impressive.

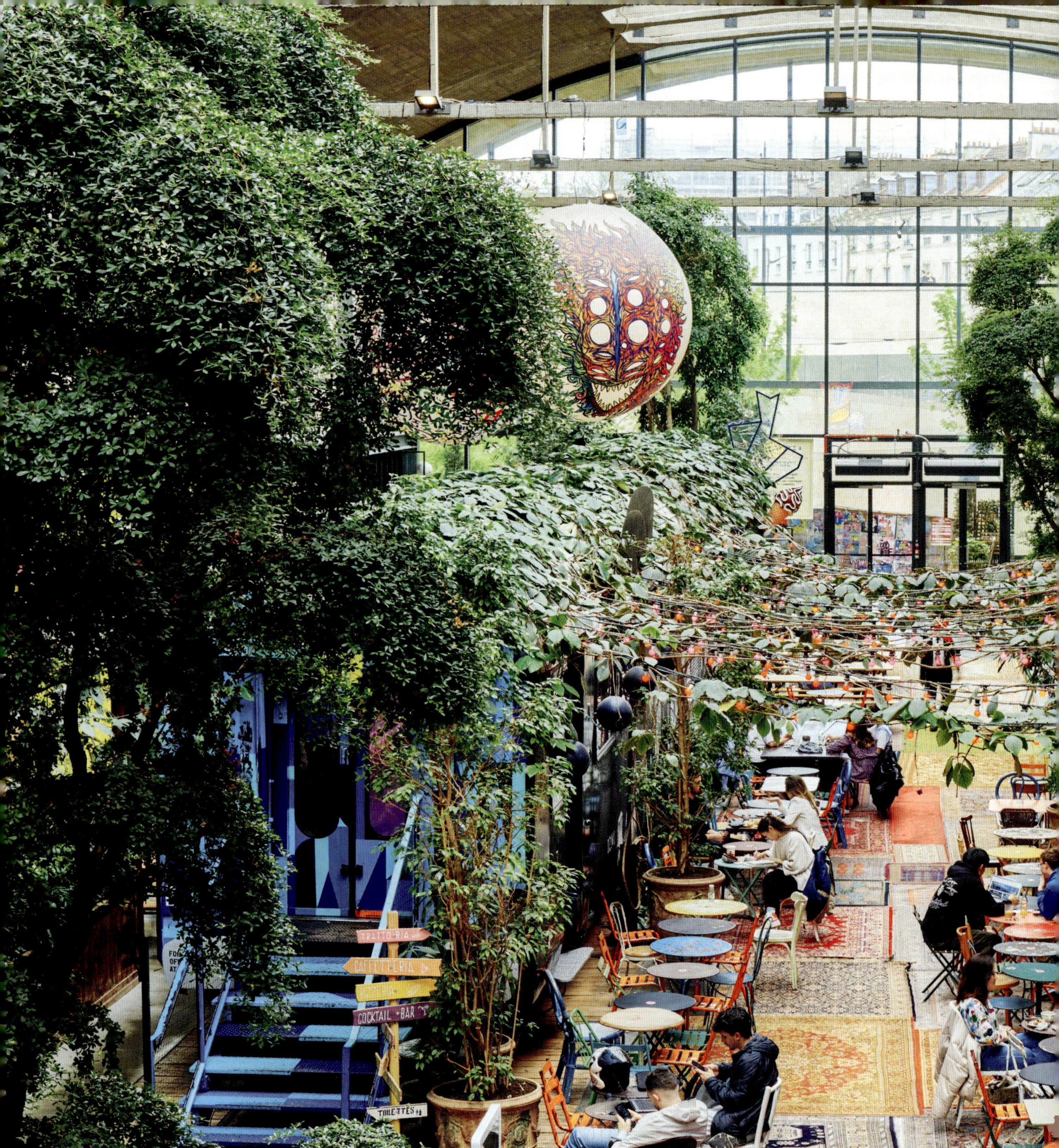

TRATTORIA
PASTICCERIA
PIZZERIA
COCKTAIL + BAR
TOILETTES

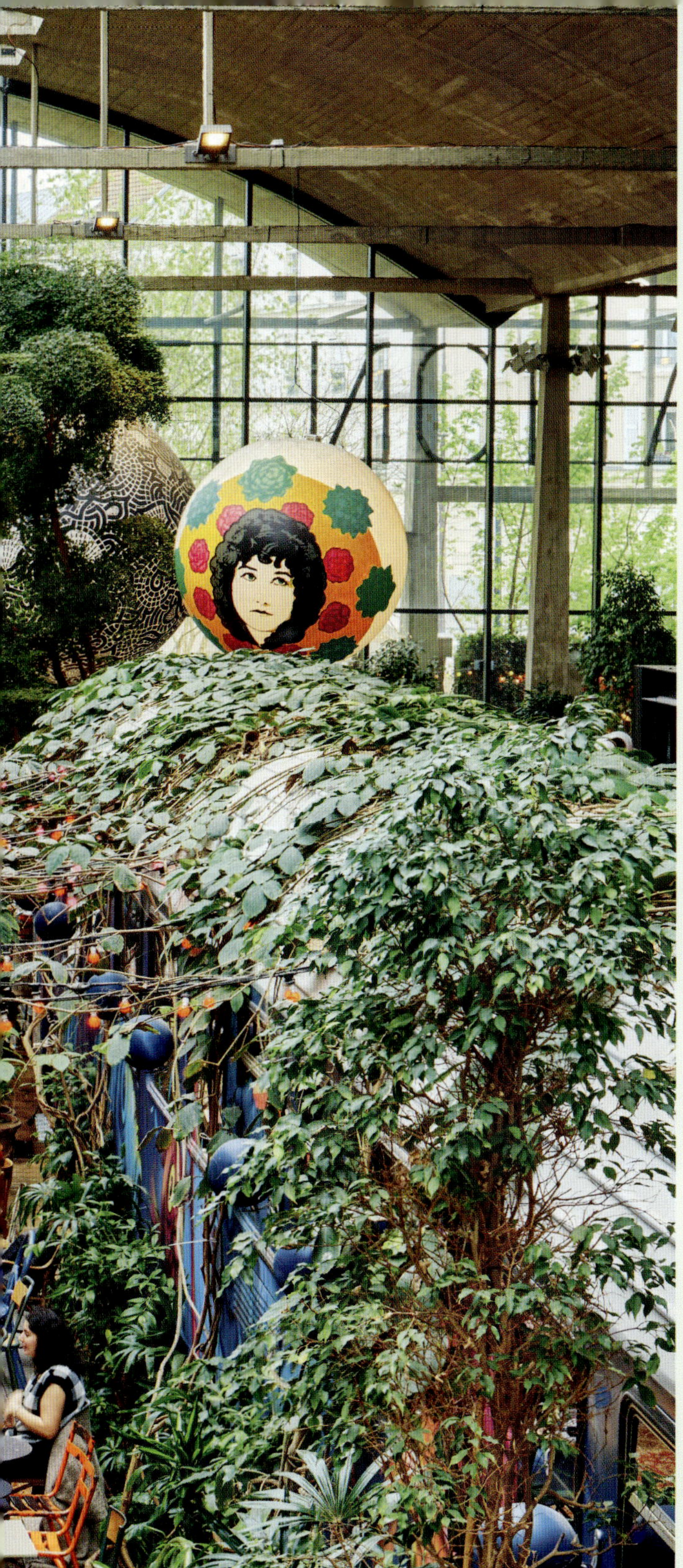



## ADAPTIVE REUSE: OLD BUILDINGS WITH A NEW PURPOSE

### *La Felicità* at *Station F*
13th arrondissement
2018

La Felicità was created by Victor Lugger and Tigrane Seydoux as part of their line of successful restaurants under the Big Mamma Group. A former property of SNCF, the national rail company, la halle Freyssinet was almost destroyed on more than one occasion, but it was also saved on more than one occasion, both by public objections and government intervention. It finally received protected status in 2012. Its concrete, arched structure, developed by the engineer it was named after, Eugène Freyssinet, originally opened in 1929, and it now holds Station F, a startup incubator, and La Felicità. The building was adapted and modernized by the team of architects at Wilmotte & Associés. The interiors by Studio Kiki, the in-house design team of Big Mamma Group who are behind the design of La Felicità, take a something-for-everyone approach, yet it doesn't feel like a traditional food hall. It is a collection of experiences, each one designed to be cozy and intimate. It seems impossible that a space that holds one thousand seats can have the intimacy of a café. The hall is divided. The middle section, which starts at the entry, offers small tables and chairs between two 1970s train cars, each covered in street-art-like works. Live trees and vines grow on and next to the trains. In the outer sections, a biergarten has a trellis support system that is covered in live plants, and a burger joint has its own space, defined by an overhead canopy of lights. On the right side, there is a bar with glass shelving that holds one thousand bottles of wine and alcohol, as well as a cafeteria and a pizza restaurant, from which orders are placed on a smart phone, with pickup alerts by text. Upstairs, there is another bar. La Felicità may appear to be a crowded jumble, but the underlying theme is pure joy.

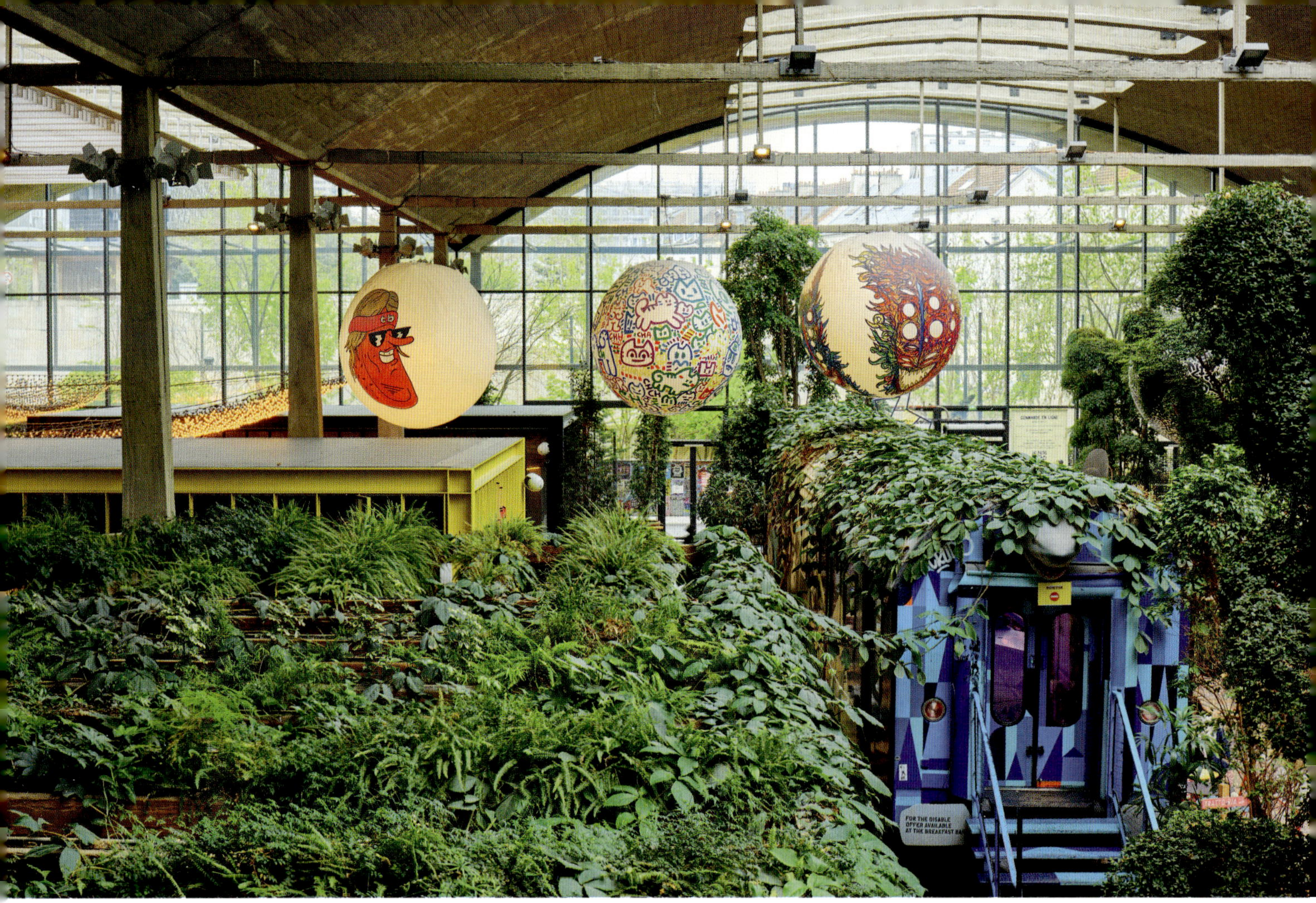

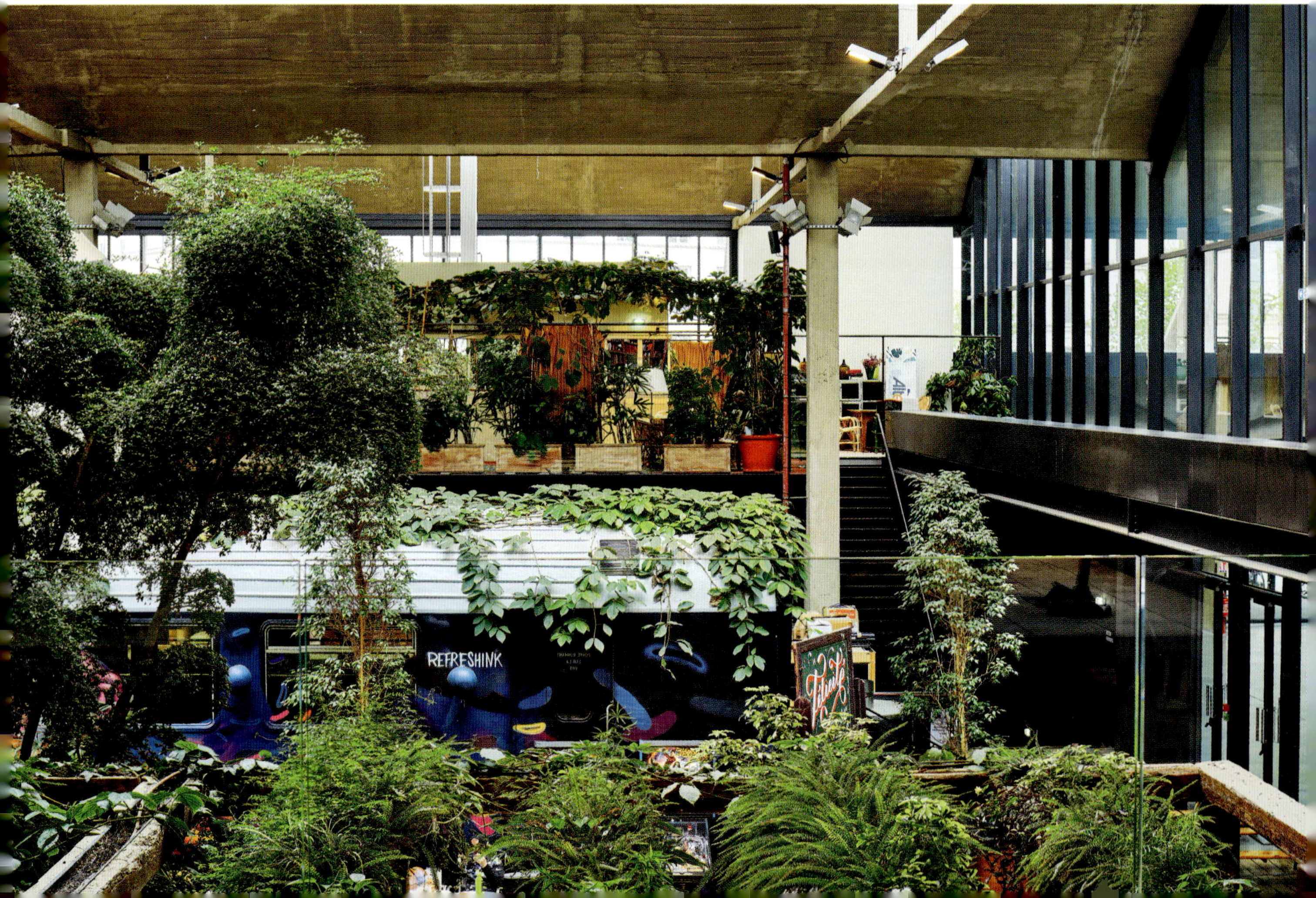

FOR THE DISABLED
OFFER AVAILABLE
AT THE BREAKFAST BAR

REFRESHINK

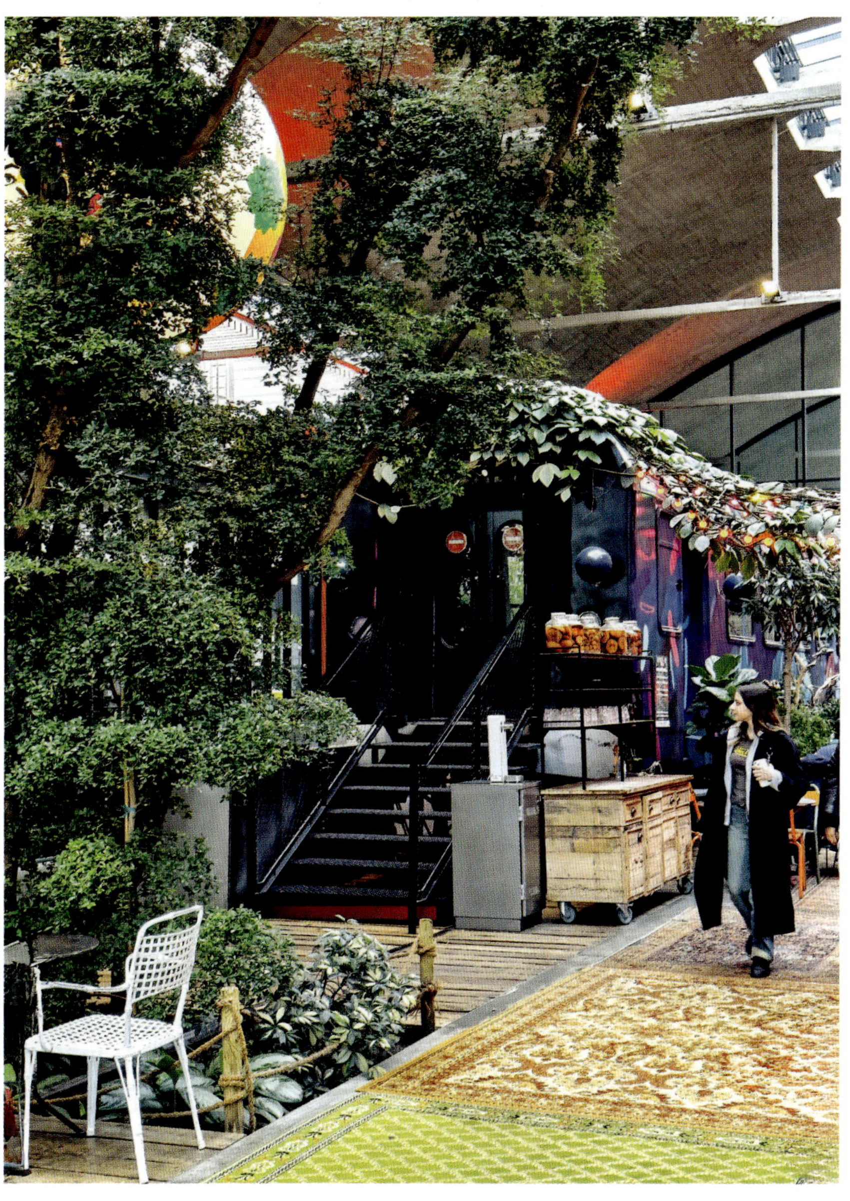

OPPOSITE ABOVE
The glass ceiling above the pergola of the biergarten brings in natural light to the plants inside. Local street artists, including Le Chat, painted the non-backlit balloons, which are periodically changed out for different designs. They bring an air of levity to the space.

OPPOSITE BELOW
The vaulted concrete ceilings are part of the original 1929 design. Plants grow among the train cars and on the wooden trellis of the biergarten.

ABOVE
Trees are planted directly into beds of dirt. A collection of layered carpets conceals a concrete floor, making the room even more color filled and cozy.

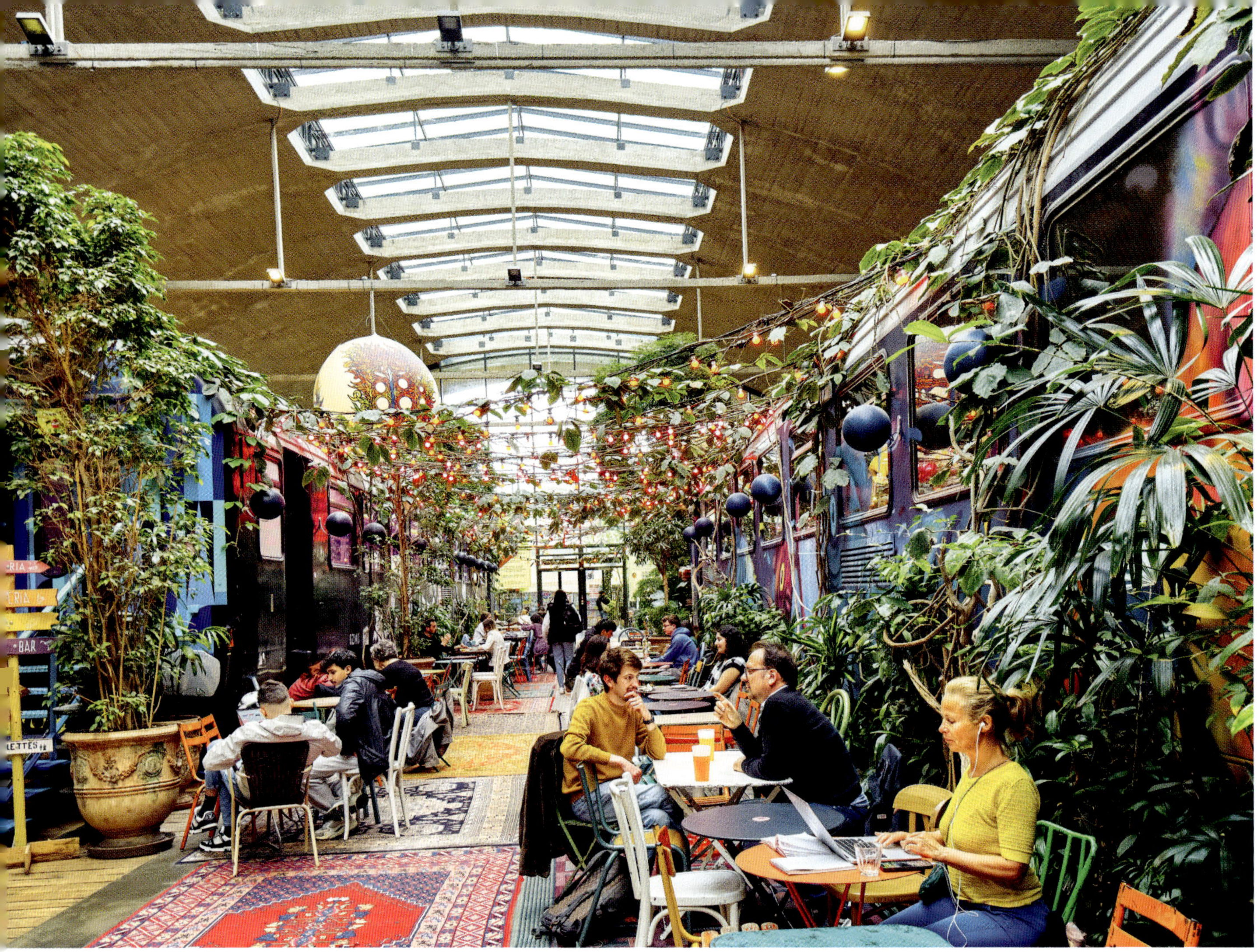

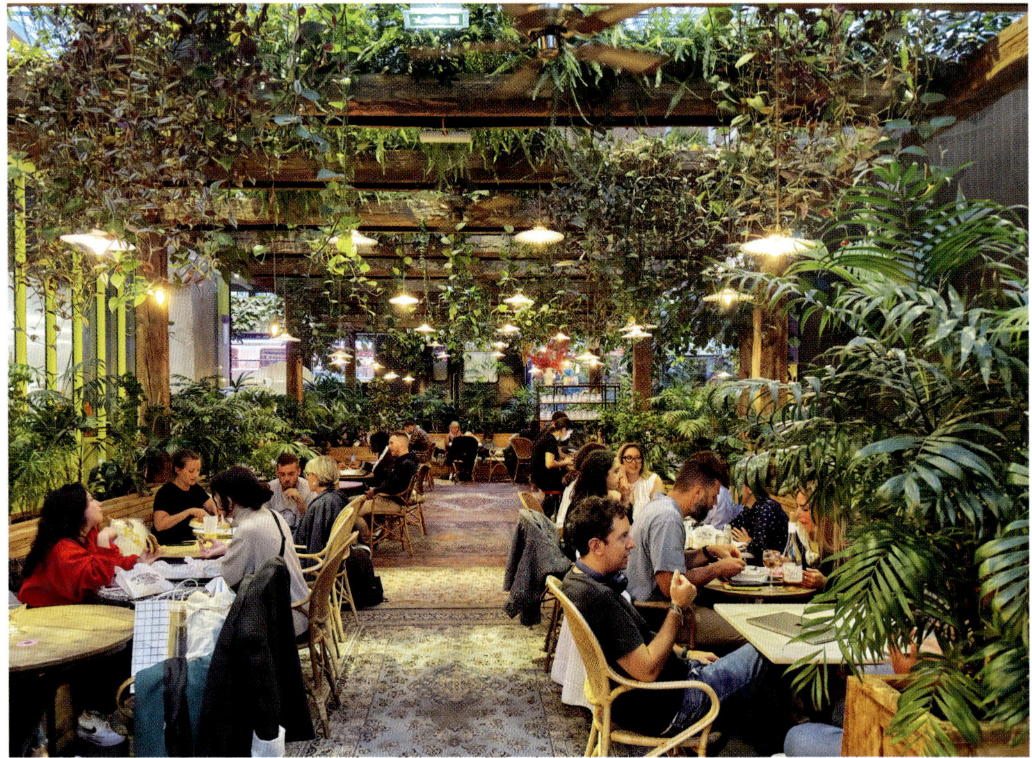

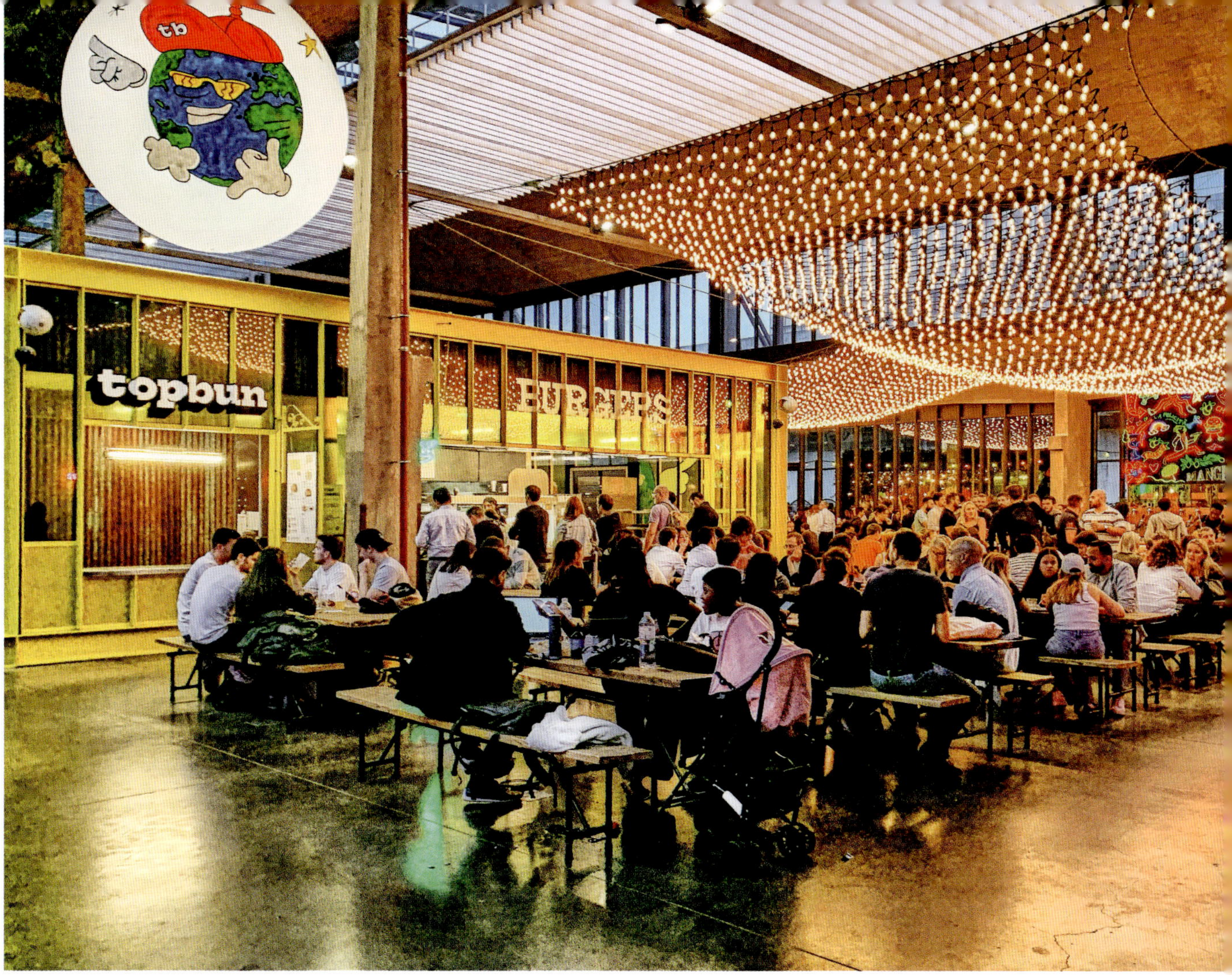

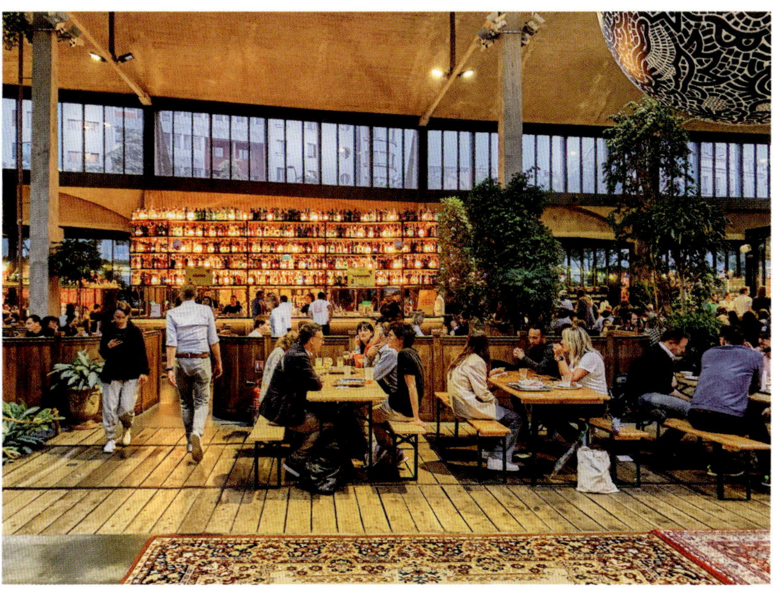



**OPPOSITE ABOVE**
The main corridor is created by two train cars. The space is conducive to remote working as well as to drinks and food whose ingredients skew toward Italian, including pizza.

**OPPOSITE BELOW**
The numerous plants in the biergarten create a feeling of an outdoor terrace.

**ABOVE**
A canopy of fairy lights illuminates the tables near the burger restaurant.

**LEFT**
The cocktail bar glows with more than one thousand bottles backlit and placed on glass shelves. Windows starting at the ceiling run the length of the building and add openness to the space.

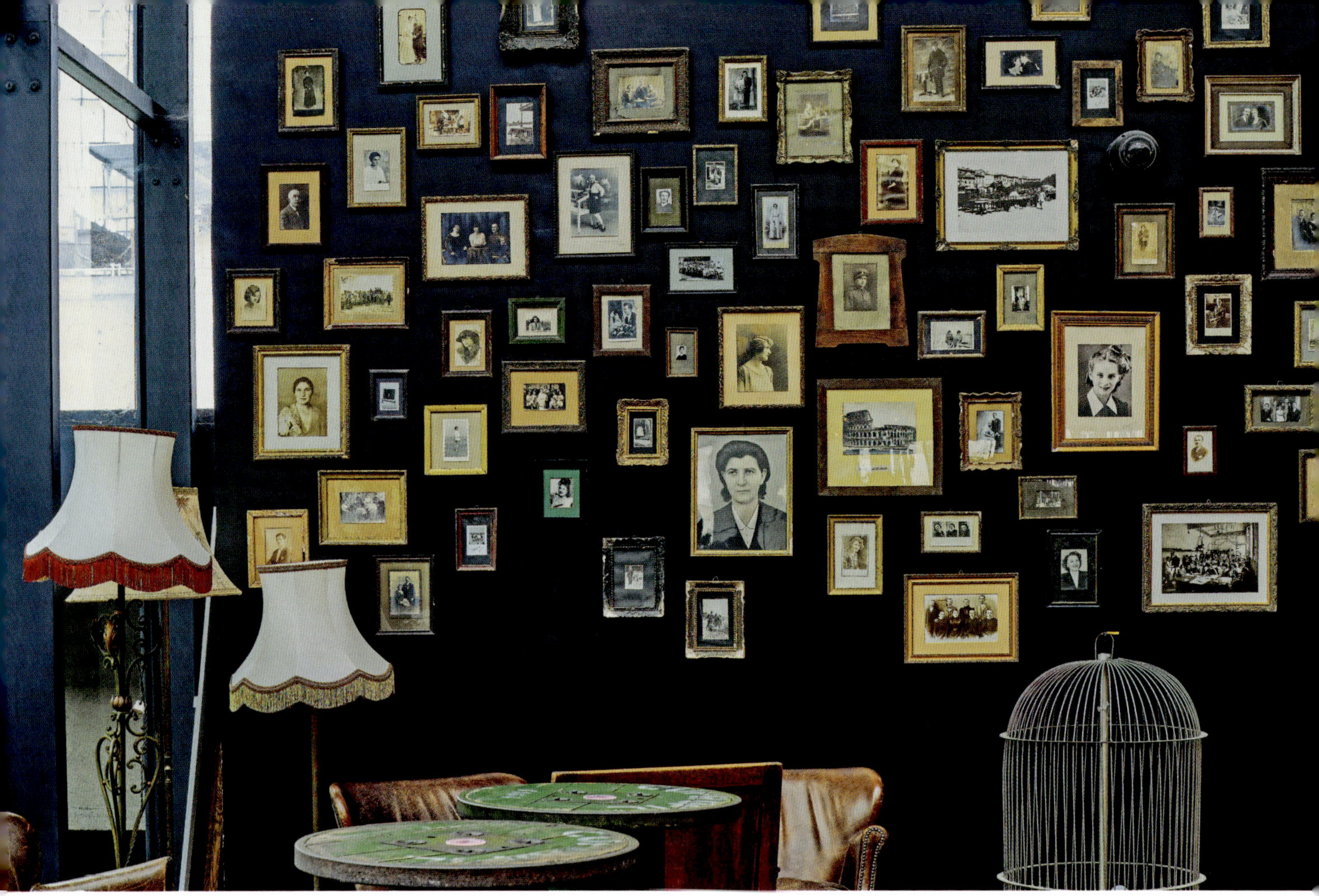

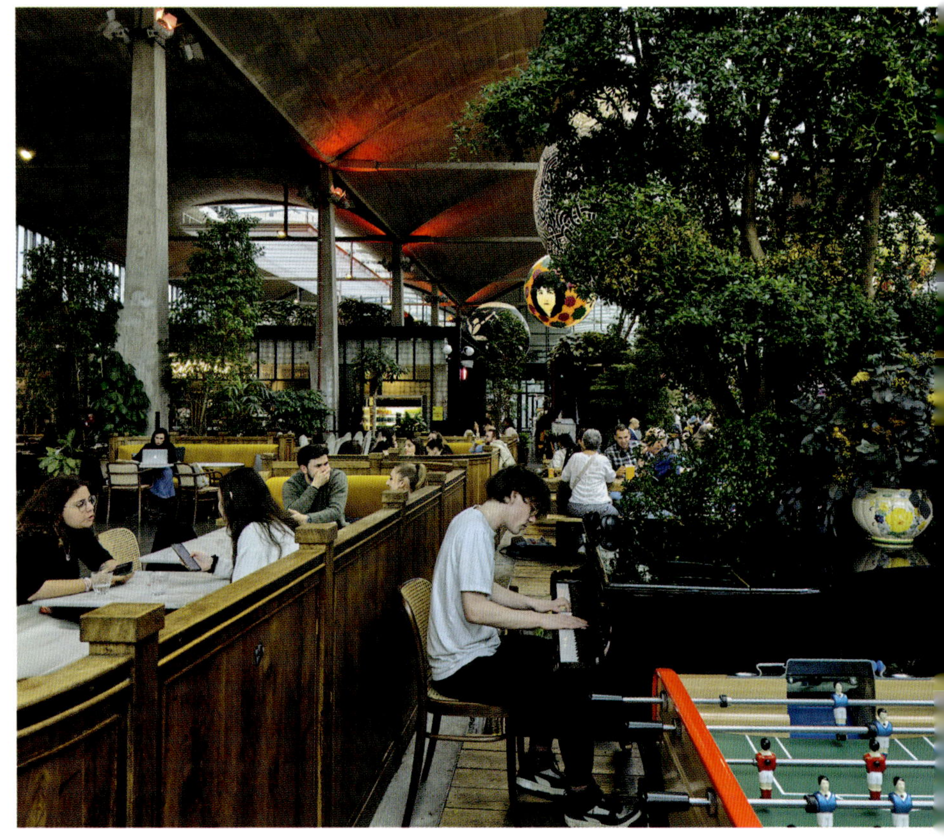

ABOVE
An upstairs bar is decorated with antique furnishings and a collection of random framed images.

RIGHT
Downstairs, near the entry, a piano is placed near the *table de baby-foot*, or foosball table.

OPPOSITE ABOVE
A collection of potted plants by one of the train carriages.

OPPOSITE BELOW
The ice cream shop inside the train car has neon lighting.

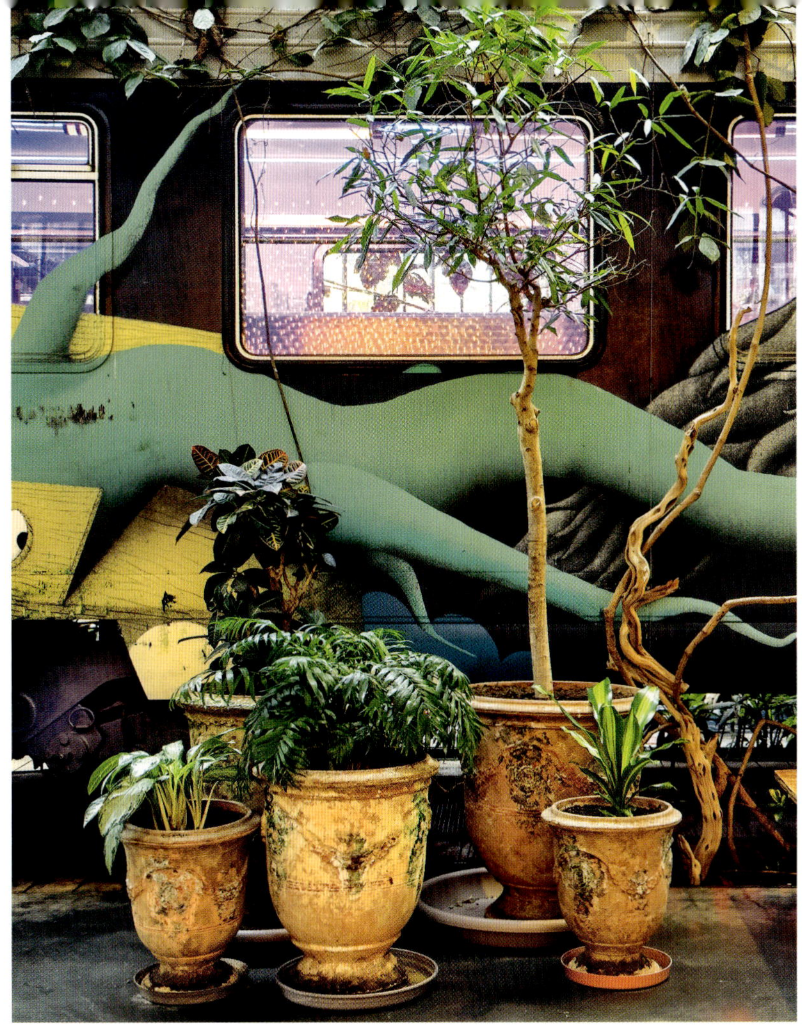

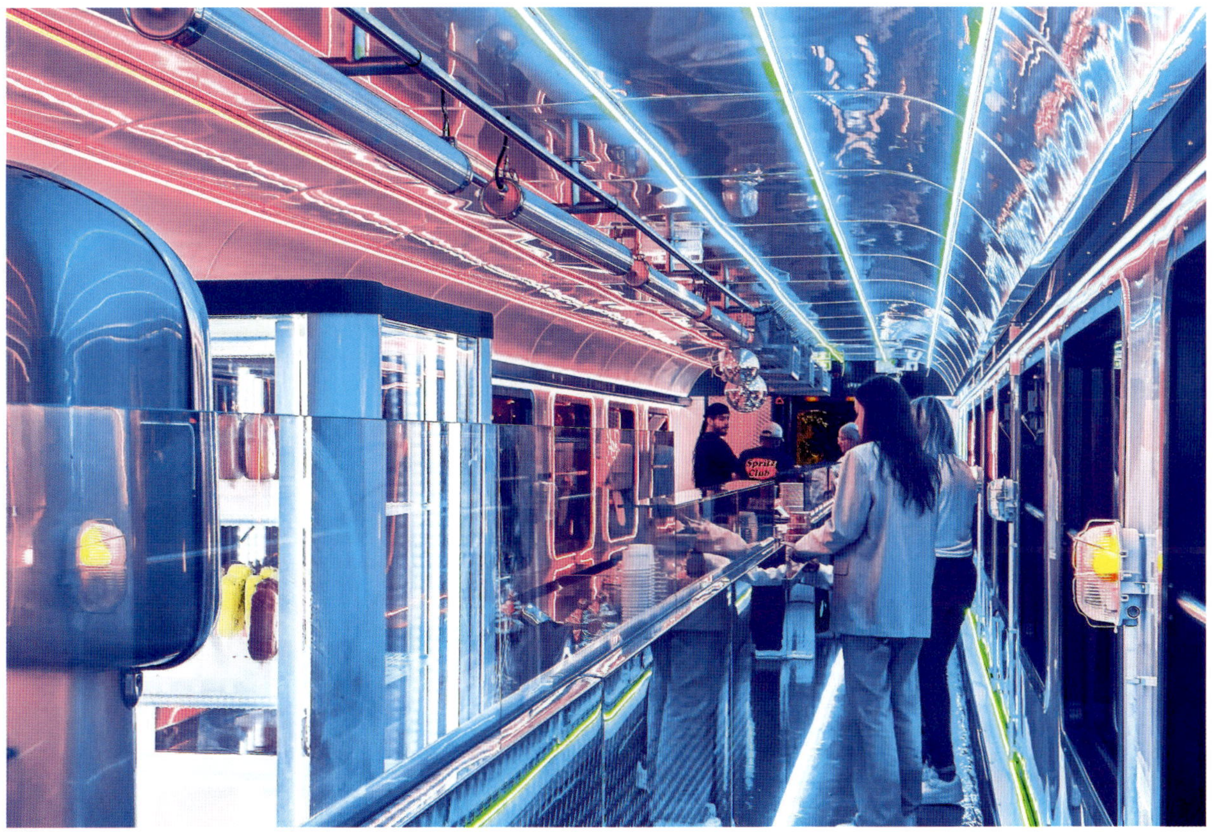

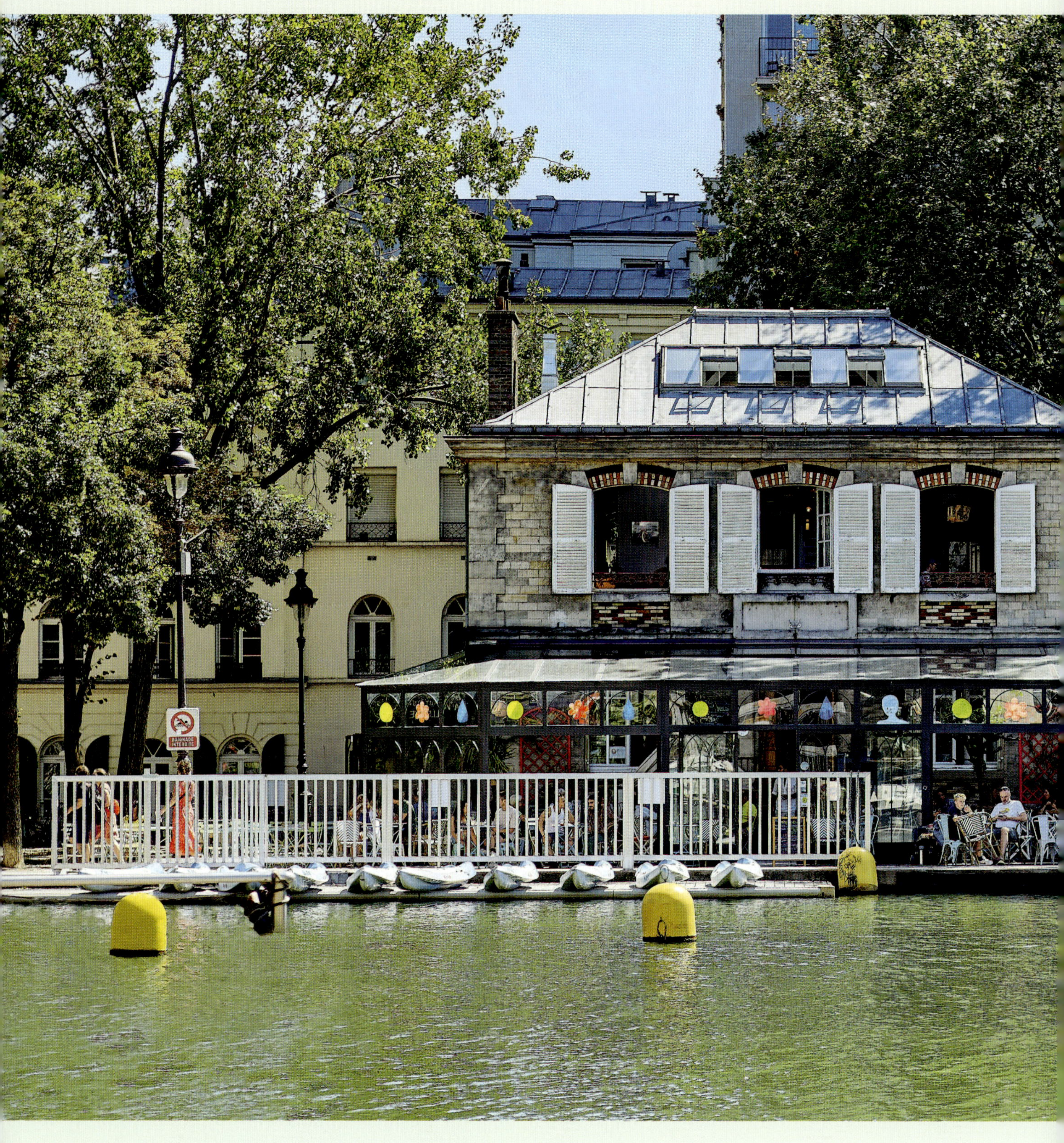

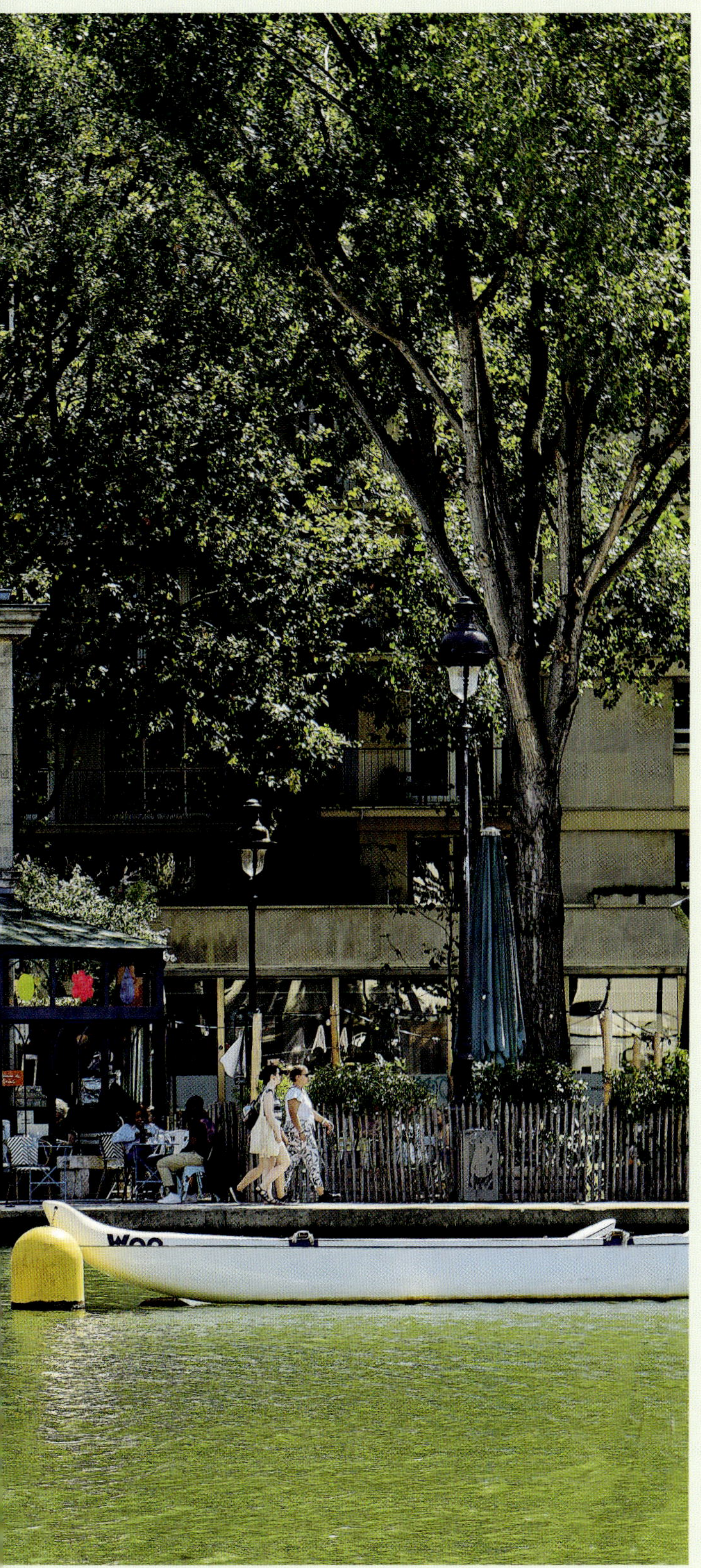

An abandoned nineteenth-century building on the banks of le bassin de la Villette has been revived as a café, restaurant, coworking space, and culture hub.

## *Le Pavillon des Canaux*
19th arrondissement
2015

Alockkeeper's house on the banks of le canal de l'Ourcq, now called le bassin de la Villette, has been transformed into a *tiers-lieu* (or third space) with a restaurant, coworking areas, and a community space with an active calendar of cultural events. The restaurant extends from the enclosed glass façade extension to a terrace under the trees. Inside, each room has been decorated with recycled furnishings, the more colorful the better. Even the bathroom was converted into an office, with a bathtub as a desk looking out over the water. The property was renovated by Sinny&Ooko, a company that has reclaimed several historic properties in Paris, transforming these old buildings and giving them a new life. The design of each project they take on considers the site's location and the building's history as well as the socioeconomic demographics of the neighborhood's residents. Le Pavillon des Canaux is a member of Éco-table, an association of restaurants committed to sustainable practices in their business operations. Patrons must order drinks at the bar. There's a convivial feeling of belonging in the act of fetching your own drinks.

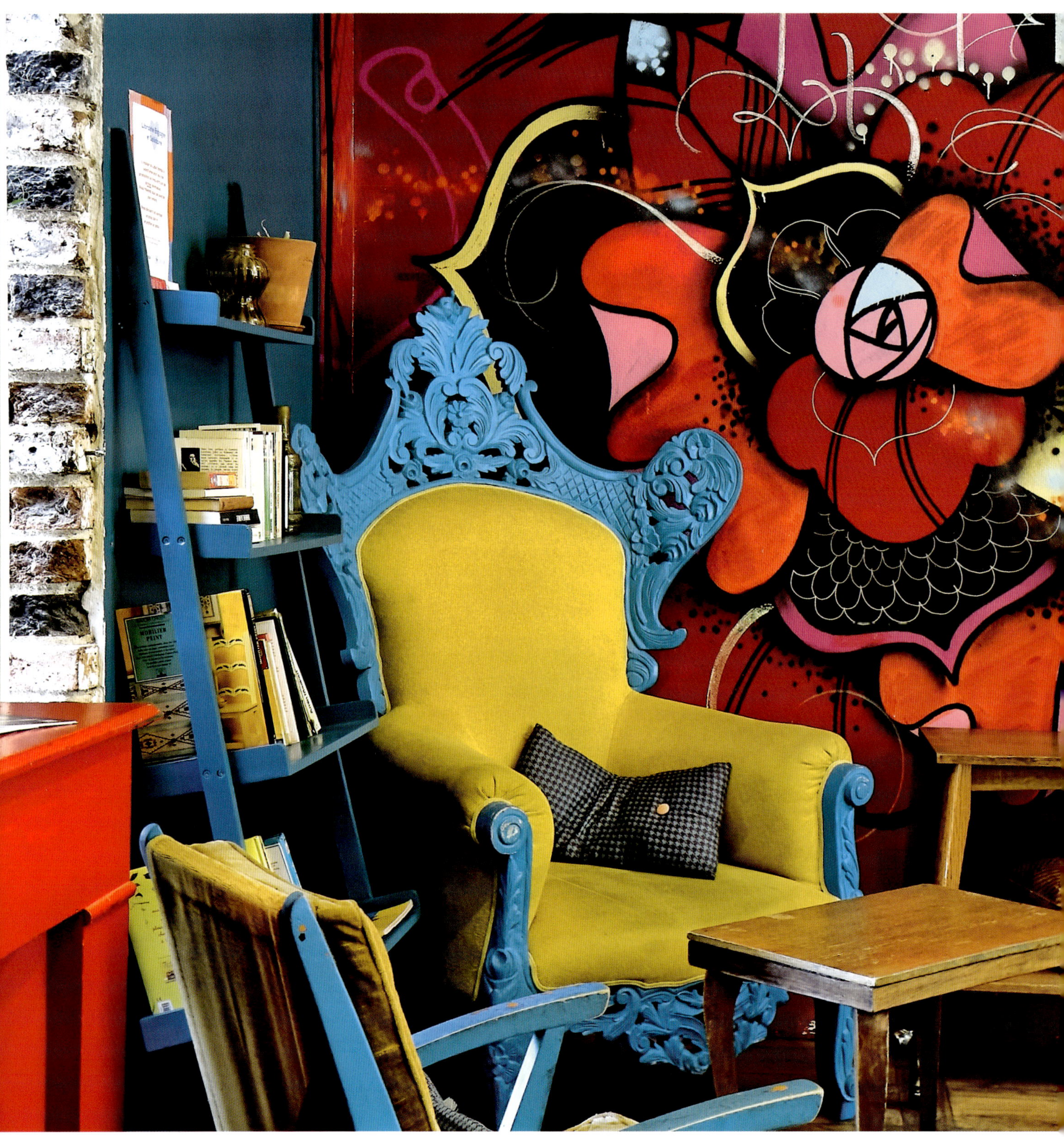

  *LE PAVILLON DES CANAUX*

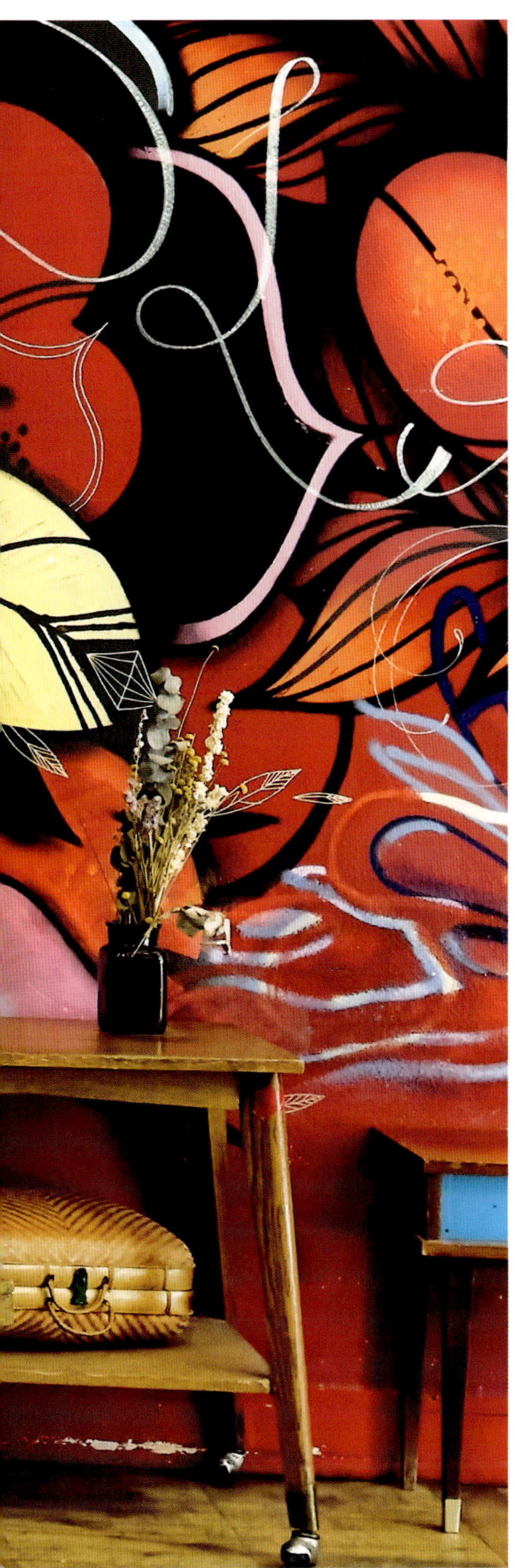

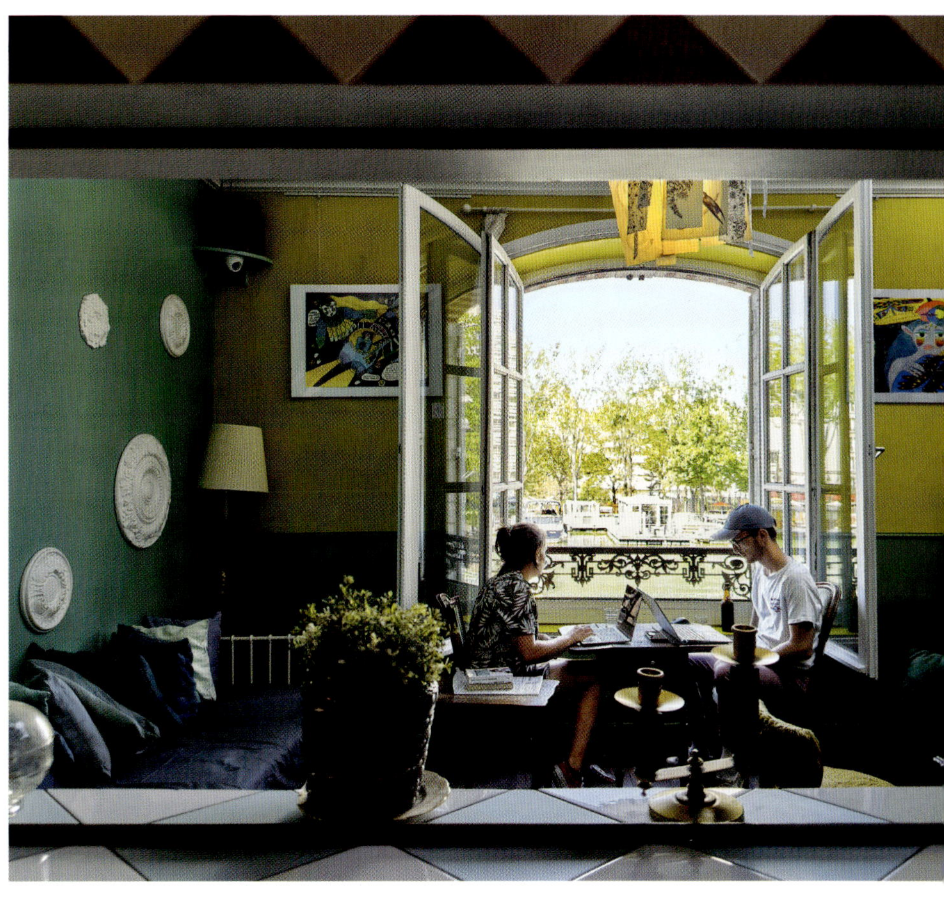


Bold colors on the recycled furniture
and artwork combine in another shared
workspace. Part of the sustainability
program is to create rooms using only
recycled and repaired furnishings.


One of the coworking spaces is painted
yellow and green. Seating is a small bed
by the wall or a desk by windows that
open onto a view.

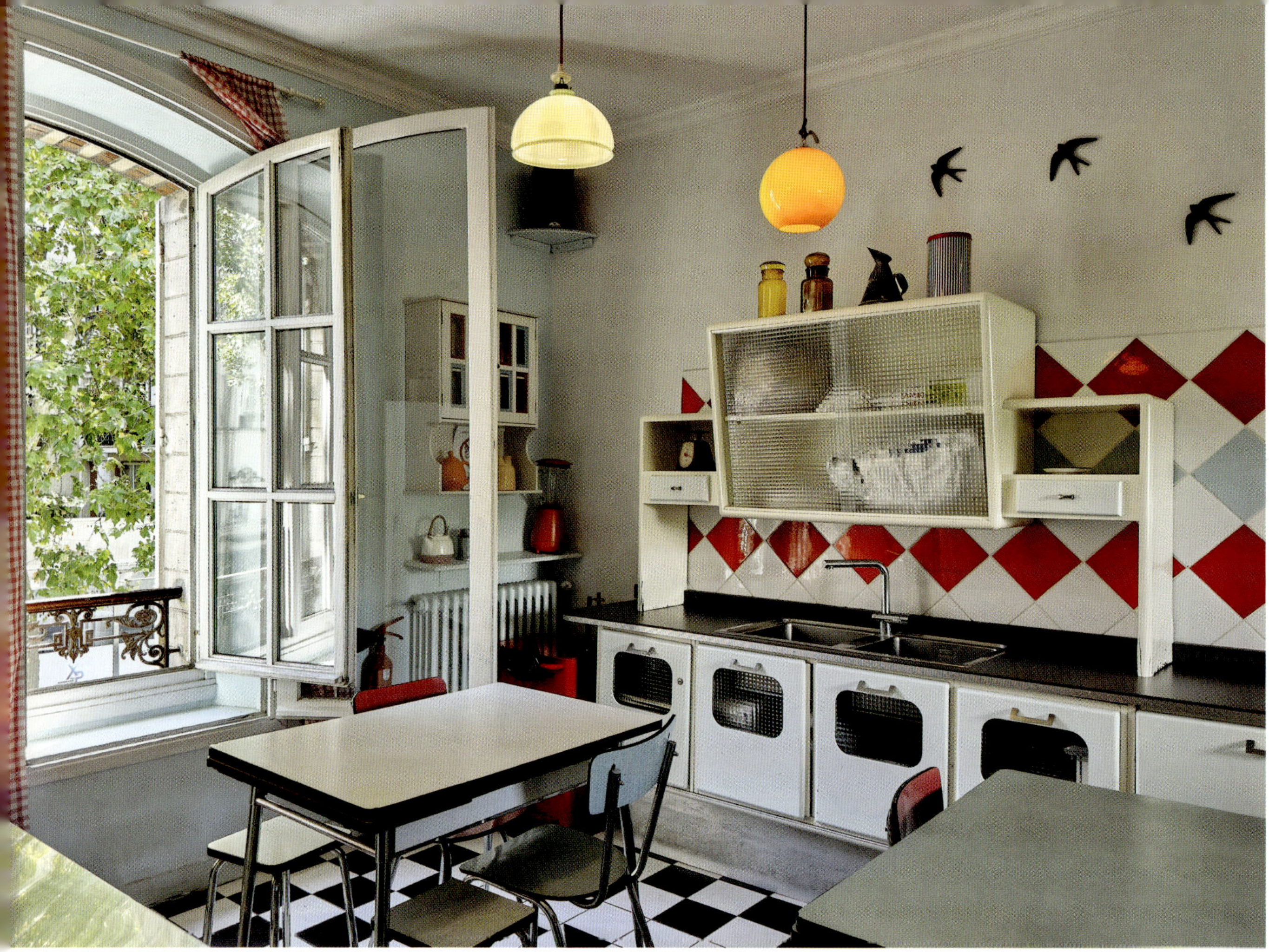

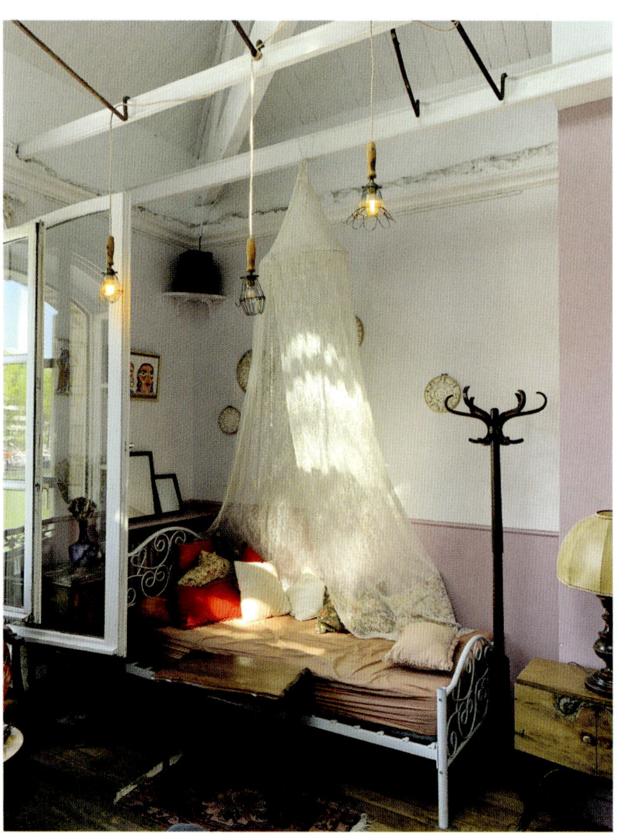

ABOVE
A red-and-white kitchen is another available workspace upstairs.

RIGHT
The communal spaces, such as the bedroom, are meant to have a homelike sensibility.

OPPOSITE
A bathroom on the second floor is also used as an office. The bathtub has a portable desktop.

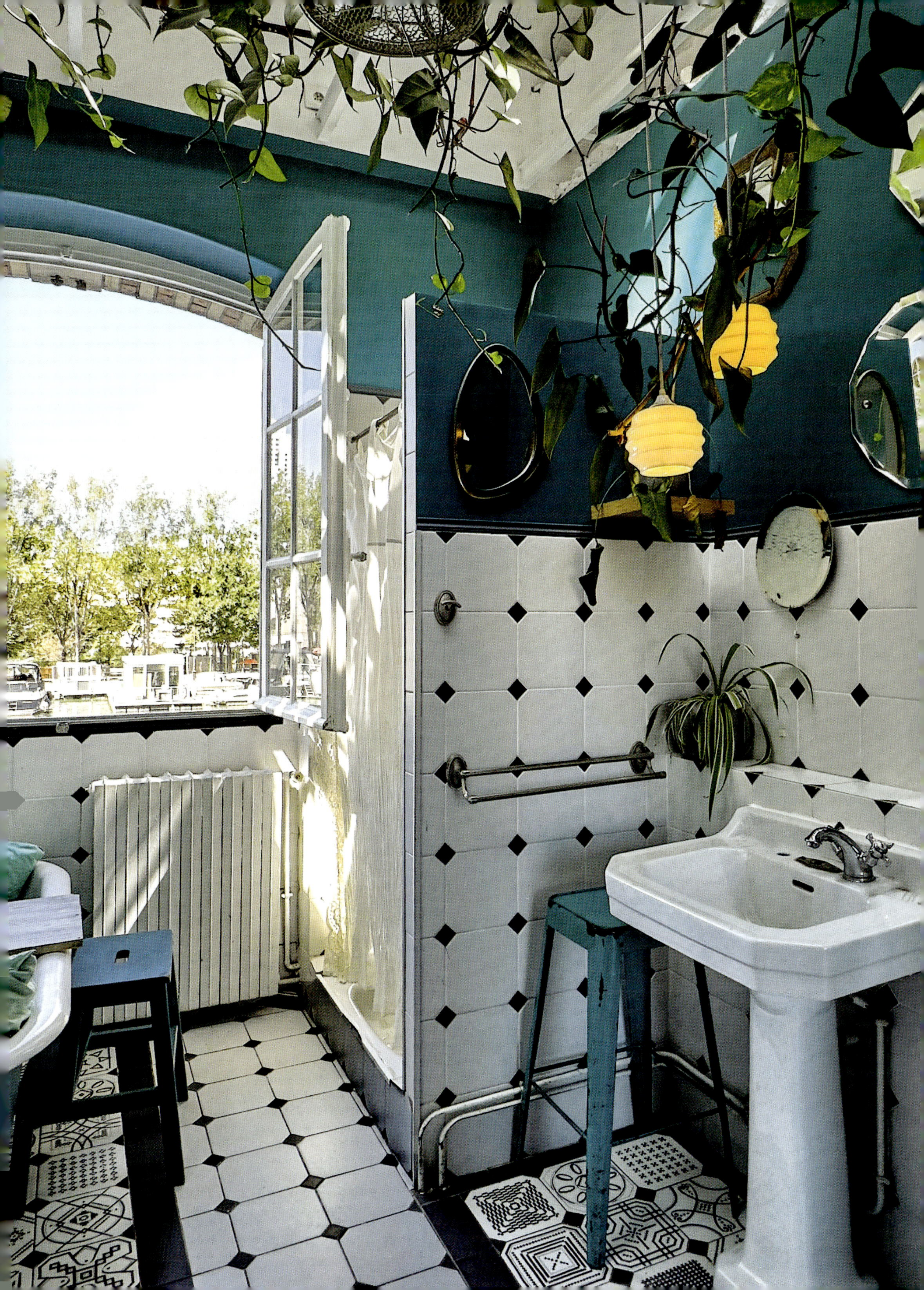

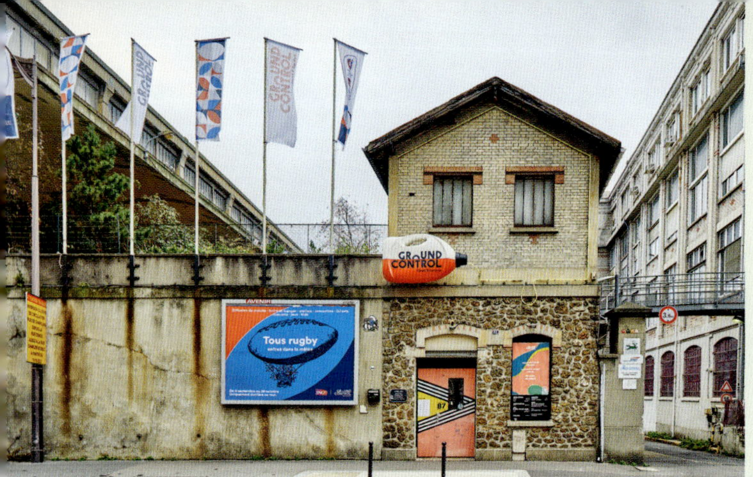

# Ground Control
12th arrondissement
2014

The entrance to Ground Control has a security guard at a roped line. It almost feels like a nightclub. Once above street level, past the murals of train cars in the stairwell, there's an open outdoor space that is an ad hoc garden; plants of all kinds are grown in pots and containers. Between the potted olive trees are tables of all shapes and sizes, chairs, benches, and food trucks with a variety of cuisine from burgers to noodles. Even old train cars and shipping containers have been converted for use, either as sites for restaurants or as shelter for diners. The vibe is urban chic in a French way. The site is a former postal sorting facility owned by the national railroad company, SNCF, near la gare de Lyon. Every bit of the space has been reconsidered and reused. On the weekends, the place is packed inside and out with families or friends, travelers or locals. Inside the 6,200-square-meter (65,000-square-foot) space are more small restaurants, a huge area for seating, a bookstore, a used clothing shop, a games shop, a production studio for podcasts, and spaces for musicians to play and practice. There is a regular program of conferences and speakers that discuss ideas ranging from architecture to a sustainable future. Ground Control is a world of its own making—an intersection between culture and food, and a gathering place of ideas, images, movement, and sounds.

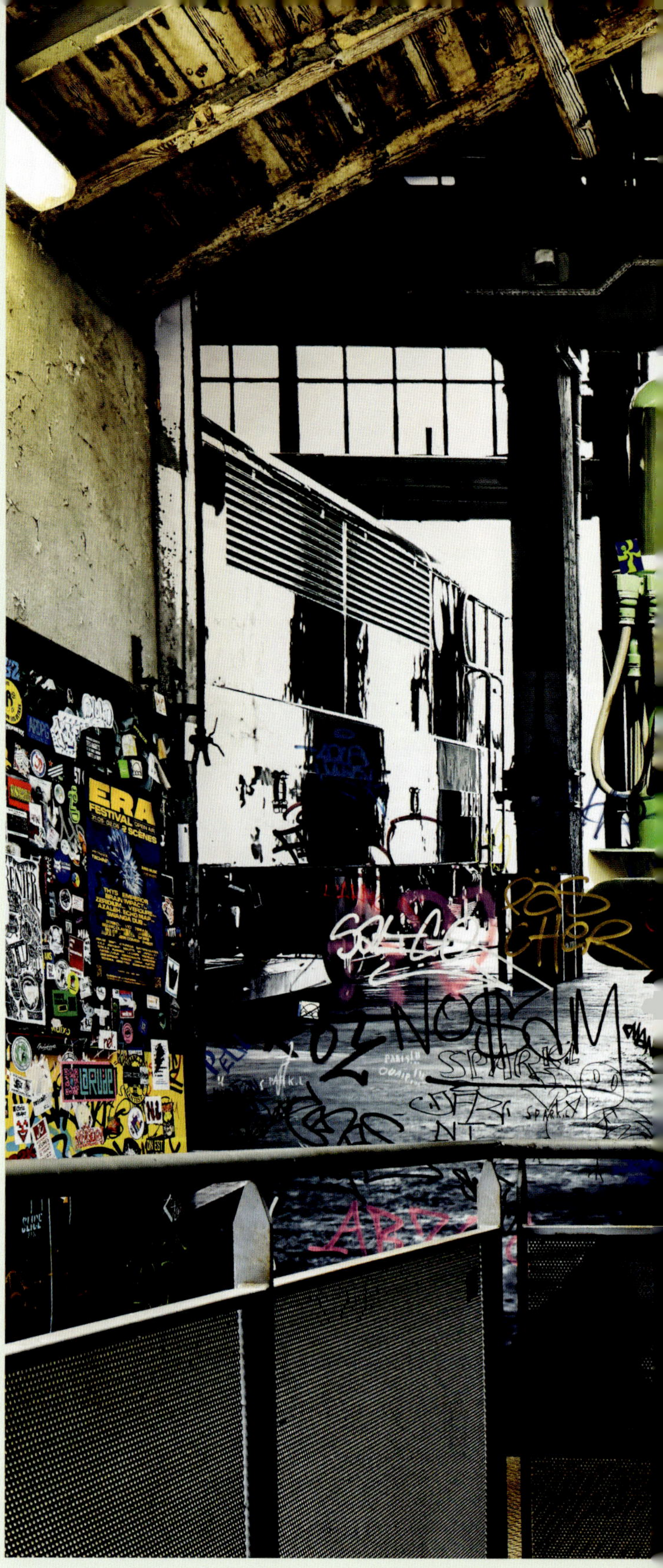

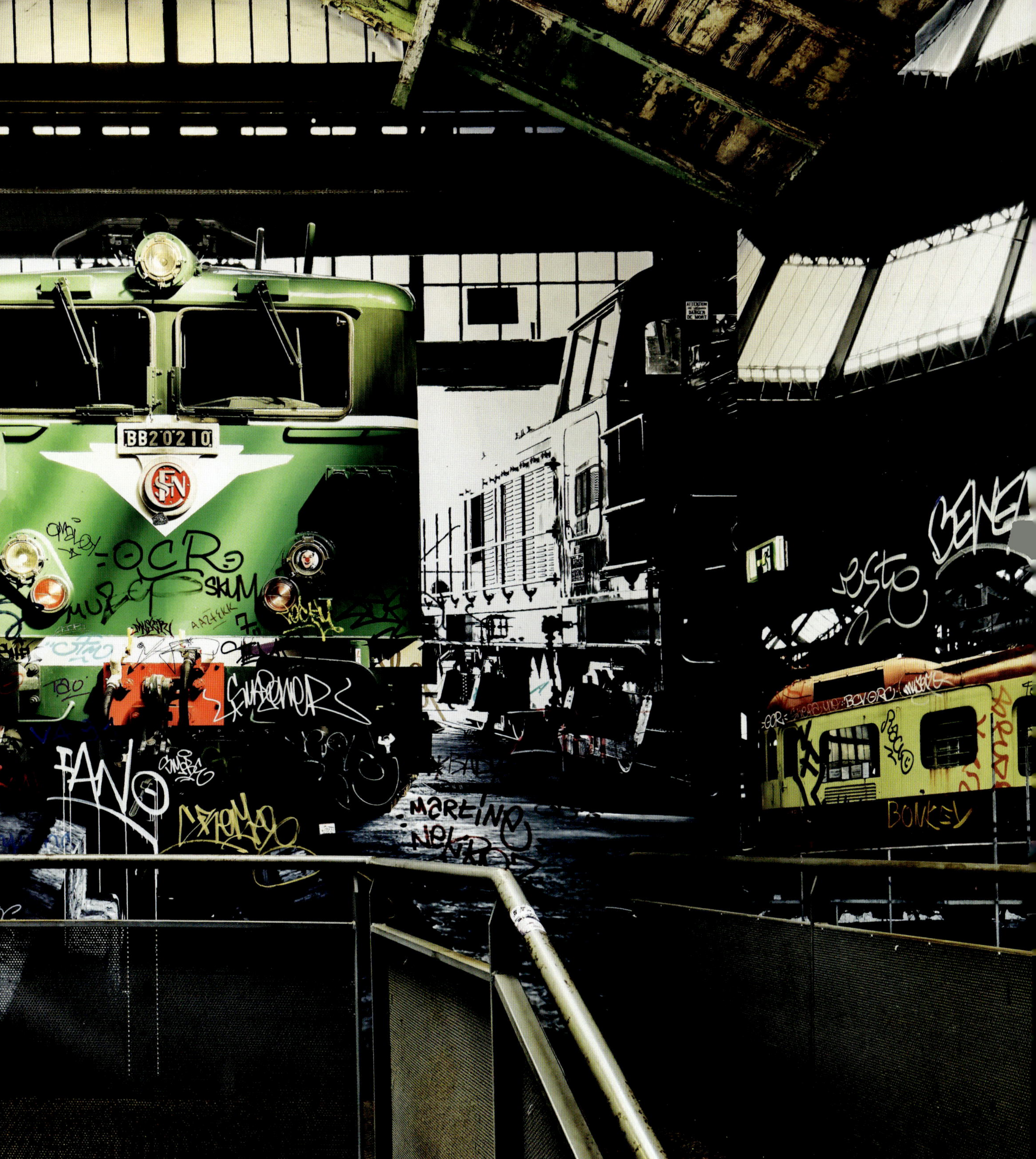



**ABOVE**
The stairwell to the second floor has images of trains and the old station, acknowledging the site's history as an SNCF property.

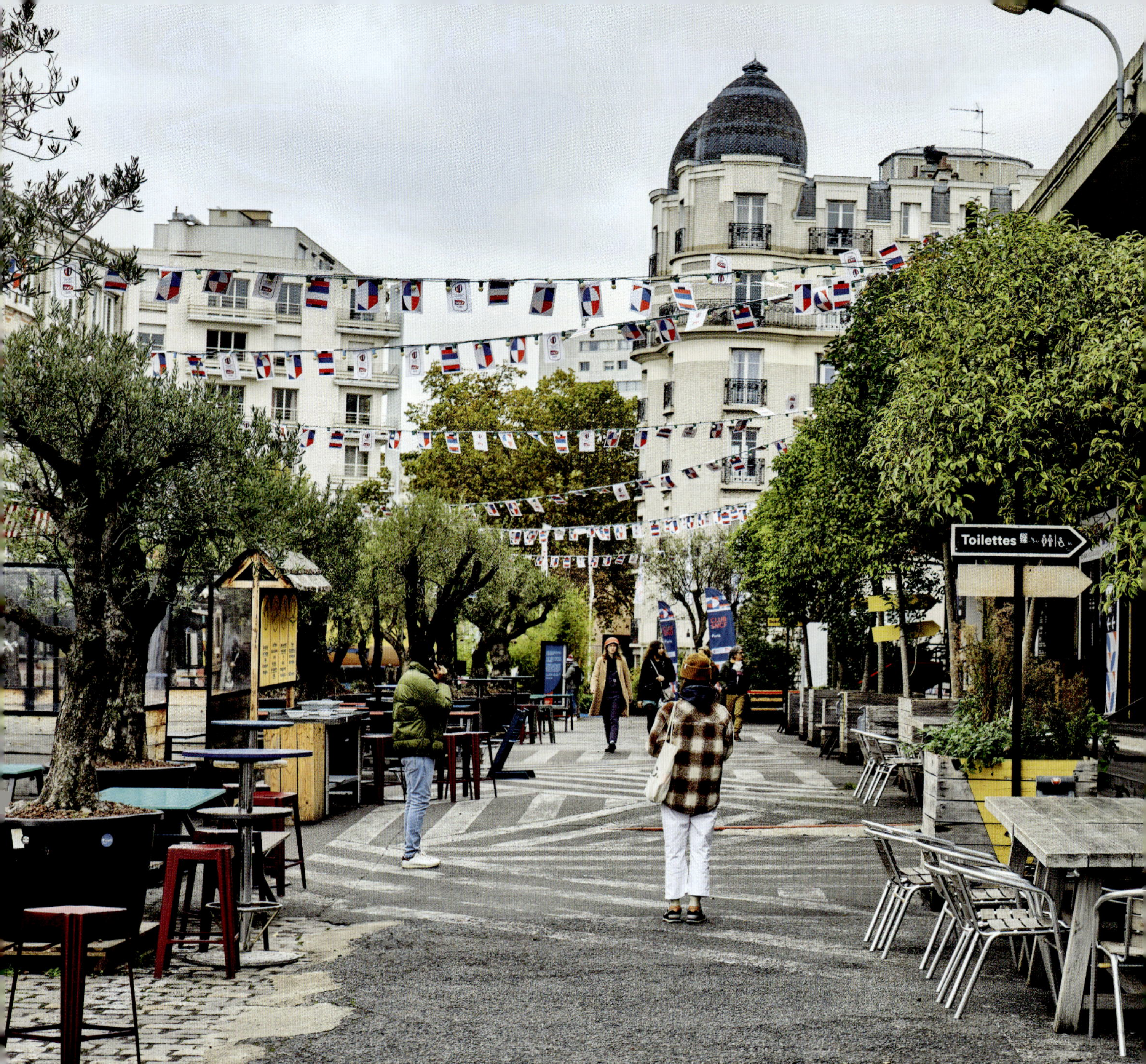



**ABOVE**
In cooler temperatures, there is still space to sit outside. A festive feeling prevails. Located across the street from la promenade plantée, it is possible to see the trees and plants of the elevated park from the terrace.

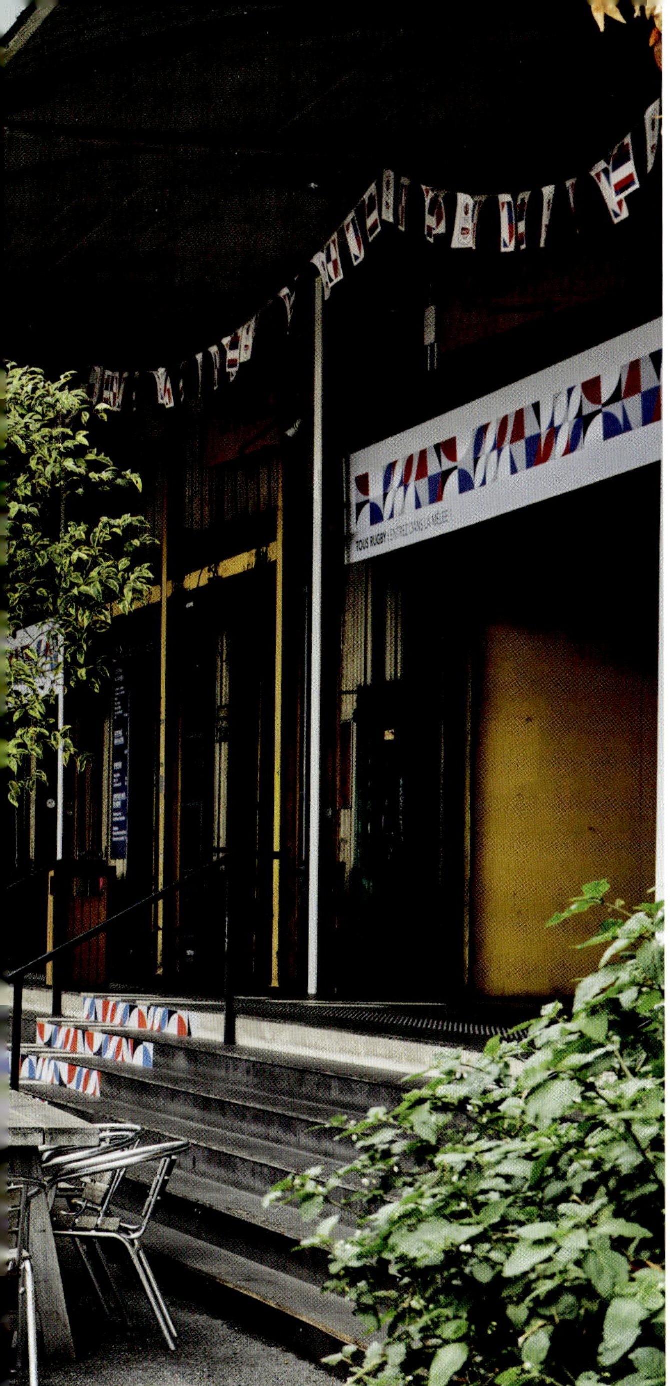

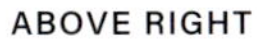

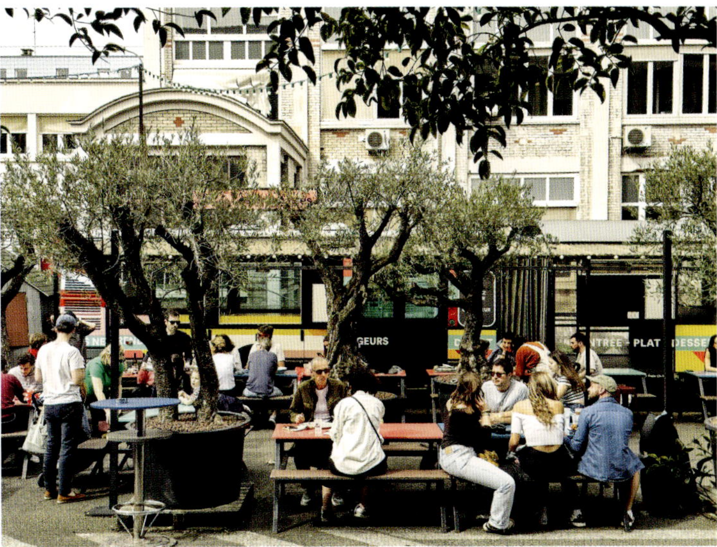

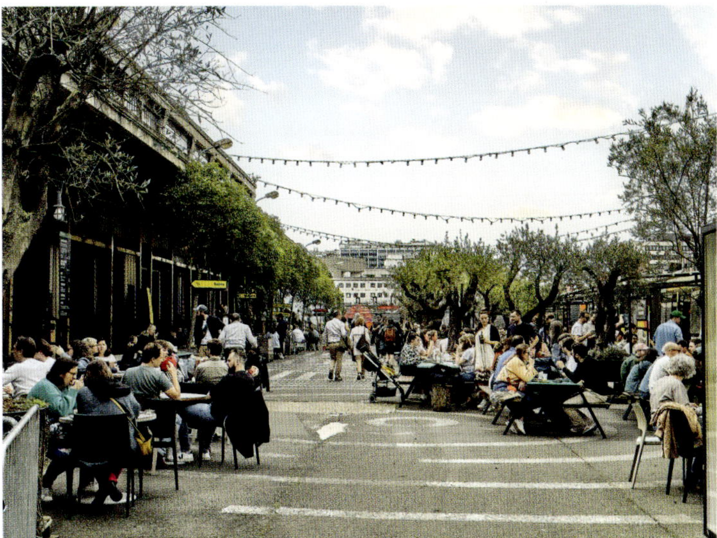

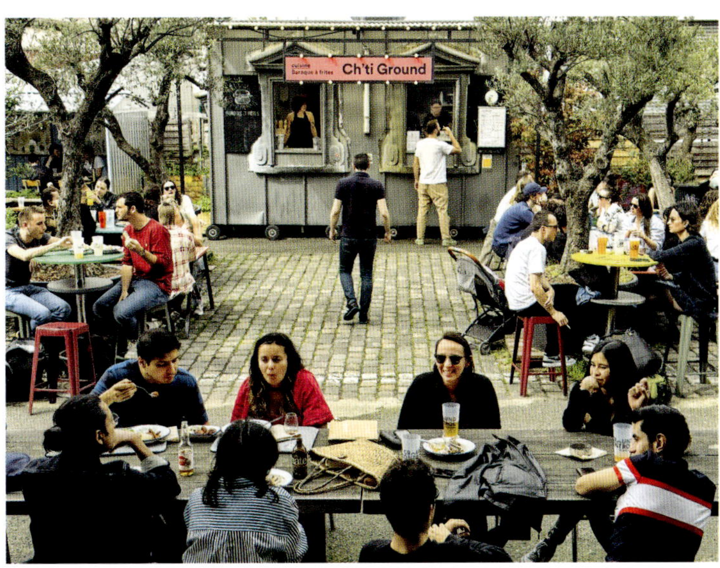

**ABOVE RIGHT**
Olive trees in huge containers on moveable pallets are placed throughout the garden. They provide some shade in the summer.

**CENTER**
The upstairs terrace of Ground Control is usually busy and crowded in warmer weather.

**RIGHT**
One of several food trucks that service diners outdoors.

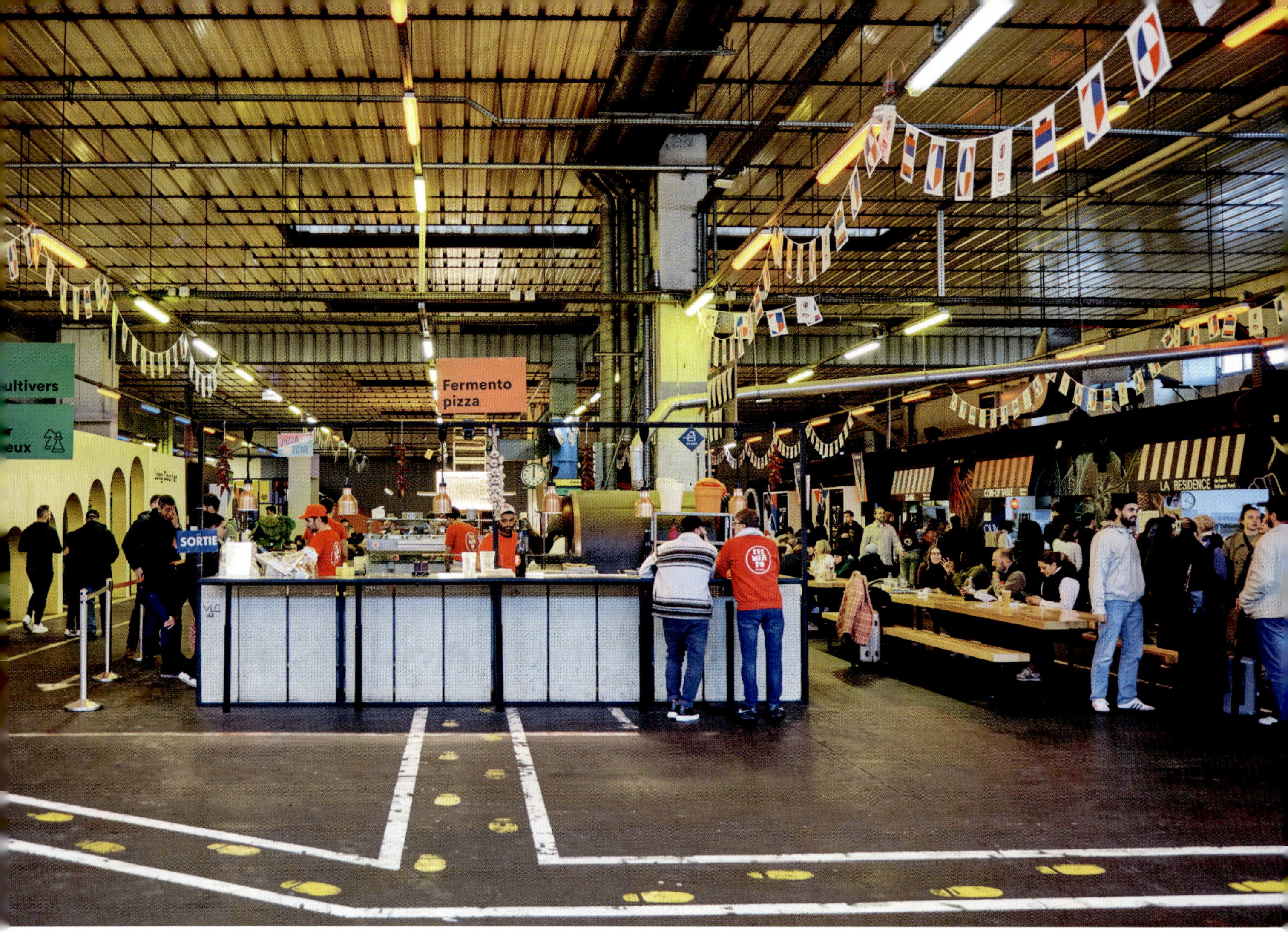

ultivers
eux
SORTIE
Fermento
pizza
LA RESIDENCE

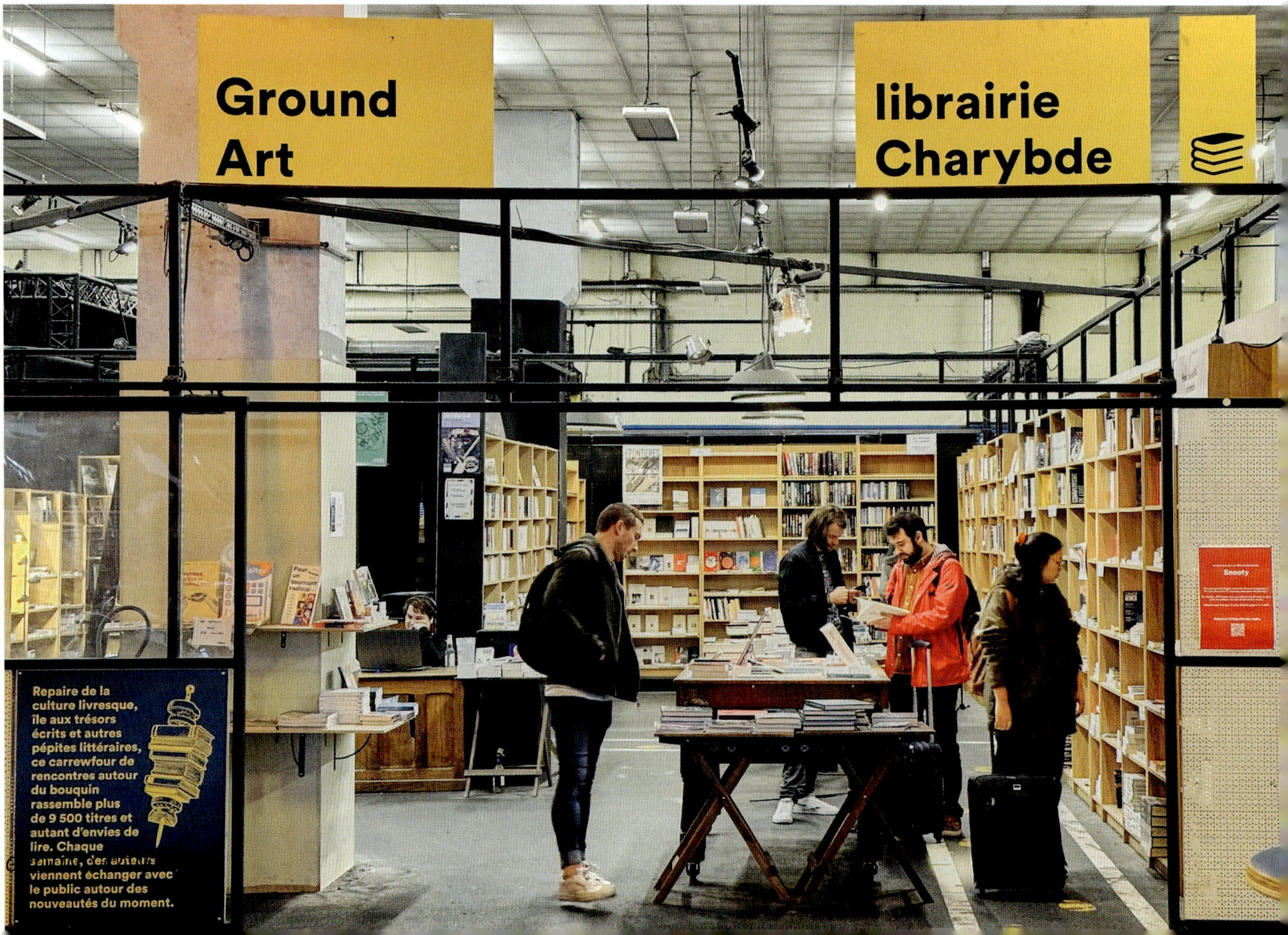

Ground
Art
librairie
Charybde
Repaire de la
culture livresque,
île aux trésors
écrits et autres
pépites littéraires,
ce carrewfour de
rencontres autour
du bouquin
rassemble plus
de 9 500 titres et
autant d'envies de
lire. Chaque
semaine, des auteurs
viennent échanger avec
le public autour des
nouveautés du moment.

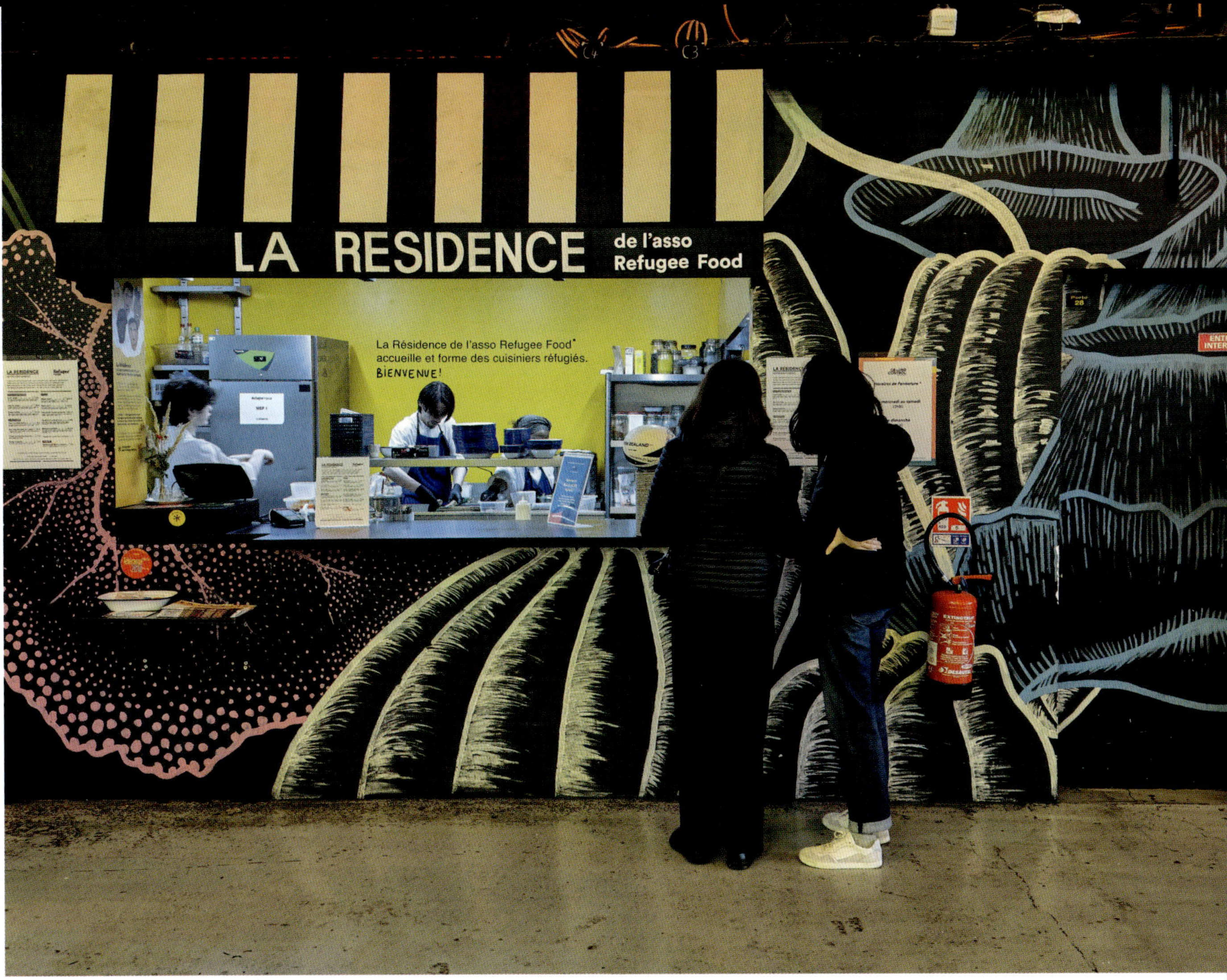

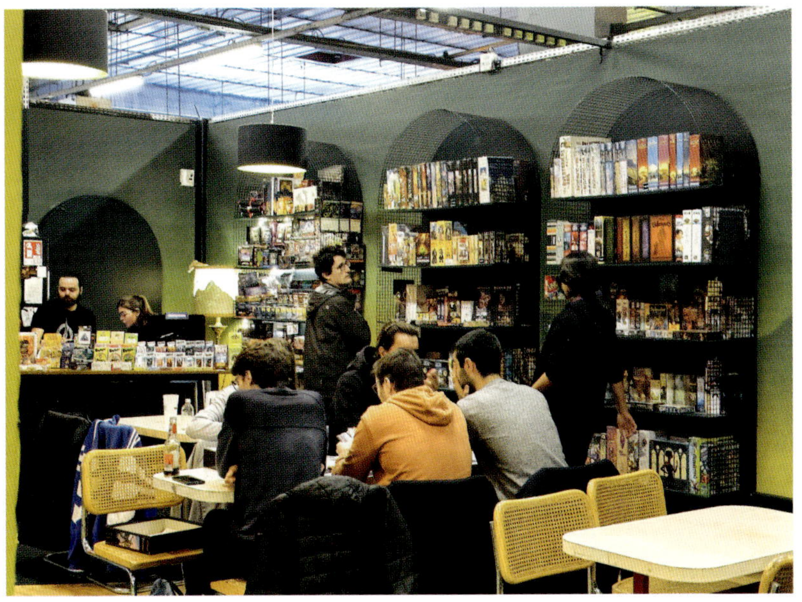



**OPPOSITE ABOVE**
Ground Control's gigantic interior has a pizza kitchen in the center of the dining area and rows of restaurants on the right side against the wall.

**OPPOSITE BELOW**
The bookstore Charybde and an art gallery share a space.

**ABOVE**
Individual restaurants, such as La Résidence and Solina, serve different types of cuisine, from fresh pasta to food made by refugee chefs who now live in France. All the restaurants are part of the Écotable system, recognizing sustainable business practices. The bars promote smaller producers and artisanal beers and wines. Drinks are served in reusable glass pitchers. Cutlery is also cleaned and reused, not disposable plastic. The food hall has a compost system for food waste.

**LEFT**
The shop Multivers sells and rents games, so a group of friends can meet to play in their café, just off the main dining area.

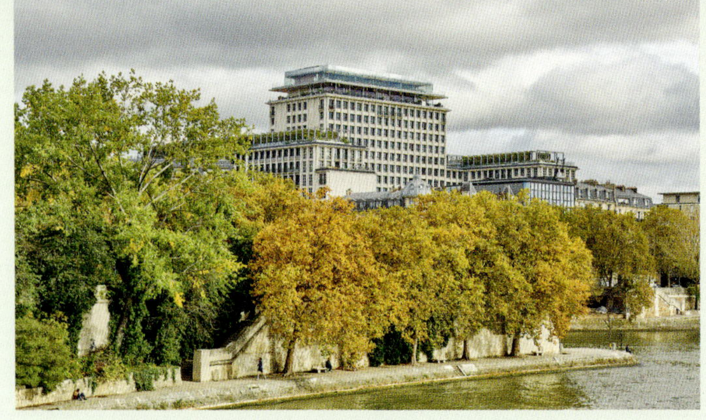

## *La Félicité Paris Sully-Morland*
4th arrondissement
2022

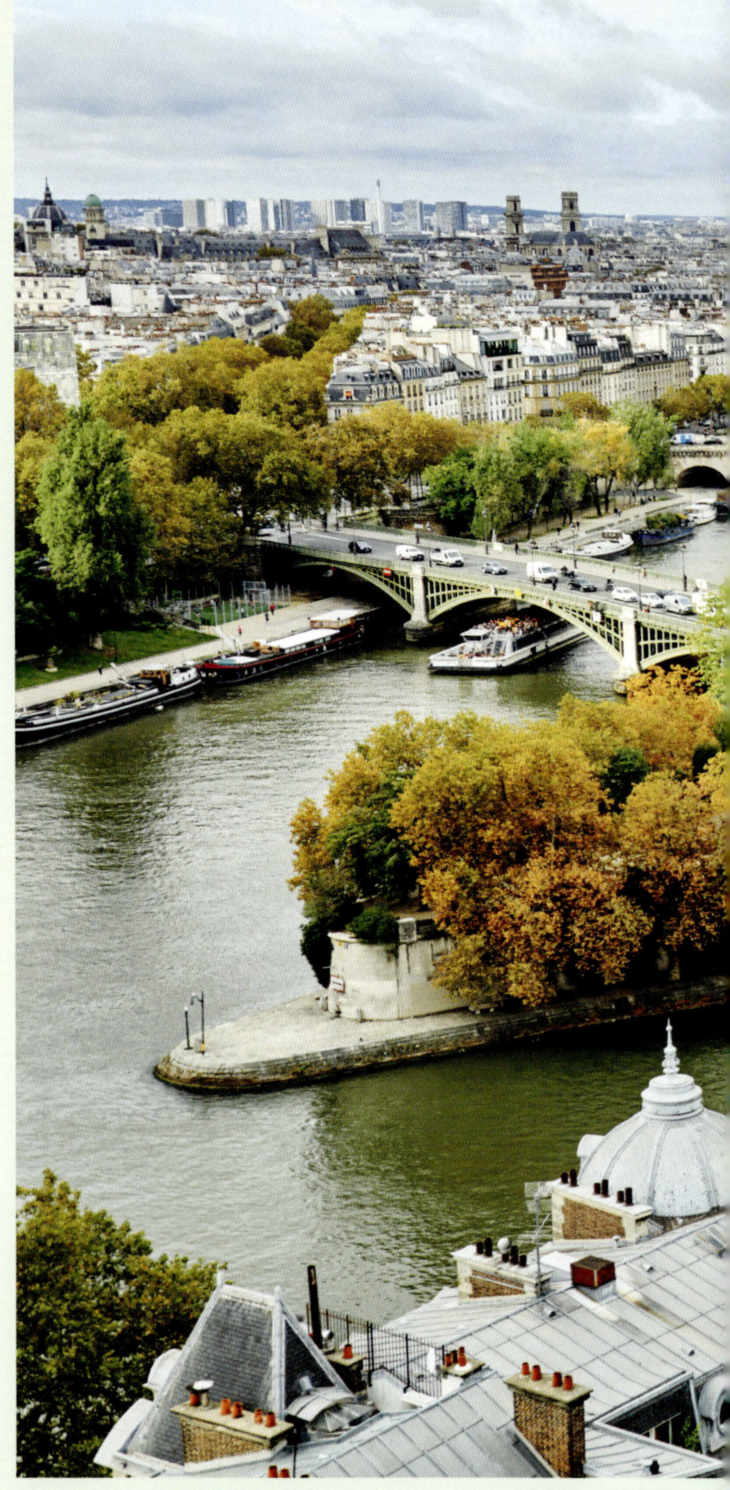

In 2014 the City of Paris initiated a program named Réinventer Paris. The plan was to accept proposals that rethink and repurpose buildings and sites owned by the city. The architecture offices of David Chipperfield Berlin and CALQ won the international competition to repurpose an office building known as the Cité Administrative (Préfecture) de la Ville de Paris. Designed by Albert Laprade, Pierre-Victor Fournier, and René Fontaine, the 1966 building complex was composed of a central high-rise tower with two nine-story buildings on either side, which created a largely empty plaza closed in by metal fencing, facing boulevard Morland. The revitalization design enclosed the courtyard, making a new streetscape—a modern glass building with a classical concrete arcade as its base and another glass building facing the river. The project was known as Morland Mixité Capitale, for its address on the right bank of the Seine and for the ideas behind its reinvention. Truly, it is a mixed-use development with so many different types of housing and accommodations: from a hostel to a hotel, from luxury apartments to affordable housing. But that was just the beginning of the innovations. Art is installed in the now intimate courtyard garden and on the balcony of the restaurant on the top floor of the central building. A rooftop farm grows on the smaller original and new buildings. A bakery and a bar face the courtyard. On Saturdays, there is a flea market under the arcade, bike storage is filled to the brim, guests relax in the hotel lobby, visitors at the hostel congregate around its entrance, and residents come and go. At the opening in 2022, the complex was again appropriately renamed La Félicité Paris Sully-Morland, now that life there has been transformed.

**ABOVE LEFT**
The complex of buildings that comprise La Félicité Paris Sully-Morland rises above the banks of the Seine.

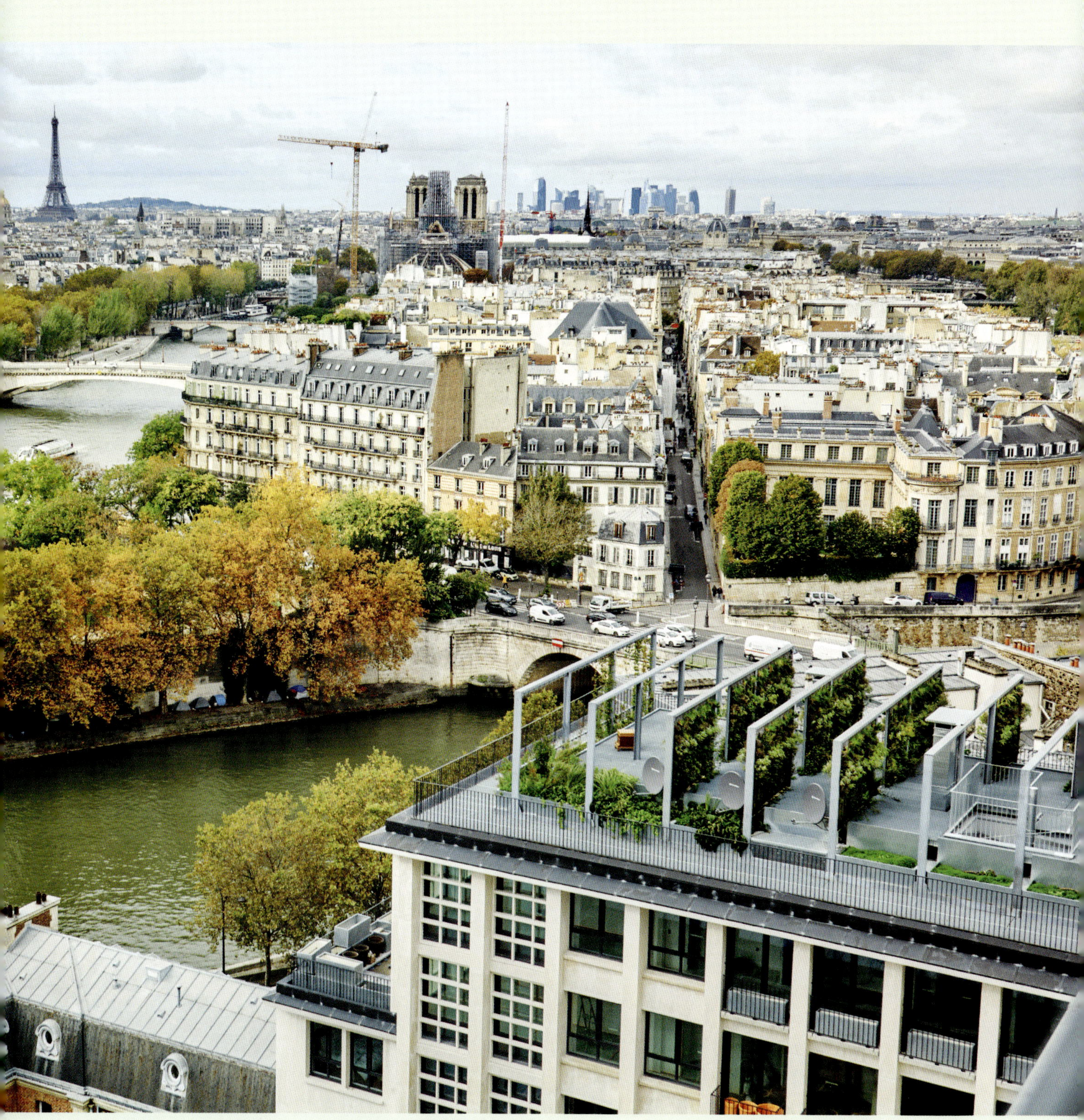

**ABOVE**
The La Félicité Paris Sully-Morland is one of the tallest buildings on the right bank of the Seine. The vertical gardens on the rooftop overlook le square Barye at the end of Île Saint-Louis, with the Cathédrale Notre-Dame de Paris and la tour Eiffel in the distance.

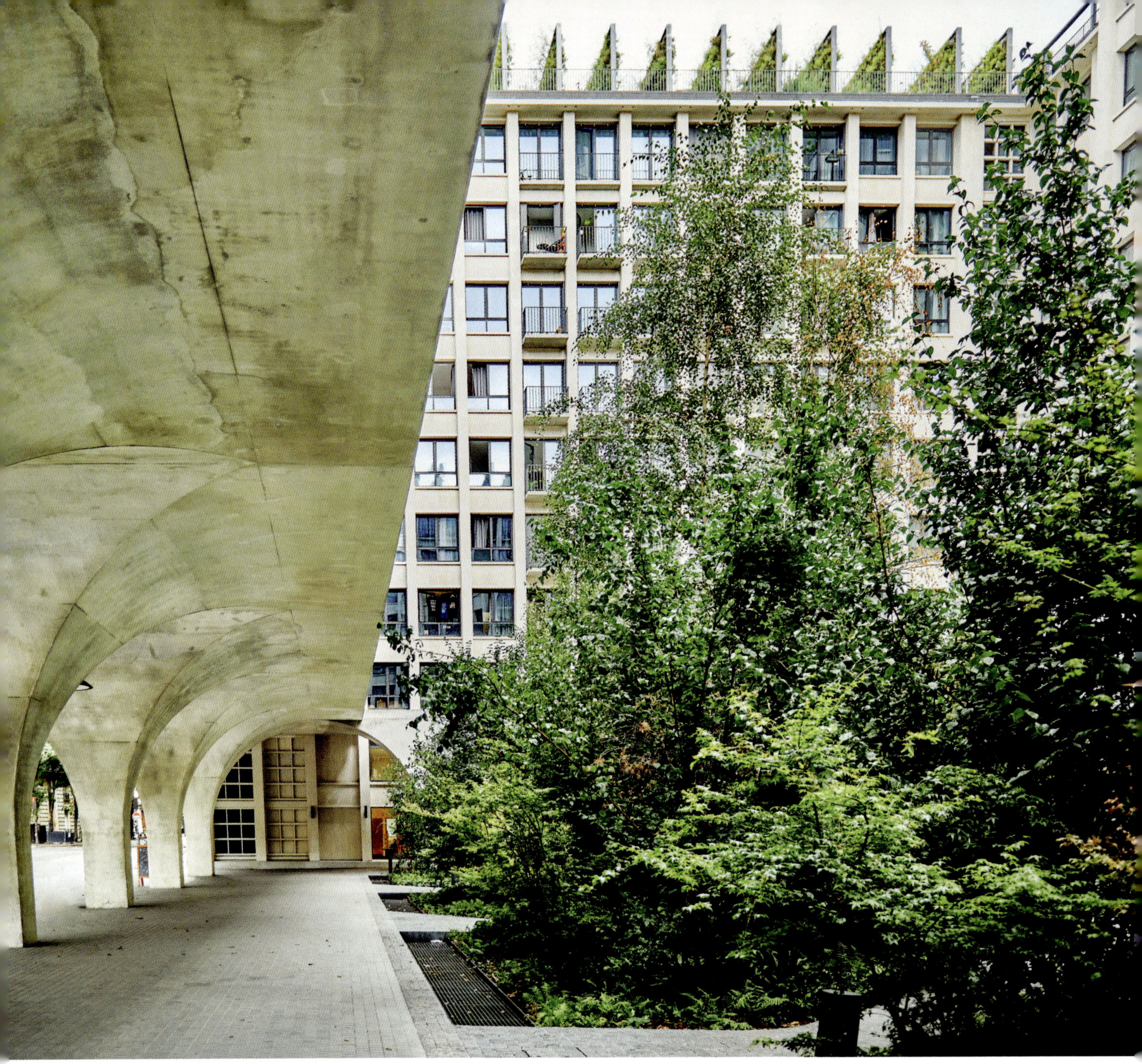

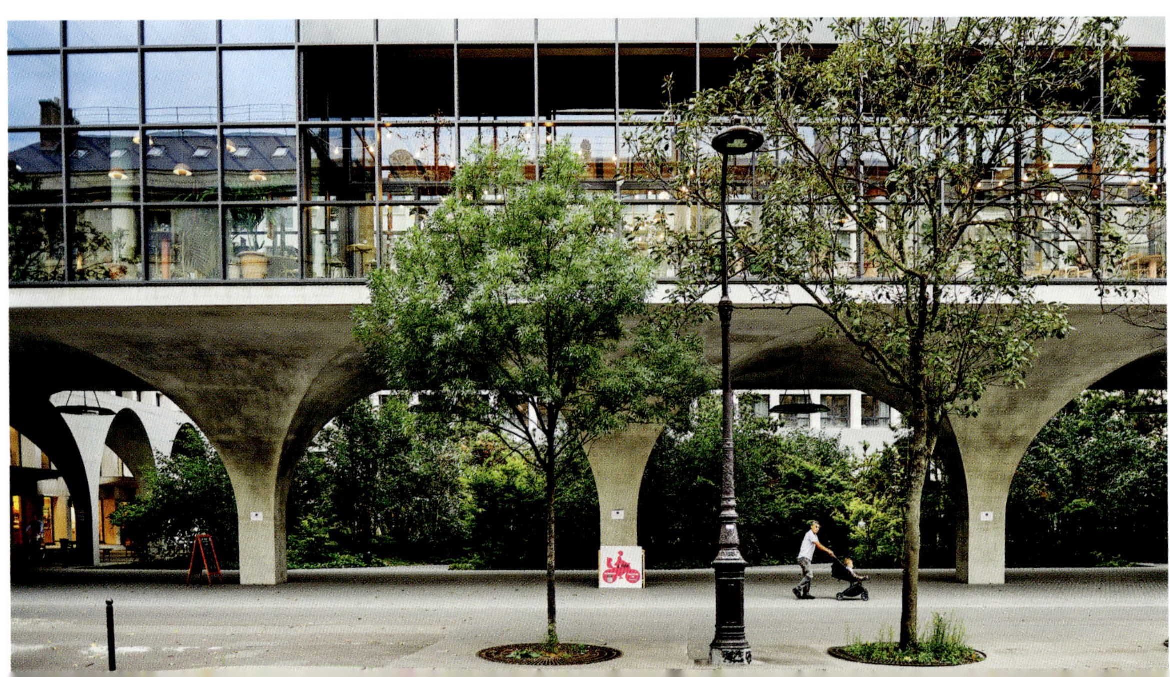

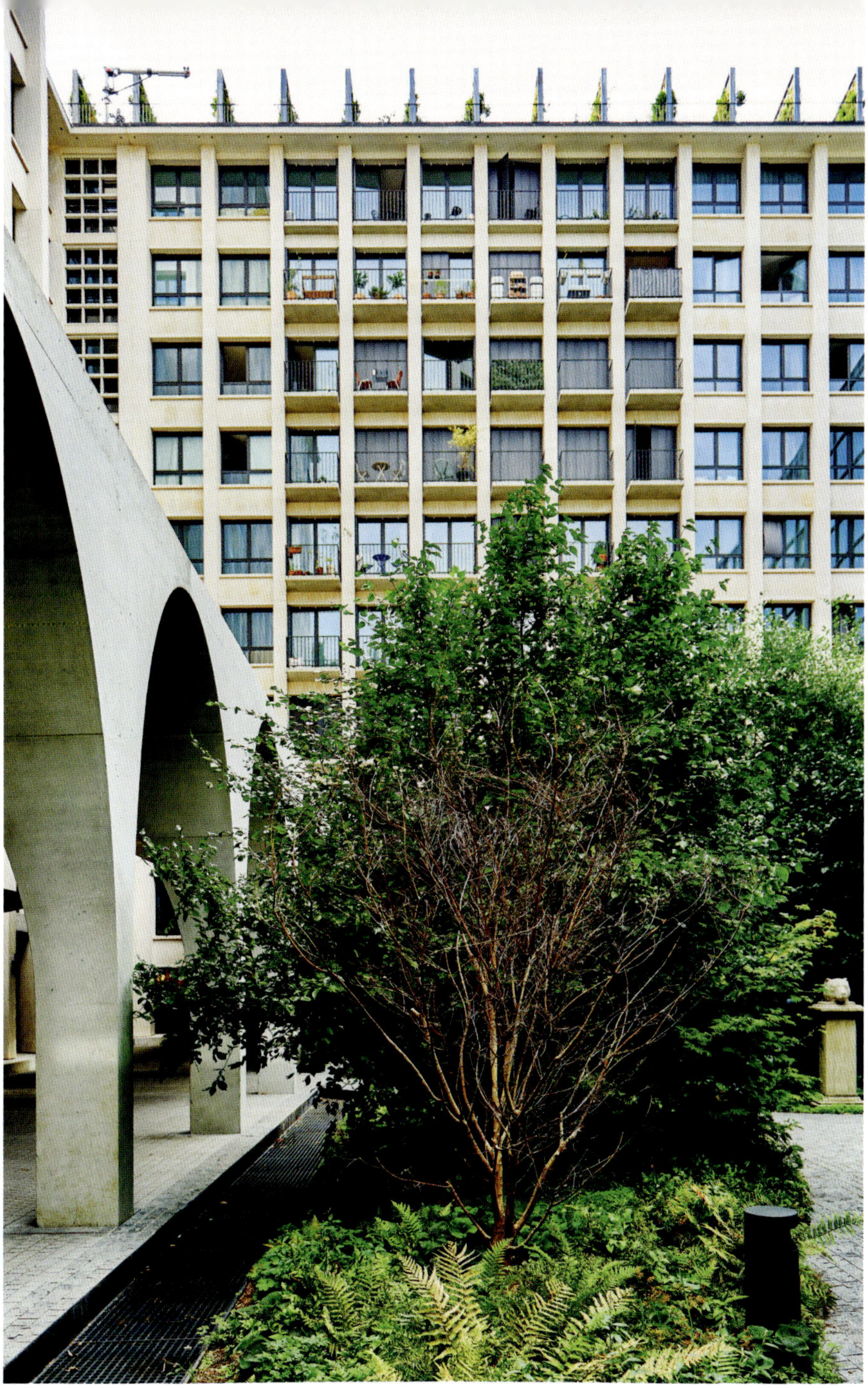

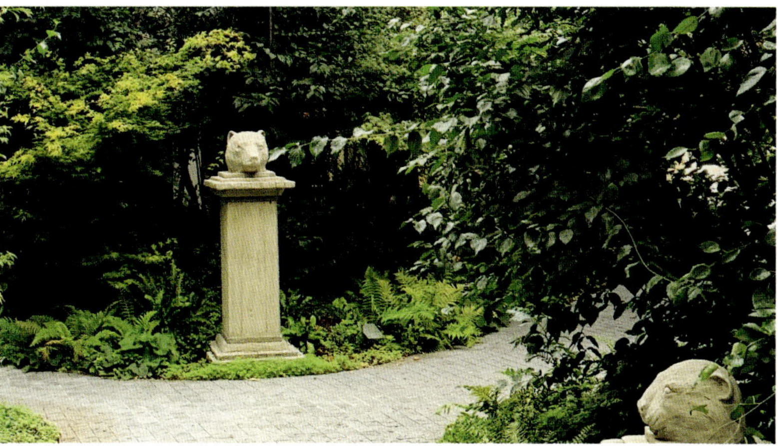

OPPOSITE ABOVE AND LEFT
As part of its former plan, trees were relegated to the edges of the open plaza of the administrative campus, but in the renovation, landscape architect Michel Desvigne brought a mini urban forest to the center courtyard. A path meanders through the trees.

OPPOSITE BELOW
The arcade at the base of the new building by David Chipperfield Berlin and CALQ not only creates a new streetscape but also an intimate garden and corridors against the backdrop of the original mid-century modern office building. The arches humanize a former corporate façade.

LEFT
Sculptures by artist Laurent Le Deunff, *Tête d'ours* and *Tête de castor* (2020) are placed along the pathway through la cour de l'Île-Louviers.

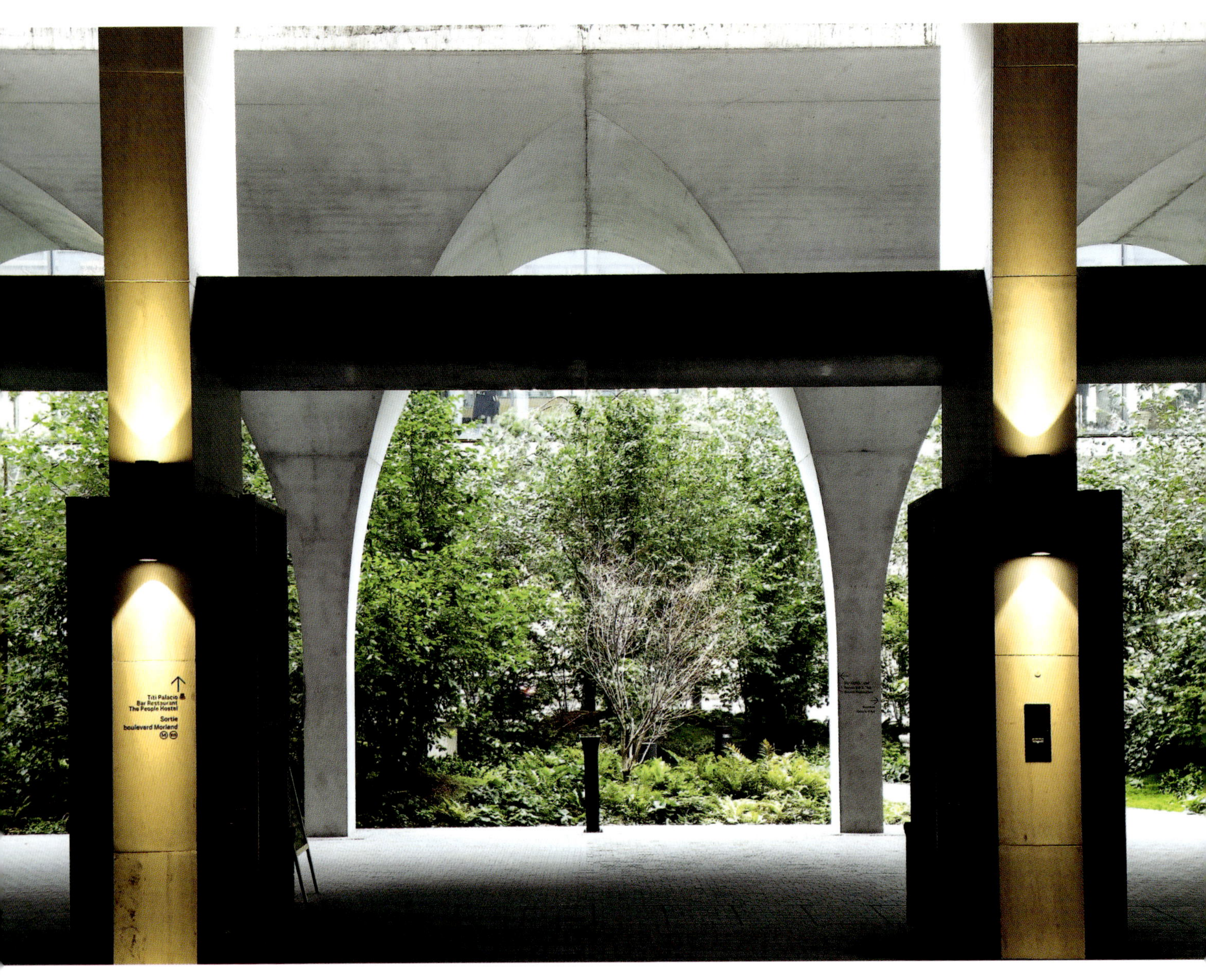

A view of the arcade and garden
through the hotel lobby.

 *LA FÉLICITÉ PARIS SULLY-MORLAND*

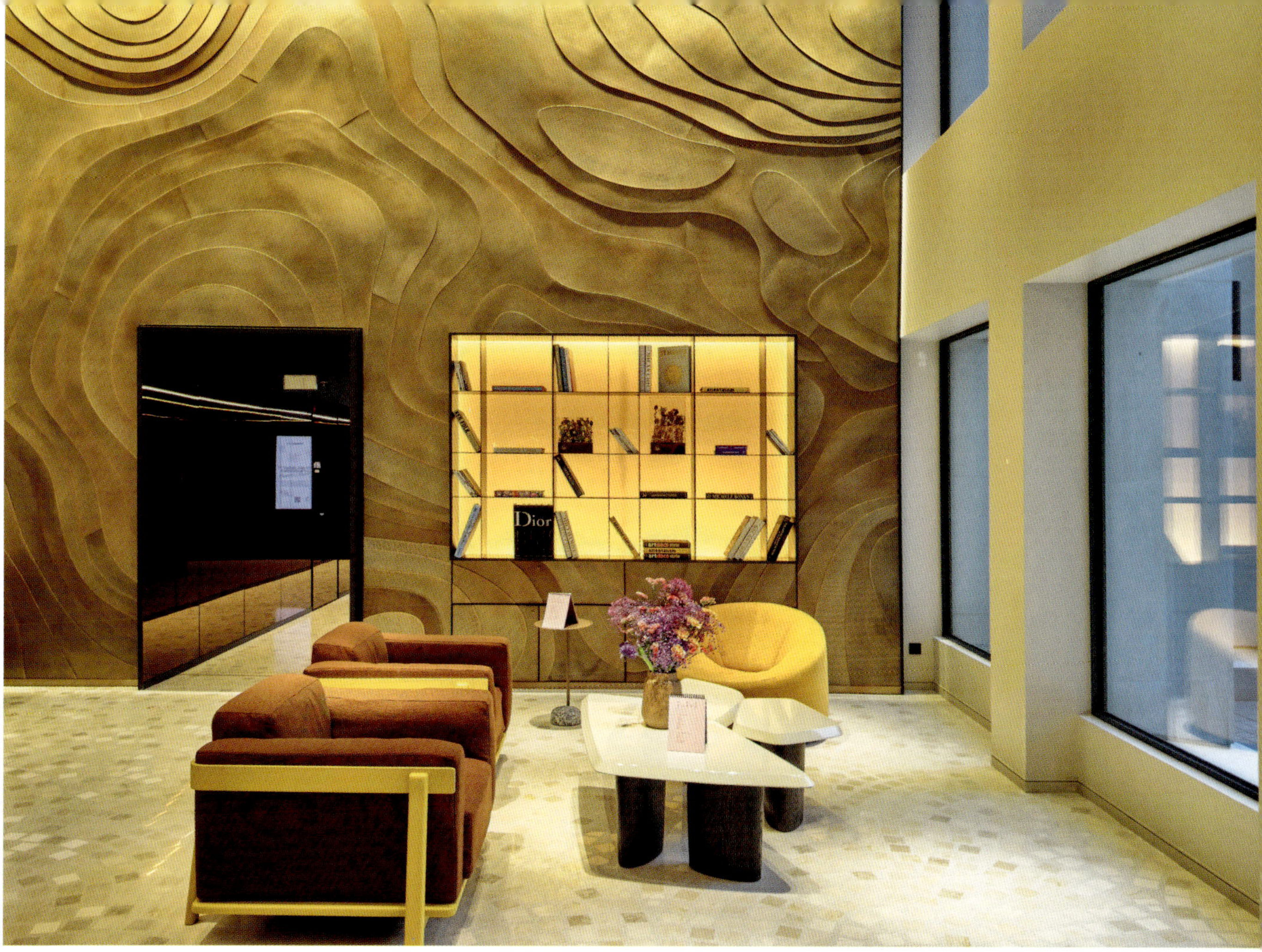

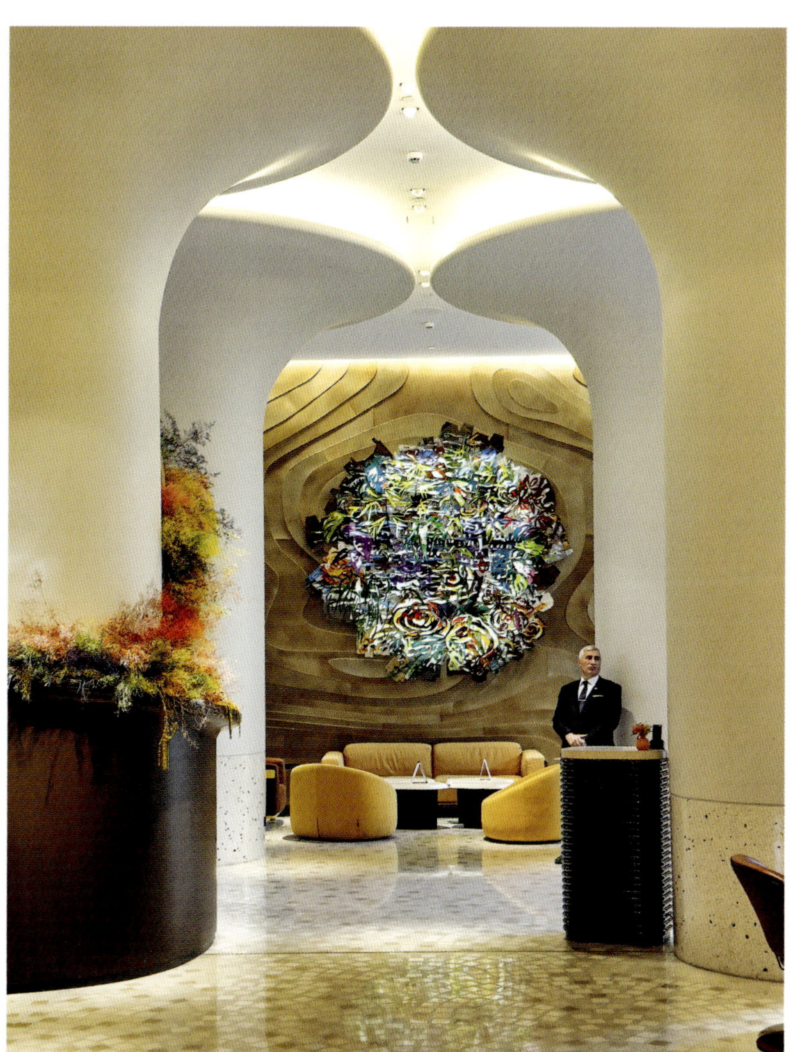


One wall of the lobby of the SO/ Paris hôtel is covered in undulating perforated sheet metal.


An artwork by Neil Beloufa, *Le Phare de Paris* (2021), is the focal point of the lobby. Sculptural dried floral arrangements by Studio Maison Ciero are positioned at the base of one of the four floor-to-ceiling columns. Several groupings of seating are placed in the hotel lobby.

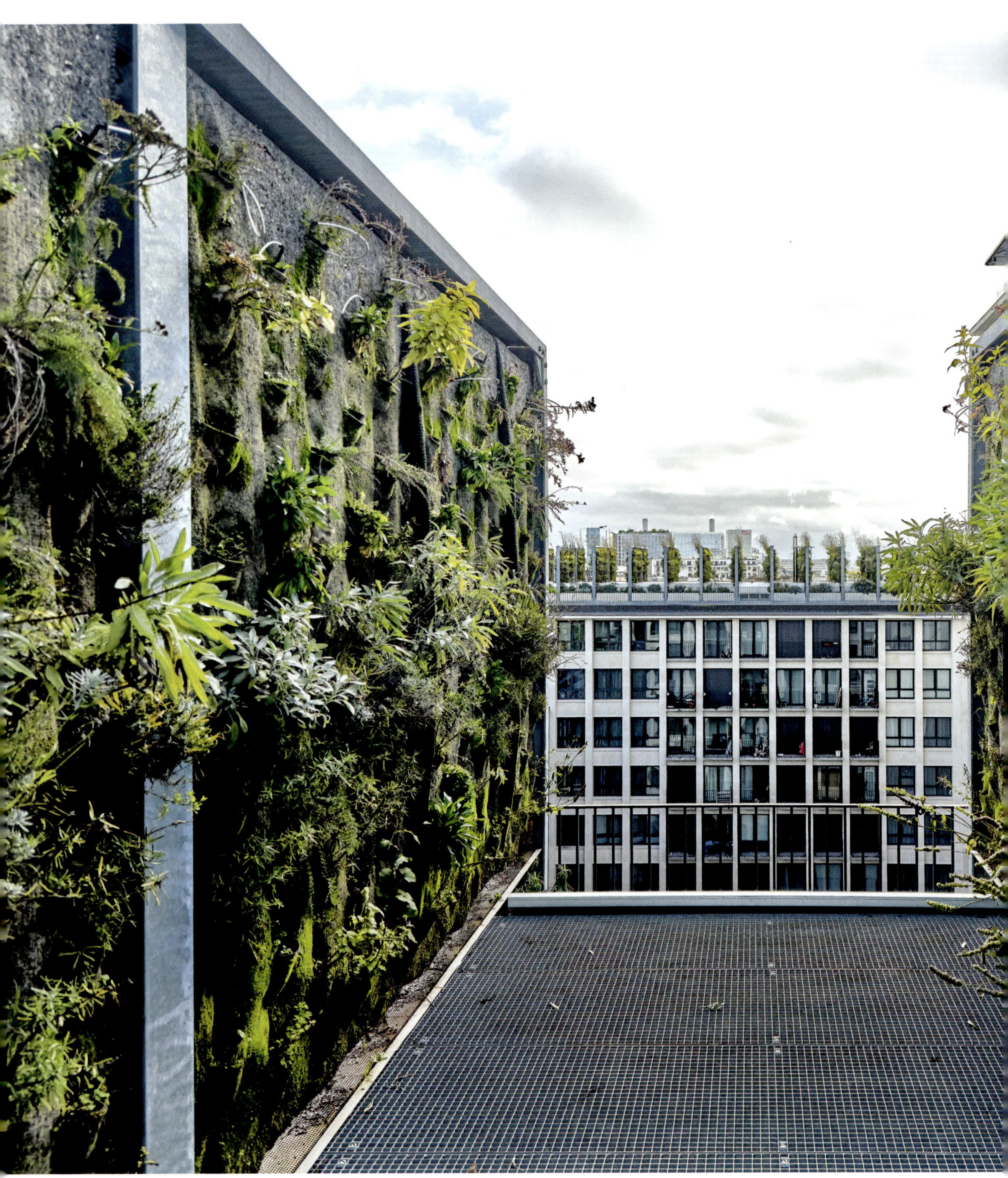

 *LA FÉLICITÉ PARIS SULLY-MORLAND*

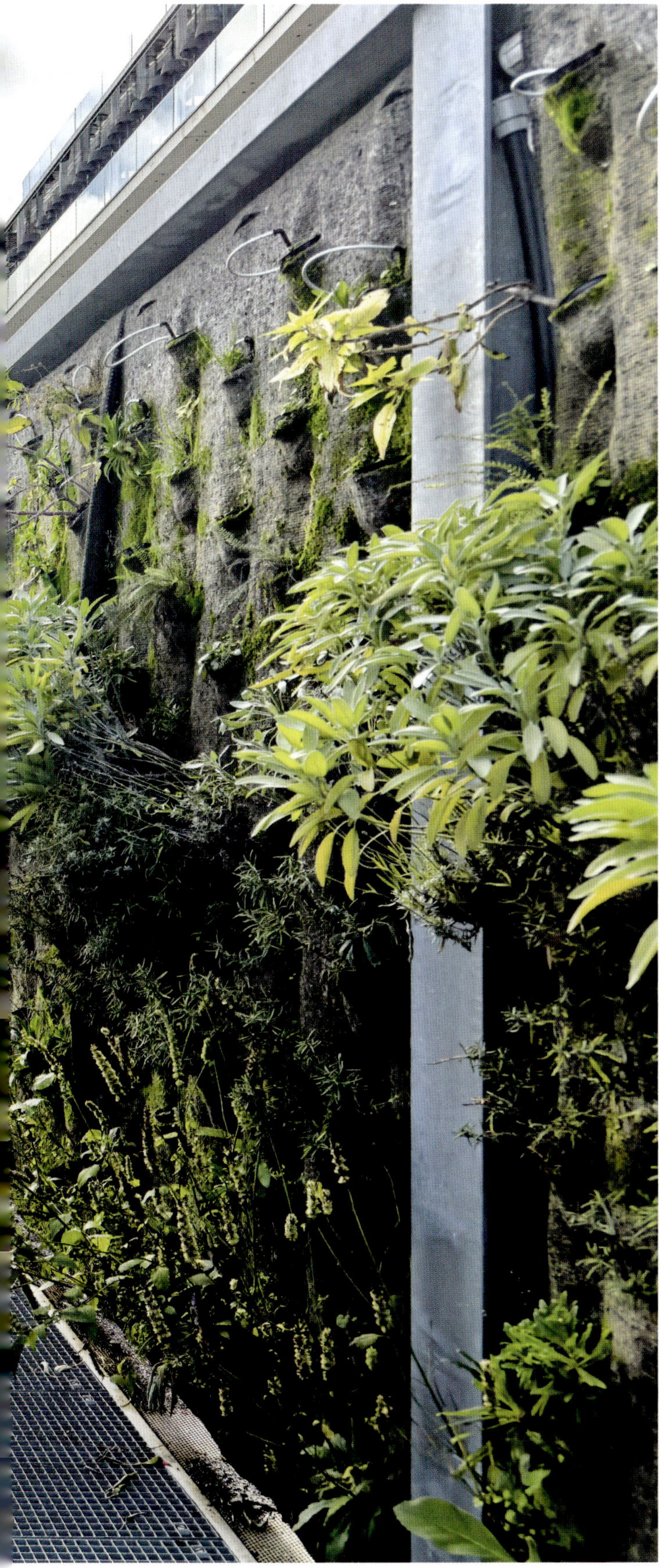

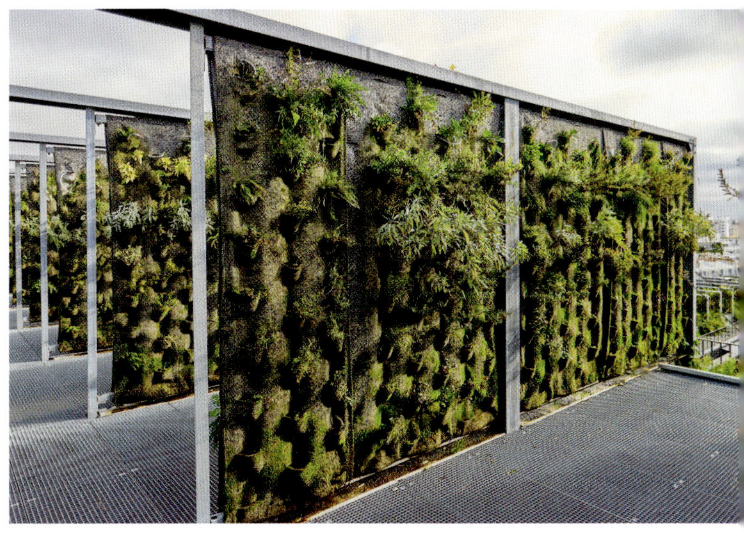

The landscape company Sous les Fraises built and planted the vertical farm on the rooftops of the complex. There are 150 different kinds of vegetables, fruits, and herbs grown on the rows of metal structures. Recycled filtered water is used for irrigating the urban farm.

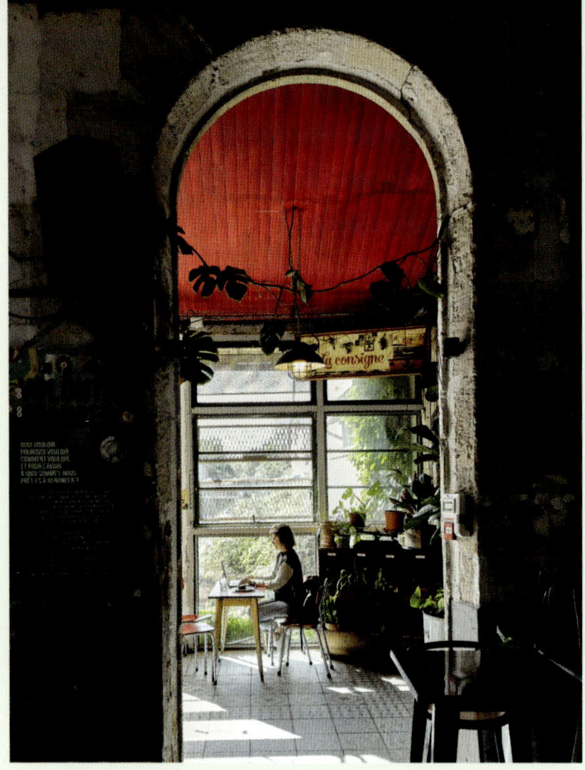

## La REcyclerie

18th arrondissement
2014

In the late 1990s, Stéphane Vatinel, Martin Liot, and Peggy Szkudlarek were creating underground music venues in Paris. By chance, in 2008, they were approached by an investor, Olivier Laffon, to produce a new model of a *tiers-lieu* (or third space) named Comptoir Général. The place was a success, and it gave the group a fresh perspective. They founded a new company, Sinny&Ooko, and they began to research places to develop their new business plan to rehabilitate and reuse old spaces. La REcyclerie, a former train station on the Petite Ceinture, opened in 2014. The entrance is on the corner of two busy boulevards in the 18th arrondissement. But inside, the quiet station is divided into multiple spaces that encourage privacy in the smaller areas and gathering spots in the larger areas. There is a multipaned wall of glass windows in the main restaurant that overlooks the urban farm and their neighbor, les jardins du Ruisseau, a local community garden. The concepts of the *tiers-lieu* (or third space), which not only offers another place to go but also a multiactivity space, guide the program. Despite the place being in a hub of activity with so many possibilities available to do and see, one of the simplest pleasures of being at La REcyclerie is simply sitting by the window, enjoying the beautiful garden views.

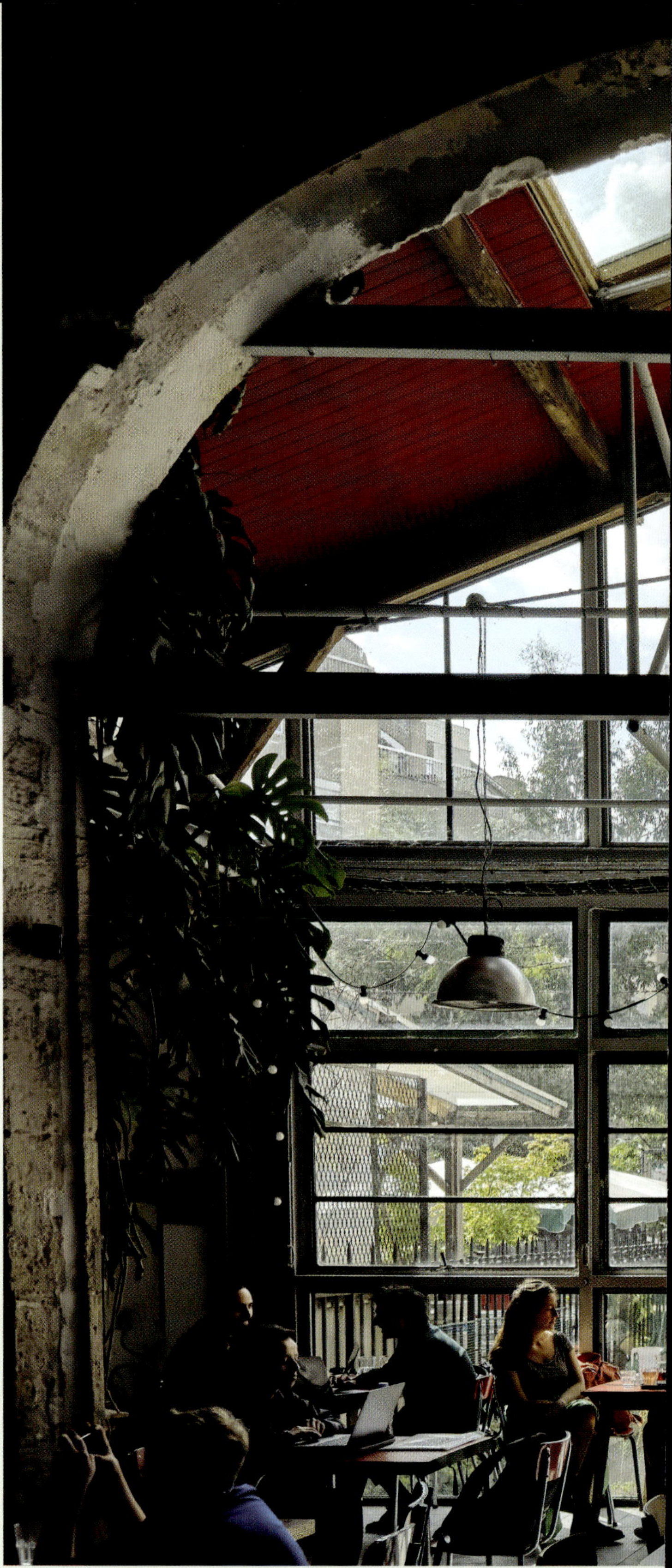

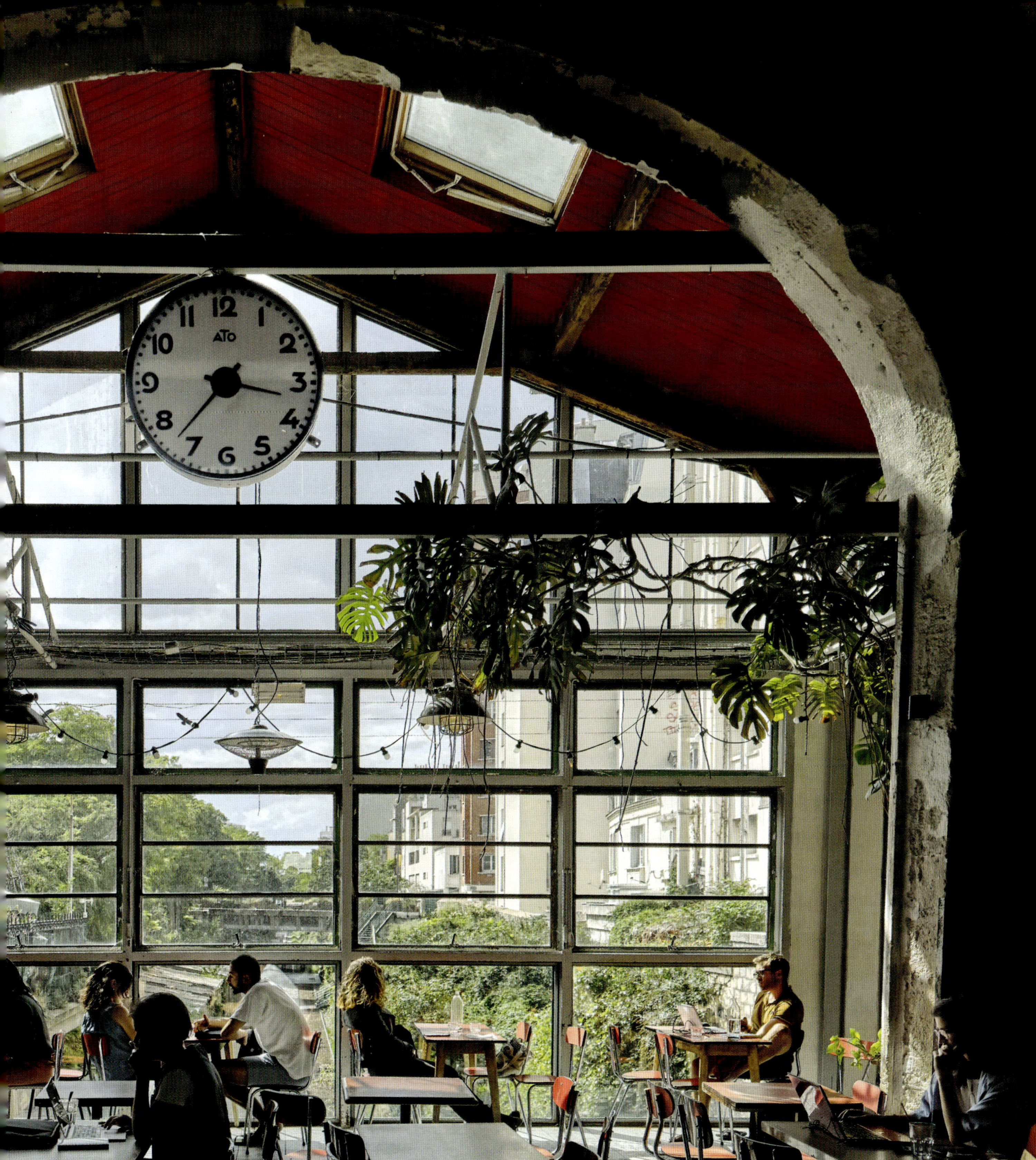



**ABOVE**
The restaurant's wall of windows looks over the gardens on the tracks of the Petite Ceinture.

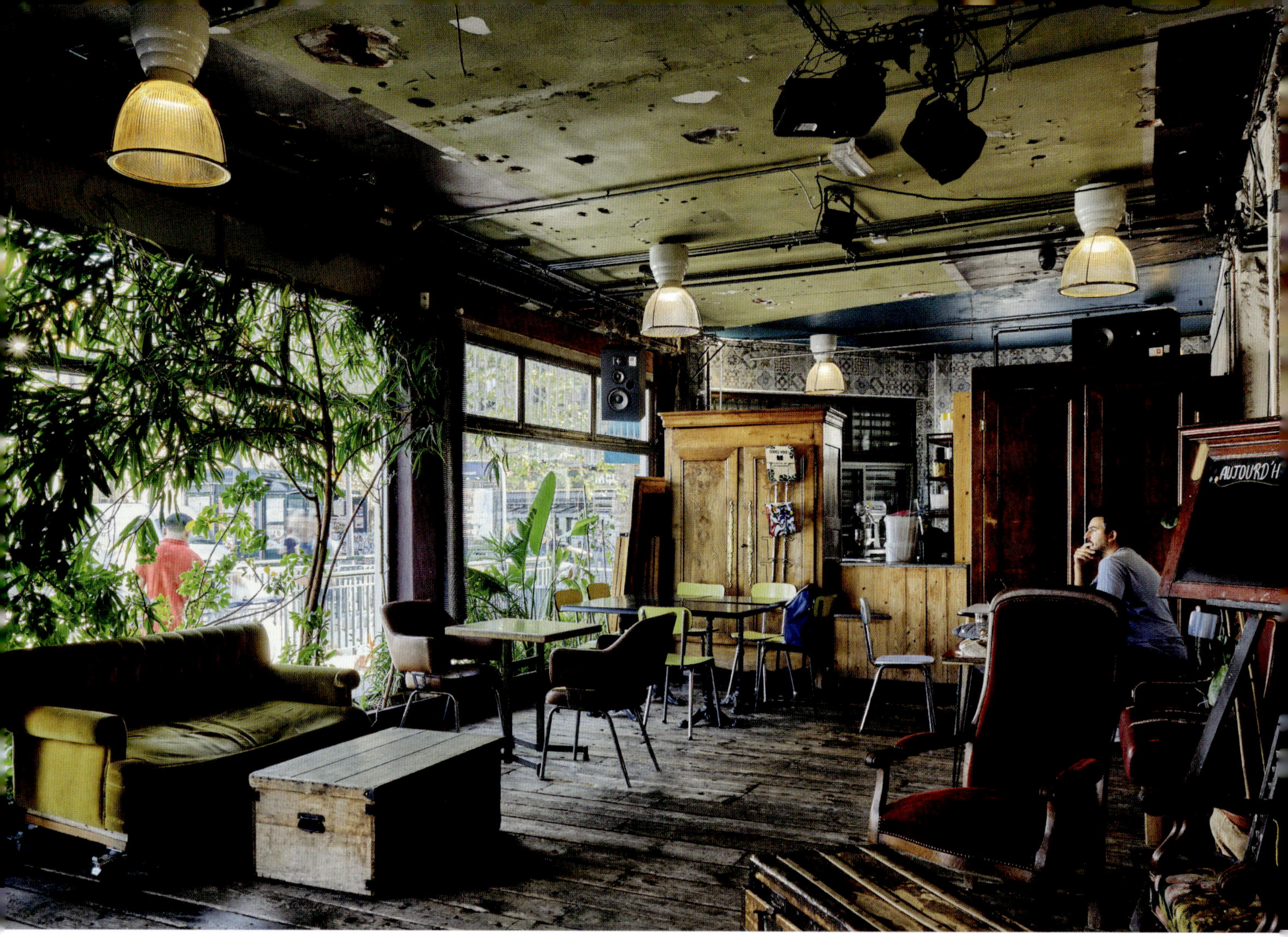

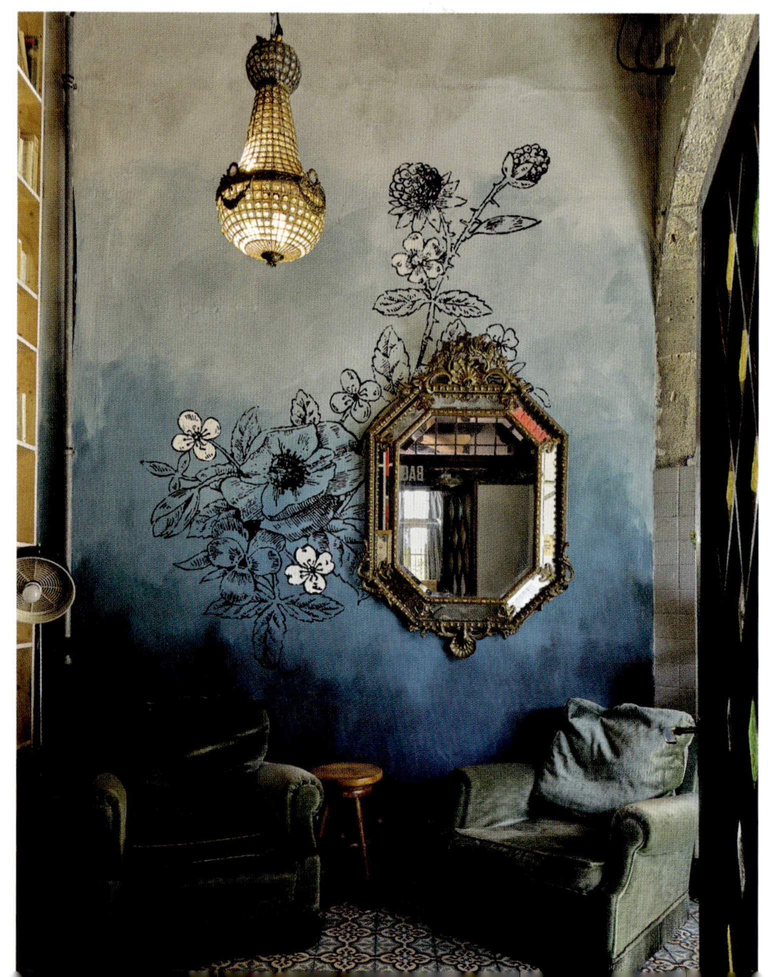

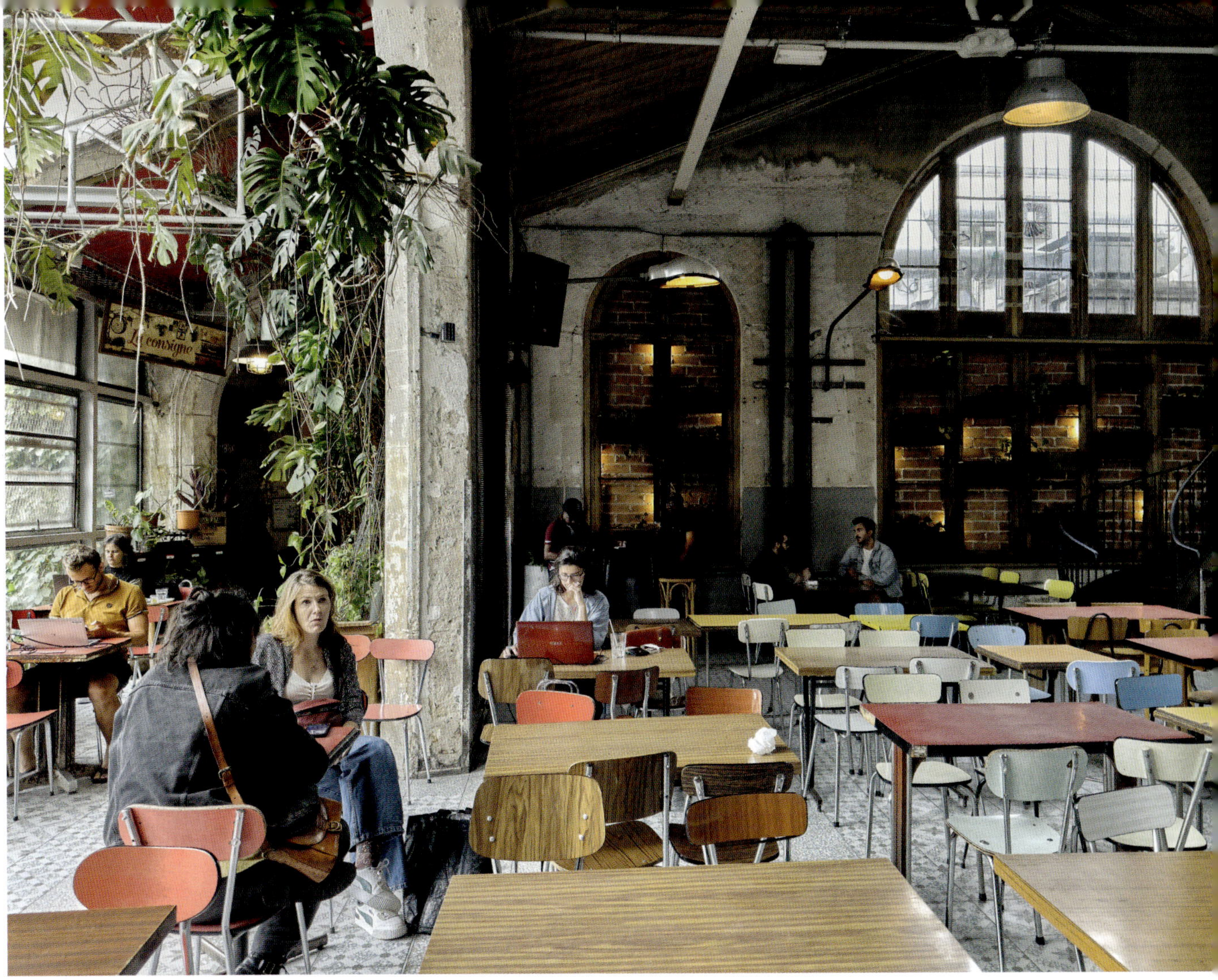

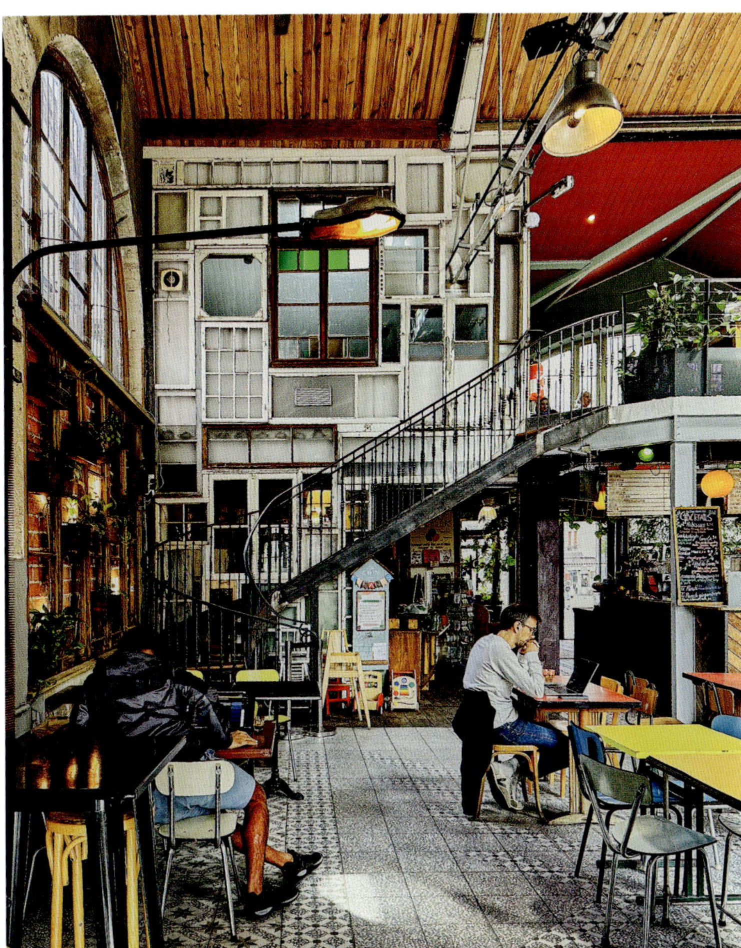



**OPPOSITE ABOVE**
Large windows at the entrance of La REcyclerie allow in natural light from the street. The room is decorated with used furnishings. The flooring is reclaimed wood from freight cars.

**OPPOSITE BELOW**
A quiet corner for reading near the library.

**ABOVE**
Philippe Peiger, an expert in urban agroecology, designed the interior plantings and the urban farm on the railway tracks. Planters are placed near the windows of the restaurant. A green wall is installed near one of the staircases.

**LEFT**
Another staircase in the restaurant, past a wall made with found mirror, window, and door frames, leads to an upstairs office.

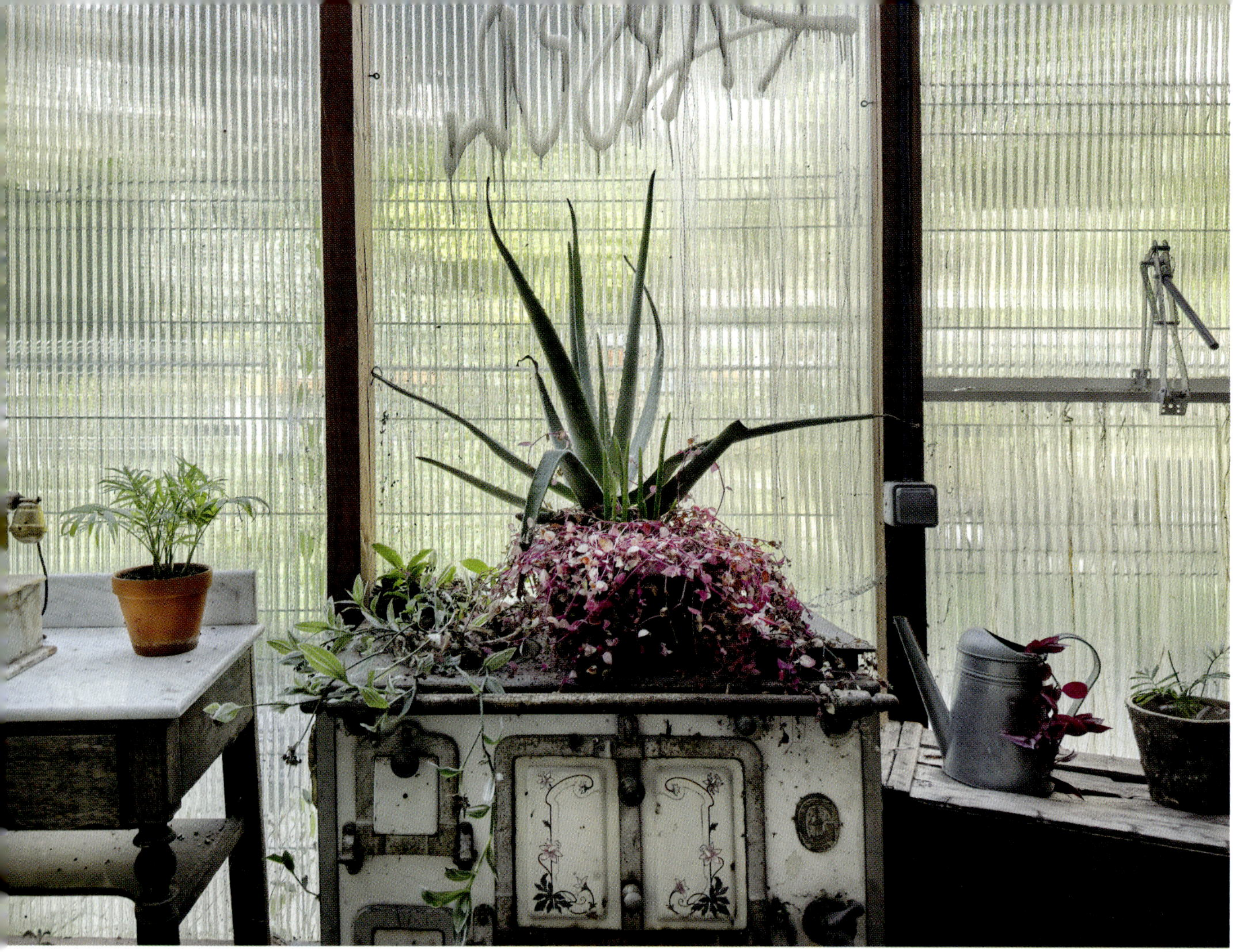

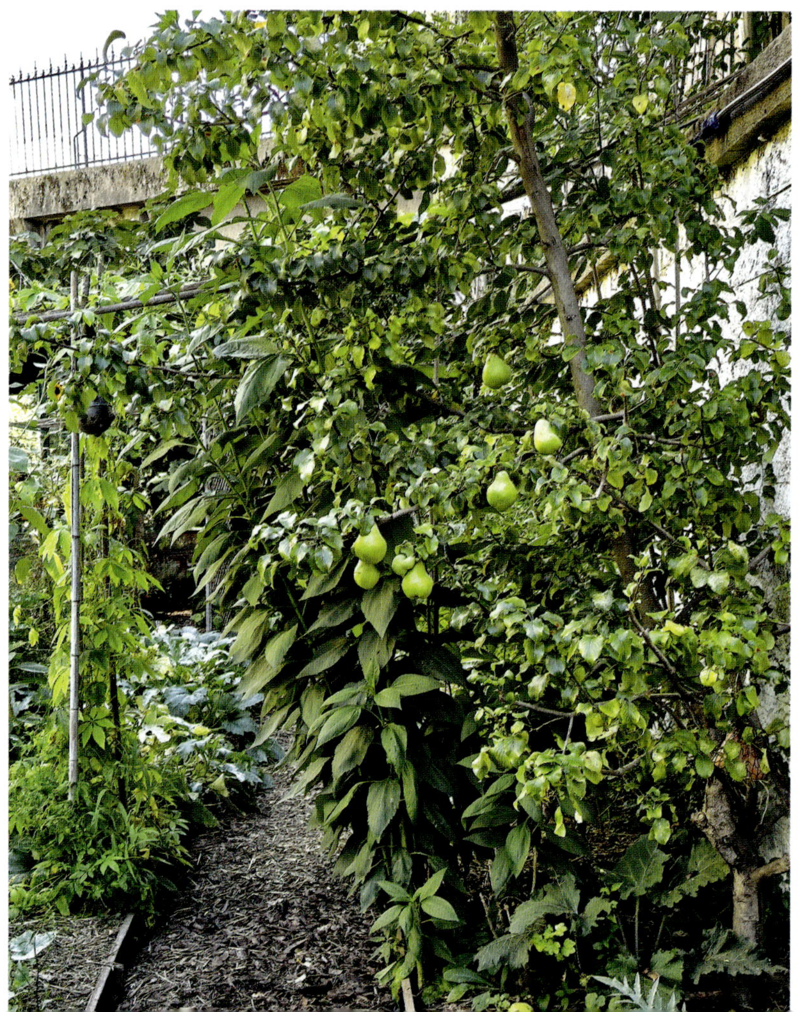

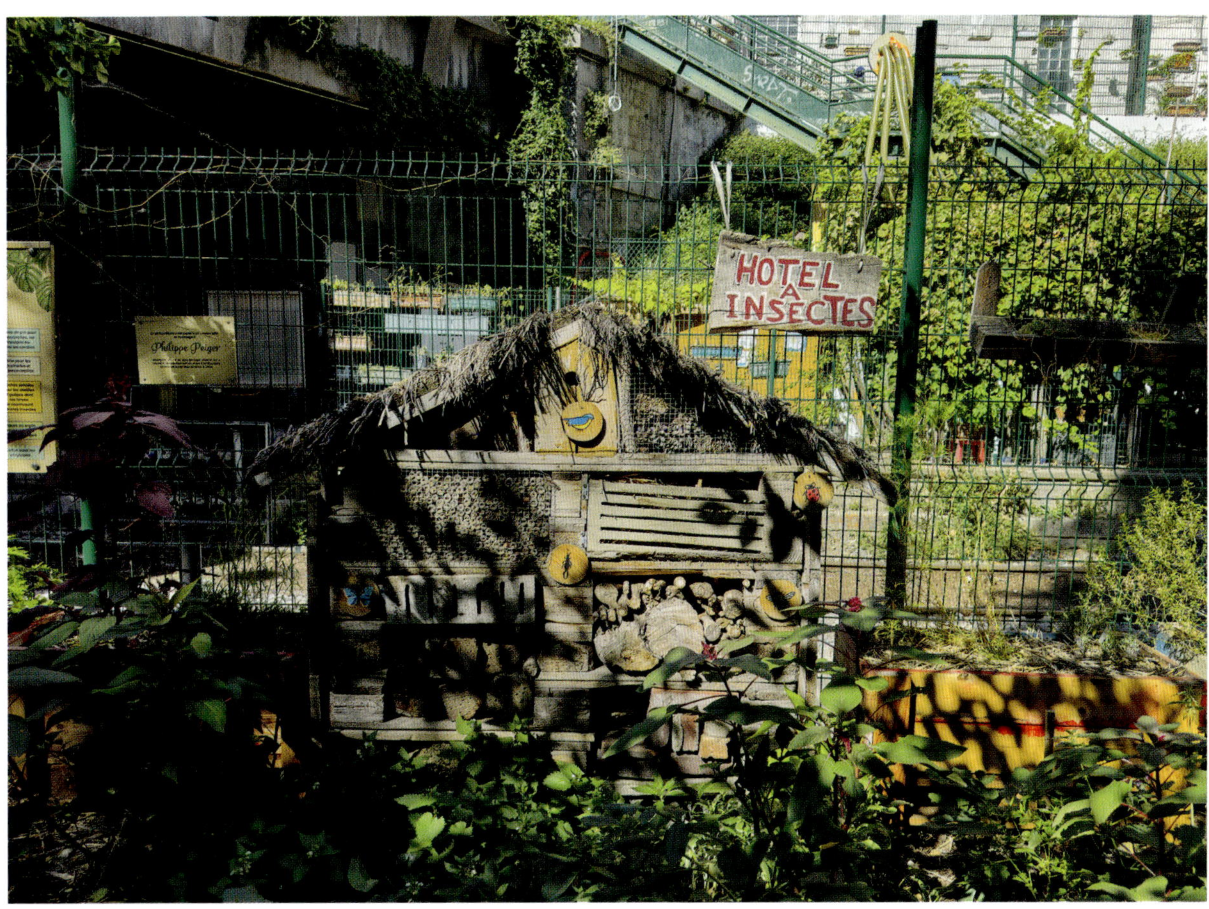

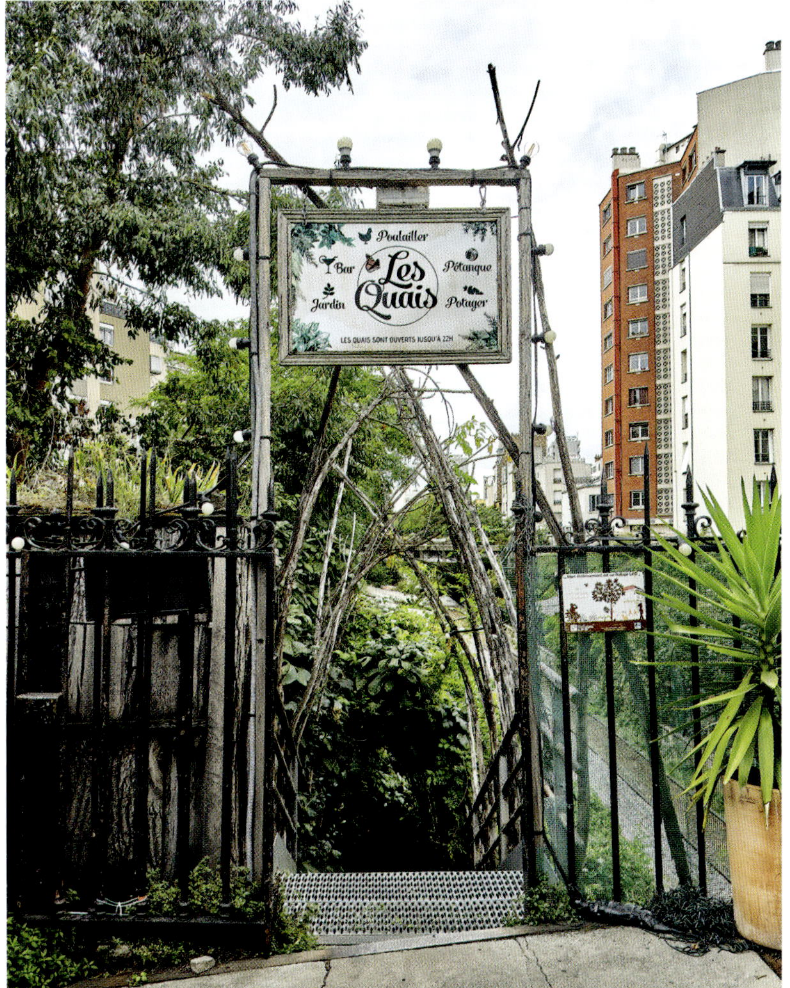


**OPPOSITE ABOVE**
Used furnishings like this old stove and these tables are incorporated into the garden.

**OPPOSITE BELOW**
Pear and other fruit trees grow on the garden path.

**ABOVE**
The gardeners created an "insect hotel" to promote the biodiversity of the site.

**LEFT**
The entrance to the urban farm, which is below street level.

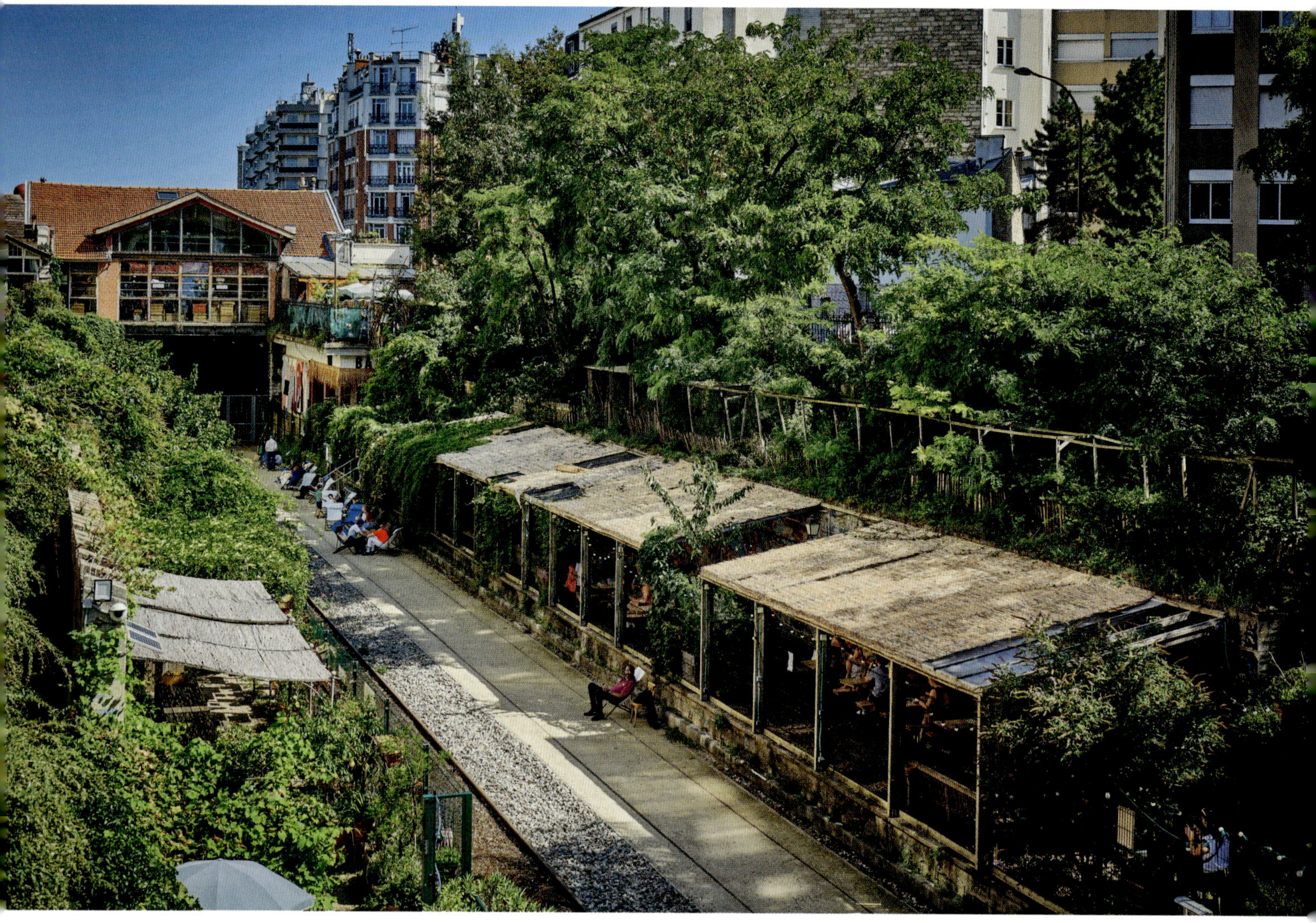

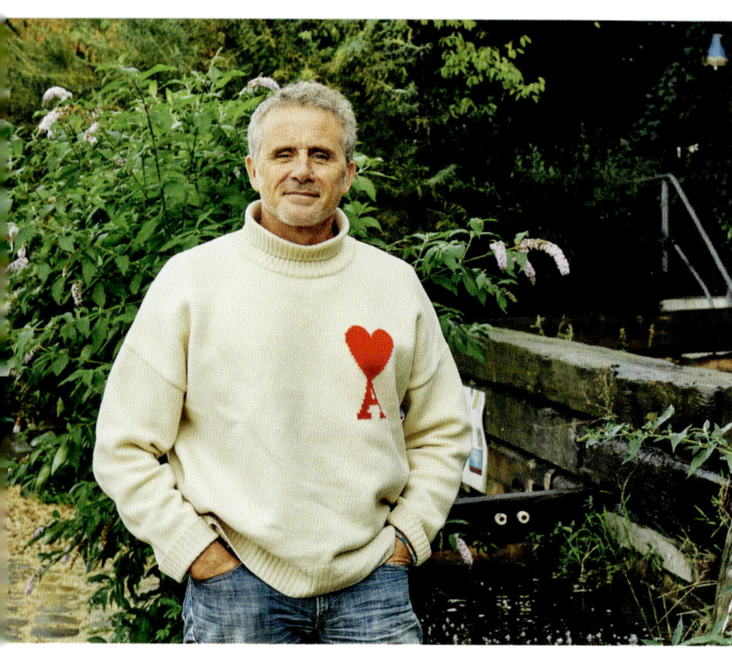

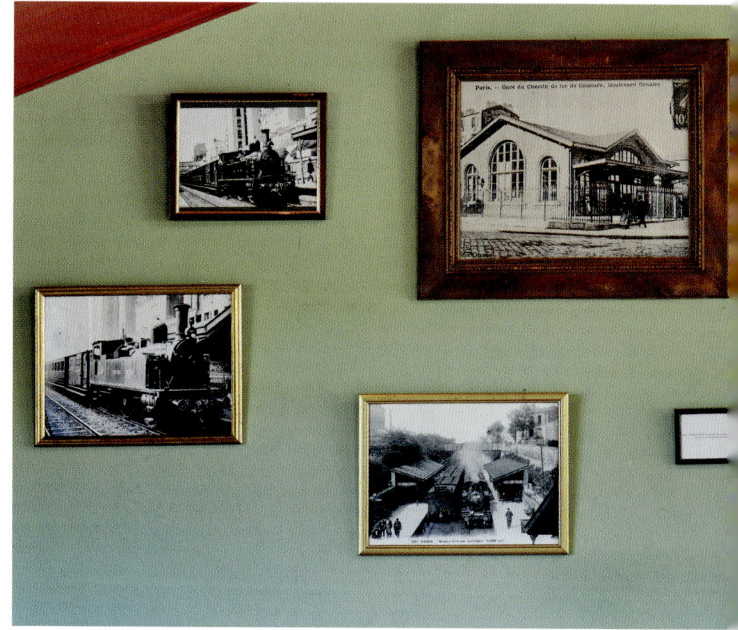

# an interview with Stéphane Vatinel, president of Sinny&Ooko

**M**ichel Arnaud: How did you start La REcyclerie?

**Stéphane Vatinel:** La REcyclerie, to give credit where it's due, started through an amazing guy, Olivier Laffon. He made his fortune building shopping centers in the suburbs. At the dawn of his sixtieth birthday, he decided to seek redemption and asked us to create a place called the Comptoir Général for him. He told us, "I want a place that talks about ecology and denounces France-Afrique relations." It was the first time we responded to an external commission. We would never have dared to dive into a theme so different from what we were doing with our artistic and cultural venues. We opened in 2008. If it hadn't been for this good Samaritan who said, "No matter if it works or not, I'll finance this project," we would never have come up with the idea of La REcyclerie. Four years later, when his son told us, "Comptoir Général is working beautifully," I met with Olivier Laffon and I said, "Listen, there's a train station for sale in the 18th arrondissement, and the mayor [of the 18th arrondissement] wants to know if we can buy it from SNCF." I suggested we propose a unique project that would resonate with the 18th arrondissement, and specifically porte de Clignancourt.

Porte de Clignancourt and porte de Saint-Ouen have a history with les Puces de Saint-Ouen, the oldest flea market [in Paris]. From the sixteenth to the nineteenth centuries, people who went to the wealthy districts to pick up what the nobles and bourgeoisie discarded were called *biffins*. They would sell furniture and clothes, giving a second life to what the bourgeoisie no longer wanted. Over the centuries, the Puces de Saint-Ouen, also known as the Clignancourt flea market, became a meeting place for Parisians from all socioeconomic backgrounds. After World War II, antique dealers began opening shops with rare pieces, attracting wealthy decorators, aristocrats, and people from around the world. Thus, the Puces de Saint-Ouen became a mix of people from everywhere.

The first idea [of a connection to the flea market] inspired us in 2012. At the time, we became aware of overconsumption, which leads to overproduction and the disposal of unused goods, creating what we might call aberrations. We started to realize that this [system] wasn't morally acceptable.

The second element that led us to finalize the La REcyclerie project was that [the site] is an old train station on the Petite Ceinture, a railway circling around Paris created to supply all the gates of the periphery. Finally, in the 1970s, it closed due to the influence of car manufacturers and oil companies that wanted to promote individual car use and dismantle public transport, similar to what happened in some American cities.



**OPPOSITE ABOVE**
Visitors to the garden can walk on the path of the Petite Ceinture, the defunct railway line that was preserved.

**OPPOSITE BELOW LEFT**
Stéphane Vatinel in Paris, 2024.

**OPPOSITE BELOW RIGHT**
Photographs of the old train station document the history of La REcyclerie.

The fabulous thing is that [the Petite Ceinture] remained closed for over fifty years. If these lands had been given to property developers, Paris would have been surrounded by buildings. But SNCF, which wasn't in a hurry and had a commitment to safeguard the city in case of war, left this 30-kilometer [19-mile] ring railroad to flourish. This [situation] created a biodiversity hotspot with foxes, raptors, martens, and lush vegetation. Our interest in the former Ornano station, with its rich biodiversity, led us to consider creating a symbolic place that addressed both biodiversity and recycling. Porte de Clignancourt symbolized reuse and recycling.

We proposed the project to the mayor of the 18th arrondissement, Daniel Vaillant, a former minister of the interior, suggesting a basic economic model. We aimed to create a place based on the three Rs: Reduce, Repair, Recycle. We would create a workshop where people could bring their broken items, borrow tools for free, and repair their belongings. On the other side, we would focus on biodiversity and urban agriculture, building greenhouses. We told the mayor, "This model will resonate with the 18th arrondissement, a working-class district." We would offer affordable food, with meals costing ten to twelve euros, including a dish and dessert, with wine *en vrac* [in bulk] and free water access. Importantly, we wouldn't force anyone visiting La REcyclerie to consume anything. They would have free Wi-Fi access without needing to buy a coffee. We drafted this beautiful dossier, which the mayor of the 18th arrondissement loved. Once approved by city hall, we purchased the building from SNCF with Olivier Laffon and another investor.

We bought the place in 2012, and it opened in 2014.

**MA:** Did you have help with the interior design of the station? What was your inspiration?
**SV:** We always work with decorators who we love. Two decorators worked on La REcyclerie, with the main decoration done by Pierre Ferrari. The station had been completely mistreated by the three previous activities that had taken place inside this old building. There was a bank, a brasserie, and a store a few years before. They all had put up false ceilings and plywood everywhere to hide everything. The main work we had to do was to strip away all that to find the original building. We found floorboards from livestock transport wagons.

**MA:** How did you use them?
**SV:** We recovered all the floorboards, which were already over one hundred years old in the time when they were made into wagons. We used them to make our own floors. The entire kitchen was made from recycled materials. When Pierre Ferrari started, our directive was, as much as possible, do not buy anything new, much like the *biffins* who prioritized recovery. I can say that the only things that weren't recycled were the paint and maybe some tiles. All the sales equipment at the bar, the kitchen, was made with secondhand ovens, fridges, and what we call a "piano," where you have gas burners. All of it was equipment that we had bought secondhand. The chefs were quite angry because they wanted to work with new equipment. But if we call ourselves La REcyclerie, we must truly embrace that approach. Recycling everything is essential to the coherence of the project.

It worked very well for two or three years, but eventually, the equipment started to become obsolete, and we had to replace it. In the kitchen, new equipment tends to last longer than old, despite everything.

**MA:** When you look toward the staircase leading to the offices, on the wall, there are wooden plant containers.
**SV:** We worked with a landscape architect, Philippe Peiger, who put a lot of greenery inside La REcyclerie and arranged all the gardens on the train platforms. It was one of my desires; I really wanted to put green in the place as much as possible for two reasons. First, the site is a biodiversity corridor, the Petite Ceinture. It was important to me that we make the vegetation visible. So, we put a lot of plants on the platforms. We have almost 2,500 square meters [27,000 square feet] of green outdoor space on the platforms, and all the roofs were covered in greenery as well. The green roofs help in winter and especially in summer to reduce the impact of heat waves. Vegetation acts as a screen against the sun's rays.

The second equally important point is that you realize vegetation has an extraordinary ability to calm people. The more you immerse humans and animals in a densely vegetated space, the softer their gestures, voices, and expectations become. It makes them a bit more serene. It's a beautiful metaphor for what nature can truly do when we listen to it. For a long time, we had a great capacity to deny nature in our cities. Now, we are bringing back green spaces. The city of Paris, for a long time, was very under-vegetated, everything was paved over. In the last twenty years, we've started to recognize the importance of vegetation for quality of life. I wanted to bring vegetation inside La REcyclerie, and I think it has significantly contributed to its huge success since it opened.

One of our concerns was to offer people who came to La REcyclerie a green space that creates better energy, a calming energy compared to the hustle and bustle of porte de Clignancourt. As soon as you pass [through] our door and go down to the platforms along the Petite Ceinture, you suddenly find yourself in an oasis of tranquility. You are no longer in Paris. Just a 4-meter [13-foot] descent and 30 meters [98 feet] of teleportation to the west, and suddenly you feel like you are in a small, quiet provincial town where you can hear the birds. This, in my opinion, is of crucial importance. If all our cities had such spaces where you can easily recharge and escape from the hyperconcentration of people, which generates a lot of stress and excitement, it might help us be more serene in these big metropolises.

**MA:** I have photos of pear trees and fig trees, and I wanted to talk about the French version of the *tiers-lieu*.
**SV:** Figs and pears, of course. Plus, we grow our own hops that we take to a brewery to make our own beer. We have chickens that produce around five thousand eggs a year, fed fifty percent from kitchen waste, plus corn and wheat that we give them. We also produce vegetables in our greenhouse. We have [large meeting] rooms, and all this leads to the concept of the *tiers-lieu*, which is very important to us because we believe La REcyclerie is an extraordinary example of a place that can be replicated anywhere in our cities and villages. It thrives on something extremely basic: A place can host a multitude of activities. The more diverse these activities are, the more they feed each other in a way that wouldn't necessarily be economically viable if they were standalone activities in a single location.

In this multifunctional place, at certain times of the day, certain days of the week, and in different parts of the same location, you can have coffee roasting, vegetable production, woodworking, bike repair, a medical center, office spaces—and all these activities bring in different populations for different reasons. These populations together support its fixed costs, and then the activities can develop their own financial balance, creating a positive economic ripple effect.

The *tiers-lieu* concept will allow our cities and villages in France or any other country, like the United States, to re-create an economy, reopen businesses, and create jobs, because these places are open seven days a week, at least twelve hours a day minimum. But really the minimum should be from nine A.M. to two A.M. La REcyclerie is open seven days a week, 365 days a year, from nine A.M. to two A.M. This also helps create social bonds between people who wouldn't have access to this diversity of activities if there were no such place. People might not meet otherwise and would be isolated at home.

Once I've said that I haven't said anything new. The concept of the good old mall was invented in 1956, and we saw the first example in Minnesota, USA. Ultimately, shopping malls are a form of *tiers-lieu* that was implemented cleverly by merchants.

If you remove the strictly commercial aspect and include sentiment, generosity, the notion of community, and are not greedy but instead want to share this gain, which is emotional, social, economic, and psychological, the *tiers-lieu* becomes a shared space where there is a place for everyone who goes there and uses it. It's the generosity aspect of the *tiers-lieu* that needs to be highlighted.

We have many villages that have become ghost towns because the bakery closed, the hairdresser closed, the general practitioner retired, and the post office closed. We say, create a *tiers-lieu*, bring back a general practitioner, a hairdresser who also sells drinks, put it all inside, and you'll gradually see the village come back to life thanks to this type of place. Make sure there is as much time dedicated to work as to leisure, because for too long, some people considered coworking spaces where people worked together as a *tiers-lieu.* We say no, no, no. The *tiers-lieu* is meant to bring together both those who work and those who don't. It should be open on weekends and evenings because you shouldn't be bored in your village, and there should always be leisure activities available.

All the programming that we organize inside La REcyclerie—the markets, theater, flea markets; all the weekend bike rallies for people in the neighborhood who are delighted to take a tour around the area or Paris on the Petite Ceinture—we are here to help you find a job and to bring you happiness through leisure activities. All of this together makes for wonderful *tiers-lieu*.

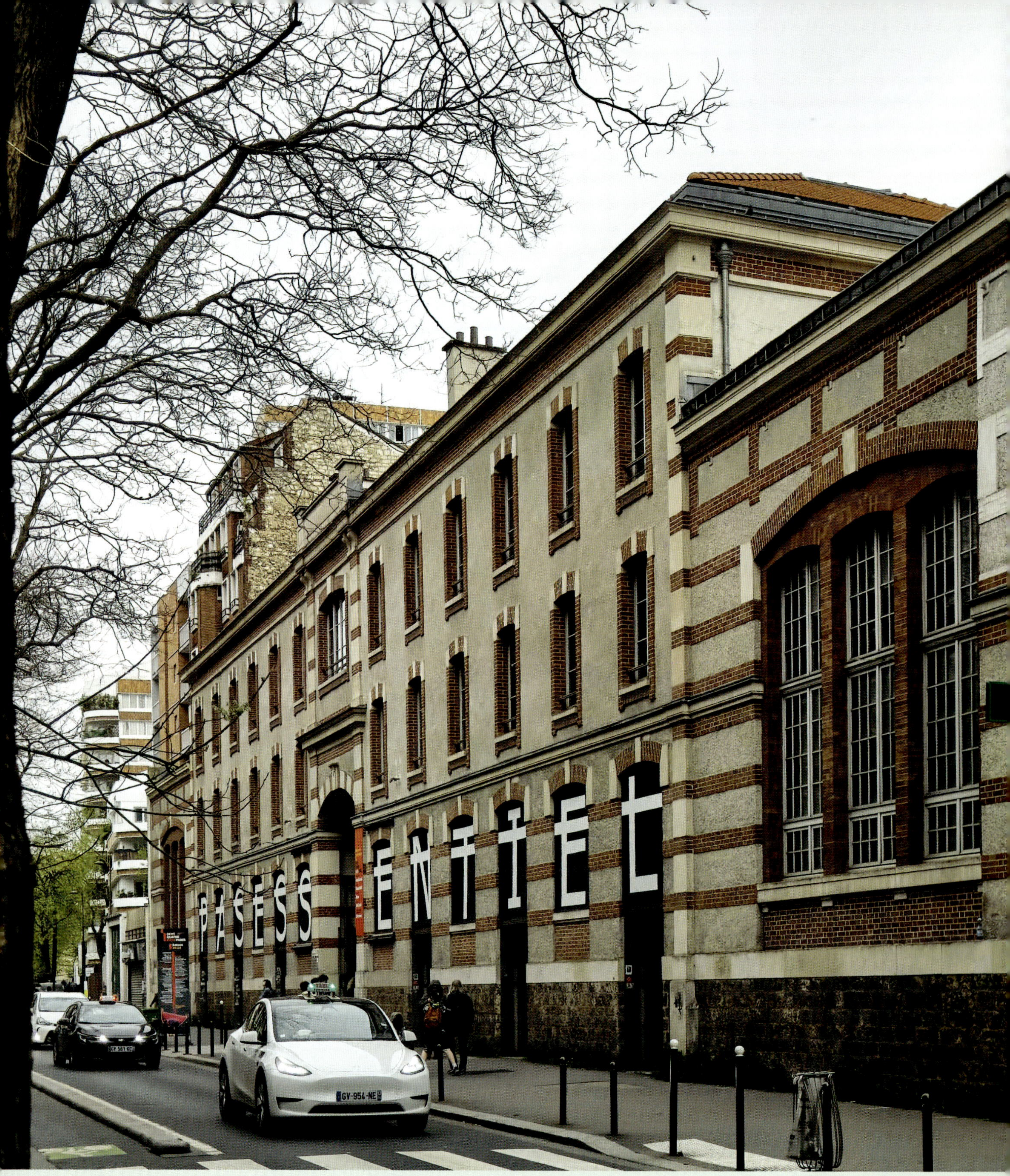



**ABOVE**
The address 104 rue d'Aubervilliers wraps around the exterior corner of Centquatre-Paris.

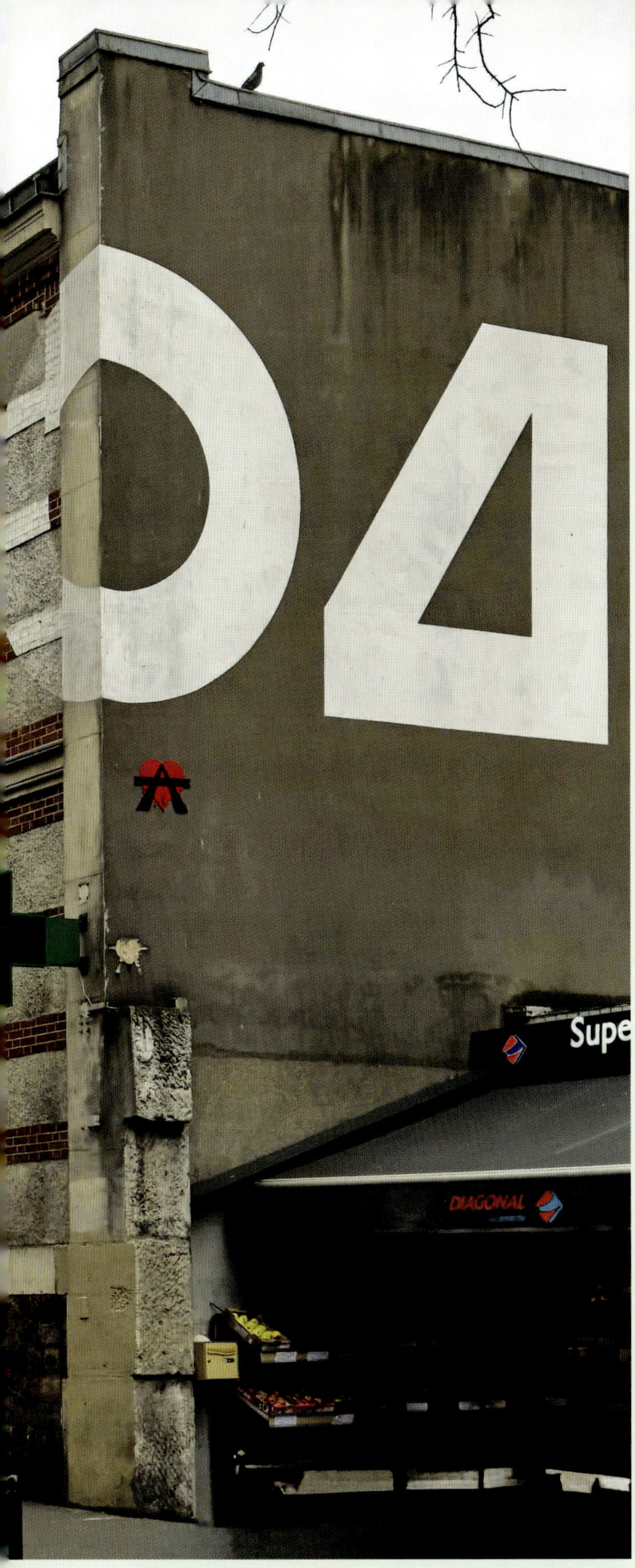

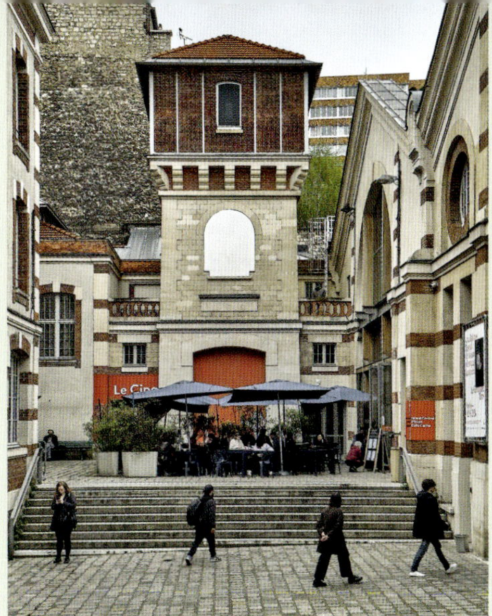

## Centquatre-Paris
19th arrondissement
2008

An 1890s black-and-white photograph of a luxury funeral cortege, posed inside a giant warehouse, was taken as they prepared to march in procession. That warehouse was once the funeral home of the City of Paris and is now home to the vibrant Centquatre-Paris art center. Even in the 1980s, rue d'Aubervilliers, near the edge of the 19th arrondissement, was bleak. It was a warehouse district, near the police compound lot at la porte d'Aubervilliers, named for the suburb at its border. In 2008, after a complete renovation led by architects Atelier Novembre, it was transformed. There are two buildings on-site. One entrance is on rue Curial, and the other is on rue d'Aubervilliers. At the Curial entry, an interior courtyard with a café on its terrace welcomes visitors to the space. Beyond a glass wall is an enormous hall. There is a second set of windows over columns and an arcade below. Natural light and dancers fill the center floor. An instructor leads a group numbering more than a dozen people. Not far away, other dancers are working independently, making moves, then resetting and starting again. Centquartre-Paris has a myriad of programs and spaces. A restaurant and bookstore are on site. There are two theaters, gallery spaces, and production and rehearsal rooms. The second building, an open-air warehouse, also hosts dances, a farmers' market, and events. There is no hint of its former use as a preparation place for funerals; only the impression of exuberance and motion remains.



**ABOVE RIGHT**
A brick-and-stone tower stands over the courtyard and café of the nineteenth-century building.

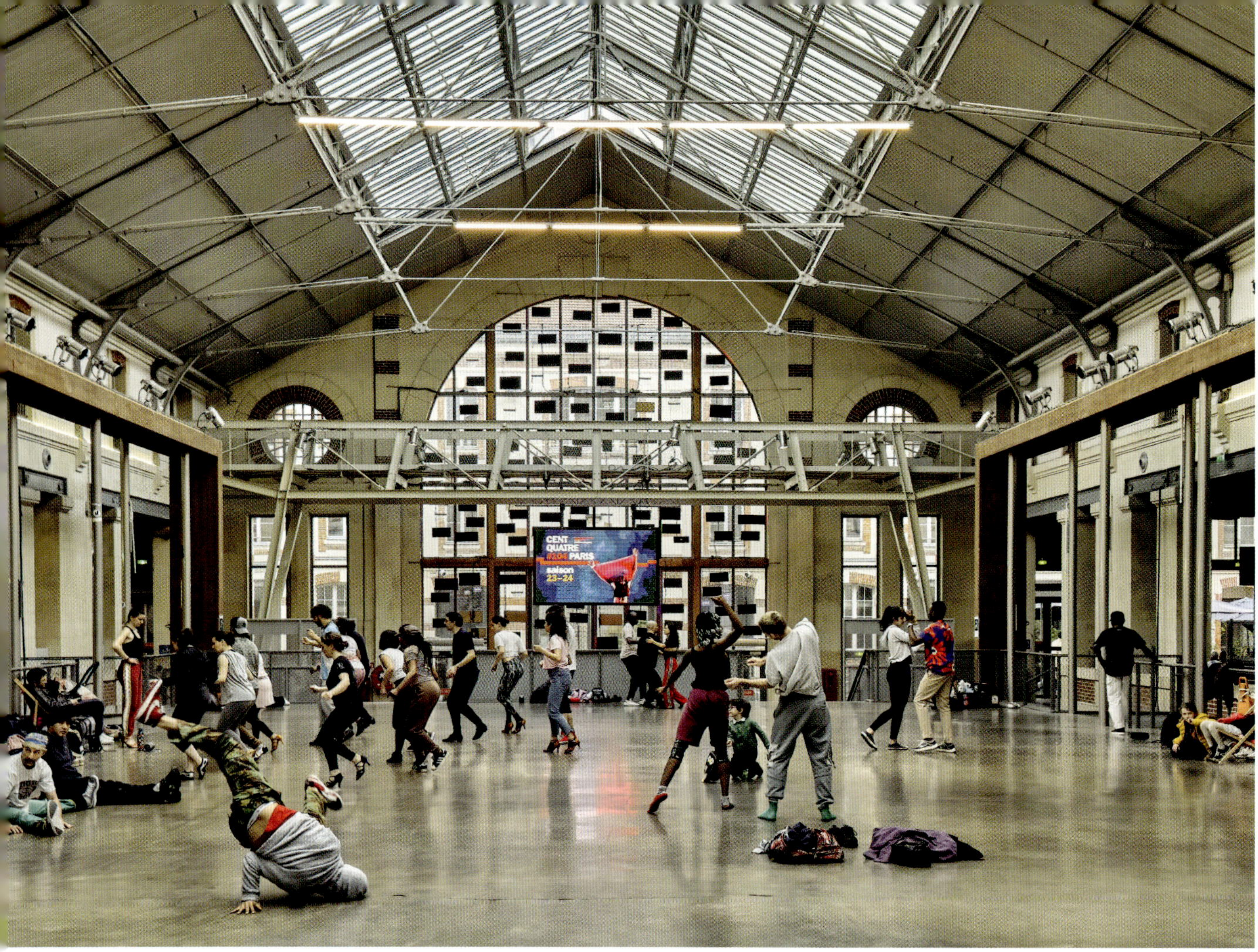

CENT
QUATRE
104 PARIS
saison
23-24

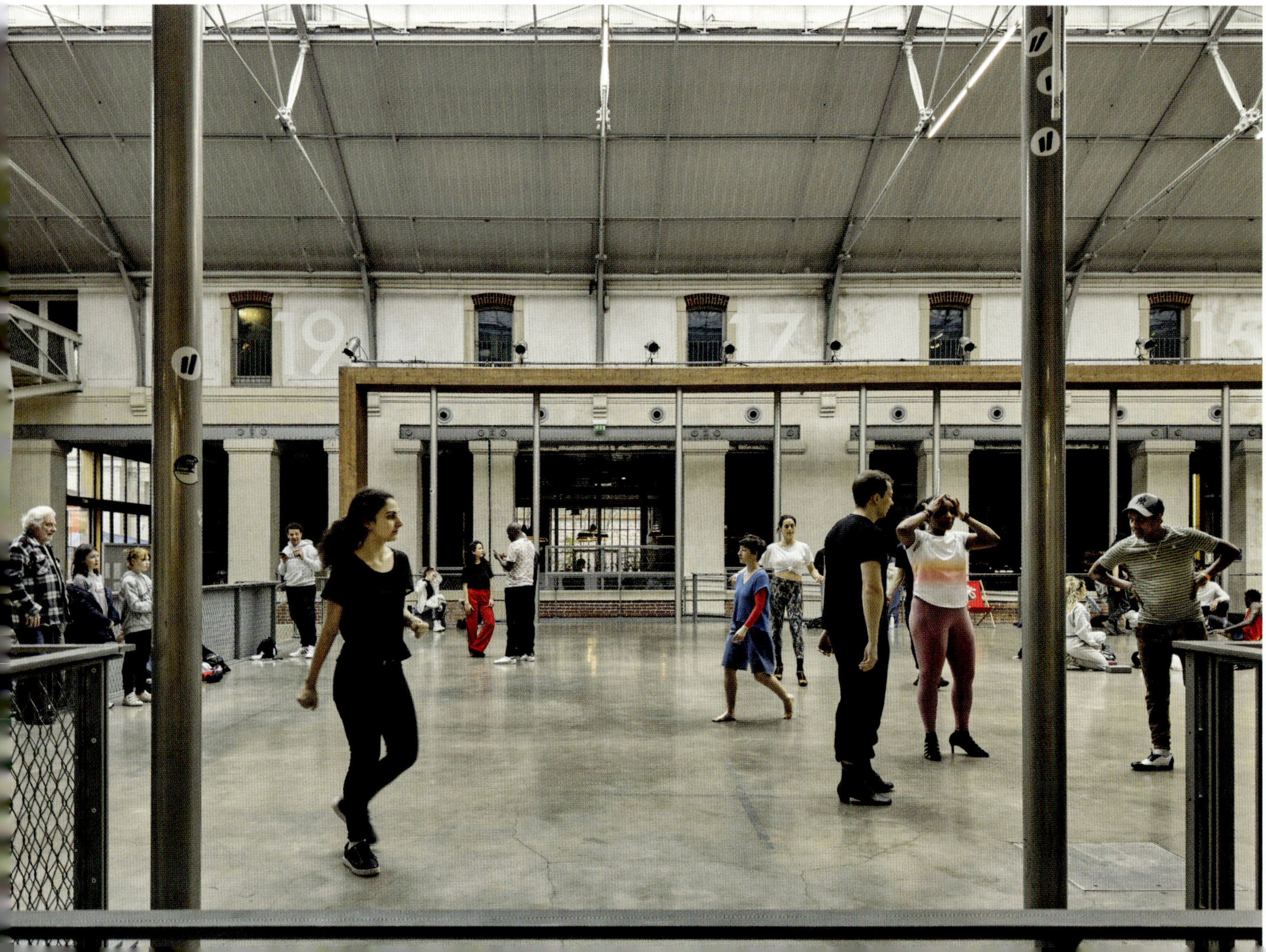

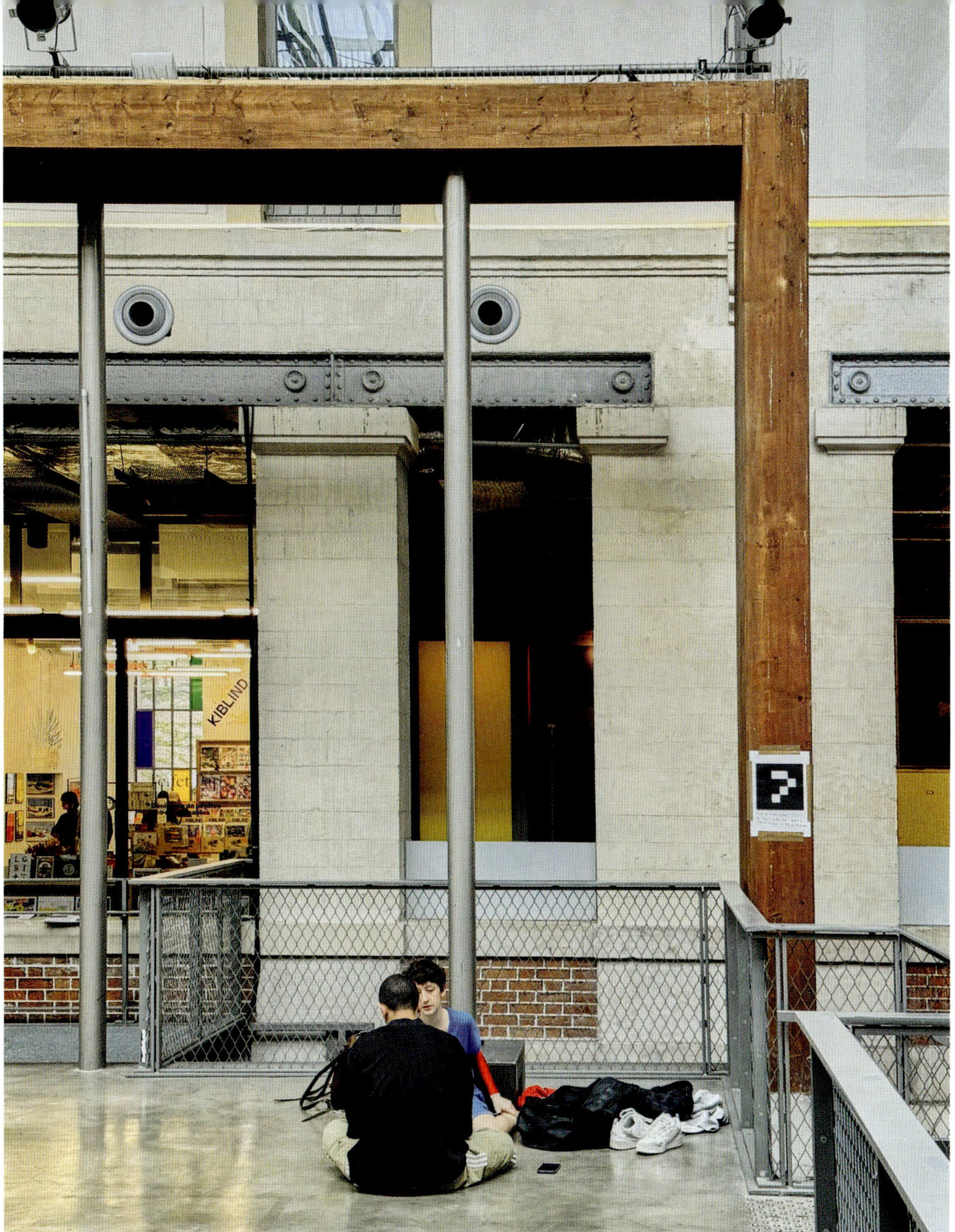



**OPPOSITE ABOVE**
The steel framing supports the skylights above the dancers. The arched window and doorway and the skylights above flood the space with natural light. Additional lighting is installed on tension wiring and new steel beams from the renovation in 2008.

**OPPOSITE BELOW**
A diverse group makes up performers and their audiences in the main front hall of Centquatre-Paris. The center has programing for everyone, from children to older people.

**ABOVE**
Wooden beams frame the dance floor activities and offer additional structural support. Just beyond is the bookstore.

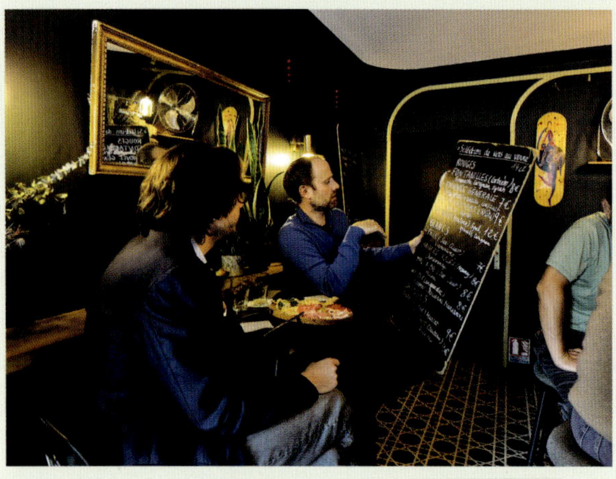

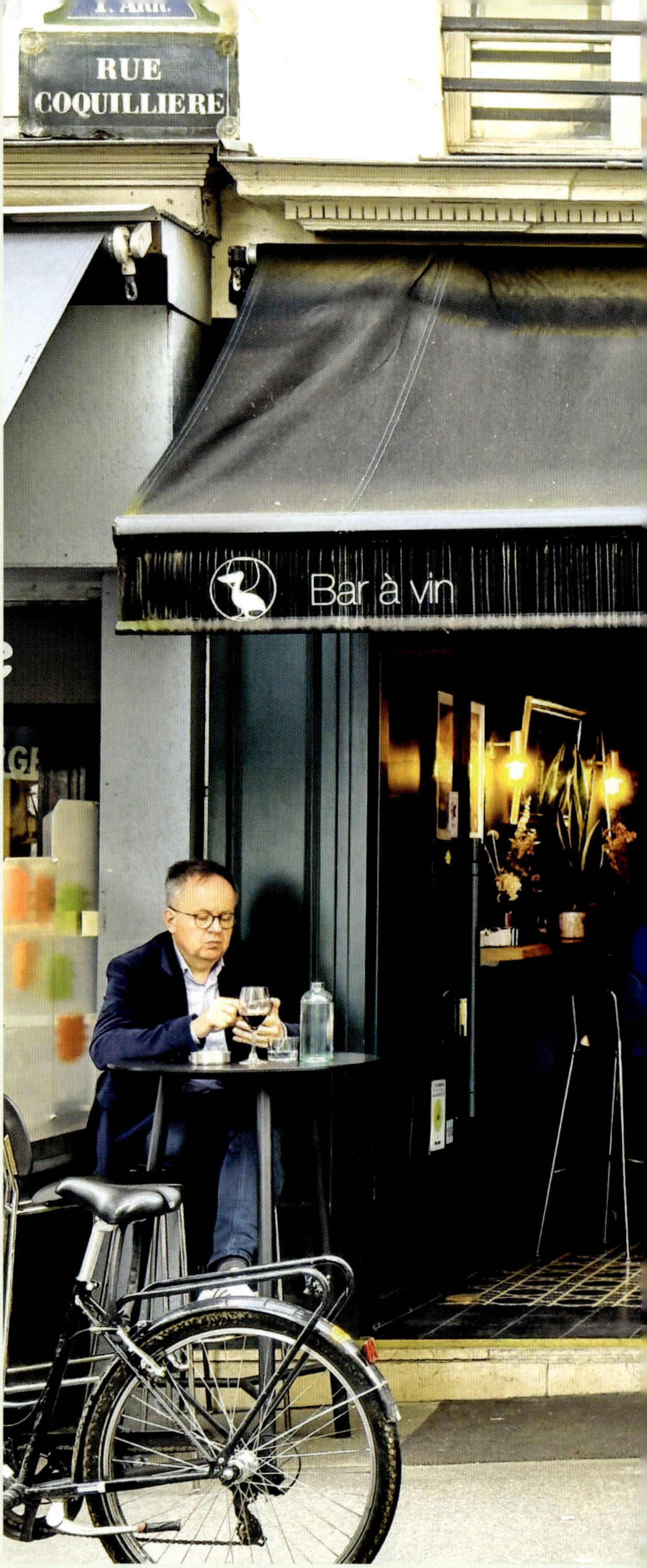

## *Au Naturel*: Food and Wine
## *L'Envers*

1st arrondissement
2019

Olivier Moglia created a charming wine bar, L'Envers (or The Reverse), out of a former Chinese restaurant. A few years later, his partner, Nikos Talbi-Lykakis, joined him in the business. Their program is only natural wines with a specific focus. The natural wine designation within the overall wine industry is complicated. Only one certification, Demeter, named for the Greek goddess, is officially recognized. Olivier and Nikos decided to create their own list of natural wine distinctions. They only select wines from winemakers who respect the *terroir*, or the land, where the grapes are grown. Also, the growers must use less than 7 grams (0.2 ounces) of sulfites and have land parcels of a manageable size (10 to 15 hectares, or 25 to 37 acres, maximum). They feel wines with these parameters will reflect the winemaker's and *terroir*'s personality. With six seating spots inside and another three table tops outside, the space is intimate. Be forewarned vegetarians, most of the bar food is charcuterie boards. But the concentration on natural wines is serious, and the selection is excellent. Natural wines are grown in line with sustainable and/or organic farming methods and produced with no other chemicals. The natural wine movement started in France in the 1980s and has grown exponentially in the last twenty years.

**ABOVE LEFT**
A blackboard of the specialties of the day is passed from table to table.

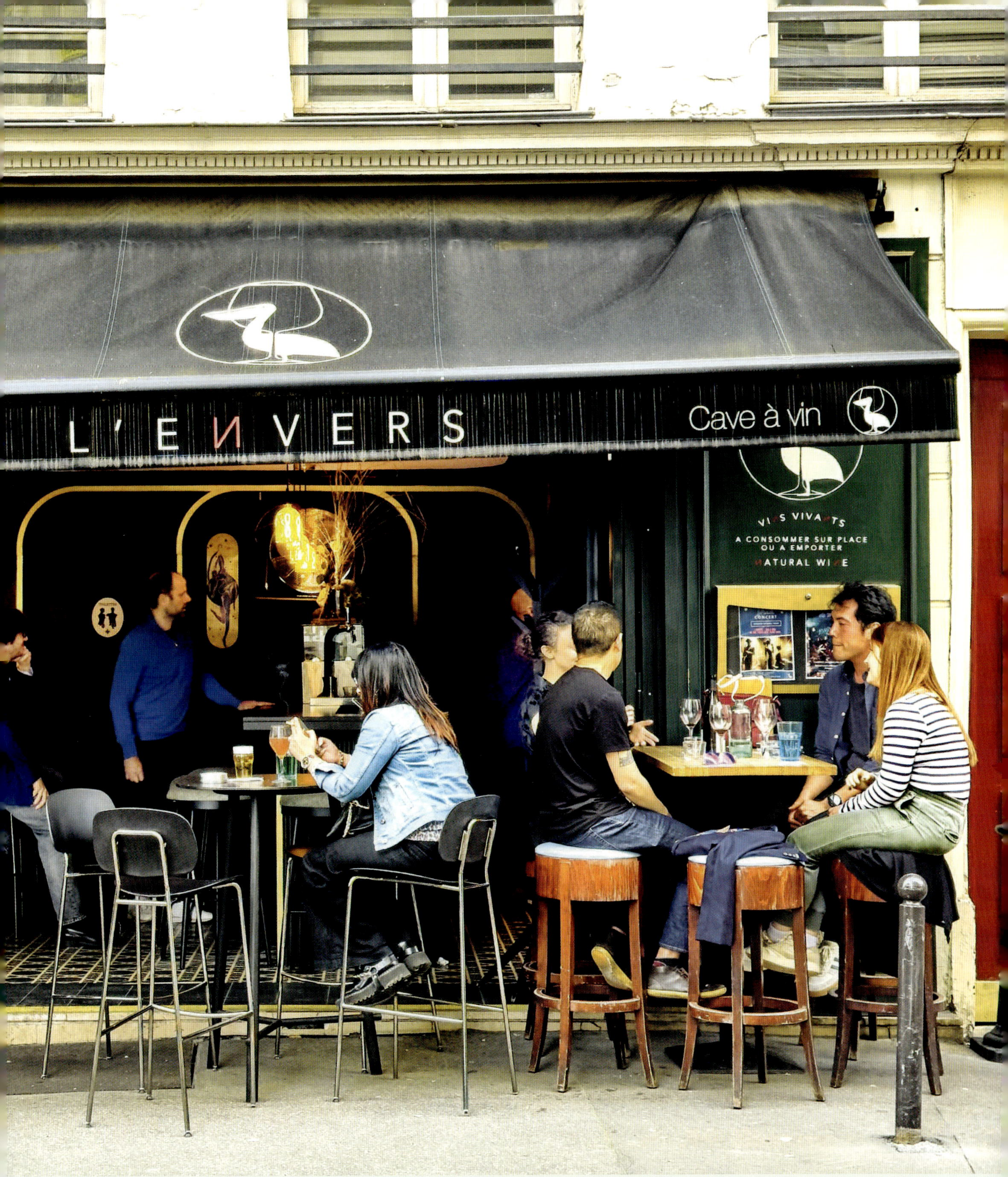



**ABOVE**
Streetside drinks at L'Envers, a natural
wine bar.

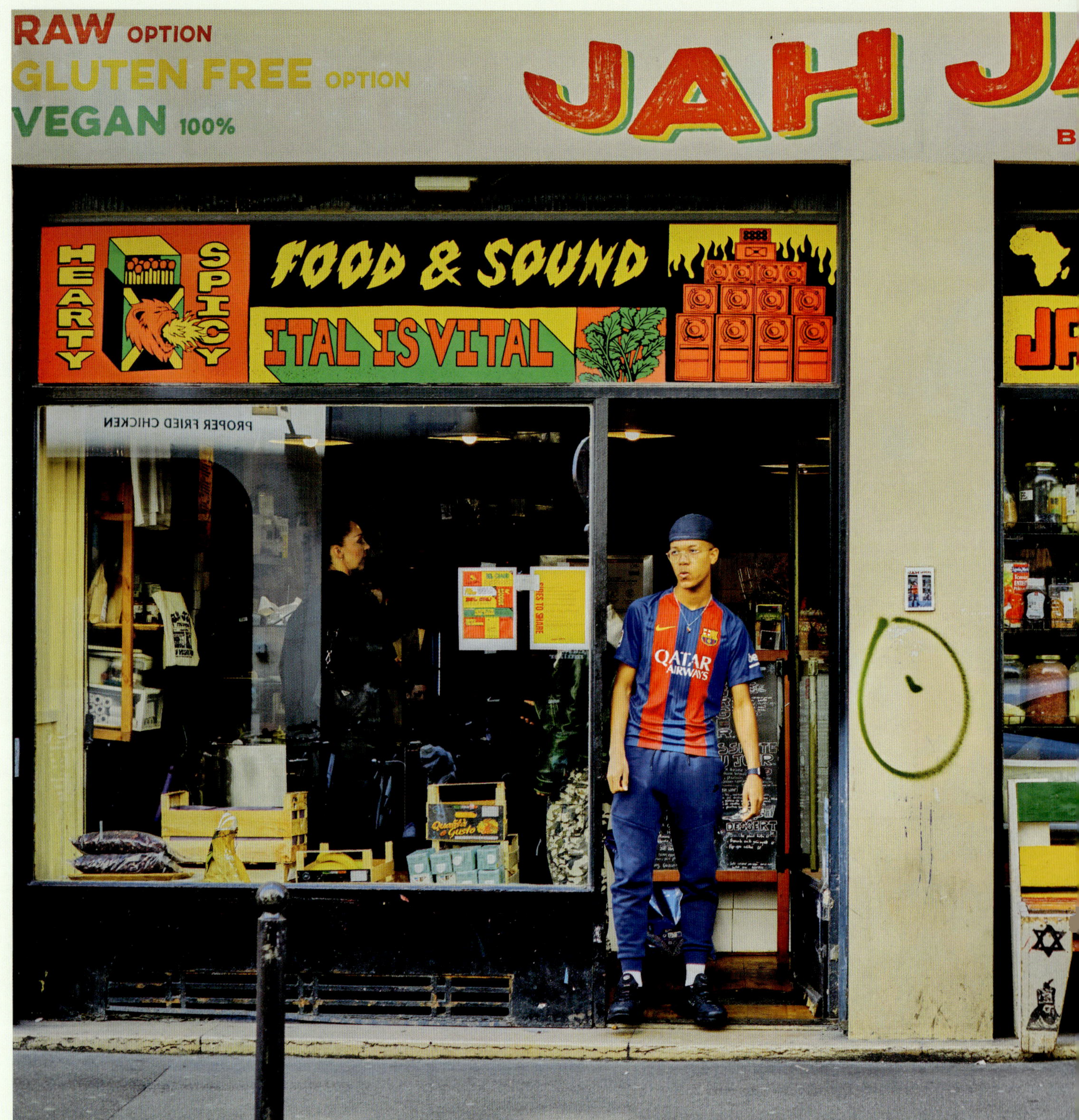


**ABOVE**
Jah Jah, outside.

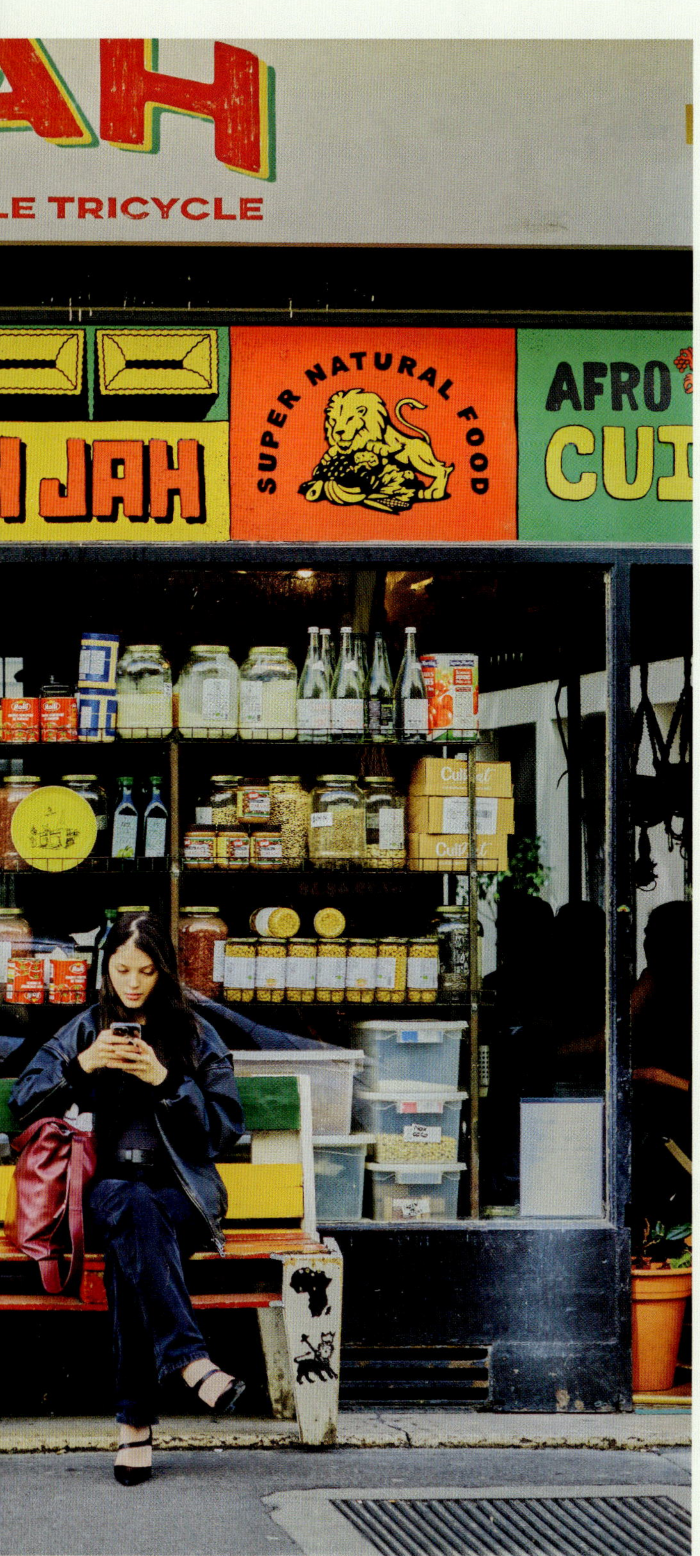


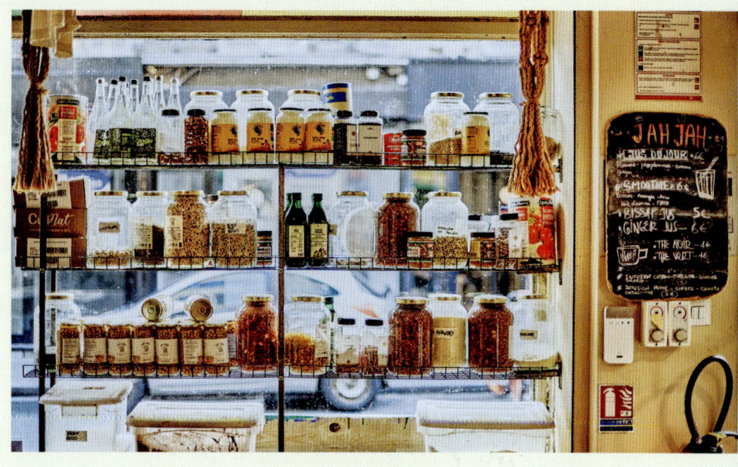

### *Jah Jah* by *Le Tricycle*
10th arrondissement
2017

Daquisiline Gomis and Coralie Jouhier are partners in both life and their businesses, including Jah Jah by Le Tricycle, a vegan restaurant with a Caribbean influence. They started out making vegan hot dogs and selling them on a cargo bike. The restaurant has developed into a community hub with activities like yoga, hiking, music, and dance. Even the exterior of the restaurant has a colorful, cheerful vibe—it stands out on the block. Bright signage in neon orange, blue, and yellow matches the bench in front. Shelving lined with glass jars can be seen from the street, so the storefront looks like a bodega. People are constantly coming and going or hanging out on the bench. Jah Jah is not typical. Inside, the story is the same. Lots of bright colors and images—on tables and chairs, on the walls, and in the ingredients of the dishes. The food, too, reflects the colors of the sea, sky, foliage, and fruits of the islands. The range and depths of the flavors is surprising for what seems to be a simple meal! On one hand it's a quiet café, but on the other it is an homage to Afro-Caribbean history, politics, and sport.

**ABOVE RIGHT**
Pantry items that are used in the dishes
are also for sale.

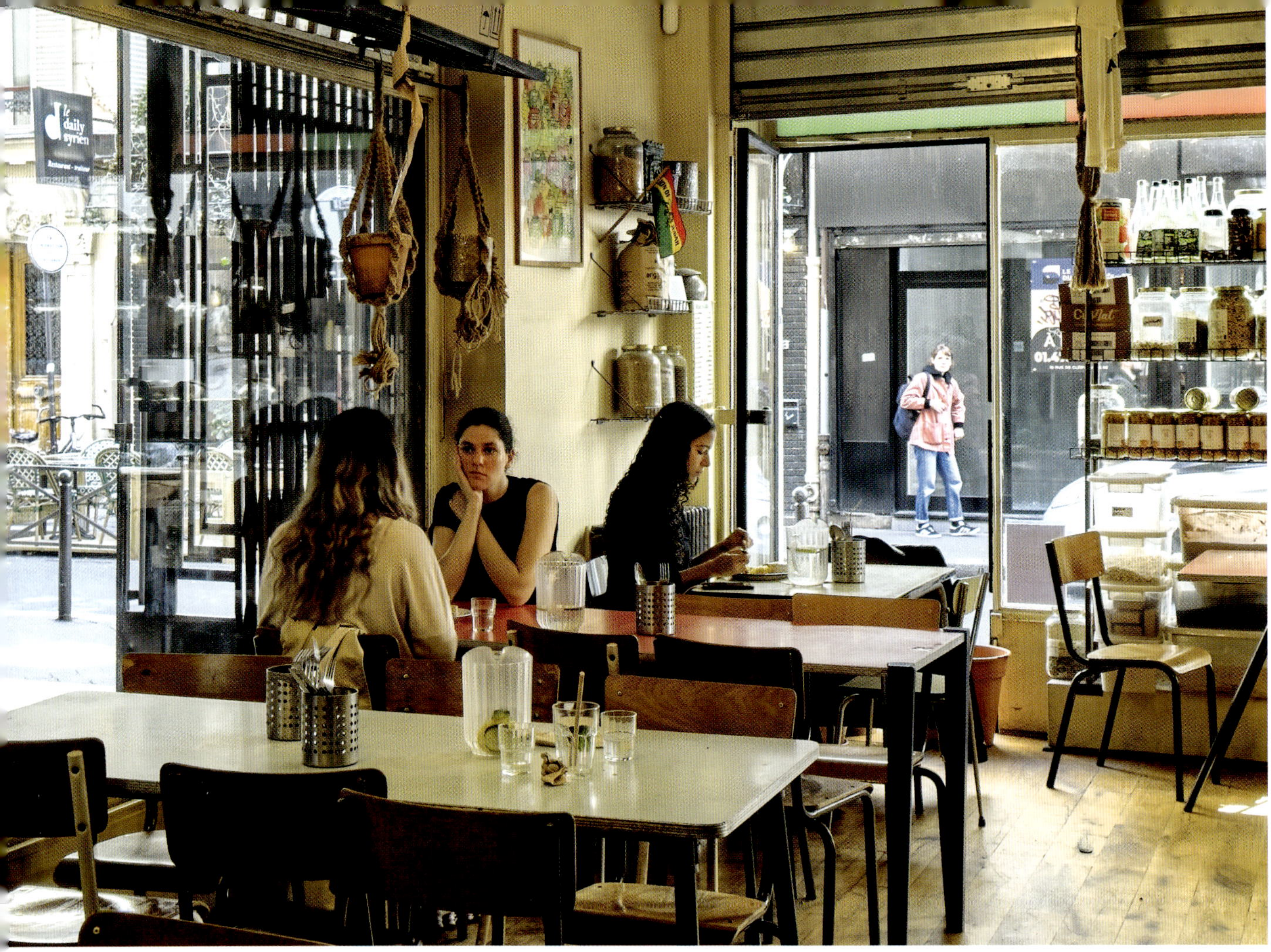

ABOVE
The restaurant is on the corner of a
building that has a courtyard. One wall
is a length of windows.

RIGHT
At the front counter, the chalkboard
menu leans against the half wall that
separates the kitchen from the dining
area.

OPPOSITE ABOVE
A view of the kitchen and the chef in
action.

OPPOSITE BELOW LEFT
The back dining area displays images of
Jah Jah's heroes.

OPPOSITE BELOW RIGHT
Most plates are brightly composed with
a combination of cooked dishes, rice,
and fresh and pickled vegetables.

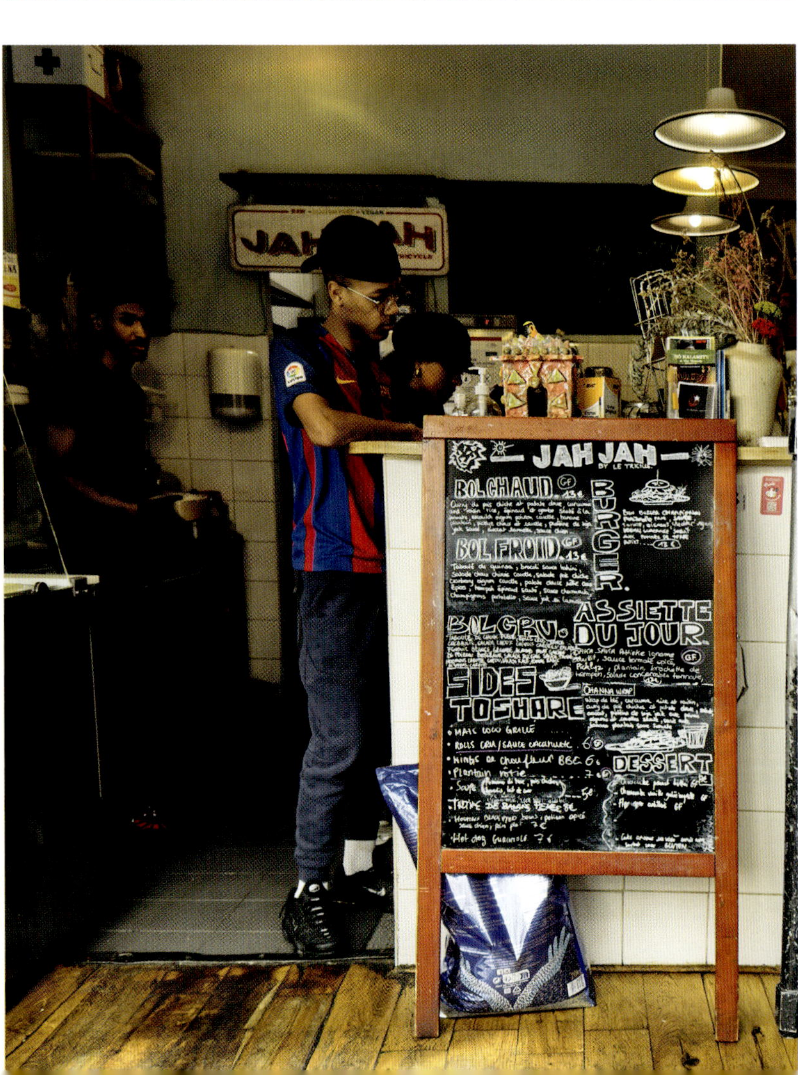

   *JAH JAH BY LE TRICYCLE*

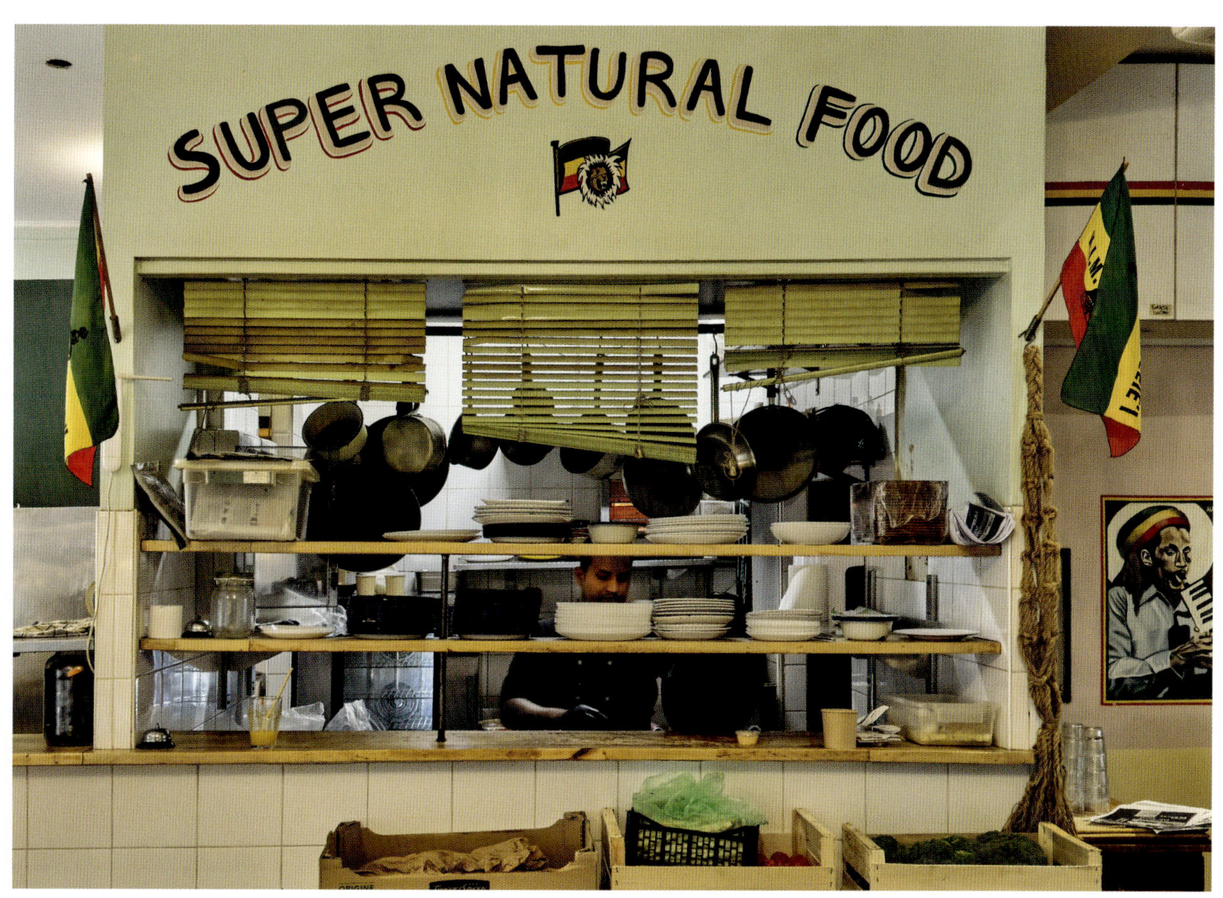


SUPER NATURAL FOOD


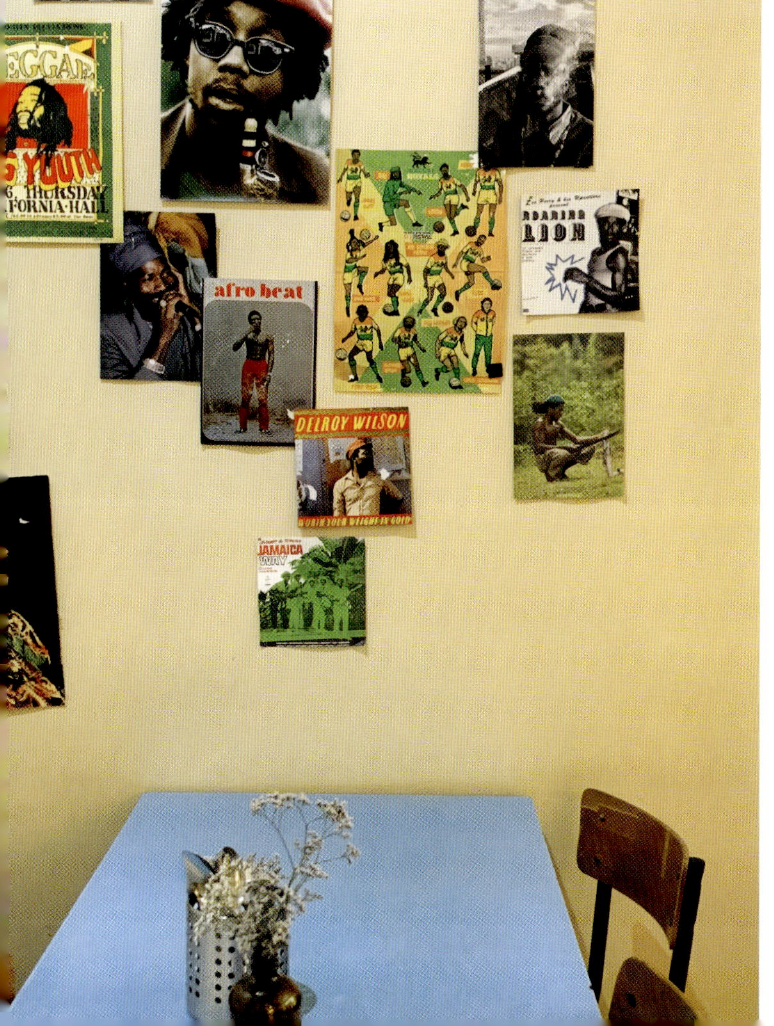


afro beat
DELROY WILSON
JAMAICA


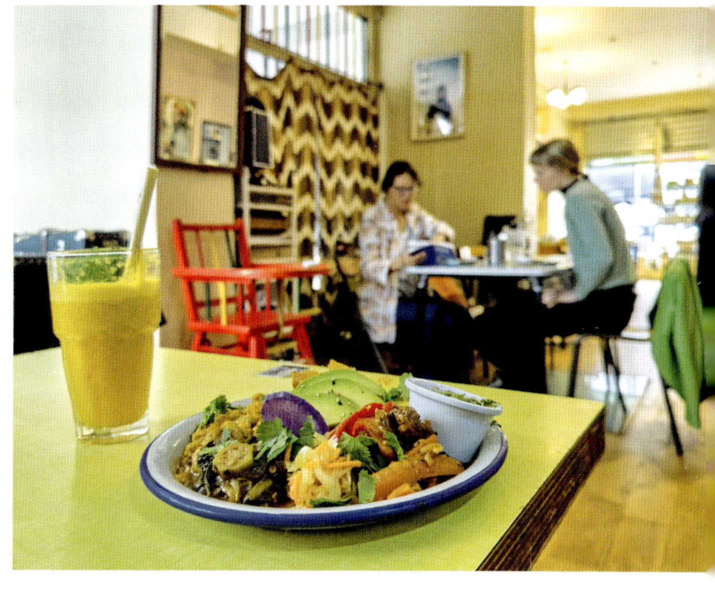

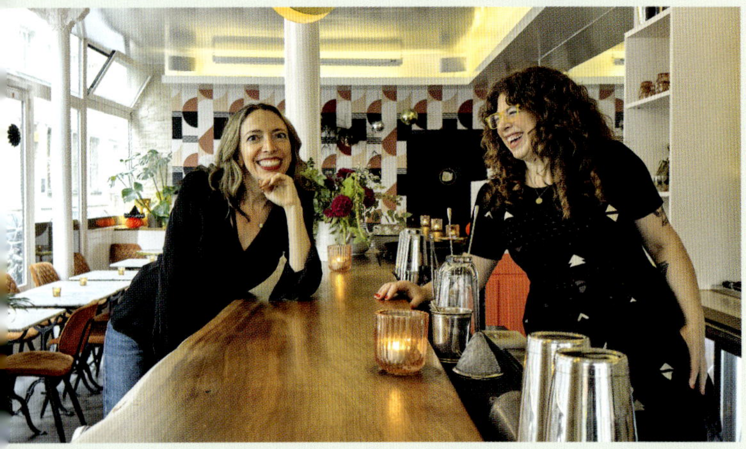



---

### *Abricot*
10th arrondissement
2023

What started as an idea to bring cocktails to everyone stuck at home during COVID lockdown turned into a vegan bar three years later. After building a delivery business serving handmade plant-based drinks in recyclable glass jars, Jennifer Crain and Allison Kave decided to give their love of vegan food and cocktails a permanent place. In February 2023, they opened the bright and hip Abricot. The room reflects both their personalities and their hometowns, Brooklyn and San Francisco. While most of their patrons are from the neighborhood (aren't all good bars local joints?) the vegan community also stops by, and everyone is welcome. Abricot is the first vegan bar in Paris. They don't use any animal products in their drinks or food. Both Crain and Kave have lived in France for more than six years. They felt moving to Paris would be a great fit with their passions for vegan food and drinks, given the value French culture places on fresh food and produce. The emphasis is always on taste, flavor, and fun.

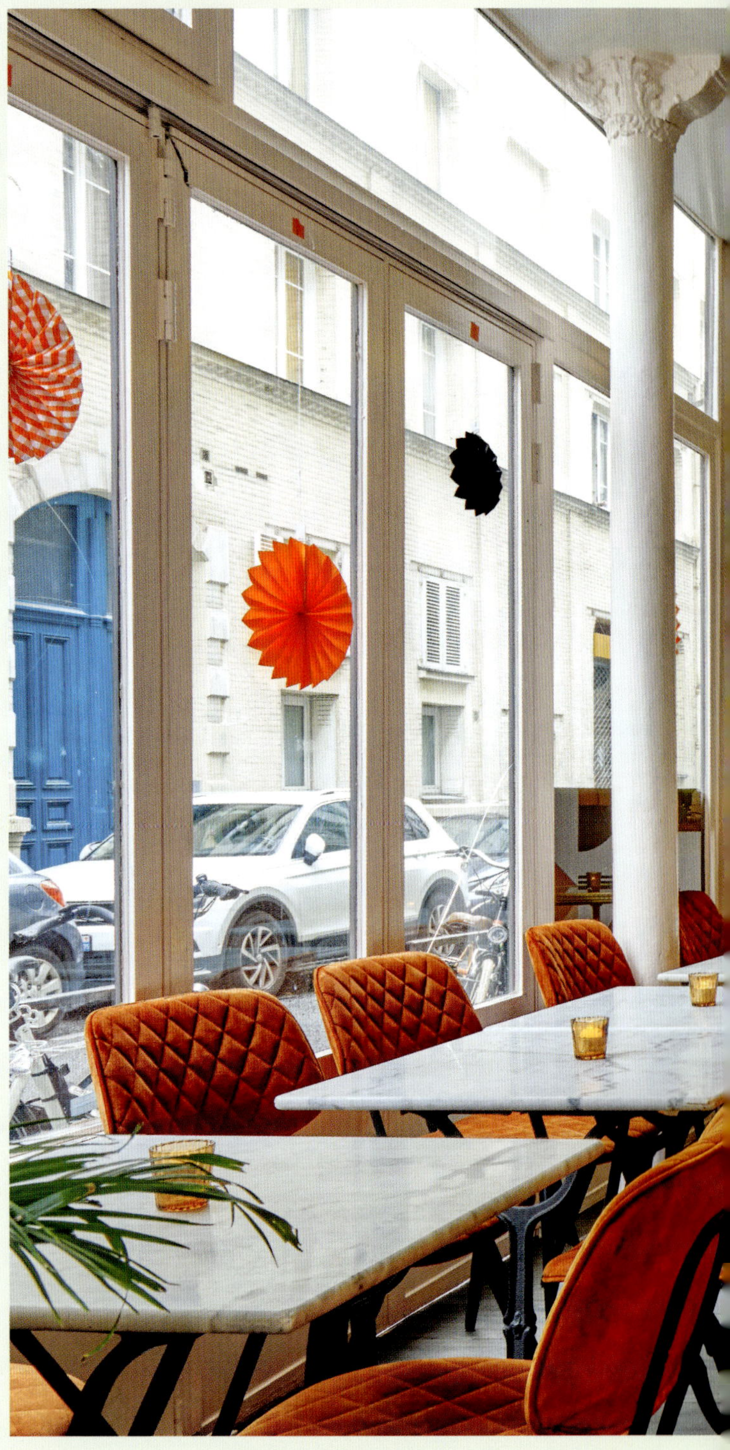

**ABOVE LEFT**
Owners and business partners Jennifer Crain and Allison Kave serve an eclectic and creative list of cocktails, natural wines, beers, and cider.

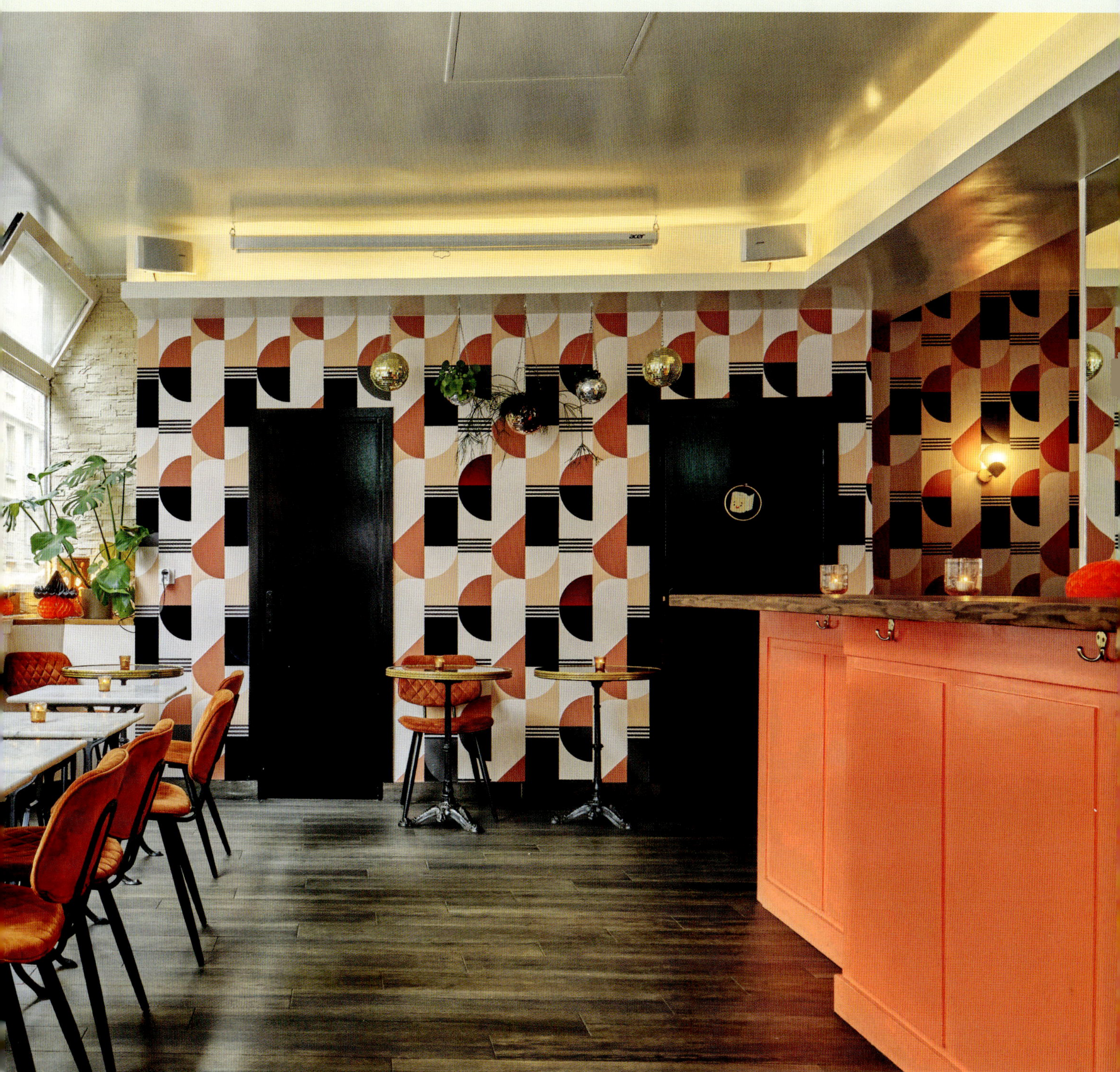


**ABOVE**
The bar is a cheery place with its graphic wallpaper, mirror wall, and orange seating. Each interior design element simultaneously has the optimistic elements of California sunshine, Brooklyn cool, and Paris sophistication.

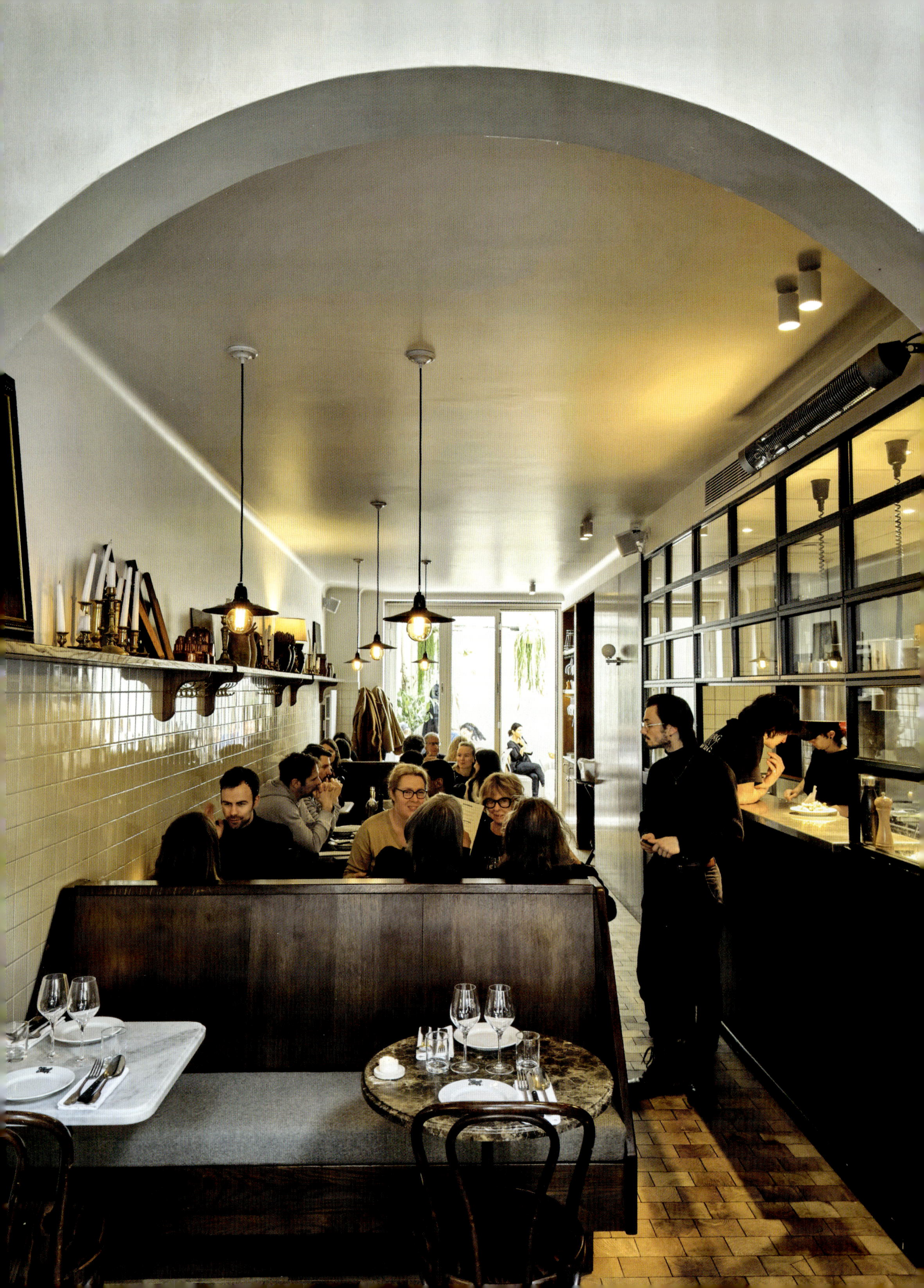

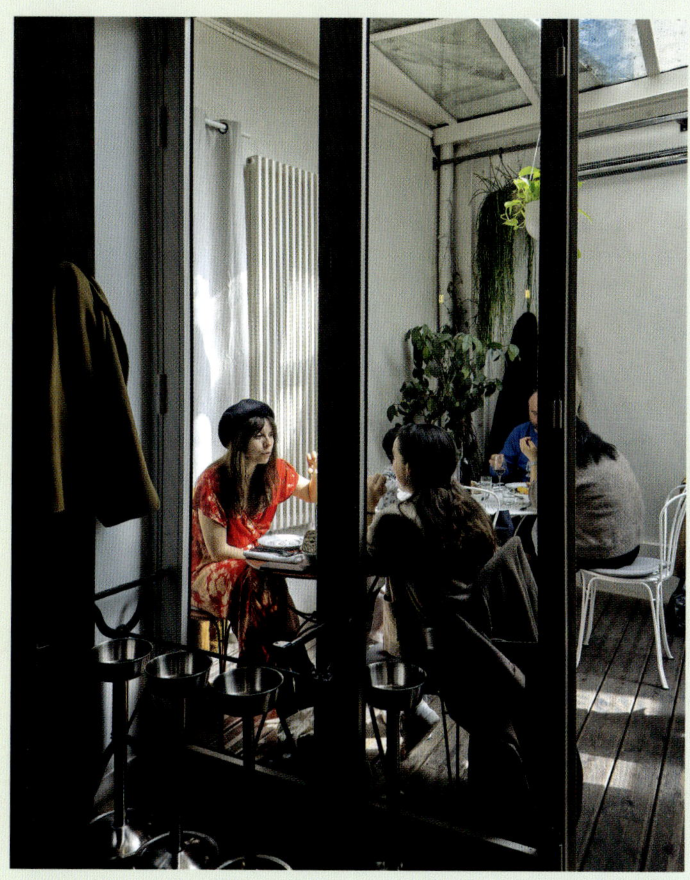



## *Faubourg Daimant*
### 10th arrondissement
### 2023

Nothing seems to be missing from Faubourg Daimant's classic interior decoration: banquettes, a few tables by the window, a courtyard garden, and an open kitchen. But it is what is happening in the kitchen that is making waves. Alice Tuyet, owner, has created a fine-dining vegan experience in Paris. Alice is the granddaughter of Vietnamese immigrants, and she was raised in a restaurant, where her French mother taught her to cook. Alice noticed that in traditional French cooking there is an emphasis on sauces. As a vegan and someone who is passionate about animal welfare and the environment, she began to rethink not only the menu of her restaurants—the other is a sandwich shop named Plan D—but also her own lifestyle. While the restaurant is not grand-scale, the experience is magnified. The open kitchen fills the room with wonderful smells. The wall of street-facing windows fills the room with light. The beautifully plated food arrives, and the outdated image and taste of vegan food is transformed.

**OPPOSITE**
An arched wall at the entrance leads to the main dining room and kitchen of Faubourg Daimant.

**ABOVE**
Guests can also enjoy lunch or dinner in the intimate courtyard garden.

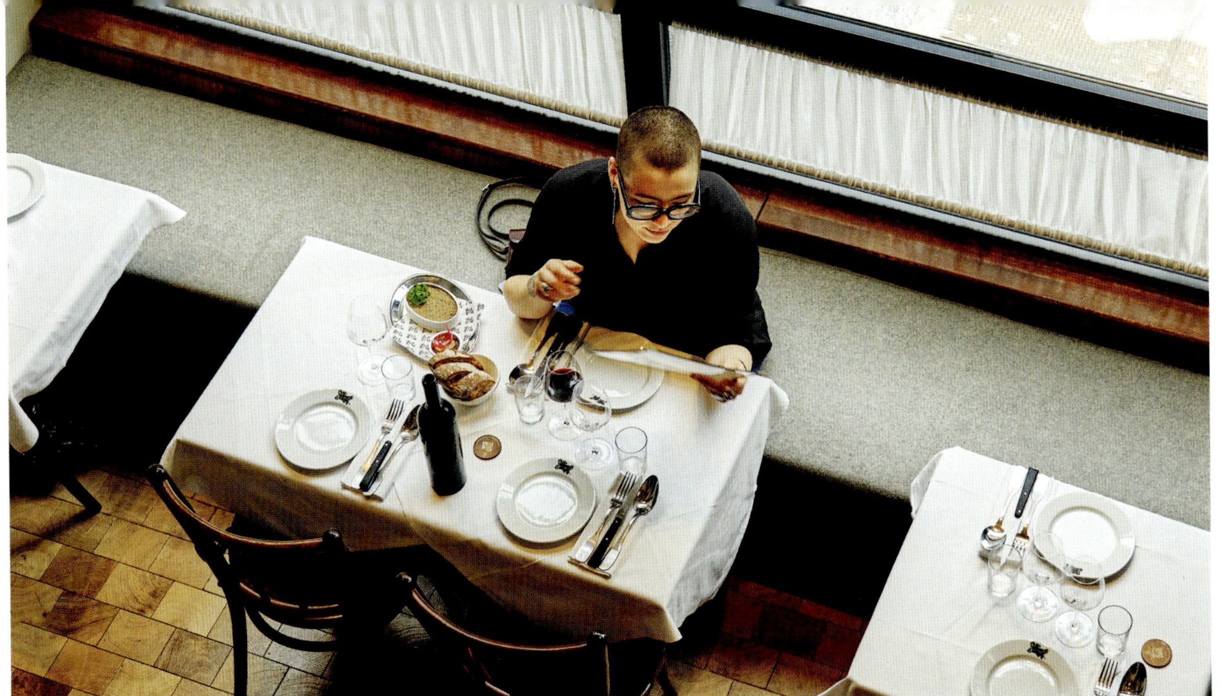

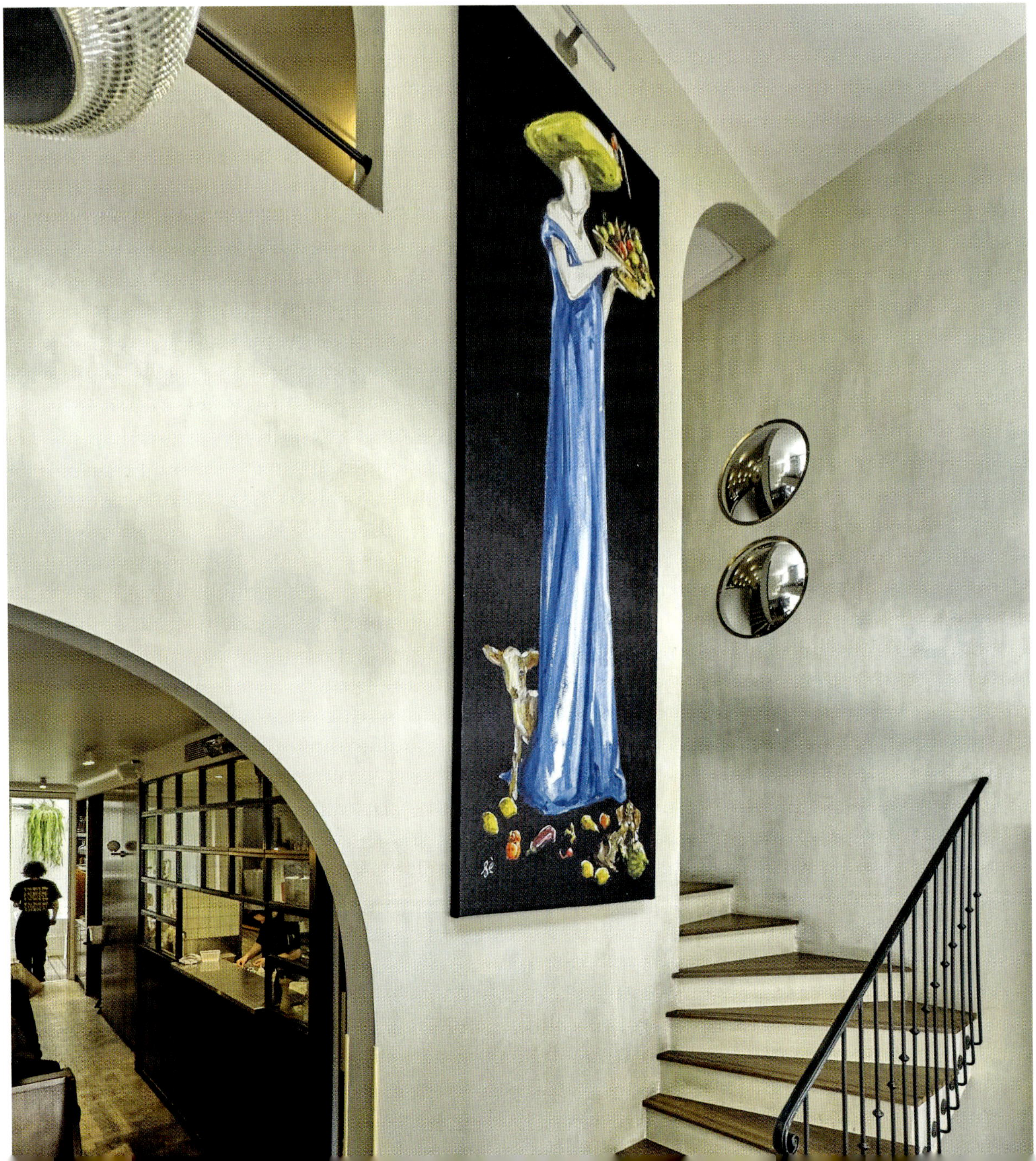

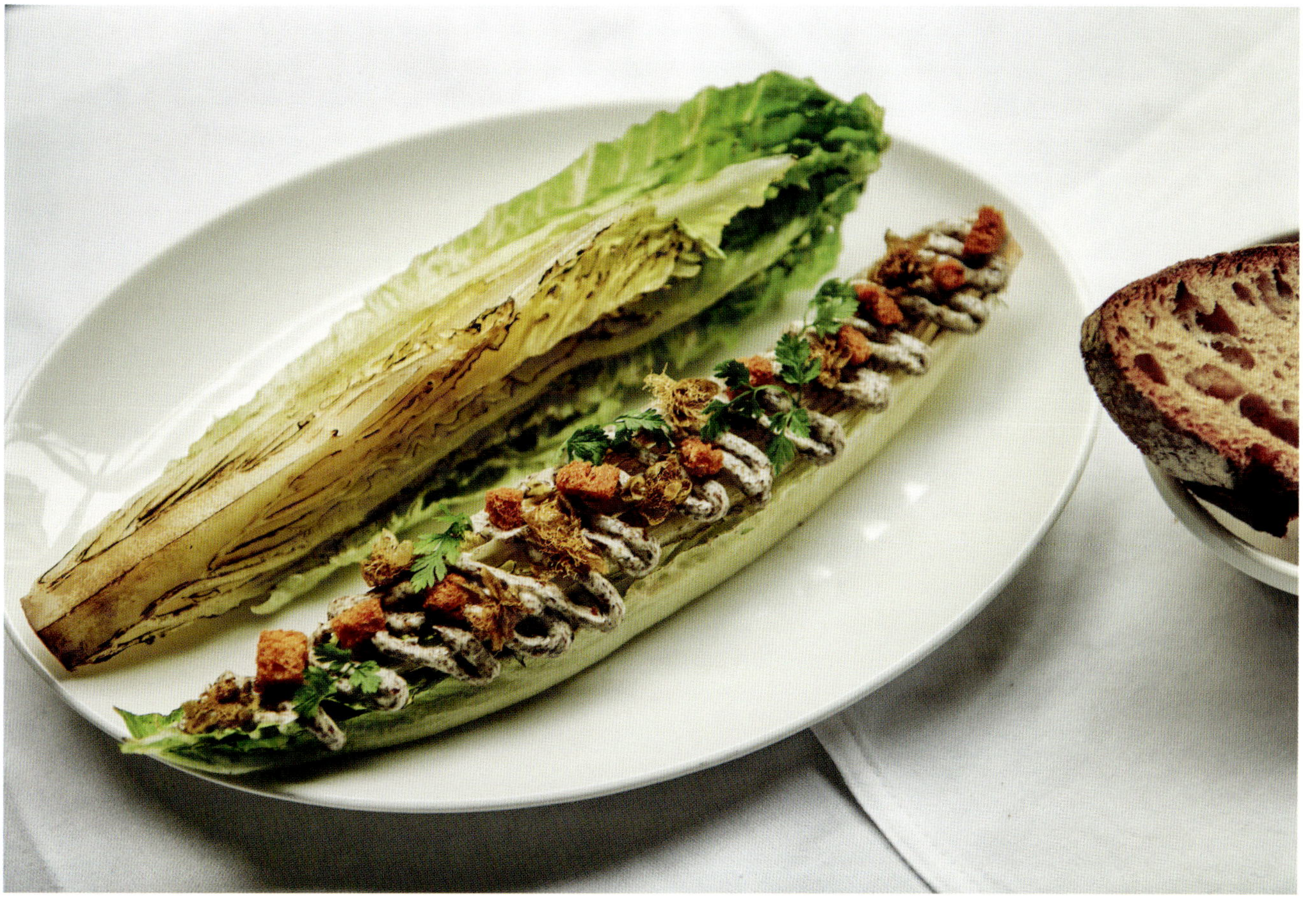

OPPOSITE ABOVE
A long bench in the window provides
seating in the front of the restaurant.
Table service is simply but elegantly set.

OPPOSITE BELOW
Upstairs there is a bar area and
additional seating. A painting by Sophie
Estève graces the staircase wall.

ABOVE
One of the signature dishes of the
restaurant, romaine brûlée Caesar, is
made with seaweed, not anchovies.

RIGHT
Chefs Lou Joguet and Alexandre Sans in
the downstairs kitchen that is divided by
a glass wall.

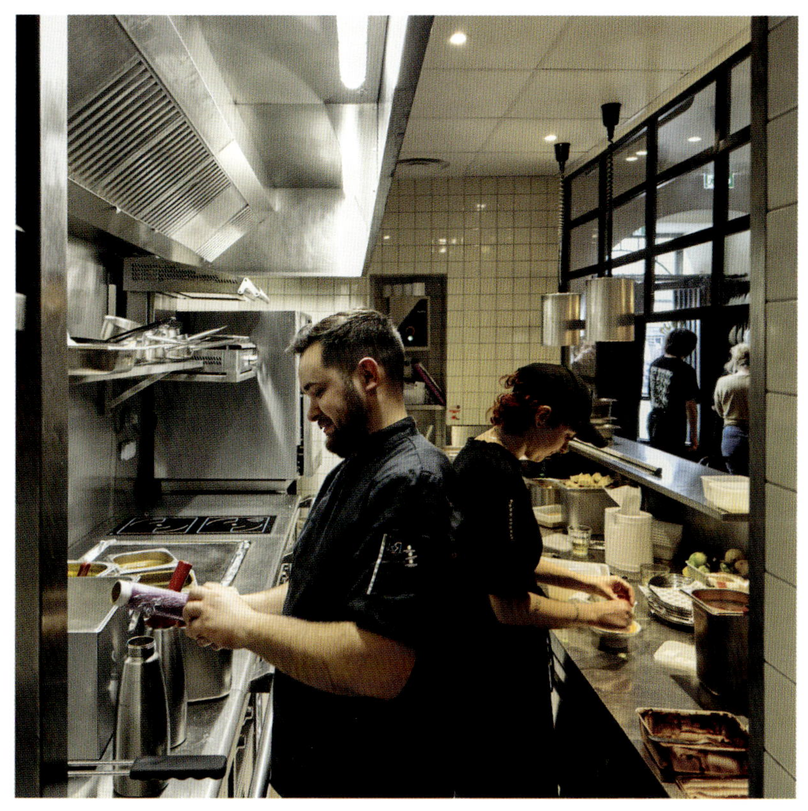

# an interview with Alice Tuyet, Faubourg Daimant

**A**lice Tuyet: The purpose of the restaurant was to be able to reconcile two worlds that don't necessarily communicate today. One is an extremely committed world. I come from the animal rights cause, which is the beginning of plant-based cuisine.

Reconciling that with the ideas of hedonism, expertise, and the pleasure of dining, which is very important, especially for us French. The dining moment is extremely important. I couldn't find places that joined these two worlds. The idea was to build a bridge between the two so that when people come to Faubourg Daimant, they don't think, "We're in a vegetarian restaurant, we're going to deprive ourselves." On the contrary, it's a restaurant like any other. We wanted to show that [vegetarian dining] could be as beautiful, as sexy as any other restaurant where you feel good and can have a great time.

**Michel Arnaud:** That's what interested me in your approach, which I found different from the image of a classic vegetarian restaurant. You also have a small restaurant that makes sandwiches?

**AT:** Yes, it's small. It was the first project that came about during COVID, almost by accident. We called it Plan D. It's a small 19-square-meter [205-square-foot] shop where we serve street food. Takeout was ninety percent of sales, and it always had the same theme: making something indulgent, generous, with a lot of work on the sauces, even if it's street food. It's the common thread between the two restaurants.

It's very important to tell people about the fears for the future of the world, about what's happening, about all the horrors, and that in fact, climatically, our world and we might not survive.

Next is how to make people want to change. We need to rethink models that are desirable. Restaurants like ours are part of that because we're offering a plant-based experience that's good without excuses.

Yes, it's a slightly different position, but it's interesting. It's very important to make [it] sustainability desirable. And to note how it works well.

**MA:** Who is your clientele?
**AT:** Frankly, [our clientele] is quite varied, and that is what's cool. We have many customers who follow our articles or funny videos on social media. We also cater to a more established, older clientele, and that's quite nice.

What's also great is that we don't have an exclusively vegetarian or vegan clientele. That was always the goal. It's not about creating an exclusive community and making vegan food for vegans. It is about food that can speak to everyone because it has that quality of seasoning, of cooking, in a beautiful place with a service that's both elegant and warm. It's all these incredible factors mixed that allows us to appeal beyond a purely vegan or vegetarian clientele. We are lucky to have a super diverse clientele. We noticed this fact even at Plan D, the sandwich shop. There, the clientele is more masculine than feminine. It's always a bit of a cliché that vegetables are for women, but we are very happy to have this clientele.

Our cuisine was designed with a clear focus on health and diet. We can say we eat vegetables because they don't make you fat, they are full of vitamins, and they are simple. We don't have that approach to plant-based cuisine at all.

**MA:** Do you want to develop other restaurants?
**AT:** Yes, and we are currently looking for other locations. Yes, we want to develop more places, because today when we serve several hundred meals a day, that's something that will change the world in a way that is better toward sustainability. The more restaurants we have, the more meals we can serve, the stronger our social, ecological, and ethical impact will be, quite simply. And yes, we are ambitious.

**MA:** Do you develop the dishes yourself, or do you make acquisitions?

**AT:** I am simply a self-taught cook. My grandmother had a restaurant, and I grew up in one. My Vietnamese grandmother fled the Vietnam War. They were near Paris, in Garches. They had intellectual professions in Vietnam, and they found themselves with nothing when they arrived in France. My grandmother didn't speak a word of French, which she never learned. It happened because she stayed within the community. I was also lucky to have my French mother who cooked a lot and taught us this bourgeois cuisine.

**MA:** The recipes?

**AT:** For me, recipes are really about the moment of creation. I work hand in hand with our chef to conceive the recipes. I bring the vision and knowledge of plant-based cuisine. I did all the initial tests at home.

I work with a chef who is fifty thousand times better than me. He refines all the techniques and allows us to scale them for two hundred clients a day. It's not the same thing to cook one dish at home as it is to serve it in a restaurant. That's why I am a cook, but I am not a chef.

Regarding the environment, today I hardly ever fly. I aim for zero flights for my carbon footprint. Maybe if a special event in my family requires me to travel quickly, but I am very conscious of my movements. I don't take the plane as casually as buying a chocolate croissant. In fact, I've changed my lifestyle.

**MA:** What other forms of transport do you use?

**AT:** In Paris, I only walk. On the street, you are free. I find it great because you take the time to look around, and you see scenes of life that you wouldn't see otherwise.

At home, it's about balance. My husband became vegetarian because I cook at home. Initially, I always cooked different dishes for him, and when I had friends over, I cooked with meat because I thought it shouldn't be a social barrier. One day, he told me to stop making separate dishes for him and that he wanted to eat like me because it was simpler. So, I stopped, and I did the same for my friends. Then I realized that we could please everyone by cooking only plant-based food.

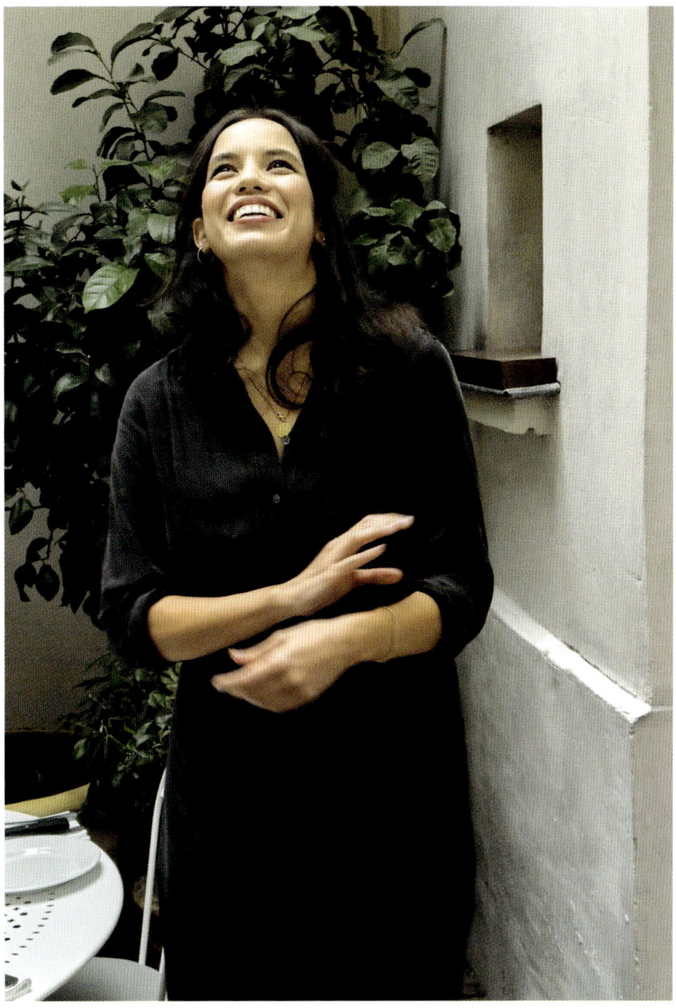

Alice Tuyet, owner of Faubourg Daimant.

# Boneshaker Donuts & Coffee

2nd arrondissement

2016

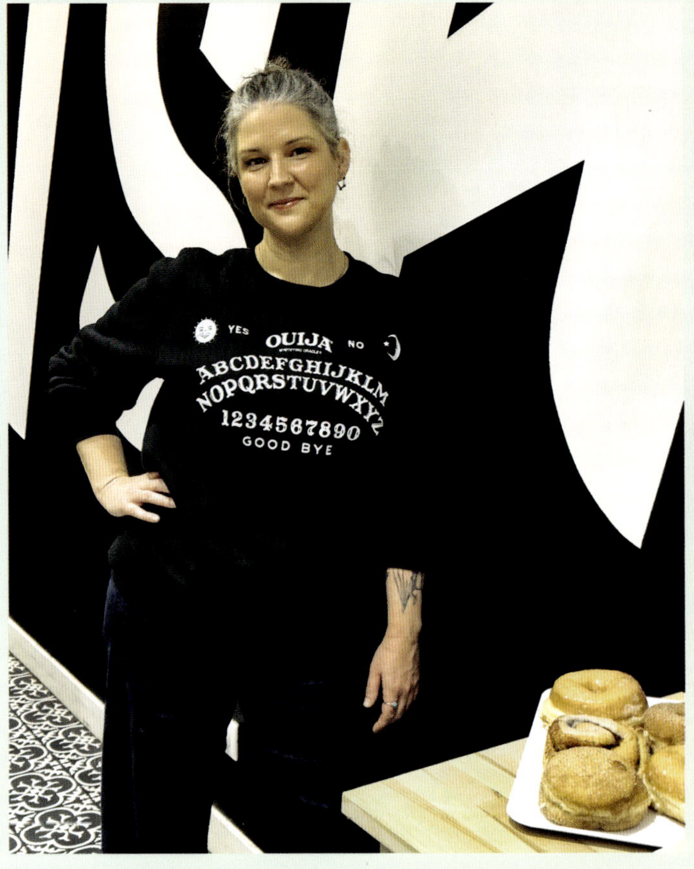


Coffee and donuts in Paris? In the land of café and croissants, that possibility seems far-fetched. Undaunted, American expat Amanda Bankert set up her vegan bakery off a busy street. At first, she didn't share the news that the donuts were vegan, but now she does. After all, French pastry chefs often reinvent the classics creating new flavors of éclairs, so why not rethink an American classic? As Amanda developed her recipes, she experimented with not only creating different flavor profiles, but she also took a careful look at the ingredients. What she perfected is a texture that isn't heavy or too cake-like. The pastry is light, the flavors have interesting combinations, and the feelings of regret after eating a whole donut (in this case one named No Sleep Till Brooklyn, after a Beastie Boys song) aren't there either.

**ABOVE**
Owner and pastry chef Amanda Bankert in her modest shop in Paris.

**OPPOSITE ABOVE**
The simple storefront of Boneshaker Donuts & Coffee. The pink door gives a hint at the confections inside.

**OPPOSITE BELOW**
The bakery is just the place to take a break from croissants. All the donuts are made with vegan ingredients.

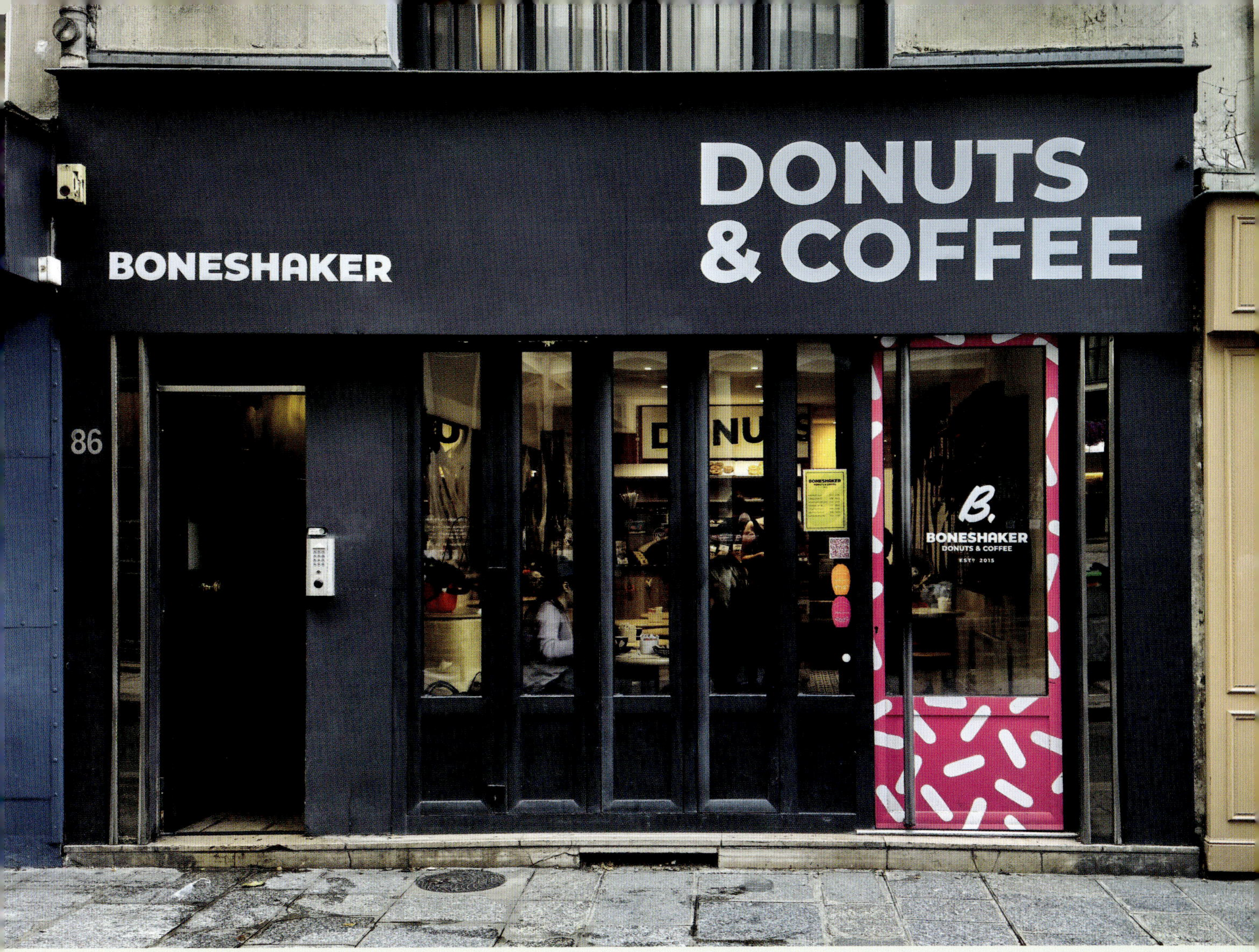

BONESHAKER
DONUTS & COFFEE
86
B.
BONESHAKER
DONUTS & COFFEE
ESTD 2015

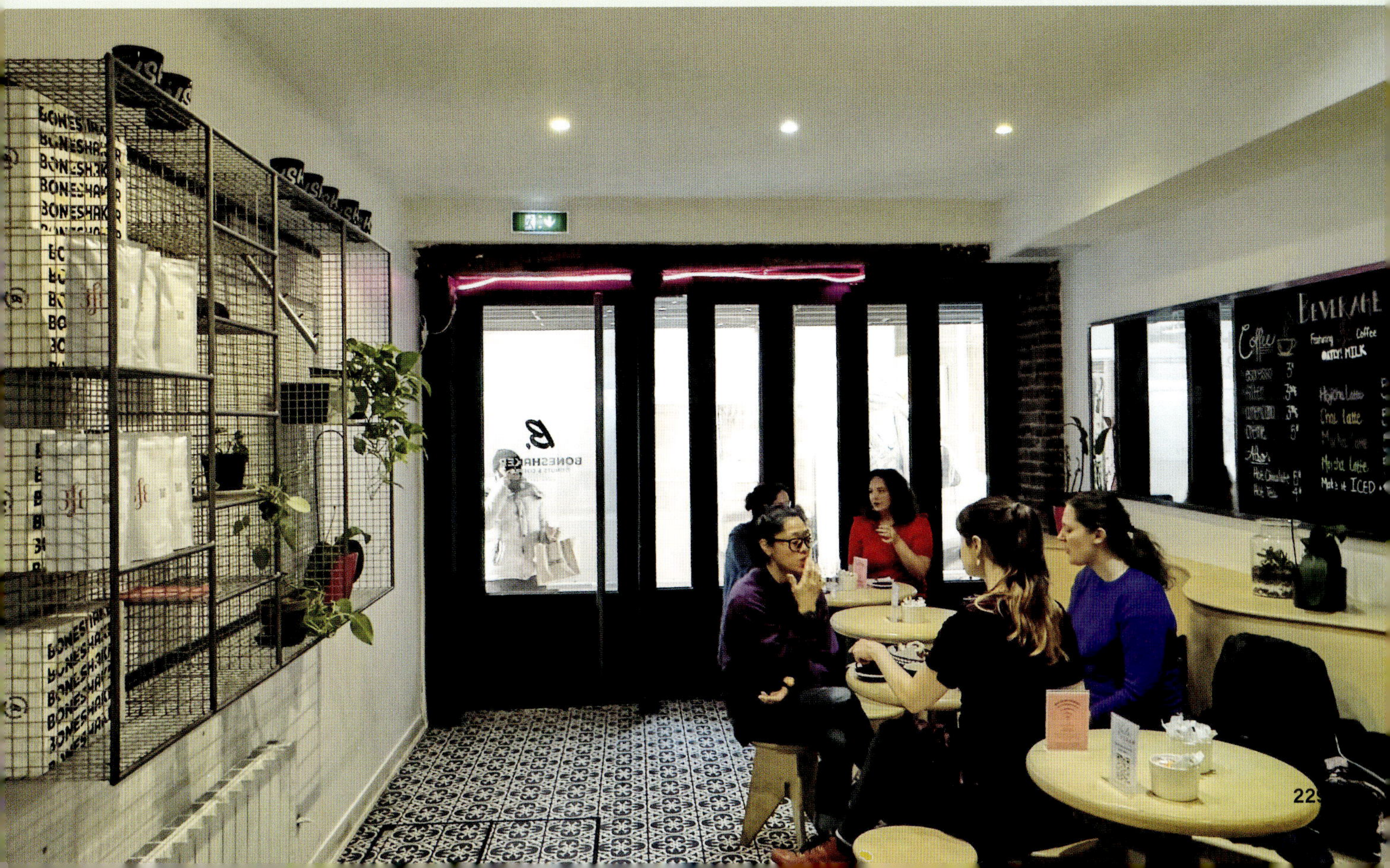

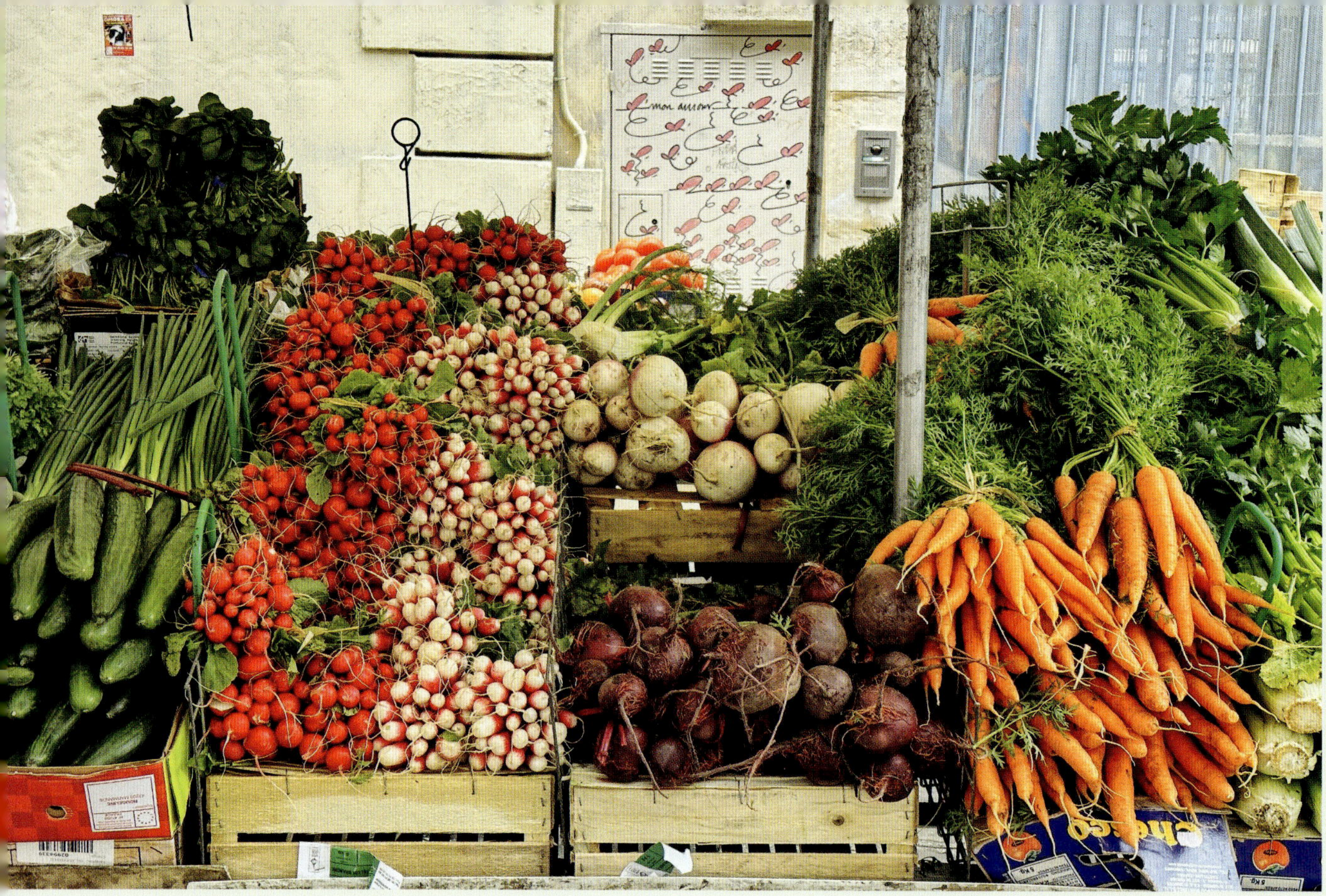

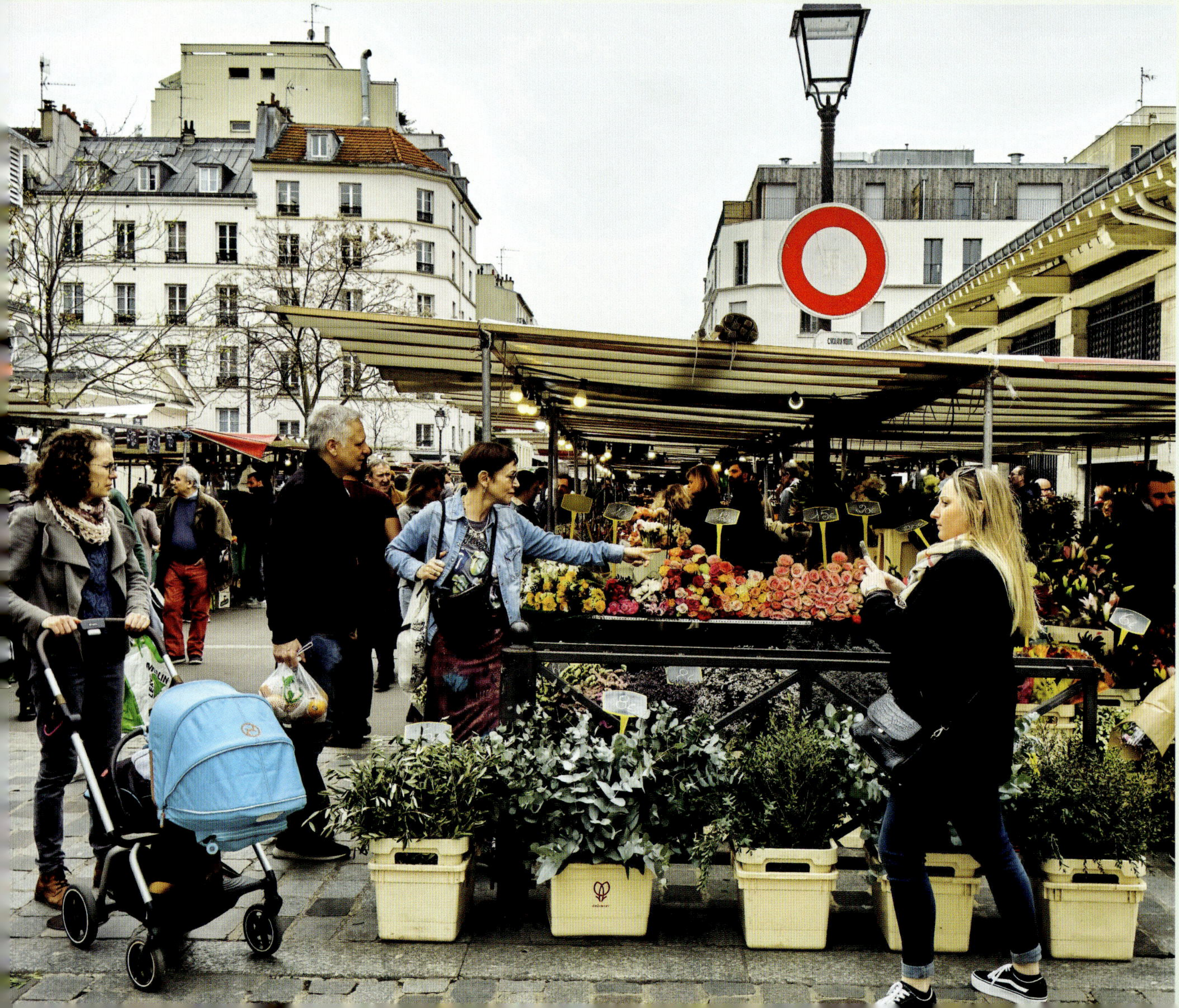

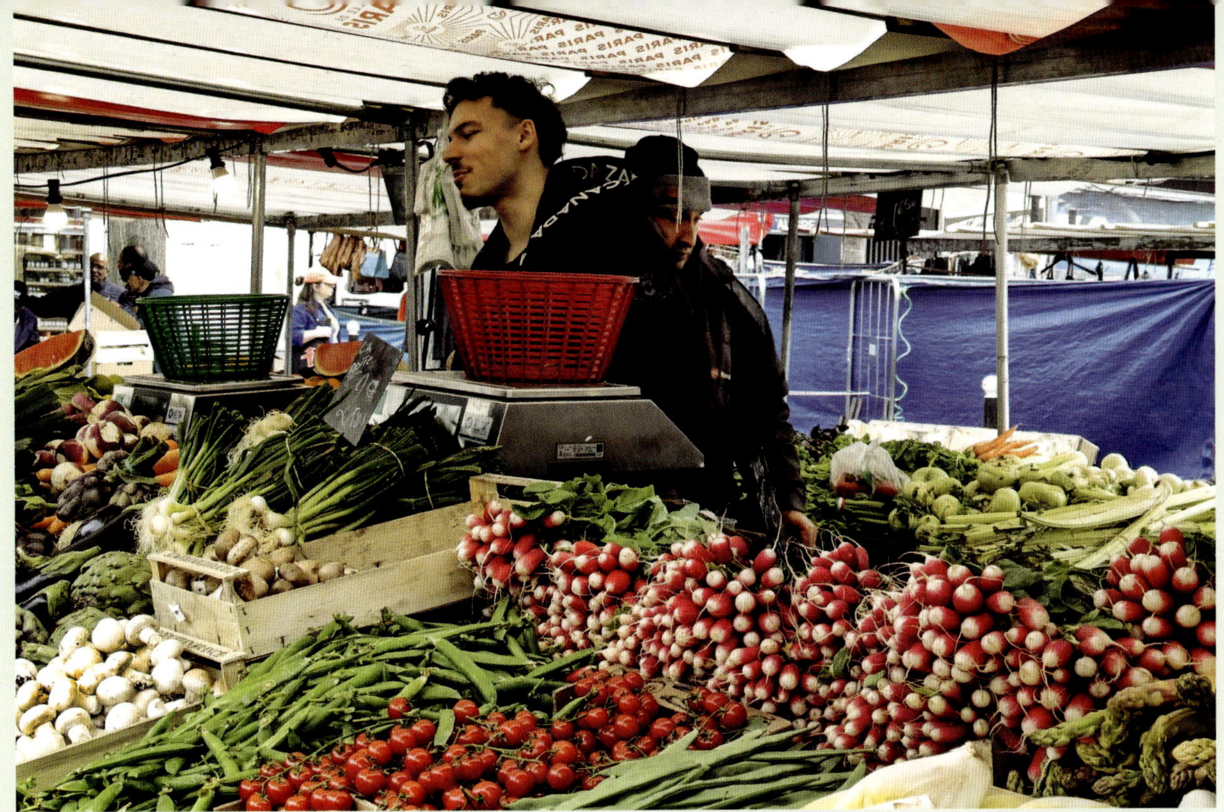

## *Marché d'Aligre*
### 12th arrondissement
### 1741

Although most French markets are busy and chaotic, marché d'Aligre seems especially so. Three markets share la place d'Aligre: a covered market known as le marché couvert Beauvau, an open market with stalls for vendors, and a flea market with secondhand books, clothing, and more. Market activity at this location dates to the middle 1700s. The covered market was built in 1843. As more modern buildings have grown up around the site, the vendors have increased in number and the market street has extended. The outside stalls are primarily vegetable and flower vendors selling both fresh seasonal and specialty products. Inside la halle Beauvau, established merchants and shops include a patisserie, seafood sellers, cheesemongers, and butchers. Sampling their wares or stopping to eat a dozen oysters from Normandy is one of the pleasures of shopping there. At the end of the day, vendors offer fresh but unsold food at discounted prices. In addition, aid organizations gather donated food items from vendors to distribute to those in need. A city program manages the waste from the markets by either composting or turning it into biofuel.

**OPPOSITE ABOVE**
Fresh vegetables available at the open-air market.

**OPPOSITE BELOW**
A flower vendor's stall at le marché d'Aligre in October.

**ABOVE**
There are multiple vendors selling similar products, so shoppers have a choice between vendors.

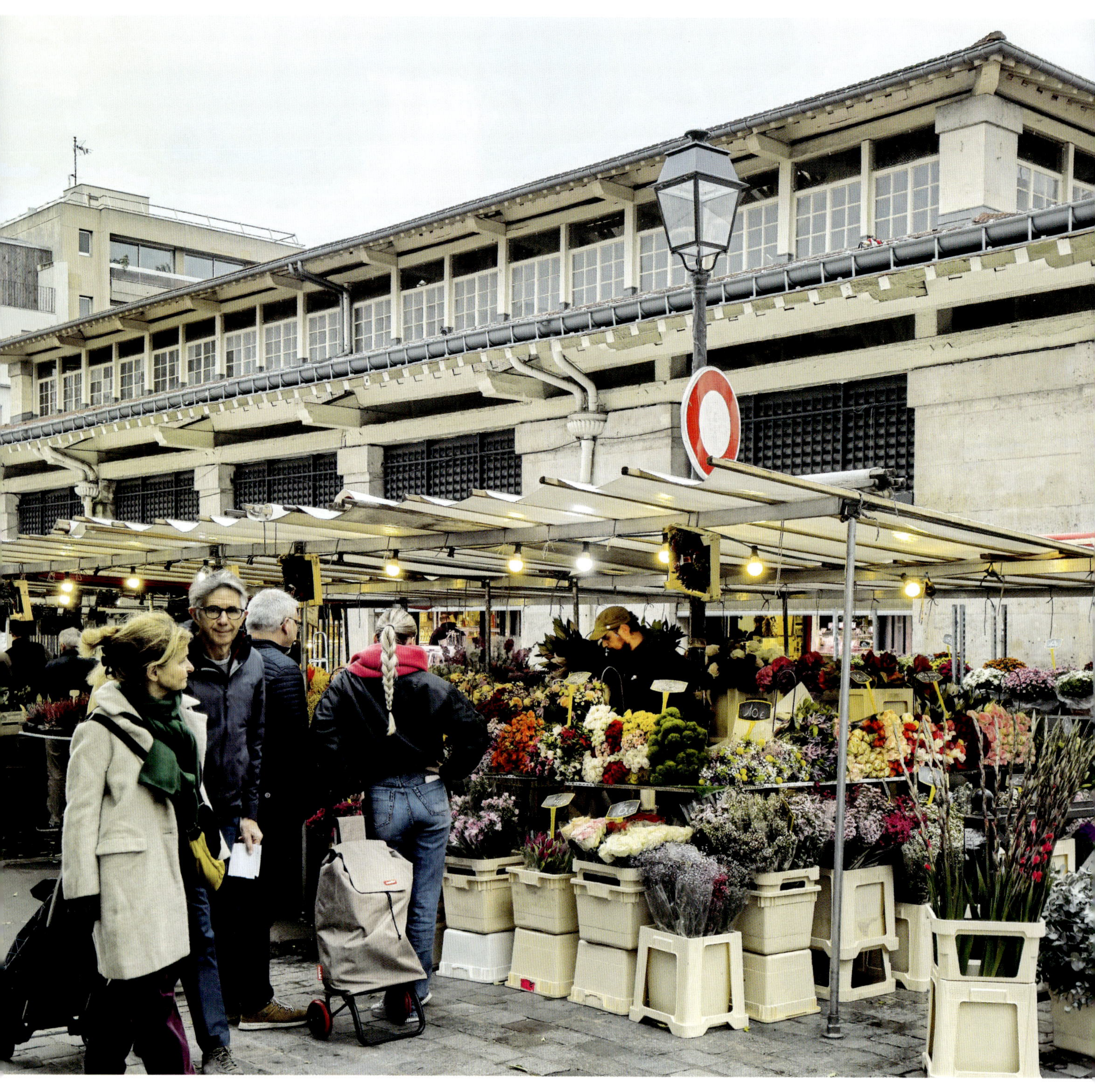


La halle Beauvau has been an active
covered market since 1843.

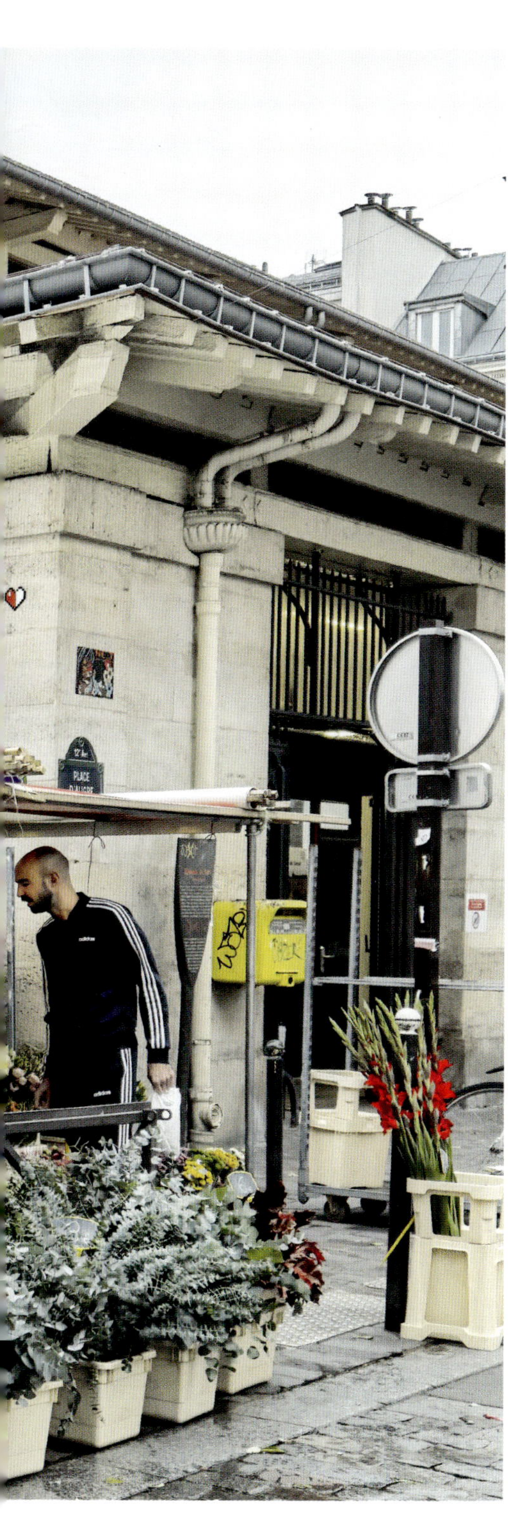

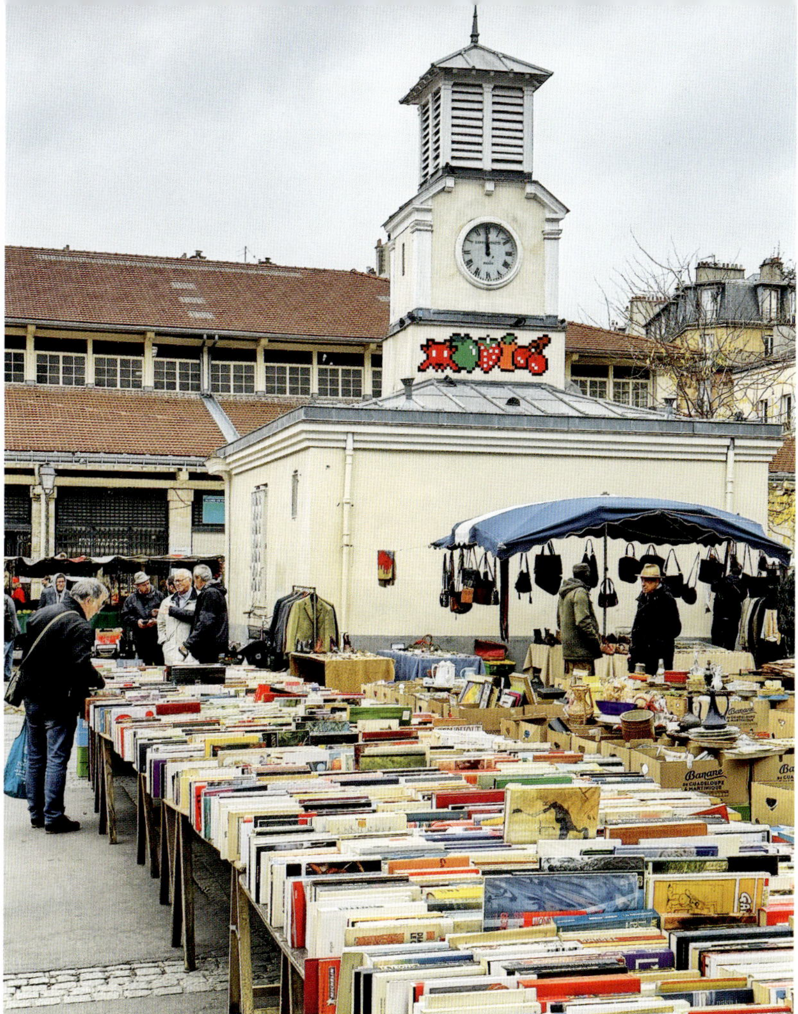

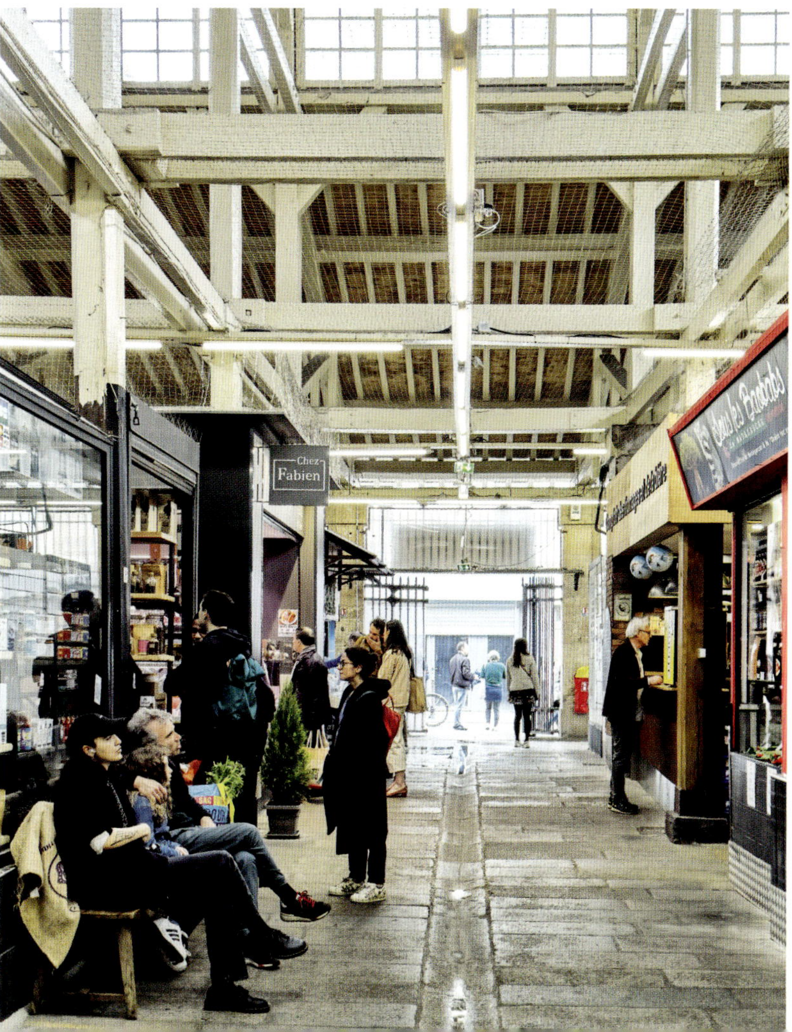

**ABOVE RIGHT**
A clock tower is at the center of the market, between the hall and the flea market.

**RIGHT**
Inside the covered market, various food vendors and shops are off the center of the shopping alley.

## *Rue Mouffetard*

5th arrondissement
Twelfth century

A long, hilly, and narrow pedestrian street, rue Mouffetard is one of the oldest market streets in Paris. It is so beloved that it even has a nickname, la Mouffe. Images by photographers Charles Marville, from the 1860s, and Eugène Atget, from the 1900s, attest to its historical significance and document its staying power as a place for food in Paris. Unlike a market with stalls or a covered market, shops are filled with a wide variety of provisions. Restaurants and traiteurs selling all kinds of cuisines also line rue Mouffetard. The street is busy even in August, when many residents leave Paris for vacation. In 2023, a plan was voted on to add plant beds to the streetscape, so changes are on their way.

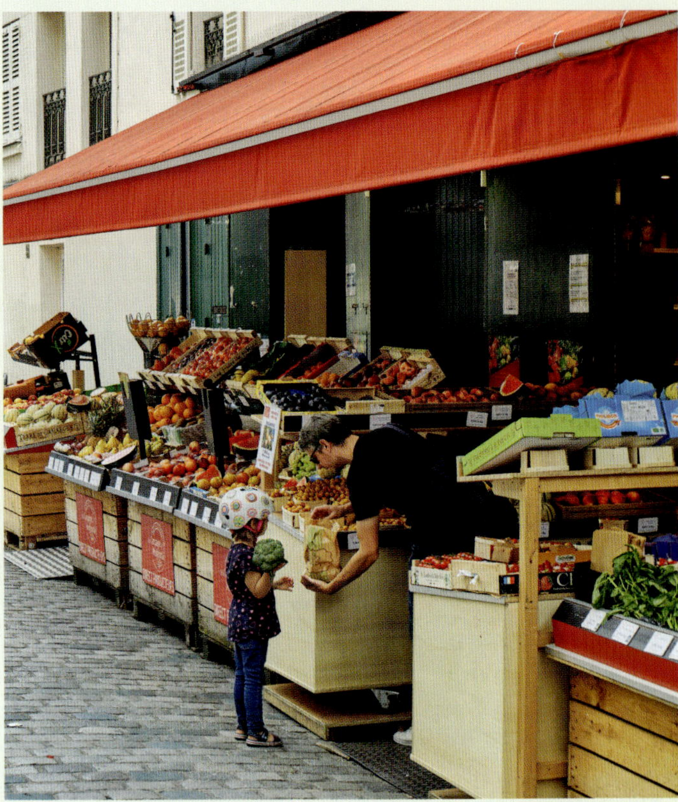

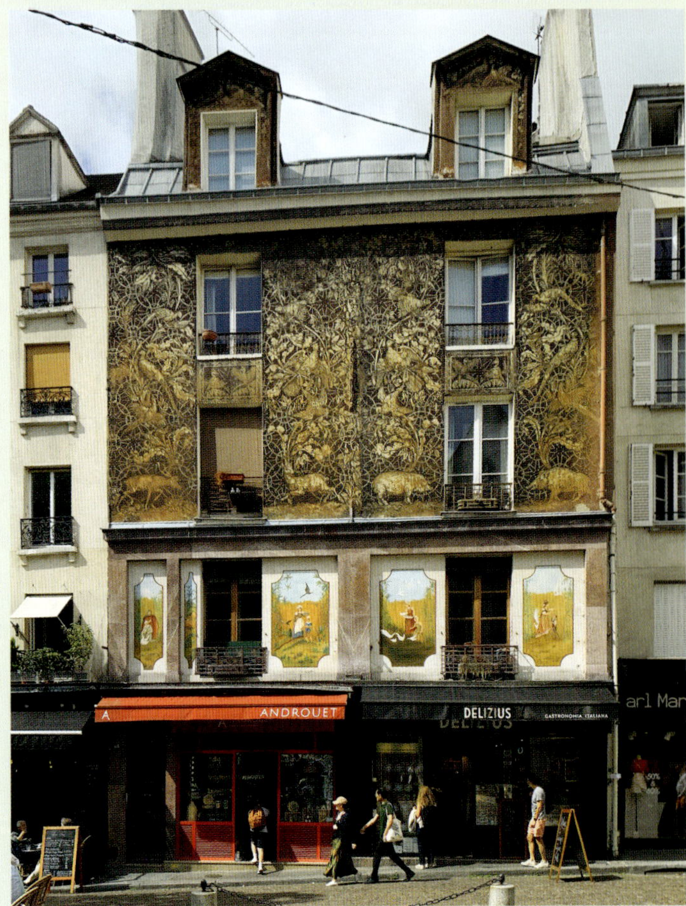

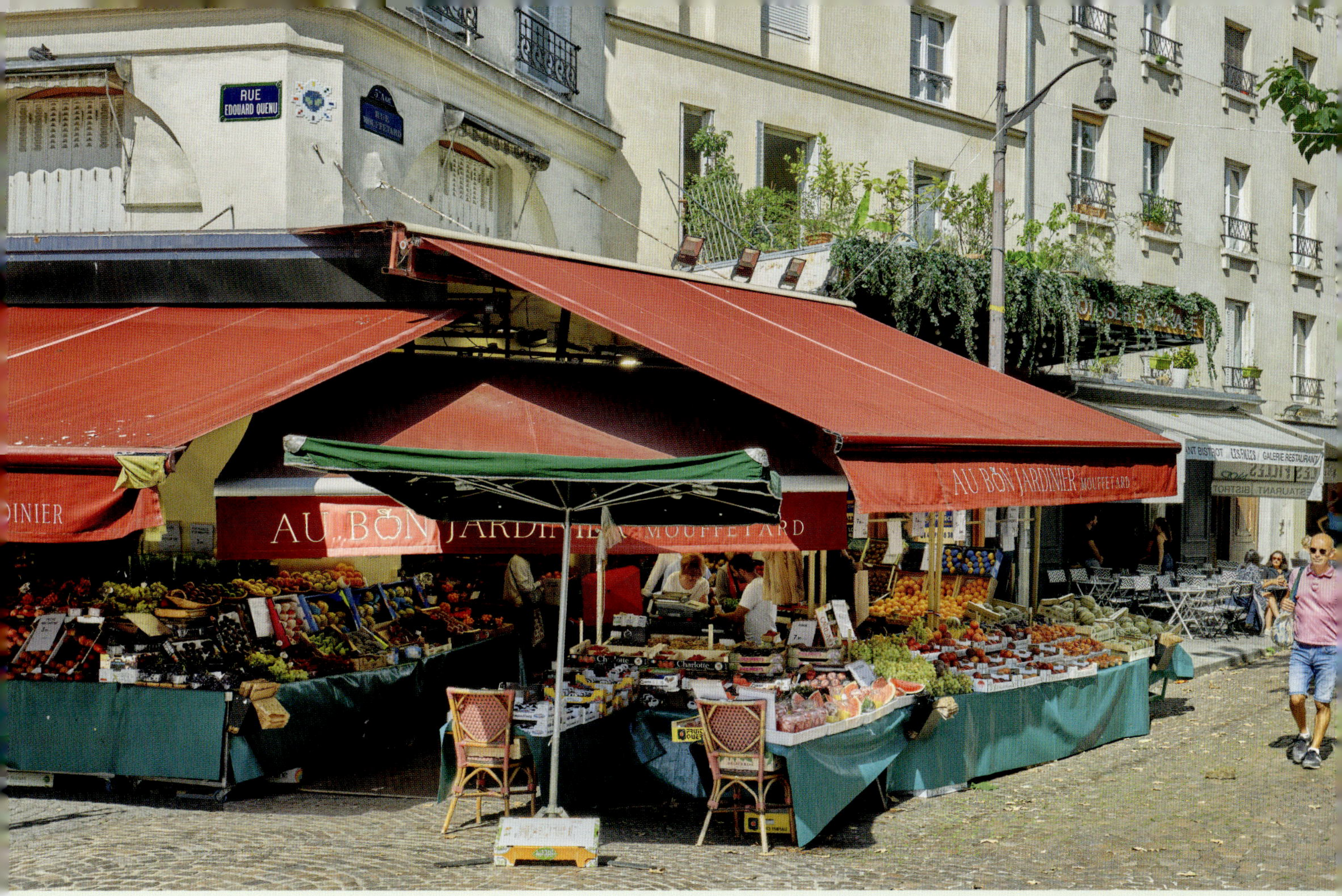

**OPPOSITE ABOVE**
A centuries-old tradition of buying food here continues with a new generation.

**OPPOSITE BELOW**
One of the most famous shops on the street is Androuet, a *crémerie*, or cheese and dairy shop. The building at 134–136 is covered in an Italian art technique called "sgraffito," applied to the building around 1930, that depicts not only seasonal harvests but also flora and game of the woods. A butcher shop commissioned the work.

**ABOVE**
The corner market at rue Mouffetard and rue Censier is a vegetable stand.

**RIGHT**
Le square Saint-Médard is at the bottom of rue Mouffetard, across from the church for which it is named. Cafés of several restaurants give shoppers a place to sit and relax.

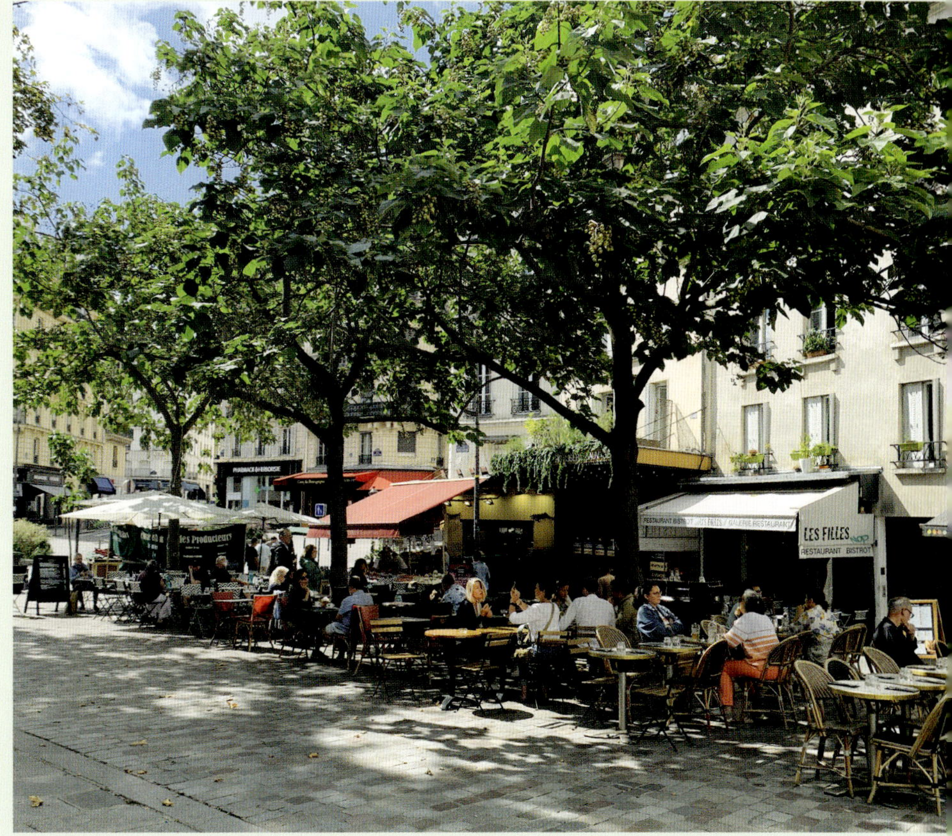

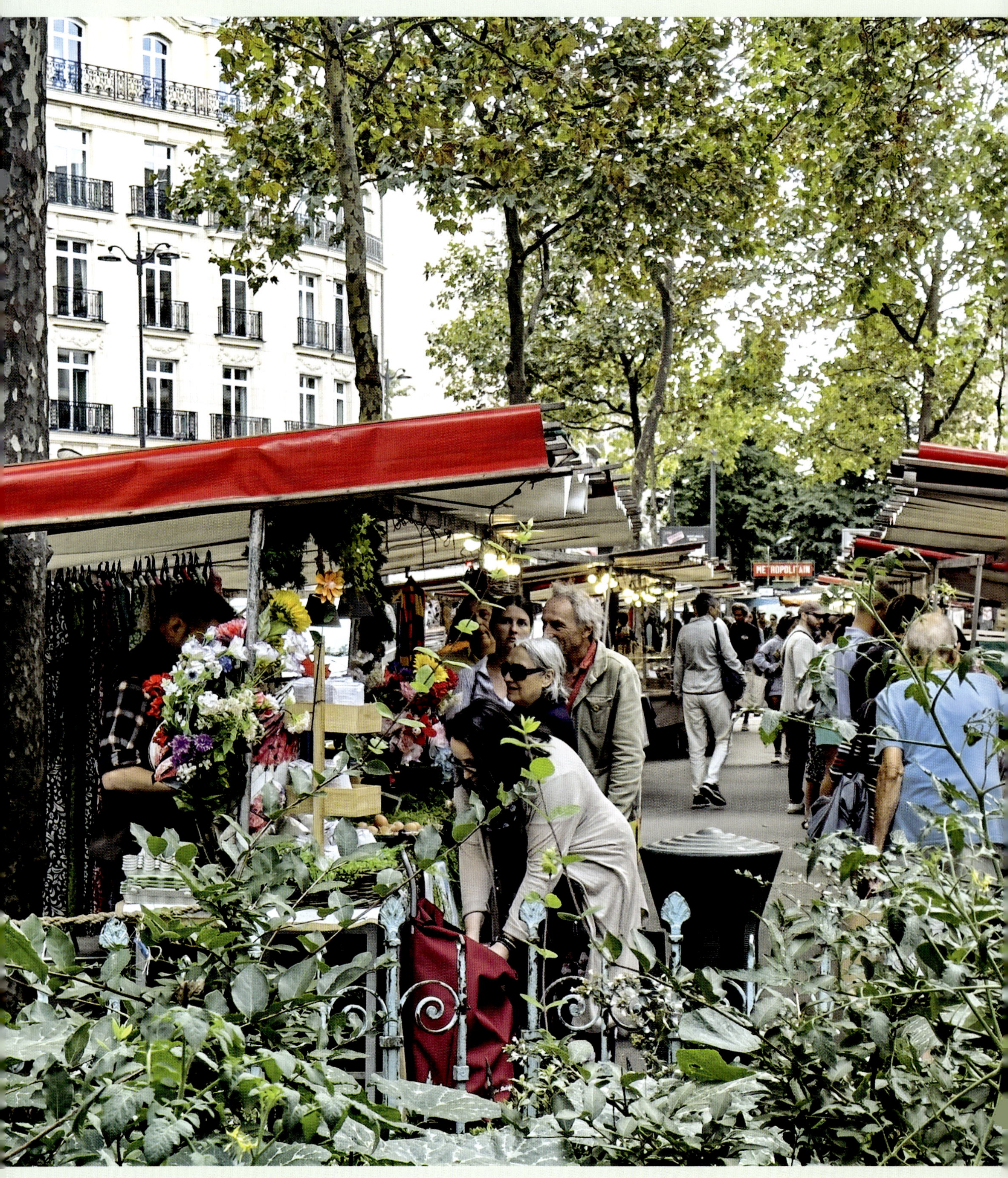

MÉTROPOLITAIN

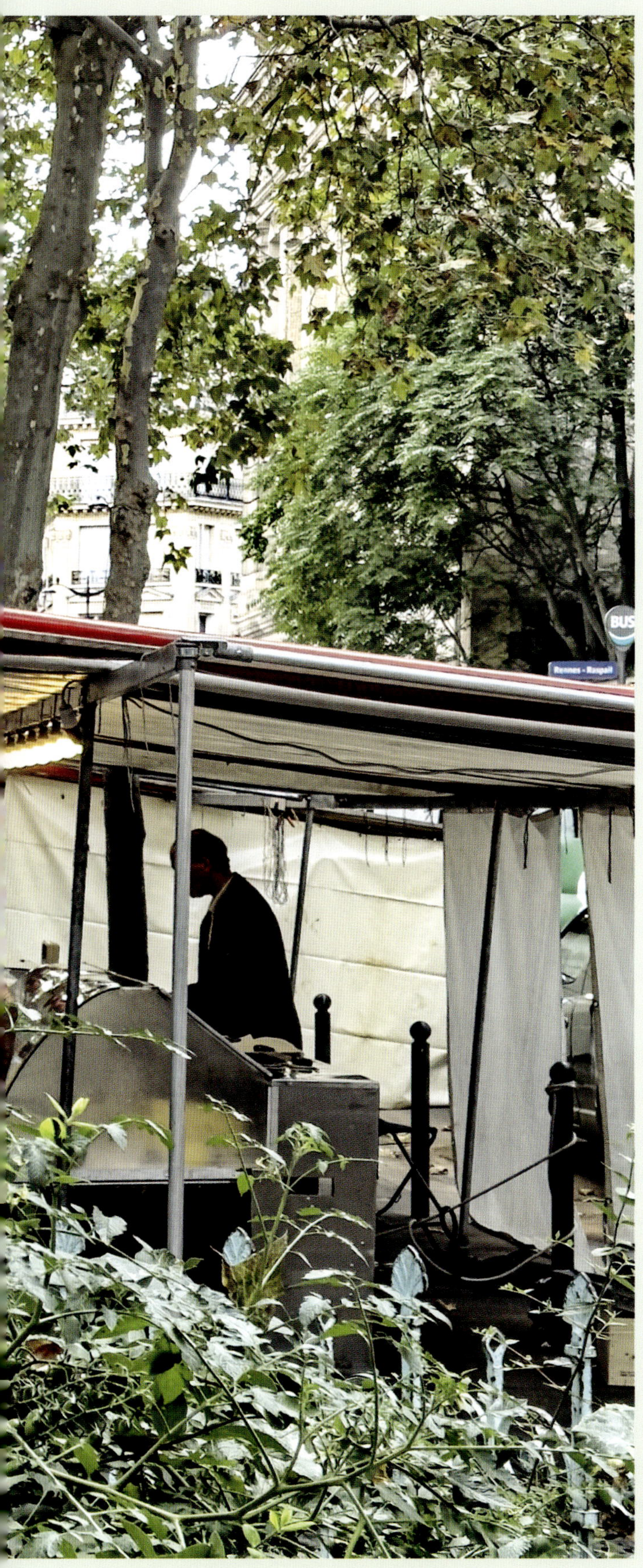

## *Marché Spécialisé Biologique Raspail*

6th arrondissement
1989

On any given Sunday, you can leave square Boucicaut, turn right on boulevard Raspail, and you will find an open-air market in the median. Many of the thirty to forty vendors have local produce, and all the food products are one hundred percent *biologique* (organic). The market proceeds down allée Sonia-Rykiel to rue de Rennes. (Fashion designer Rykiel's original boutique was just around the corner on rue du Cherche-Midi.) Among the roses in the green spaces there are stalls on either side of the allée. It is a regular shopping area for people who live in this fashionable district. There are only four markets in Paris that are totally organic. The French ministry of agriculture regulates organic labeling of food according to European Union standards.

Each Parisian street market has a different style and ambience that matches its surroundings and neighborhood. This market in the 6th arrondissement is no exception.

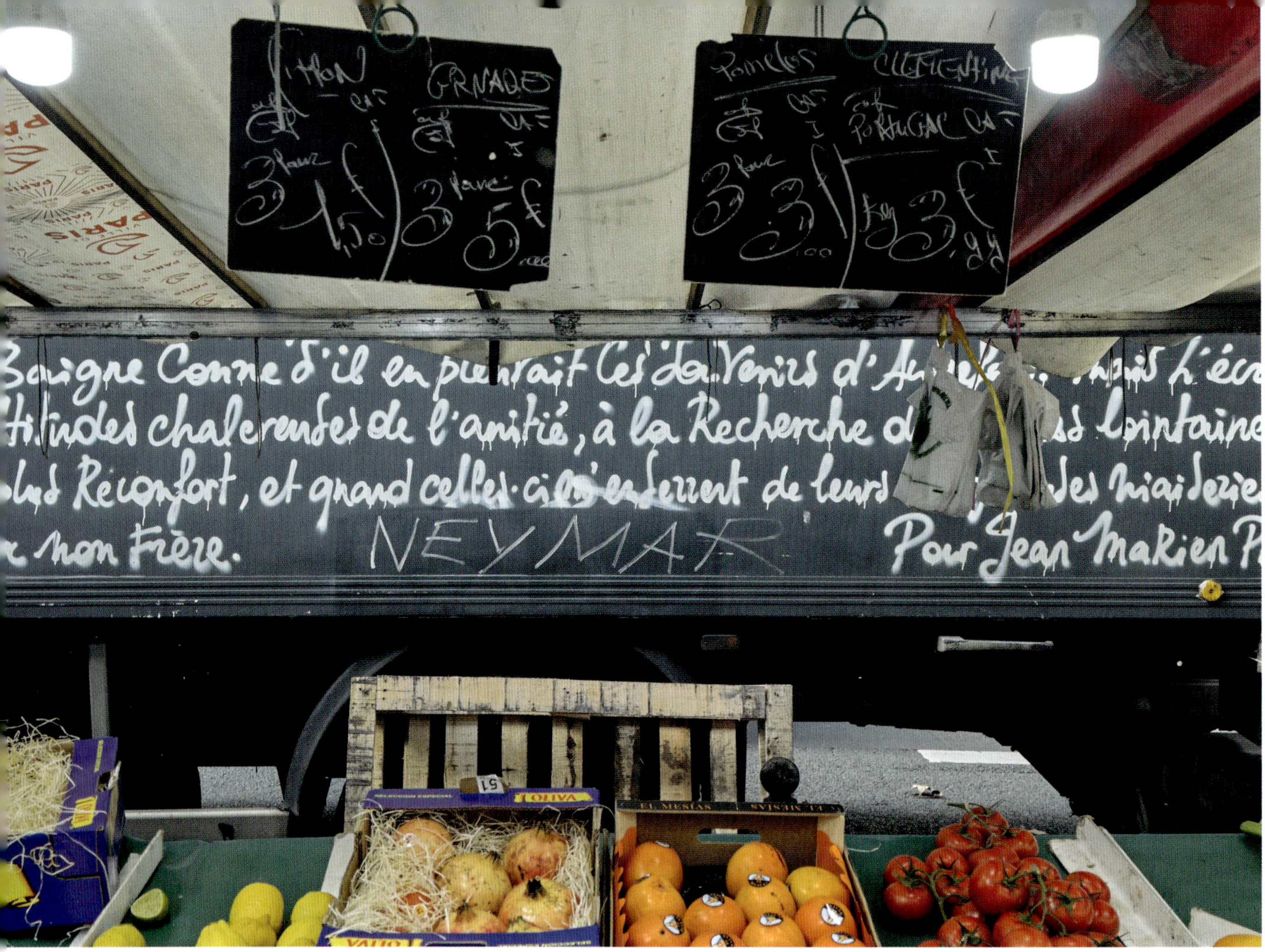

Baigne Comme s'il en pleurait Ces Souvenirs d'Au... mais L'écr...
...tudes chaleureuses de l'amitié, à la Recherche d... ...s Lointaine...
...lus Réconfort, et quand celles-ci s'esserrent de leurs ... Des mai...
...n non Frère.   NEYMAR   Pour Jean Marien P...

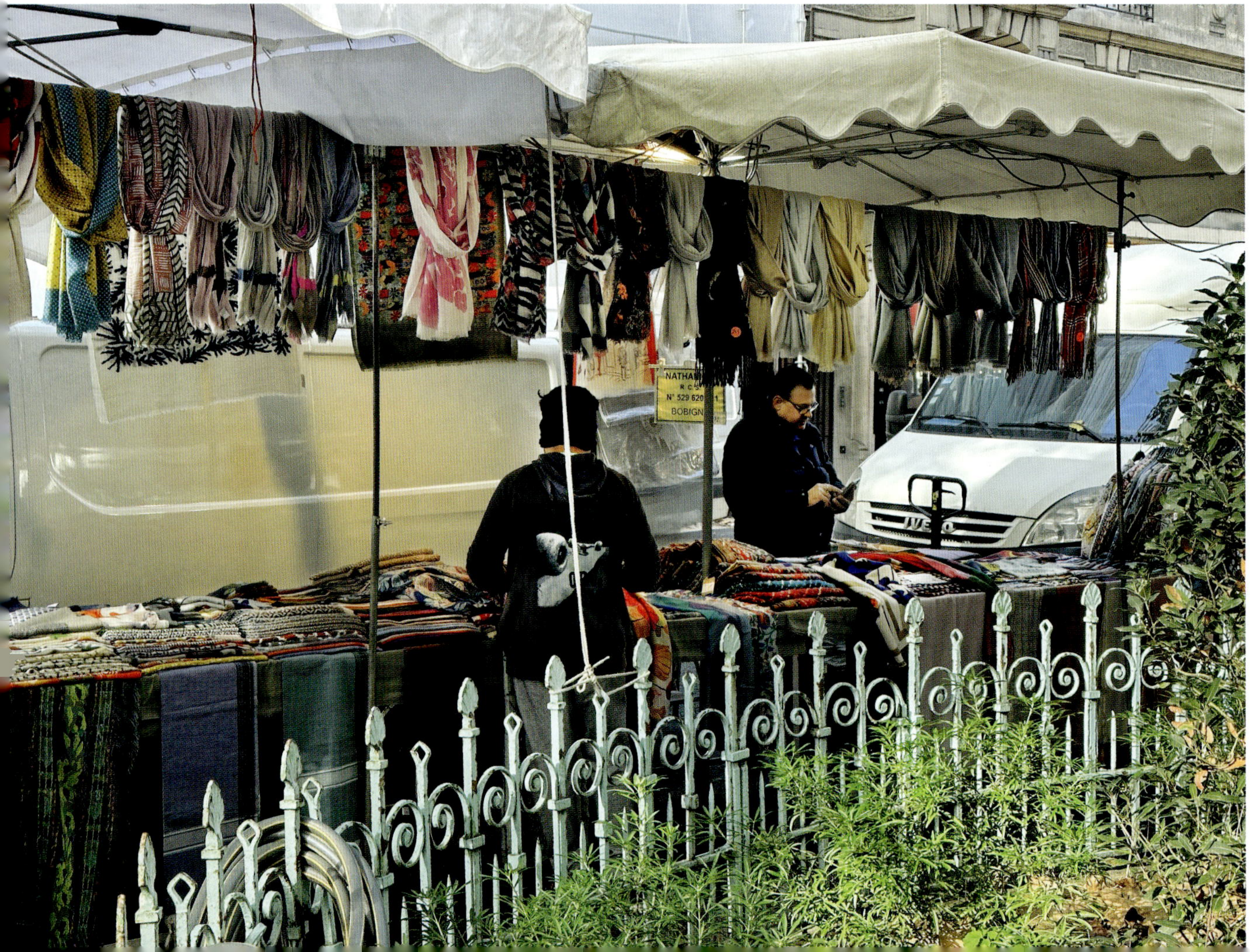

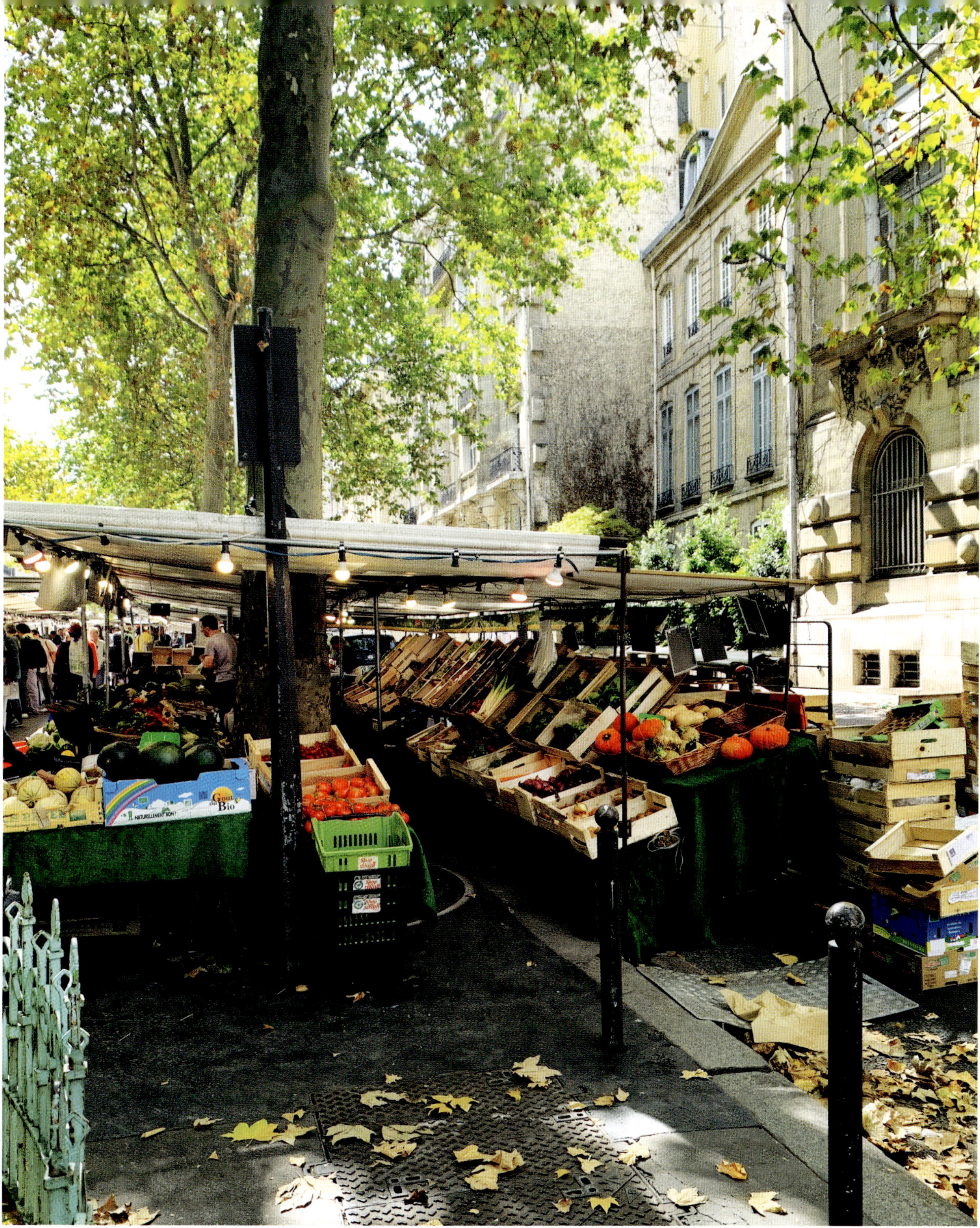



**OPPOSITE ABOVE**
The metal-frame structures remain on the site even when the market is not in session. Prices are handwritten on black slate and hung in each stall.

**OPPOSITE BELOW**
Among the aisles of produce are sellers of vintage clothing, household goods, and accessories, such as this scarf vendor.

**ABOVE**
As with most markets, the range of choices is varied and plentiful, unless of course you arrive at the end. While most items are displayed in crates, others are shown in baskets.

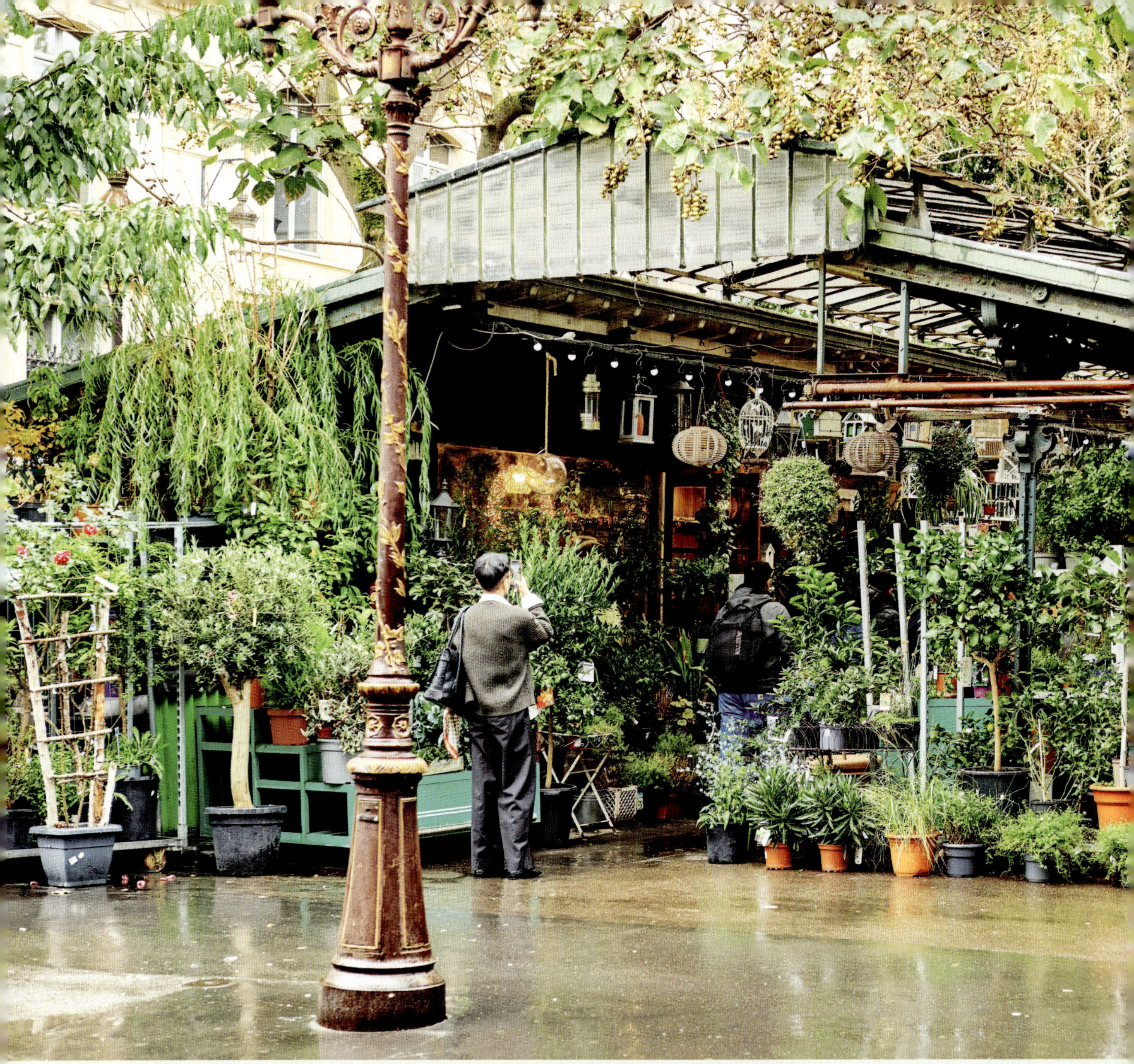

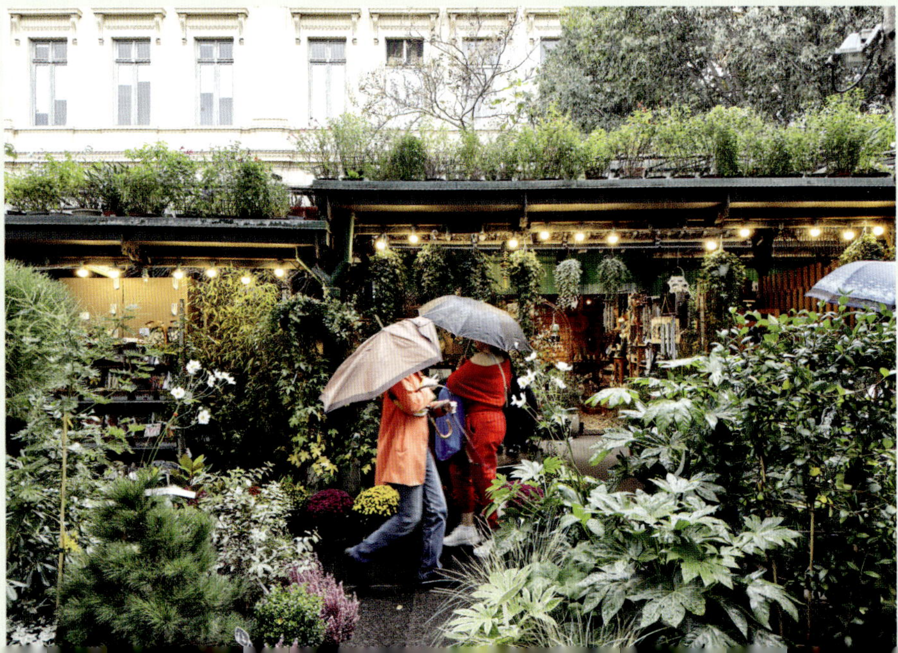

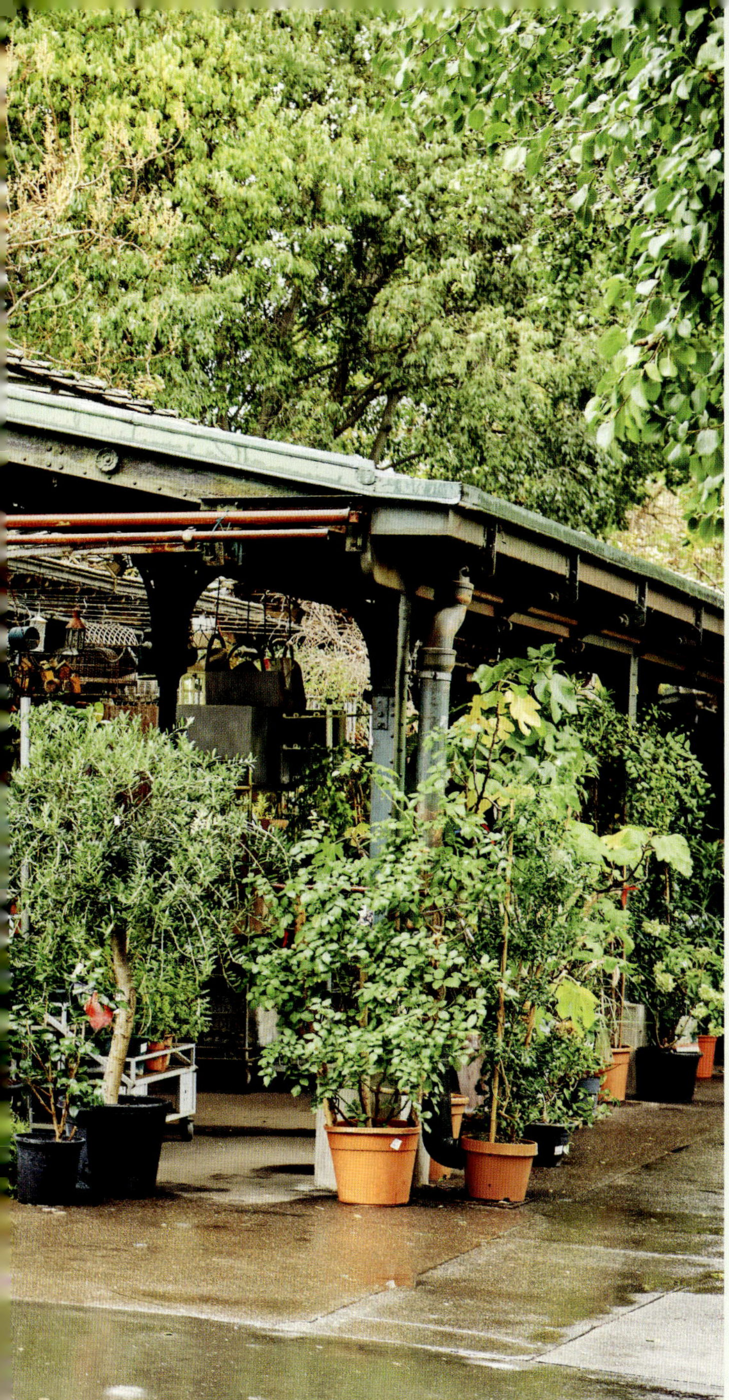

## Marché aux Fleurs Reine Elizabeth II

4th arrondissement
1808

Established in 1808 as the flower market of the city, the current location on l'île de la Cité and its buildings are survivors. The market was moved in the 1920s to make way for the metro station, Cité. Visitors exit the Hector Guimard–designed art deco station entrance onto place Louis-Lépine, at the flower market's three rows of steel-and-glass halls overlooking the Seine. Parisians buy plants from fifteen vendors here to take home to their apartments and terraces. Throughout its long history, many plans have been made to update the buildings and the place. Finally, a new renovation is due to be completed in 2025. When Queen Elizabeth II and Prince Phillip visited the market in 2014, the City of Paris decided to rename the flower-filled destination in her honor.

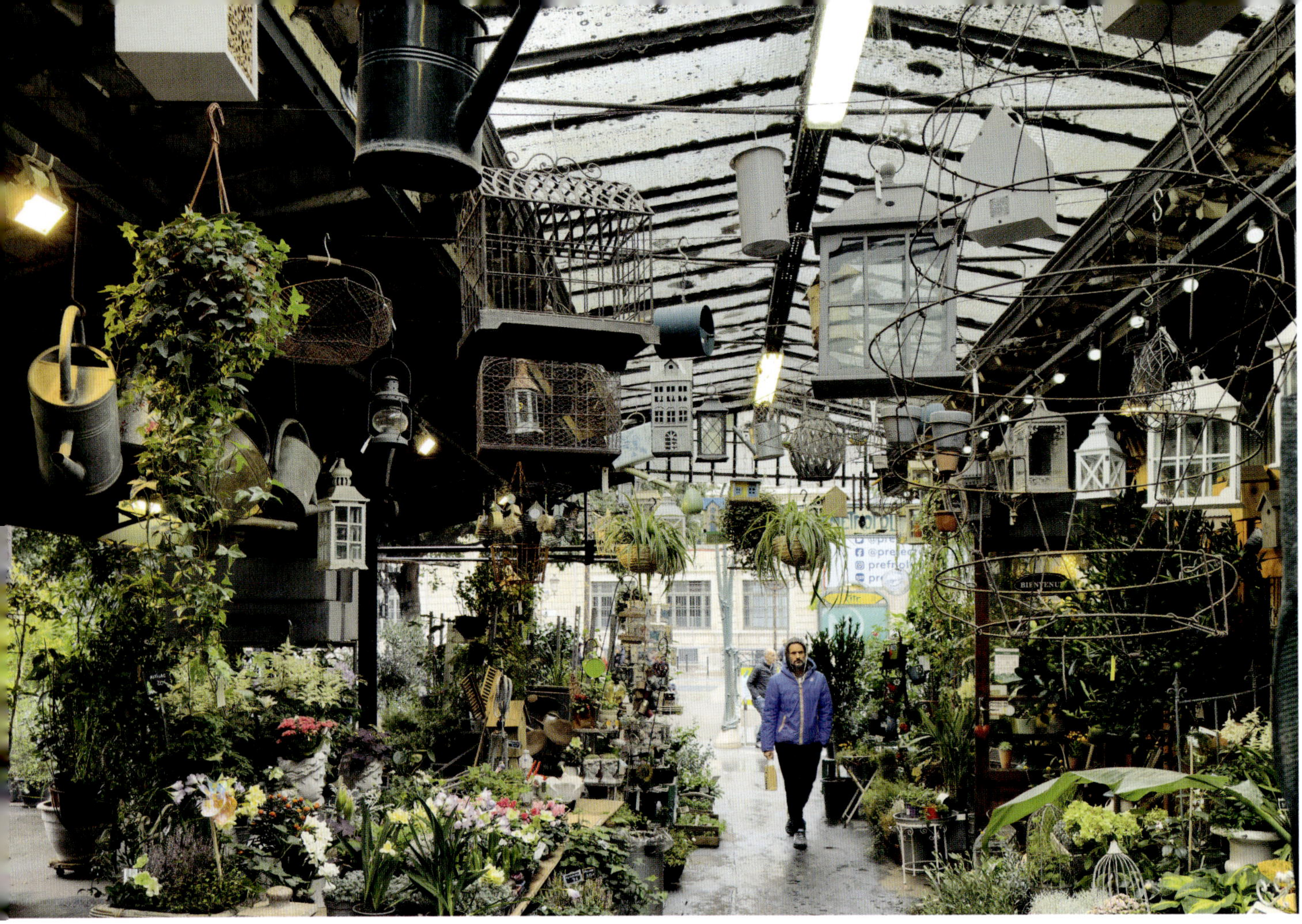

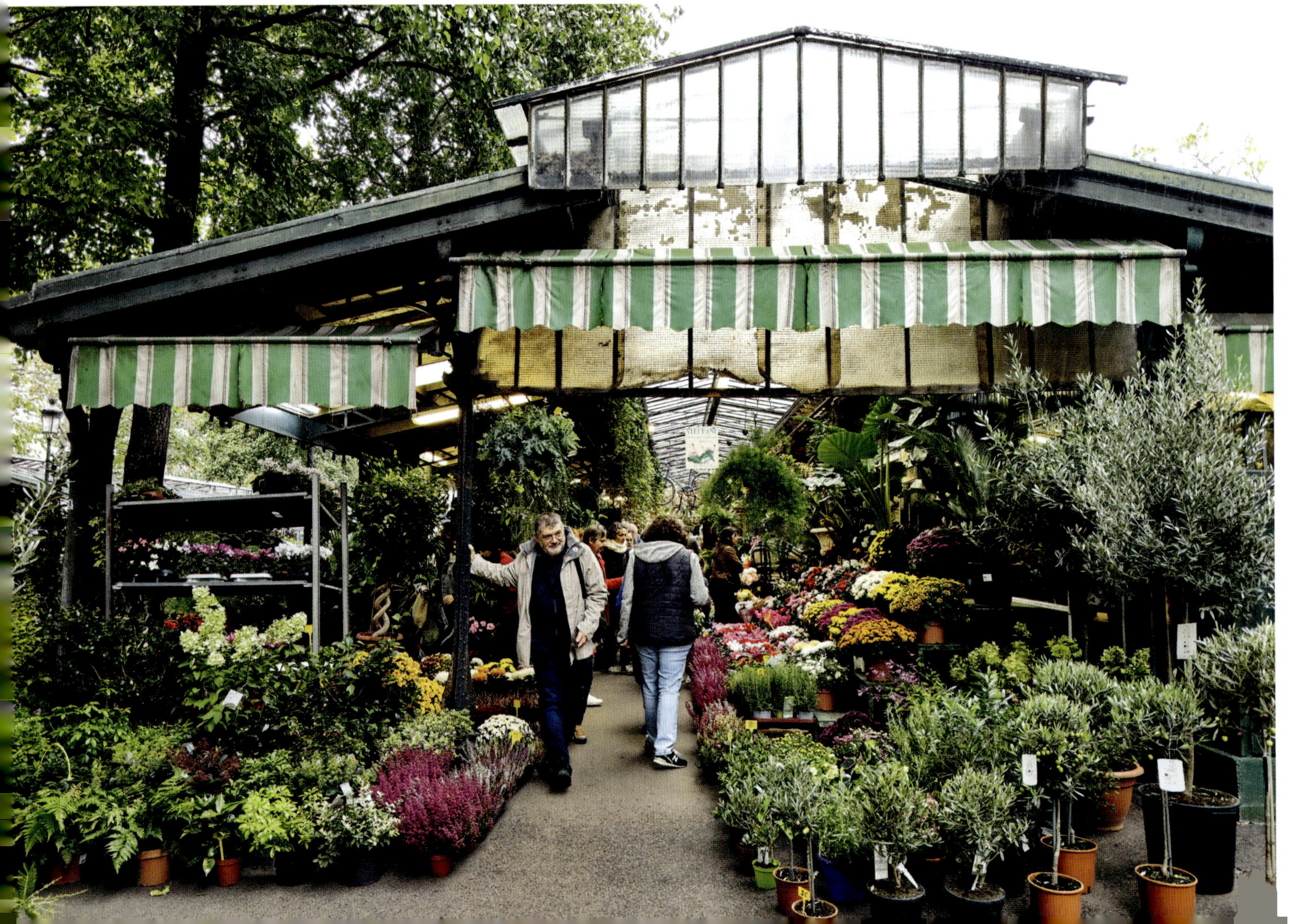

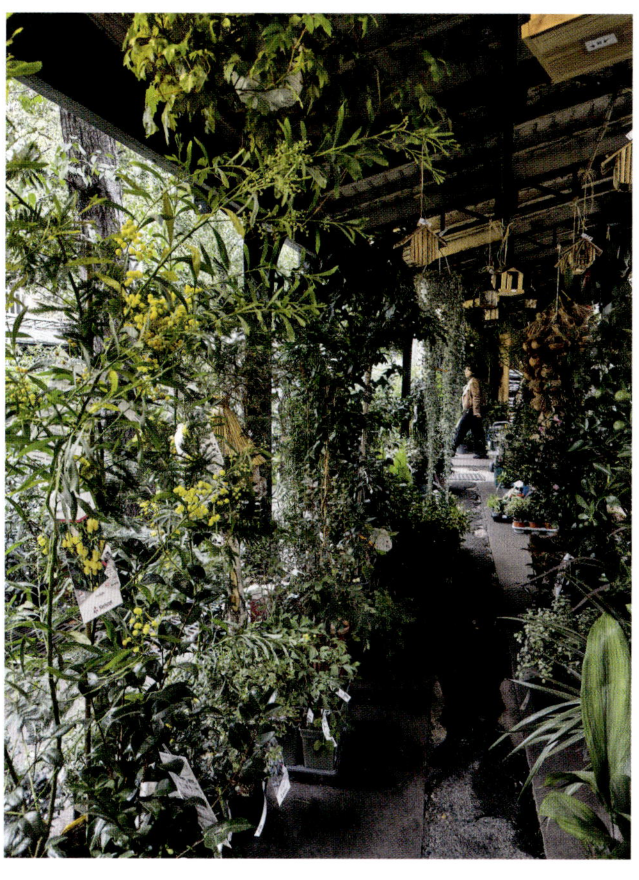

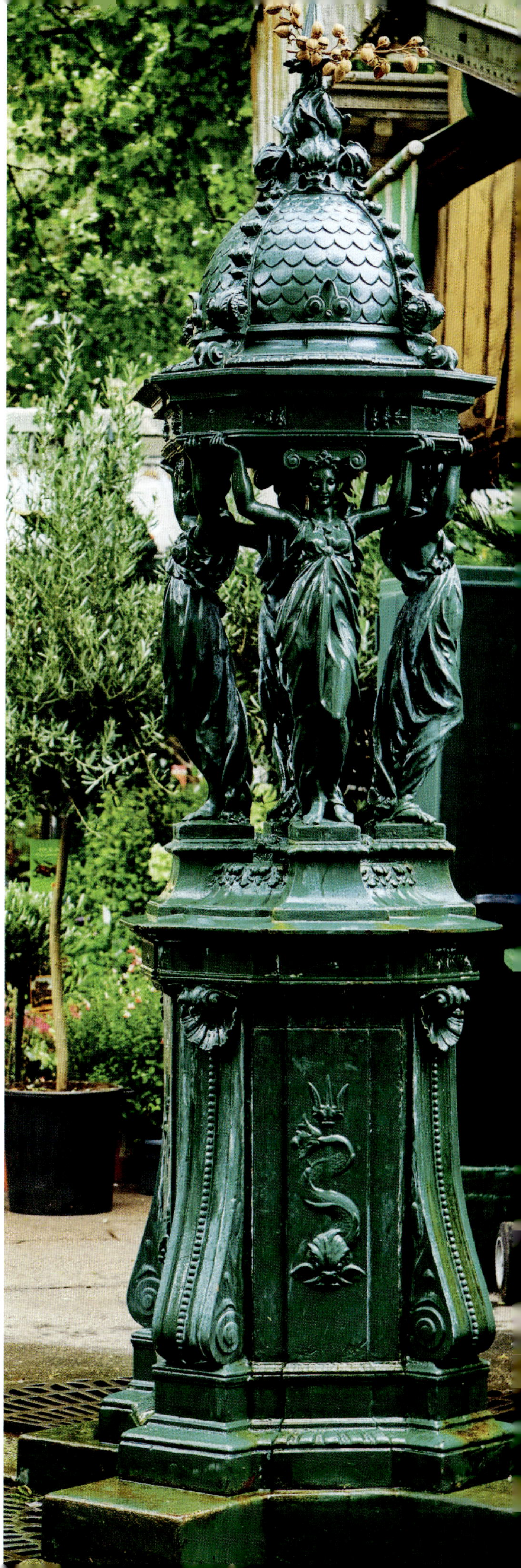

OPPOSITE ABOVE
Lanterns, watering cans, and bird cages
hang from wires and rafters inside the
market. Useful tools and decorative
garden items are sold by flower vendors.

OPPOSITE BELOW
Green-and-white-striped awnings
provide shade in the summer and
protection in the winter.

ABOVE
The overgrown outdoor corridors
offer inspiration to garden lovers
and designers.

RIGHT
A Wallace fountain on the grounds.

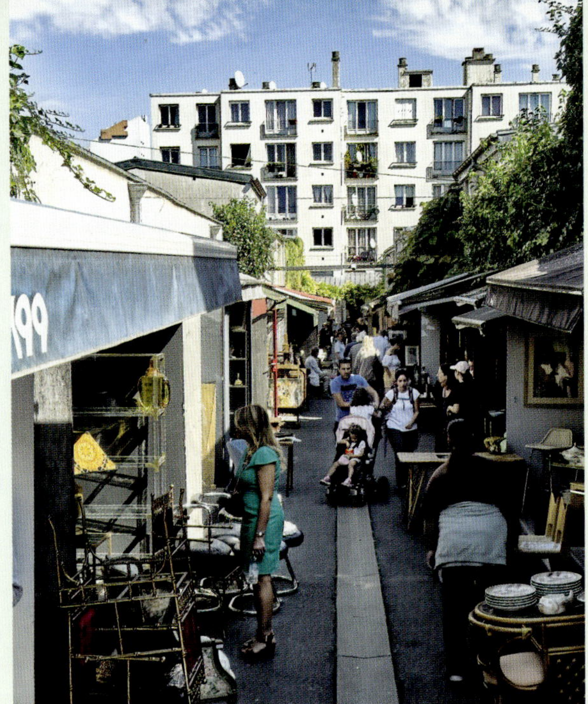

# RECYCLING: FASHION AND FURNISHINGS

## *Marché aux Puces de Paris Saint-Ouen*

Saint-Ouen-sur-Seine
1870

Recycling, repairing, and reducing are known as the three Rs, and in France this is not a new concept. In fact, Parisians have been practicing the three Rs for centuries—gathering used or previously owned clothing, furnishing and household items, and artworks and reselling them. The *puces*, or flea markets, moved outside of the city to the area right over le boulevard périphérique in Saint-Ouen-sur-Seine in the 1860s. As antiques dealers began to set up shops in the old stalls, valuable artworks, jewelry, and antiques became available for sale. The tenor of the place changed, upgraded, and expanded. Deals became fewer but quality rose. In modern times, a visit to the French flea markets is for many a must-do Parisian experience. For others, it is a business and source of income. These days younger dealers and buyers have started to appear with the hopes of supporting and participating in a circular economy. There are eleven official *marchés*, or covered markets, plus open-market streets on the 7-hectare (17-acre) site. Walking through the markets' galleries and stands provides a view of French life through objects and collectibles.

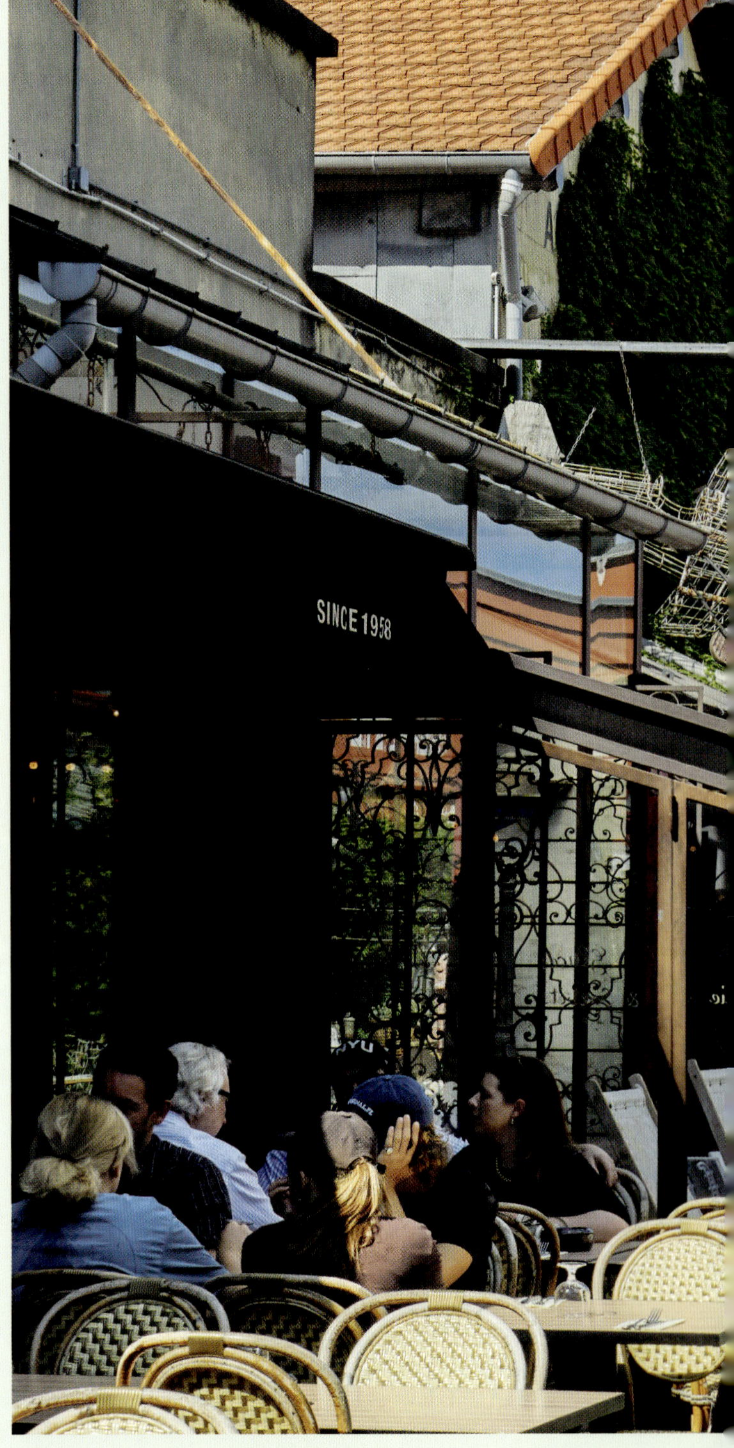



**ABOVE LEFT**
Families have been strolling the markets' *alleés* for more than 150 years.

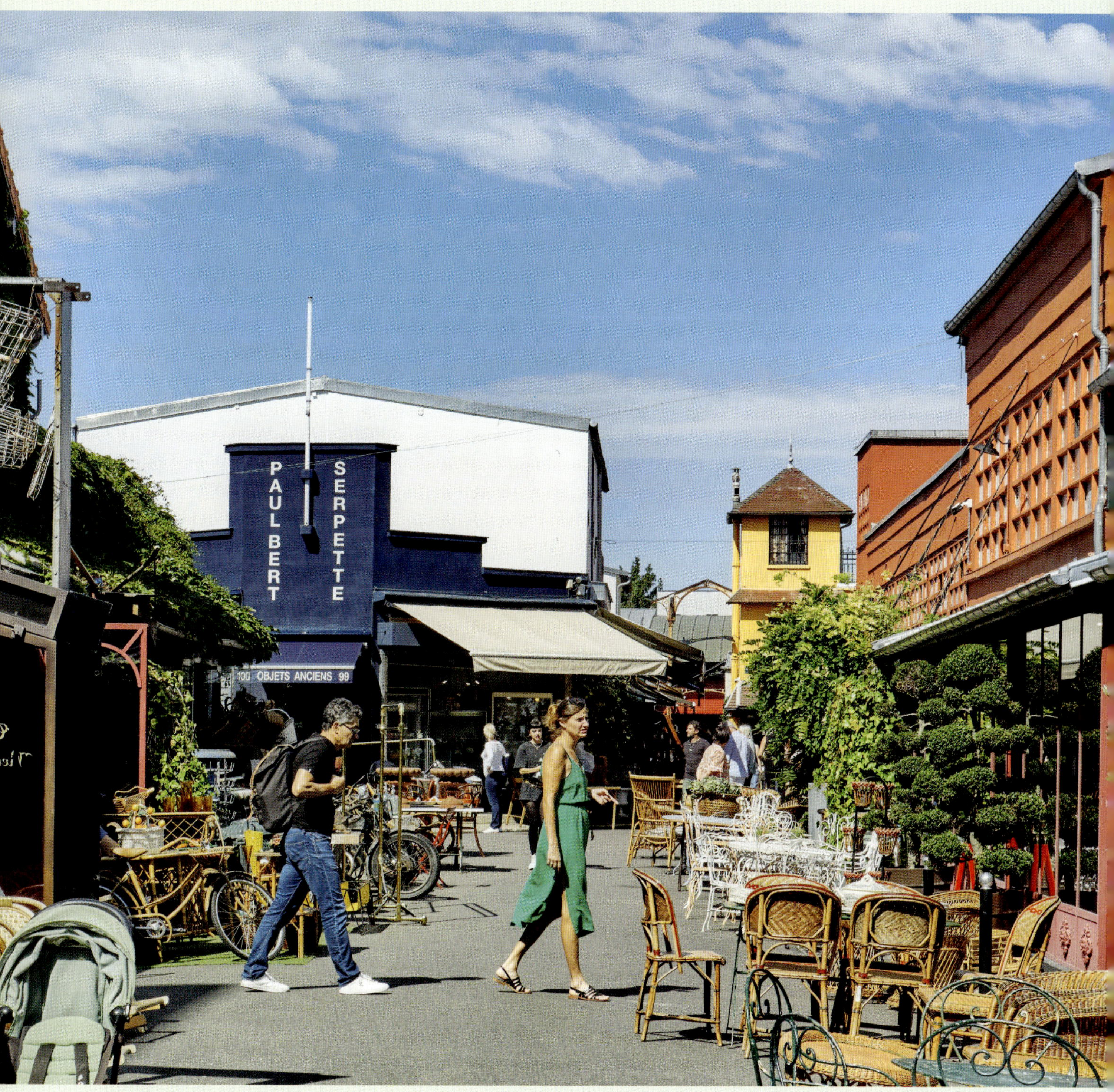



**ABOVE**
La rue Paul Bert, one of the oldest and most well-known market streets, in front of the Paul Bert Serpette, a covered market that sells high-end objects from antiquity to the 1970s. Chairs and other furniture are displayed outdoors. Visitors can take advantage of the café at the market to reflect on their purchases.

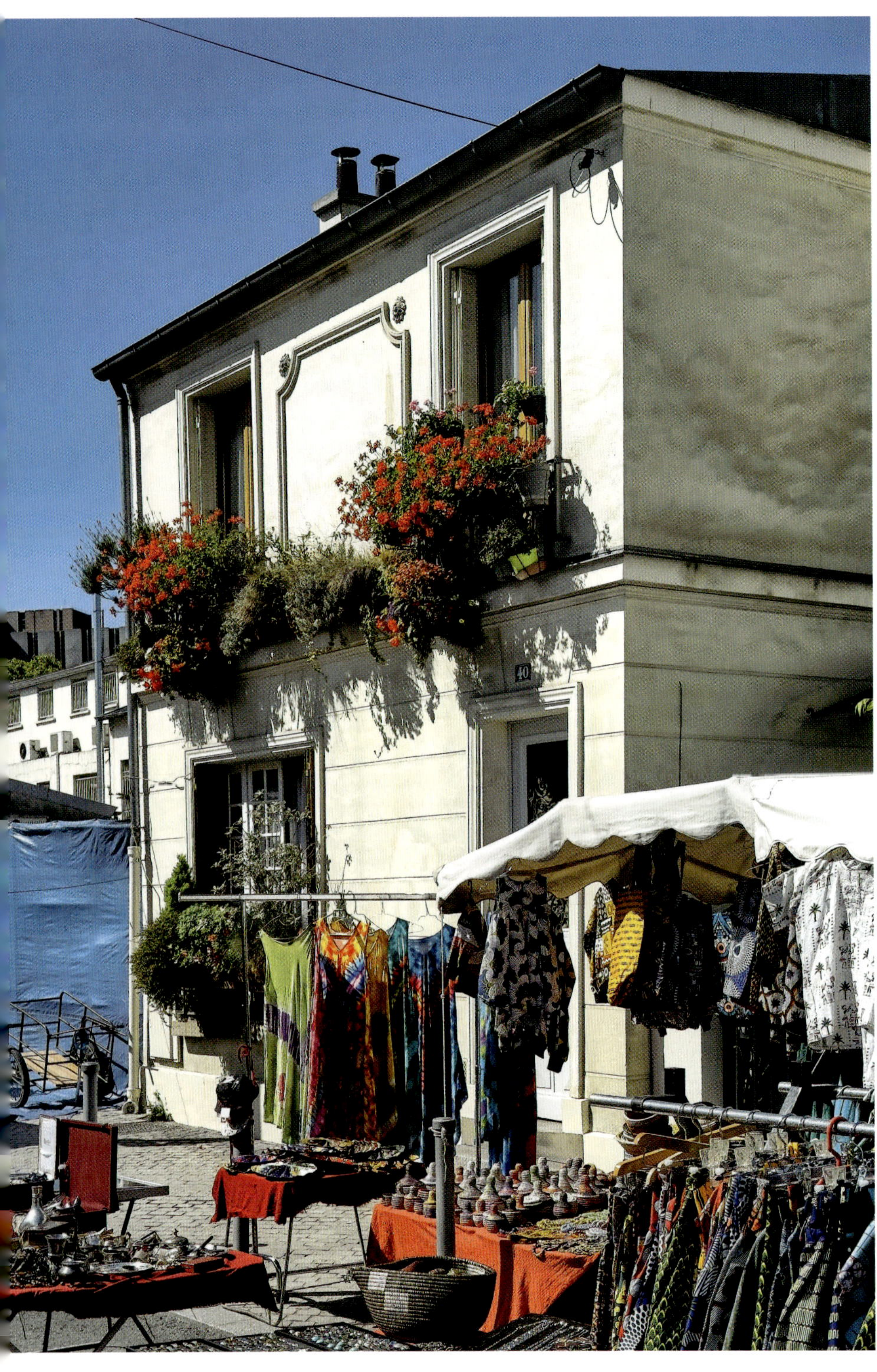



**LEFT**
On la rue Jules-Vallès, a frippery (or old clothes) stand is set up. The overgrown flowers cascading over the balconettes add a charming backdrop.

**OPPOSITE ABOVE**
Le marché Dauphine is a two-story covered market off la rue des Rosiers. Antiques dealer stands are also located on the second floor of the nineteenth-century building, with its steel, brick, and glass structure.

**OPPOSITE BELOW**
Finnish architect Matti Suuronen first designed the Futuro house as a holiday house. One example now sits in le marché Dauphine.

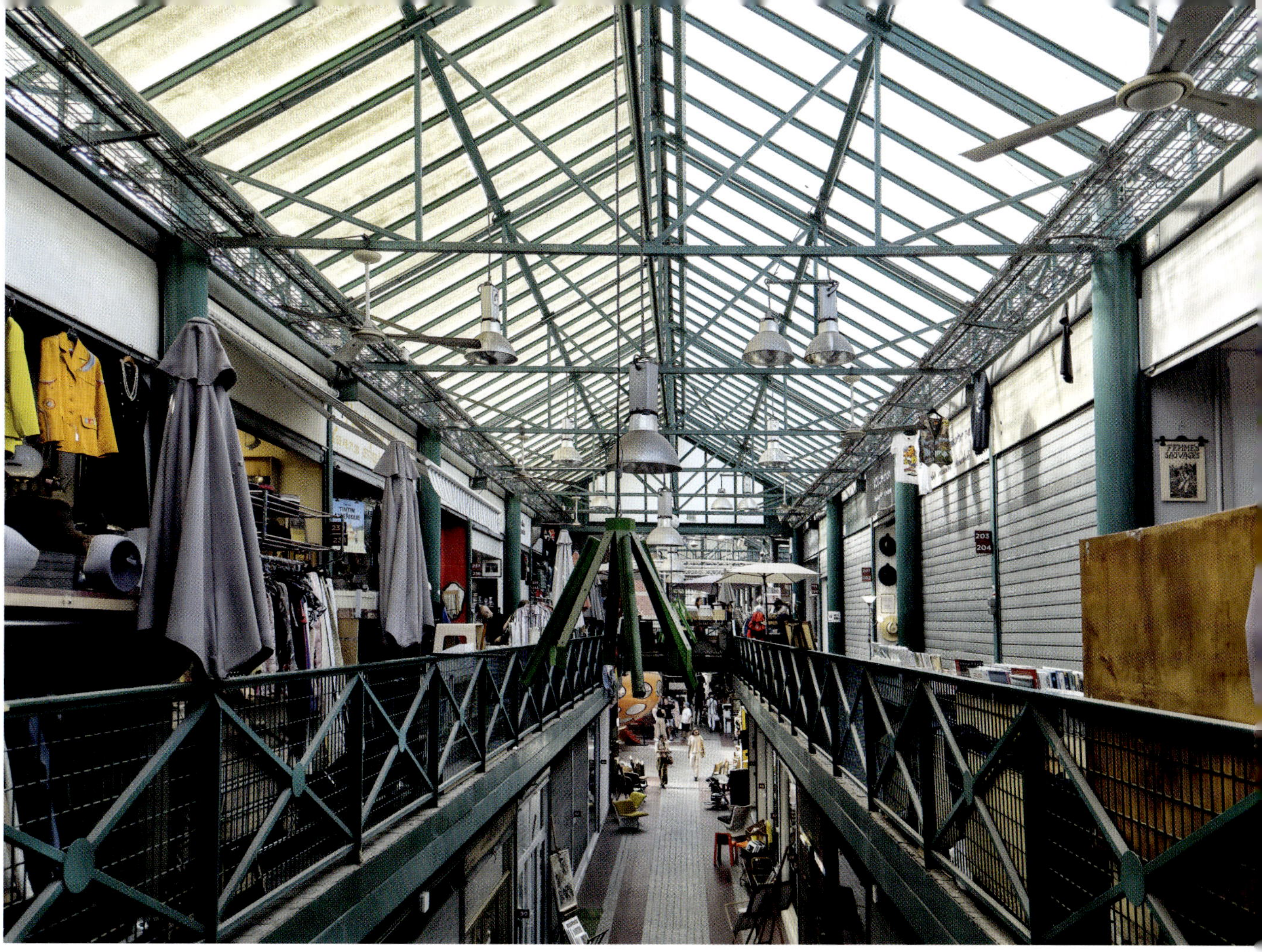

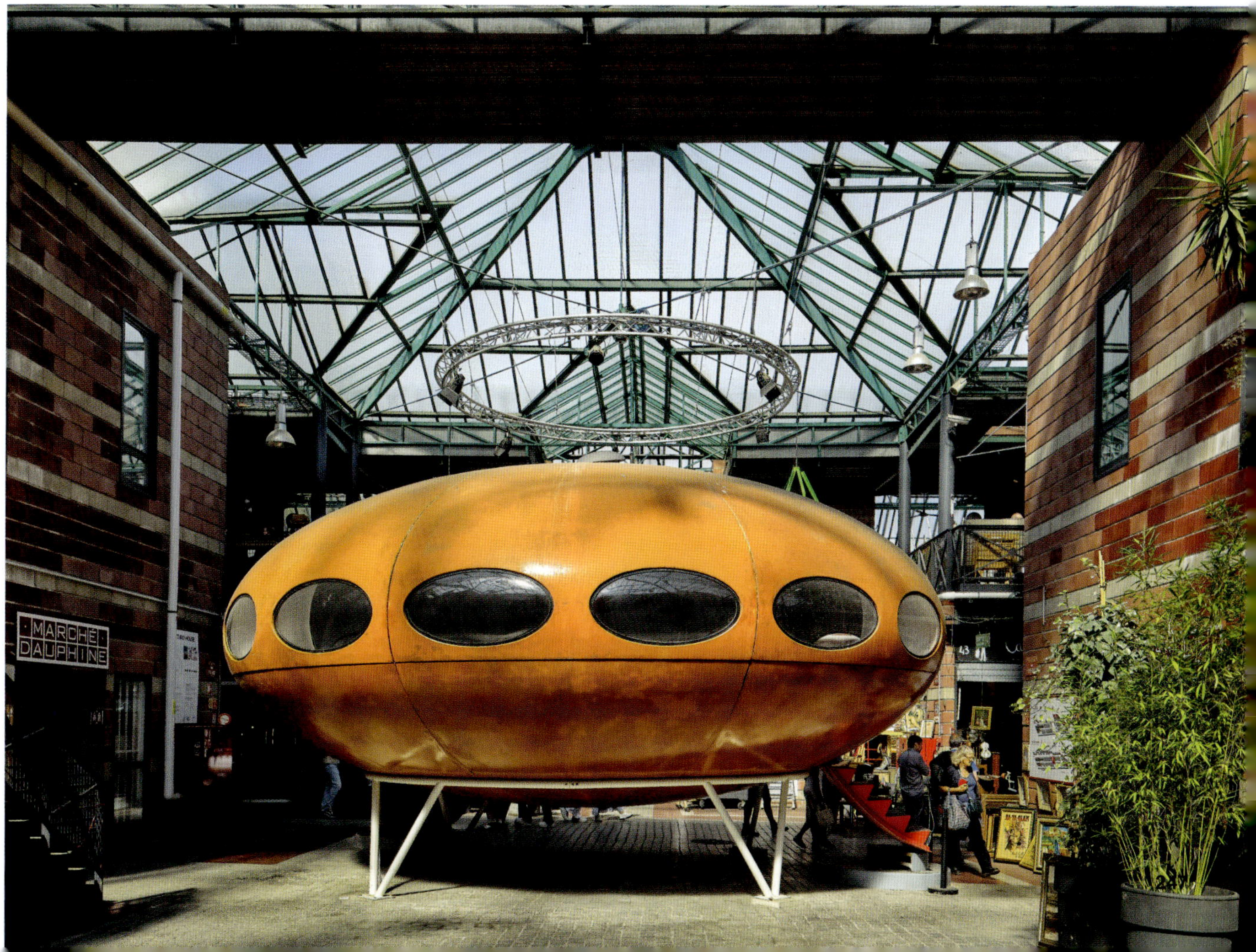

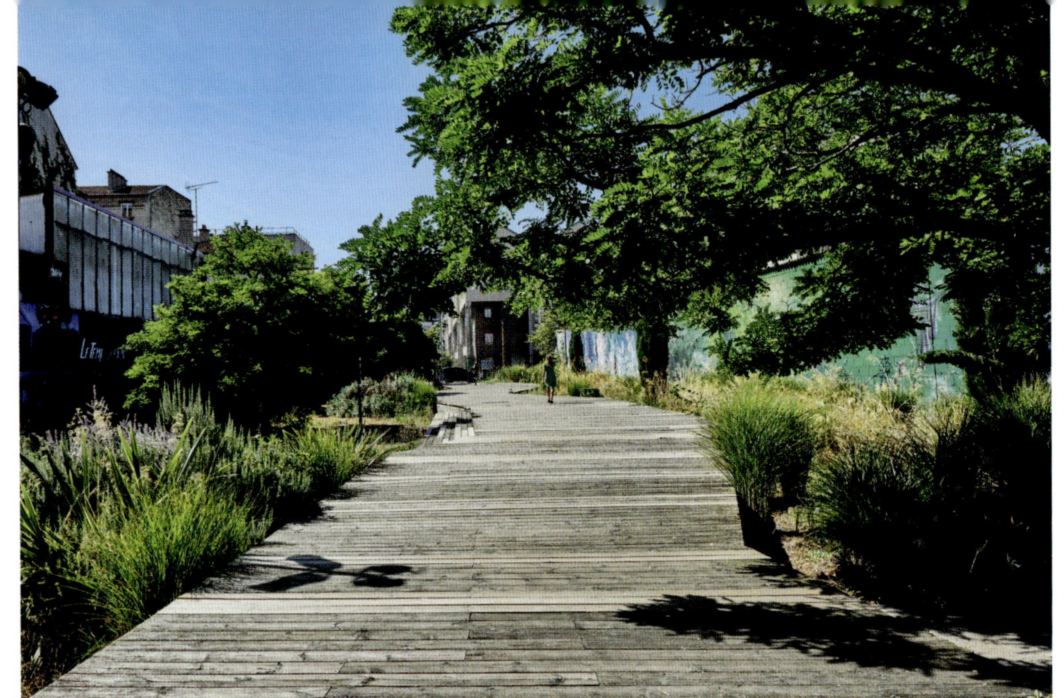

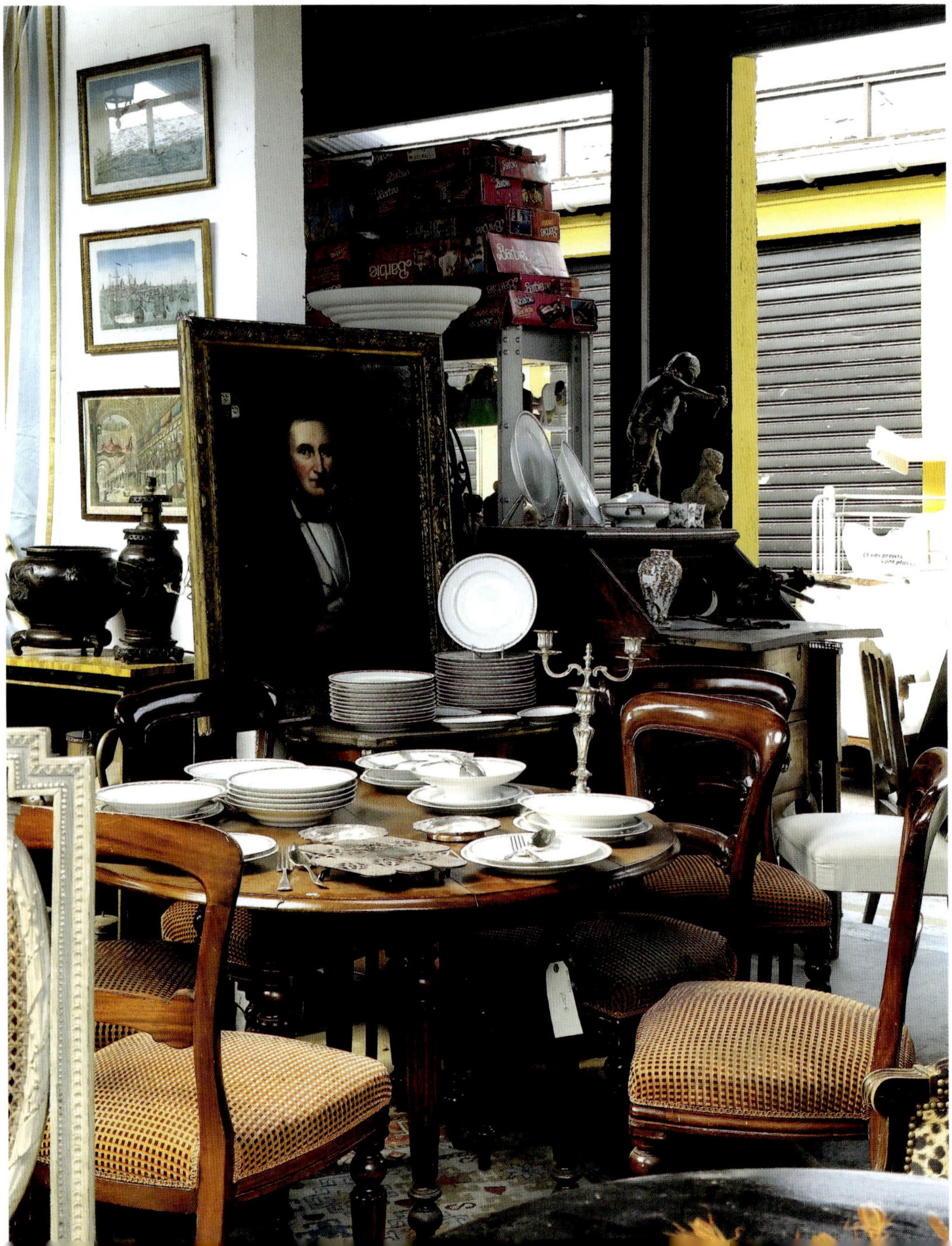

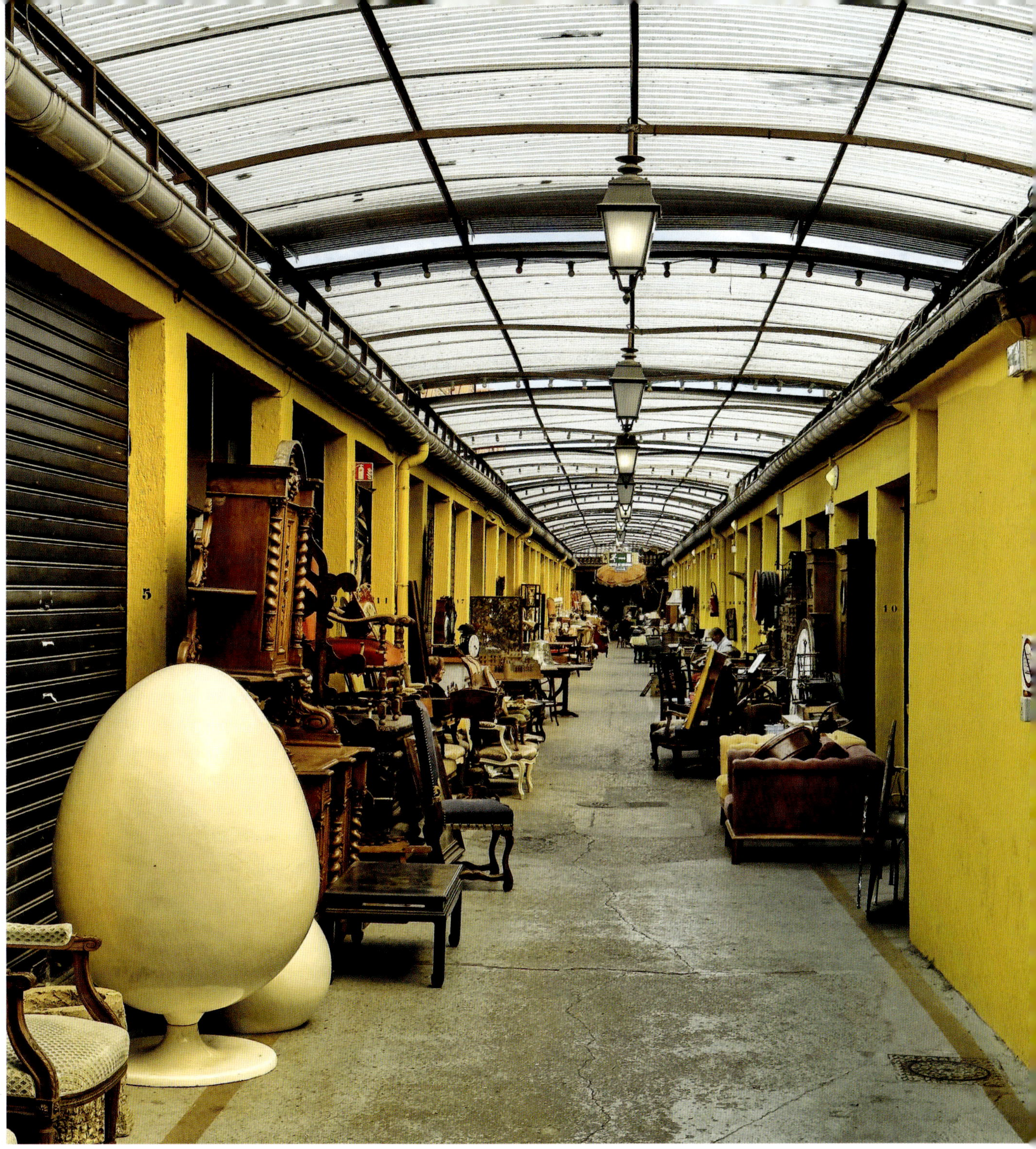



**OPPOSITE ABOVE**
Along one of the back walls of the marketplace is a restorative garden called le Jardin éphémère (the ephemeral garden). It is a much-needed respite from the sometimes-overwhelming nature of the market.

**OPPOSITE BELOW**
You never know what you will find at the flea market, including a stack of Barbies behind a more formal table setup.

**ABOVE**
An allée in bright yellow in le marché Jules-Vallès.

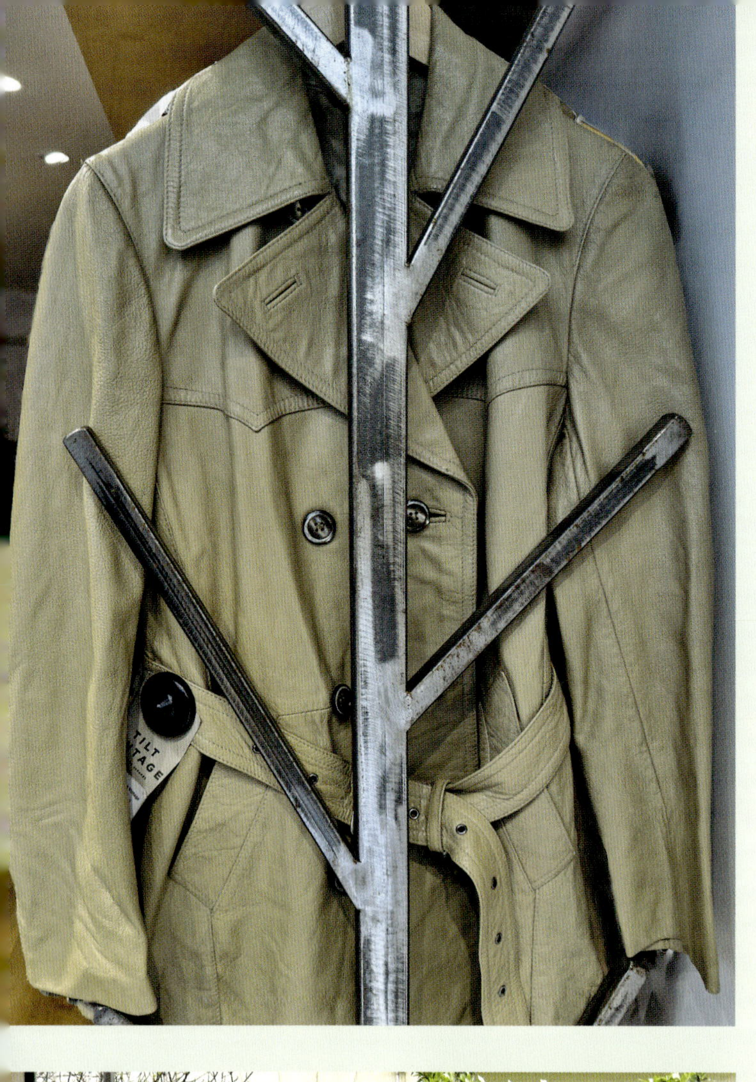
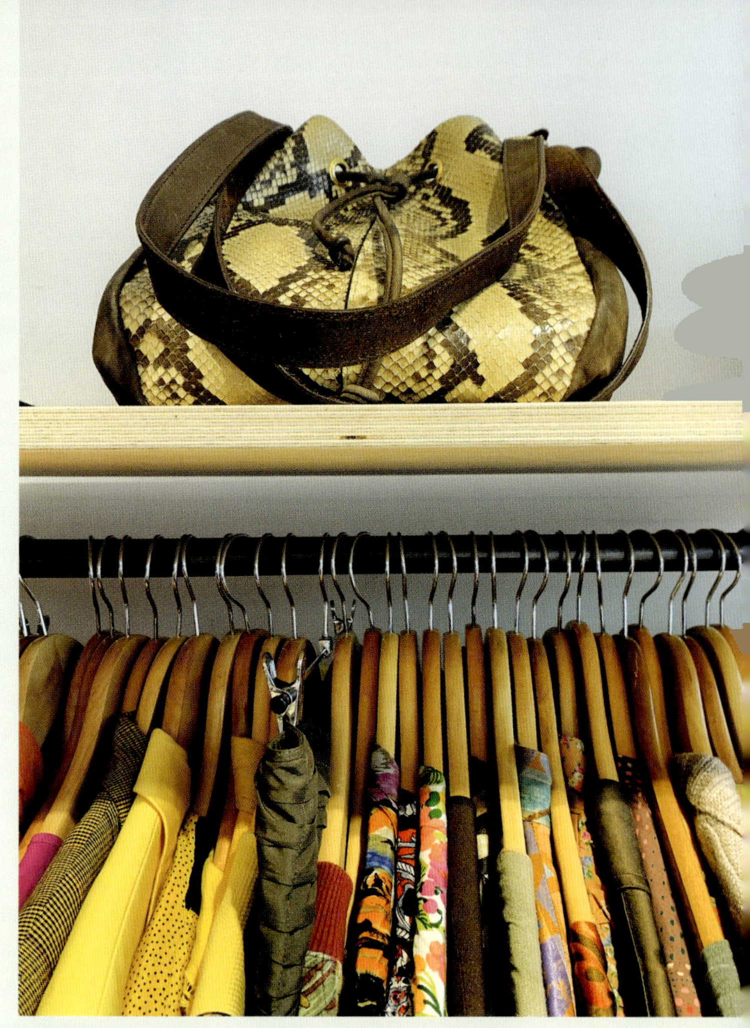
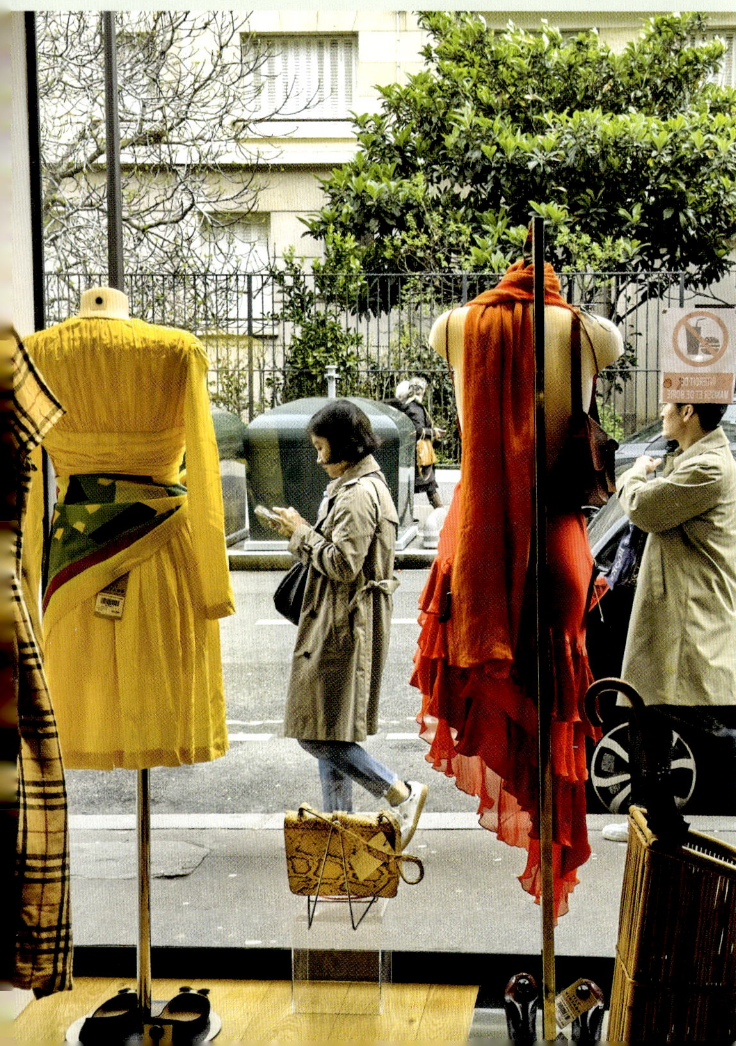
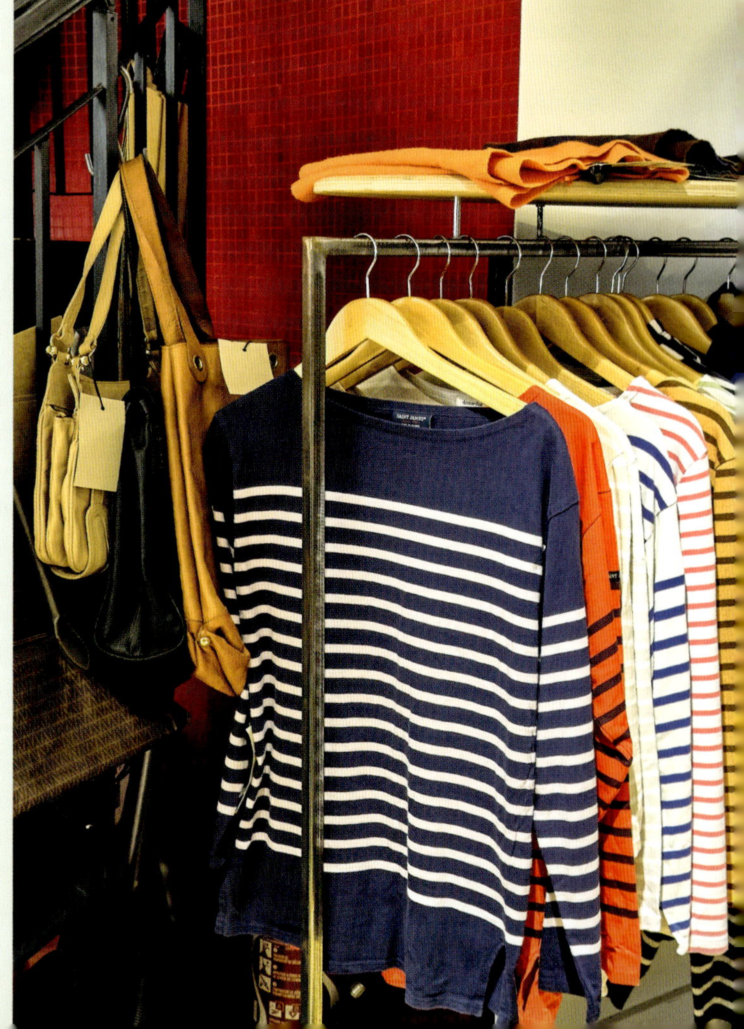

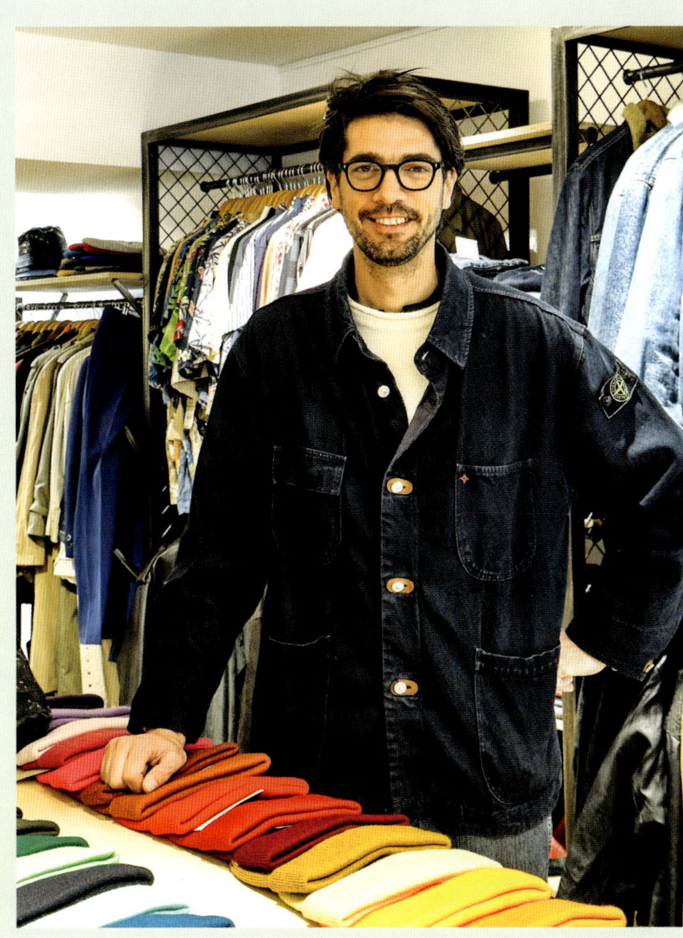



# Tilt Vintage
4th and 6th arrondissements
2011

Jonathan Sabban was born into the clothing business. From the time that he was a small boy, he lived in the world of selling vintage clothes. His parents have a stand in le marché aux Puces de Saint-Ouen specializing in French workwear and vintage clothing from the 1920s, 1930s, and 1940s. So, he started in the family business, but in his own way by going to vintage fashion trade fairs or salons and selling on the internet for three years. Then he decided to take a different tack: to start a chain of vintage stores. He opened his first store in 2010 in Lille. He has developed seven boutiques throughout France with locations in Paris, Lille, Lyon, Bordeaux, and Rouen. He works with his wife, Éléonore, and together they work with contacts and resources they've developed over the years to buy unique pieces that are highly curated. He doesn't buy clothes from individuals (nor does he shop for individuals), only from his trusted sources. Their vintage pieces are sourced mainly in Europe. Shopping trips last a week at a time, a few times a year, with the goal of buying substantial amounts of clothing, but they don't buy vintage clothes in bulk. The shops and websites carry only two percent new stock, such as hats and gloves. At the same time, they have recently created a label called Atelier Tilt Vintage with About a Worker, a company that facilitates fashion collaboration and upcycling. Clothes that are damaged and unable to be repaired are sent to About a Worker to be transformed. Their first collaboration was to create a *sac banane*, or belt bag, with recycled jeans. Tilt Vintage also does some upcycling itself with a few products, mostly jeans and T-shirts. Tilt Vintage's mission is maximum recycling that is good for business and the environment.

**OPPOSITE ABOVE LEFT**
The store's bestseller is an icon vintage trench coat.

**OPPOSITE ABOVE RIGHT**
Vintage luxury handbags and shoes are sold alongside clothing for both men and women.

**OPPOSITE BELOW LEFT**
Tilt's window display is constantly revolving with vintage finds. Each shop is curated for the neighborhood's clientele.

**OPPOSITE BELOW RIGHTT**
*La marinière*, or the sailor, is a wardrobe staple and a popular item at Tilt.

**ABOVE**
Jonathan Sabban, founder of Tilt Vintage

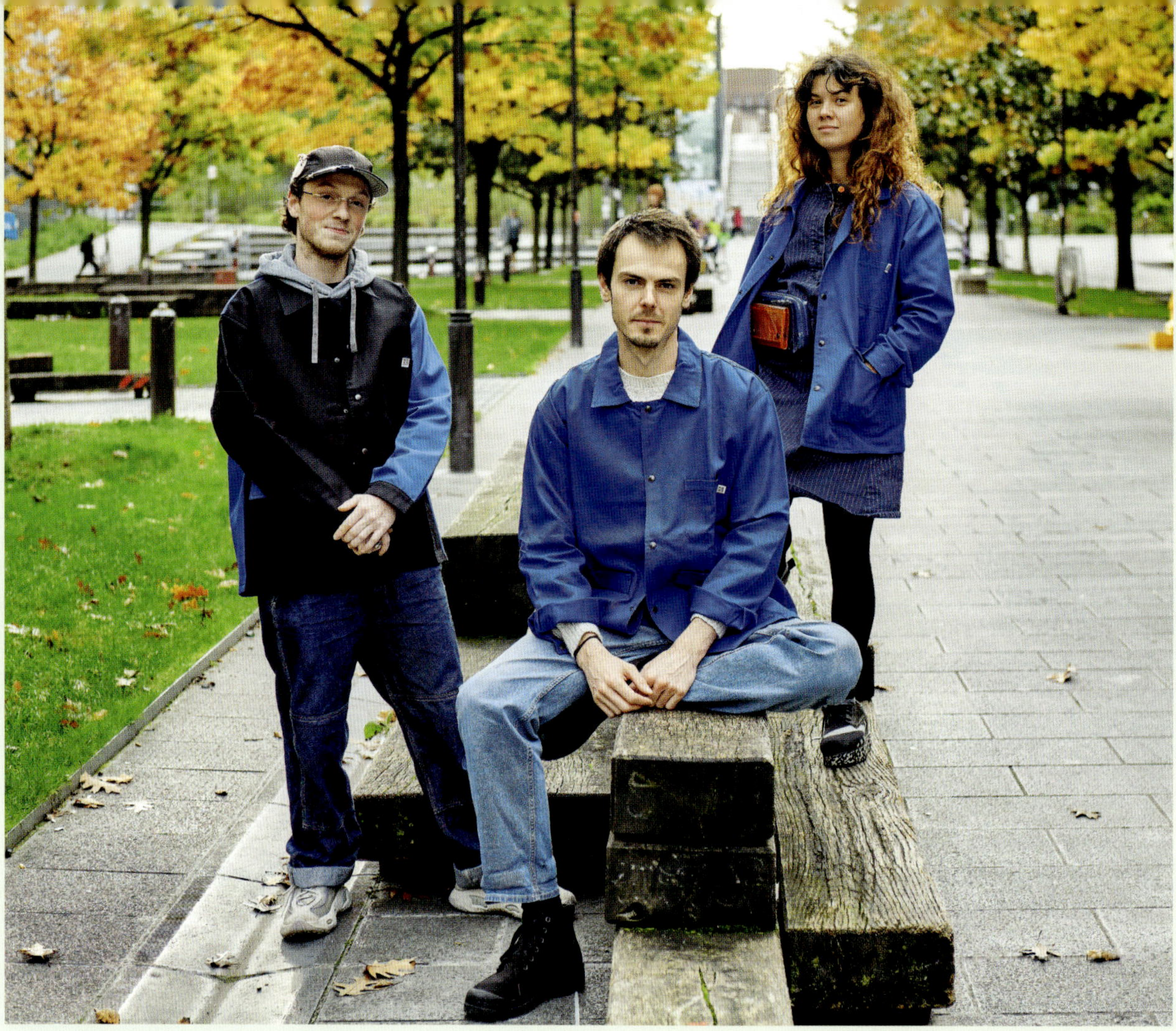

## About a Worker

13th arrondissement
2017

Kim Hou and Paul Boulenger are rethinking the fashion industry. They first met in London when they were both studying at Kingston School of Art. They reconnected years later and decided to create a company around an idea that grew from Kim's graduate studies and Paul's expertise in the business side of fashion. The concept was to include fashion factory workers in the clothing design process. For their first line, they collaborated with workers to give the classic French worker's jacket a fresh redesign in a shocking blue fabric. They produced and sold three hundred pieces; each different model had a label with a picture and the story of its designer/worker sewn on an inside seam. As their company has grown, they have explored how other traditionally French apparel was designed and made; for example, charentaises,

or bedroom slippers. There are only a few French factories that still make the slippers using traditional methods. Kim and Paul collaborated with workers to create a new design and use new techniques. The limited run of fun, brightly colored slippers sold out. As their company, About a Worker, drew attention, Kim and Paul started to work with fashion businesses and cultural institutions to educate the public on upcycling. Adidas asked About a Worker to host a workshop in their main store in Paris. Adidas supplied the materials, and the About a Worker team guided people as they transformed the materials into trendy fanny packs and hats on-site. The first morning, a line of five hundred people turned up to participate in the workshop, and Adidas ran the workshop for a month. Kim and Paul are working with their clients/partners to educate a new generation of consumers on the importance and possibilities of recycling. They are expanding their company with a research division that is focused on manufacturing. About a Worker is working from within the fashion industry to improve the system and to be inclusive, transparent, and eco-conscious.

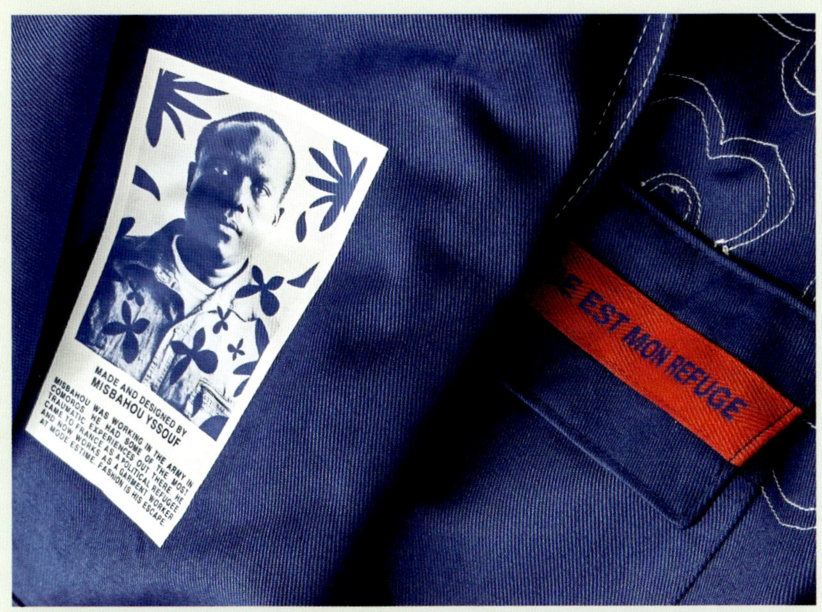



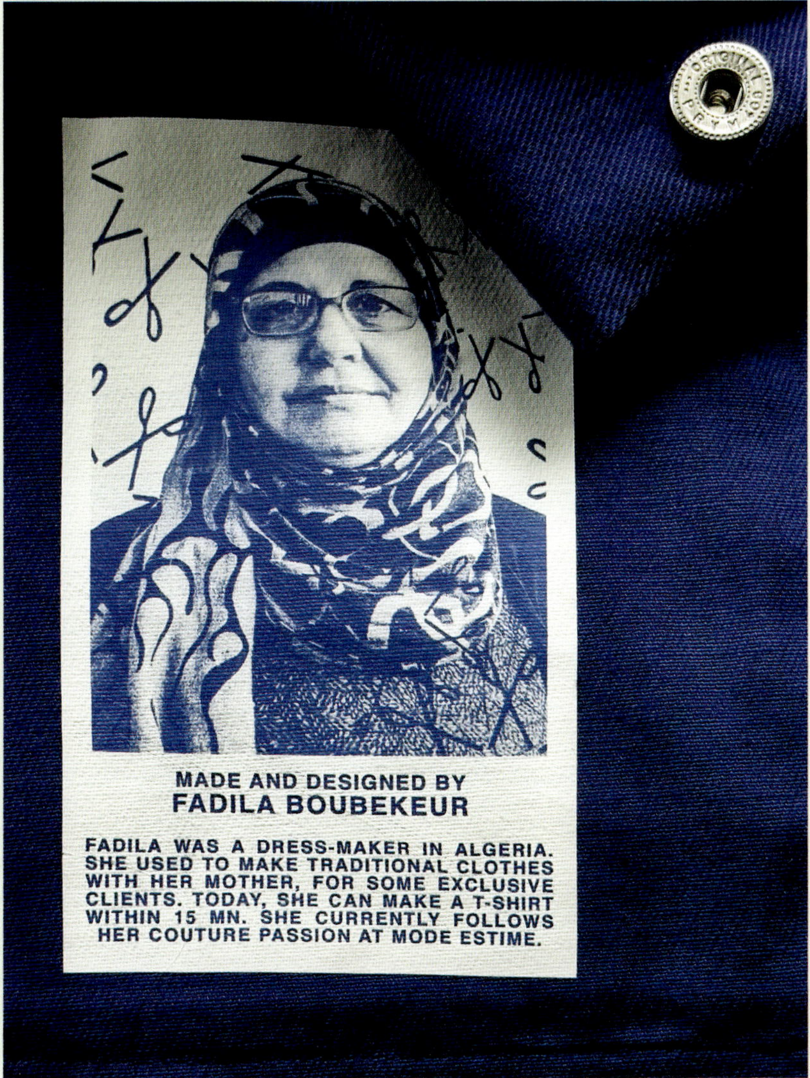



**OPPOSITE**
Members of the About a Worker team, left to right: Alaïnn Menoni, Paul Boulenger, and Kim Hou. All are wearing their first line of worker's jackets.

**ABOVE**
The interior label on one of the About a Worker jackets. It shows the person who designed the jacket and made it, bringing a personal element to the clothing brand.

**LEFT**
Many of the workers have immigration stories that are made even more poignant when told in connection to a garment.

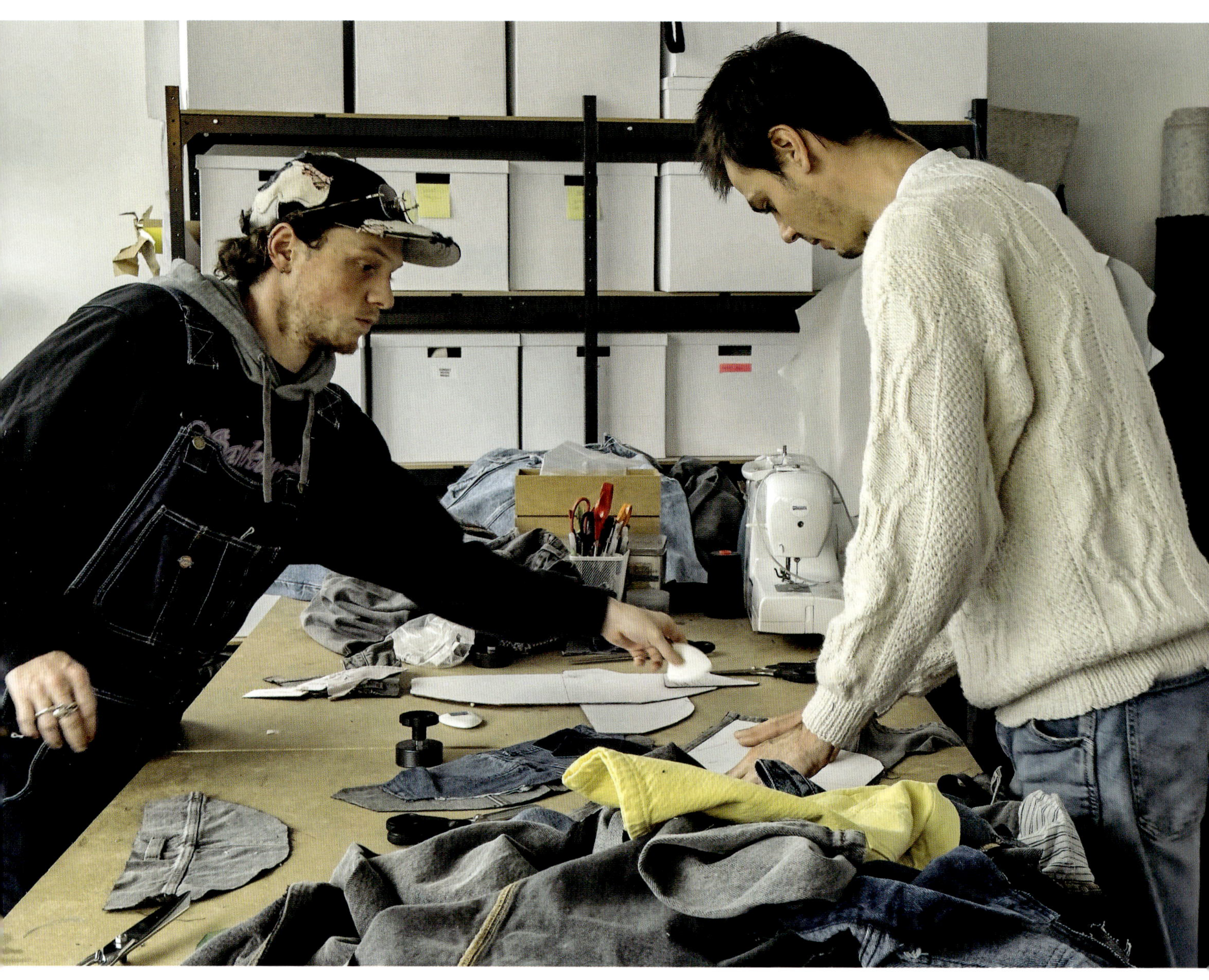

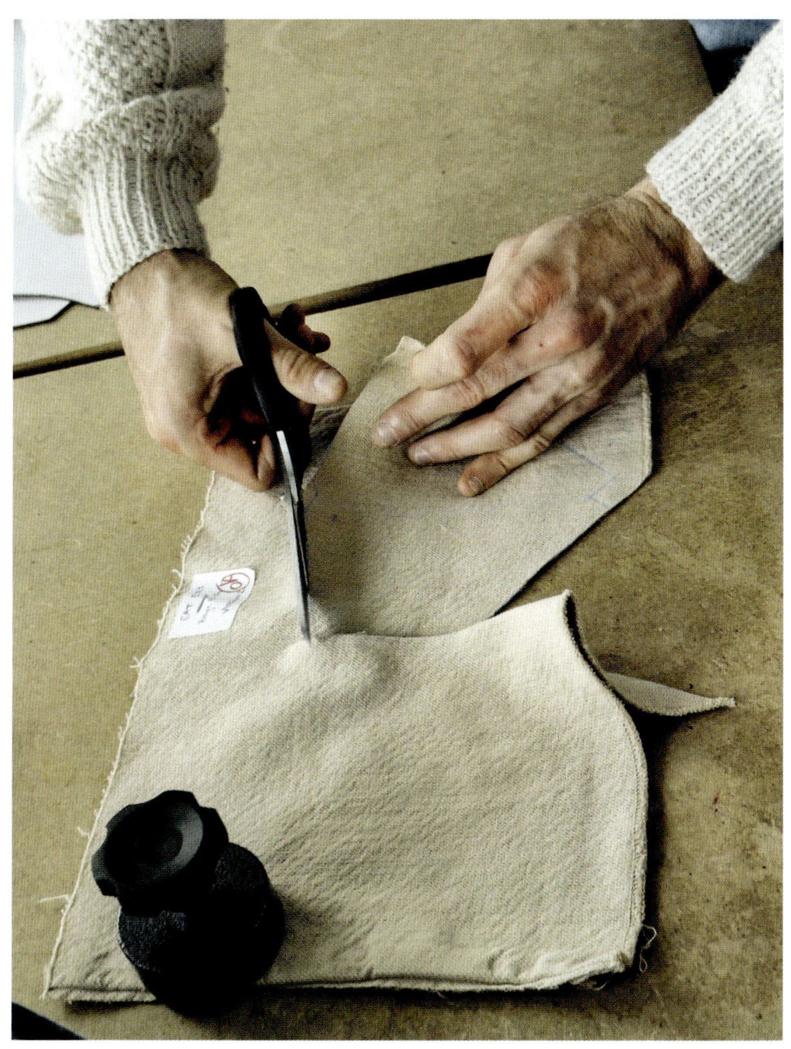

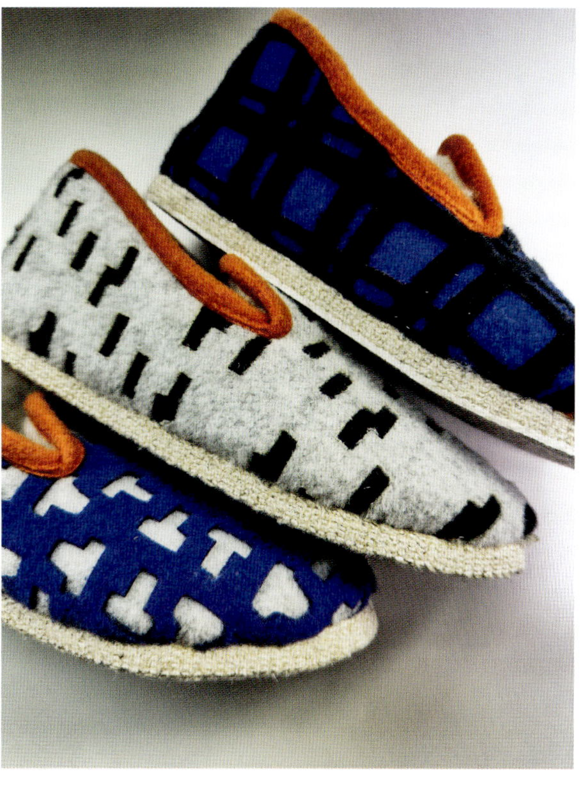

**OPPOSITE**
Paul is working with Alaïnn to create a simple model of a fanny pack that can be sewn by the public in a workshop.

**ABOVE**
Paul cuts recycled material for one of the company's projects—a *sac banana*, or belt bag. They source their materials from textile companies' dead stock.

**ABOVE RIGHT**
A sample of French slippers that About a Worker collaborated with factory workers to make. The graphic patterns are an update from the traditional patterns generations of French people know from their grandfather's favorite pair.

**BELOW RIGHT**
A display of some of the accessories made from recycled materials.

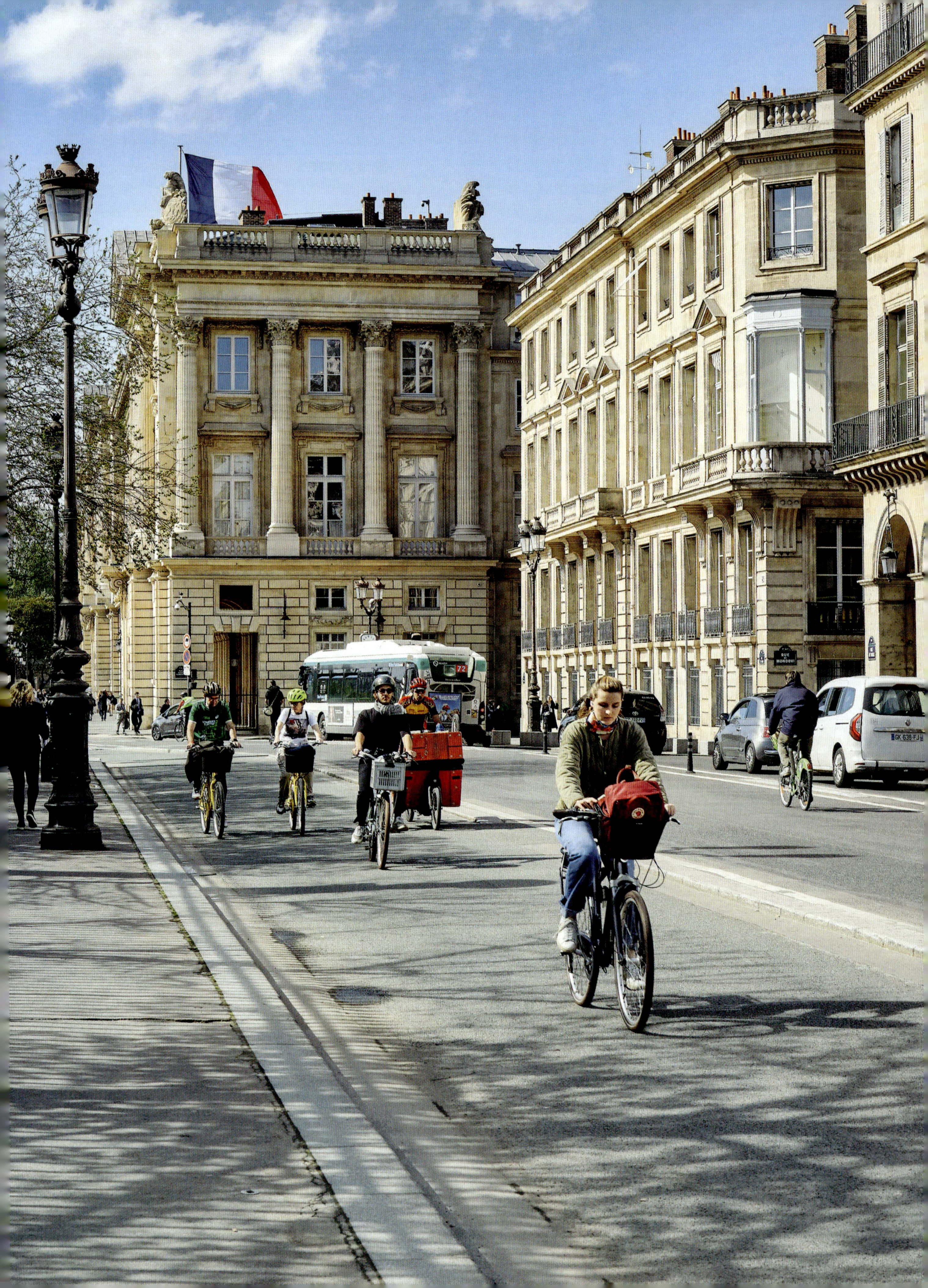

# Alternative Transportation

How Parisians are changing the way they are getting around is impacting the environment. Between riding bicycles, taking the tram, or walking, the effect on the air quality is noticeable. La rue de Rivoli is perhaps the best example of the changes in the City of Paris's mobility plan. At one time carriages went up and down this illustrious street, then cars were packed five or six across, often stopped in traffic going west. It was, and still is, a main artery of central Paris that starts at la place de la Concorde and ends with the merger of rue Saint-Antoine near la place de la Bastille. Since 2019, rue de Rivoli has been transformed into two large bike lanes and one lane for taxis and buses. Another good example of the plan to decrease the number of cars in the center of Paris was the closing of le quai de la Seine to traffic. At one time not long ago, it was possible to ride in a taxi along the banks of the Seine. Cars were so prevalent that the roads looked like parking lots. Those areas have now been pedestrianized and host Paris Plages in the summer. In 2007, the bike-sharing plan Vélib' (now known as Vélib' Metropole) was first introduced on the streets of Paris, making affordable bikes available for everyone. A 2024 study by l'Institut Paris Région revealed that 11.2 percent of trips were made by bikes, compared to 4.3 percent by car. Parisian streets are filled with bike riders, from kids to couples, some riding in tandem. The plan to extend the network of biking paths is on track to create total bike-lane coverage throughout the city. Paris is becoming a cyclist's dream city.

The Île-de-France tram system has also expanded. Paris had a comprehensive tram system in 1925, based on a system that was developed in New York City by a French engineer, Alphonse Loubat. The French trams were slowly dismantled under pressure from the oil and car industries. Buses replaced the trams. But the modern trams run on electricity, and they began to return to the city in 1992. Tracks have been integrated into new design projects and neighborhoods, such as Rosa Parks in the 19th arrondissement, where the T3b runs. The system is easy to navigate. Access is street level, unlike the metro, which has staircase entrances more often than not.

Walking in Paris in some areas is a different experience than it used to be. Fewer cars have made an impact on that feeling of freedom. While the rise in biking has grown exponentially, and more than 9.4 million people travel per day on bus and tramway, the primary mode of transportation in Paris remains walking. Strolling in Paris has a romantic association, but most Parisians walk to simply get to work. More streets and areas in the city are being pedestrianized, which makes walking in Paris safer. La place de la République has been reclaimed for walking, and la rue du Faubourg-du-Temple, which is perpendicular, has been pedestrianized, so when exiting the metro, there is plenty of room to walk to the square. The plan to create a walking path on the former rail lines of the Petite Ceinture is proceeding. By 2025, it will be possible to walk around the city of Paris on the linked path and to experience section by section the city's wild ecosystem, uninterrupted.

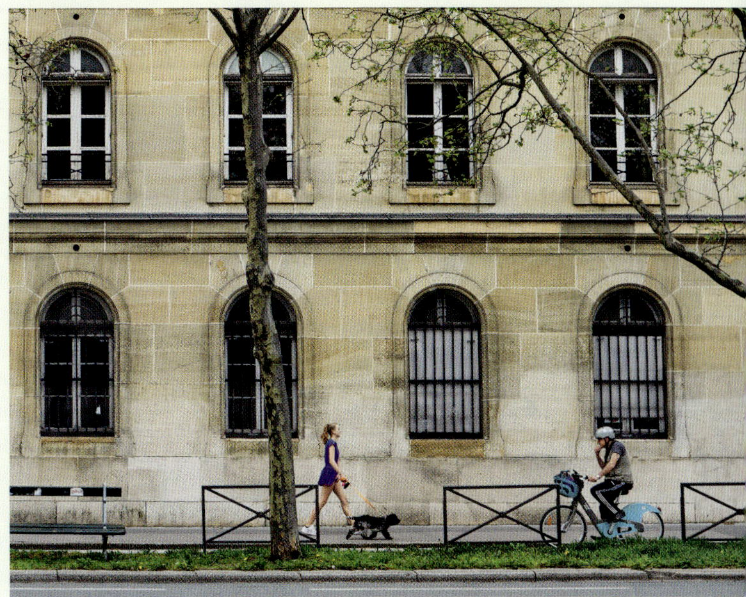

**OPPOSITE**
Heading west on la rue de Rivoli, toward la place de la Concorde, at 4:00 P.M. The bidirectional bike pathways are wide enough for many riders.

**ABOVE**
On boulevard des Invalides in the 7th arrondissement, walkers and bikers coexist.

## *En Vélo*

**BELOW LEFT**
La place de Catalogne was once
a roundabout, but now the flow of
traffic of both cars and bikes has been
changed with the addition of a new
urban forest.

**BELOW CENTER**
Some bikes are rented, and others are
personal bikes. There is more than one
bike rental company in the city. Bike
businesses are proliferating. Near place
de la République, bikers enjoy a street
now closed to car traffic

**BOTTOM LEFT**
Bike riders are in the parks, such as the
Champ-de-Mars, where there are wide
pathways.

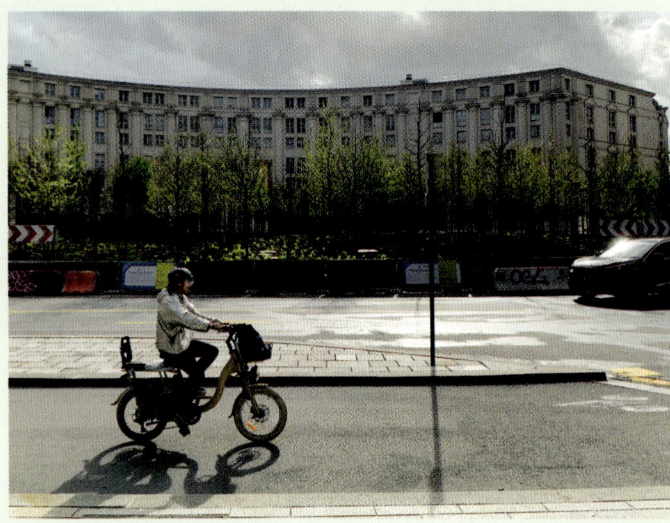

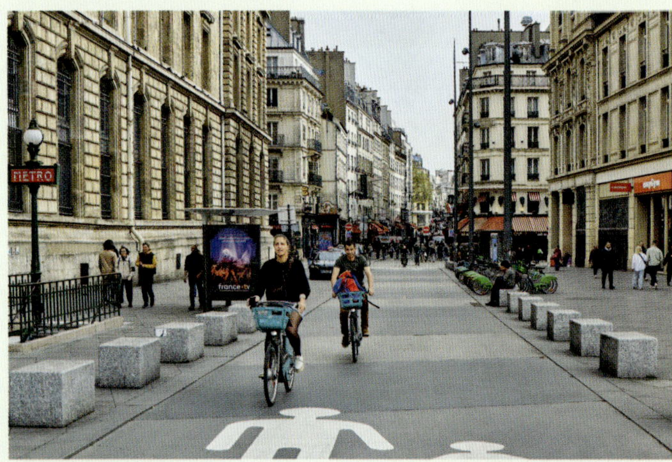

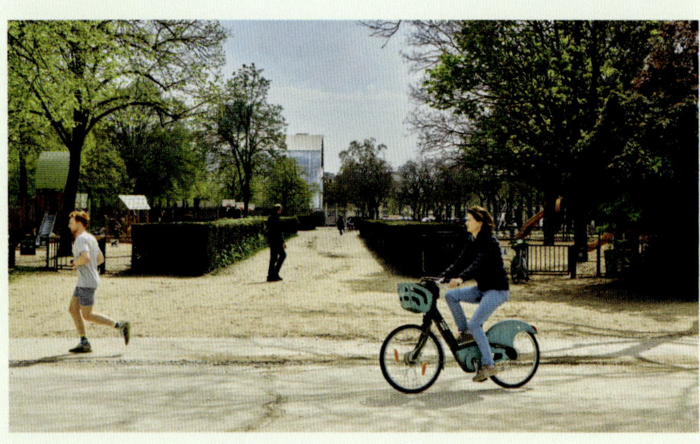

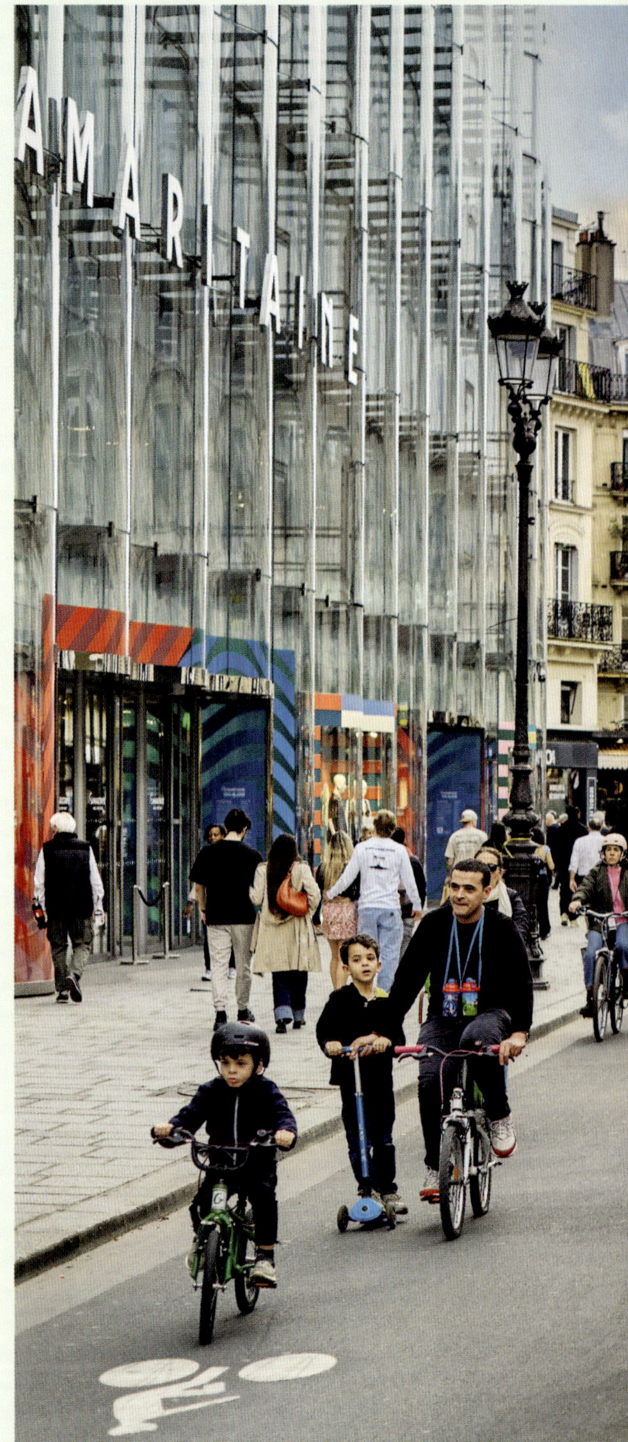

BELOW
On la rue de Rivoli, with the famous
department store La Samaritaine on
the left. Families ride together either on
bikes or with scooters.

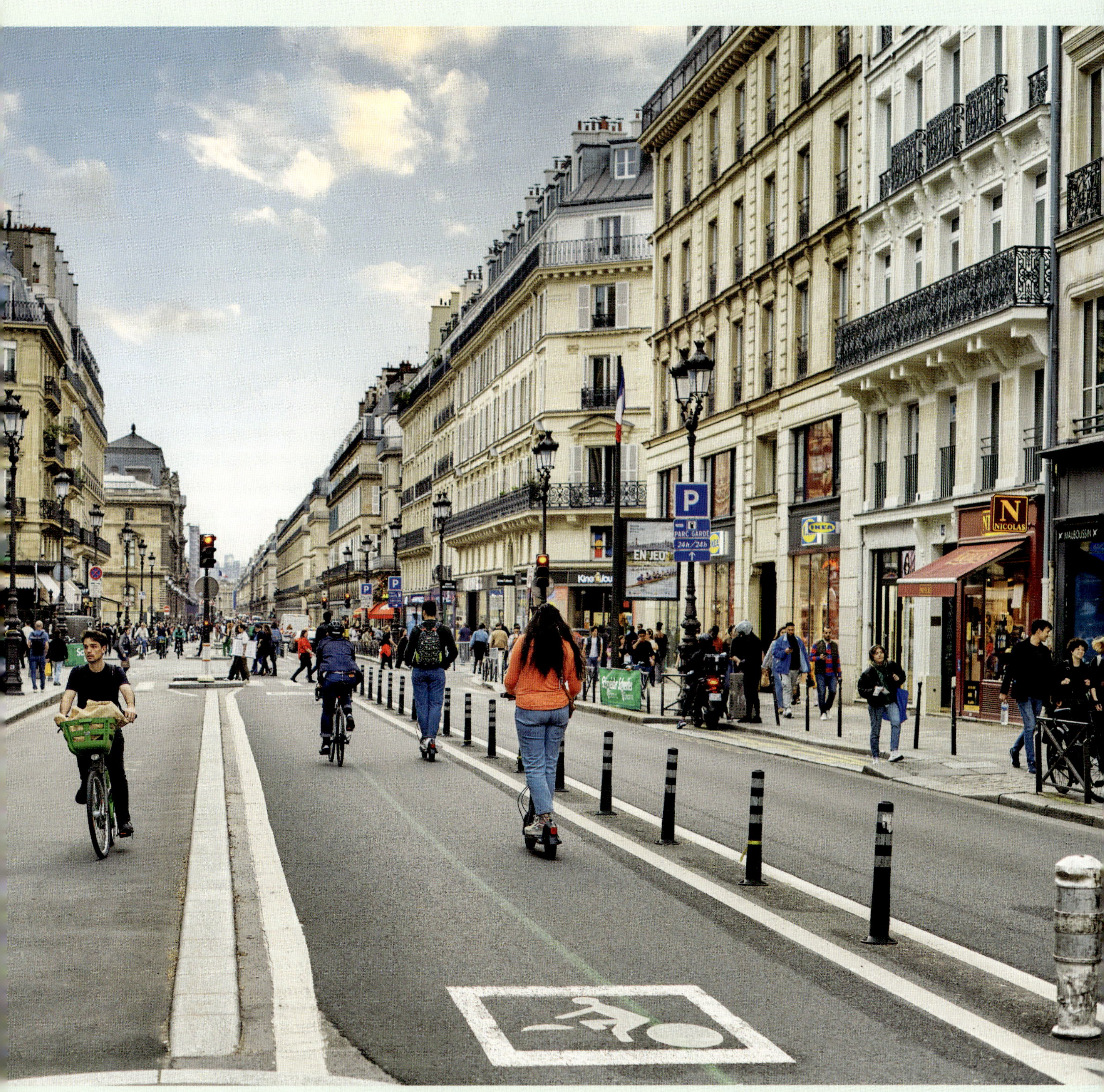

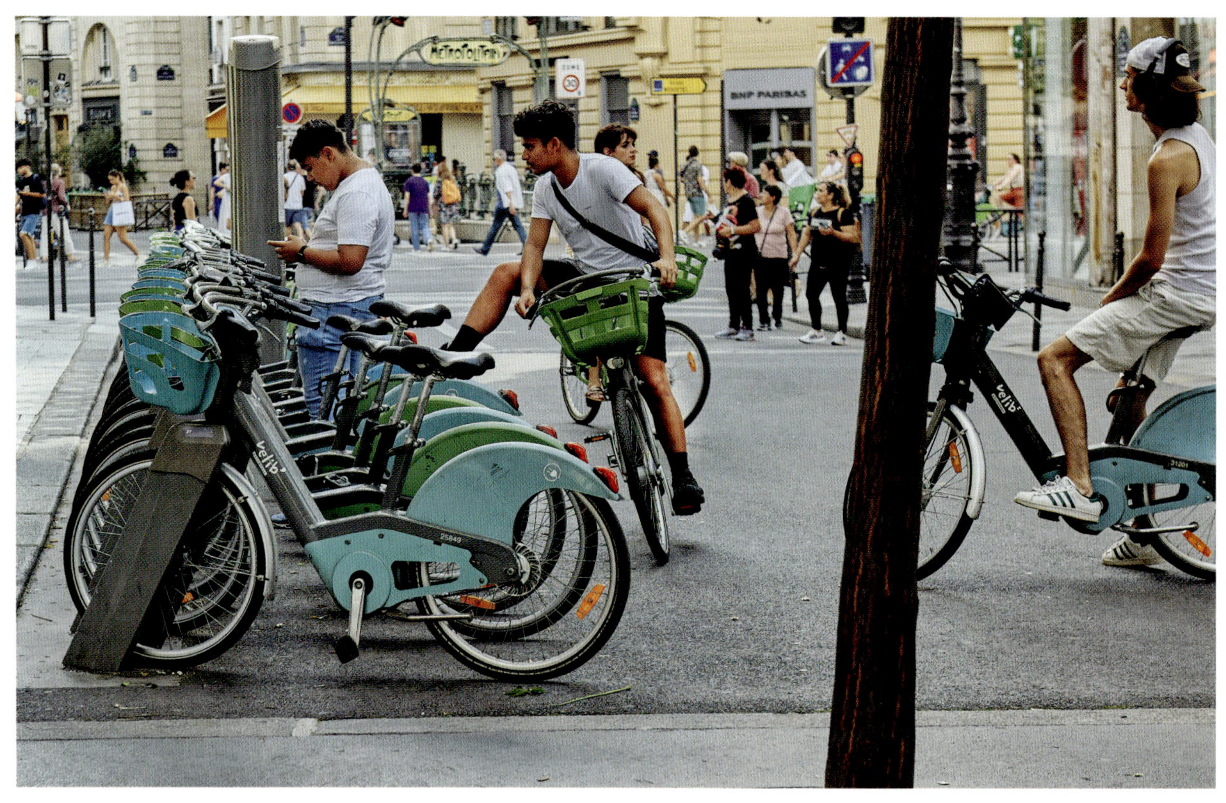

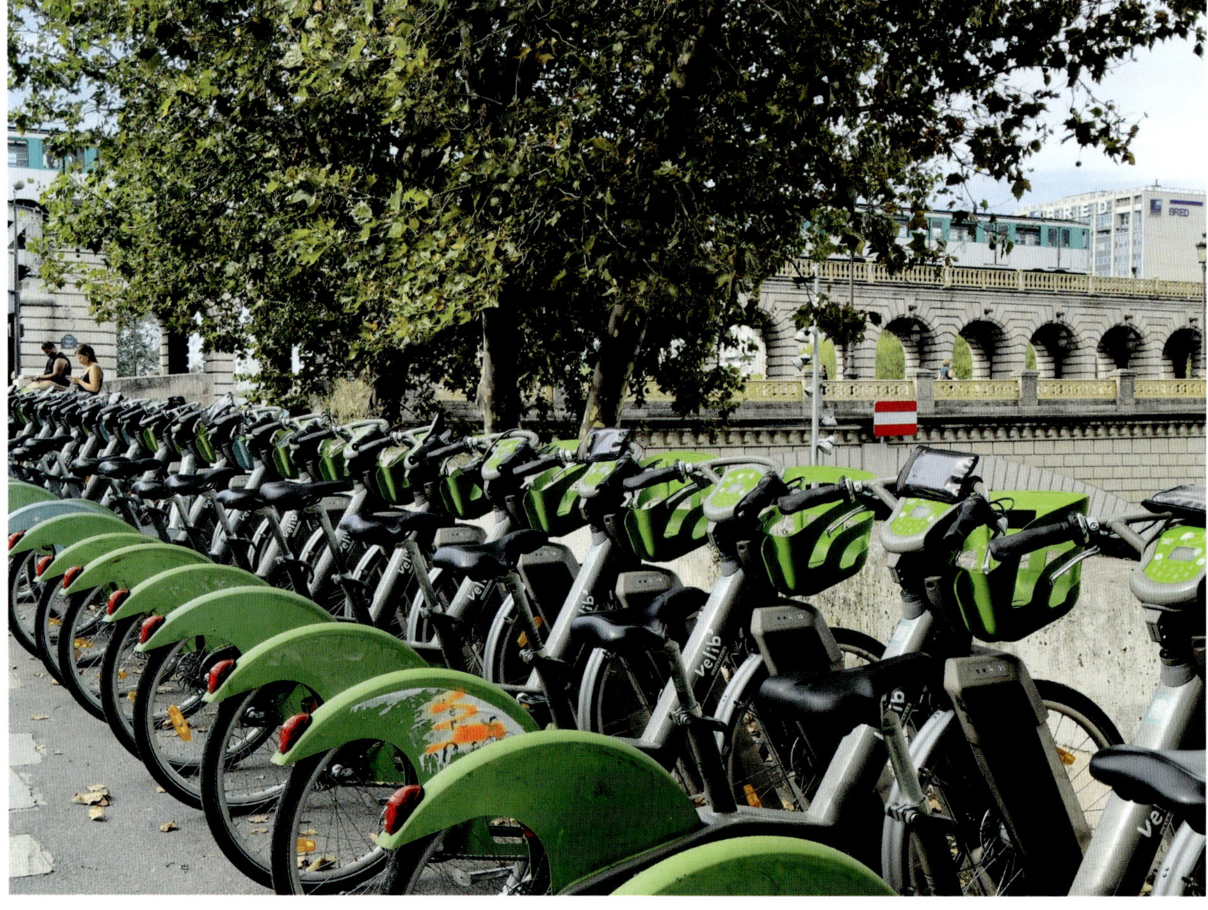

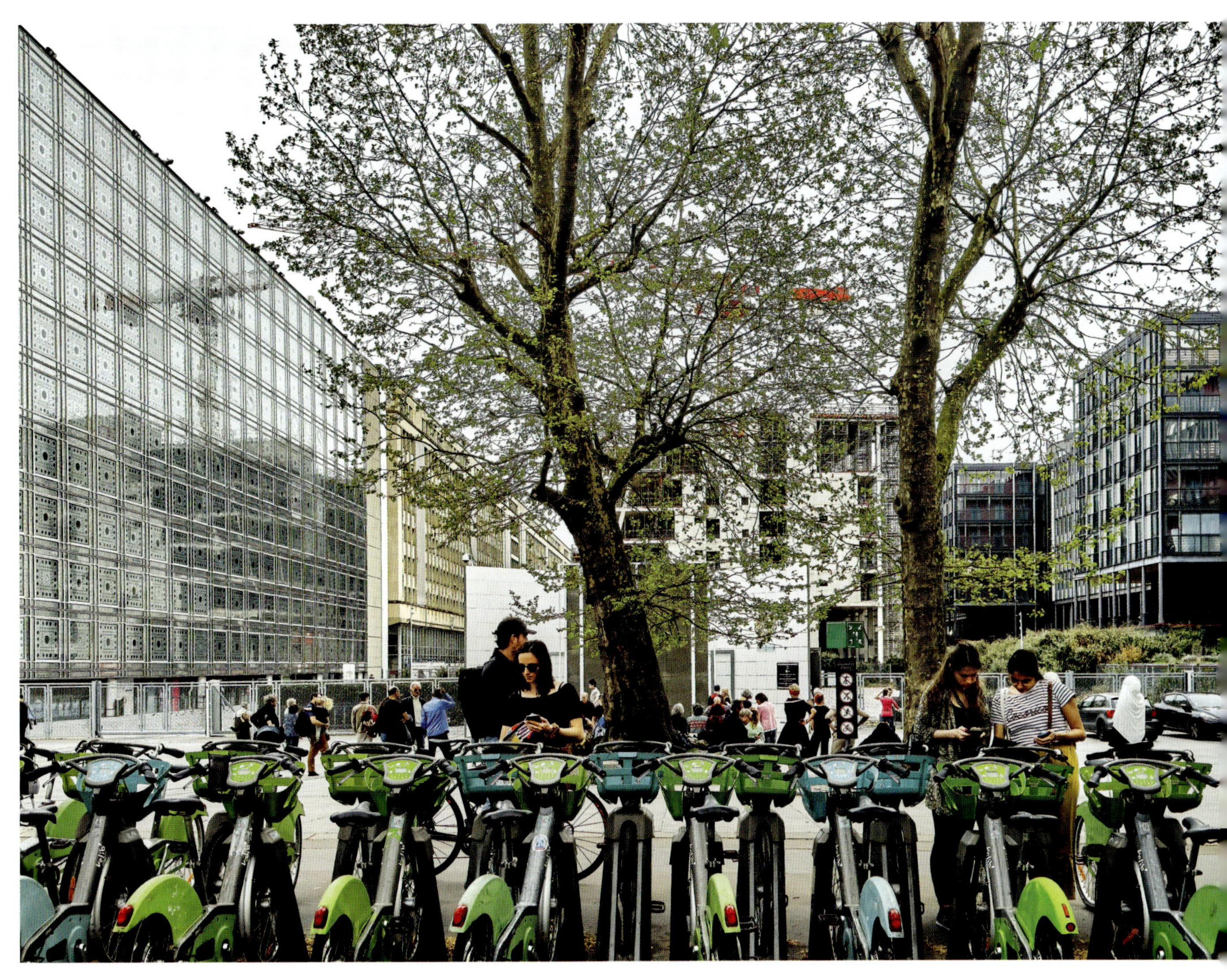



Vélib' Métropole was the first bike-sharing program in Paris. Now there are other companies that offer ride sharing and bike rentals. The bikes have different colors associated with the companies.

**ABOVE**
Bike parking has also become an important issue in the city.

# Tramways d'Île-de-France

**BELOW**
The T3a line near le parc Georges-Bressans that
runs on boulevard Lefebvre. Even the tram tracks
are an opportunity for a green space in Paris.

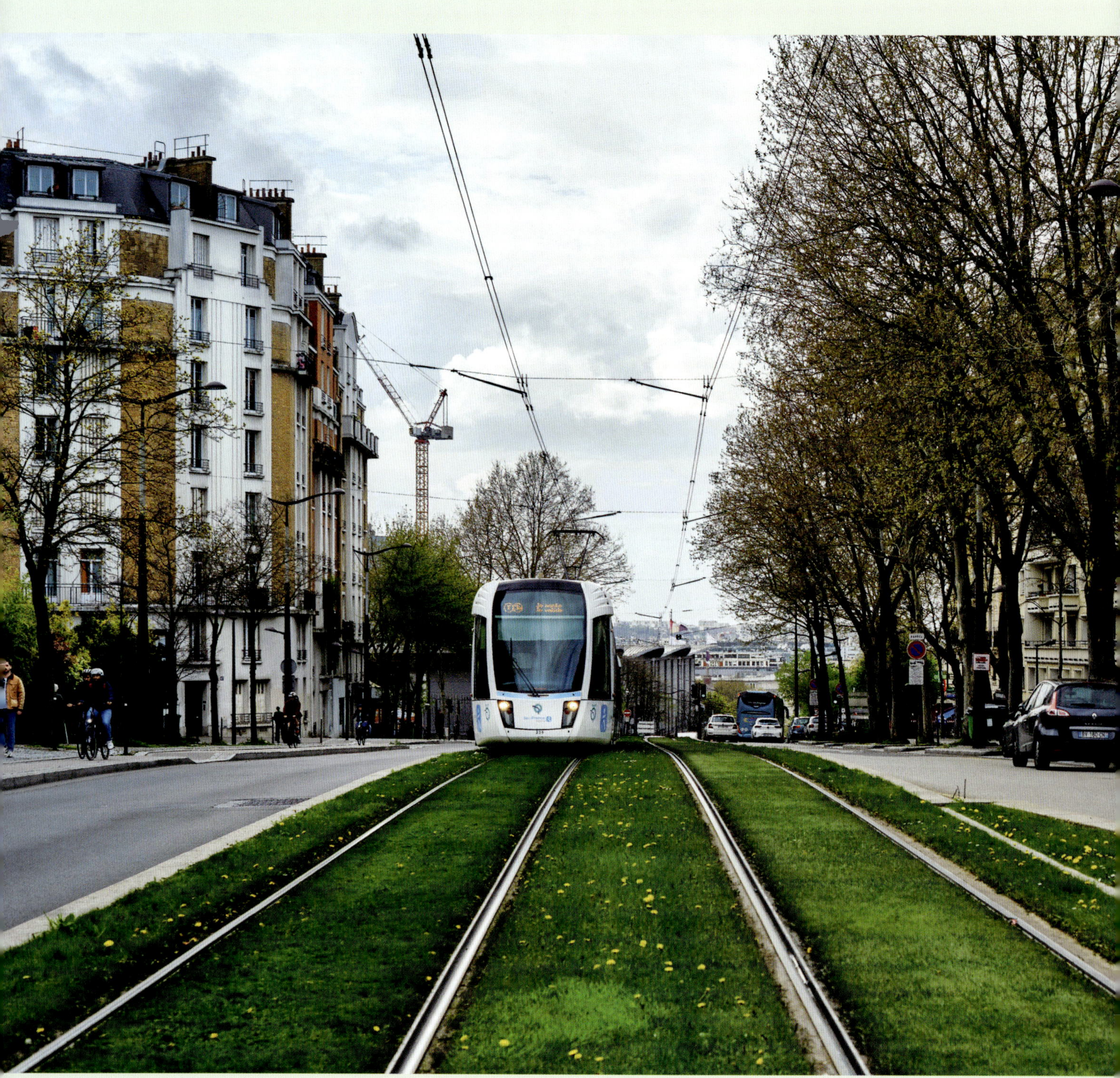

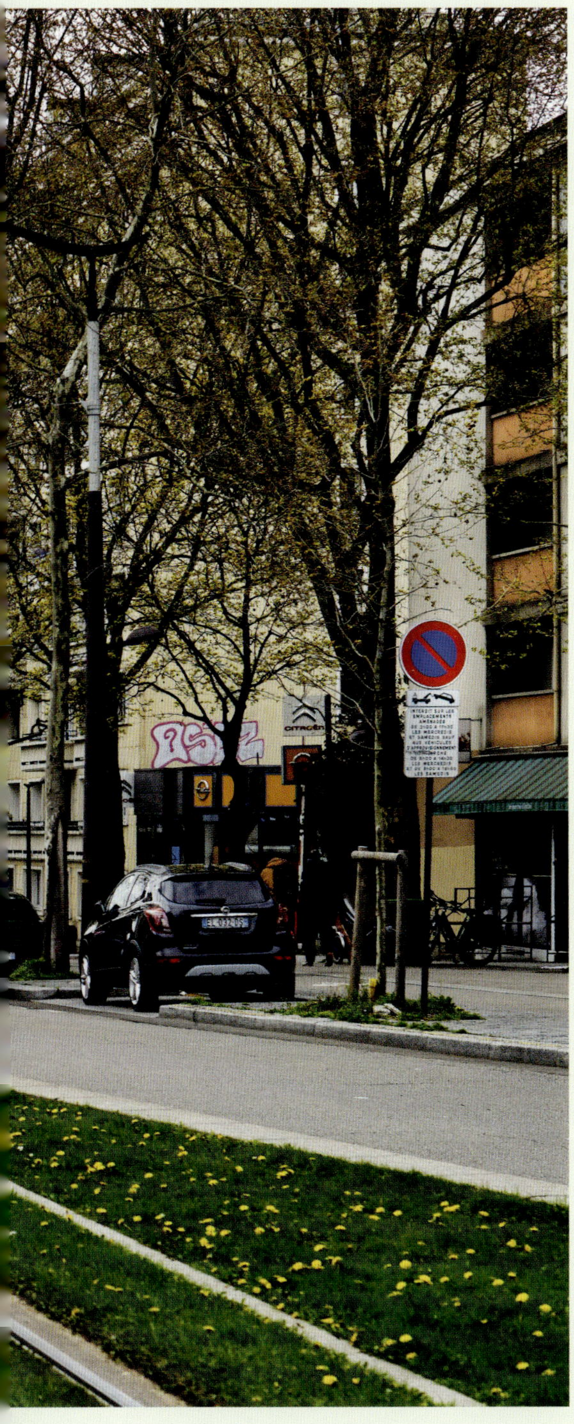

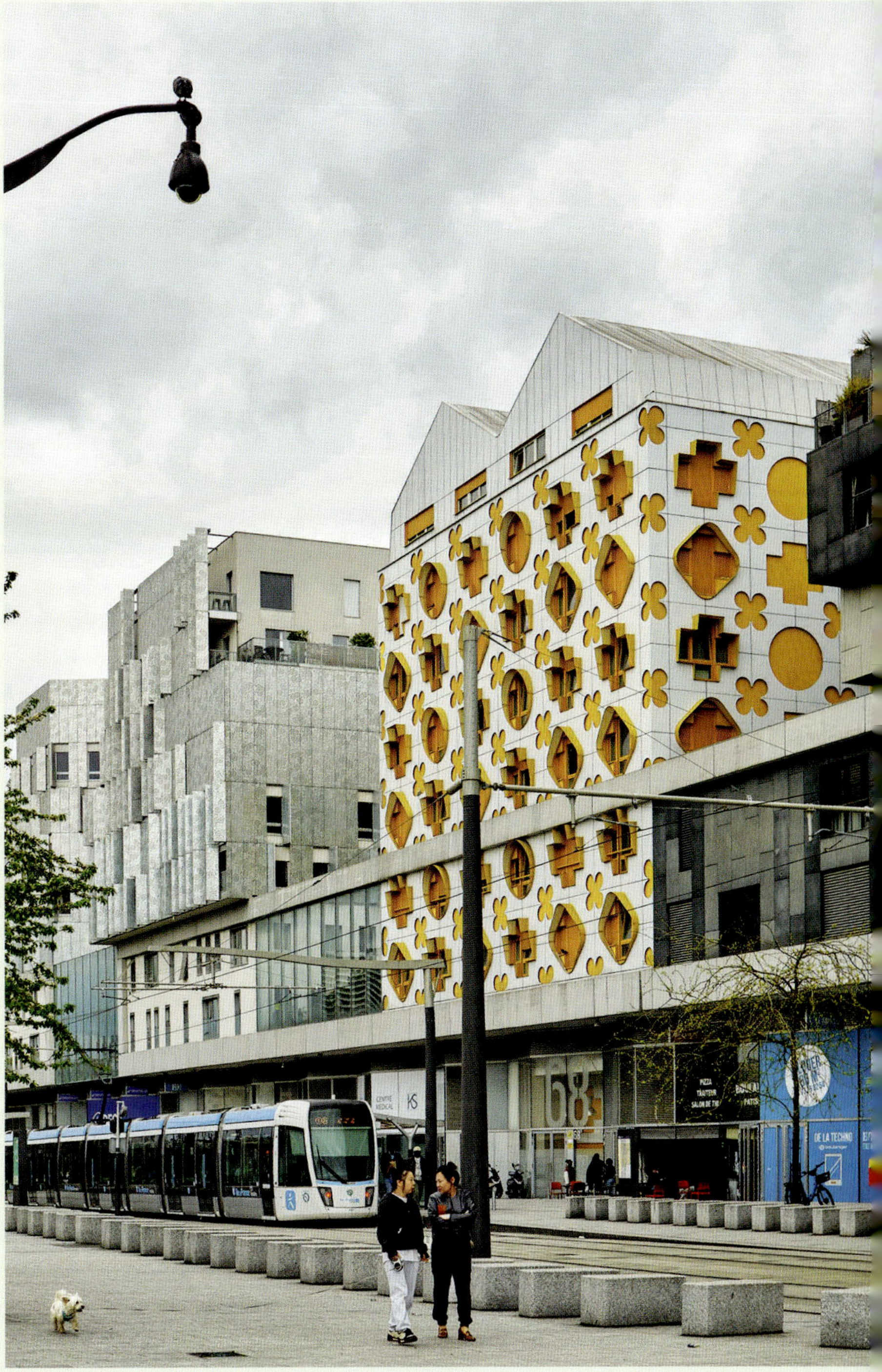

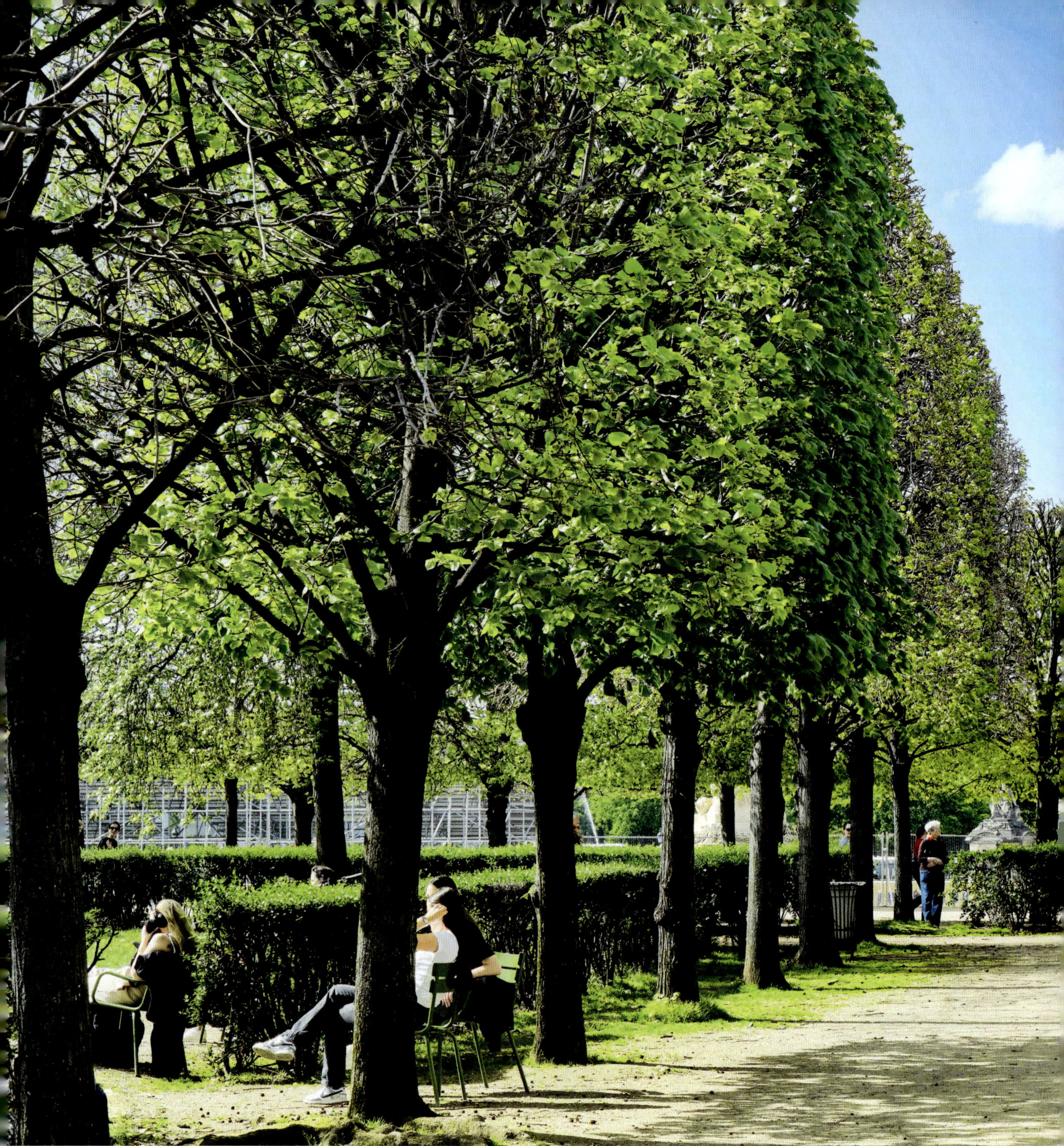

## *Promenade*

Walkers in le jardin des Tuileries. The trees are heavily trimmed in a technique called "pollarding" that limits their growth.

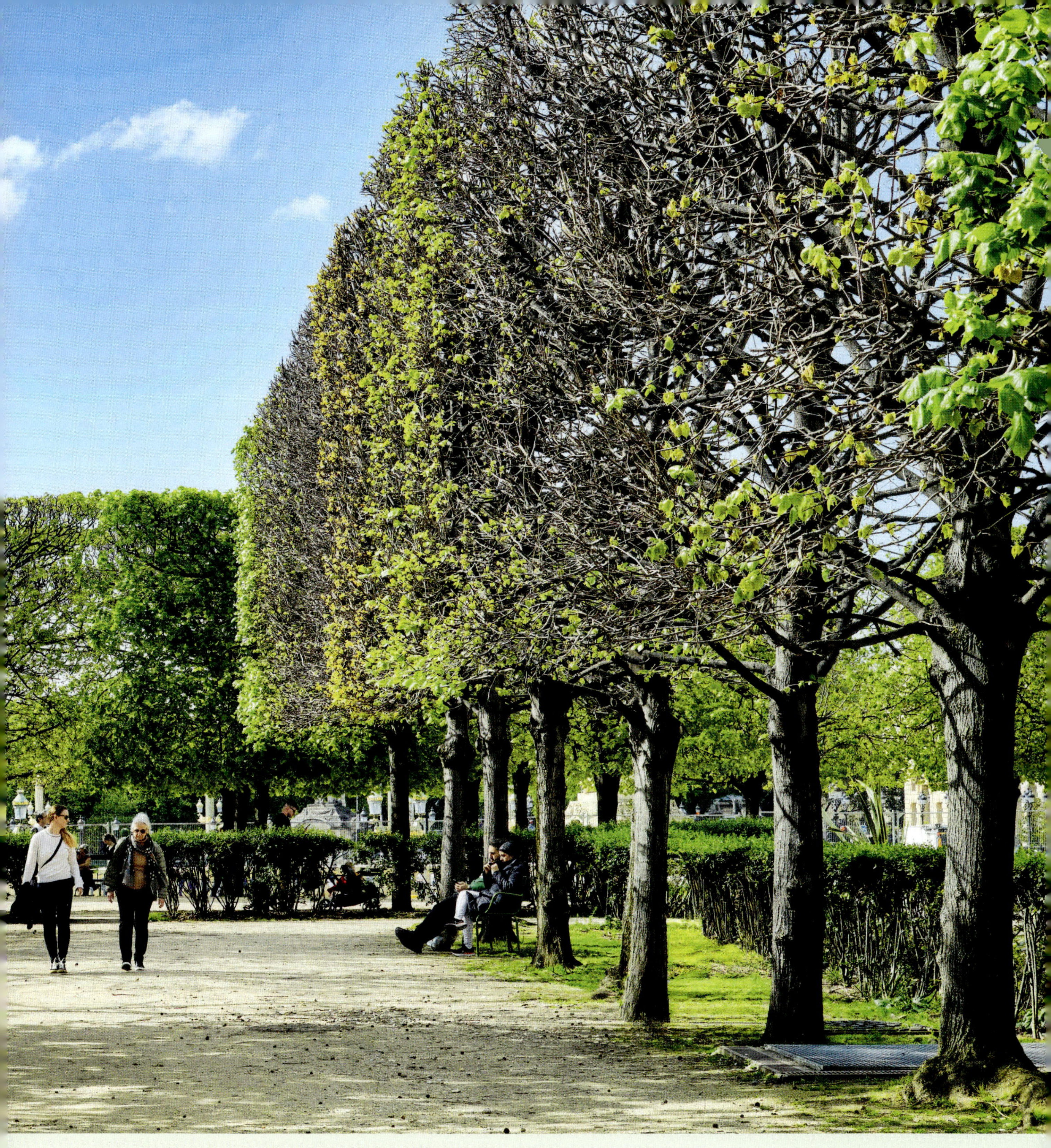

# Walking Itineraries

The following itineraries are meant to inspire the reader to connect stories featured throughout the book and to discover these places by foot. Some routes are longer than others, some involve taking a bus or a tram along the way, and all start with the metro as a beginning point. Purchasing a Navigo Travel Card is highly recommended for seamless travel throughout the city's public transportation system. Addresses are also provided so walkers can set their own courses using a smartphone app.

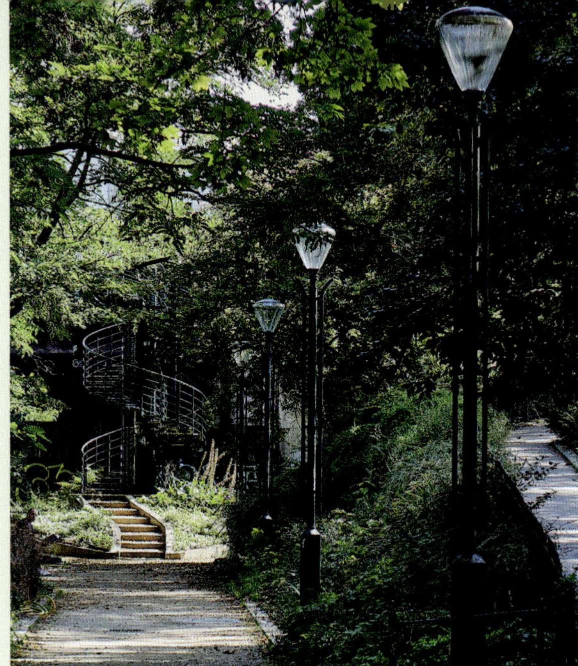

**Itinerary 1:** A stroll on la coulée verte René-Dumont, also known as la promenade plantée; stop for lunch at Ground Control; walk to marché d'Aligre; and finish at rue Charles-Baudelaire.

- Approximately 1.7 miles (2.7 km). Note: Staircases are on the path, near the elevated section of the park.

1. Take public transport to the start of the walk: From metro stop Nation (lines 1, 2, 6, 9), walk to the Fabre d'Églantine stop for bus line 29; exit the bus at the Porte de Montempoivre stop; and walk 100 feet (30.5 m) to the entrance of la coulée verte.
2. The park entry is near boulevard Périphérique at 21 avenue Émile Laurent. Follow the park path west toward allée Vivaldi (approximately 0.9 miles/1.4 km).
3. Proceed to jardin de Reuilly–Paul Pernin; from there, take the elevated walkway of the coulée verte toward place de la Bastille. Exit the park at the staircase at passage Miriam-Makeba and avenue Daumesnil. Walk to Ground Control (page 186) at 81 rue de Charolais for lunch or an aperitif (approximately 0.3 miles/0.5 km).
4. After lunch, exit Ground Control, turn left along avenue Daumesnil, cross over rue de Rambouillet at the light, and then cross over avenue Daumesnil, continuing straight on the path to passage Hennel. From the passage, take a left on to rue de Charenton.
5. Turn right on to boulevard Diderot, then take a left on to rue Beccaria, proceeding straight to place d'Aligre, where the marché d'Aligre (page 231) takes place every day except for Monday (approximately 0.5 miles/0.8 km). During the week, the covered market is open in the afternoon and evening from 4:30 until 7:30 P.M., but check times while planning your walk.
6. After shopping, walk to the corner of rue de Cotte and place d'Aligre. Turn left, walk 500 feet (152.4 m), and turn on to rue Charles-Baudelaire (pages 100–101). Check out one of the *rues aux enfants* projects (page 100).

**Itinerary 2:** After-lunch walk in the 10th arrondissement from Jah Jah to Boneshaker Donuts & Coffee, and then to place de la République, finishing at le canal Saint-Martin.

- Approximately: 3 miles (4.8 km)

1. Start at Jah Jah (page 217) for lunch at 11 rue de Petites Écuries (metro stop: Château d'Eau, line 4). It is an 800-foot (244 m) walk from the metro station to the restaurant.
2. After lunch, leave the restaurant, turn right on rue de Petites Écuries, walk toward rue du Faubourg Saint-Denis and turn left. Walk down the street until you reach a fork in the road. Move right and continue on rue Faubourg Saint-Denis, following the road as it goes around Porte Saint-Denis. Then take a right on rue d'Aboukir (approximately 1.6 miles/ 2.6 km).
3. Proceed to 83 rue d'Aboukir. Discover the Oasis d'Aboukir (page 87). After admiring over two hundred species of plants that make up the green wall, stop at Boneshaker bakery (86 rue d'Aboukir; page 228) for a doughnut and coffee.
4. Leaving the bakery, turn right on rue d'Aboukir, walking to the left to follow rue Saint-Denis. After about a block, turn right on boulevard Saint-Denis. Take a left on place de la République (page 33; approximately 0.8 miles/1.3 km).

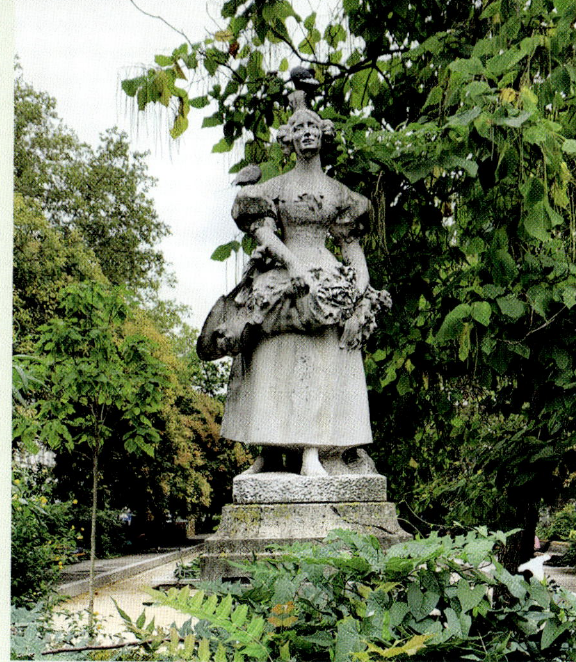

5. At place de la République, walk around the Monument à la République to admire the work of François-Charles and Léopold Morice, the brothers who created the monument, which was placed in the square in 1883. Enjoy people watching on the benches placed throughout the park.
6. From the plaza, turn right in front of the café at the Fluctuat Nec Mergitur pavilion to cross over the street place de la République. Turn right on the rue Léon Jouhaux toward quai de Valmy (approximately 0.6 miles/0.9 km). At quai de Valmy, turn either left or right to enjoy a walk along le canal Saint-Martin. If you turn right and walk toward the Seine, at the intersection of rue du Faubourg du Temple and quai de Valmy, there is a statue titled *La Grisette de 1830*, an homage to working women (approximately 0.2 miles/0.3 km).

**Itinerary 3:** Contemporary art and natural wines in the 1st arrondissement.
- Approximately 0.5 miles  (0.8 km). Note: This is an adult–only walk.

1. Take public transport to the start of the walk: exit the RER at the Châtelet–Les Halles stop (lines A, B, D).
2. Exit the Châtelet–Les Halles station under the Canopée (page 133), taking the escalators to the plaza at rue Baltard. On the right will be the Saint-Eustache church; on the left will be the Jardin Nelson Mandela. Walk straight toward the Bourse de Commerce (approximately 0.2 miles/0.3 km).
3. Walk to the entrance of the Bourse de Commerce–Pinault Collection at 2 rue de Viarmes. Spend some time taking in the transformation of the stock exchange into an art gallery. The collection is closed on Tuesdays.
4. After touring the exhibition, leave the building and turn right on rue du Louvre. Cross the street and turn left on rue Coquillière (approximately 0.2 miles/0.3 km). The wine bar L'Envers (page 214) is on the left at 41 rue Coquillière.

**Itinerary 4:** Sunday brunch and walking in the 19th arrondissement at Le TLM on the Petite Ceinture, a visit to the cultural center Centquatre-Paris, and on to la Galerie du 19M for an exhibition.
- Approximately 2 miles (3.2 km)

1. Take public transport to the start of the walk: exit the RER at the Rosa Parks stop (line E).
2. Exit the station and turn left, walking along rue Gas-

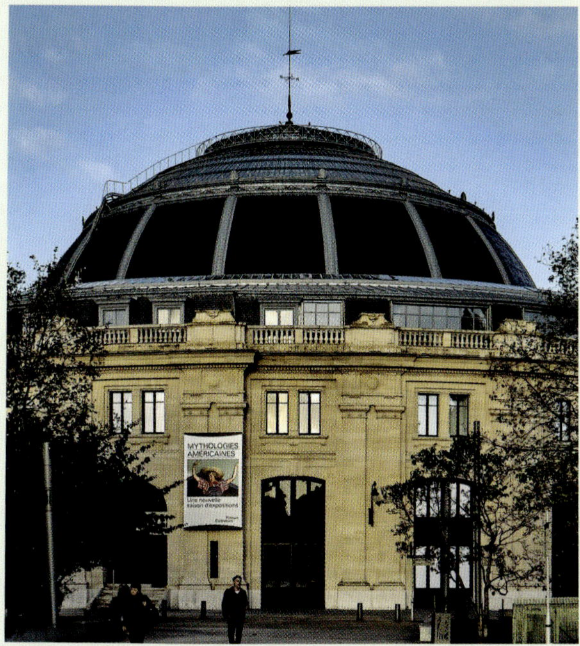

**TOP**
Jean-Bernard Descomps created the sculpture of a young woman holding flowers with her skirt.

**ABOVE**
The Bourse de Commerce museum exhibits the collection of one collector, François Pinault. The building dates back to the eighteenth century.

**OPPOSITE ABOVE**
At one entrance of la coulée verte, there is a spiral staircase, where one can access the park or have a bird's-eye view of the pathway.

**OVERLEAF**
The 19M building was designed by architect Rudy Ricciotti.

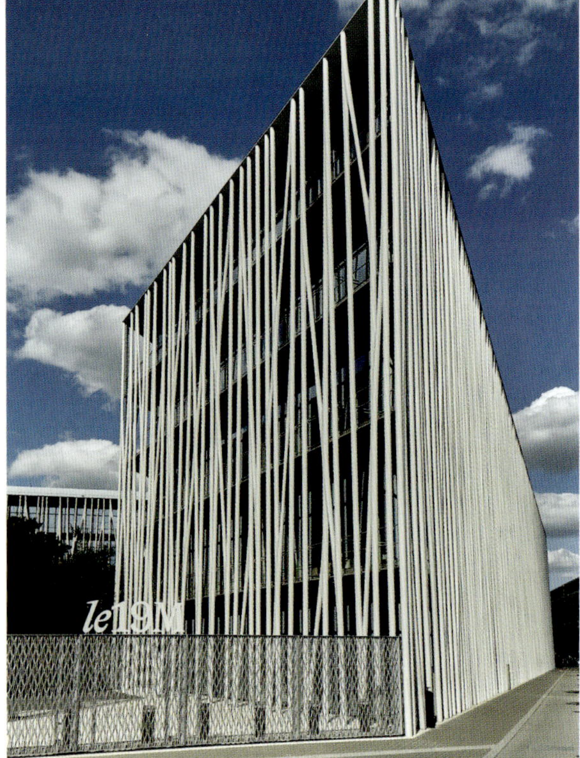


ton Tessier. Take the ramp up the hill of the Petite Ceinture, where you will find Le TLM (page 148) at 105 rue Curial on the right. Brunch is served on Sundays. There is both inside and outside seating.

3. After brunch, return to rue Curial. Walk to Centquatre-Paris (page 211) at 5 rue Curial (approximately 0.6 miles/0.9 km). Check out an exhibition, browse in the bookstore, watch the dancers practice their moves, or let the kids play with a building set and books.

4. Leaving Centquatre-Paris, turn left on to rue Curial. Walk to rue de Crimée, turn left, and continue straight (approximately 0.3 miles/0.5 km). Then turn right on to boulevards des Maréchaux and take a left on avenue de la Porte d'Aubervilliers. Cross place de Skanderbeg and arrive at 19M at 2 place Skanderbeg to see an exhibition.

- Alternative directions from Centquatre-Paris to 19M: Bus line 45 stops at rue Curial; exit at the Skander-beg stop and walk a short distance to 19M.

**Itinerary 5:** From the vineyard in parc Georges-Brassens in the 15th arrondissement to Villa Santos Dumont, a charming street hidden nearby.
- Approximately: 1 mile (1.6 km)

1. Take public transportation to the start. Metro: Porte de Vanves (Line 13).
2. From the metro station, turn right on to boulevard Lefebvre and walk to rue Brancion. Another option is to board the tram T3a at the Porte de Vanves stop across from the metro station. Exit the tram at the Brancion stop.
3. Turn right on to rue Brancion and continue. Cross the bridge over the Petite Ceinture and proceed straight. Enter the park at 104 rue Brancion (approx-imately 0.3 miles/0.5 km). On Sunday, stalls selling antique and used books fill the old horse market. Inside the park, follow the signs to the vineyard, Clos des Morillons (approximately 0.2 miles/0.3 km).
4. Make your way from the vineyard to the corner of rue des Morillons and rue Brancion (approximately 0.3 miles/0.5 km).
5. Continue straight on rue des Morillons, crossing rue Brancion. Turn left on rue Santos-Dumont (approx-imately 0.1 miles/0.2 km). Georges Brassens, the legendary singer-songwriter who the park is named for, lived at 42 rue Santos-Dumont. Take a left on to the impasse Villa Santos-Dumont (approximately 700 feet/213 m).

**Itinerary 6:** A Sunday walk in the 7th arrondissement, shopping in an organic market, searching for a vin-tage French trench coat, and stopping a quiet park.
- Approximately: 0.8 miles (1.3 km)

1. Take public transportation to the start: Exit the metro at the Rennes stop (line 12).
2. Exit the metro station on rue des Rennes, arriving in the median of boulevard Raspail (approximately 150 feet/46 m). The organic market tents (page 237) are organized in the center of the road and are open on Sundays from 9 A.M. to 3 P.M.
3. Walk through the market, down boulevard Raspail to Square Boucicaut (approximately 0.3 miles/ 0.5 km). Walking through the park, see if you can locate the *margousier*, or Indian lilac, one of the rare trees of Paris, planted in 1699.
3. Afterward, walk across the street to La Grande Épicerie de Paris (38 rue de Sèvres). Order a café au lait and sit at one of the tables in the café near the entrance.
5. Crossing rue de Sèvres, head over to Tilt Vintage (page 251) at 10 rue Saint-Placide to search for a vintage trench coat (approximately 200 feet/61 m).
6. Leaving Tilt Vintage, turn left on rue Saint-Placide, then turn right on rue des Sevres, crossing boule-vard Raspail and continuing on to rue des Sevres (approximately 0.3 miles/0.5 km). Turn left on rue Juliette Récamier. Finish at square Roger-Stéphane (page 64) at 7 rue Juliette Récamier: Enjoy the solitude.